ECONOMIC HISTORY

STUDIES ~~ ~~ IN
TH~ ~~NTURY

ANCIENT, MEDIEVAL AND EARLY MODERN

STUDIES IN ENGLISH TRADE IN THE 15TH CENTURY

Edited by

EILEEN POWER AND M.M. POSTAN

LONDON AND NEW YORK

First published in 1933

Published in 2006 by
Routledge
2 Park Square, Milton Park, Abingdon, Oxfordshire OX14 4RN
711 Third Avenue, New York, NY 10017

First issued in paperback 2014

Routledge is an imprint of the Taylor and Francis Group, an informa business

© 1933 Eileen Power and M.M. Postan

All rights reserved. No part of this book may be reprinted or reproduced or utilized in any form or by any electronic, mechanical, or other means, now known or hereafter invented, including photocopying and recording, or in any information storage or retrieval system, without permission in writing from the publishers.

The publishers have made every effort to contact authors and copyright holders of the works reprinted in the *Economic History* series. This has not been possible in every case, however, and we would welcome correspondence from those individuals or organisations we have been unable to trace.

These reprints are taken from original copies of each book. In many cases the condition of these originals is not perfect. The publisher has gone to great lengths to ensure the quality of these reprints, but wishes to point out that certain characteristics of the original copies will, of necessity, be apparent in reprints thereof.

British Library Cataloguing in Publication Data
A CIP catalogue record for this book
is available from the British Library

Studies in English Trade in the 15th Century
ISBN 0-415-38266-1 (volume)
ISBN 0-415-37680-7 (subset)
ISBN 0-415-28619-0 (set)

ISBN13: 978-1-138-86536-5 (pbk)
ISBN13: 978-0-415-38266-3 (hbk)

Routledge Library Editions: Economic History

STUDIES IN
ENGLISH TRADE IN
THE FIFTEENTH CENTURY

STUDIES IN ENGLISH TRADE IN THE FIFTEENTH CENTURY

EDITED BY
EILEEN POWER
AND
M. M. POSTAN

LONDON
ROUTLEDGE & KEGAN PAUL LTD
BROADWAY HOUSE, 68-74 CARTER LANE, E.C.4

First published 1933
Second impression 1951

Reissued 1966
by Routledge & Kegan Paul Ltd.

No part of this book may be reproduced
in any form without permission from
the publisher, except for quotation
of brief passages in criticism.

TABLE OF CONTENTS

		PAGE
	PREFACE	xvii
I.	ENGLISH FOREIGN TRADE FROM 1446 TO 1482 . . .	1
	By H. L. Gray, Ph.D., Professor of History at Bryn Mawr College.	
II.	THE WOOL TRADE IN THE FIFTEENTH CENTURY . .	39
	By E. E. Power, M.A., D.Lit., Professor of Economic History in the University of London.	
III.	THE ECONOMIC AND POLITICAL RELATIONS OF ENGLAND AND THE HANSE FROM 1400 TO 1475	91
	By M. M. Postan, M.Sc. (Econ.), Lecturer in Economic History at the London School of Economics and Political Science (University of London).	
IV.	THE ICELAND TRADE	155
	By E. M. Carus Wilson, M.A.	
V.	THE OVERSEAS TRADE OF BRISTOL	183
	By E. M. Carus Wilson, M.A.	
VI.	THE GROCERS OF LONDON, A STUDY OF DISTRIBUTIVE TRADE	247
	By S. Thrupp, M.A., Ph.D.	
VII.	THE FINANCIAL TRANSACTIONS BETWEEN THE LANCASTRIAN GOVERNMENT AND THE MERCHANTS OF THE STAPLE FROM 1449 TO 1461	293
	By W. I. Haward, M.A., Ph.D., late Lecturer in History at Bedford College (University of London).	
VIII.	TABLES OF ENROLLED CUSTOMS AND SUBSIDY ACCOUNTS, 1399 TO 1482	321
	§ 1. INTRODUCTION	321
	By Professor H. L. Gray.	
	§ 2. TABLES	330
NOTES TO THE TEXT		361
APPENDIX A. VARIATIONS IN ENGLISH FOREIGN TRADE, 1446 TO 1482. ANNUAL AVERAGES BY PERIODS . . .		401
APPENDIX B. TOTAL ENGLISH FOREIGN TRADE, 1446 TO 1482 .		402
APPENDIX C. BROADCLOTHS EXPORTED BY THE HANSEATIC MERCHANTS, 1406 TO 1480		407
	LIST OF ABBREVIATIONS USED IN THE NOTES AND TABLES	409
	BIBLIOGRAPHY	411
	INDEX	417

MAPS

		PAGE
I.	THE PRINCIPAL NAVIGATION ROUTES OF NORTHERN EUROPE IN THE FOURTEENTH AND FIFTEENTH CENTURIES	92
II.	PLAN OF BRISTOL, *c.* 1480	184
III.	THE REGIONAL TRADE OF BRISTOL DURING THE FIFTEENTH CENTURY	186

SYNOPSIS OF CONTENTS

	PAGE
I. ENGLISH FOREIGN TRADE FROM 1446 TO 1482	1–38
§ 1. THE EVIDENCE OF THE CUSTOMS ACCOUNTS	1–10
(1) A period of general depression	1–2
Subdivision into twelve periods, the trade for each being indicated by annual averages derived from the enrolled customs accounts.	
(2) The main branches of English trade and the groups of merchants participating in it as reflected in the imposition of various duties	3–10
(i) The specific duties	3–4
The export duties on wool, hides, and cloth. The import duties on wax and wine. The tunnage and butlerage on the import of wine.	
(ii) The *ad valorem* duties on imports and exports	5–10
The petty customs. The subsidy of poundage.	
§ 2. ENGLISH TRADE IN THE YEARS 1446 TO 1448	10–20
(1) Its volume, value, and distribution among denizens, Hansards, and other aliens	10–17
(i) The wool trade. Its decline	10–13
(ii) The cloth trade	13
(iii) The wine trade	13–14
(iv) The trade in miscellaneous merchandise	14–15
(2) Comparison between the trade of the Staplers and that of the Merchant Adventurers	15–17
(3) The value of the trade of each of the four groups of merchants in 1446–8. Table	18
(4) The balance of trade	19–20
§ 3. FLUCTUATIONS IN ENGLISH TRADE DURING THE PERIOD 1448 TO 1492	20–38
(1) The wool trade. Fortunes of Staplers and aliens	20–23
(2) The cloth trade. Fortunes of denizens, Hansards, and other aliens. Causes of depression	23–29
(3) The trade in miscellaneous merchandise	30–31
(4) The wine trade	31–32
(5) General comparison between the trades of denizens and that of aliens	32–36
(6) The value of the trade of each of the four groups of merchants in 1479–82. Table	36–37
(7) Changes in the balance of trade	37
(8) General conclusions	38

ix

SYNOPSIS OF CONTENTS

	PAGE
II. THE WOOL TRADE IN THE FIFTEENTH CENTURY	39–90
§ 1. THE DIRECTIONS OF THE TRADE	39–48
(1) Importance of the wool trade	39–40
(2) Direction of the trade	41–48
(i) To Calais	41–43
The Staple monopoly. The wool ports	41–43
(ii) To the Netherlands	43
North Country wool going via Berwick and Newcastle-upon-Tyne	43
(iii) To Italy	43–47
The land route	44
Direct shipment via the Straits of Marrock	44–45
The Italian merchants	45–47
(3) Evasion of the Staple monopoly	47–48
(i) By licences	47–48
(ii) By smuggling	48
§ 2. THE TECHNIQUE OF THE TRADE	48–72
(1) The purchase of the wool	48–58
(i) Grades of wool	49–51
(ii) Wool dealers	51–56
(iii) Wool packers	56–58
(2) The transmission and sale of the wool	59–72
(i) Transport from the Cotswolds to Calais	59–60
(ii) The customers of the Staple	60–62
(iii) Credit sales	62–66
(iv) Collection of money at the marts and transmission to England by bills of exchange	66–70
(v) The profits of the trade	70–72
§ 3. THE STAPLE AS AN ORGAN OF STATE FINANCE	72–90
(1) Loans, the wool customs and the garrison of Calais	72–79
(i) The Staple loans on the security of the customs	73–74
(ii) The Act of Retainer of 1466	74–75
(iii) Financial transactions between the Company and its members	75–79
(2) Bullion regulations	79–90
(i) Use of the Staple to carry out the bullionist policy of the government	79–82
(ii) The Ordinance of Partition, 1430	82–89
(iii) Withdrawal of the Ordinance of Partition and of the bullion regulations, 1443	89–90
III. THE ECONOMIC AND POLITICAL RELATIONS OF ENGLAND AND THE HANSE FROM 1400 TO 1475	91–153
§ 1. THE RIVALRY	91–105
(1) The position of the Hanseatic League	91–96
(i) Economic foundation of Hanseatic monopoly	91–93

SYNOPSIS OF CONTENTS

	PAGE
(ii) The necessity for political protection of that monopoly from the mid-fourteenth century	93–95
(iii) Hanseatic policy in the late fourteenth century. The League, under Lübeck, standing for rigid protection and the individual towns for exclusion of aliens from the local market.	95–96
(2) The English penetration into northern markets	96–98
(i) Importance of the trade with Prussia	97
(ii) Inevitability of conflict with the Hanse	97–98
(3) Hanseatic privileges in England and the reciprocity programme	98–101
(4) Reason for English failure: weakness of the government. The policy of the government.	101–105

§ 2. THE THREE SUCCESSES (1400 TO 1437) . . . 105–120

 (1) The crisis of 1385 to 1388 105–108
  (i) First emergence of the reciprocity programme, 1375–80 106–107
  (ii) Piracy, the crisis of 1385 and the treaty of 1388 . 107–108
 (2) The crisis of 1405 to 1408 108–111
  (i) Causes of the crisis 108
  (ii) Treaty acknowledging the principle of reciprocity, 1408 110–111
  (iii) Development of English trade in Danzig . 111
 (3) The crisis of 1431 to 1437 111–119
  (i) Causes of friction 111–115
  (ii) The conflict breaks out again, 1431 . . 116
  (iii) The Hanseatic delegation of 1434–64; the treaty of 1437 116–119

§ 3. THE FAILURE (1437 TO 1475) 120–138

 (1) The treaty of 1437 as the climax of English success . 120
 (2) Reasons for English failure in the subsequent conflicts . 121–123
  (i) The political situation in England . . 121–122
  (ii) The outburst of privateering brings Lübeck into the struggle 122–123
 (3) The course of the struggle 123–136
  (i) The anti-foreign measures in England in the forties 125–127
  (ii) Capture of the Bay fleet, 1449, and events of 1449–68 127–132
  (iii) The arrests of Hanseatic goods, 1468 . . 132–133
  (iv) The Hanse united against England and the outbreak of naval war . . . 134–136
 (4) The Conference of Utrecht, 1474, and the Treaty of 1475 136–138

§ 4. THE TRADE 138–153

 (1) Exchange of Baltic goods for English cloth . . 139–145
  (i) Hanseatic imports 139–141
  (ii) Export of cloth by Hanseatics and English . 141–145

		PAGE
(2) Business organization		145–150
(i) The combination of wholesale and retail trade		146
(ii) The "integral" firm and the system of commission trade		147–148
(iii) The Hanseatic factories in England; the Steelyard		148–149
(iv) The English association in Prussia; the Danzig factory		149–150
(3) Connection between the eclipse of the Society of English merchants in Danzig and the rise of the Merchant Adventurers in the Low Countries		150–153

IV. THE ICELAND TRADE 155–182

§ 1. The Establishment of the Trade 155–171

(1) Early connections between Ireland and Iceland . . 155–156
(2) Reasons for the isolation of Iceland at the end of the fourteenth century 157–159
(3) Reasons for the revival of English enterprise to Iceland . 159–161
  (i) The need for new markets for cloth and new supplies of fish 159
  (ii) The advance in English shipbuilding . . 159–160
  (iii) The Hanseatic control of Bergen . . . 161
(4) Development of a flourishing trade in the first half of the fifteenth century 161–169
  (i) First arrival of English fishermen and merchants, 1412 161
  (ii) The prohibition of direct trade and its development under the licence system . . 162–169
(5) English bishops in Iceland 169–171

§ 2. The Trade at its Height 171–177

(1) Commerce of Iceland completely under English control in the mid-fifteenth century . . . 171–172
(2) The fishing doggers 172–174
(3) The merchant ships from Bristol, Hull, and Lynn . 174–176
(4) Seasons for the Iceland trade 176–177

§ 3. The Decline of the Trade 177–182

(1) Reasons for the decline of the trade in the second half of the fifteenth century 177–181
  (i) Effect of English civil struggles on commercial policy 177
  (ii) Rise of Hanseatic competition . . . 177–181
(2) Turmoil and confusion in the Iceland trade in the eighties 181–182
(3) The voyage to the New Found Land . . . 182

V. THE OVERSEAS TRADE OF BRISTOL . . . 183–246

§ 1. The Port of Bristol 183–191

(1) Importance of Bristol as a port and a manufacturing city 183–187
(2) The inland trade of Bristol 187–190
(3) The quays 190–191

SYNOPSIS OF CONTENTS

		PAGE
§ 2. IRELAND		191–201
(1) Trade of Bristol chiefly with the South and West of Ireland		191–195
(2) The Irish in Bristol		195–196
(3) Imports and exports		196–201
§ 3. GASCONY		201–214
(1) Imports and exports		201–208
(i) The wine trade with Bayonne and Bordeaux		201–206
(ii) Other imports, especially woad		206–207
(iii) Exports to Gascony		207–208
(2) Fortunes of the Gascon trade in the fifteenth century		208–214
§ 4. THE IBERIAN PENINSULA		214–220
(1) The trade with Spain		214–220
(i) Imports and exports		214–216
(ii) Bristol trade with the Castilian ports		216–217
(iii) The pilgrim traffic to Compostella		217
(iv) Spanish merchants and ships trading to Bristol		217–218
(v) Piracy and war		218–220
(2) The trade with Portugal		220–224
(i) Imports and exports		220–221
(ii) Bristol trade with Portuguese ports		222
(iii) Piracy		222–224
§ 5. THE MEDITERRANEAN		224–230
(1) Occasional Italian ships in the Severn		224
(2) The career of Richard Sturmy		225–230
(i) The voyage of the *Cog Anne* to the Mediterranean, 1446		225–227
(ii) The voyage of the *Katherine Sturmy*, c. 1457		227–230
§ 6. THE MERCHANT OF BRISTOL		230–237
(1) The merchant		230–237
(i) Houses and furniture		231–233
(ii) Investments in land		233–234
(iii) The Canynge family		234–235
(iv) Apprentices, factors, and attorneys		235–237
(2) The shipowner		237–242
(i) Bristol shipowners		238–239
(ii) Bristol ships		239–241
(iii) The risks of sea voyages		241–242
(3) Women traders		242–243
(4) Some general characteristics		243–246
VI. THE GROCERS OF LONDON, A STUDY OF DISTRIBUTIVE TRADE		247–292
§ 1. INTRODUCTION		247
The general problem of the economic functions of the London Livery Companies		247

SYNOPSIS OF CONTENTS

		PAGE
§ 2. Early History and Constitution of the London Grocers' Company		248–262
(1) Early history		248–250
Amalgamation to form the Grocers' Company by :—		
(i) The Pepperers of Soper Lane		248
(ii) The Canvas Dealers of the Ropery		249
(iii) The Spicers of Cheap		249
(2) Constitution and membership		251–257
(i) Constitution of the Company		251
(ii) Corporate trading and the use of common funds		252–253
(iii) The Livery and the subordinate freemen		253–255
(iv) Apprenticeship		255–257
(3) Civic functions		257–259
(i) Nomination of the Weigher of the King's Beam		257–258
(ii) Nomination of the Garbler of Spices		258–259
(4) The fourteenth century		259–262
(i) The Act of 1363, forcing merchants to deal in one commodity only		259–260
(ii) The charters of the Fishmongers, Drapers, and Vintners of London		260–261
(iii) The London Ordinance of 1365 and its interpretation		261–262
§ 3. The Main Branches of the Grocers' Trade		262–265
(1) The wool and cloth trade		262–269
(i) The Grocers and the wool trade		263
(ii) The Grocers and the cloth trade		263–265
(2) The victualling and mercery trades		265–272
(i) The victualling trade		265–268
(ii) The mercery trade		268–269
(3) The trade in grocery		269–272
(i) Metals		269
(ii) Dye		270
(iii) Spices		270–272
§ 4. Wholesale and Retail Trade		272–284
(1) Wholesale trade		272–277
(i) Controversy over the problem of mediaeval wholesale trade		272–273
(ii) London as the centre of distribution for the country		273–277
(2) Retail trade		277–284
(i) Importance of retail trade		277–278
(ii) Relations of the Grocers with :—		
the victualling crafts		278–279
the industrial crafts		279–282
other importers		282–284
§ 5. Division of Function among the Companies		284–292
(1) The London Companies		284–288
(i) Rough division of function but some overlapping		284–286
(ii) Obligations of craft membership		286–288

SYNOPSIS OF CONTENTS

		PAGE
(2) Provincial merchant companies	. . . .	288–292
(i) No specialization of function	. . .	288–291
(ii) The typical provincial mercer	. . .	291–292

VII. THE FINANCIAL TRANSACTIONS BETWEEN THE LANCASTRIAN GOVERNMENT AND THE MERCHANTS OF THE STAPLE FROM 1449 TO 1461 293–320

§ 1. THE LOANS FROM THE MERCHANTS OF THE STAPLE AND THEIR REPAYMENT 293–301
    (1) The general policy of the Staplers . . . 293
    (2) The crisis of 1449 294–295
    (3) The resumption of licences and the loan of £10,700 . 295–296
    (4) The loans of 1451 and their repayment . . . 296–301

§ 2. THE FINANCING OF CALAIS BY THE MERCHANTS OF THE STAPLE 301–307
    (1) The payment of the garrison in Calais . . . 301–302
    (2) The mutiny of 1454 302–306
    (3) The settlement of 1456 306–307

§ 3. INCREASING DIFFICULTIES, 1454 TO 1459 . . . 307–315
    (1) The king resumes the right to grant licences . . 307–309
    (2) The anti-Italian movement of 1456–7 . . . 309–311
    (3) The Guildhall inquiry into breaches of the wool statutes, 1458–9 311–312
    (4) The Staplers' loan for the Household, 1457 . . 312–314
    (5) The Mediterranean trade and the king's Italian creditors, 1459 314–315

§ 4. THE STRUGGLE FOR THE THRONE, 1459 TO 1461 . . 315–320
    (1) Calais becomes the Yorkist headquarters . . 315–318
    (2) Neutrality of the Staplers in the struggle . . 318–320
        (i) Heyron's case 318–320
        (ii) Conclusion 320

VIII. TABLES OF ENROLLED CUSTOMS AND SUBSIDY ACCOUNTS, 1399 TO 1482 321–360

§ 1. INTRODUCTION 321–330

§ 2. THE TABLES OF ENROLLED CUSTOMS AND SUBSIDY ACCOUNTS . 330–360
    (1) Boston 330–331
    (2) Bridgewater 332–333
    (3) Bristol 333–335
    (4) Chichester 335–337
    (5) Exeter and Dartmouth 337–339
    (6) Ipswich 339–340
    (7) Kingston-upon-Hull 341–342
    (8) London 342–346
    (9) Lynn 347–348
    (10) Melcombe and Poole 349–350

SYNOPSIS OF CONTENTS

		PAGE
(11)	Newcastle-upon-Tyne	350–352
(12)	Plymouth and Fowey	352–354
(13)	Sandwich	354–356
(14)	Southampton	356–358
(15)	Yarmouth	359–360

NOTES TO THE TEXT 361–399

APPENDIXES 401–407

LIST OF ABBREVIATIONS 409

BIBLIOGRAPHY 411–416

INDEX 417

PREFACE

THE subject of this book is the result of something more than that almost accidental choice, which often decides the direction of historical research. The writers whose work is here united were drawn into the field by two irresistible attractions. On the one hand they were tempted by the unusual abundance of the material awaiting investigation in the collection of customs accounts preserved in the Public Record Office, on the other by the great importance and almost equally great obscurity of the history of English trade in the century before the accession of the Tudor dynasty.

The pioneer work of Schanz and Dr. Hubert Hall, and later of Professors N. S. B. Gras and H. L. Gray, had long revealed the customs accounts as a fertile source of new historical information; and a preliminary survey made independently some years ago by Professor H. L. Gray and by a London seminar under the leadership of the editors of this volume, showed that for no other period was the material as copious and as complete as for the fifteenth century. But it was the subject itself, and the various problems suggested by it, which tempted the writers most. Of all the activities of the most neglected century in English history, England's trade has received the least attention in proportion to its importance. It was obviously in the course of the later Middle Ages, and more particularly in the fifteenth century, that there took place the great transformation from mediaeval England, isolated and intensely local, to the England of the Tudor and Stuart age, with its world-wide connections and imperial designs. It was during the same period that most of the forms of international trade characteristic of the Middle Ages were replaced by new methods of commercial organization and regulation, national in scope and at times definitely nationalist in object, and that a marked movement towards capitalist methods and principles took place in the sphere of domestic trade. Yet beyond a number of general accounts of the activities of the Staplers and the Merchant Adventurers, little has been written concerning either the development or the organization of English trade in the last century of the Middle Ages.

It is hoped that this volume may do something to fill the gap. We can claim at least to have performed one task which is indispensable to the future historian of English trade, in compiling statistical tables of the enrolled customs accounts from 1377 to 1482. These accounts provide an essential measure of the nature, volume, and movement of English foreign commerce. How exact the measure is, and when and why its exactness varies, can be determined only after the history of the administration of the customs has been studied. The lack of such a history constitutes an obvious gap, which we hope later to be able to fill; meanwhile we have had to bring to bear on the interpretation of the figures knowledge painfully acquired as a result of work on the accounts themselves. For the rest, we make no claim to have written the history of English trade in the fifteenth century; these studies are to be regarded merely as prolegomena to such a history. All we have been able to do is to " sample " the field of investigation, confining our work to certain geographical regions and to certain particular problems.

A brief preliminary survey of the geographical area covered by English foreign trade will make clear exactly what we have done and what we have perforce had to leave undone. In the fifteenth century that area was coextensive with the whole of North-Western and Western Europe. The most ancient and most active channel led along a short sea route to the Low Countries, England's nearest continental neighbour and the commercial hub of Europe, but throughout the Middle Ages, and especially throughout the late fourteenth and fifteenth centuries, other channels, possibly less active but certainly most promising, led English merchants to the regions outside the Low Countries. To the west of Flanders lay Normandy and Brittany, trade with which, though constantly interrupted by war and piracy, never completely ceased; even in the war decades of the fifteenth century, intercourse with the North of France remained one of the principal occupations of the seafaring population of the southern and south-western ports, from Chichester to Plymouth and Fowey. Beyond Brittany stretched the great vine-growing districts of the Atlantic sea-board, and if England's commercial connections with the wine lands of Poitou were fitful and irregular, her links with Aquitaine and Gascony remained close and extremely important until quite late in the second half of the century. The occupation of Aquitaine by the English provided the necessary political conditions for the trade; the exclusive specialization of the region in wine-production and its dependence on foreign supplies of grain and other foodstuffs, provided the necessary economic basis. Consequently the Gascon trade ranked next to that with Flanders as the most important branch of English commerce during this period. Beyond Bordeaux and Bayonne there opened the lands of the Mediterranean South, the source of sweet wines, exotic fruits, and oriental luxuries. The English attempt to enter these regions began quite early and English merchants maintained constant and close connections with the western coast of the Iberian peninsula, especially with Portugal. Beyond the Straits of Morocco, however, they could not penetrate; their attempts to do so were defeated by the Italians, and it was through the medium of the Italians that

English trade with the Mediterranean continued to be conducted until the end of the Middle Ages. This western wing of the English commercial system (which for some purposes included Ireland) was matched in importance by the commercial routes which ran to the east and north of Flanders. The English had traded in Scandinavia throughout the Middle Ages, and if their trade there suffered in the fifteenth century, the loss was to some extent compensated by a new extension to Iceland. It was in the late fourteenth and fifteenth centuries, too, that English merchants first penetrated into the Baltic and Prussian lands, and were thus brought face to face with the political and economic machinery of the Hanseatic League.

In the light of this survey it will be plain that only a very incomplete description of English foreign trade is given in this book. In so far as a comprehensive picture is discernible in the Customs Accounts, it has been attempted by Professor H. L. Gray, who suggests an interpretation of the statistical evidence relating to the whole field during a limited period (1446 to 1482). But the other studies are concerned only with isolated sections. The wool trade, still the principal branch of English commerce in Flanders, is described by Professor Power, Mr. Postan's essay on England and the Hanse traces the fortunes of English trade in the Eastern Baltic, and Miss Carus Wilson deals with the Iceland trade; but the trade to Scandinavia still awaits an historian. Even greater is the amount of work which remains to be done before the history of English commerce in the West and South of Europe can be written. In so far as the Mediterranean trade was concerned with wool, it has been touched upon in the above-mentioned essay, and some aspects of the Gascon wine trade and of the Irish trade are investigated in Miss Carus Wilson's study of Bristol; but the French trade as a whole, the Iberian trade, and the commercial relations of England and Italy remain unexplored and largely unexplained.

Turning from foreign to domestic trade, and to those problems concerning the organization and method of domestic and foreign commerce which present so much more difficulty than a mere description of its area and scope, we have been obliged to proceed by the same method of taking samples. Professor Power has analyzed the business organization of the wool trade, both at home and abroad; Miss Carus Wilson has made a regional study of the trade of an important provincial port; Dr. Thrupp has investigated some aspects of distributive trade in London; Mr. Postan has touched upon one side of the evolution of the Merchant Adventurers, and Dr. Haward has sought to elucidate a complicated phase in the relations between the Crown and commercial interests. How many and how important are the problems left untouched will be evident to every student of the period. Further regional studies, the analysis of local and inter-regional trade, the investigation of transport and communications, the explanation of commercial routine and of the financial organization of commerce are all necessary before a satisfactory history of English trade during the later Middle Ages can be written. It is our hope in the course of time to fill some of these gaps ourselves, and some of the necessary investigations are already in process.

It remains only for the editors to express their gratitude to those who have helped them in the preparation of this book. Their chief obligation is to Professor H. L. Gray, without whose collaboration it would have been almost impossible. Finding that their London seminar was working in a field related to that of his own labours, he not only gave its members valuable advice and assistance in the initial phases of their work, but handed over to them the statistical tables which he had compiled for his own purposes from the customs accounts, and acceded to their request to provide those tables with an explanatory introduction, and to contribute an essay on English trade during the period covered by his investigations. Thus the statistical tables for the period 1399 to 1445 have been jointly compiled by the London seminar and those for the period 1446 to 1482 are Professor Gray's own work, as are Appendixes A and B. The thanks of the editors are also due to a member of the seminar, whose work is not here represented by a separate study, Miss Doris Leech. It was hoped to include an essay by Miss Leech, on Anglo-Hanseatic relations during the reign of Richard II, but circumstances have obliged us to postpone its publication to a later volume. Meanwhile her help in the collection of material, compilation of statistics and preparation of the book for the Press has been invaluable, and she has also compiled the index. It is difficult for the editors to imagine what they would have done without her. Finally, our thanks are also due, for help received by various contributors at various times, to Dr. Hubert Hall; to Mr. C. McFarlane; to Mr. A. H. Thomas, Deputy Keeper of the Records of the City of London; to the Worshipful Company of Mercers and to Colonel F. D. Watney, Clerk of the Company; to Mr. L. Hickman Barnes; to the Town Clerk and the Archivist of Bristol; and to the Town Clerks of Hull and Lynn.

It should perhaps be added, in conclusion, that all contributors are individually responsible for the views expressed in their essays. It will be observed that on certain points they are not in entire agreement; but it has been thought best in such cases to allow each contributor complete freedom in the statement of his or her own opinion, and to leave students of the period to judge between them.

EILEEN POWER.
M. M. POSTAN.

STUDIES IN THE HISTORY OF ENGLISH TRADE IN THE FIFTEENTH CENTURY

I

ENGLISH FOREIGN TRADE FROM 1446 TO 1482

§ 1

THE EVIDENCE OF THE CUSTOMS ACCOUNTS

So far as the fortunes of English foreign trade in the fifteenth century resembled the fortunes of one of its branches, the export trade in woollens, they admit of simple description. They take on the aspect of two similar cyclical movements. The first began with a depression appearing at the opening of the century, persisting more or less through the first quarter of it, but succeeded by a recovery which was characteristic of the two or three following decades. This period of prosperous trade, in turn, gave way to a second depression which lasted throughout the third quarter of the century; but, as before, prosperity was restored in the following twenty-five years.[1]

The third of these periods is the one here under consideration. Since it coincides in a measure with the years of conflict known as the War of the Roses, a causal sequence between civil war and declining trade might be inferred. Other causes, however, may have played a part. In any event economic disorder antedated somewhat the first battle of St. Albans and economic restoration antedated Bosworth Field. One explanation of this may be that shortly before 1455 there had been years of ruinous foreign war, while for some time before 1485 there had been years of peace. At least the depression of trade actually began at the time of the opening of the final conflict of the Hundred Years War. To appraise the extent of it, comparison should be made with the last years of the preceding period of prosperity; and, in the same way to appreciate the eventual recovery, conditions at the beginning of the last quarter of the century should be described. The period under survey, therefore, is extended to thirty-six years, reaching backwards and forwards into periods of prosperity.

The final phase of the Hundred Years War opened in the summer of 1449, and was to endure until the autumn of 1453. It had been preceded by five years of truce, dating from Suffolk's arrangement for the marriage of Henry VI with Margaret of Anjou. Although military operations were not entirely suspended after the spring of 1444 (indeed, the occasion was represented to Parliament as furnishing opportunity " to stuffe . . . alle maner Fortresses . . . in the parties of Normandie and Fraunce "[2]), there was an approximation to conditions of peace. In trade, restorative effects were presumably felt at least during the last two years of the truce. These years, Michaelmas, 1446 to Michaelmas, 1448, have, therefore, been chosen as representative normal years of undisturbed trade, so far as any two years of the second quarter of the century may represent such. The exportation of English cloth, for instance, was very like what it had been six years before.[3] The trade of the two years, just because they were years of peace following upon a long period of war, probably reveals the full degree of expansion reached by English foreign commerce in the second quarter of the fifteenth century.

In a study of fluctuating trade the records of single years are usually not so informing as are annual averages based upon the records of a longer period.[4] How many years should be represented by one average depends upon how rapidly the volume of trade fluctuated. In the middle of the fifteenth century averages for from two to five years are best, since a longer period is likely to embrace changes worthy of note. For the thirty-six years under consideration it has, therefore, seemed desirable to ascertan averages for twelve periods, several of them, as it happens, having limits which correspond roughly with periods of political change. In every delimitation of years, here and hereafter, the years referred to extend from Michaelmas to Michaelmas, these termini being imposed by the financial records upon which it is necessary to rely. The averages are given in Appendix A, and the periods may be briefly characterized as follows :—

(1) 1446–1448, years of truce and normal trade.
(2) 1448–1450, years of active fighting in France, ending with the loss of Normandy.
(3) 1450–1453, years marked by expeditions sent to save Guienne, ending with the loss of the province.
(4) 1453–1456, years of the administration of the Duke of York.
(5) 1456–1459, years of the administration of the Queen's party.
(6) 1459–1462, years of sharp civil war, attending the change of dynasty.
(7) 1462–1465, years of exhaustion and of the establishment of the Yorkist régime.
(8) 1465–1469, years of increasingly stable conditions under Yorkist rule.
(9) 1469–1471, years disturbed by the attempted restoration of Henry VI in 1470–1471.
(10) 1471–1476, years of political stability and domestic peace, culminating in treaties with the Hanse and France.
(11) 1476–1479, years reflecting the increase of prosperity under the Yorkists.

(12) 1479–1482, years characterized by the culmination of this prosperity.

The records which furnish continuous data for a study of English foreign trade during these periods are the enrolled customs accounts. Their characteristics and limitations are described elsewhere in this volume.[5] Although, in the appended tables, exports and imports have been tabulated by ports they can equally well, at least for the second half of the century, be arranged by years. For the purpose of this paper such an arrangement has been made; but instead of presenting the results year by year, the averages for the periods indicated above are presented in compact form in Appendix A. The character of the enrolled accounts dictates to a slight degree the delimitation of the periods outlined above, and it entirely determines the method of discussion. Restrictions in delimitation arise because the returns from the ports, although in general extending from Michaelmas to Michaelmas, do not always do so. The periods, for instance, which have been divided from each other in 1476, might well have been divided in 1475. In August, 1475, was signed the treaty of Picquigny with Louis XI of France, and a year earlier the treaty of Utrecht with the Hanse. But it happens that the account for Southampton, always important, disregards Michaelmas, 1475, and runs on for another year. The next Michaelmus thus becomes the preferred point of division apart from the fact that the expansion of trade did become somewhat more noteworthy thereafter than before. At times, accounts which similarly influence totals end awkwardly in the spring. Were it desirable to draw a line between 1478 and 1479, it would be difficult to do so, since the petty customs and the poundage accounts for London end in June, 1478. Irregularities of this sort cause no marked inconvenience if the grouping by years is made as has been indicated. In the third period, to be sure, the London wool account ends in April, 1453, and shipments of wool for 1450–3 are to this extent underestimated. So serious is the irregularity caused by the ending of the London wool account in March, 1471, that the period 1469–71 has been extended, for exports of wool only, to 1469–72. Apart from these instances, awkward endings of accounts for the most part fall within the periods as defined and, since irregularities are thus repaired, the averages become closely representative of prevailing conditions.

While the form assumed by the enrolled accounts does not seriously affect the delimitation of periods, it does determine the information available and sometimes compels the positing of assumptions in order to supplement the record as it stands. For certain branches of trade there is no difficulty whatever. The imposts levied in the fifteenth century required of the records a precise quantitative statement regarding exports of English wool, hides, and broadcloths, and regarding imports of wine and aliens' wax. For the exports in question there was further differentiation between denizen and foreign exporters and, in the case of broadcloths, also between Hanseatic merchants and other aliens. Shipments of hides during the period under consideration were negligible, averaging less than five lasts a year, these being worth about £100.[6] In addition to the broadcloths a certain number of worsteds were shipped abroad, upwards of half of them by denizens and most of them doubles. Along with some 200 singles, the total exportation of doubles in the first half of the period was about 1,000 a year, in the second half of it about 1,800. Since they were worth about 30*s*. each, and the singles about 15*s*. each, both sorts of worsteds will henceforth be dismissed as contributing, inclusive of 500 doubles exported by Hansards, at first some £1,600, and later some £2,900 to the total value of the annual export trade.[7] Far surpassing hides and worsteds in volume were the outstanding exports of England, wool and woollen cloth, regarding both of which the enrolled accounts yield admirable information. Of the two specified imports, wax was a secondary item in English commerce. Since only alien imports of it were noted, the total traffic in it cannot be precisely ascertained; but it is safe to assume that the recorded imports, largely Hanseatic, represented the greater part of the trade. Wine ranked with wool and woollens as a major factor in commerce both in the number and in the value of the tuns imported.

As it happens, the tunnage accounts which record the imports of wine, do not always distinguish denizen from alien importers, but usually content themselves with separating sweet or Malmsey wine [8] from the non-sweet red or white wines of Gascony, France, and the Rhineland. The former, it appears, seldom amounted to more than one-tenth of all wine imported and was brought in almost entirely by aliens; the latter, usually called by the generic term red wine, constituted the bulk of the trade and was imported by denizens as well. To estimate the respective shares of denizens and aliens in the traffic recourse must be had to the accounts of the chief butler. These are at times enrolled with the customs accounts of the period.[9] The record is brief, merely noting that during periods of two or four years the butler received two shillings from every tun of " sweet and red " wine imported by aliens. If we assume that all the sweet wine recorded in the tunnage accounts was brought by aliens and subtract the amount of it from the chief butler's figures, there remains the red wine imported by aliens. This, in turn, subtracted from the tunnage total of red wine, leaves the wine imported by denizens. Tunnage accounts and butlerage accounts, in thus supplementing each other, yield considerable information about the wine trade. Neither, unfortunately, records any distinction between alien importers.[10]

All items of the enrolled customs accounts are not so revealing as are those relating to wool, hides, cloth, wax, and wine, the duties

ENGLISH FOREIGN TRADE

upon which were specific. Upon other commodities the duties were *ad valorem*, and it is in connection with them that perplexities arise. The first of such duties was the petty custom of $3d.$ in the £, levied upon the value of alien exports and imports. Only the commodities just mentioned were exempted. No distinction was made between imports and exports; but from the enrolled accounts of the time of Henry VIII and from the particulars of accounts it is clear that imports greatly predominated. This arose because, apart from wool and cloth, exports from England consisted principally of corn, tin, tallow, and fat, the value of which was small compared with the value of alien imports. During the years 1522-33, when alien exports and imports paying the custom of $3d.$ in the £ were separated from each other in the accounts, exports averaged 10·6 per cent of the combined total.[11] It is not unlikely that something like this percentage was characteristic of the fifteenth century.

While it is desirable to separate alien exports from imports, it is even more important to distinguish between the trade of Hansards and that of other aliens. The latter differentiation is significant in itself and, as will appear, is essential to the determination of the general volume of the trade of denizens. Fortunately the accounts themselves make it during the last seven years of the periods under consideration. These were years following the treaty of Utrecht, which brought to an end in July, 1474 a six-years war between the Hanse and the English government. During the war all trade had been interrupted save such as was carried on by the merchants of Cologne, who kept out of the conflict and whose trade throve at the expense of that of other Hansards. By the terms of the treaty the Hansards, other than those of Cologne, recovered their privileges, and, in lieu of £15,000 assigned them as compensation for injuries, were to be credited with all customs due from their exports until the amount should be paid. The collectors, therefore, entered separately the petty custom of $3d.$ in the £ due from Hansards that it might later be remitted. Since Cologne had continued its trade while the other members of the Hanse were at war, the latter in 1474 demanded the penalization of the seemingly disloyal city. Not until 1478 was it allowed to share in the recovered privileges and trade.[12]

The entries on the enrolled accounts reflect both the restricted trade of the years of war and the provisions of the treaty. The former will be referred to later.[13] The latter account for the separation in the petty customs of the trade of Hansards from that of other aliens during the years Michaelmas, 1474, to Michaelmas, 1482. Since Hanseatic trade was not well restored until after Michaelmas, 1475, the statistics of the last seven years of our period are of most interest. These record that during the first three of the seven the share of the Hanse in shipments of commodities paying the petty custom of $3d.$ in the £ was about 25 per cent of the total valuation (£31,862 out of £128,161), and that during the last four years it increased to about 44 per cent of the corresponding total (£98,462 out of £226,338).[14] Since the first three years, 1475-8, were those during which Cologne merchants were largely excluded from English trade, the last four represent more accurately the normal trade of the Hanse. It would seem permissible, therefore, to assume that this was about 40 per cent of the total alien trade which paid the petty custom of 3d. in the £.[15]

If the Hanseatic share in miscellaneous alien merchandise imported and exported may in general be estimated at 40 per cent, there is no hint in the enrolled accounts as to how much of the remaining 60 per cent should be attributed to Italians and how much to other aliens. The particulars of accounts show that very much of it, rated according to value rather than according to bulk, was Italian. Among other merchants men of the Low Countries predominated, though there were a few Frenchmen and a few Spaniards, the latter increasing in number toward the end of Edward IV's reign. In the following discussion only the distinction between Hansards and other aliens will be attempted.

The second important *ad valorem* tax levied upon exports and imports was the subsidy of poundage. The merchandise subject to it comprised heterogeneous elements, the separating of which from one another necessitates further estimate and computation. Theoretically, poundage was levied on all exports and imports of denizens and aliens saving only wool, hides, and wine. Woollens and worsteds were included; but denizens and Hansards secured exemption for their shipments, leaving only the cloths of non-Hanseatic aliens burdened by the subsidy. The privileges of the Hansards extended further—to the exemption from poundage of all their exports and imports. Denizens and non-Hanseatic aliens continued to pay the subsidy on merchandise other than that mentioned above. The residuum valuation upon which poundage was levied comprised, therefore, three elements: the value of woollens exported by non-Hanseatic aliens; the value of merchandise, other than wool, hides, cloth, and wine, exported and imported by them; and the value of merchandise, with the same exceptions, exported and imported by denizens.

The second of these elements is already familiar as the value of non-Hanseatic merchandise subject to the custom of 3d. in the £, and remaining after the value of Hanseatic merchandise is subtracted from the totals of the petty customs accounts. For the last seven years of our period the value of this Hanseatic merchandise is known; for the other twenty-nine years, it may be estimated at 40 per cent of the total, leaving 60 per cent as the value of non-Hanseatic merchandise. By deducting this in any year from the total poundage valuation, we are left with the two remaining elements comprised therein.

The first of these is the value of broadcloths exported by non-Hanseatic aliens. To ascertain it would seem easy, since the number of such cloths appears in the accounts of the petty customs. But a value must be put upon each cloth and the determination of an appropriate one brings perplexities. It might be expected that the collectors of poundage would have followed the usage of the petty custom in making no distinction between broadcloths other than separating the rare scarlets and cloths of half-grain from cloths without grain. Had they done so, they would have valued all sorts, except the two, at a uniform price. This, however, is what they did not do. Although normally their accounts, like the petty customs accounts, give no detail about the valuation of broadcloths, yet at times, in connection with exemptions granted to persons who would otherwise pay the subsidy, values are noted. These show pretty wide variations and no uniformity as to ports, years, or periods.[16] Occasionally they are as low as £1 the cloth and not infrequently they rise to £3 or even £4. By far the greatest number are a little more or a little less than £2 the cloth. Sixty-eight entries in the enrolled accounts between 1446 and 1482 record the values of 57,193 cloths. The number is large enough to serve as basis for an average and the average value of a cloth works out at £1 15s. 1d.

Most of the entries relate to remissions made upon cargoes exported from London or from Southampton. In general the value of cloths shipped from London was lower than that of cloths shipped from Southampton; and the contrast reappears in a comparison of the entries in the particulars of accounts of the two ports. In the London tunnage and poundage account of 10th June, 1449, to 30th November, 1449, in which forty-two entries record the values of 2,181 cloths, the average value of a cloth is £1 10s. 6d.; and in the Southampton account of Michaelmas, 1443, to Michaelmas, 1444, in which 208 entries record the values of 4,254 cloths, the average rises to £2 6s. 8d.[17] The contrast suggests incidentally that the London market drew heavily upon cheaper stuffs, whether of the west or of the south-east, and supplied foreign markets less exacting than those supplied by Southampton. Entries relative to kerseys and Essex straits, manufactured in East Anglia and Essex, illustrate their relative cheapness. The three kerseys and the four straits, which for the customs were equivalent to a broadcloth,[18] were never rated at more than £2 and often at less. Broadcloths of much this quality, shipped from East Coast ports other than London, were valued at less than 30s., and in one case below £1.[19]

Although Schanz argued that cloths, even before the price revolution of the sixteenth century, should be rated at an average of £3, he scarcely did justice to the precision shown by the enrolled accounts. He seemed to think that their ratings were usually £2 or less.[20] The frequency, however, with which cloths shipped from

Southampton were rated at high prices and the great variety of the valuations here and elsewhere tend to show that the customs officials were attentive to differences in the values of the cloths in each bale before them. None the less, it is permissible to conjecture that the prices of the enrolled accounts, while discriminating, were artificial or antiquated; and to discover whether they did correspond with current prices attention should be given to the ulnage accounts and the valuations which are there assigned to cloths forfeited. Since the farmers of the ulnage shared with the exchequer the proceeds of the sale of these cloths, it is likely that they tried to sell them for the best possible price.

For the years 1432–63, the ulnage returns for London note 190 instances of forfeiture and sale in which the descriptions are precise enough to permit of an estimate of the value of the *pannus*, prices being affixed to *panni*, to dozens, and to yards.[21] The outstanding feature of these entries is the variety of cloths offered for sale and the corresponding diversity of price. The ulnagers realized from 4*d.* to 6*s.* a yard and from 7*s.* to £7 4*s.* 8*d.* a *pannus*. Even the same sort of cloth sold for rather widely divergent prices. Most valuable were cloths called murrey, puke, mustrevillers, and marble, the value of these being usually from 2*s.* to 6*s.* the yard, or above £2 the cloth.[22] The sorts of cloths usually confiscated and sold, however, seldom brought the ulnager more than £2 the cloth, or the equivalent of 20*d* the yard. Cheapest of them apparently were the " russets called Welsh frises " worth from 7*s.* to 16*s.* the *pannus*, 4*s.* the dozen, and 5*d.* to 8*d.* the yard. Very like them was a russet called cogware worth 18*s.* to 20*s.* the *pannus*. Even if these cloths were " straits " of a kind equivalent to only half of a *pannus*, the value of two of them was less than £2. Kerseys varied in value from 8*s.* to 24*s.* 6*d.*, the latter being the price of a red one containing 21 yards. Smaller pieces of kersey brought 8*d.* and 9*d.* the yard for the white, 10*d.* for the black, 13*d.* for the red, and 20*d.* for the crimson. Since kerseys were eighteen yards long,[23] and were equated for the customs at three kerseys to one broadcloth, the value of three sometimes exceeded £2. Perhaps the typical cloths were the white and the red, the *pannus albus* and the *pannus sanguinis coloris*, the latter usually called " blod ". Although there were white cloths valued as low as 5*s.* 9*d.*, and as high as 46*s.* 8*s.*, the usual price was not far from 20*s.*[24] The same was true of white cloths called " Westernes " and " Bastards ", numerous entries valuing white cloth by the yard at from 8*d.* to 16*d.* Cloths of " blod " were worth between £1 and £2, occasionally less than £1. Smaller pieces sold at from 14*d.* to 40*d.* the yard, the average being rather above 20*d.* The " medleys ", red, green, and blue, were worth from 24*s.* to 78*s.* the cloth, and from 16*d.* to 28*d.* the yard. Black cloth " de lire ", or Blakalyre, brought £2 the *pannus*, and from 21*d.* to 28*d.* the yard.

While, therefore, it appears that many cloths, especially the coloured ones, sold in the local market at rather more than £2 the cloth, it is likely that the greater number, especially the white cloths and the russets, brought scarcely so much. Of the 190 specific entries in the ulnagers' accounts of 1432–63, thirty-five indicate a selling price above £2 the cloth, while 155 indicate one below £2. Several of the costly cloths were in the hands of Italians and were thus representative of Italian exports. The cheaper ones were of the sort shipped to northern markets. The evidence of the ulnage accounts thus confirms that of the customs accounts, whether these be particulars or enrollments. In the three groups of records it appears that, while many English cloths, especially those shipped by Italians or from Southampton, were worth more than £2 the cloth, a greater number, including most of the shipments of denizens and Hansards, were worth less than £2. In the computations which follow, therefore, the value of £2 will be adopted for cloths exported by denizens and Hansards, £2 10s. for cloths exported by non-Hanseatic aliens. An immediate use of the latter valuation will be to multiply it by the number of cloths exported annually by non-Hanseatic aliens. The product will be the first element in the annual poundage total, to ascertain which this lengthy discussion about values has been undertaken. Since the second element in the poundage valuation has already been ascertained, we may now proceed to compute the third element.

This third element is the value of denizen exports and imports other than wool, hides, cloth, and wine, and to ascertain it is of fundamental importance in a survey of English trade. Nowhere in the enrolled customs accounts does such a value appear as a recorded item; and nowhere is there ground for an estimate of it save here in the poundage record. A method for determining it has just been sketched, the essence of which is the elimination from poundage values of the two items touching aliens. In practice the method involves (1) subtracting from the value of all merchandise paying poundage 60 per cent of the value of all merchandise paying the petty custom of 3d. in the £, i.e. the value of the merchandise of non-Hanseatic aliens, and (2) subtracting further the value of the broadcloths recorded in the cloth custom as exported by non-Hanseatic aliens and valued by estimate at £2 10s. the cloth. From the annual values of miscellaneous denizen exports and imports so computed, averages have been derived, as they have been in the case of sacks of wool, broadcloths, and tuns of wine, for each of the periods into which our thirty-six years have been divided. These averages, too, are included in Appendix A.

This completes the description of the branches into which the enrolled customs accounts divide English foreign trade of the fifteenth century. The broad divisions of it were the wool trade, the cloth trade, the wine trade, the trade in other and miscellaneous merchandise. Each in turn was subdivided into denizen and alien traffic. Alien traffic again was either Hanseatic or non-Hanseatic, both in the cloth trade and in the trade in general merchandize. In the wool trade all alien shipments were non-Hanseatic, since the Hanse did not ship wool. Estimates are necessary to ascertain the share of each of the three groups of merchants in the wine trade and in the trade in miscellaneous merchandise. The division between exports and imports is automatic in the case of wool, hides, woollens, and wine; but for general merchandise estimates are again necessary, whether the trade be that of denizens or of aliens. So far as the various estimates are valid, the exports and imports of each group of merchants in each branch of trade can be valued and comparison between the trade of the different groups instituted.

§ 2

ENGLISH TRADE DURING THE YEARS 1446 TO 1448

It is best to attempt to make these valuations and comparisons first for years of normal trade. As such the two years, Michaelmas, 1446, to Michaelmas, 1448, have, for reasons already indicated, been selected. Succeeding fluctuations in total values, attendant upon disordered political conditions, will be traced later and some contrasts with normal years will be noted.

Of the branches of English trade, the wool trade was foremost in antiquity, in volume, and in traditional importance. By 1446, however, it had greatly declined from its high estate. For the years 1446-8, the average exportation of wool was only 7,654 sacks, and this despite the extension of the London account to January, 1449. Although a two years' average, the amount is perhaps a slight understatement. Exports of wool have the appearance of fluctuating from year to year rather more than did other exports, a phenomenon due at times to the termination of the account within the financial year rather than at its close. The average of the exports of the next two years was 8,412 sacks; and for each of three succeeding three-year periods 7,760, 9,290, and 7,664 sacks respectively. Throughout the thirteen years, 1446-59, therefore, exports fluctuated above and below 8,000 sacks with considerable regularity, averaging 8,175 sacks. The amount which best represents normal exportation in 1446-8 is thus about 8,000 sacks.

The extent of the decline which had taken place in the wool trade before 1446 is best realized by recalling that, in the days of Edward I and still at the beginning of Edward III's reign, the average annual exportation of wool was about 32,000 sacks. Decline began in the second half of the fourteenth century. After 1363, annual shipments dropped below 30,000 sacks, the average for the years Michaelmas, 1392, to Michaelmas, 1395, falling to 19,359 sacks.[25] During the first half of the fifteenth century the shrinkage was more rapid. From Michaelmas, 1410, to Michaelmas, 1415, annual shipments averaged 13,625 sacks, a decline of 5,700 sacks, and a contraction of 30 per cent in twenty years.[26] A further loss of almost the same number of sacks brings us to 1446.

No precise estimate of the causes of this decline can be undertaken here. In part it may have been due to the effect of warfare upon sheep-raising and upon trade. During the years 1446-82, the exportation of wool, as will appear, twice fell off markedly and each decline coincided with the outbreak of civil war. Neither depression, however, was long continued and, in general, the wool trade suffered little from the disturbed conditions of the period. Its experience in this respect was in contrast with that of the cloth trade, which did suffer severely and for a long time. In the second half of the fourteenth century, also a period of warfare, the experiences of the two had been different; then the wool trade declined while the cloth trade prospered. Again, in the earlier years of Henry VI this happened. The contrasted experience suggests that not warfare primarily but some other cause or causes lay behind the 30,000 sacks of 1363 becoming the 8,000 of 1446.

One contributing factor is, of course, obvious. English wool ceased to go to the Continent in large quantities because it was used at home in the manufacture of cloth. In the second half of the fourteenth century the economic revolution which reduced by one-third the exportation of wool increased ninefold the exportation of broadcloths. The 10,000 sacks of wool which were no longer exported in 1392-5, should, if still produced, have furnished material for the manufacture of perhaps 43,000 pieces of cloth.[27] As a matter of fact about 30,000 more broadcloths were exported annually in these years than had been exported in 1363, when shipments of wool were still 30,000 sacks. If the domestic market absorbed 13,000 cloths, as is not improbable, the production of wool did not fall off noticeably between 1363 and 1392.[28]

After the retrocession in the exports of both wool and woollens in Henry IV's reign, exports of woollens once more rose until in 1437-40 the annual average was 56,000 broadcloths, an amount greater by some 13,000 than in the days of Richard II. Meanwhile, exports of wool had fallen by another 10,000 sacks and more. This shrinkage is difficult to attribute altogether to enhanced industrial activity; for the 13,000 additional woollens exported represented about 3,000 sacks of wool, while an expanding domestic market can scarcely have absorbed the woollens which could have been made from 7,000 sacks. The conclusion seems to be that, although expansion of industry accounted for much of the decline in the exports of wool in the fourteenth century, a restriction of sheep-growing also played a part in the fifteenth century. Whether this in turn was due to a decline in agriculture or to a development of arable farming at the expense of sheep-growing cannot here be discussed.

In 1446-8 about four-fifths of the wool trade, or 6,400 sacks, was in the hands of denizens; for the most part in the hands of the powerful group of Staplers. Italians exported annually about 1,000 sacks on their own account; and in their galleys went upwards of 600 sacks more, shipped by denizens presumably employing Italians as factors. Sometimes such employment is noted; sometimes it is merely said that denizens exported *ad partes exteras*, the phrase *ultra montana* being occasionally added. Custom and subsidy were nearly always imposed at alien rates. Shipments of this sort were characteristic of the later years of Henry VI, favoured licencees being permitted to export wool elsewhere than to Calais with the duty often wholly or in part remitted. Although these exports were nominally made by denizens, and sometimes by the king, alien factors must have been employed and perhaps bought the licences.[29] For this reason and because of the rate of duty imposed, all such shipments have been treated as alien ones. Of denizens' wool some 500 sacks were sent yearly by the burgesses of Newcastle largely to Bruges and Middleburgh. It was the wool of the northern counties and of inferior quality.[30] All remaining shipments were taken by denizens to the Staplers' mart at Calais, there to be sold to continental buyers.

To ascertain the investments of Staplers and of aliens in the English wool trade, it is necessary to determine the average cost of a sack of wool in the middle of the fifteenth century. What was paid the grower may be estimated from a parliamentary petition of 1454, and from the purchases of the Celys at the close of our period. The petition laments the decay of the cloth industry through excessive exportation of wool and would have the situation remedied by requiring that all wool intended for export be bought at an indicated scale of minimum prices. Since the implication is that these prices were not then received, they were, from the growers' and buyers' point of view, maximum prices. According to the schedule, the wool of the south-eastern counties was poorest, being worth from £2 10s. to £4 the sack, that of the midlands and eastern counties of medium quality, worth from £4 to £5 10s., that of Herefordshire, Shropshire, and the Cotswolds best and worth from £8 to £9.[31] The prices were not unlike those paid by the Celys. For Cotswold wool they paid £8, and considered £8 13s. 4d. a "grete pryse". They were content to sell in Flanders the best "Cotts." for £12 13s. 4d., and "Middle Cotts." for £8 13s. 4d., implying that for the latter they had paid considerably less than £8.[32] Without doubt most wool shipped abroad was of either best or medium quality; and shipments of the latter from East Coast ports were large. Probably an average price paid the grower was between £6 and £7. Although Schanz adopted £6, we shall not be far astray if we include expenses of carriage and accept £7 as an average cost of the sack of wool delivered at Calais.[33] In addition to this, denizens paid customs and subsidies amounting to 40*s.* the sack, aliens in normal times, 53*s.* 4*d.* With an average total investment of £9 the sack, merchants like the Celys could afford to sell wool of the best grade to their Flemish customers at £12 13*s.* 4*d.* the sack, and wool of middle grade at somewhat under £9. They must have been content with a profit of £2 to £3 the sack. On the assumption, therefore, that denizens invested on the average of £9 the sack for wool, and aliens £9 13*s.* 4*d.*, the total annual investment of English wool merchants in 1446-8 was about £57,600 for their 6,400 sacks, and of aliens about £15,500 for 1,600 sacks.

The cloth trade stood in such close relations with the wool trade that the volume of the one in 1446-8 may fittingly be contrasted with the volume of the other. At this time the average annual exportation of cloth was 53,700 broadcloths, including perhaps 100 scarlets and cloths of half-grain, and neglecting 200 single worsteds and 1,000 doubles. The value of exported worsteds has already been estimated at £1,600.[34] As the average value of a broadcloth we have adopted £2 for those exported by denizens and Hansards, £2 10*s.* for those exported by non-Hanseatic aliens. Of the export trade in broadcloths, 55 per cent was in the hands of denizens, 21 per cent in the hands of Hansards, and 24 per cent in the hands of other aliens. The total investments of the three groups, including customs charges of £1,700, £600, and £1,700, and including the value of denizen and Hanseatic worsteds, amounted to about £61,800, £23,900, and £33,700 respectively. It may perhaps be permissible to apply in the fifteenth century to English merchants trading in cloth and in various commodities other than wool and hides the generic term Merchant Adventurers; and it will be convenient to designate merchants trading in wool by the generic term Staplers. Employing this abbreviated terminology, we may say that by 1446 the annual investment of Merchant Adventurers in English cloth (£61,800) had come to surpass slightly the investment of the Staplers in exported wool (£57,600). Viewed commercially, the outcome of the industrial revolution of the preceding hundred years was the creation of a second powerful group of merchants, a fraction of whose trade was already the largest item in English commerce.[35] The other fractions of it were the wine trade and the trade in miscellaneous commodities, in both of which, as in the cloth trade, they had alien competitors.

As has been noted, the tunnage accounts give an incomplete view of the wine trade, but can be supplemented by the accounts of the chief butler. Tunnage was paid during the years Michaelmas, 1446, to Michaelmas, 1448, on an average importation by denizens and aliens of 10,234 tuns of red wine, and on an average importation by aliens of 766 tuns of sweet wine. From the butlerage accounts, it appears that the average total importation of both red and sweet wine by aliens during the four years Michaelmas, 1446, to Michaelmas, 1450, was 1963 tuns.[36] Since the period comprises two years characterized by war, the average is probably lower than it would have been for the first two years alone; and the same account reveals that for the eight preceding years the average was 2,150 tuns or for the last six of them 2,814. It is best, therefore, to assume that the average alien importation of wine in times of peace or truce was about 2,500 tuns. Since some 800 tuns of this were sweet wine, the red wine imported by aliens must have been about 1,700 tuns annually. In contrast, the remaining red wine imported during 1446–8, constituting as it did the denizen share in the trade, amounted to about 8,500 tuns or some five times the share of aliens.

The contrast between the value of denizen imports of red wine and the value of alien imports of both red and sweet wine was somewhat less marked. Values of red and of sweet wine are recorded in household accounts of 1446–53, but by no means at an unvarying price per tun. In the account of household stores noted at the beginning of each year and in the record of wine given to religious houses or to officials whose perquisites included wine, the value per tun is entered as £5 14s. 10d. or £5 9s. 4½d. Malmsey wine was valued at twice as much, £5 15s. the butt. From these entries alone we should be led to value red wine at £5 10s. the tun. In the same household accounts, however, there are other entries recording sales by the chief butler of a part of the wine which he was privileged to pre-empt from native merchants at the rate of £1 the tun. For this wine he received prices varying from £3 to £4 10s. during the years 1446–53.[37] The price was lowest before the loss of Guienne and rose thereafter. These must have been the market prices for wine of ordinary grade, whereas the wine of the royal cellars, probably of superior quality, was rated much higher. In 1478, a petition to king and council touches upon the sale of 16 tuns of the red wine of Gascony by Bordeaux merchants to John Hall of Salisbury at £4 the tun.[38] It may not be wide of the mark to choose £4 the tun as an average price for red wine and £8 the tun as the corresponding price for sweet wine.[39] Since these were prices in the English market they included costs of transportation and customs charges. Adopting them, we find that the average annual value of denizen imports of wine in 1446–8 was about £34,000, that of alien imports, both red and sweet, about £12,900.[40]

To determine the third item in the trade of the Merchant Adventurers, viz. the value of commodities other than wool, hides, cloth, and wine, recourse has been had to the enrolled accounts of poundage. The poundage totals yield this item if there is subtracted

ENGLISH FOREIGN TRADE

from the value of all commodities paying poundage the value of non-Hanseatic alien exports of cloth and of other merchandise. Cloths exported annually by non-Hanseatic alien merchants in 1446–8 were worth, apart from customs, about £32,000, if valued at £2 10s. the cloth. Other merchandise exported by them, it has been estimated, was 60 per cent of all alien merchandise paying the petty custom of 3d. in the £. Since this total in 1446–8 averaged £54,484, the non-Hanseatic share was about £32,700. The two items to be subtracted from the poundage of 1446–8 are, therefore, £32,000 and £32,700. Inasmuch as the value of all commodities, both alien and denizen, paying poundage in these years averaged £121,800, there remains as the value of denizen trade in miscellaneous commodities £57,100. If to this, as well as to the non-Hanseatic miscellaneous trade of £32,700, is added the 5 per cent customs charge for poundage, the total investments become £60,000 and £34,300 respectively.

Before drawing final conclusions regarding the total trade of the Merchant Adventurers, it is necessary to inquire whether this trade may properly be juxtaposed to the wool trade; for it is possible that wool merchants may have been also exporters of cloth, importers of wine, or exporters and importers of miscellaneous merchandise. To ascertain to what extent they were it is necessary to turn for a moment to the particulars of accounts. In so far as these reveal in any year the individual merchants engaged in each branch of trade, a comparison of names and shipments should furnish the information desired, provided all traders were active in the year in question. Unfortunately the particulars of accounts in the fifteenth century are too fragmentary to permit of precise comparison. Seldom does there survive a satisfactory account from any port extending over precisely a year. From London, however, accounts are intact which enable us to ascertain approximately the names of London merchants engaged in the four branches of trade in certain years between 1438 and 1450.

Exporters of wool are enumerated in the particulars of the wool account of London for Michaelmas, 1439 to Michaelmas, 1440.[41] Sixty-five shippers are noted, but twenty-seven of them shipped fewer than three sacks of wool each. These small traders were probably not Staplers, and may be disregarded.[42] Although some of the remaining thirty-eight may likewise not have been Staplers, most of them probably were. Except for a half-dozen, they shipped upwards of ten sacks of wool each, and twenty-six of them exported more than forty sacks each. This list of thirty-eight wool-merchants, largely Staplers, may be supplemented by the names of undoubted London Staplers, who in October, 1449, and March, 1450, received writs ensuring payment of two loans which they had made to the crown. Eight of the creditors had been exporters of wool ten years earlier, but twenty names were new. Thus fifty-eight men shipping wool from London in the years 1439–50, are identified. Exporters of English cloth are enumerated in the particulars of the petty customs of Michaelmas, 1438, to Michaelmas, 1439, an account antedating by a year the wool account just described. Finally, exporters and importers of miscellaneous merchandise and importers of wine are set down at great length in the London particulars of tunnage and poundage for the year Michaelmas, 1442, to Michaelmas, 1443.[43] Thus three London particulars of accounts, falling within the five years 1438–43, furnish information pertinent to our inquiry.

From a comparison of the three it appears that nine denizens, each shipping more than three sacks of wool to Calais in 1439–40, engaged in other branches of trade as well. In addition, commodities other than wool were imported and exported by three Staplers, who in 1439–40 shipped no wool from London, but in 1449–50 loaned money to the king. They were William Cantelowe, Robert Horne, and John Malvern. Perhaps in 1439 they were not yet members of the Staple or exporters of wool. If, however, they were, but for some reason shipped no wool from London in 1439–40, their shipments other than wool may be added to those of the nine merchants who did ship wool in that year. The shipments of the twelve were as follows :—

	Exports.			Imports.
	Cloths. No.	Misc. Commods. Value. £ s. d.	Wine. Tuns.	Misc. Commods. Value. £ s. d.
Badby, Thos.	—	—	—	9 0 0
Bolle, Jo.	9	4 15 0	15	99 12 5
Cattsworth, Thos.	—	—	—	25 0 0
Felde, Jo.	83	—	—	139 16 8
Holt, Wm.	—	7 10 0	—	—
Johnson, Alan	11	11 3 4	14	45 12 6
Olney, Jo.	3	14 10 0	—	160 0 0
Selby, Rich.	—	—	11	—
Sharp, Rich.	40	3 8 4	—	—
Cantelowe, Wm.	9	—	—	—
Horne, Robt.	87	—	—	202 0 0
Malvern, Jo.	26	60 16 8	—	111 1 4
Total	268	102 3 4	40	792 2 11

Four of these wool merchants, it appears, trafficked in commodities other than wool only within a limit of £25, or less than the value of three exported sacks of wool. The annual trade of each of the eight others averaged 32 cloths, 5 tuns of wine, and miscellaneous commodities worth £100, a total investment of about £200. To view these shipments in their proper light, however, they should be compared with the total trade of all denizens in similar commodities. Such denizen totals, as we now know them, averaged in 1446–8, 29,633 broadcloths, 8,740 tuns of wine, and miscellaneous commodities worth £57,100. Expressed in percentages, the trade of the twelve wool merchants together amounted to about ·9 per cent, ·4 per cent, 1·6 per cent respectively of these totals. If the percentages are increased, because wool merchants in ports other than London may sometimes have shipped commodities other than wool, they still remain small. Despite the somewhat restricted character of our data, therefore, it seems safe to conclude that, in general, the share of wool merchants in the exportation and importation of commodities other than wool in the middle of the fifteenth century was not much more than 2 per cent of the total.[44] The Staplers restricted their ventures almost entirely to shipments of wool.

It is, therefore, possible to juxtapose the trade of English woolmerchants, largely Staplers, with that of other exporting and importing Englishmen, designated briefly as Merchant Adventurers. Men of the former group trafficked to only a small degree in commodities shipped by men of the latter. Another aspect of English foreign trade, however, has to be kept in mind in making this juxtaposition; for the Staplers, while not to any extent investing in the import trade, yet did indirectly facilitate the conduct of it. This they were able to do as a result of the part played in English foreign commerce by instruments of credit, primarily by bills of exchange. Although purchases and sales abroad, owing to deferred payments and widely scattered markets, were in fact somewhat complex, the principles involved were simple. Staplers, having bought wool in England and having sold it abroad at a profit, stood ready to repeat the venture as soon as their money could be returned to them. At times the government required that a part of the returns should be paid into the mint in the form of bullion; but the regulation could not always be well enforced. To a large extent the returns from sales of wool came back to the Staplers indirectly, precisely as would happen in modern trade. Importing merchants borrowed Staplers' money abroad, invested it in commodities to be imported, and repaid their creditors in England, using therefor the proceeds from the sales of their imports. Actually these transactions were carried on through the sale and purchase of bills of exchange. Richard Cely had his money given over " be exschange to mersers . . .".[45] Had the Staplers themselves seen fit to utilize the available returns from their sales of wool in the purchase of imports, the amount of capital so invested would have to be subtracted from the total value of the import trade and combined with the value of their exports to indicate the extent to which they carried on English foreign commerce. Inasmuch as they did not but preferred to lend their money to importing merchants,[46] the latter may be credited with almost all the denizen import trade, as the men whose enterprise made it possible.

With a differentiation between Staplers and Merchant Adventurers established, we may, at length, glance at the relation existing in 1446–8 between the investments of the four groups of merchants who carried on English foreign trade. These relations will become clearer if they are considered from the point of view of exports and imports, and such a consideration will make possible inferences regarding the actual balance of trade. In the following table the values of exports and imports have been set down both with and without the customs imposed upon them, so that a purely commercial balance of trade appears in the second group of figures. At one point an estimate has been necessary. Inasmuch as the collection of poundage involved no distinction between exports and imports, the customs accounts do not trouble to separate the value of exported miscellaneous commodities from that of imported miscellaneous commodities. Actually imports greatly predominated, and exports may be estimated at as little as £4,000 for denizens, £2,000 for Hansards, and £5,000 for other aliens.[47]

VALUE OF THE EXPORT AND OF THE IMPORT TRADE, 1446 TO 1448.

			Including Customs. £	Without Customs. £	Customs. £
Staplers . . .	Exports.	Wool	£57,600	£44,800	£12,800
Merchant Adventurers.	Exports.	Cloth	61,800	60,100 [48]	1,700
		Misc. Mdse.	4,200	4,000 [50]	200
		Total	£123,600	£108,900	
	Imports.	Wine	34,000	32,700	1,300
		Misc. Mdse.	55,800	53,100 [50]	2,700
		Total	£89,800	£85,800	
Hansards . . .	Exports.	Cloth	23,900	23,300 [49]	600
		Misc. Mdse.	2,000	2,000 [50]	
		Total	£25,900	£25,300	
	Imports.	Misc. Mdse.	20,100	19,800 [50]	300
		Wax . .	1,000	1,000	
		Total	£21,100	£20,800	
Non-Hanseatic Aliens.	Exports.	Wool	15,500	11,200	4,300
		Cloth	33,700	32,000	1,700
		Misc. Mdse.	5,300	5,000 [50]	300
		Total	£54,500	£48,200	
	Imports.	Wine	12,900	12,400	500
		Misc. Mdse.	29,400	27,700 [50]	1,700
		Total	£42,300	£40,100	£21,800

As between Staplers and Merchant Adventurers it appears that, if customs charges are included, the investment of the latter in the export trade was slightly the greater, and that, apart from customs, it was considerably the greater. Since practically all of the import trade is to be ascribed to Merchant Adventurers, some three-fourths of all denizen trade was in their hands. For imports they utilized the Staplers' capital as well as their own, but their own was the larger in amount. In comparison with the Hansards they expended more than twice as much annually in the export trade and perhaps four times as much in the import trade. In comparison with non-Hanseatic aliens they invested somewhat more in the export trade and twice as much in the import trade. In comparison with the three groups combined, they carried on one-third of the export trade and more than one-half of the import trade.

No emphasis should be placed upon precisely the figures given above as representing the value of denizen and alien exports and imports in 1446–8. All of them depend in some degree upon estimates. Such are the estimates of current prices of wool, cloth, wine, and wax, the estimate of the respective shares of Hansards and of non-Hanseatic aliens in the trade in commodities paying the petty custom of $3d.$ in the £, and the estimate of what fraction of the trade of denizens, Hansards, and other aliens in miscellaneous commodities was export trade and what fraction was import trade. A change in any of these estimates would change one or more of the valuations; and new information may easily prove an estimate incorrect. Any changes necessitated, however, would not be far-reaching, and would not invalidate the general conclusions reached. Of these the most significant is the ascertaining of the share of the English Merchant Adventurers in the trade of 1446–8. The extent of this, both absolute and relative, was the outstanding feature of English commerce at the moment. It had probably been in large measure the development of a century or even of a half-century; and it marks the period of the Hundred Years War as the creator of a new commercial aristocracy in England more important to the trade of the country than Staplers, Hansards, or Italians, and almost as enterprising as all of them combined.

To estimate the balance of trade as between the exports and imports of denizens and of aliens, the values already assigned to commodities may be retained. Although merchants' profits enhanced the actual receipts of both exporters and importers, it must be assumed that these profits respectively balanced each other, and that the lower purchase prices furnish a basis for an estimate of trade balances. It will be best, also, to consider the commercial balances apart from customs paid by each group, as these have been noted in the table given above.

The export trade of denizens comprised shipments of wool valued at £44,800, of cloth valued at £60,100, and of miscellaneous commodities valued conjecturally at £4,000. The total was £108,900. The denizen import trade comprised cargoes of wine valued at £32,700, and of miscellaneous commodities valued at £53,100. The total of £85,800 left a favourable balance of £23,100. Similar balances characterized the trade of Hansards and that of other aliens. To the cloths exported by Hansards and valued at £23,300, may be added a conjectural £2,000 as the value of their other exports. To their imports of miscellaneous commodities worth £19,800 (if the £2,000 is correct) is to be added £1,000 as the value of their imported wax.[51] The export balance was thus £4,500. Non-Hanseatic aliens exported wool and cloth worth respectively £11,200 and £32,000, together with miscellaneous commodities worth perhaps £5,000, a total of £48,200. The value of their imports of miscellaneous commodities was £27,700 (if £5,000 is attributed to exports), and of wine £12,400, the total being £40,100. Again there was a favourable balance, this time of £8,100.

In the trade of denizens and in that of both groups of aliens, the balances of trade were thus favourable export ones, the total of the three amounting to £35,700. It may be, of course, that the values adopted for exported wool and cloth are too high, and that for this reason the estimated balance is too favourable.[52] Another explanation, however, is possible, one arising from the political situation of the time. In 1446–8 the English government was maintaining garrisons in France and in preceding years had waged war there as well. Calais alone cost £9,000 a year, and other military expenditure amounted to more than as much again. Not only was it assumed that a part of the customs revenue should be used for the defence of the realm, but for some years parliament had added for the protection of the continental conquests the half of a tenth and fifteenth, amounting to some £15,000 annually. In addition, half of a clerical tenth, yielding perhaps £7,000, was usually granted. In general, therefore, the government may have expected to use on the continent upwards of £20,000 a year. A glance at the table shows that customs due from the export and import trade amounted each year to about £28,100. Military needs in France, therefore, could have been met by an expenditure equivalent to perhaps three-fourths of the total customs revenue. This in turn, paid by denizen and alien merchants, was well within the trade balance estimated above. An explanation, therefore, of the use to which the trade balance was put might be that it served the government, through the medium of customs payments, for the maintenance of English garrisons and troops in France.

§ 3

History of the Trade during the Period 1448 to 1482

We are at length in a position to examine the fortunes of the trade of each of the four groups of merchants during the last five years of the French war, the succeeding civil war, and the years of political stabilization under Edward IV. The periods into which the thirty-four years may be divided have already been indicated. The earlier of them will presumably be periods of declining trade, the later periods of recovery. In Appendix A averages by periods are given for the outstanding subdivisions of the customs accounts, viz. the wool trade, the cloth trade, the wine trade, the foreign trade subject to the petty custom of 3*d*. in the £, and the trade subject to the payment of poundage. To utilize the last item, the value of denizen trade incorporated therein has been extracted from it in accordance with the assumptions indicated above, and has been averaged and noted by periods as have the other items. Apart from the union of Hanseatic and non-Hanseatic merchandise in the petty customs entry, two groups which have to be separated by inference except during the last seven years, the table summarizes pretty well the course of English trade from 1446 to 1482.

Most stable perhaps of all its branches throughout the thirty-six years was the wool trade, although on two ocasions it, too, manifested momentary sensitiveness to civil war. It showed no decline until after Michaelmas, 1459. Up to that time it fluctuated, as has been noted, in cycles of two or three years with annual averages ranging from 7,700 to 9,300 sacks. This was only a slight deviation from the 8,000 sacks which appear to have been normal in 1446–8. Of the total, aliens shipped during 1448–53 about 1,200 sacks yearly, but during the next six years twice as much (an average of 2,557 sacks). At this time they acted more extensively than before as alien factors of denizens or of the king.[53]

During the years Michaelmas, 1459, to Michaelmas, 1462, years of sharp civil war, the wool trade shrank to what was probably its lowest ebb during the century. Exports fell to an average of 5,000 sacks annually. The accounts show that there was an almost entire suspension of the trade during the ten months before August, 1460, at which time the Yorkists came into control. In the next year there was a forwarding of retarded shipments,[54] but the number of sacks dropped off again a year later. Aliens suffered as did denizens, their shipments declining to an average of 859 sacks during the three years.

The first recovery came in 1462–5, when exports rose to an average of 7,000 sacks. This in turn was a prelude to the noteworthy advance of the years 1465–9, when the annual average became 9,316 sacks. Shipments of this magnitude were a tribute to the Yorkist policy of providing well for the security of Calais and of ensuring to the Staplers a safe and garrisoned market. It was in 1466 that final form was given to the policy by setting apart £10,000 annually from the wool custom and from Calais tolls and rents to maintain the garrison there, and by providing that the money pass directly from the merchants to the treasurer and victualler of Calais.[55]

The warfare of Michaelmas, 1469, to Michaelmas, 1471, attendant upon the restoration of Henry VI, depressed the wool trade somewhat, but less than might have been expected. During Michaelmas, 1469, to Michaelmas, 1470, exports were still at their best with a total of 9,600 sacks. The London account for the next year ends in March, a circumstance contributing to the apparently remarkable shrinkage of exports to 1,560 sacks. Shipments belonging in this year appear in the following year, the total exports of the latter becoming 12,275 sacks. The nature of the accounts thus force us to employ an average for three rather than for two years, and this average for Michaelmas, 1469, to Michaelmas, 1472, was 7,811 sacks. What the second civil war meant to the wool trade, therefore, was a contraction of some 1,500 sacks from its recent prosperity and a return to the condition of the fifties. The economic shock was much less severe than that of 1459–62, both in the degree of the depression (a decline of 1,500 sacks instead of 3,000), and in the level to which exports fell (to 7,800 sacks instead of to 5,000).

Once more the rebound was prompt and this time somewhat better sustained. It carried the annual average for the years 1472–6 to 9,091 sacks, nearly to where it had been before the recent warfare. During the next three years the average fell again to the level of 7,500 sacks, only to recover once more to 9,784 in the last three years of Edward's reign.

What may be called the cyclical character of the wool trade is noteworthy. Just as exports fluctuated during the last thirteen years of Henry VI's reign in periods of two or three years, the averages of which were alternatively about 7,700 and 8,400–9,300 sacks, so under Yorkist rule, after the three lean initial years, cycles of three or four years show successively averages of 7,044, 9,316, 7,811, 9,091, 7,502, and 9,784 sacks. These are fluctuations of from 1,000 sacks below to 1,700 sacks above 8,000; and, indeed, the average annual exportation for the last twenty years of the reign was 8,448 sacks. If the three preceding years of civil war are included, the average for twenty-three years was 8,074 sacks. Hence, despite the rise and fall of the curve of period averages, the median of the wool trade remained under Edward pretty much what it had been in the last years of Henry VI. A difference, however, appears in that thrice, when political circumstances favoured, exports rose during periods of three or four years to a level of more than 9,000 sacks. They had only once thus risen in the later years of Henry VI. It is correct, therefore, to say that, after twenty years of Yorkist rule, wool merchants were in general exporting 9,000 sacks annually instead of the 8,000 of the last decade of the Lancastrians. To this extent, at least, Edward IV's government not only repaired the damages of civil war but put the wool trade on a firmer basis than the one on which it rested at the end of the Hundred Years War.[56]

Among wool merchants it was, on the whole, the Staplers rather than Italians who profited by the new régime. Alien exports of wool had dropped from an average of 1,329 sacks in 1446–53 and from one of 2,557 sacks in the six years following to one in 859 in 1459–62. They never recovered the larger volume. Instead, they declined further to an average of 515 sacks in the next three years. But they rose at once thereafter for four years to a level of 1,250 sacks a year;

and, after the depression of 1469-72, they continued for six years at 1,000-1,100 sacks until in the last three years of the reign they rose to 1,456 sacks. With respect to alien shipments of wool, therefore, Edward's reign, for the most part, differed little from the last thirteen years of that of his predecessor. In both periods 1,200 sacks a year was often the normal exportation. From 1454 to 1459 it was exceeded, probably because the government leaned heavily upon foreigners; and in 1480-2 a similar increase was probably due to the general expansion of trade which affected all traders and all commodities. Relatively, however, denizens were the beneficiaries of whatever expansion occurred; and, if it may be said that exports of wool in general rose during the reign of Edward IV from 8,000 to upwards of 9,000 sacks, it should be added that denizen exports rose from 6,400 to nearly 8,000 sacks.

The fortunes of the cloth trade during our period differed considerably from those of the wool trade; for they were depressed more quickly, more violently, and for a much longer time. The figures of the appendix show that the depression had taken place at least before 1450. The exports of broadcloths, which in 1446-8 were nearly 54,000 annually, averaged for the next two years only 35,000. It was a decline of 35 per cent. This severe restriction of the most valuable branch of English foreign trade continued with little relief, and sometimes with added severity, for twenty-eight years—until 1476. Exports sometimes averaged a little more than 35,000 woollens, often somewhat less. Only in the last six years of the reign did they take a decisive turn for the better.

In the cloth trade it is possible to distinguish the respective activities of denizens, Hansards, and other aliens, but in the last group not possible to distinguish those of Italians from those of other non-Hanseatic aliens. As between the distinguishable groups, the share of denizens in the trade of 1446-8 was 55 per cent, that of Hansards 21 per cent, that of other aliens 24 per cent. In the last three years of our period, 1479-82, years characterized by a restoration of the cloth trade, the respective shares were 59 per cent, 22 per cent, and 19 per cent. The close similarity of the percentages, separated from each other by some thirty years, suggests that they represent the normal division of the trade in time of peace between the three groups of traders. Divergences from them in the intervening years are likely to have arisen through peculiar circumstances affecting one group more than another.

On the whole such divergences were relatively slight; which is equivalent to saying that all traders suffered in much the same way. Nevertheless, there were divergences. The share of denizens in the cloth trade at one time dropped to 50 per cent of all exported cloths, at another, rose to 64 per cent; the share of the Hansards at one time rose to 31 per cent, at another, fell to 11 per cent; the share of non-Hanseatic aliens fluctuated between 14 per cent and 32 per cent of the total. There is not sufficient correspondence between these fluctuations and the fluctuations of the cloth trade in general to indicate that one group always suffered in the blackest years more acutely or less acutely than did the others. In the three unfavourable years 1459-62, for example, the share of denizens was only 50 per cent, but for the next three equally unfavourable years their share was 59 per cent. It is best, therefore, to glance at the fortunes of each group of traders and then endeavour to explain them.

In 1446-8, denizens exported annually 29,633 broadcloths, worth presumably £59,300. During the two following years the annual average dropped to 18,774 cloths, and for the next nine years fluctuated around 20,802. Throughout the three years of civil war, 1459-62, and the three years following, the annual average fell once more, this time to 15,614 cloths, about one-half of the normal exportation and the worst showing of the Merchant Adventuers. In the years 1465-9, the average rose to 22,000,[57] then dropped back for two years to 17,532, rose again for five years to 25,000,[57] and in the last years of the reign became for three years 33,000, and for another three 36,728. In general, it may be said that for twenty-two years exports were not far from 20,000 cloths, for the six worst years 15,600, and for the last six years of Edward's reign were, at first, a little above the average of 1446-8, and then 7,000 cloths above it. The value of the exports of cloth of the Merchant Adventurers after 1448, therefore, became for many years about £40,000, at one time dropped to £31,000, but finally recovered to £66,000, and then to £73,000.

Broadcloths exported by Hansards in 1446-8 averaged 11,289. In 1448-50 this number was reduced by nearly one-half, a loss of trade relatively greater than the concurrent losses of denizens or non-Hanseatic aliens, and one not recovered until after 1453. For the nine years 1453-62, however, a period of general decline for other branches of trade, the average rose to about 10,000 cloths, approaching its pre-war standard. Gradually during the years 1462-8 it fell away to between 6,000 and 7,000 cloths, and then dropped until it was scarcely more than 3,000 for the next seven years. Thereafter a prompt recovery for four years brought the average to 9,400 cloths, and a final advance in the last three years of the reign carried it to 13,900.

Non-Hanseatic aliens, for the most part Italians and Dutchmen, were exporting, in 1446-8, 12,777 woollens annually. After the outbreak of war the number declined only moderately, and for eight years annual exports averaged 9,200 cloths. After 1456, however, they fell away for six years to an average of 5,500 cloths, and then for the years 1462-5 to 3,420, their lowest point. As soon, however, as Edward began to exploit the cloth trade for his own advantage, the Italians, shipping nominally for him and for other denizens as well as professedly for themselves, brought the non-Hanseatic average for 1465-9 to 12,642 cloths, precisely what it had been in 1446-8.

During the two following years of civil war it was reduced to one-half this amount, only to rise again from 1471–6 to 13,481, its highest point. At the end of the reign it became for three year 9,704 woollens and for three more 11,951, the last only 1,000 cloths below the level of 1446–8. On the whole, the non-Hanseatic alien cloth trade suffered for a shorter time than did that of denizens or even that of Hansards. Although it was reduced to less than one-half its accustomed volume for six years, and to less than one-third of it for three years, it was, during the remaining twenty-three years, seldom below 75 per cent of the level of 1446–8, and was often on a par with this or above it.

From the fact that the cloth trade as a whole was greatly depressed from 1448 to 1476, a depression in which the three branches of it shared, although in varying degrees, it might seem that the fundamental cause was the French war which was resumed with vehemence in 1449, and the civil war which followed. It will be recalled, however, that the wool trade was not at all depressed by the outbreak of the war. Until 1459, it showed no falling away from the exports of 1446–8, and, except for 1459–62, little recession at any time from that total. Are we to conclude that the cloth trade was the more sensitive barometer of the disorder attendant upon war and the loss of continental possessions? Was a trade dependent upon agriculture more stable than one dependent upon industry? Or were there other influences which affected one trade but not the other?

An outstanding difference between the trade in wool and that in cloth in the fifteenth century lay in the conditions under which each commodity was marketed. Except for Italian shipments, wool was sold to continental buyers by Englishmen at Calais, a mart in English possession, and professedly cherished by the government. In contrast, cloth, sold on the continent by aliens as extensively as by Englishmen, was marketed in regions extending from Prussia round the western coast of Europe to Italy. This outspread and unprotected market-area was more exposed to disturbance than was the concentrated and sheltered wool market at Calais with its supplementary Italian trade. The larger markets for English cloth were the Baltic regions, especially Prussia and Poland, the Low Countries and the lower Rhine, finally northern France and Guienne. It happened that, during the period 1448–76, not only was Guienne lost to England, but the markets of the Baltic and of the Low Countries were unsettled through political dissentions. The condition of the three market areas should therefore be noted in assessing responsibilities for the decline in the cloth trade.

From our export figures it is not possible to ascertain at all precisely what was the condition of each of these markets at a given time. The Baltic and Netherlandish markets were served by both denizens and Hansards, and the latter by non-Hanseatic Dutchmen as well. We should expect to find disturbances of the Baltic trade reflected in the exports of denizens, but more particularly in the exports of Hansards. The latter may, therefore, be scrutinized with this in mind. Disturbances in the market of the Low Countries were reflected imperfectly, but perhaps better than elsewhere, in the exports of denizens from London; for, although London exporters of cloth supplied German markets as well, any considerable stoppage of their Burgundian trade could not fail to reveal itself in smaller export totals. Denizen exports of cloth from London may, therefore, be taken tentatively as indicative of conditions in the Netherlandish markets. Lastly, the fortunes of the Guienne trade should appear in denizen exports of the South Coast ports from Southampton to Bristol. Hansards seldom trafficked in these ports and Italians carried their cloths to the Mediterranean. A scrutiny of the cloth trade of the Hansards, of denizens from the port of London, and of denizens from the ports of the South Coast respectively, should reveal roughly to what extent unsettled conditions in the Baltic market, in the Netherlandish market, and in the Guienne market, contributed to the decline of the English cloth trade.

In the late forties there developed one of the many crises in the rivalry between English and Hanseatic merchants. The slow but constant deterioration of the political situation in England, reacting upon the anti-Hanseatic agitation in Parliament and elsewhere, led first to the English ultimata of 1442 and 1446, and then to the suspension of the Hanseatic privileges in 1447 and the capture of the Bay fleet in 1449. It was only with difficulty and after a whole year of disturbances in foreign trade that a prospect of settlement appeared again. The High Master of the Prussian Order vetoed the proposals of other parts of the Hanse, and above all of Lübeck, for violent reprisals. It is true that his attempts at separate negotiations with England came to nothing and true also that throughout the fifties Lübeck persisted in its opposition to England; by arrangement with Denmark it closed the Sund to English shipping, and prohibited the passage of English cloth to the East. Nevertheless the crisis seemed to be getting less acute as the fifties drew to an end. The other parts of the Hanse were showing every sign of an accommodating temper. The Prussians, ever since the abortive attempts at separate negotiations with England in 1451, had continued to be friendly disposed and to maintain the English trade. The same is true, in a still greater measure, of the English trade with the Western towns and especially with Cologne. In the end Lübeck had to give way and raise the embargo in 1454 and subsequently trade could continue under the eight years' truce proclaimed in 1456.[58]

These dissentions and their provisional settlement are reflected in the export of cloth by Hansards from East Coast ports. Such exports, which amounted to 13,157 cloths from Michaelmas, 1446, to Michaelmas, 1447, declined in the following year, during the winter of which Hanseatic privileges in England were suspended, to 9,421 cloths, and in the two following years, affected by the Bay capture, to 5,929. For the next three years the average did not rise above 7,420.

In 1453, when the acuteness of the crisis had passed away, exports somewhat expanded again, and for the nine years 1453-62 the average became 10,000 cloths. It thus seems clear that the cause of the decline in the English cloth trade for five years after 1448 was the dispute with the Hanse, and that the partial healing of the latter in the late fifties contributed a great deal to the partial restoration of this branch of the trade for almost a decade.

In 1462 the renewal of agitation against Hanseatic privileges again disturbed the relations of England and the Hanse and in 1468 the arrests of Hanseatic goods under the famous " verdict " of the Council very nearly produced a complete cessation of trade.[59] During the six years exports of cloth averaged 6,000-7,000, and after 1468 declined during the six years of war to scarcely more than 3,000 cloths. That exports were maintained even to this extent was due to the schism within the Hanse whereby the Cologne branch refused to join in the conflict. The accounts for the six years attribute exports not to Hansards but to merchants of Cologne. With the treaty of July, 1474, intercourse was slowly resumed, and, after a year, Hanseatic exports rose to an average of 9,133 cloths for three years and then to one of 13,907 in 1479-82. Under Edward IV as under Henry VI, dissention with Hansards was thus responsible for a restriction of the Hanseatic cloth trade amounting at times to 4,000-8,000 cloths. Inasmuch as denizen trade to Baltic regions must have suffered correspondingly,[60] a noteworthy share in the general decline of the cloth trade between 1448 and 1475 must be attributed to conflict with the Hanse.

In 1448 the trade in English cloth encountered other difficulties, probably as serious for a time as the misunderstandings with the Hanse. The parliament of the spring of 1449, complaining that for some time English cloth had been excluded from Brabant, Holland, and Flanders, asked that merchandise from these countries be excluded from England unless " due contynuell reformation be made " before Michaelmas next, the ordinance to endure until the next parliament. The king assented, but by the next parliament no " reformation " had been made. Consequently, in the summer of 1450 parliament petitioned and secured that the retaliatory measures be continued for seven years unless redress were offered earlier.[61]

Some sort of understanding with Burgundy seems to have been reached in 1451. By writ of 2nd June of that year collectors of customs were instructed to remit the subsidy on wool to certain Staplers who had advanced a loan of £2,000 to be paid to the Duke. Payment had been made to recover English merchandise in Burgundy arrested because of the seizure by Englishmen of two Burgundian ships.[62] If the loan may be regarded as one feature of a settlement, we may infer that early in 1451 Burgundy was again to some degree open to English cloth.

Denizen exports of cloth from London, which we have assumed

to be roughly indicative of the prosperity of the Netherlandish trade, seem to confirm this surmise. In ten months of the year Michaelmas, 1446, to Michaelmas, 1447, these exports were 8,827 cloths. In the twelve months following, however, they dropped to 4,413, and during the next two years they were only about 6,000 a year. From Michaelmas, 1450, to Michaelmas, 1451, they were again 8,048, and in the next two years averaged 9,826. Although there was a sharp recession during 1453–4 to 4,113 cloths, the average during the next five years was maintained at from 8,000–9,000 cloths. It seems, therefore, that the falling away of the London denizen average by 2,000–4,000 cloths during the three years Michaelmas, 1447, to Michaelmas, 1450, may have been due to the closing of Burgundian lands to English cloth. The recovery of the normal exportation in 1451, and its maintenance thereafter probably signified that intercourse was to a considerable degree resumed until at least the end of 1459.

During the two years of sharp civil war, 1459–61, denizen exports of cloth from London again declined to 6,000 a year, but after that there was full recovery until 1464. For the ten months from December, 1464 to September, 1465, however, exports suddenly dropped to an insignificant 776. It was the time when the Merchant Adventurers, owing to renewed misunderstandings with the Duke of Burgundy, removed from Antwerp to Utrecht.[63] There they stayed until 1467, but meanwhile London denizen shipments regained the usual total of 8,000 cloths. The treaty with Duke Charles in 1467[64] seems to have galvanized these exports, which suddenly expanded to 15,000 cloths. At about this figure they remained for ten years until in the last four years of the reign they rose above 20,000 cloths. Markets supplied by London cloth merchants included, of course, others than Burgundy; but in so far as their trade reflected the conditions of the Netherlandish market, it appears that the closing of this in 1447–50 brought a contraction of exports from which there was only a hesitant recovery during the next sixteen years. On the renewal of friendly relations with Burgundy in 1467, it is not unlikely that exports thither nearly doubled, and in the last four years of the reign expanded still further.

We have assumed that the fortunes of the third market for English cloth, that of Northern France and Guienne, can be discerned in the denizen trade of South Coast ports from Southampton to Bristol inclusive. In the years 1446–8, which presumably saw the cloth trade with France and Guienne at its best, 15,040 cloths were exported from these ports annually. From Michaelmas, 1448, to Michaelmas, 1449, the number contracted sharply to 8,370, and during the next decade fluctuated between 6,400 and 8,500 a year. The outbreak of war in 1449, its continuance for four years, and the final loss both of Normandy and Guienne thus reduced the denizen cloth trade of these ports to about one-half of its normal volume. In the civil war of 1459–62, it contracted further to an average of 5,300 cloths, and thereafter for ten years tended to sink even below this level. From 1469-71 its average was only 3,565 cloths. After 1471 it revived, but just how rapidly cannot be discovered, since the accounts for Bristol are missing until Michaelmas, 1477. The average exportation for these six years was probably about 8,000 cloths. During the last five years of the reign it was 11,000 cloths, or rather more than three-fourths of its volume in 1446-8.

Disturbances in each of the three principal continental markets for English cloth thus contributed to the decline in the export trade which began in 1448 and lasted until 1475. Restriction of Hanseatic privileges in England and the corresponding restriction of English privileges in Prussia depressed it from 1448 to 1453, and again in the early years of Edward IV. The war with the Hanse in 1468-74 cut off the entire Baltic trade, nor was prosperity restored until after the treaty of Utrecht. Exclusion of English cloth from Brabant, Holland, and Flanders, ordered and effected in 1447, lasted for at least two years, and the Netherlandish market during the next sixteen years was subject to occasional depression. If we may judge from the sudden expansion of denizen exports of cloth from London in 1467 and the maintenance of this larger volume, it would seem that the market at no time between 1448 and 1467 was exploited to its full capacity. The new vitality of the London denizen trade, caused in part, apparently, by a completely recovered market, was not, however, promptly reflected in the total exportation of broadcloths; for it came at the very moment when Hanseatic trade to the Baltic was cut off. What probably happened was that much of the Baltic cloth trade was diverted to the Netherlands and the Rhine, so that the total of exports did not greatly increase for some years after 1467. The change came when, in 1475, not only the Hanseatic trade but also the trade with France was restored. The latter market, affected at the beginning of our period but a year or so later than the markets of the Baltic and the Low Countries, proved very susceptible to the disasters of war. Its absorptive power probably shrank to one-half or one-third of its former capacity, and this shrinkage was the greatest factor in the general decline of the cloth trade. The ports of the south-west suffered most. Relief came with the restorative year 1475, when the treaty of Picquigny did for the French market what the treaty of Utrecht did for the Baltic market.[65] Thenceforth these two as well as the Netherlandish market were open as they had been before 1448. The subsequent expansion of the cloth trade carried exports well beyond the volume which they had attained in that year.

Domestic strife probably contributed to the misfortunes of the cloth trade much as it did to the contraction of the wool trade. Just as the latter in 1459-62 and again in 1469-71 responded to years of civil war, so the cloth trade on both occasions fell below its already depressed levels. At both times relations with France were unfriendly, and the hostility of the Hansards during the later period may have been in part counterbalanced by lukewarm intercourse with Burgundy during the first. If no change in foreign relations seems to account for the two sharpest depressions in the cloth trade, it is likely that these were the outcome of civil war.

From the fluctuations in the cloth trade of the three groups of merchants, we may now turn to the fluctuations in the trade of each group in merchandise other than wool, hides, cloth, and wine. For denizens the value of this trade is derived, as has been indicated, from the poundage totals by a process of exclusion; and for Hansards and other aliens, it is derived from the petty custom of 3*d*. in the £ by dividing this, wherever the accounts fail to make division, in the ratio of two to three.

The value of denizen trade in what may be called miscellaneous merchandise in 1446–8 averaged £57,162. After 1448, it fell away for two years to an average of £38,546, or 67 per cent of its recent volume. The corresponding shrinkage in the denizen cloth trade was to 63 per cent of its usual exports. The two branches of the trade of the Merchant Adventurers thus suffered in much the same degree. We have seen that at least three depressing influences in foreign markets contributed to the decline of the cloth trade— dissension with the Hansards, exclusion from Burgundy, and the renewal of the French war. Probably the same influences brought about the contraction of the denizen trade in miscellaneous commodities. If English merchants lost a third of their export trade in one or the other of those markets, their import trade, drawn largely from the same sources may well have been affected similarly. Since the figures of the enrolled accounts do not admit of a precise assessing of responsibilities for the decline of the trade in miscellaneous commodities, we must be content with this assumption that the two trades were susceptible to the same influences and we may proceed to inquire whether they continued to be similarly depressed and similarly recuperative.

From 1450 to 1453 both recovered a little, presumably owing to some accommodation with Burgundy. But after the final loss of Guienne both of them, despite better relations with the Hanse, declined again, the trade in miscellaneous commodities the more severely. In 1453–6 it fell to an annual average of £32,636, and in 1456–9 to one of £24,653, or only 43 per cent of what it had been in 1446–8. During the six years 1459–65, it recovered slightly, becoming 51 per cent of the trade of 1446–8, while the cloth trade was now 53 per cent of what it had been in the same years. Both trades shared, but in different degree, in the recovery of 1465–9, the percentages relative to the standards of 1446–8 becoming 56 per cent and 70 per cent respectively. In 1469–71 they fell again to 38 per cent and 59 per cent. From 1471, however, expansion began. The percentages for 1471–6 became 91 per cent and 84 per cent, for 1476–9 109 per cent and 111 per cent, and for 1479–83 203 per cent and 124 per cent. In general the two branches of denizen trade fared similarly, although from 1453 to 1471 the trade in miscellaneous commodities was usually the more severely depressed. After 1471, on the other hand, it recovered the more rapidly, soon surpassing the cloth trade in its expansion. Its volume during the last three years of Edward's reign became £116,300, a remarkable testimony to the beneficence of Yorkist rule for merchants adventuring abroad.

There was need that native merchants expand their traffic in cloth and miscellaneous merchandise beyond the compass of 1446-8 if the full value of their pre-war trade was to be recovered. For one fraction of it had deteriorated without hope of complete restoration at least in Yorkist days. This was the wine trade, likely, of course, to be crippled by the loss of Guienne. Evidence has been advanced to show that about five-sixths of the import trade in red and non-sweet wine in and before 1446-8 was in the hands of denizens, that their share amounted to 8,500 tuns a year, and that the value of it was about £34,000. To what extent this trade declined and recovered must now be noted.

For certain years after 1448 no butlerage accounts are enrolled on the customs rolls, and for these years it is necessary to be content with an estimate of the share of denizens in the red-wine trade. Such are the years May, 1458, to March, 1461, Michaelmas, 1468, to May, 1475, and Michaelmas, 1481, to Michaelmas, 1482. Since for a decade before May, 1458, the share of denizens varied from 76 per cent to 88 per cent of the total traffic in wine, it will be assumed that they continued during the next three years to control as much as 85 per cent of it. Since, however, in the years March, 1461, to Michaelmas, 1468, their share was from 44 per cent to 80 per cent of the red wine imported,[66] it will be assumed that from 1468-75 they controlled only 66 per cent of it. If these ratios are applied where specific information is not available, the fortunes of the denizen trade in red wine appear to have been somewhat as follows.

For a year after the outbreak of war the trade changed little. In 1450, however, with the loss of Guienne, it suddenly fell away to about one-half of its usual volume; for, during the seven years 1449-56, the annual imports of red wine by native merchants averaged only about 5,000 tuns a year. Yet worse was to come. Throughout the period 1456-62, the average dropped to about 3,000 tuns. These were the six years when the trade of denizens in miscellaneous merchandise and their trade in cloth were both also at almost their lowest ebb, first the one, then the other.

Just as the other branches of denizen trade began to recover after 1462, or at least after 1465, so did the wine trade. But the recovery here was far more modest. During the years 1462-8, when the butlerage accounts reveal that only two-thirds of the total trade in red wine was in the hands of denizens, the share of these merchants averaged about 4,000 tuns a year. During the next seven years, for which the butlerage accounts are wanting and for which it must be assumed that the share of denizens continued to be two-thirds of the total, there was another decline and another recovery. Denizen imports of wine averaged little more than 2,100 tuns in 1469–71, but rose to an average of about 3,600 tuns in 1471–6. Finally, in the last seven years of the reign, years so prosperous for every other branch of denizen trade, the denizen wine trade too, recovered. For the years 1476–8 the average of imports rose to 4,774 tuns and for 1478–81 to 6,639 tuns.[67] While this amount was considerably below the 8,740 tuns which denizens had imported when Guienne was still under English rule, it was an advance upon the average imports of any period since 1450. It was perhaps the largest volume of trade which could be expected under the changed political conditions.[68]

Briefly put, therefore, denizen imports of wine from 1450 to 1482 fluctuated between 3,000 and 6,600 tuns annually, most often being about 4,000 tuns. Always this trade was relatively worse off than denizen trade in cloth or in miscellaneous commodities, being at 30 per cent of pre-war standards when the latter were at about 50 per cent of them, and at 40 per cent when they were at about 60 per cent of them. At the end of the reign when the two trades had recovered and exceeded their standards, the wine trade was about two-thirds of what it had been in 1446–8.

If tuns are translated into pounds sterling at the rate of £4 the tun, the £34,000, which represented the value of the denizen wine trade in 1446–8, shrank at one time to £12,000, was throughout much of the period worth about £16,000, and at its close had risen to about £24,000. In its failure to recover its pre-war volume, the wine trade might have prevented the full restoration of the value of denizen trade, if the other branches of it had been content with mere recovery. It is at this point that the remarkable expansion of denizen trade in miscellaneous merchandise becomes pertinent. No longer did native merchants, even while becoming more prosperous than their predecessors of 1446–8, import wine to the same degree as before. Some £10,000 of the old trade was sacrificed. For it was substituted an increase of £68,000 in imports of miscellaneous merchandise. The new prosperity of the Merchant Adventurers was on a basis different in some respects from that of 1446–8.

Now that the entire course of denizen trade has been surveyed, it is appropriate to compare with it the fortunes of the trade of aliens. As regards exports of wool and cloth, this has already been done. There remain the imports of wine, of wax, and the imports and exports of miscellaneous merchandise.

The normal annual importation of red wine by aliens before the renewal of war in 1449 has been estimated at 1,700 tuns. Since the two years of war, Michaelmas, 1448, to Michaelmas, 1450, are grouped in the butlerage accounts with the two preceding years, the average for the four years was depressed to 1,140 tuns. Succeeding butlerage accounts show that it rose in 1450–2 to 1,290 tuns and in 1452–4 to

1,812 tuns. During the period, therefore, in which efforts were still made to retain Guienne, the trade in red wine tended to recover. With 1454-6, however, years in which the loss of the province had been virtually recognized, the average dropped to 616 tuns. In 1456-8 it was perhaps 800 tuns and in 1458-62 about 600 tuns.[69] Like the denizen trade in red wine, it shrank to about one-third of its normal volume.

The general recovery of trade, which in some cases began slowly after 1462 and in all cases definitely after 1465, was prompt and pronounced in the alien red wine trade. In 1462-4 annual imports averaged 2,107 tuns; in 1464-6, 3,051 tuns; in 1466-8, 1,485 tuns. This was not merely a recovery of pre-war prosperity, but a passing beyond it. It was paralleled only by the improvement in the wool trade of denizens, the cloth trade of non-Hanseatic aliens, and the alien trade in miscellaneous merchandise. These four were the seeming beneficiaries of the first decade of Yorkist rule.

From 1468-76 it is necessary, in the absence of specific information, to assume that the alien red wine trade continued to be about one-third of the total red-wine trade, and that it experienced the same fortunes as the latter. If so, it declined to an average of 1,100 tuns in 1469-71, and rose to one of 1,600 tuns in 1471-6. This last average and the inference upon which it is based may be unwarranted; for, as soon as the butlerage accounts again take up the record, as they do after Michaelmas, 1476, annual imports of red wine are seen to be smaller than 1,600 tuns. For the year 1476-9 they averaged 1,196 tuns, and for 1479-81 only 474 tuns. The experience of alien importers during these last two years was in sharp contract with that of denizens. While the trade of the latter expanded to two-thirds of its pre-war volume, that of the former shrank to less than one-third of what it had then been. It is possible that the treaty of Picquigny was in a measure responsible for the shifting fortunes of the importers of red wine.

The general experience of the alien trade in red wine was, therefore, somewhat different from that of other branches of trade, either alien or denizen. Serious contraction of it was delayed until after 1456, although, when this did occur, the trade was, like that of denizens, reduced to one-third of its pre-war volume. Recovery characterized the early years of Edward IV, being even more marked than in other branches of trade. It was not maintained, however, during the second decade of Edward's reign, when alien imports of red wine dropped at first to an average of from 1,100 to 1,600 tuns, and finally to one of less than 500 tuns. The contraction was in contrast with the almost universally expanding trade of these years.

While red wine was brought to England by Dutch, French, or Spanish merchants, sweet wine was brought by Italians and Spaniards. Imports of it fared differently from imports of red wine. In 1446-8 they averaged 776 tuns a year. In the two following years of war the average actually rose to 934 tuns only to drop back for three years to 734 tuns. Apparently 700 tuns was a normal importation at the beginning of our period. After 1453 the average for three years declined to 622 tuns and thenceforth, except for the wartime years, 1469–71, continued to be from 500 to 600 tuns until the last six years of Edward's reign, when it dropped to 332 tuns. Such an experience is different from any thus far encountered. The sweet-wine trade resembled the alien trade in red wine in its sharp decline in Edward's last years, but it differed in experiencing little depression from 1456 to 1462. Why imports of sweet wine declined little during days of adversity but shrank in years of prosperity is difficult to explain. Its high cost and the consequent consumption of it by the wealthy, who in time of depression would not necessarily be forced to retrench, might explain the first circumstance. Its restricted importation in prosperous years, however, points either to a change of taste or to some impediment in production or transportation.[70]

The only other commodity imported by aliens relative to which the accounts give details was wax. The normal importation of it in 1446–8 was 531 quintals. That nearly all of this was brought in by Hansards is evident from the circumstance that, when their Baltic trade was shut off during 1468–74, alien imports of wax shrank for six years to 48, 20, 9, 51, 159, and 146 quintals respectively. The record of fluctuations in this branch of alien trade, therefore, is practically the record of one branch of Hanseatic trade. Its fortunes were in general similar to, but in details slightly different from, those of the Hanseatic cloth trade already noted.

During the years 1448–53, when the cloth trade of the Hansards reflected considerably their dissension with the English government, alien imports of wax declined by only 20 per cent—to an average of 432 quintals; and, when for nine years after a settlement had been made their cloth trade recovered a part of its losses, the trade in wax fell further to an average of 326 quintals.[71] With the renewal of dissension between the Hanse and the government from 1462 to 1468, the average continued to decline, becoming 268 quintals. This time it reflected the decline in the exportation of cloth by Hansards during these six years. The almost complete cessation of alien importation of wax during the following six years of war (1468–74) has been noted above. With the restoration of peace in July, 1474, the trade was so restored and expanded that the average imports of 1475–9 were 1,107 quintals, and those of 1479–83, 2,750 quintals. They were twofold and fivefold those of 1446–8.

Of alien imports and exports, all except wool, cloth, wine, and wax formed the miscellaneous group which paid the petty custom of 3*d*. in the £. The value of these in 1446–8 averaged £54,484 annually; and, in default of specific information, it has been assumed that the Hanse's share in them was 40 per cent of the total.[72] In considering the fluctuations of this trade until 1475, the assumption is, therefore, implicit that its vicissitudes were the same for Hansards and for other aliens and that the ratio of 40 per cent to 60 per cent as between the two was unvarying, as of course it was not. The following observations, therefore, refer to the trade as a whole and only approximate to a description of what befell the trade of each group separately. Especially during 1468–74 the Hanse was somewhat worse off and other aliens were somewhat better off than the combined figures suggest; for, throughout the war with the English government, the Hanse's trade in miscellaneous merchandise, like its trade in cloth, was reduced to whatever fraction of it was maintained by the merchants of Cologne, who had refused to join in the war.

Of all branches of English foreign trade the alien trade in miscellaneous merchandise suffered less throughout the period than did any other except the Staplers' trade in wool. Described in percentages relative to the average of 1446–8, it declined to 82 per cent in 1448–50, to 78 per cent in 1450–3, rose to 86 per cent in 1453–6, fell to 67 per cent in 1456–62, fell further to 56 per cent in 1462–5, rose rapidly to 92 per cent in 1465–9, dropped to its lowest in 1469–71 with 47 per cent, regained 89 per cent throughout 1471–9, and in the last three years of the reign rose to 109 per cent. For only five years did the average fall below 67 per cent, and for only eleven below 78 per cent. This relative good fortune was indeed a little greater than that of the cloth trade of non-Hanseatic aliens, which except for eleven years maintained exports at 75 per cent or more of the standard of 1446–8. Nor did the Hanseatic cloth trade fare much worse except for the six years during which there was war between the Hanse and the government. Alien imports of sweet wine, too, were maintained at 75 per cent of the pre-war standard except during 1469–71, and during the last six years of the reign.

From the combined experience of Hanseatic and non-Hanseatic merchants in the different branches of their trade certain broad contrasts with the experience of denizens emerge. Like denizens they suffered from the disorders of the period 1448–82. Often their trade was only 75 per cent or 85 per cent of what it had been in 1446–8. From 1456 to 1465 the percentage declined to perhaps 60–65 per cent, and in 1469–71 dipped below 50 per cent. Throughout the period, however, they nearly always suffered less than did the Merchant Adventurers, the standard of comparison in each case being the trade of 1446–8; for denizen trade in cloth often fell to some 65 per cent of this standard, and for six years was only 53 per cent of it, while denizen trade in miscellaneous merchandise was frequently about 55 per cent and sometimes no more than 38 per cent of its former volume.

The principal cause of the divergence between the experience of Merchant Adventurers and aliens was probably the English loss of Normandy and Guienne. We have seen how the cloth trade and the wine trade of denizens was gravely impaired after 1453. Each,

36   ENGLISH TRADE IN FIFTEENTH CENTURY

especially the latter, was dependent upon the French connection and each revived after the French treaty of 1475. The denizen trade in miscellaneous merchandise may have been less closely related to France. Its depression may have been more largely due to interruptions in the Baltic or Netherlandish trade. Denizens probably suffered, too, more than did aliens from civil strife. They were not only merchants, but were citizens upon whom requisitions were levied for political and military ends. Their home market may have been impaired for the same reasons. The sharp depressions of 1459–62 and 1469–71 indicate that civil war could bring disaster and the less violent strife of other years during the fifties and sixties must have had effects similar in kind if slighter in degree.

Just as the adversities of native merchants, except the Staplers, were in general greater than those of aliens throughout three-fourths of our period, so their good fortune in the last six, and especially in the last three, years of Edward's reign was more pronounced. A comparison of the respective values of the trade of each of the four groups of merchants engaged in English commerce has been hazarded for the years 1446–8. It tended to show the Merchant Adventurers possessed of about one-third of the export trade and more than

VALUE OF THE EXPORT AND OF THE IMPORT TRADE, 1479 TO 1482

			Including Customs. £	Without Customs. £	Customs. £
Staplers	Exports.	Wool	74,600	58,000	16,600
Merchant Adventurers.	Exports.	Cloth	77,600	75,500 [74]	2,100
		Misc. Mdse.	6,300	6,000 [76]	300
	Total denizen exports		£158,500	£139,500	
Merchant Adventurers.	Imports.	Wine	24,000	23,100	900
		Misc. Mdse.	121,800	116,300 [76]	5,500
	Total denizen imports		£145,800	£139,400	
Hansards.	Exports.	Cloth	29,300	28,600 [75]	700
		Misc. Mdse.	3,000	3,000 [76]	
	Total		£32,300	£31,600	
	Imports.	Misc. Mdse.	23,300	23,000 [76]	300
		Wax	5,500	5,500	
	Total		£28,800	£28,500	
Non-Hanseatic Aliens.	Exports.	Wool	14,500	10,500	4,000
		Cloth	31,600	29,900	1,700
		Misc. Mdse.	5,300	5,000 [76]	300
	Total		£51,400	£45,400	
	Imports.	Wine	5,200	5,000	200
		Misc. Mdse.	29,800	28,100 [75]	1,700
	Total		£35,000	£33,100	£34,300

one-half of the import trade. A second comparison, applicable to the years 1479-82 will reveal whether the passing of a third of a century wrought material change. To make the comparison pertinent, it is best to retain the valuations already adopted for wool, cloth, wine, and wax. The results are shown in the table on p. 36, which may advantageously be compared with the one showing the export and import trade of 1446-8.[73]

From this summary it appears that the merchants who in 1479-82 had barely recovered their earlier trade were the non-Hanseatic aliens. Owing to a shrinkage in their cloth trade, their wine trade, and in the shipments of wool which they made as factors of denizens, the value of their combined exports and imports, excluding customs payments, had become less by nearly £10,000 than the £88,300 of 1446-8. The Hansards, on the other hand, had advanced an earlier trade of £46,100 to one of £60,100; and the wool exported by the Staplers increased in volume until its value became £58,000 instead of £44,800. It was the Merchant Adventurers, however, whose activities had increased most. While the value of their exports had arisen by about £17,400, that of their imports had expanded by £53,600. Their share in the combined denizen export and import trade had changed from 77 per cent to 79 per cent, or, if customs payments are included as part of the capital investment, from 73 per cent to 75 per cent. Their exports were now worth two and one-half times those of the Hansards, and their imports were five times as valuable as Hanseatic imports. Their exports in comparison with those of non-Hanseatic aliens were greater by 79 per cent, and their imports were worth more than four times the imports of non-Hanseatic aliens. Their export trade was equal to the export trade of both groups of aliens, and their import trade was twice the import trade of both groups. Their combined investments in both branches of trade were greater than the combined investments in both branches of Staplers and of all aliens, and this whether customs payments are included in the computation or not.

From a further comparison of the exports and imports of 1478-82 with those of 1446-8, certain changes may be noted in the balance of trade. It will be remembered that in the earlier years both denizen and alien trade showed a favourable balance, the total amounting to some £37,700. Computed in the same way the denizen balance of trade in 1479-82 had become precisely adjusted, imports and exports balancing each other. The alien balances, however, remained favourable, that of the Hansards amounting to £3,100, that of non-Hanseatic aliens to £12,300. As a whole the balance of trade was favourable to the extent of £15,300. At the same time customs payments were due from denizen and alien merchants amounting to £34,300. From its income the government had, as before, to provide some £9,000 for the maintenance of the garrison at Calais, but it no longer had to expend its resources upon troops elsewhere in France. For its reduced needs the smaller export balance of trade somewhat more than sufficed, just as the larger balance of 1446–8 had then been somewhat more than adequate. The new balance of trade, therefore, reflected the changed political situation. Much more of the government's revenue could now be retained in England, and the commercial aspect of this was the possibility of increased imports and a smaller favourable balance of trade.

As a result of the examination of the record of thirty-six years of the enrolled accounts, certain general conclusions seem warranted. At the end of the first half of the fifteenth century, just before the final conflict of the Hundred Years War, English trade, with the possible exception of the wool trade, was prosperous. Most noteworthy was the value of the exports and imports of the English merchants to whom the name Merchant Adventurers is broadly applicable. In many respects their trade was a relatively new one, concerned with varied commodities and exposed to misfortune because of the widespread markets upon which it depended.

With the renewal of war in 1449, concurrent, as it happened, with disturbances in the German and Burgundian markets, all foreign commerce, except the trade in wool and in sweet wine, declined. In particular the trade of the Merchant Adventurers contracted to about two-thirds of its recent volume. Throughout the following twenty-three years all branches of trade continued at one time or another to suffer from adversity. Even the wool trade, which in general changed little, shrank in 1459–62 to 65 per cent of its pre-war volume; and the trade of aliens, usually not greatly affected, did likewise and for even a longer period. It was, however, the trade of the Merchant Adventurers, already diminished to about this extent, which now contracted further until for six years and later for two years their cloth trade and their trade in miscellaneous merchandise became little more than 50 per cent of the volume which each had attained in 1446–8.

For all branches of trade there was some degree of recovery from 1465 to 1469; and after 1471 the movement was resumed except in the case of Hanseatic trade, which halted until 1475. In this recovery the trade of the Merchant Adventurers in miscellaneous merchandise was at first more laggard than their trade in cloth; but during the last six years of Edward's reign both were fully restored, and in the last three years of it were considerably more prosperous than they had been even before 1448. While non-Hanseatic alien trade scarcely recovered its pre-war volume, that of the Hanse did recover and even expanded by some 30 per cent. The trade of the Staplers, too, expanded by 25 per cent. The wool trade, however, was already relatively decrepit and the total trade of aliens was now equivalent to only 63 per cent of that of the Merchant Adventurers. The period 1446–82 ended, as it began, with the predominance of these English merchants, a predominance at length considerably enhanced and a testimonial to the restorative effects of Yorkist rule.

II

THE WOOL TRADE IN THE FIFTEENTH CENTURY

§ 1

THE DIRECTIONS OF THE TRADE

The wool trade in the fifteenth century, though already steadily declining, was yet the oldest, the largest, and by tradition the foremost of all branches of English commerce. The basis of its importance was the immense pre-eminence of English wool in the European markets, owing to its superior quality. Other countries, notably Spain, exported wool in large quantities, but it was everywhere admitted to be inferior to that of England, and the great cloth-making towns of Italy and the Netherlands were thus mainly dependent upon English wool for the manufacture of all their finer cloths. Hence the political importance of this commodity, which played a leading part in the diplomacy of the Hundred Years War, and hence, too, the reiterated complaints of cloth-manufacturing towns that an interference in the supply of English wool meant unemployment and misery for their inhabitants.[1] It was not for nothing that the lord chancellor of England was seated on a woolsack, and that poets such as Gower,[2] Lydgate,[3] and the author of the *Libelle of Englyshe Poylcye*,[4] praised the queen of raw materials (" O belle, o blanche, o bien delie ") in verse more remarkable for economic enthusiasm than for poetic fire :—

>Off Brutis Albion his wolle is cheeff richesse
> In prys surmounting avery other thyng
>Sauff Greyn and corn : merchauntis al expresse
> Woolle is cheef tresoure in this land growyng :
>To Riche & poorë this beeste fynt clothyng :
> Alle Naciouns afferme up to the fulle
>In al the world ther is no bettir wolle.[5]

From the earliest times the need for wool had brought foreign merchants to England, but if they at first predominated in the export trade native merchants soon began to wrest it from them. Already in 1273, English merchants were exporting 11,415 sacks out of a total of 32,743, or 34·9 per cent of the whole ; of the rest, the Italians took 8,000 sacks (24·4 per cent), merchants from Northern France 5,280 (16·1 per cent), and Brabanters, 3,678 (11·2 per cent). The remainder was exported by German, Lettish, South French, and

Spanish traders.[6] The English continued to make rapid headway, until by the end of the fourteenth century the only foreigners taking any part worth speaking of in the export trade were the Italians, and they were confined to a single branch (the trade with Italy by sea) comprising only about a fifth of the whole trade; even in this English merchants began to compete with them before the fifteenth century ended.

The immense importance of the trade to the Netherlands had led to the evolution of the famous Staple system in the interests partly of mercantile convenience and partly of royal finance, and to the formation of the first of the great English trading companies, which had a practical monopoly of the wool trade with Europe, north of the Alps. By the beginning of the fifteenth century the Staple had been finally fixed at Calais, and the privileges and organization of the Fellowship of the Staple had been clearly defined. Nor did the national importance of the wool trade rest solely on the fact that English graziers and merchants (both wool dealers and exporters) were enriched by it. The government had a direct interest in it, not only because it formed a diplomatic lever in negotiations with foreign powers, but because the custom and subsidy on wool was one of the most valuable sources of national revenue. By the beginning of the fifteenth century the evolution of the customs revenue was complete; custom and subsidy had to be paid on every sack (364 lb.) of wool or 240 woolfells. The rate of the custom duty was 6s. 8d. per sack for denizens, and 10s. for aliens. The rate of the subsidy varied from time to time, but the normal rate was 33s. 4d. for denizens; for aliens the rate varied during the century between 43s. 4d. and 100s.; but when it reached the last figure they were usually able to secure a remission, which sometimes amounted to the added 66s. 8d. Thus denizen merchants normally had to meet a total payment of 40s. per sack and aliens one of 53s. 4d. In addition, a small tax known as "Calais penny" was levied at the rate of 8d. per sack upon all wool exported elsewhere than to Calais. The direct interest which the government thus possessed in the wool trade led to important results, for in the course of time the Staple became, as Schanz has termed it, "an organ of the English financial system,"[7] by means of which the Crown was able to enforce its bullion regulations and anticipate its revenue by loans raised on the security of the customs, and which soon after the middle of the century had become entirely responsible for the collection and administration of the customs revenue on wool, and for the payment of the garrison and other expenses of the upkeep of Calais.

It is proposed in this paper to describe the technique of the English wool trade and the function and activities of the Fellowship of the Staple during the fifteenth century. Before proceeding to a detailed consideration of these subjects, it will be well to give some account of the direction of the trade at this time and of the merchants engaged in it. The English wool trade in the fifteenth century fell into three sections according to destination. With two exceptions, the law forbade wool to be shipped elsewhere than to the Staple town of Calais and to Calais the bulk of it went, for the most part shipped by members of the Fellowship of the Staple, though a small quantity was exported by non-staplers to that town, where, however, it had to be sold under the Company's regulations. Calais was obviously a convenient place, being a town in English possession, defended by a strong garrison and within easy reach of England's best customers, the cloth-making towns of Flanders, Brabant, Holland, and Zealand, and of the great international marts of Bruges, Antwerp, and Bergen op Zoom. Entry into the Fellowship of the Staple was obtained by apprenticeship or by purchase.[8] It was a large body and it controlled roughly about four-fifths of the total export of wool from the country.[9] No complete list of its members at any one period has as yet been found, but by collecting the names of merchants described as Staplers in the customs accounts and in lists of royal creditors and of persons receiving general pardons a rough idea can be formed of their number. Documents belonging to the reign of Edward IV yield a total of over three hundred, and in the early part of the sixteenth century the Staplers themselves estimated it (possibly with some exaggeration) at "four hundred shippers",[10] so that it would probably be safe to put the number between those two figures. The majority were Londoners, provincial Staplers being not only less numerous, but as a rule in a smaller way of business than those of the metropolis. Some provincial Staplers, however, were very wealthy, as was John Barton of Holme beside Newark, who set as a posy in the window of his house the motto:—

> I thank God and ever shall
> It is the sheep hath payed for all.[11]

Provincial Staplers are to be found among those taking part in loans made by the Company to the Crown, and the mayor of the Staple was sometimes chosen from a provincial port.

The most important ports of shipment for Calais were London, then Boston, and then Ipswich and Hull. Wool was sometimes shipped from Southampton and Sandwich for Calais, but they were chiefly important for the Mediterranean trade. Occasionally odd cargoes or part cargoes of wool are also recorded from Lynn, Poole, Chichester, and Yarmouth. Much information about the wool fleets and the merchants shipping by them is furnished by the customs accounts (particulars) and by the accounts sent in to the Exchequer by the Company of the Staple from 1466 onwards, when it was administering the custom and subsidy on wool. One of the latter accounts, running from 6th April, 1470, to 6th April, 1471, will illustrate a typical series of sailings.[12]

Date.	Port.	Wool.			Wool-fells.	Custom and Subsidy.	No. of Merchants Shipping.*
						£ s. d.	
April 11	Ipswich	590½ sacks	5½	cloves	18,041	1,431 14 10¼	24
April 12	Boston	259¼ ,,	5	,,	8,750	591 12 9	62
May 4	Ipswich	241¾ ,,	5	,,	6,984	541 19 0	19
May 9	Boston	1,373½ ,,	5	,,	18,056	3,106 3 9¾	87
May 15	Ipswich	134 ,,	6	,,	12,924	375 19 6	20
May 26	Hull	{467½ ,,	11	stones 1 cl.	2,209	159 1 0¼	34
		{373 ,,	7 ,,	1 cl.†	31,866†	1,009 5 10½†	45†
June 10	Ipswich	102½ ,,	3	cloves	11,866	304 0 0	17
August 4	London	2,113½ ,,	2	,,	257,914	6,376 7 2¾	67
Oct. 29	London	490½ ,,	10	,,	27,196	1,208 0 4¾	41
Nov. 12	Boston	36½ ,,	2	,,	768	79 9 7¼	11
Nov. 28	London	939½ ,,	5	,,	1,792	1,894 2 6¼	36
Dec. 22	London	238 ,,	5	,,	5,180	519 7 2¼	22
Jan. 29	Boston	145¾ ,,	11	,,	1,000	300 5 3	23
Feb. 12	London	1,021½ ,,	17	,,	5,526	298 0 9	52
March 10	Hull	183 ,,	14	stone	8,000	373 14 0¾	16
March 28	London	1,160½ ,,	23	cloves	80,722	2,994 11 4¾	42

In addition to these shipments from the regular ports of Calais, a Stapler, Ralph Gerald (who also did a large business shipping wool to Italy), shipped 3½ sacks 12 cloves of wool and 886 wool-fells from Sandwich to Calais and another, John Elyngton, shipped 2 sacks 2 cloves from the same port, their custom and subsidy amounting to £18 18s. 5¾d., shipment being made on 10th April, 19th January, and 31st August.

The survival of the London customs account for the period 5th July, 1478, to Michaelmas, 1479, enables us to follow the shipping of wool from London in even greater detail for over a year.[13] The first wool fleet recorded sailed on 20th July, and consisted of thirty-eight ships, carrying between them, in all, 1,160½ sacks 12 cloves of wool and 268,227 wool-fells. All the merchants divided their wool among several ships to lessen the risk of loss, and as a rule between five and eleven merchants had consignments on each. After the departure of the main fleet, shipping was spasmodic; three ships sailed for Calais on 25th September, two on 31st October, six on 13th November, two on 27th November, five on 14th December, and five on 14th February, but the next big wool fleet did not sail until the Spring (27th March), and it contained twenty-four ships carrying 945½ sacks 24 cloves of wool and 111,767 wool-fells. On 18th May a smaller fleet of fourteen ships sailed with 589½ sacks

* Some of these were partners shipping together, and some shipped on several occasions and from more than one port.

† Part of these were shipped on 14th April but the account groups the two dates together.

5 cloves and 46,829 wool-fells and on 9th September another fleet of eighteen with 446⅓ sacks 12 cloves and 104,594 wool-fells. The Boston and Ipswich fleets sailed less often and were usually smaller, but the Boston account for 1466-7 shows a fleet of twenty-two ships sailing on 15th October with 1,886½ sacks 7 cloves and 34,923 wool-fells, and in 1473 the July fleet from Ipswich numbered sixteen.[14]

Apart from evasions of the law, only two exceptions were recognized to the rule that all wool must go to Calais. It was, in the first place, relaxed in favour of merchants shipping wool of the growing of certain northern counties straight to the Netherlands. The merchants of Berwick enjoyed the privilege of so shipping wools grown between the Cocket and the Tweed and in Teviotdale and other parts of Scotland. More important, the merchants of Newcastle-on-Tyne were allowed to export wool of the growing of Northumberland, Cumberland, Westmorland, and Durham, together with Richmond and Northallerton and the lands lying between the Tees and the Tweed, sometimes to any part of the Netherlands, usually to the specified ports of Bruges and Middleburgh. The North Country wools for which exception was thus made were of inferior quality and their employment in the manufacture of the fine cloth of the Netherlands was forbidden. A Leyden ordinance classes them with Scottish, Irish, Spanish, Dutch, and Flemish wools, and cloth-makers mixing Newcastle and Staple wool in their cloth were severely punished; there were separate dealers and separate wool-combers for Staple and non-Staple wool.[15] Nevertheless, there was a good market for Newcastle wool in towns which specialized in cheap, coarse cloths, and the Newcastle merchants valued their licence. The Staplers, however, constantly complained that advantage was taken of it to export the finer wools of neighbouring counties, especially "Yorkeswold", Lincs, Notts, and Derby.[16] The fixing of a staple for North Country wools at Middleburgh or elsewhere was an attempt to control this; and the Calais Company continually tried to get coarse as well as fine wool under its own control. Whether for this reason or another, the volume of Newcastle exports, about 500 sacks per annum in the middle of the century, declined steadily thereafter.

The other exception to the rule which made Calais the Staple was more important, since it involved fine wool and a different market. The cloth-manufacturing towns of Italy had always been among the largest customers for English wool and Italians had from early times visited England to collect and export it; their letters and memoranda are, indeed, among our earliest sources of information for the conduct of the trade. In the fifteenth century Italian merchants still purchased a certain amount of wool at Calais or in the marts of the Low Countries, and carried it back to Italy, either shipping it from Sluys to go by sea,[17] or taking it by one of the land routes over the Alps. A regular toll was levied on English wool passing through the duchies of Luxemburg and Brabant (*licentia lane lombardorum vehende per Brabantiam ad partes superiores et ad Lombardiam*).[18] Great efforts were made by the Company of the Staple to secure that Italians buying wool at Calais should not sell it in the Netherlands. An ordinance of 1376, confirming the privileges of the Staple, lays down that Italians may purchase wool at the Staple and take it to Italy, if they do it up in sacks and give a guarantee not to sell it "on this side of the mountains".[19] Licences were sometimes granted by the English Crown to Italian merchants allowing them to export wool to the Netherlands "and soo fro thens to be ladde and caried over the mountains into Lumbardie", under a similar guarantee not to sell it *en route*.[20] The Privy Council, granting such a licence to Benedict Barromei, merchant of Florence, was careful to add "First to commune with the maistre of the staple herupon", and heavy sureties had to be found against the sale of the wool before it reached its destination —in one case two staplers standing surety for £500 each. Nevertheless, there were complaints that "somme persounes yat shuld by thaire Licence have caried thaire Wolls over the Mountaynes have sold theyme in Brabant and in other places, to suche men as were wonte to bye thaire Wolls at the Staple of Calais".[21] Certainly plaints recorded at Bruges show Italians selling wool to each other there,[22] and the *Libelle of Englyshe Polycye* complains that they were accustomed to buy wool on credit in Calais and sell it below cost price for ready money at Bruges.[23]

The main channel of export between England and Italy was not, however, the land route. It was far more convenient for Italians to buy wool in England and ship it the whole way by sea, by way of the Straits of Marrock (Morocco), or as we should say, the Straits of Gibraltar. This wool was mainly shipped by Italians; it is true that from Henry VI's reign a certain amount was shipped under licence and nominally by Englishmen, but it seems probable that in most cases the real exporters were the alien "factors", to whom the licences had been sold, for the wool was taxed at alien rates. At the beginning of the fifteenth century the chief ports of shipment for the Straits of Marrock were London, Southampton, and Sandwich, but by the middle of the century the famous "Flanders galleys" of Venice had almost deserted London, and Southampton and Sandwich were the great ports for export to this market. Two or more of these Venetian galleys put in there every year and from the moment that the fleet left Venice until two months after its return, the Venetian Senate forbade any wool to be brought into the city by the land routes.[24] Genoese and Florentine ships also regularly visited England (for Florence, whose wool was usually carried in Genoese bottoms at the beginning of the century, began to build herself a fleet after her acquisition of the port of Leghorn) and Lucchese and Milanese merchants likewise exported wool. The customs accounts and patent rolls afford considerable insight into the dealings of the more important Italian exporters, who are to be found acting on their own behalf or (increasingly in the last part of the century) under the guise of factors for the King and other great English personages. In Edward IV's reign the most active were the Florentine, Gerard Caniziani, sometime factor and attorney of the Medici Company, factor to the king, citizen and mercer of London, and merchant of the Staple, who took out letters of naturalization,[25] and Jerome Contarini, who acted at different times as factor for the king's mother (Cecily, Duchess of York), his sister (Margaret of Burgundy), and Sir John Astley, and who brought down the wrath of the Signory of Venice upon his own head by trying to make a corner in the wool cargo of the galleys that year.[26]

Wool going by the Straits of Marrock was usually shipped in Italian galleys and carracks, but Edward IV occasionally sent one of his own great ships southward with a cargo of wool and cloth. His *Antony* sailed from London for the Mediterranean on 26th August, 1478, carrying wool shipped by a wealthy alderman, William Heryot, and on 28th May, 1482, his *Mary de la Towre* left Southampton with a similar cargo.[27] The expenses of the journey were extremely heavy; they are estimated in the minutest detail in a handbook compiled by an English merchant in the last part of the fifteenth century (later than the reign of Henry VI), who may have been in the habit of shipping wool not only to Calais but to Venice. He gives first the expenses entailed in carrying the wool from the growers to Southampton or London, packing, warehousing and weighing it there, including the payment of custom and subsidy, and then the expenses of freight in a galley from Southampton to Venice and the cost of customs, etc., there. His conclusions are summarized thus: " The first bying of a sacke woll of Cotswold ys worthe aftre the Rate of the yere one with anodyr xii marke: viij*li*. The Reysing of the price for cause of the costes that Rennyth uppon a sacke into the tyme that hitt is in the galey aforesayd: iij*li*. vj*s*. viij*d*. The Reysing of the price for Freyght of a sacke withe oder costes aforesayd: iij*li*. iiij*s*. iiij*d*." Thus the total cost of a sack of wool to the exporter (apparently an alien paying custom and subsidy at 53*s*. 4*d*.) would be £14 11*s*.; but the profits of the trade were good, for the writer estimates that the wool would sell at Venice at the rate of £20 per sack.[28]

The Italian merchants were, as in previous centuries, favoured by the Crown as a source of frequent loans, secured as a rule upon the custom and subsidy due on their wool. These were sometimes forced loans and the king experienced some difficulty in raising them. On 25th May, 1415, for example, the Privy Council summoned before it six members of the Florentine companies, four Venetians, and two Lucchese dwelling in London, and the chancellor informed them that it was usual for merchants trading in any other country than their own to render to the sovereign thereof, in case of necessity, such sum as they could afford, or else be committed to prison, and that in aid of the king's expedition to France he expected these merchants, who through his grace enjoyed great privileges and acquired much money by the exercise of their trade, to lend him specified sums, on sufficient pledges of gold, silver, and jewels.[29] All refused and were committed to the Fleet, but subsequently a Lucchese merchant, Paul de Milan, lent 200 marks and credited the king's wardrobe with a large sum for goods, and the Venetians (Nicholas de Muleyn and his fellows) and the Florentines (Laurentius de Albertis and four of his fellows) lent 1,000 marks each for the expedition, to be repaid out of the custom and subsidy.[30] These loans were usually thus made by individual merchants or companies, but the Venetians had a factory in London under a consul and the officers of the factory sometimes advanced the money, with permission to repay it out of the custom and subsidy of Venetian merchants, in much the same way that Staple loans were made. An interesting decree of the Venetian senate in March, 1449, recites that three years ago £200 was lent to the king to be so repaid, from which time all merchants of Venice had exported wool not in their own name, but in that of Englishmen (who paid a lower rate) in order to benefit themselves, and in 1456 another decree ordered that, in future, loans were to be made by the merchants and not by the factory.[31]

But although favoured and, whenever possible, protected by the king, on account of the loans which they made to him, the Italian merchants were the object of a good deal of opposition among Englishmen, and from time to time there were anti-Italian riots. The mercantilist theories of the day imposed restrictions on their trade, and the English exporters looked upon their rivals with an unfriendly eye. It was complained that they rode about the country and bought up the wool.

> In Cotteswolde also they ryde aboute
> And al Englande and bien wythouten doute
> What them liste wythe fredome and fraunchise
> More then we Englisshe may getyn in any wyse.[32]

"I have not bought this year a lock of wool," writes old Richard Cely in 1480, "for the wool of Cotswold is bought by Lombards," and his son reports that there is little wool in Calais for the same reason.[33] Certainly they were among the best customers of the Cotswold and London wool dealers.[34] Complaints were made that the Lombards smuggled wool and indulged in "clacking and bearding" and other devices to evade the payment of customs, which

THE WOOL TRADE

is certainly true, for the Memoranda Rolls abound in such cases,[35] and the Venetian Senate, with complete frankness, passed a decree in 1456 stating that the English factory was not to be burdened with more than the usual £20 given to the customers for putting a low price on goods.[36] It was also complained that they evaded the laws prohibiting aliens from buying staple wares on credit and their astute financial dealings were resented. A Staplers' petition of 1437 set forth that " Lombardes and straungers beying in yis land, at yair comyng first into yis Roialme, bringe with them lytel goode or noght, and within short time after, yai byen notable substance of gode to apprest and to long dayes [at credit for long terms], to content for ye same with Merchandise at ye same dayes. And yef ye Merchandise faille and come not at ye dayes, yan yai take newe dayes, muche lenger yan ye first daies were, to paie for ye same gode redy money, thurgh whiche apprestes yai have been and yet beth daily gretly enriched."[37] It was only a year before this petition was presented and rejected that the writer of the *Libelle of Englyshe Polycye* was making his vigorous and amusing attack on the usurious practices of the Lombard wool merchants, who bought wool on credit both in the Cotswolds and in Calais, selling it for ready money, and employing that money to make loans at a high rate of interest to English merchants :—

> And thus they wolde, if ye will so beleve
> Wypen our nose with our owne sleve.[38]

Thus wool was going out of England in three directions, to Calais, to Holland and Zealand, and to Italy; and the monopoly of the Staple was legally waived only in the case of inferior wools shipped from the Northern Counties via Newcastle, and wools going the whole way by sea to the Mediterranean. Nevertheless, there were means of eluding that monopoly and the most effective of these was the Crown's freely exercised right of licensing individuals to export wool to places other than Calais. The sale of such licences was a lucrative source of income and an easy way of paying debts, and both Henry VI and Edward IV made extensive use of it, in spite of the constantly reiterated complaints of the Staple, which waged a steady war on the practice and rarely granted a large loan to the Crown, without coupling it with a request for the withdrawal of licences to ship elsewhere than to Calais. These licences were almost always given to ship wool by the Straits of Marrock, sometimes paying customs and sometimes custom free. They were granted to all sorts of persons to whom the king owed money, and they were sometimes held by Staplers.[39] The activities of the licencees can be followed in detail in the customs accounts, but since the licences were clearly transferable, it is sometimes difficult to say whether the grantee is actually trading himself or not. The customs accounts during Edward IV's reign show the Duchess of York and a number of other important persons apparently exporting cloth and wool by means of both native and alien factors, but it seems certain that in most cases the factor was the actual exporter, having bought the licence from the grantee and covered the transaction by representing himself as the grantee's agent.[40] It is significant that when the export is made by an alien factor, custom and subsidy is almost always charged at alien rates, which would seem to be conclusive. The same difficulty applies to the question of royal shipments. Henry VI from time to time exported wool on his own account, and Edward IV nominally exported wool, cloth, and tin in large quantities through a number of factors, of whom Caniziani and Alan Mountayn were the most active. Hardly a year passes without a shipment of wool in this king's name appearing in the customs accounts, but a study of the details makes it plain that some at least of these shipments were made by his factors on their own behalf.[41]

In the matter of licences the interests of the king and the Staplers were opposed, but there was another means of evading the Staple monopoly concerning which their interests were identical, to wit, smuggling, whereby if the Staple lost its rights the king lost his customs. Smuggling (chiefly to the Low Countries) went on continually from little creeks, where the customs officers could be avaded. In 1423 it was asserted that the Abbot of Furness had for five years loaded a ship of 200 tons with wool in a place called " le Peele de Foddray " in Lancashire, and sent it to Zealand without paying customs,[42] and shipmen strangers from the Low Countries were alleged to carry away wool and wool-fells trussed up in tuns, pipes, barrels, sacks, and fardels, or hidden under wood, wheat, oats, and seacoal,[43] while some ingenious merchants rolled wool up in their bales of cloth, which paid a much lower duty.[44] The Mayor of the Staple was authorized to search at sea for ships containing uncustomed goods and on land the duty fell to the customs officials, but although a large number of cases of smuggling are recorded in the Memoranda Rolls, it is exceedingly difficult to form any exact estimate of the extent to which it took place, since only cases which were detected found their way into the records.[45]

§ 2

THE TECHNIQUE OF THE TRADE

1. *Purchase of the Wool*

A great mass of evidence concerning the English wool trade is preserved in the Public Record Office and in the archives of certain towns of the Netherlands (notably Leyden). Of particular importance is the survival of the letters and business memoranda of the Celys,

THE WOOL TRADE

a family of merchants of the Staple, covering the years 1475 to 1488.[46] From these materials it is possible to reconstruct the whole technique of the export trade as it was carried on by the Staplers, from the purchase of the raw wool in England, through its carriage to London or one of the provincial ports, its shipment to Calais and sale there, to the final collection of the money due from the foreign purchaser at one of the seasonal marts of the Netherlands and the transmission of that money home by means of bills of exchange.

The first stage was the purchase of the wool in England. English wool varied considerably in quality according to the district where it was grown, and was very carefully classified. Two lists of wools, graded according to price, have survived from the last half of the fifteenth century. The earlier in date is to be found in a schedule attached to a petition in Parliament (1454), setting forth a project, which was abortive, for fixing a maximum price for the exporter in the interests of the native cloth industry.[47] The prices given are those payable in England, and fifty-one grades are distinguished. From this it appears that the most valuable wool came from the March of Shropshire and Leominster Soke (14 marks per sack)—"March" wool is often mentioned in English and Dutch documents—Leominster in Herefordshire (13 marks), and Cotswold (12½ marks). Since the wide district of the Cotswolds produced the largest supply, the term "Cotes" or "Cotswold" was used as a technical term to denote wool of the finest quality.[48] After these came a drop of 4 marks and then High Lindsey in Lincs (8½ marks), Low Lindsey, young Cotswold, and Herefordshire outside the Leominster district (8 marks), Cley, Newark, Lindsey Marsh, North Holland (Lincs), Banstead Down, and Gloucestershire (7½ marks). Then followed Kesteven (Lincs), Wilts, Hants, Notts, Berks, and South Holland (7 marks). Thirty other grades are specified, ending with those of Southray, Middlesex, Yorkshire, and Kent (4½ marks), and Suffolk and Sussex (£2 12s. and £2 10s. respectively). The list does not include the North Country wools which went by Newcastle, nor the wools of the Western peninsula, which were almost too coarse to be worth exporting, Cornish wool being contemptuously known as "Cornish hair".[49] The other schedule belongs to some date in the fifteenth century later than Henry VI, and occurs in the remarkable treatise entitled *The Noumbre of Weyghtes* to which reference has already been made.[50] It contains "the prises sett at Caleys uppon woll of dyvers countreys in Yngelande" and distinguishes thirty-five grades, with March wool (20 marks), Cotswold fine (18 marks), Lindsey and Berks (16½ marks), Norfolk (11½ marks), and Yorks (10½ marks) at the bottom.[51] The most notable divergence between the two lists lies in the position assigned to Berks wool, which is much higher in the second schedule; Kesteven and Wilts are also ranked higher and Lindsey Marsh and Hants lower in this list.

Of these wools the finer grades [52] were in demand for all the fine cloths of Italy and the Low Countries, but the poorer qualities were also much used for coarse cloth, and were exported both to Italy and to Calais; Edward IV, for example, made large shipments of Kentish wool from Sandwich to the Staple by his "attorney", the Stapler Ralph Gerald, in 1480–1 and 1481–2, and a Genoese merchant, Ralph Pynell, who dealt largely in fine wool, also shipped it regularly for the Straits of Marrock between 1479 and 1483.[53] These "slight" or coarse wools were also either smuggled or taken under licence direct to the Low Countries, and efforts were made from time to time to free them from the obligation to pass through the Staple. A petition of 1393–4 from the "commons" of Hants, Wilts, Somerset, Dorset, and Berks asserts that the cost of the passage to Calais and the small value of the wool, made it impossible for the "slight" wools of these counties to be sold at a profit to the Staple, and begged that they might be exported direct to Normandy, and that Norman merchants bringing goods to England might be allowed to recharge their vessels with these wools.[54] It is difficult to see on what principle the wools of Berks and Hants could be classed as "slight" and the influence of the Company of the Staple sufficed in any case to secure the rejection of the petition. But licences to export "slight" wools continued to be granted, and in 1423 the Staple, protesting against the practice, specially mentions the "slight wools" of Hants, Sussex, Kent, and Yorks, and denies the argument that such wools could find no sale at the Staple: "on the contrary, if all the slight wools of the realm were to come to the Staple, as great a crowd of merchants would come to seek them as would come for the good wools, for the slight wools be as necessary for the drapery of some towns as the good be for others, because there be several towns in Flanders and Brabant that be accustomed to make cloth of slight wools, and they have their gain and living thereby; so that if their cloths were made out of fine wools and sealed with their seal, as is accustomed, they would not sell them dearer, for by the seal of each town the cloths are known and so perforce they would be obliged to have as well slight wools as good."[55] The answer to this argument would seem to be that put forward in another petition from dealers in coarse wools against holding the Staple for such wools at Calais, pointing out that "the wools of Scotland that pay but half a mark of custom and the wools of Normandy, Picardy, and Flanders that pay nought in custom, be like to the coarse wools of England that pay 50s. to the king in custom and subsidy, [wherefore] it seemeth that if the coarse wools of England shall pass to Calais no merchant of Flanders will come there to buy them save to the great damage and loss of those Englishmen that own them, for since a man may have wools of like sort more cheaply at home, he will not go far away in order to buy such wools more dear."[56]

THE WOOL TRADE

The wool was exported in the form either of shorn and wound wool from the clip, which was sold by the sack, or of wool-fells (i.e. sheepskins with the wool on them, collected after the Martinmas slaying), 240 wool-fells being accounted equal to a sack of shorn wool for purposes of taxation. It was classified as " good " or " middle " wool, and in contracts for the purchase of wool the proportion of good to middle wool was often specifically laid down. " Young " wool was also specially classified, " young Cotswold " being less valuable than " Cotswold ".[57] " Clift " wool, which constantly occurs in the documents, seems to have been an inferior quality classed with middle wool.[58] Sometimes fells were classified as " summer ware " and " winter ware ".[59] Outside the good and middle wool came a miscellaneous assortment of inferior wools and skins, morlings or moreins (skins of sheep found dead from murrain or other causes), scaldings (skins of scabby or " scald " sheep), shorlings (skins recently shorn), brecklings (broken fragments), pell-wool (plucked from the skins of dead sheep), flesh-wool (possibly the same), and locks (the lowest class of remnant, after the removal of the fleece, consisting of the shortest wool from the legs and belly of the sheep). These were usually classed as " refuse " and cast out by the wool packers as they made up the sarplers of wool and fells, but all were exported.[60] There was also an export trade in lambs-wool and lamb-fells, milk-fells (possibly the skins of unborn lambs), morkins (the skins of dead lambs), and " laslades and mesandes " (diseased or damaged lamb-fells). Usually (though apparently not at all times) lambs-wool, shorlings, and morlings paid only poundage and were exempt from the great custom and subsidy on wool and wool-fells, not being rated as staple ware. Henry VI (especially between 1439 and 1453) granted a number of licences for the export of all three direct to Holland, Zealand, and Brabant from various English ports, usually specifying that no staple wool should be shipped under colour of the licence,[61] but such licences were opposed by the Staple, on the ground that they were often a mere excuse for shipping uncustomed good staple wool under colour of " newe feyned names, as Morlings and Shorlings ".[62] These inferior wools and fells were shipped chiefly from Newcastle and from Sandwich, going direct to the Netherlands and to Italy, though they were also exported by Staplers to Calais.[63] Refuse and lambs-wool are often found as part of mixed cargoes exported by general merchants, or by masters of ships plying across the Channel, and there was a good market for lamb-fells among the Lombards.[64]

Wool could be purchased either direct from the grower or from a middleman, the " woolman ", " woolmonger ", or " brogger ". It was an important part of a Stapler's business to ride about purchasing wool from dealers and growers in the Cotswolds and other wool producing districts from which they drew their supplies. The Celys usually had two representatives riding in the Cotswolds in the spring and autumn. When the correspondence opens old Richard Cely himself interviews the dealers, and his brother John is employed in gathering wool from the farmers, sometimes going as far afield as Lancashire and being paid at the rate of 5*s*. a sack. A statement of accounts for 1482 show the firm making payments to a big Northleach dealer, William Midwinter (from whom they got the bulk of their wool), to John Cely for wool collected by him, and to a group of persons, who are probably local growers, from whom fells were purchased; these include William Syger of Camden, from whom 458 were bought, Margaret Caenes and Margaret Pynner of Chipping Norton (4098 and 1224 respectively), Richard Coolys of Preston (454), and others.[65] That Staplers dealt directly with growers is likewise shown very pleasantly by the will (1435) of John Russell, a well-known Yorkshire Stapler and sometime mayor of York, who leaves " for distribution among the farmers of Yorkes Walde from whom I bought wool 20*l*, and in the same way among the farmers of Lyndeshay, 10*l* ".[66] The Italian merchants also, besides dealing largely with "woolmen", maintained those direct relations with wool-growing monastic houses which had characterized their trade in the thirteenth century. They still bought up the whole clip of certain monasteries, and these probably still continued to act as dealers, collecting and selling the wool of the countryside with their own. Some light is thrown upon these transactions in the fifteenth century by the Views of Hosts, in which is reported the business of Italian merchants during their sojourn in England. Thus in the six months between Michaelmas, 1443, and the following Easter, Laurence Marconovo of Venice purchases forty sacks of wool for £400 from the abbots of Gloucester, Oseney, and Winchcombe, and the prior of Gloucester; and two other Venetians, between Easter 1441 and Michaelmas, 1443, buy Cotswold wool from the abbot of Dorchester, " divers gentz de Cotyswold " and Robert Page, who was probably a dealer.[67]

    The business of riding round and collecting wool from individual farmers and monastic houses was, however, a cumbersome one for the foreign exporter, and the middleman wool-dealer made his appearance at an early date. By the end of the fourteenth century both Staplers and Italians, though continuing to buy some of their wool direct from the farmers, were getting the bulk of their supplies from these woolmen. In the fifteenth century they formed one of the richest and most important trading groups in the country, supplying not only the export trade, but also the native cloth industry with wool. It is possible to distinguish two classes of persons engaged in this business. The most important and interesting group is formed by the local dealers of the Cotswolds and other wool growing districts; the other group is composed of London merchants (and a certain number of merchants belonging to other large towns), who dealt in wool among other commodities.

The local dealers of the Cotswolds lived on the spot and organized the collection of wool from all the sheep farms round, buying the produce of the manorial home farm and the substantial yeoman's holding, the clip of the peasant's small flock and the rector's tithe-wool. The villages which once resounded with their traffic—Northleach and Stow, Campden and Lechlade, Burford and Cirencester, and many another—are now fast asleep; the clatter of packhorses bringing in the bales of wool to their great barns, the valuing and packing and cording, the vociferous bargaining with Lombard and Stapler, are silent; but the memory of the woolmen is still preserved in some of the most beautiful churches of England, where their brasses lie still in proud immortality upon the stone pavement. Their memory is also preserved as enduringly, if less pleasantly, in those historical records which deal with their misdemeanours, in petitions for breaches of contract (in which, however, they are as often sinned against as sinning), and in entries upon the Memoranda Rolls, concerning their offences against various statutes regulating the sale of wool.

From the Memoranda Rolls, extremely interesting information can be derived as to the general economic activities of the Cotswold wool-dealers. During the years 1455-60 a large number of dealers were prosecuted under the statute of 8 Hen. VI [68] for various offences against the wool statutes, and most of them extricated themselves by the expedient of purchasing general pardons from the crown. The full descriptions given in these pardons are very significant, and some may be quoted :—

(1) "John Briddoke de Northleache in comitatu Gloucestrie, Wolman, *alias* Johan Briddok nuper de Northlache, husbandman." [69]

(2) "Johannes Lenard, nuper de Campden in comitatu, Gloucestrie, dyer, *alias* . . . Wolleman . . . *alias* . . . yoman, *alias* merchaunt." [70]

(3) John Stokes of Ceryngnorton (Oxon), woolman, *alias* mercer, *alias* draper.[71]

(4) John Fortey, of Cirencester, dyer and merchant.[72]

(5) John Thame of Fairford, junior, husbandman, *alias* merchant, *alias* gentleman, *alias* woolman, *alias* yeoman.[73]

(6) Hugh Calcote of Calcote (Glos), chapman, *alias* merchant, *alias* mercer, *alias* yeoman.[74]

(7) Thomas Arnold of Cirencester, gentleman, *alias* clothman, *alias* woolman, *alias* chapman.[75]

(8) John Elmes of Henley, merchant *alias* gentleman.[76]

From these descriptions it is plain that the activities of some of the more important woolmen were by no means confined to the business of "gathering" and selling wool. They are here seen to combine this function with one or more of three others; first, they are husbandmen and yeomen, settled on the land and undoubtedly graziers, growing on their own farms some at least of the wool which they sold; secondly, they are dyers, drapers, or "clothmen", engaged in some branch of the cloth industry, and equally without doubt setting a more or less large number of employees to work on making up some of their wool into cloth for sale; thirdly, they are mercers and chapmen, i.e. general merchants on a large or small scale, engaged in selling other commodities besides wool.

The history of some of the more important of these families is well worth the attention of the historian. The best known are the Tames of Fairford,[77] but the Fortey family, though less famous than the Tames afterwards became, were in the mid-fifteenth century no less considerable personages in the Cotswold district. The John Fortey of Northleach, who died in 1458, and lies buried in Northleach church, with one foot on a wool-pack and the other on a wool-fell, was a well-known wool dealer, and is to be distinguished from the John Fortey of Cirencester, dyer and woolman, mentioned above, to whom he left a legacy in his will, and who was one of his executors.[78] The will,[79] which contains exceptionally numerous and large legacies to churches and charities, also mentions Nicolas and Thomas Fortey of Hamendon and William Fortey of Harwell. John Fortey's son Thomas died in 1474, and his brass, with woolpack at feet, likewise adorns the parish church of Northleach. Two other Northleach dealers, known to us through the *Cely Papers*, are John Busshe and Thomas Widwinter. The Busshes and the Midwinters intermarried and flourished exceedingly on the trade. William Widwinter left £600 and lands in Northleach when he died in 1501, but it is in the next generation that we can best see how profitable a wool dealer's business might be, when combined with that of a grazier. John Busshe had owned lands in Northleach only, but when his son Thomas died in 1526, he was able to leave his wife (Thomas Midwinter's daughter) £400 and lands in three Cotswold villages, and his sons £100 apiece and lands in Oxfordshire, Wiltshire, Gloucestershire, and Berkshire (all wool-growing districts) including one farm let on a stock and land lease to a London Stapler, and another stocked with 300 sheep and also let.[80]

The dimensions of the trade which some of these woolmen were doing can be gauged from such records of their bargains as have chanced to survive. Richard Cely's account books show that his firm purchased from Thomas Midwinter wool to the value of £558 11s. in 1482, and £753 5s. 11d. in 1487.[81] John Elmes of Henley (one of the dealers whom we meet in the Stonor Papers) [82] made a bargain with an Italian for £840 worth of wool on 12th May, 1457.[83] John Townsend of Lechlade (Glos.) contracted to supply wool to the value of £1,078 to two aliens on 27th September, 1452.[84] William Willey of Campden was granted letters of marque against the Florentine Company of the Albertini in 1442, because they owed him £1,180 for wool, which they had not paid.[85] These large sums represent only single bargains, and all these dealers were undoubtedly entering into contracts with other customers at the same time. It is greatly to be regretted that Midwinter's or Fortey's accounts have not survived, to enable us to form as exact an estimate of their annual turnover as we can form of that of the Celys.

These great local woolmen form the first group of men interested in the business of supplying the wool exporters; and, as we have seen, they sometimes combined the functions of graziers, clothiers, and general merchants with that of wool gatherers. The second group interested in the business is composed of London merchants, for whom the wool trade was only one among several interests. A number of these men also got into trouble for selling wool to aliens, contrary to the Statute, and their descriptions in the Memoranda Rolls are equally interesting. They are all designated as citizens of London, two of them being aldermen; among them are six drapers, four grocers, three mercers, a skinner, a brasier, and a girdler; and one, John Bolt, is described as "tailor, *alias* draper, *alias* mercer".[86] Membership of the city companies did not at this date necessarily imply that a man was engaged in the trade with which that company was particularly concerned, and probably the most cautious conclusion would be that many big London merchants dealt in wool among other commodities. Their position as middlemen was at one remove from that of the Cotswold woolmen; they bought their wool from the latter and sold it either to the clothmakers at home or to the Italian exporters. They did not export it themselves unless, as sometimes happened, they were also merchants of the Staple. They appear most frequently to have been drapers or mercers. By this date the term mercer was used to denote a general merchant, engaging in an import and export trade in various commodities and not in mercery alone. Sales of wool to and by mercers are frequently recorded;[87] we hear of a partnership between a Stapler and a mercer;[88] and some of the most important members of the Stapler's Company throughout the century were also mercers, although such a combination of rôles was not common.[89]

The procedure followed in sales of wool can be reconstructed from a large number of documents. The purchaser "cast a sort" (i.e. took a sample) of the wool proffered for sale, and an agreement was drawn up for the supply by the dealer of a certain quantity of wool of the same quality at a specified price. An indenture between an Oxfordshire woolman and a London mercer published by Mr. Kingsford is typical. The woolman binds himself in September to supply the mercer with twenty-five sacks of young Cotswold, guaranteed of sufficient packing and true winding, twenty sacks being of fine and five of middle wool, and fifty fleeces, the wool to be packed and wound at the woolman's house by "an indifferent persone of the ffelishp of Wolpakkers of London", assigned thereto by the buyer. The woolman agrees to convey 'it to London before Candlemas (2nd February), and deliver it to the purchaser at the king's beam at the Leadenhall, which was the place appointed for the tronage or weighing of wool in London, and the usual place of delivery specified in wool contracts by London merchants. For this consignment the purchaser agrees to pay £140, of which the woolman acknowledges receipt of £81 17s. down, the residue being payable the day after delivery of the wool.[90] Usually, however, the dealer allowed the merchant a rather longer term of credit; a Cely contract with Busshe, made in August, 1476, stipulates that a third of the sum shall be payable at the weighing, a third in the following May, and the remainder in September, and another Cely contract with Midwinter (24th November, 1478) makes the same arrangement.[91] The prosecutions for selling wool on credit to aliens, to which reference has already been made, show that much longer credit was sometimes allowed by the woolmen. In these contracts with Italians it seems to have been usual for payment to be spread over about two and a half years,[92] but sometimes longer terms even than this are allowed. John Austyn, of Woodstock, woolman, sold the Venetian John da Ponte on 1st December, 1458, wool to the value of £116 10s., payable at the four following Easters (i.e. over a term of $3\frac{1}{2}$ years,[93] and John Claymond, a London draper, sold another alien fifty sacks to be paid for in the course of four years.[94]

The "indifferent person of the fellowship of wool-packers" mentioned in the indenture quoted above, played an important part in the trade. The wool-packers were not only packers but valuers of wool, and a number of statutes deal with their business and the peculiar temptations to which it was liable. They had to cast out the refuse wool and be wary to detect deceit by the owners "by putting in Flecez, lokkes of Wolle and peces of moche worse Wolle than of the same Fleze and also puttyng in the same Flecez erthe, stones, sonde, donge or heere, to grete hurt of the byer".[95] On the other hand, they were forbidden to practise devices which would assist the exporter to elude the king's customs, such as "inwinding", or winding in good with inferior wool [96] (a trick euphemistically known in the trade as "good packing") [97] or clacking, bearding, and forcing the wool, i.e. removing impurities, especially the tarry marks on fleeces and clipping away inferior parts, so that, as custom was charged on the sack, the wool paid lightly in proportion to its value; a sack so clacked or bearded was estimated to be worth three times as much as a sack not so treated.[98] The wool-packers had to value the wool as they packed it, marking each sarpler with its place of origin and grading it as good or middle wool; the further to prevent frauds it was enacted that wool must be packed in the shire in which it was grown.[99] The wool-packers had a craft gild of their own,[100] and were employed and paid by the buyers in the Cotswolds as a check on the dealers and by the royal officials and the Staple at the ports as a check on the merchants. We hear of them travelling to the wool-growers with the dealers, and sampling wool from farm to farm on behalf of the London merchants. A petition in the Early Chancery Proceedings records a bargain between a Bucks woolman named Dayson and John Croke, a merchant in a large way of business and member of a well-known family of London Staplers, by which Dayson undertook to supply twenty or forty sacks of good Cotswold wool, and Croke to accept it when seen by him or his packer, paying on delivery. Croke thereupon sent his packer to Dayson to view the wool, with £25 to deliver " for his erneste penyes ", upon receipt of which Dayson, and the packer, went " to dyverse men of the contre for to see wolles " and such wool as the packer approved was bought to Croke's use, £17 out of the £25 being " leyed erneste thereon in divers places ".[101] The packer most usually employed by the Celys was one William Breton, who travelled about between the Cotswolds, the English ports, and Calais. George Cely writes from Calais (5th August, 1481) to tell his father that his wool has been awarded as " good cottes " by William Breton and Harry John, and Richard reports in March, 1482, that he has been to Abingdon to engage Breton to go into the Cotswolds with him " but he myte go no fardar wt me for packyng of Lombardes wholl at Hamton [Southampton], the qwheche muste departe into Gean [Genoa] at thys Ester in the Kynges schypys, and he has promysed to met wt me at Norlache [Northleach] on Low Sonday ", which Breton did, and reported the sample of Midwinter's wool to be " the fayreste woll that he saw thys zeyr ".[102]

These wool-packers were, however, by no means always " indifferent persons ". They sometimes carried on a business as wool dealers side by side with their function as packers and valuers, and among wool-packers pardoned for fraudulent packing in 1458 occur the names of Henry John, late of London, " wolman, *alias* wolpakker, *alias* wollegaderer, *alias* merchaunt," Thomas Faukes, late of London, " *civis et* wolman, *alias* wollepakker ", and William Breton, " wolman *alias* wolpakker ", two of whom are the packers mentioned in George Cely's letter quoted above.[103] Two years before a petition to parliament had asserted that the " subtill labour and grete pollicie " of merchant strangers and English wool-packers buying wool to their use had greatly brought down the price of wool, and that " the said Wolle Packers of right be and owe for to be Juges betwyx the buyer and the seller, for to discerne the fyne Wolle from the myddell Wolle, and the Myddell Wolle from the refuse. Whiche Wolle Packers may not than in any wise by raison be partie as buyer and Juge togeder, whiche maner of buying hath be oon of the grete causes of the seid amenuting the prices of the seid Wolles and overe grete empoverysshing of the growers of the same". For these reasons it was asked that no wool-packer should hereafter be allowed to buy more than four sacks a year, " for to make Cloth therof for his Houshold."[104] The bill was not passed; in 1473 the Staplers succeeded in procuring an act forbidding any packer of wools to buy or sell wool or wool-fells within the realm for himself or for any other person.[105]

The reason for the concern of the Staplers in preventing wool-packers from trading in wool is to be found in the close relation which sometimes existed between these packers and alien buyers. Not only did the wool-packers buy wool for Italians, but they seem to have conspired freely with them to break the laws against clacking, bearding, and forcing, and to defeat the king's customers by fraudulently packing wool-fells as wool and "slight" wool as Cotswold. Some cases on the Memoranda Rolls throw a light upon their activities. On 17th December, 1455, William Bert, alien merchant, and William Denys of London, wool-packer, caused 8,000 wool-fells to be taken secretly from the Woolquay to a suspicious place called Knolles Alley in Sevedon Lane, in the parish of All Saints, Barking (Tower Ward), near the banks of the Thames by John Bolle,[106] servant of William Breton (the Celys' packer again) and three of Denys' servants, who cut off the feet and legs of the fells, and packed them in twenty-eight sarplers " in the guise wherein merchants be wont to pack wools called Coteswold wools " and were about to smuggle them over to Flanders, when they were caught. The same William Denys was involved in another amusing case of fraudulent packing of wool-fells on behalf of an Italian merchant, and some years later he was again detected packing 220 sacks of " sleyght wool " into packets under the guise of fine Cotswold for a London draper and assisting him to smuggle them over to Holland in two alien boats.[107] William Breton and John Bolle seem to have been hardened sinners, for on 28th May, 1454, they had been found assisting Simon Reame and two Lombards, in Simon's house in the Vintry Ward, to cut off the feet of 800 wool-fells and pack them as Cotswold wool, afterwards causing them to be carried to Sandwich, where they were fraudulently exported as wool,[108] and William Breton on another occasion was accused of bearding twenty-five sacks of wool for one of the Bardi of Florence.[109] In view of these cases it is not surprising that on 18th June, 1481, the king appointed two men " to the mistery or occupation of discretores of wools within the town of Calais, commonly called ' wolpakkers ' with full power and authority to examine all sacks, packs, piles and sarplers of wools brought to the Staple of Calais from any part of the realm, on account of the losses to the king and the merchants of the Staple through the infidelity of divers persons exercising that occupation ".[110]

2. *Transmission and Sale of the Wool*

We may now return to the wool purchased in the Cotswolds by our Stapler and follow the further stages of its progress to Calais. After being packed in great canvas sarplers (for which the Celys were constantly buying Arras canvas and packthread at the marts of the Netherlands) it was loaded on to packhorses and, accompanied by the dealer or wool-packer or by both, carried to the port of shipment, where it was taken over by the purchaser. After having been weighed for custom and subsidy, the wool was sometimes warehoused for a time at the wool quay if no fleet were sailing or if business were slack, otherwise it was shipped off by the next fleet, the sarplers being divided among several ships to minimize loss; and there were at the ports skilled persons, whose business it was to stow the wool aboard.[111] All these operations can be followed in detail from the Cely accounts and other sources. George Cely on one occasion records money delivered for packing, canvas, and packthread, carriage to London, portage at the Leadenhall, cartage from the Leadenhall to the wool quays, " houshire " for the wool at the Leadenhall and the quays, payments to the customers' clerk, to the Mayor's clerk and the " tellers of fells " for their labour in weighing the wool (at 1*d*. per sack or 100 wool-fells), to porters on the wool quay (4*d*. per sarpler and 3*d*. per 100 wool-fells), to the chalkers on the wool quay for writing with chalk on the sarplers ($\frac{1}{4}d$. per sarpler), to the wharfagers of the wool quays for wharfage and to labourers for drying and mending fells damaged by sea-water and landed again after shipment " because of trouble on the sea and in Zealand ".[112] He also, several times, records payment of " conduit " or conduct money to the convoys of the fleet; it seems to have been levied at a varying rate, for on one occasion he pays 3*s*. 4*d*. per sarpler, and on another only 1*s*. $6\frac{3}{4}d$.

On the arrival of the wool in Calais, the Calais representative of each firm would have to receive it, supervise its disembarkation, examine its quality, and have it repacked and warehoused. Moreover, here again it was subjected to a careful examination by the Company to see if it had been properly valued and marked in England. The inspection by the Company's packers was done by selecting one sarpler of each consignment to be unpacked and examined, but no vigilance was sufficient to prevent a certain amount of fraud. On one occasion, when the Lieutenant of the Staple had selected sarpler No. 24 of the Celys' wool to be examined, and their agent knew it to be middle wool and " very gruff ", he privily caused the packer to " cast out " another sarpler, No. 8, of fair wool and exchanged the wool of the two sarplers, being able to report in his next letter : " Sir, your wool is awarded by the sarpler that I cast out last." [113] It is no wonder that there were constant complaints of fraudulent packing on the part of buyers. During the negotiations between English and Burgundian envoys at Lille in 1478, the English produced in writing the regulations which existed in regard to packing both in England and at Calais. At Calais, they asserted, there was a commission to inquire into breaches of the ordinances governing the inspection of wool there and to confiscate wool incorrectly labelled before it was exposed for sale; there were two sworn packers to unpack and repack wool on its arrival; customers and controllers had to deliver their books and certificates to the Exchequer as did those in England; and the commissioners were empowered to punish delinquencies on the part of customers, controllers, and packers with the utmost severity. Upon this the Burgundian envoys remarked " that they believed the ordinance to be such, but that it was by no means observed, for the merchants asserted that frauds in the packing of wools had been found since the time that the aforesaid ordinance had been in force ".[114] These complaints of fraudulent packing were destined to continue long after the end of the century.

When the wool had been inspected, repacked, and warehoused, the only thing which remained was to sell it. The sales had to take place at Calais and merchants resorted to the town from all parts of the Netherlands and elsewhere. Those from Flanders and Brabant were still among the best customers, though the cloth industry was beginning to decline there. The Celys dealt largely with a Bruges merchant, Gyesbryght van Wynsbarge, who seems to have been one of the biggest customers at the Staple, for when in March, 1484, certain townsmen of Calais wished the Lieutenant of the town to arrest him as surety for goods of theirs, which had been arrested at Nieuport, the Lieutenant of the Staple opposed such action on behalf of his fellowship, saying that " if so be that Gyesbryght should be arrested here and troubled, it should cause at [*sic*] great inconvenience to the Staple, for Gyesbryght and his fellow be the men that doth greater feat of any merchants that cometh hither, for the goods that they have bought here this year draweth above £25,000 sterling, wherefore if they should be stopped there would come no more merchants hither, the which should cause a great stop, and if merchants strangers might not resort hither that men might make sale of their goods, they could make no payment unto the soldiers of their wages, and also should cause men to land again such goods as they were a-shipping withal ".[115] Gyesbryght seems to have been in partnership with one John Delopys (presumably de Lopez), who may have been a Spaniard and the *Cely Papers* are full of financial dealings with them.

At this time, however, the Dutch cloth industry was beginning to outstrip that of Flanders, and merchants from Delft and Leyden were among the most important buyers at the Staple, which accounts for the anxiety displayed in the Cely letters when the Hollanders failed to arrive at the expected time. The Leyden merchants mainly bought fells, and if the annual import of Calais wool-fells registered in the Leyden archives be compared with the annual export from England, it would appear that the Leydeners in the last half of the fifteenth century were buying up about half the total number of wool-fells exported.[116] They used to form themselves into syndicates for the purchase of fells and pool their capital, sometimes one, sometimes three members of each group being entrusted with the money and the business of making the journey to Calais. Stringent regulations controlled these Staple *vairders*, on whom the whole industry of the town depended; in the interest of their co-partners, they were obliged to have at least 100 nobles of their own money involved in each deal, the amount which they might buy on credit was limited, all their transactions had to be officially attested, and they were subject to strict rules of partition.[117] They usually went first to Antwerp and Bergen op Zoom to dispose of their cloth, going on to Calais afterwards to purchase wool with the proceeds, and the *Cely Papers* constantly record transactions with these Delft and Leyden fellowships.[118] At the bargain making the seller had to disburse small sums for " telling out " the fells, for brokerage at the rate of 4*d.* per 100 fells, sometimes for entertainment: " Item, spent at bargyn making," is a common entry.[119] Occasionally there were disputes : " Item, " runs one entry, " John Egengton with Elderbecke with Adam Moy, whereat a [he] dined for to see the said fells, for the merchants said it was Conyswaye [i.e. old fells] and not Cotswold fells. So spent upon them at wine 12*d.*" [120]

Relations between the Staple and its customers were not always peaceful, and Calais was thrice closed to Leyden merchants as a measure of coercion, once in 1421 over a dispute as to the validity of obligations under the Staple seal in cases of debt, and again in 1449 and 1468, over the protectionist policy of the Leyden town government, which tried, in the interest of the native cloth industry, to prevent its merchants from selling wool in the marts by forbidding them to buy more than could be made into cloth in Leyden. But closing the Staple to Leyden was too much like cutting off their nose to spite their face to be done often by the Staplers, and the two parties henceforth usually managed to settle their difficulties by negotiation. Some of the more common causes of complaint are preserved in the Leyden negotiations of 1458, 1467-9, 1473, 1482, and 1486,[121] and in the negotiations between English and Flemish envoys at Lille in July, 1478.[122] There were complaints against wool of inferior quality and against fraudulent weighing and packing in 1473. The Leydeners obtained a treaty acceding to their demands that tellers of fells should be sworn to do their work without fraud, that Leyden merchants might view fells and remove unsuitable ones, such as " bacons " or winter fells found among summer ones (subject to the mediation of valuers appointed by the Staple) and that they should not be forced to take more than five grey or black fells to the hundred; finally, that every sack should be plainly marked with the quality of the wool which it contained and the seller's name, and that if the wool were found to be of inferior quality, it might be returned to Calais.[123] The negotiations of July, 1478, were largely taken up by a struggle between the Burgundian and English envoys over the rule of the Staple which obliged its customers to take a sack of old wool with every three sacks of new, whether they wanted it or not, which led to an entertaining debate on economic principles. The English refused to do more than modify their regulations on this subject, but Leyden got exemption by a treaty in 1486. There were also constant difficulties over the exchanges, into which it is unnecessary to enter here; and from time to time difficulties arose over the practice, universal in the wool trade, of allowing a considerable amount of credit to the wool buyers.

Indeed, one of the most interesting aspects of the mediaeval wool trade is the extent to which, from beginning to end, it rested on a credit basis.[124] Dealers like the Midwinters bought on credit from the growers and sold on credit to the Staplers, who in their turn sold on credit to the foreign buyers. In each of these transactions, however, a larger or smaller sum (often a third of the whole) had to be paid down at once, and therefore when buying wool in England, a Stapler would have to have some money in hand for this "earnest penny" and be ready to pay the instalments of the balance when they fell due. For this he was dependent on receiving remittances in time from Calais, or else he would have to borrow money on interest in London, at a loss to himself. The *Cely Papers* show that merchants often found themselves in considerable difficulties when their money did not arrive in time from Calais. Old Richard Cely remarks on one occasion that he is obliged to forgo bargains in fells for want of cash, and on another writes to his son that his wool is home from the Cotswolds and ready to be weighed, and that he must have money sent over for it. In June, 1480, Richard Cely the younger writes urgently to his brother George that he has bought £91 13s. 4d. worth of fells from Midwinter, and must pay within five days £40 and at Bartholomewtide £20, and at Hallowtide £20; " Sir, I pray you have these days in remembrance; my poor honesty lies thereupon." In November he is going to the Cotswolds again, and is waiting for £10 in "Carolus groats", which he is expecting from Calais; he writes three letters about those groats and, after a fortnight, is still awaiting them and can tarry no more. " Sir, I pray you send me the £10 that ye wrote to me ye had purveyed in Carolus groats; . . . but it come within this twelve days I am half shamed else for my promise, and therefore I pray you for God's sake remember my poor honesty." [125]

A good illustration of the difficulties which sometimes arose

THE WOOL TRADE

occurred in September, 1482, when the dealer Midwinter, having made a contract to supply wool to the Celys, found that he had misjudged the market and could not buy it as cheaply as he had reckoned, and that the growers, who usually allowed him long credit, were demanding their money before the date at which he had agreed to take payment from the Celys. An incoherent letter to Richard Cely explains the situation :

"Right reverent and worshipful Sir, I recommend me unto you, desiring to hear of your welfare. Furthermore I thank you of the great cheer that ye did me at my last being with you. Sir, I made a bargain with you at that season, the which I would I had slept the whiles, for theke [those] customers that I trusted most to a [have] sold them, and I trusted that I should not a [have] bought their wool above 13*s*. 8*d*. a tod, and now I cannot buy their wool under 14*s*. and 13*s*. and 6*d*. a tod ; the price is, that I buy at, above that I sold you right much and to reckon the refuse I shall lose, by my troth, a noble or 10*s*. in every Sarpler. And, as my troth help me, and they must have ready money by and by—they that were wont to leave in my hand most part of their money—now they must needs have all their money. And now I must trust to your courtesy and I pray you consider this well, as ye may have my service, for I must trust to you that I may have the £200 that ye said I should not have till November. I pray as heartily as I can that ye make it ready within fourteen days after Michaelmas, or else I am hotly shamed, for I made myself never so bare without money, and therefore I pray you that ye make it ready. No more to you at this time, but Jhesu keep you. Written at Northleach the 20 day of September.

By William Midwinter." [126]

This bombshell arrived at a peculiarly inconvenient moment for the Celys, and Richard sent it on to George in Calais, with the comment : "I wot not how to answer it, and our father's tomb a-setting up and our eme [the uncle John Cely, who was one of their wool gatherers] is here for money and this day I depart into Cotswold and how soon they will call upon [us] for the 20*s*. of the sarplers [custom and subsidy] I cannot say. I am at my wits' end without your comfort." A fortnight later he is writing, "I pray God send us a merry world. It is ruel for a man to charge him far nowadays, for I hear of no utterance [sale]. If I may depart fair from the bargain with William Midwinter that ye and I made, I will do my best. Methink it will be well done, for good debtors are slow payers." [127]

These and similar difficulties in paying for wool were, of course, due to the fact that the Celys themselves were selling wool on credit and had to collect the sums due to them by their Dutch and Flemish debtors before they could remit money to England. The usual custom in the trade was to divide the purchase price into three parts, one of which was payable at Calais on the spot, while the purchaser gave the seller bills for the balance, payable at two later terms, sometimes at the marts next forthcoming, but sometimes " at six months and six months ", or over a period of eighteen months or even longer, for the terms of credit were a subject for haggling and depended (as will be seen) on the condition of the market. The custom of the trade was plainly set forth (probably by the fellowship of the Staple) in a series of notes for the use of the English ambassadors who were negotiating a renewal of the treaty with the Flemings in 1411. It is pointed out that if the Staple be held at Calais, peace with Flanders is a necessity, otherwise the Flemings will not allow the Germans, Brabanters, Lombards, and others to pass through their land to the Staple; but " if it be urged that the Staple might be at Calais, even if we be at war with Flanders, the merchants making delivery of their wools there for cash down, that may not be; for all they that be wont to buy wools cannot buy them for cash down; and if the substance of the wools of the realm once in the year be not sold, the wools of the new year will be unable to maintain their price and value within the realm . . . Seeing that the wools cannot be sold at any value without they be lent [i.e. on credit] and if the merchants of the Staple were thus to lend to the folk of Flanders and Brabant and Holland and the Easterlings, while the king and Flanders were at war, his lieges would be unable to pass through Flanders to collect their debts in the other aforesaid parts; wherefore the Staple cannot well be at Calais if there be war with Flanders. Nathless, there is no merchant frequenting the aforesaid Staple who desires to have the Staple removed from the aforesaid town of Calais." [128]

The credit transactions thus referred to were cloaked by the device of representing them as a loan from the seller to the purchaser. A good example occurs in a deed of 1445, in the Leyden archives. between two Dutch merchants and William Cantelowe, a member of a well-known family of Staplers: " Be it known to all that we, Jean Bertout and Duic Florijszon, merchants of Leyden, are bound to Cantelo [*sic*], merchant of the Staple of Calais or to the bringer of this letter, in £100 sterling, which he paid for us [i.e. for which he gave us credit] for the wool and fells which we bought at Calais and the money is to be paid at the Pinxstermaret [Synchon Mart] at Antwerp next coming." [129] The phrase " lent to " the buyer occurs over and over again in the Cely accounts,[130] and is used in a passage in the *Libelle of Englysche Polycye*, concerning long credits to the Lombards and the use which they made of them :—

> Now lestene welle how they made us a baleys [birch],
> Whan they borowed at the toune of Caleys,
> As they were wonte, ther woll that was hem lente;
> For yere and yere they schulde make paymente,
> And sometyme als for too yere and too yere.

THE WOOL TRADE

This was fayre lone; but yett woll ye here
How they to Bruges wolde her wolles carye
And for hem take paymente wythowten tarye
And sell it faste for redy money in honde
(For fifty pounde of losse thei wolde not wonde [shrink],
In a thowsande pounde) and lyve therebye
Tyll the day of paymente easylye,
Some gayne ageyne in exchaynge makynge,
Full lyke usurie as men make undertakynge.
Than whan thys payment of a thowsande pounde
Was well contente, they shulde have chaffre sounde
Yff they wolde fro the staple at the full
Reseyve ageyne ther thousande pounde in woll.[131]

On these deferred sales interest was charged, but this also was cloaked under a convenient device, being expressed in the rate of exchange at which the sums due on the bills had to be repaid. Credit being regarded as a loan made in Flemish currency to the purchaser, the longer the term allowed the more English pounds would the seller expect to obtain for the same sum of Flemish money, and the interest chargeable on sale credits was always thus expressed in terms of the exchanges. For example, on 20th October, 1478, Richard Cely records the sale to John Delopis and a group of his fellow-merchants of thirty-one sarplers of good Cotswold wool at 19 marks. He receives the "third penny" in ready money, at 25*s*. 4*d*. Flemish to the pound sterling, and the other two-thirds are payable at 24*s*. Flemish to the pound sterling on 20th April and 20th October, 1479, respectively.[132] This sale of time also served to keep prices steady. Mr. Postan points out the remarkable fact observable in the *Cely Papers* that, although both the supply of and the demand for wool varied from year to year, prices at Calais remained substantially the same. From 1472-82 fine wool was selling at 19 marks per sack; in 1483 it rose to 20 marks, and remained steady until the end of the period covered by the accounts (1488). The Staplers were able thus to keep prices at the same level by adjusting terms of credit to the state of the wool market; if the market value of wool fell, a longer term of credit would be allowed to customers, or the rate of interest as expressed by the exchanges would be adjusted, or both adjustments would be made simultaneously. Old Richard Cely's advices to his son at Calais concerns not the price of wool, but the terms of credit. On 23rd May, 1477, for example, he writes to say that he has heard that there is little sale for wool at Calais, and tells his son to find some sure and true buyers "to adventure some of my wool and fell in their hands by the mean of sale at long days, for I feel men shall do so at this season . . . Spare not for a long day, for I fear me it will come thereto, for I understand well there be divers men of the fellowship of the Staple of Calais have sold wool for three year day the last payment, and the price kept and the money 22s. 8d. for the pound; also for money by exchange at London is 7s. 10d. Flemish for 6s. 8d. sterling, and to receive at London in hand and for to deliver at Bruges at a month day after 7s. 10d. Flemish for 6s. 8d. sterling; for the which I can think money will be better this mart no" [i.e. a month's interest on exchange is nil, which portends a rise in the English rate].[133]

There were official attempts to put a stop to these credit transactions, as will be seen later, all through the first half of the fifteenth century. It was laid down that the Staplers were to sell for ready money, a part of which they were to deliver to the mint, either in Calais or in London, to be coined into English money. On the other side the town government of Leyden was also doing its best to prevent or to limit purchases on credit by its *Calisvairders*. At the beginning of the century an attempt was made to establish a fixed ratio of 10 per cent between the capital of the wool merchants and the amount of credit which they were allowed to receive from the Staple. In 1406, this was apparently modified to apply to wool-fells only, and they could buy as much shorn wool as they liked; but wool-fells were, as we saw, the most important article of purchase for Leydeners. In 1437 it was laid down that "those who go to Calais to buy fells or wool shall not lend or borrow money [i.e. give or take credit] nor give letters of exchange (*brieve van wissel*) to buy wool therewith", and in 1446 the prohibition was confirmed again and merchants were from time to time fined for breaking the ordinance. Merchants going to Calais were, however, later specifically allowed to receive credit for a fixed sum. In the 1446-51 regulations, for instance, each member of the group had to adventure at least 100 nobles of his own in the deal and might "borrow" 50 nobles. The real object of the regulation was probably to protect the interests of the merchants who entrusted money to the *Calisvairders*. The regulations, however, seem to have had little effect upon practice.[134]

The Staplers thus received only the "earnest penny" or first instalment of the money due to them at Calais. The balance had to be collected at the marts of Antwerp, Bruges, Bergen op Zoom (Barrow), or other much frequented cities. These "marts" were the great seasonal fairs of the Netherlands, which were held at four periods, "Cold mart" in the winter, "Pask mart" round about Easter, "Synchon" or "Pinxster mart" round about Whitsuntide, and "Balms mart" round about St. Bamis' day in October. On these occasions the chief representatives of all the wool firms in Calais would be riding round to the marts, presenting their bills and collecting their debts, as well as arranging for the transmission of their money home; for all kinds of financial transactions were carried on at these marts, and the Stapler met there the Dutch, Flemish, or Lombard customer, whose bills he held, and the mercer-importer by whose bills of exchange he could transmit his money to London. The correspondence in the *Cely Papers* is often a triangular one, between the senior partner Richard in London, the junior partner George at the mart, and the factor, William Cely, at Calais. The money was collected by methods which we are apt to consider much more modern than they really are. The discounting of debts by " assigning " or transferring them was common, and bills passed from hand to hand as freely as they do to-day. When, for example, Lowes Lyneham, attorney of a well-known London Stapler, John Feld,[135] sold Peter Laurencon, a Bergen merchant, wool to the value of £247 11s. 11d. on 31st October, 1447, he apparently took no earnest penny, but received two " letters of payment ", one for £124 7s. 5½d. payable at the Whitsun mart, the other for £123 4s. 5½d. payable the following Michaelmas. The sum which he actually received was made up out of (1) a load of white salt, (2) three bills of exchange drawn by Laurencon on two London mercers and a firm of Flushing merchants respectively, (3) a letter of payment of an Easterling merchant payable at Bruges at two terms. This left £67 5s. 2d. still owing on the second of Laurencon's bills in June, 1451, in which month Lyneham being at Calais, a mercer named John Petyt came to see if he had any bill of Laurencon's, and another Stapler, in Lyneham's name, delivered the bill to him, on condition that Petyt should return it to Lyneham or Feld if it were not executed by 1454, in surety for which Petyt delivered a statute staple of £80. Lyneham's story was that Petyt then bought merchandise from several Flemish merchants and paid them with Laurencon's bill, but that his master Feld never received the £67 5s. 2d. owing to him, and so got execution of the statute staple against Petyt, who sued Lyneham. But Petyt's version of the affair was that he and Colard de May, on Feld's behalf, had sued for the unpaid balance in the court of Bergen against Peter Laurencon, who had eventually paid it to Feld.[136]

English merchants were constantly obliged to sue for debts in the courts of the Low Countries, as Petyt and Colard de May were alleged to have sued at Bergen, and a number of such cases are entered in the *Register Calaisstapel* in the archives of Leyden.[137] The increasing disturbances in the Low Countries in the last quarter of the fifteenth century were a considerable hindrance to trade, and there are several references in the *Cely Papers* to the tardy payments of the Hollanders, and accounts of attempts by Dutch merchants to obtain longer credit and to evade paying anything in hand in cash. On 1st March, 1478, Leyden wrote to the Staple asking that, owing to the extreme insecurity of the roads in wartime, " our townsmen may be free to deposit their money in Bruges and to do their trade in the Staple of Calais with bills of exchange (*litteris de Cambio*), as was wont to be done in times past, their payments to be made in Bruges."[138] Here the attempt of the Leydeners is to dispense with the payment of cash on the first instalment and to pay the whole sum by bills payable at Bruges at a later date, in order to avoid carrying money with them; and the Staple agreed to their request, except in the case of purchases of wool (as distinct from wool-fells).[139] On 14th May of the same year, however, the Fellowship of the Staple held a full congregation to decide on the minimum sum in cash which should be payable as a first instalment for each grade of wool, and laid down that for every sarpler of " endewolt " the third penny should be paid in ready money, for every sarpler of " cliftwolt " £7 sterling, or its equivalent in Flemish money and for every 100 wool-fells at least £1 sterling or its equivalent, thus withdrawing its previous concession. The decree was communicated to Leyden on 20th October.[140] Apparently the Staple was trying to tighten up the terms of credit again. Six years later the Staple complained that the Leydeners constantly came late to the marts at which they had to meet their bills, whereby the English merchants were incommoded, and threatened that if this were not remedied the sale of wool and woolfells would be permitted only for cash down.[141]

Suppose, however, that the Calais representative of a firm of Staplers had duly secured payment of the bills due to him. There remained the problem of getting the money home. Obviously there were three possible ways of doing this. The first was by transferring cash, towards the employment of which the regulations of the government were directed, but it was obviously cumbersome and unlikely to commend itself to the mercantile community. The second was by bestowing the money made by selling wool on the purchase of goods for import into England, but, as has been pointed out, the Staplers were not commonly buyers in the marts of Flanders;[142] a few of them were mercers and did an import trade, but the customs accounts rarely show us Staplers engaged in anything but the export trade in wool, and the Celys seem to have kept their transactions at Calais and the voyages of their ship, the *Margaret Cely*, quite distinct. The third way by which the Staplers could transfer their money home was by means of bills of exchange drawn upon the London offices of merchants who imported on a large scale, and this was the method which they habitually employed; they " made it over," as the phrase went, usually by means of the mercers, who were importers buying heavily at the Flemish marts. The Staplers had Flemish money in Calais, where they sold, and in the marts, where they collected their debts; they wanted English money in the Cotswolds and London, where they bought. The mercers had English money in London, where they sold, and needed Flemish money at the marts, where they bought. So the Stapler on the continent delivered his money to a mercer and received a bill of exchange payable at a future date in London in English money, the interest being expressed in the rate of exchange for different terms, exactly as in the case of the wool sales.[143]

The *Cely Papers* record many such transactions, and show also that a large part in these dealings was also played by Lombard and Spanish financiers. "Item," writes William Cely to George on 12th September, 1487, "I have made you over by exchange with Benynge Decasonn, Lombard, an hundred nobles sterling, payable at usuance : I delivered it at 11*s*. 2½*d*. Flemish the noble, it amounteth £100 17*s*. 6*d*. Flemish. Item, I have made you over by exchange in like wise with Jacob van de Base 89 nobles and 6*s*. sterling, payable at London in usuance in like wise . . . it amounteth £50 Flemish ; and the rest of your £300 remains still by me, for I can make you over no more at this season, for here is no more that will take any money as yet. And money goeth now upon the bourse at 11*s*. 3½*d*. the noble . . . and the exchange goeth ever the longer worse and worse. Item, Sir, I send you enclosed in this said letter the two first letters of the payment of the exchange above written. Benynge Decasonn's letter is directed to Gabryell Defuye and Petyr Sanly, Genoese, and Jacob van der Base's is directed to Anthony Corsy and Maxy Strossy, Spaniards ; in Lombard street ye shall hear of them." [144] Sometimes, if business were bad or if the Flemish currency were falling, the Staplers experienced great difficulty in making their money over in this way, as William's letter suggests. In November —in the thick of the war between Ghent and Maximilian—he writes again, " as for making over your money, since this trouble began I could not make over a penny, saving an £48 sterling ", and reports the suggestion of one of their Dutch customers that " he aviseth you to bestow your money in gross wares now betimes at this Barrow mart, in such wares as your masterships thinketh will be best at London, whether it be in madder, wax, or fustians, but I trow madder be best ; an so be that ye will, Gomers de Sore shall buy it for your masterships and ship it in Spanish ships in his own name, for John Delowppis and he are purposed to buy much madder to send into England . . . and John Delowppis saith if your masterships will he will bestow your money as well as his own and he saith that that is the best ways to make over your money, for the exchange is right naught." [145] By February—after Maximilian's unsuccessful attempt to seize Bruges—things were worse still. " As touching making over of money at Bruges by exchange or other ways of convenience, in ready money or fine gold, there can be none till this heat be over, for every man is in harness in the market place, and so is John Delowppis and Gomers Desers both . . . Sir, the sayings is that the coins [mint] shall be set down at Bruges, and if it so be, it were best your masterships tarried in making over of your moneys, for it is now at outrageous loss." [146]

It is extremely interesting to compare the financial organization of the wool trade as it appears in the *Cely Papers* with the retrospective account of it given by an anonymous writer (probably Clement

Armstrong) some half a century later (*c.* 1519-39) in his *Treatise concerninge the Staple*.[147] His story is that up to the reign of Edward IV the Staplers sold wool at Calais for ready money and bullion, which they brought to be coined at the mint. But during this reign " soo many Staplers increased in nomber oon of a nother by meane of apprentisehode" that the price of wool rose through their competition, and increasing quantities were exported. In the later days of Edward there were so many Staplers and such large supplies of wool at Calais that the Dutch perceived that they would never lack for it, and so stopped paying ready money at the Staple and begun to " buy on respite " (credit). The mint was dissolved, and the Dutch agreed with the Staple to pay a certain sum in hand and the balance at the mart at Bruges, and, after its decline, at Antwerp, Barrow, and Middleburgh. Henceforth the Staplers no longer brought money into the realm, but covenanted with the Merchant Adventurers (by whom he means the large importers referred to in the *Cely Papers* as mercers) in London, to deliver the money arising out of wool sales to them by exchange, and the Adventurers, receiving it at the mart from Staplers, bestowed it there upon foreign merchandise, which they imported. The writer argues that " Theis two kyndes of exchaunges ", the sale of wool on credit at the Staple and the exchange between Stapler and Adventurer in London, were a double loss to the realm, since the Adventurer, instead of bestowing his stock of money upon English cloth for export and paying custom on it, delivered it to the Stapler and went over the sea with empty hands, while the Stapler, instead of importing his money in bullion gave it to the Adventurer to import in the shape of foreign goods. He finds the root of the evil in the fact that, whereas before Edward IV's reign the Staplers had been comparatively few and had dwelt abroad in the country, then " the staplers toke into ther folish [fellowship] adventurers of London by redempcion " and these Adventurers had so great an advantage over the country Staplers that in a short time they " begane to were owt all the Staplers abrode in the reame ". In spite of demonstrable misstatements, an exaggeration of the extent to which the bullion laws were operative prior to Edward IV's reign and a considerable post-dating of the use of credit, which had certainly prevailed for centuries, the treatise is an interesting expression of the traditions current in Armstrong's day as to the relations between Staplers and Adventurers, which can be studied at first hand in the *Cely Papers*.

In conclusion, it may be of some interest to try to estimate the average profit which a Stapler expected to make on his wool. The best sources of evidence on which such a calculation may be based for the latter part of the middle ages are the late fifteenth century treatise entitled *The Noumbre of Weyghts*, to which reference has already been made, and the Cely accounts. The *Noumbre of Weyghts*, as has been pointed out, estimates the total cost from the grower to the port, including packing, transport, and custom and subsidy at £3 6s. 8d. per sack, but custom and subsidy is apparently calculated at the alien rate (53s. 4d.), which would bring the costs down to £2 13s. 4d. for the Stapler paying the 40s. rate. On to this there has to be added the freight from London, or another wool port, to Calais, and the conduct money; in 1478, the Celys paid 6s. 8d. per sarpler from London to Calais, with " premage " at a penny a sarpler.[148] Thus if the estimate of *The Noumbre of Weyghts* be accurate, the total cost per sack would amount to something over £3. The average cost of a sack of wool in the Cotswolds was estimated at £8 (though the Celys occasionally had to pay as much as £8 13s. 4d. and even £8 15s.), so that the merchant would have to make his profit on an investment of about £11 per sack of the best Cotswold wool. *The Noumbre of Weyghts*, in its list of prices set in Calais on the wools of different counties, puts the sale price of March wool (the most expensive variety) at £13 6s. 8d., and of fine Cotswold at £12. The Celys sold for £12 13s. 4d. from 1474 to 1482, and for £13 6s. 8d. from 1482 to 1488. On these estimates, therefore, the Stapler must have expected to make a clear profit of between £1 and £2 per sack of fine wool. Middle wool, of course, sold at a lower rate; when the Celys sold " good cottes " at £12 13s. 4d. they sold " middle cottes " at £8 13s. 4d., and in general the difference in value of the two quantities was reckoned at £4. On occasion, however, they bought both together from the grower at the same rate, as when in 1476 Richard Cely contracted with John Busshe of Northleach, to supply him with " 40 sacke of good cottys wolde woll, good woll and midde woll of the same pryse the sacke of bothe good and medde, 13 marks 20d." (£8 15s., a very high rate, but 1476 was a dear year).[149] In cases such as this the profit per sack was obviously lower.

A clear profit of £1 to £2 per sack seems very little, when it is considered that out of it the Stapler had to keep up his offices on both sides of the Channel, warehouse his wool at Calais, and ride regularly to the Cotswolds and to the marts in the Low Countries several times a year. The explanation seems to be that certain rebates and differences in the weight of a sack in England and in Calais gave the Stapler a series of advantages, out of which he was able to meet a part at least of his expenses. Our information on this subject derives in the main from a series of memoranda drawn up for the government by various interested persons during the middle years of the sixteenth century, and has to be used with great caution (apart altogether from the fact that it is half a century later in date than the documents with which we have been dealing), because these memoranda were hostile to the Staplers and intended to make their profits appear high in relation to their taxation. It would be beyond the scope of this study to subject them to the criticism necessary in order to judge of the degree of truth in their estimate of Staplers' profits, but since the system to which they refer was certainly in existence in the latter part of the middle ages, they may safely be used to indicate the points at which the Staplers profited by rebates or differences in weight. The fullest account occurs in a memorandum of which several copies are in existence, and to which Schanz (who prints it from the Cotton MS. Tiberius D viii) assigns the date *c.* 1527, though it is more probable that it belongs to 1547.[150] The author enumerates five advantages enjoyed by the Staplers. First, a sack of wool in England contains 52 nails and a sack of wool in Calais 90 nails; but the Calais nail is only half the weight of the English nail, and therefore 45 nails in England make a sack in Calais, with 7 nails advantage in every sack. Secondly, the wool dealer has to allow the buyer 4 nails of wool in every sarpler and a nail at the draught, i.e. 5 nails (in this document the sarpler is estimated to contain nearly three sacks). Thirdly, when the wool is customed the King's Weigher has to allow the owner 8 nails in every sarpler. Fourthly, after the weighing the canvas in which the sarpler is packed is sold for wool, and is worth 10*s*. 8*d*. a sack, which after rebating the original cost of 4*s*. for the canvas, amounts to a gain of 6*s*. 8*d*. on every sarpler. Lastly, merchants buy fells in England by the long hundred (120) for £3 6*s*. 8*d*. per hundred, and sell them in Calais by the short hundred (100) at £5 per hundred. The author estimates that the Staplers gain through these advantages enough to pay all their customs and other charges. This is certainly an exaggeration, but no estimate of profits would be exact without taking into consideration this system of rebates and allowances.

§ 3

THE STAPLE AS AN ORGAN OF PUBLIC FINANCE

1. *Loans, the Wool Customs and the Garrison of Calais*

The organization and privileges of the Fellowship of the Merchants of the Staple were fully defined by the beginning of the fifteenth century, and received confirmation at the beginning of each reign. It was during this century (when in reality the basis of its power was being undermined by the shrinkage of the export trade in wool) that it played the most active part in English public life. The functions which the Staple performed were manifold. It was a legislative body within its own sphere, making all the regulations which governed the sale of wool in Calais, save such as were imposed upon it by Parliament, and these were often due to its own inspiration. It was a judicial body, holding one of the most important courts administering the law merchant in Europe. It was an administrative body, organizing and maintaining an elaborate machinery for the inspection of wool and keeping a watch at the ports against smuggling. It was a financial body, engaged in extremely complicated financial transactions with its own members on the one hand and with the Crown on the other, out of which transactions there grew up a whole group of financial instruments, which were legal tender among merchants, just as negotiable paper is in our own day. Finally, it was in some sense a political and diplomatic body too. In Calais itself, it had to maintain relations with two other bodies having rights and powers in the town, the burgesses under their Mayor and Aldermen and the garrison, under its Captain and Treasurer. It was continually engaged in negotiations with the government in England, settling the terms on which it would make loans, pursuing an incessant warfare against the grant of licences and against smuggling, presenting petition after petition to Parliament. At the same time it frequently carried on negotiations with the towns of the Netherlands and (as we have seen) concluded a series of commercial treaties with Leyden, while in all general negotiations for peace between England and Burgundy, high officials of the Staple were always to be found among the English commissioners, and the conduct of the wool trade at Calais was always one of the subjects under discussion.

So far as the Staple was concerned with the regulation of the wool trade, its relations with its own members and its customers have been sufficiently illustrated in the preceding section of this essay. It is necessary now to consider another aspect of its activities, to wit, its financial relations with the Crown and their reaction upon its relations with its own members; for it was as an organ of public finance that the Staple played its most conspicious part in public affairs during the fifteenth century. Three things in particular demand some explanation, first, the series of loans by which the Staplers established themselves as among the most important financiers of the Crown, secondly, the part which they came to play, as a result, in the collection and administration of the custom and subsidy on wool, and thirdly, the use made of them by the government in enforcing the bullion regulations.

The position which the Fellowship of the Staple came to occupy in the fifteenth century as financiers of the Crown was one to which the circumstances of their trade and its relation to taxation foredoomed them. At the beginning of the fifteenth century they were a wealthy and well-organized body, " reputed and taken the most worshipfull company of merchantis subiectis to a king that any prince christned hath had," [151] and the custom and subsidy on wool was one of the most important sources of the royal revenue. This inevitably marked them out as a body from which loans could conveniently be raised on the security of the customs, and such financial transactions between the king and the wool-merchants had been frequently resorted to in the past. In the fifteenth century, however, there was a new element in the situation. The Staple was now permanently fixed at Calais, and the maintenance of the fortifications and payment of the garrison at that town constituted a heavy annual charge on the revenue. It was natural to assign a part of the custom and subsidy on wool to meet this charge, since the merchants of the Staple could, when required, make a part of the payment due from them at Calais, and thus facilitate the payment of the Treasurer and Victualler there. But the Crown was constantly in arrears, and on more than one occasion the soldiers, refusing to wait any longer for their unpaid wages, forcibly seized the wool of the Staplers. This seems first to have happened in 1407, and the Staplers, in order to regain their wool, advanced the king the sum necessary to pay the garrison.[152] From this time there begins a long series of loans from the Staple to the Crown, usually secured upon the custom and subsidy, and employed for the payment of the garrison. These loans seem usually to have been raised by a group of between fifty and sixty of the wealthiest members of the Company, trading both from London and from provincial ports. In return they were allowed to retain a part or the whole of the custom and subsidy on wool shipped from certain ports, sometimes taking part of the custom and subsidy due from non-Staplers and shipping freely themselves, until they had repaid themselves. A common arrangement was for the Treasurer and Victualler of Calais to give the Company obligations or receipts for the sums which they had received, these being written upon the bills of custom and subsidy due from the Staplers who had provided the money, when these fell due. Such loans were advance payments of customs, but others were " prests " raised by the Staple from its members, and payable by assignments upon other sources of revenue.

It is unnecessary to consider here the loans made by the Staplers to Henry VI and the terms upon which these were granted; they are considered in detail in Miss Haward's essay. By the reign of Edward IV the situation had become acute. Like his Lancastrian rival he continued to raise loans from the Staple, at first providing for their repayment by arrangements similar to those which had prevailed under Henry VI.[153] But the accumulated debt of the Crown to the Staplers was now very large (in 1464, they put it at £32,861), and the hold of the Company upon the custom and subsidy had grown steadily closer. This led, in 1466, to an entirely new arrangement, which became known as the " act of retainer ", and which was the logical outcome of the development of the last fifty years. So intimate had become the connection of the Company with the collection of the custom and subsidy on wool on the one hand, and the payment of the garrison on the other, that there was an obvious convenience in handing both over entirely into its control. The arrangement entered into was as follows.[154] The Mayor of the Staple became Treasurer and Surveyor of the Works of Calais, and his Lieutenant became Victualler. The Company was to take (1) all revenues, fees, and profits arising to the king in Calais and the Marches, and (2) all the custom and subsidy on wool, wool-fells, shorlings, and morlings shipped from England, with the exception of those going by the Straits of Marrock. Out of these revenues the Company undertook (1) to pay the wages (two-thirds in cash and one-third in victuals) of the garrison of the town of Calais, the Tower of Rysbank, and the castles of Guines and Hammes (for which £10,022 4s. 8d. was to be set aside annually), and to maintain the fortifications and artillery there ; (2) to retain a sum of £3,000 a year for themselves, until they should be fully repaid the debt of £32,861 owed to them by the King ; (3) to pay £100 a year for the fees of the Customers and Controller of the Great Custom in the Port of London, and 1,000 marks for the salaries of the king's judges, sergeants, and attorney ; and (4) to meet the expenses of the convoy of the wool-fleet to Calais twice a year.[155] If, however, the revenues from Calais and the customs exceeded the sum of £15,022 4s. 8d., they had to pay the surplus into the Exchequer. This arrangement was to last for eight years ; and it was renewed for another sixteen in 1473, when the royal debt to the Staplers stood at £28,000.[156]

These financial transactions between the Company of the Staple and the Crown were naturally reflected in further transactions between the Company and its members. In order to meet the demands of the Crown and to pay the garrison, the Company was often obliged to borrow money from its members, either by calling in advance instalments of the custom and subsidy due at a later date, or by imposing a forced loan on the value of each man's merchandise.[157] These " chevisances " bore interest, and there is an interesting reference to the losses incurred thereby by the Staple in the ordinance of 1473, which renewed the arrangement by which the Staple took and administered the custom and subsidy on wool. Here it is enacted that, " where the said Maire, Feliship and Merchauntes have susteyned dyvers lostes and charges by means of chevisaunce and otherwise for the wele and saufgarde of the said Toune of Caleys and Marches," all persons having debentures under the Staple seal for " apprestes " or loans made in the Staple, are to share the loss in proportion to the amount owed to them, bringing their old debentures into the Staple, so that these deductions may be made and taking out new debentures for what is left, the Company being in no wise constrained to pay the deducted sums. This regulation, however, is not to extend to obligations under the Staple seal, nor to any " Bille delyvered for partition of Debentours " (usually called a warrant), nor to " the duetye of apprest of xiid. of the pownd last born in the Staple " (i.e. to the most recent loan).[158]

This ordinance is interesting for its enumeration of various financial instruments issued by the Treasury of the Staple in its dealings with the members of the Company. The debentures and warrants, or bills of partition, have recently been elucidated by Mr. Postan :—

> The debts of the Staple to its members, incurred principally in connection with loans to the King, were often recorded on certificates of debt handed over to each lender in lieu of an obligation or a receipt, and identical in economic use and diplomatic construction with the debentures employed by the clerks of the King's Wardrobe to certify the debts from the Wardrobe to various individuals. The debenture states in an impersonal form that a sum of money is owing (*debentur*) to the person named therein ... The warrant of the Staple was a document subsidiary to the obligations and certificates of debt. Whenever the Staple was in a position to make payments on account of its floating debt to individual Staplers, in settlement of state loans or in connection with the compulsory pooling of profits, it made a partition, or in other words declared the size of the next payment and issued to the holders of obligations and debentures of the Staple warrants of payment setting out the fraction of the pound to be paid as the next instalment. The warrant was thus neither a bond nor a certificate, but an order for payment and was akin to the bill of exchange. All these Staple documents ... were legal tender for payments to the Staple and circulated among the merchants in Calais and the other towns in a manner very similar to modern negotiable paper.[159]

A very interesting light on the financial relations of the Staple and its members during the last quarter of the fifteenth century, is thrown by the letters and business memoranda of the Celys. The custom and subsidy on wool formed the main item in these relations. For the Stapler it was a considerable charge which he had to be ready to meet at stated times, for the officers of the Staple it was the chief source of income out of which they had to meet heavy expenses on both sides of the Channel, and they had to arrange for it to be paid at those times and places which would be most convenient from this point of view. It was usual for the custom and subsidy to be paid partly in England and partly in Calais, the first instalment being usually due when the wool was shipped and the others at specified terms. In *The Noumbre of Weyghtes* it is stated that " the custome of woll and the subcyde of woll be all on[e] except that the custome ys payd in hand and the subsyde ys payd att days ".[160] Sometimes the Stapler handed over to the Company a certificate of debt payable to the Mayor, Constable, and Fellowship or bearer at pleasure, and on this would be written off the sums paid until the payment was complete.[161] At other times payment was made in the form of bills payable at specified dates, according to direction. A note, by George Cely in 1478, of sums disbursed in payment of custom and subsidy on 116½ sacks 13 cloves of wool, and 5,568 fells (amounting to

THE WOOL TRADE

£279 18s.) illustrates the way in which these obligations were met partly in cash and partly in negotiable paper. He sets down first of all a sum of £167 1s. 8¼d. paid in London as follows:—

(1) "by the menes of our wharreant of lone money lent be me the xx day of nouembyr" (1476)—£50;

(2) "by the menes of my sayd fadyrs debenture of our portyssyon of ivs. of the pound" (see the explanation of warrants of the Staple given above)—£20 3s. 4d.;

(3) "by one portyssyon of William Olwys debenture" (which, these warrants being negotiable, had come into the Celys' hands)—£19 0s. 9d.;

(4) 'be my fadyr at London for xvis. viiid. of the sarplers" (i.e. for the instalment payable in cash on shipment)—£47 18s. 4¼d.; "be my fadyr by an nodyr byll of my bond whiche most be paid at the syght allso"—£30. He then proceeds to note how the balance has been paid by himself in Calais in coins of various denominations (crowns, "royals," etc.) bought in Flanders, with a note of the rate of exchange.[162]

The correspondence of William Cely, factor to the Cely brothers after their father's death, gives a particularly full account of his transaction on their behalf at Calais and his letters during the summer of 1482, report in detail the financial arrangements made between the Staple and the Crown, and the arrangements between the Staple and its members, which were dependent on these. On 5th May he writes to tell George Cely, at the mart in Antwerp, that negotiations have been going on in London between the King's Council and the Fellowship about the payment of the garrison's wages for this half-year; the Council demands that the sum due shall be paid at Calais in sterling money, but the Fellowship has finally agreed to pay half in sterling in London on the last day of July and the other half in Flemish money (at 26s. 8d. Flemish to the pound sterling) at Calais by midsummer. Staplers must therefore send bills over to London for one half of the custom and subsidy due from them, but if anyone prefer to pay in sterling in Calais it will be deducted off his bill in England.[163] Two days later William writes to report further details. The Fellowship in London has been in negotiation with the king over his "surplusage" (i.e. the surplus left over each year from the customs and subsidies, after the Staplers had met the various charges which they had undertaken, which sum had to be paid into the Exchequer) and it has been fixed at 6,000 marks. The Fellowship in Calais has just held an assembly and agreed that all the wool and fells shipped from London at the next shipping shall be cocketed before the 6th April last (i.e. before the end of the last financial year), and shall pay custom in England "at such days as they can get of the king", and be set towards the payment of the surplusage, anything over and above the sum required being cocketed after the 11th April and paid at Calais. All the wool and fells shipped at the other ports are to pay custom at Calais, and this is to be used for the payment of the next half-year's wages. William adds that, in spite of the arrangement for paying half the wages in England by 31st July, and half in Calais by midsummer, he now understands that they will have to pay the whole sum in Calais in Flemish money by Whitsuntide, " for the soldiers had liever been paid here at 26s. 8d. than have in England sterling money, for they trust not their payment there." [164]

The faithful William now sets about trying to get together some money to meet the first instalment of the customs when it falls due, and tries first to get in the money owed to his master by the Staple; " John Dalton and I," he writes on 10th May, " have spoken many times unto Master Lieutenant for payment of your warrants of 15s. of the pound, and he hath drawn us off many times and desired us to forbear but 6 or 7 days and we should have payment, but as on the 10th day of this month we spoke to him again and desired him that we might have payment of them or else that they might be set upon your bills of custom and subsidy and he desired us to tarry till ye come and then they should be set upon your bills of custom and subsidy." [165] On 13th August he writes to his masters in London to announce that the King's Council demands that the garrison be paid its half-year's wages in Nimuegen groats at an exchange rate of $4\frac{1}{2}d.$; much inferior money was current in the marts, and the Crown insisted on specifying the currency in which payment was to be made and sometimes fixed a rate of exchange very favourable to itself. " Sir, it will be a shrewd loss to receive the Nimuegen groats at 5d. and pay it into the place [the Staple] at $4\frac{1}{2}d.$ " says William Cely. He adds that he understands the goods now coming from London and Ipswich are to pay part of the sum, and that neither he nor any other holders of the warrants of 15s. in the pound can get anything but promises out of the Court. [166]

A week later he sends further details; a letter has been received from Sir William Stocker, Mayor of the Staple in London, and read in the Court at Calais, announcing that the king demands £2,000 for the surplusage of wools shipped during the half-year between 6th April last and the coming 11th October, for which there have been made under the Staple seal six obligations " at six months and six months ", i.e. three payable in February and three in August next year (1483). [167] Another letter, written on 29th August, reports that " the 28th August it was agreed here by Court that any man that had any goods comen from London or Ipswich with this last fleet should bring in his bills of custom and subsidy of the said goods as that day sennight, pain of 12d. of the pound; and that we must make two bills, each of them of the half, the t'one payable the 19th day of October next and the t'other payable the 20th day of February next, and we must make a bill of 20s. of the sarpler, made payable at pleasure, which shall be sent over to England and written upon one of the bills before rehearsed." He adds a list of the coins in which payment towards this half-year's wages is to be made, " and as for an[y] other golds and other silver, they will none." [168] A week later he reports the steps taken by the Fellowship to try and get in the money required for this payment. " Here is an ordinance made by all the fellowship the last court day that we shall receive from that day forward ready money in Calais at 26*s*. 8*d*. Flemish for the pound sterling [the rate fixed for the payment of the garrison] . . . for all wool and fell that shall be sold at Calais from henceforward "; but the men of Leyden and Delft are to be allowed their usual credit, paying half in hand at 26*s*. 8*d*. and the rest by bills " at six months and six months " at 28*s*.; (this project, like so many attempts to interfere with the normal custom of credit sales, seems to have been abortive, and it is significant that the Staple's best customers are exempted). He informs his master that he has taken into the Staple Cely's " bill of 20*s*. of the sarpler, payable at pleasure" and amounting to £35 10*s*., and that it is written upon his last bill payable on 20th February, " as all other men's is in like case and the bills of 20*s*. of the sarpler shall be sent into England to the Solicitor shortly." As to Cely's other bill of custom and subsidy payable on 20th October, it amounts to £79 13*s*. 5½*d*., and must be provided for when George collects the money due to him from his customers at the next mart. " For your warrants of 15*s*. of the pound," he concludes, " I can have but £14 Flemish yet, for it have been spoken of in Court, and there be divers that be in case like as you and the Court saith they can take no direction of it till it be grown in treasury, for the which they say ye must forbear a season." [169] At the end of the month he writes again to George Cely, who is riding to collect money at the marts, to remind him that his second bill will soon fall due : " Item, sir, your mastership must remember to bring home with you £106 fleming for to pay your custom and subsidy." [170]

2. *Bullion Regulations* [171]

The advance of loans, the payment of the garrison at Calais, and the collection of the custom and subsidy on wool were not the only public functions performed by the Company of the Staple in the fifteenth century. The government also made use of it to enforce upon its members a long series of bullionist regulations, which intimately affected the way in which business was carried on between merchants in the wool trade. The object of the government was to secure a plentiful supply of money for purposes of circulation, and to prevent the export of good English money and the import of foreign coins of inferior standard. This object it attempted to carry out by forbidding the export of gold and silver on the one hand, and on the other by trying to secure that a certain proportion of bullion should be brought into the mint, as a result of all sales by aliens in England or by Staplers at Calais; for the convenience of the latter a mint was usually maintained at Calais as well as in the Tower of London. From time to time, as part of the same policy, it tried (naturally without great success) to interfere with the normal conduct of business between merchant and merchant by forbidding credit sales and bills of exchange, and by insisting that payments should be in cash. Attempts were also made to force Lombard merchants in England to export merchandise against the merchandise which they imported.

A study of these regulations so far as they affected the trade of the Staplers may perhaps conveniently begin with Richard II's *Ordinance de la Bullion* of 1397, which laid down that each merchant, whether denizen or alien, who wished to export wool was to bring for each sack or 240 wool-fells an ounce of gold of foreign coinage into the mint in the Tower, within six months of the time when the wool was cocketed, or else pay to the king 13s. 4d. for each sarpler of wool or 240 fells, over and above the ordinary custom and subsidy; the merchants were to find surety with the customers at the ports for the production of the bullion according to the ordinance.[172] The promulgation of this act immediately brought about a petition from the Staplers, pointing out that since the king had a mint master in Calais, bullion brought there for the purchase of wool was delivered to him to be struck into English money and the petitioners received only English money for their wool, but that they were nevertheless bound by the ordinance to bring foreign gold into the mint in the Tower. They asserted that the Duke of Burgundy, in view of this ordinance, refused to allow bullion to be brought out of Flanders or through Flanders to Calais and was making a rigorous search for it, to the great damage of the Staple and of foreign merchants coming through Flanders, with the result that the Staplers were unable to get bullion wherewith to obey the new regulation. They added that whereas merchants from divers parts of the realm shipping wool to the Staple, " some 10 sacks, some 20 sacks," had been accustomed, after selling their wares, to go straight back to their own part of the country by sea, they were now forced to go to London for the sake of ten or twenty ounces of bullion, and wait there until it had been struck into coin, " whereby they spend all that they have gained from their merchandise and more." For these reasons the petitioners asked to be relieved from taking bullion to the Tower and allowed to take it to the mint in Calais, as they had been accustomed to do in times past, and they asked that merchants in arrears with their payments at the Tower should be pardoned and released, and their obligations with the customers at the ports annulled.[173]

This petition was granted and immediately on his accession Henry IV confirmed the arrangement thus made.[174] But the next year the Commons complained that merchants at Calais were still taking Flemish nobles in payment for their wool, and bringing them into England, " the which are current here in such numbers that a man cannot take a sum of 100s., wherein there will not be three or four of such Flemish nobles, and each piece is worse and less worth than the English noble by 2d.", and it was enacted that foreign money should be voided out of the realm or sent to the mint as bullion before Christmas, and that merchants at Calais should send it to the mint there, import being forbidden and search being made for it at Calais and the ports.[175] Complaints that the bullion statutes were being evaded, especially by Italian merchants, continued,[176] and the whole question came to the front again in 1420, when the Commons brought in a bill embodying extremely elaborate regulations for the conduct of the wool trade in Calais from this point of view, but succeeded only in obtaining a reaffirmation of former statutes and ordinances.[177] It is clear that at this time the mint in Calais was closed, for the bill contains a clause asking that English merchants should be discharged from the obligation to bring bullion " to the value of two marks for each sack of wool " to the master of the mint in London. Moreover, the next year the Calais mint was re-established in accordance with a bill, founded upon a petition from the Mayor, Constables, and Merchants of the Staple, setting forth that the Treasurer and Victualler of Calais refused to accept payment of the subsidy on wool due to them except in nobles, which the Staplers, being unable to take nobles out of England, could provide only if the mint were set up again at Calais.[178]

A letter written by the Lieutenant and Constables of the Staple to the Mayor, Richard Whittington, at this time (November, 1421), gives interesting details as to the predicament in which they had been placed. They announce that business is bad, for the Dutch merchants dare not venture to Calais (and in any case have of late been so unreliable that the Staplers are unwilling to have many dealings with them) and the Flemings are prevented from doing as much business as usual by the regulation that they must pay ready money for their wool.

> " Moreover the small amount of money coming in here, or that we are able to obtain with great difficulty in the aforesaid regions for our debts, is all in florins of Guelders or of other lords on this side the Rhine, and also of Holland, the which the Victualler of Calais and others having our obligations of customs will in no wise accept or receive, for they will have all in English nobles, which it is not in our power to do, seeing also that the whole payment for this town and march falls upon us in obligations [payable] here, which is great duress and discomfort to us, and oftentimes causeth many of us to ride about Flanders, for to buy English nobles at very great cost and expense. God knoweth how and by what persons they be carried thither and pray God it be amended, for

we cannot long endure in this discomfort, nor find nobles wherewith to meet our obligations over here and pay our debts in England, seeing that we receive but few of them from our merchants over here, save a remedy be set thereto. Wherefore we beseech you to speak to the lords of the Council, that at the coming of the new wools here a mint may be ordained to continue at Calais in the manner of old accustomed and that the foreign gold which comes here may be brought there and turned into nobles . . . for then their money will be brought into the realm and we shall have money to meet our obligations, understanding, if it please you, that unless this thing be provided we know not how we shall make any payment of our debts." [179]

The bogy of an export of bullion continued to be a source of anxiety and in 1423 the Commons brought in a bill, again founded upon a petition from the Company of the Staple, setting forth that the establishment of the mint at Calais had already brought much gold and silver into England, but that money was still being taken out of the country to Bordeaux, Flanders, and elsewhere, and numbers of English nobles were always to be found being sold by the exchangers at Bruges, "the which thing, if it be not remedied, will be the destruction of the said mint, for if nobles were not so plentiful in Flanders, more plenty of bullion would come into the said mint, which is unlikely hereafter, if the said nobles that pass out of the realm are current there. For the merchants of the Staple at Calais have there no power over their gold or silver, until they have passed over the sea into England, and they are not commonly purchasers of merchandise in Flanders, and also it is little enough to pay for their wools, customs, and subsidy, which they owe within the realm." As a result, the laws against the export of bullion were re-enacted and alien merchants were ordered to find surety not to break them.[180]

It was in connection with the regulations for bringing in bullion to the Calais mint that an extremely interesting experiment was shortly afterwards inaugurated in the organization of the Staple. Its origin and objects are obscure, but it seems to have been connected in part with an attempt on the part of a small group of large dealers to get the control of sales into their own hands. This experiment was initiated by ordinances made in the Staple in 1429. In that year the Commons presented petitions against the export of bullion, for the confirmation of Staple privileges confirmed in 2 Henry VI, for additional restrictions on wool sales in favour of the Staple and for the just observance of " ye ordinaunce and appointement nowe late made in the said Staple at Caleys " in certain points, which they enumerated. The whole payment for wool, wool-fells and tin was to be made in gold and silver at the time of purchase, and of the money so obtained about one-third was to be brought into the mint at Calais as bullion, to be melted down and struck into English coins. Furthermore, every man selling wool at the Staple was to " make trwe and even partition of ye money yerof, with hem yat have Wolle or Felles of the same Contrees yat his Wolle or Felles is of and yat he is adjoined and associed to make partition with, withouten fraude or male engyne ". All merchant sellers were to give their customers acquittances, sealed with the Staple seal, so that no Stapler should henceforth be able to allow credit to a buyer, " and yat ye same money mowe be brought in to yis Roialme, withouten subtilite or fraude." [181] This bill became law (8 Henry VI, c. 18), and the regulations contained in it were to last for three years from the following Lady Day (1430); it was re-enacted for another three years in 1433 (11 Henry VI, c. 13).

This partition ordinance embodied notable alterations in the prevailing organization of wool sales. Hitherto the price had been dictated by the market, and it had been customary to receive only a portion of the sale price by cash in hand, the balance being payable by bills at different terms, fairly long credit being allowed. Moreover, there was certainly no division of profits among all the members of the Fellowship. The Staple was what would later have been called a " regulated " company; its members entered by apprenticeship, paid certain dues, and conformed to its rules, but apart from this they traded freely as individuals. Now, however, it appears that the price of wool was fixed by the Staple, merchants being obliged to sell at the price ordained, while all credit transactions were prohibited. Each member had to pool the money which he received with that of other members dealing in wool of the same growth as himself, and the total sum was distributed among all the members of each group, according to an assessment based upon the quantity of wool which each had brought to the Staple, whether they had actually sold all, or only a part, or none at all of their stock. The effect of the ordinance was, in fact, to convert the Fellowship of the Staple from a regulated into something not unlike a joint-stock company.

A very hostile picture of the results of the partition system is to be found in the complaints made by the towns of Holland and Zealand, during negotiations in London, in the early summer of 1438, for a peace treaty between England and Burgundy. These towns were, by now, the best consumers of the Staple, and their attitude is interesting. First, they say, the Staplers have set one price on all wool and wool-fells and have been raising that price steadily in the course of the last ten years. Moreover, the money that they receive from sales is divided among those who have and those who have not sold alike, according to the quantity of wool and fells which each has in the Staple, with the result that the merchants who sell their wool first have to wait for three or four years before they receive the last penny for their goods, and are naturally obliged to charge much more than they did when payment was made twice every year. Secondly, they declare that there is an ordinance at the Staple, whereby, in order to be in a partition, goods have to be brought in during a short specified period, after which no merchant is allowed to bring any more wool for sale until the partition has been entirely completed. The result is that six or seven years often elapse before " common merchants " are able to do business, and the whole management of the trade has now fallen into the hands of twenty or thirty merchants, who rate the value of the wool " at the third or fourth penny " above the customary price. The Dutch towns furthermore declare that the result of these practices is to delay goods for so long in England that they are sold in a rotten condition, that the amount of wool sold at the Staple has fallen from 7,000 or 8,000 sarplers to 3,000 or 4,000, and that thrice as much Scottish and Spanish wool is now being sold in towns where English wool used to be sold for great sums.[182] In the course of the same negotiations the Dutch also furnished their ambassadors with a statement of the conditions which had prevailed in the Staple before the ordinance and which they desired to see re-established. Then, they say, all merchants at Calais were free to sell their goods " high or low ", without all being priced alike, and every man sold as dearly as he could, and was paid as much as he desired for his satisfaction. All wool was then brought " a third or fourth penny " more cheaply than now, and not more than ten pounds per sarpler used to be given in ready money, the rest being " allowed for a long day ".[183]

It is evident that foreign buyers felt themselves severely hampered by the new arrangement. They deeply resented the obligation to pay cash in hand for the whole of their purchases, which was a breach of the long standing system by which commercial transactions were conducted and was particularly inconvenient in times of political disturbance, when it might be dangerous to carry large sums of money to Calais. It is, indeed, difficult to believe that the regulation forbidding credit can have been rigidly observed, but the new order was sufficiently firmly enforced to give rise to constant complaints among the wool-buying towns of the Netherlands. In March, 1430-1, after it had been in force for under two years, the communal accounts of Bruges show that a delegate was sent to Calais, " together with the deputies of the other Members of Flanders " to confer with the Mayor of the Staple concerning an English ordinance of wool, which was deemed to be contrary to the interests of the " drapery of Flanders ". On 20th October, 1431-2, there is a further notice that two delegates have been sent to take part in a conference of the towns of Flanders, Brabant, Holland, and Zealand about the English ordinance on wool. In 1433 (the year in which the partition act was re-enacted for another three years) there was renewed activity among the towns of the Netherlands. On 20th October, the Four Members of Flanders, assembled at Bruges, directed a letter to the Diet of the Hanse League, informing it that, by an agreement with neighbouring provinces under the rule of the Duke of Burgundy, they had prohibited the passage of English cloth in retaliation for the English conduct of wool sales. "We would inform you," they write, "that the English at Calais enacted several years ago great, sharp, strict, and unjust (*groote, schaerpe, strenge ende onredelike*) ordinances concerning wool, which are being stiffened from year to year, so that it is impossible to procure English wool save at heavy cost, which is a great loss not only to the inhabitants of Flanders, and likewise to those of Brabant, Hainault, Holland, and Zealand, who cannot obtain wool because of its dearness (*diersten*), but also to the merchants of your Hanse, who are forced to pay a high price for cloth," and they ask for the support of the Hanse in the matter. On 6th December of the same year a deputation was sent to England to try and obtain a withdrawal or modification of the new Calais ordinances, and on 28th July, 1434, a delegation went to Bruges to bring the matter to the notice of the Duke of Burgundy.[184]

The representations of these delegations had the result of causing the English king on 14th February, 1435, to nominate a commission to inquire into and bring about a modification of the Staple regulations in favour of the Flemish towns, and on 5th July, Cardinal Beaufort was given the same charge,[185] but nothing seems to have been done and the next year was full of political disturbances, in the course of which Calais was besieged and commercial relations with Flanders were cut off. In the peace negotiations between England and Burgundy in 1438, the complaint of the Dutch towns against the new ordinance was (as we have seen) brought forward. They asked : (1) that trade should be as free at the Staple as it had been fourteen or sixteen years previously, according to the old custom which then prevailed ; (2) that the merchants of Leyden should be free to buy wool or woolfells as they desired, without restraint ; (3) that the towns should be warned eighteen months in advance of any new ordinance ; (4) that the question of bullion and payments should be settled ; and (5) that there should be no more forced purchases of old wool.[186]

Thus the new ordinance was consistently opposed by the customers of the Staple in the Low Countries. Meanwhile, what attitude was being adopted by the English wool merchants ? It is clear, if there be any truth in the account given by the Dutch towns in 1438, that the partition ordinance was proving disadvantageous not only to the foreign buyer, but also to the smaller English exporter. A Stapler trading with a small stock of wool would normally rely on a quick turnover, selling out his stock at once, collecting payment at the two appointed terms, and meeting the bills of his wool-growers at home when they fell due, with the money thus in hand. Now, however, at the end of each season, he could count on only a proportion of the total sum gained by all merchants dealing in the same class of wool as himself, and that proportion was based, not on his sales, but on his stock. This was a serious consideration, for if business were slack, he might, even if he had disposed of the whole of his small stock early in the season, receive a sum too small to enable him to meet his obligations at home and lay in his stock for the forthcoming season. He might have to wait a long time, too, before getting the whole of what was due to him on his sales, much longer than he had been accustomed to wait under the old arrangement, by which he had allowed credit for a limited period to his customers. He was, moreover, disallowed from bargaining as to prices, which were fixed over his head by the large dealers, who controlled the machinery of the Staple. These large dealers, on the other hand, had plenty of capital, and could afford to tie up their money for a long period before receiving full payment for any one consignment, and in bad seasons they were secure of a large percentage of the sum partitioned, however poor their sales might have been. The partition plan would thus favour, as the Dutch towns pointed out, the practical monopolization of the trade by a small group of large exporters.

It is clear that there were internal dissensions in the Staple during the period in which the partition ordinance was in force, and as early as 1431, the Mayor, John Reynwell, referred to a settlement of disputes. As time went on the breach between rich and poor widened, bringing with it conflicts concerning the election of the Mayor and the membership of the Company. Attempts were made to evade the restrictions both by smuggling and by the purchase of licences, and in 1435 a petition was presented in Parliament against both practices. It was complained that certain persons, in destruction of the good ordinance of partition and abasement of the price of wool, purchased licences " to shippe Wolles to Caleys, yere to be solde afore alle other Wolles beyng there, and been bounden neither to kepe ye pris, ne to receive no Bullion, ne to make partition ne distribution of thaire money, like as all the marchauntz of England thider repairyng be streitly bounded by ye saide statutz to doo ".[187]

The petition was granted, but, as might be expected, the King continued to raise money, of which he stood in urgent need, by granting licences in contravention of the partition order, and among the licencees were to be found such wealthy and important Staplers as Hugh Dyke, Hamo Sutton, and William Cantelowe. The case of Hugh Dyke is particularly interesting. In the winter of 1436, he and two other merchants, William Estfeld and Hamo Sutton, lent the King the sum of 8,000 marks; on 2nd December, they received letters patent licensing them that in selling their wools at Calais " they should be preferred before all other merchants there to the value of the sum aforesaid, and that they, or every of them, or others in their name whom the said William, Hamo and Hugh should name thereto, might freely sell their wools to the value aforesaid within the aforesaid town of Calais, to what person soever and howsoever they should wish, before the other merchants aforesaid, and retain by them the sums forthcoming thence, lawfully and without interference, without any restriction or partition to be made thereof in the Staple of Calais among the merchants of the same, any statute or ordinance made to the contrary notwithstanding ".[188] The Mayor of the Staple at this time was Thomas Thurland, who was determined to enforce the partition ordinance. What happened is contained in a petition to Chancery from Hugh Dyke, setting forth that under the protection of his licence his servant, Thomas Ketyll, had on his instructions sold a sarpler of wool to a stranger for £12 5s., " to have and enjoy to him without any restriction or partition to be made thereof, as parcel of the sum aforesaid," but Thomas Thurland, Mayor of the Staple, because Ketyll " would not deliver the said sum of £12 5s., to put the same in partition in the Staple " cast him into prison and kept him there for a long time; wherefore Dyke asks that Thurland should be subpœnaed to appear in Chancery to answer concerning the matter.[189] The fact that a similar licence was granted to Cantelowe appears from an entry in the proceedings of the Privy Council (29th November, 1441), recording that a warrant was to be sent to the Mayor of the Staple commanding him " that notwithstanding any lettres patentes of licence graunted to the said Cantelowe by the which he may ship certain wolles to Caleys and from thens selle hem withoute departisan ayenst thordenance of thestaple, that he suffer not the said Cantelowe, his assignes nother deputees, to have or selle in or from Caleys any wolles that he shal shippe thider by vertue of the said licence unto the tyme the kyng geve him other in commandment ". This revocation was probably due to the fact that the Staple had offered the king a loan, for it is explained that such a sale by Cantelowe would be prejudicial to the Staple, because it would hinder the sale of their wools now at Calais, upon which they had an assignment of four nobles out of the subsidy on every sack, to repay a loan of £10,000, which they had made to the king.[190]

The bullion regulations, however, were even more difficult to maintain than the partition and in consequence a petition was presented in the Parliament of 1437, seeking a modification of the act of 1429, by which a third of the price for each sack had to be brought into the mint. England's alliance with Burgundy had come to an end two years previously, and war had interfered with the wool trade and with the supply of bullion. The English were appreciating the importance of the Dutch trade and now pointed out the difficulty of complying with this regulation in time of war, " in so meche y^t where late certeins Merchantz of Leyden, Amsterdamme and oyer parties of Holland and Seland, beyng of ye special amiste of oure Soverain Lorde, come yider to have boght a gret part of ye said Wolles and Wolfell, offring suffisant contentement, plein agrement and redy paiement yerfore, the pore Merchaunts of this Royalme yan beyng yere, myght ner durst not enclyne yerto, because of ye Statut aforsaid." The king in Parliament is therefore asked, in order to promote the sale of wool, to modify the bullion ordinance and to ordain that " for ye reste of the said Wolles and Woll-fell over the moderation aforesaid ye Merchauntz of youre said Staple mowen lieffully receyve alle maner payement, suche as partition may be made of, answeryng to ye paiement in England ". At the same time it is requested that merchants of Holland, Zealand, and other lands in the king's amity repairing with merchandise to England, should not be bound by the statute requiring them to employ the money gained thereby in this country, but should be allowed to buy wool at Calais with it, giving surety to the customers and taking a certificate of having done so from the Staple, this ordinance to endure until the wools then at Calais were sold and delivered. Complaint is also made that whereas the Merchants of the Staple were forbidden to sell on credit, Lombards habitually broke the laws in this matter and it is asked that no Englishman should henceforth sell to a stranger any merchandise except woollen cloth, save for ready money, or merchandise for merchandise. The usual request for the suppression of smuggling and licences was also made.[191]

This petition was refused, except for the article against smuggling, but it was only the prelude to a more serious attack on the whole principle of partition. The years from 1442 to 1447, were a period of internal dissensions in the Staple, about which it is difficult to obtain any exact knowledge, beyond the fact that a quarrel was still going on between a group of rich men, standing for oligarchical government, the partition ordinance, and high prices, and the commonalty of smaller wool merchants, standing for democratic control, hostile to the partition ordinance, and in favour of lower prices. It was clearly these small men who were responsible for a petition presented to Parliament in 1442, in which it was stated that the ordinance had decreased the customs and subsidies and caused merchant strangers " to labour unto their lords " to make strict search for bullion coming into the mint at Calais, so that the conveyance of bullion had been hindered; moreover that the merchants of the realm were forced to give up their business " be cause they may not be rulers of their owen goodes " and divers men, " the which may not abide the streite rule of the saide partition, bribe and stele out of your saide Roialme Woll and Wolfell, without paieng any Custom or Subsidie." The result was said to be a great decrease in the shipping of wool " and that the price and valugh of Wolles and Wolfell [i.e. at home] by the saide streit rules and ordinaunces of partition is ovir gretely decrecid and amenusyd ". The king was asked to ordain that all wool shipped thereinafter to Calais by merchant denizens should be put to sale by the owners thereof,

THE WOOL TRADE

or by their attorneys, under due form and rule of the Staple and at the price set by Staple ordinance, the third part of the price being brought as bullion to the mint at Calais, to be coined and delivered to the owners for transmission by them to England, "without eny partition of the money that shall come of the said Bullion or of eny paiement of the other partes of the valugh of the said Wolle and Wollefelles to be hadde or made." This was to last for seven years. The royal answer was an order to the Mayor and Fellowship of the Staple to reform the partition among themselves before the first of August next coming, for the period of seven years specified in the petition, "and if thay do it noght, thanne the kyng wolle as to the petition and the remenant in the same petition conteyned, that it be as it is desired."[192] The petition became law in the act of 20 Henry VI, c. 2.

It is clear that the democratic party had now got control at the Staple, and shortly afterwards the government granted Hamo Sutton (who was now Mayor and whom we have already seen contravening the partition by means of a royal licence in 1436) confirmation of all Staple liberties and power to execute them, on the ground that great commodity of wool had deteriorated and diminished both in the Staple and in the kingdom, by reason of defective government "and ordinances, as it is supposed, for the reform and increase of the price".[193] This grant, together with the act of 20 Henry VI, c 12, marks the end of the partition ordinance. Meanwhile the government had been obliged to withdraw the bullion regulations, which were impossible of enforcement in face of the hostility of the Duke of Burgundy, who continued to search merchants on their way to Calais, in order to prevent them from carrying cash there.[194] After 1443, neither partition nor bullion ordinances were in operation, but the internal dissensions in the Staple continued, several attempts were made by the big men to get control of the machinery of government again, and in 1454 a petition was brought into Parliament demanding the reintroduction of both ordinances. The Company, however, sent in a counter petition, promising a loan for the payment of the garrison at Calais if the royal consent were refused to this bill, and to another, introduced at the same time, which aimed at fixing the price of wools within the realm, in the interest of the home buyer; and the bills consequently did not become law. A final attempt was made to enforce the bullion ordinances under Edward IV in 1464, by an act which was to last for three years.[195] But it was not renewed; the usual difficulties had arisen, and the Duke of Burgundy had retaliated by prohibiting the sale of English cloth in the Netherlands.[196] The legal restrictions on "exchange" between merchants were specifically removed in 1473.[197]

There is an echo of the partition ordinance in the negotiations between English and Flemish envoys at Lille in 1478. The Flemings say that they are aggrieved in that when they wish to buy wool they are not allowed to offer less for it than the price fixed by the ordinance of the Staple, and that if they do, they are compelled to make their purchase entirely from the man to whom they made the offer (doubtless at the regulation rate). The Staple even compels buyer and seller to take a solemn oath that they have not broken the ordinance of price fixed by the Staple. They complain " that the money paid was wont to be delivered into the hands of the Treasurer of the Staple and distributed among others not selling wools, to each according to the size of his stock, which was harmful alike to the English merchants and to those of the Duke ", and that " the Merchants of the Staple exact and will have part payment for the wools sold in bullion, and if they cannot do so, they oblige the buyers to pay a higher price (*ad aliquam Recompensam Pecuniarum*) instead of Bullion ".[198] All these complaints were met with an immediate promise that the matter should be remedied; the English do not seem to have argued the points, as they argued such matters as the obligation to buy old together with new wool, and yet if the customs prevailing at the Staple had been those described by the Flemish envoys, to give them up would have involved important changes of organization. It seems more probable that the Flemish towns (as was a not unusual practice in negotiations of the kind) brought up all the grievances from which they had suffered at the hands of the Staple within memory of man, irrespective of whether those grievances still prevailed, in order to obtain a final repudiation of them as part of a lasting *intercursus*.

III

THE ECONOMIC AND POLITICAL RELATIONS OF ENGLAND AND THE HANSE (1400 to 1475)

§ 1

THE RIVALRY

The subject of Anglo-Hanseatic relations is something more than just one chapter in the history of English expansion. All through the Middle Ages the activities and policies of the Hanseatic towns dominated the economic configuration of Northern Europe, and thus affected everything the English did, or failed to do, in the Baltic and the North Sea. The Hanse formed a background to English commercial development, as inevitable and sometimes as unaccountable as the weather itself.[1]

Over the greater part of the middle ages that background was far from favourable to English commercial development. Every attempt of English merchants to expand their trade with the other countries of Northern Europe was bound to bring them into conflict with the economic system established and guarded by the Hanse. The main currents of northern trade in the later Middle Ages ran from east to west, between the recently opened markets and sources of raw materials in Eastern Europe, and the older countries in the west. It was to their position on this current that the towns of the German Hanse owed their greatness. The two poles, Novgorod in the extreme east and Bruges in the west, were just outside the racial and political limits of German expansion, but all along the intervening route there grew up a chain of purely German towns, each commanding an important halt in the route or a junction with a contributory stream of traffic. In the centre there were the great cities of Lübeck and Hamburg, both situated at points where the coastal shipping going east or west struck the projecting coast of Jutland, and goods had to be unloaded for transportation by land across the peninsula. Like their Saxon and "Wendish" neighbours (Bremen, Wismar, and Rostock) they were also natural foci of the northward and southward traffic: northward to the fishing centres of Skania on the Sund, and the principal ports of Scandinavia, and southward to the cornlands of Eastern Saxony, Brandenburg, and Mecklenburg. The western section of the route was served by the towns of Westfalia, the Zuider Zee and the Rhine, and dominated by the ancient and proud city of Cologne. It was the function of Cologne to connect the

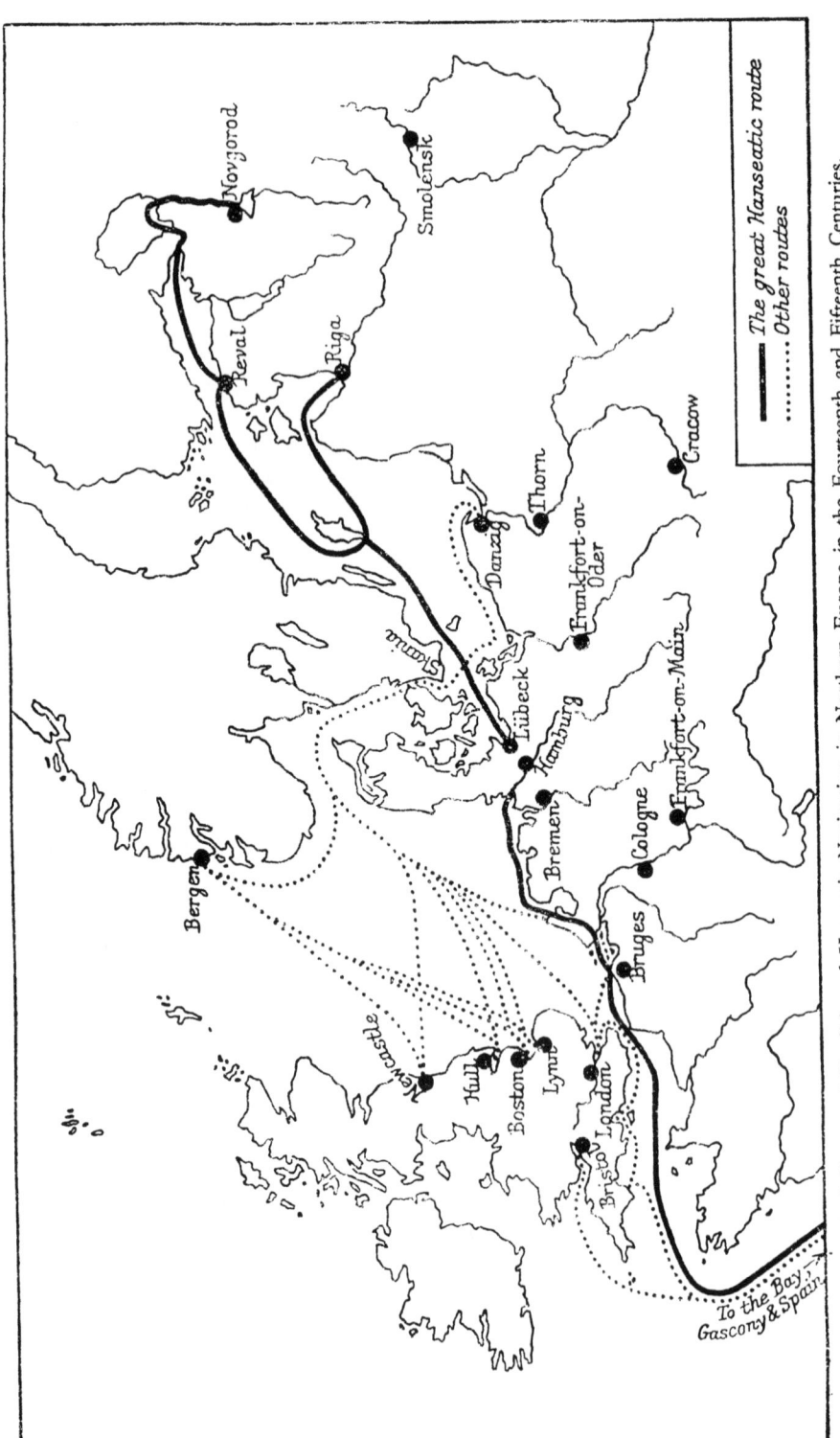

The Principal Routes of English and Hanseatic Navigation in Northern Europe in the Fourteenth and Fifteenth Centuries.

great transcontinental current with reservoirs traditionally her own —the Rhine valley, England, and the Netherlands. To the east of the Lübeck-Hamburg combination there were the towns of Prussia clustering round the new and rapidly growing port of Danzig. These formed the next stage in the journey through Livonia to Russia, and tapped the interior of Prussia and Poland. In the extreme northeast were the towns of Livonia guarding the approaches to Novgorod and the intermediate regions of westernmost Russia.[2]

These towns lived on, and by, the great route. They exploited it not only directly, but also indirectly, by the power it gave them in foreign fields. The industrial centres of Western Europe were badly in need of the East European markets; the industrial, wool-growing and fishing regions of the west were badly in need of East German corn and of the sylvan products of Poland and Russia. As long as the North German towns dominated the route to the Baltic East they possessed a virtual monopoly of trade to the east, and as long as they possessed that monopoly their merchants were welcome and indispensable in more than one foreign country. In England the merchants of North German towns acquired, by the end of the thirteenth century, liberties and privileges, which in some matters placed them well above all other foreigners, and even above the English merchants themselves. In Flanders they formed, from the middle of the thirteenth century, a privileged body of merchants occupying an exceptional place in the commerce of Bruges and well protected by treaties with the Dukes and the " four members " of Flanders. In Novgorod they succeeded a generation earlier in ousting their Scandinavian predecessors, and establishing a monopoly in Russian trade. But nowhere was their power greater than in Scandinavia. In the course of the late thirteenth and early fourteenth centuries they acquired a hold over the mineral wealth of Sweden, the fisheries of Skania, and the fish and fur trade of Norway, established their domination in the municipal government and law of Sweden and Denmark, and came very near to ousting the Norwegian merchants from their own port of Bergen. The four great German factories: the " Steelyard " in London, the Hanseatic " commonalty " in Bruges, the Court of St. Peter in Novgorod, and the German Bridge in Bergen, were outlying termini of a commercial system spreading, in centipede formation, all along the great route and all over Northern Europe.[3]

An economic domination so thorough over a territory so vast was bound to be inimical to the maritime and commercial enterprise of outsiders, English, Dutch, or Scandinavian. But at no time was its enmity more pronounced than at the end of the fourteenth and the beginning of the fifteenth centuries. The very emergence of the Hanseatic league as a political organization in the middle of the fourteenth century was symptomatic. The war against Denmark in 1367 was the first of the great trade wars which the Hanseatic towns were to wage in defence of their economic position in northern trade, and it was also the first official debut of the Hanse as a political and military league. Throughout its subsequent career the league remained true to the objects of 1367. It existed in order to defend the economic foundation of the Hanseatic monopoly; its object was to organize military and political action against possible economic change and commercial competition. This policy of political resistance to economic change was forced upon the Hanseatic towns by the whole trend of contemporary developments. In the late fourteenth and the fifteenth centuries the economic positions which the Hanseatic towns had won for themselves in the course of the preceding century were rapidly changing, and could not endure without constant political protection. The changes were manifold. Some of them affected the international situation in Northern Europe, others occurred in the inner structure and mutual relations of the Hanseatic towns. But whether external or internal, they undermined the very foundation of Hanseatic prosperity, and forced upon the league a policy of rigorous and jealous protection.

In the first place, the situation in Northern Europe as a whole was no longer the same as in the first half of the fourteenth century. In the west the Flemish cloth industry was being rapidly overtaken by the English, and in the fifteenth century also by the Dutch industries. The day was not distant when the Hanseatic colony in Bruges would be unable to control the flow of western produce to the east. Further east and north the Dutch were showing the first signs of commercial activity. By the beginning of the fourteenth century, Holland had completed the main part of her defensive work against the sea, and was entering upon a period of rapid economic development. The native shipping which had always been very active in the North Sea was now steadily penetrating into the Baltic, and towns like Amsterdam and Rotterdam were beginning to claim a far greater share in the east to west trade than the most vital interest of the Hanse would permit. Further east and north the Scandinavian countries were undergoing an experiment in unification which threatened to emancipate them from the Hanseatic tutelage. The great Margaret was able to rule unhampered by the Hanseatic towns, thanks rather to her good sense than to Hanseatic indifference, but her predecessor and successor were led into a conflict with Hanseatic interests in the fisheries of Skania and the domestic trade of Denmark and Norway.[4] Lastly, as will be shown further, England made her appearance as a serious rival in the Baltic.

The changing international situation was in itself bound to make the Hanseatic towns fearful for their future. But their fears were made greater still by the fact that by the beginning of the fifteenth century they were already losing their mutual cohesion and sense of harmony. The towns composing the Hanse formed from the geographical and the economic point of view at least three distinct groups: the central body and the two wings. The western wing, comprising the towns of Zuider Zee, Westfalia, and the Rhine, was chiefly concerned with the trade of Western Germany, England, and the Low Countries. The eastern section, formed by the towns of Prussia and Livonia, was economically bound up with the markets of Prussia, Poland, and Russia. It was the central group, the Saxon and Wendish towns, and above all Lübeck, that gave cohesion and unity to the system. Lübeck's position was central in more than one respect. Its situation on the Jutland peninsula made it a geographical link between the eastern and western wings, and its position as a link enabled its merchants to assume the economic function of intermediaries, as carriers and traders, to the different regions of Hanseatic territory. It is therefore no wonder that Lübeck became the "head" of the Hanse, the builder and defender of its unity. As long as it kept its position of intermediary it stood to benefit by the economic development of the other sections, and could easily reconcile their interests with its own. The integrity of the Hanse was Lübeck's interest, and therefore became Lübeck's policy.

Unfortunately for the Hanse the relations between Lübeck and the other parts had begun to change towards the end of the fourteenth century. In the second half of the century the Zuider Zee towns established direct connections with the Baltic by sea, and this *Umlandfahrt* was becoming more and more popular according as the English and the Dutch were finding their way into the Baltic. This new route gave a stimulus to Dutch and English enterprise in the Baltic, but, what was equally important, deprived Lübeck's position on the Jutland peninsula of its old importance, and thus brought out a conflict of interests within the Hanse. Lübeck was the chief sufferer from the new route, and its own interests forced it to take a lead against the foreign penetration. On the other hand the towns of Prussia, with their bulky goods, availed themselves readily of the new opportunities for direct shipping to the west and of the competitive services of foreign, above all Dutch, carriers. Different, again, was the attitude of the western towns. Some of them had initiated the *Umlandfahrt*, all of them were closely bound up with Dutch trade, and Lübeck could expect no support from them for its conservative and anti-Dutch policy. The harmony of Hanseatic interests was thus rapidly becoming a thing of the past.[5]

This cleavage, or rather the threat of a cleavage, contributed greatly to the anti-foreign policies in the Hanseatic counsels. Itself a product of economic and geographical change, the cleavage justified and intensified Lübeck's resistance to what was the most conspicuous feature of the change: the rise of rivals in the west. The sacred name of unity could now be invoked on behalf of the *status quo*. The recurrent separatism of Cologne or Prussia may often have impeded and weakened Hanseatic action, but it also raised up fears and forebodings, which in the end only strengthened Lübeck's policy of rigid protection and conservation.

The spirit of monopoly and exclusiveness, so strong in the councils of the Hanse as a whole, was also finding its way into the internal policies of the individual Hanseatic towns. The middle of the fourteenth century saw the end of the pioneering era in Eastern Europe, during which the rest of the East German towns had been founded and settled. But the passing of the pioneering age meant also the passing of the pioneers. The earlier period in the history of the German towns was a time of constant expansion and adventure; its authors were men of expansive and adventurous mould. The leaders of the urban policies of the thirteenth century, the typical east-going families of Westfalian and Saxon origin, had no need to be exclusive in the local markets of their towns. Their interests were flung far and wide, all along the Hanseatic route, in Northern Europe and beyond. Their prosperity was based on their ever-growing foreign trade, and foreign trade, especially when it is growing, invariably favours free trade. But in the late fourteenth and the fifteenth centuries the influence of these men on urban policies was fast declining. With the Hanseatic expansion at the point of saturation, the interests and the policies of individual towns were turned more and more upon the local markets. The considerations of local trade began to predominate over those of foreign trade, and the voice of men whose connections and horizons were local, began to predominate in the councils of the towns. In some of the Hanseatic towns a series of democratic revolts in the second half of the fourteenth century, and especially at the very beginning of the fifteenth, for a short time delivered the power into the hands of the petty bourgeoisie. But even in those towns and in those times, in which the government of the patriciate remained uninterrupted, the prejudices and interests of the democracy dictated the commercial policy. The exclusion of the outsider, and above all the alien, from the local trade became the settled object of municipal policy. And this new policy was bound to make the Hanseatic system in the late fourteenth and fifteenth centuries even more inimical to foreign penetration than it would otherwise have been.[6]

Unfortunately for the future of Anglo-Hanseatic relations, it was in the late fourteenth and fifteenth centuries that the English penetration into northern markets began in earnest. The causes of this spurt in English commercial activity are sufficiently obvious. In the second half of the fourteenth century large quantities of cloth began to be produced in England for export. The English merchants, some of whom were themselves cloth manufacturers, possessed those local connections and contacts with production which foreign exporters lacked. They were also assisted by a mildly protective customs tariff. Thus favoured they early acquired a large share in the new branch of the export trade, and the larger their share the greater was their need of foreign markets and their power of penetration.[7]

The penetration proceeded along each of the traditional channels of English trade. The main line of traffic led to the great fair towns of Flanders, Zealand, and Brabant, the chief intermediaries in the trade with the continental interior and the Mediterranean South. Two other channels led directly to the markets of Southern Europe by way of the ports of Aquitaine and Iberia, and to the markets of Scandinavia and Central Europe by the way of the Baltic and the North Sea. In this last direction the English penetration was quite recent. Of the English trade with Scandinavia there are traces in Anglo-Saxon evidence; the connections were not interrupted in the twelfth and the thirteenth centuries, and were still active in the fourteenth century. On the great herring mart of Skania—the threshold of the Baltic—they may have been active as early as the late thirteenth century. That they traded there in the sixties and the early seventies of the fourteenth century is shown by the Hanseatic measures directed against them at the time. On the whole, the trade of the English there seems to have been fitful and irregular. Although they continued trading in the late fourteenth and early fifteenth centuries, they never acquired a footing as permanent and valuable as that of the principal Hanseatic towns or even as that of the Dutch. But their trade to Prussia, though more recent, seemed to become more and more important according as the production of cloth was providing them with an incentive and an opportunity. Prussia supplied the most important Hanseatic imports—corn, timber, pitch, tar, and ashes; Prussia was the chief distributor of English cloth in Poland and Western Russia. It was, therefore, towards Prussia that the English directed their *Drang nach Osten*. In the second half of the thirteenth and the beginning of the fourteenth centuries we find them occasionally in different Baltic ports, but in the second half of the century they planted themselves in Danzig. By the end of the century they formed a numerous and influential foreign colony, trafficked with Danzigers and foreigners, sold wholesale and retail, owned houses and warehouses, and possessed something in the nature of a corporate organization.[8]

Unfortunately this penetration, rapid and thorough as it was, was certainly ill-timed. The English were entering into the Baltic at the very moment that the direct connections between west and east were beginning to threaten the foundations of Hanseatic prosperity and unity. They tried to establish themselves in the trade of Danzig at that very time when the protection of the local market and regional monopoly was becoming the fundamental principle of municipal policy. Their penetration into the Hanseatic system would have produced a considerable conflict in any case, but under the conditions of the late fourteenth and early fifteenth centuries it was bound to result in a bitter and desperate struggle.

The struggle was further complicated and embittered by its connection with the question of Hanseatic privileges in England. Ever since their first appearance in England the merchants of North German towns enjoyed a position of exceptional favour. The merchants of Cologne and Westfalia first, the merchants of the more eastern towns later, were allowed to form in London a corporate body, the Hanse, similar and parallel to the Hanse of Flemish merchants in London. This corporate organization was soon transformed into the permanent communal settlement of the Steelyard.[9] It held property in the City, and undertook certain communal obligations in a manner which made it a partner in the municipal defence and government. Ancient custom and royal grants invested it with rights of jurisdiction over its members and valuable privileges as to the conduct of their suits with Englishmen. Its members also claimed, and over the greater part of the middle ages possessed, the right to trade with foreigners and sell retail. And then, to crown all, a series of Royal charters, and especially Edward III's *carta mercatoria*, conferred upon the Hanseatic merchants valuable exemption from the system of customs tariffs which the government was at that time building up. Under the provisions of these charters the Hanseatics were exempt from all the subsequent increases in the tariffs, so that by the beginning of the fifteenth century they paid even less than the native merchants on their cloth exported from this country, and were not liable to the payment of the additional subsidy of poundage and tunnage.[10]

The privileged position of Hanseatic merchants was bound to provoke an attack from commercial interests at home. Between the attack and the general anti-foreign movement in the English towns, there was an obvious connection. But this connection was often implemented, and sometimes even overshadowed, by issues peculiarly Hanseatic. The towns endeavoured to exclude the foreign merchants from direct contact with consumers and with agricultural producers by limiting the duration of their residence and regulating the scope and the manner of their dealings. These endeavours were directed against all foreigners alike, the Venetians, the Genoese, the Flemings, as well as the Hanseatics, but the Hanseatics provided the best and the easiest target. It was only natural to expect that their commercial connections in England, their exceptional fiscal privileges, and their proud position in the city, would draw upon them the greater share of the urban xenophobia. But what gave to the anti-Hanseatic movement a character peculiarly its own was the strength and the inspiration which it drew from the conflict with the Hanse overseas and from the rather specialized body of anti-foreign feeling among the English merchants trading to the Baltic.

It is this combination of issues, some arising from competition at home, and others from rivalry overseas, that made the Anglo-Hanseatic clashes more frequent and much stronger than they would otherwise have been. Dangerous as are speculations in the " might-have-beens " of history, one can safely say that the single issue of English trade in Prussia would never have produced a strong movement at home. The merchants habitually trading to Prussia were a limited group of men. They may have carried great weight in some of the ports on the east coast and in the neighbouring industrial centres, Lynn, Hull, York, and Norwich, but they were hardly represented in the flourishing midland towns or in the great seaports of the south and west coast. In London their mainstay was the fishmongers, and, powerful as the London fishmongers were, they seldom carried with them the main body of the London patriciate. During the greater part of the fourteenth and the fifteenth centuries the city and its government were led by men whose interests were in the distributive trade of London, or in the commerce with Flanders and Brabant.[11] At the same time the merchants of the Hanse were considerably more popular with influential opinion in England than the merchants of most other countries. They had friends and defenders among the nobility, the clothworkers, and the lower classes; even the jingo author of the *Libelle of Englyshe Polycye* had a few nice things to say about them. Their goods were all essential commodities, not luxuries, and were sold " well cheap ". Thus an agitation on the issue of Baltic trade would have provoked the opposition of the consumers' interests, without at the same time enlisting any active support from the bulk of the English merchant class. A situation of this kind apparently did arise once in the fifteenth century, when the Genoese nipped in the bud the English attempt of 1412 to trade in the Mediterranean. On that occasion the government organized reprisals against the Genoese, but in the absence of any strong pressure from organized merchant opinion, the whole conflict degenerated into a mere question of compensations, the anti-Geonese measures were revoked and the English kept away from the Mediterranean for another fifty years.[12] What made the anti-Hanseatic agitation so persistent and so effective was the fact that at one and the same time it represented the grievances of merchants excluded from the trade of Prussian towns, and the appetites of merchants anxious to exclude the Hanseatics from the trade of English towns. A common enemy produced a sense of common interest, and a sense of common interest ranged the mass of the English commercial classes behind the agitation.

This combination of interests found its natural expression in the " programme of reciprocity ". By the end of the fourteenth century the English demands finally crystallized into a formula irresistible in its logic and simplicity. As an English petition put it, all that the English demanded was that they should be given the same treatment in Prussian and other Hanseatic centres as the Hanseatics enjoyed in England, and that, as long as the Hanseatics refused to concede the English demand, their privileges in England should be revoked.[13] This demand of " parity " eventually became the constant theme of English petitions and complaints. The official spokesmen of English merchants used it with great effect whenever they felt a need to be convincing; the Hanseatics found it very hard to parry; it became the battle-cry of the anti-Hanseatic party in Parliament and the Council, and the bugbear of the Prussian die-hards. But it was not in logic alone that the strength of this programme lay. Essentially an " omnibus " programme, it imposed a tactical unity upon fundamental differences of aim. The merchants trading to Prussia were not prepared to accept a rebuff there, even if it resulted in a revocation of Hanseatic privileges in England; nor were the bulk of the London retailers likely to agree to the continuance of the Hanseatic privileges in England, even if they were accompanied by similar privileges for the Englishmen in Danzig. But as long as the claims of the former and the grievances of the latter were still unsatisfied, the demand for reciprocity provided a convenient formula for a temporary unity of front.

This unity of front added to the strength of the English attack in the same measure in which want of unity in the Hanseatic ranks weakened the effect of their opposition. On no other point of Hanseatic policy did the variance between the component parts of the Hanse manifest itself more fully than in the conflict with the English. The merchants of the Western wing, i.e. the towns of Westfalia, the Zuider Zee towns, and above all Cologne, were very active in the English export trade. The distribution of English cloth became in the fifteenth century one of the principal branches of Cologne's commerce; the Cologne *Englandfahrer* formed a very influential body of merchants in their city as well as the most numerous section in the London Steelyard. At the same time they were not concerned with the dangers of the English competition in Prussia, and not over anxious to lose their privileges in England for the sake of Lübeck's or Danzig's safety. As a result, the leaders of the Hanseatic policy had always to reckon with possible separate action on the part of the western towns. In the second half of the century, at a most critical period in the Anglo-Hanseatic relations, Cologne formally repudiated the official policy of the Hanse, and very nearly destroyed the whole Hanseatic system in the west. The attitude of the western wing had its counterpart in the independent attitudes of Prussia and Danzig. In its policy towards England Danzig was torn between two mutually exclusive objects. It wanted to keep the English out of the local market, and at the same time it was anxious to maintain the highly important commercial connections with England. Thus while Danzig's local monopoly provoked conflicts with England, Danzig's interest in the English trade prevented it from decisive action. On more than one occasion it shirked violent measures advocated by Lübeck, and on more than one occasion it was the first to break a Hanseatic blockade of England and seek separate ways out of a struggle which it had itself begun. The Prussian attitude was further complicated by the independent policy of the Prussian Order. For although the Order was formally a member and a protector of the Hanse, it often embarked on separate policies towards the other powers of Northern Europe.

In these circumstances it is no wonder that out of the several clashes in the late fourteenth and the early fifteenth centuries the English merchants emerged undefeated. Every time the Hanseatic charters came up for confirmation the whole question of Hanseatic privileges in England and of the position of the English in the Baltic was raised, and every time it was raised the pressure of mercantile interests was sufficiently strong to force the programme of reciprocity upon the Council and the Parliament. The Hanse, divided against itself, could not offer an effective opposition. More than once the English negotiators very nearly managed to detach both Prussia and Cologne from the League, and not until 1468 was the Hanse able to organize a war or a successful blockade against England. To an informed observer in the late thirties of the fifteenth century the English position would have appeared full of promise; they seemed bound to win.

As we know now they did not win. Before the third quarter of the century was over the English merchants had been definitely shut out of the Baltic, and it was left to the Dutch to fight out the problems of Hanseatic monopoly on the northern seas. The English settlements in Prussia and Scandinavia had either disappeared or ceased to play an important part in the direction and organization of English trade. The Hanseatics returned to London in full possession of their ancient privileges, and extended their share of the English cloth exports far beyond the point it had reached in the first half of the century. It was much later, in the sixteenth century, that the English penetration of the Baltic was resumed, and it was not until then that the attack against the Hanseatics in London produced the first important curtailment of their privileges.

The causes of this defeat were too many and too various to be summarized in a single phrase. They formed a chain of unforeseen occurrences of the kind that make up the story of history and upset all the schemes of cause and effect. The only generalization which the facts permit is the rough statement that the chain of occurrences was of a political and not an economic order, and was due more to the vicissitudes of government than to the action or inaction of merchants. It is not that the government was unfriendly to the merchants, ignorant of the situation, or indifferent to the needs of English trade. It never was definitely pro-Hanseatic or anti-merchant. On the contrary, as long as the fifteenth century government functioned as government, and as long as it could define its attitude to the Hanse undisturbed by other political considerations, it adopted an economic policy favourable to the interests and opinions of the merchant classes. The iconoclastic researches of Professor Unwin have cast a doubt over the whole question of the economic policy of the English crown in the later Middle Ages. Economic historians, he thinks, antedated the birth of the mercantilist and protectionist policy. Cunningham was too simple in asserting that a mediaeval king like Edward III was capable of a consistent course of economic action towards objects definitely national and nationalistic. Such a king lived from hand to mouth; most of his economic measures were produced in response to the exigencies of the moment; they had purely fiscal ends in view, were always personal or dynastic in motive and were unrelated to any underlying economic principle.[14] These views of Edward's policy are now generally accepted, and it is not the object of this essay to revise them. But at the same time they must not be allowed— and Unwin himself does not allow them—to decide our estimate of the economic policies of the late fourteenth and fifteenth centuries. In the first place, we know very little, much less than historians often assume, about the mediaeval conceptions of state and nationality; and until we know more all the discussions of economic nationalism are bound to be somewhat unsubstantial. Then, secondly, we must guard ourselves against too rigid a test of what constitutes an economic policy. " Continuous unity of purpose " is not the only test, and the motives, however hypocritical, which a government professes, must not be excluded from the discussion of its policy. Throughout the greater part of history, even in our own times, and even in *anno domini* 1932, the legislative and the administrative record of a government is often a joint product of wish and necessity, of conscious policies and of the exigencies of the moment. And inconsistencies in the record of a government are as much a measure of its want of policy as they are of the strength of the needs of the moment.

A conflict of this nature between the economic *desiderata* of the fifteenth century governments and their actual record provides the key to the Hanseatic riddle. Their *desiderata* fully reflected the nationalist bias of the times. No student of the period can fail to observe its insistent and conscious Englishry. The demarcation of things English and foreign was grounded well enough to be taken for granted in the popular parlance, literature, and political utterances of the time. And the nationalism of the age was bound to reflect upon the prevalent notions of state policy in general, and economic policy in particular. The *Libelle of Englyshe Polycye* was saturated with it, but the *Libelle* did not stand alone. We find its sentiments echoed in diplomatic and commercial correspondence, in parliamentary petitions, and let us add, in the preambles of acts of Parliament. Sarcastic as historians are apt to be about the motives alleged in such preambles, it must not be forgotten that the object of a preamble was to justify the act by relating it to those moral and political principles which could command a general acceptance; the more hypocritical they were the more conclusive they are as evidence of the spirit of the times. The author of the memorandum on the war aims of 1449 was abreast and not ahead of his time when, among the principal objects of the war in France, he included the destruction of Breton and Norman shipping, " in order that the English merchants may have the shipping of the seas." So also was the anonymous author of the rhymed memorandum on English commercial policy with his insistence on the wealth of England and his motto: *Anglia, propter tuas naves et lanas omnia regna te salutare deberent.* These sentiments were unquestioningly accepted by the draftsmen of Richard's navigation acts, the Lancastrian bills in restriction of imports from Flanders, and the bullionist acts of the fourteenth and the fifteenth century. A student of the century could find many more instances of similar mentality and phraseology, all revealing the strength of the precocious " mercantilism " of the later Middle Ages.[15]

This being the temper of the age, it was easy for the government to respond to the pressure of the anti-Hanseatic interests, and to understand their motives and language. Naturally enough the different elements of the fifteenth century government could not be expected to be more united on the Hanseatic question than they were on other diplomatic and political problems of the day. But the difference of emphasis and tactics often concealed a common attitude which was almost identical with that of the merchant community. The House of Commons was constantly prepared to voice the point of view of the urban middle classes, and its middle class bias was repeatedly exploited in the commercial interests of the merchants. The City of London had evolved in the fifteenth century an efficient machinery for propaganda in Parliament; the provincial towns sometimes elected special commissions to "make suit in Parliament against the Hanseatic privileges ". Their combined pressure seldom failed to carry the Commons, and the Hanseatics justly regarded Parliament as their chief adversary, and never expected from it any favour or concession.[16]

This attitude of the Commons was reinforced by the activities of the civil servants in charge of Hanseatic policy. There is no other subject in the constitutional and administrative history of the fifteenth century more obscure and at the same time more important for the understanding of foreign and economic policies than the functions, power, and personnel of the chief clerical offices in the government.

In the limited field of Hanseatic policy the influence of the clerks of the council responsible for the official correspondence and negotiations was much greater than a superficial view of events would suggest. Men like Russell, Hatcliff, and above all, Thomas Kent, represented definite policies towards the Hanse, and those policies were, during the greater part of the fifteenth century, fashioned on definitely nationalistic lines. Thomas Kent was apparently the moving spirit behind the negotiations with the Hanse in the middle decades of the century; his memoranda and speeches contained the clearest exposition of the programme of parity and reciprocity, and it is not surprising that the Hanseatics regarded him as their arch-enemy in England.[17]

Less obvious and certainly less definite was the policy of the lords and of the King's Council. The " lords and prelates " sometimes shielded the merchants of the Hanse from the enmity and vindictiveness of the Commons, and were often referred to in the correspondence of the Hanse as its only friends in England. It will also be shown further that in the end the triumph of personal and mercenary interests in the Council, and the conflicting claims of the foreign and military policies which it tried to pursue, prepared the way for the Hanseatic victory. Yet as long as the Council was capable of comprehending and obeying the *raison d'état*, the underlying assumptions of its policy towards the Hanse were little different from those of the merchant classes. The German historians of the Hanse have tried to explain the vacillations of the Council by the influence of the " consumers' interests ". The nobility of England were producers of wool and consumers of imported goods and their representatives on the Council were led by the interests of their class to oppose the monopolistic attempts of the English merchants to exclude foreigners from immediate contact with the English consumers and agricultural producers. Yet the importance of these consumers' influences can easily be exaggerated. Lancastrian and the Yorkist councils contained members with interests and investments in trade and shipping: men like Lord Hastings, Lord Roos, Lord Buckingham, the Bastard of Fauconberg, Lord Say, the Duke of Suffolk, and Cardinal Beaufort.[18] But to assume that the policy of the Council was dictated by the interests of the noble " merchants " would be as crude a simplification of the facts as to assume that it was dictated by the interests of the noble " consumers ". The Gloucester party, and presumably the Yorkist party in its early years, courted the favours of the merchants and defended their point of view; while Cardinal Beaufort, in spite of his commercial activities, resisted the anti-Hanseatic irreconcilables in Parliament and Council. In time of war the Council as a whole was more anxious to placate the Hanse than in time of peace, while during the anarchy immediately preceding the Civil War the lords of the Council were anti-Hanseatic for the mere reason that the Hanseatic sheep were fat, and the baronial wolves were hungry. The attitude of the Council constantly fluctuated, and the fluctuations were due to a variety of causes: the struggle of baronial parties, the relations with Parliament, the military and the diplomatic situation. But on those occasions when the personal and party interests of the magnates were not involved, and the military and political situation was favourable, it was the considerations of English trade and the interests of English merchants that determined the policy of the King and his Council. These occasions were quite frequent in the first forty and in the last twenty years of the century. Whenever they occurred the Hanseatics were as bitter about the opposition of the Council as they were about that of the Commons.[19] But they were not frequent enough to provide the English merchants with that constant and uninterrupted political and military backing which their programme of monopoly and penetration demanded. Over and over again in the course of the century, considerations of war on the continent led the Council into a conflict with the objects of its Hanseatic policy. The objects were completely neglected in the middle decades of the century, when the violent outbreak of party struggles overshadowed all other issues, Hanseatic and non-Hanseatic alike. And during that interval a foundation was laid for the Hanseatic triumph of the seventies.[20]

It is in this sense that the "vicissitudes of government" are to be considered responsible for the failure of the English offensive. It is not that the government did not possess or was incapable of conceiving an economic policy, or that the policy was inconsistent with the programme of the merchants. What happened was that a policy, nationalist in origin and objects, was partly neutralized by a political and military situation on the continent, and partly destroyed through the destruction of all policy and all government in the War of the Roses. In this light the story of Anglo-Hanseatic relations becomes one of a frustrated development, of an economic process defeated by a play of political accidents. To this story we shall now pass.

§ 2

THE THREE SUCCESSES (1400 TO 1437)

The year 1400 found Anglo-Hanseatic relations broken and confused by a conflict several years old. This troubled opening of the century was something of a forecast, but it was also something of an epitome, for it was in the preceeding twenty-five years that the issues of 1400 had matured, and the main groupings of interests formed. The first signs of an organized agitation against the Hanse appear in 1375, when the English merchants addressed a petition to the King complaining against unfair treatment at the hands of the Hanse. The petition was probably provoked by the arrival of the Hanseatic delegation in 1375, and its attempts to obtain for the Hanse an exemption from the subsidy of tunnage and poundage. Nevertheless the grievances of the English east-going merchants were real enough. In the seventies of the fourteenth century English cloth had penetrated far into the heart of the Hanseatic *Verkehrsgebiet*, and at the same time the economic policy of the Hanseatic, and especially the Prussian, towns had become definitely protectionist and anti-foreign. When in the years 1377-8 the accession of Richard II provided the English merchants with another opportunity for an anti-Hanseatic agitation, they could point to a whole series of "injustices" inflicted upon them in Danzig, Skania, and Norway.[21] Their grievances were now substantial enough to force the problem of English trade in the east to the forefront of the negotiations, and for the first time in English history the commercial monopoly at home and the English penetration abroad were exhibited as complementary parts of one and the same programme. Both were incorporated in the "four points" of the English demands. According to these demands the Hanseatics were, first, to admit the English to trade in Hanseatic regions (including "Revele, Pernowe et Cyflandia") as freely as the Hanseatics traded in England under the royal charters of privileges, secondly, to give them similar rights in Skania, thirdly, to relieve them of collective responsibility, and finally, to specify the names of the towns composing the Hanse. These four points contained the first clear statement of that programme of reciprocity which was to dominate the Anglo-Hanseatic policies in the subsequent hundred years.[22]

It is the emergence of this programme that gives importance to the negotiations. Their immediate and practical outcome was a minor victory for the English point of view. The sponsors of the anti-Hanseatic petition, led by the merchants of London, exploited well the pro-London and anti-foreign turn of national policy at the beginning of the reign. The new government, however unlikely to revoke for good and all the privileges of the Hanse, behaved as if it indeed understood and supported the principle of reciprocity. It made the continuation of the Hanseatic privileges contingent on similar privileges to the English in the Hanse towns, and in the meantime suspended the Hanseatic charters. And although a year later a Hanseatic delegation to England managed to obtain letters of protection for a year, the Government continued to insist on its condition. It was only in 1380, after the Hanseatics had formally recognized the right of Englishmen to trade in its territories, that Richard's government gave way and confirmed the charter.[23]

This outcome was not sufficiently decisive to establish anything in the nature of a durable arrangement. It merely defined the issues instead of settling them, and, with the issues clarified, a serious clash was bound to occur sooner or later. The restoration of Hanseatic privilege in 1380 did not put an end to the agitation in England or to the friction abroad. Prussia persevered in her animosity to the English, and used the pretext of English piracies to put off her acceptance of the treaty. The English on their part continued their agitation against Hanseatic trade in England. In the absence of a definite arrangement as to the principles of Anglo-Hanseatic trade, the English authorities, both national and municipal, interpreted the provisions of the charter in a way which did away with many of the fiscal liberties of the Hanse. The Hanseatic merchants were made to pay the subsidies of tunnage and poundage, additional customs on cloth, and even the subsidies of the fifteenth and tenth—all payments from which they would have been exempt if their privileges under the charter had been faithfully and loyally observed.[24]

An additional cause for mutual recriminations was provided by the activities of pirates. Piracy on the high seas in the middle ages was as constant and as inevitable a feature of the shipper's routine as inclement weather, or bribes at the ports. But at times of international friction, with its opportunities for reprisals and counter-reprisals, its accumulating ill-feeling, and its unemployment among shippers, piracy could easily assume the dimensions and do the harm of a naval war. Piratical activity of this kind went on in the seventies, and culminated in 1385 in the capture of a Hanseatic fleet off Swyn. With this capture the crisis came to a head. A series of reprisals, at first in Prussia and later in other towns of the Hanse, as well as of counter-reprisals in England, completely interrupted the trade between the two countries. In Prussia all import from England and all export of Baltic goods to England were prohibited. The English merchants moved out of Danzig to Stralsund, and the English government prohibited all journeys to the Baltic lands.[25]

The crisis was now very acute, but its very acuteness made for its healing. The Prussians had for some time felt themselves isolated in their opposition to the English "four points". In 1381 the Wendish towns demanded that the English should be allowed and tolerated in the country. They were not subject to the competition of English traders, and were consequently satisfied with an agreement embodying the English claims to parity. The friction was above all an Anglo-Prussian one, and the Prussians had to rely solely upon their own determination. Unfortunately, even their determination proved unreliable. In this, as in all the subsequent Anglo-Prussian conflicts, the merchants of Danzig found themselves torn between their fear of English competition and their need of English trade. In the end it was their need of English trade that prevailed. So that when the events of 1385 resulted in the virtual cessation of intercourse, the Prussian resistance gave out and the main obstacle to an agreement on the lines of the proposals of 1380 disappeared. The agreement of 1388 reaffirmed all the Hanseatic freedom and privilege in England, and at the same time recognized for the English their "old rights" and their freedom to come to the lands of the Hanse and Prussia, to settle there and traffic freely and undisturbed.[26]

Thus ended the first serious clash. It is its place in the evolution of issues, rather than its effect on the respective positions of England and the Hanse, that gives it importance. The treaty of 1388 produced no immediate and definite change in the position of the English in the Hanseatic regions. They continued to trade in Danzig after 1388 in very much the same manner as they had done before the troubles of the seventies broke out. Altogether the wording of the clause dealing with English "rights" was too vague and too general to stand comparison with the very definite provisions of the Hanseatic charter in England. But vague and shadowy as the English gains were, they marked the conclusion of an epoch and the beginning of a new one. The troubled period of 1375-90 provided the English with an opportunity for formulating the principles on which their subsequent claims were to be based. It also compelled every one of the protagonists—the Hanse as a whole, the Prussian towns, the English Government, the English merchants—to define and announce their attitudes. For another sixty years the successive stages of the Anglo-Hanseatic rivalry were all enacted round the same issues, and evoked the same responses. They were all variations on the themes of 1380 and 1388.

It is in the midst of one of these variations that the story of the fifteenth century begins. The nineties of the fourteenth century and the opening years of the fifteenth century witnessed a revival of friction and a second outbreak of the Anglo-Hanseatic conflict. As at the time of the first clash, the friction began simultaneously in London and Prussia. The grant of the subsidy of tunnage and poundage in the Parliament of 1381 definitely included the Hanseatic imports and exports, and provoked an immediate outcry from the Steelyard. These difficulties in England had their counterpart in the accumulating difficulties in Danzig. With the settlement in 1388 the English resumed their penetration of Prussia. The English "liggers" (i.e. resident representatives of English firms) took up what seemed to be a permanent residence in Danzig. Some of them brought over their families, and acquired houses and shops. They dominated the trade in English cloth, and also took part in some of the local trades. Their commerce and mutual relations were regulated by a corporate organization, which they seem to have possessed in the nineties, presumably with a communal house, periodical assemblies, and elected officials. To this growth of trade the Prussians could hardly remain indifferent, and they struck out against it as soon as relations with the English were showing the first signs of strain.[27]

With this feeling in the air, it is no wonder that the centre of friction, which was in the first place the English fiscal measures, was soon transferred to Prussia. Regarded from the point of view of the Hanse as a whole, the events in England did not justify anything in the nature of violent retaliation, especially as Henry IV confirmed the Hanseatic privileges within a few months of his accession. The Hanse as a whole seemed consequently unwilling to quarrel with England. The only group clamouring for retaliation was the one which would have welcomed any opportunity for a quarrel, the Prussians, and the measure of retaliation upon which they decided was the one which they would have taken in any case: the curtailment of English trade in Danzig. In February, 1398, Prussia officially terminated the treaty with England; in 1396 the diet of Prussian towns had decided to restrict the English rights of residence, and in 1402, when the conflict passed into an acute stage, the rules against the English settling with "wife and children" and trading with foreigners, or in the interior of Prussia, were singled out for immediate enforcement.[28] The Prussian towns also tried for years to organize a boycott of English cloth. At first these attempts failed through the indifference of the other parts of the Hanse, but in the end the other towns were won over. It was English piracies that decided the attitude of the non-Prussian towns. The prevailing tension provided a good incentive for mutual attacks on the high seas, and the English did not confine their exploits to Prussian shipping alone. By 1405 the successive acts of piracy had raised the whole of the Hanse against the English; and in March, 1405, the Hanseatic diet at Lubeck prohibited both the trade in English cloth and the export of Baltic goods to England.[29]

It looked as if the conflict might pass into a formal war; and if a war at this point did not break out, it was entirely due to the fact that the hostilities on the high seas had carried the dispute much farther than the real interests of both Prussia and England permitted. Whatever their respective interests had been at the time of the first skirmishes in the late nineties, they were far from warlike in 1405. The embargo on English trade was not sufficiently complete to have any immediate political effect in England, but it was sufficiently complete to produce economic difficulties in Prussia. The other parts of the Hanse evaded the prohibition of trade; and even some of the Danzig men imported English cloth from Holland and Skania and shipped Baltic goods to the west. Now, as in 1388 and again several times later, the whole purpose of Danzig's measures was defeated by the inner contradictions of its economic interests, and the determined policy of its anti-English majority was checked by the separate interests of the merchants trading to England. Within a few months of the Lübeck decision, the Prussian towns themselves began to consider the possibility of revising it. At a diet in Falsterbo they proposed the raising of the embargo, and threw the trade open at the first opportunity. It was in vain that the Hanseatic factory in Bruges exhorted the Hanse to hold out " because the Hanse can do without the English cloth much better than the English can do without Hanseatic goods ". For judging by the frequency of evasions it was Prussia, and not England, that found the cessation of trade in 1405 difficult to bear. As a Prussian ambassador to England had himself to acknowledge some time later, the Prussians " der Engelschen nicht entbehren mögen ".[30]

Important changes had also occurred in the English position. England was in conflict with Burgundy, and John, Duke of Burgundy, had been trying to draw the Hanse into an anti-English alliance. An alliance of this kind, apart from its political and military danger, also threatened to close to England that channel of Flemish and Dutch trade, which was then the only alternative in Western Europe to the troubled Hanseatic routes.[31] In the circumstances there is no wonder that the English Government appeared more anxious than before to proceed with the negotiations which had been lazily dragging on since the beginning of the century. In 1405, an English delegation arrived in Prussia, and in October of the same year a draft treaty was ready for confirmation. Before the confirmation could take place—and the English were still somewhat dilatory—a new complication was created by an English capture of five Hanseatic boats on their way to Spain.[32] But Prussia was now too anxious for peace to be put off by a piratical attack. The negotiations for the renewal of trade continued much to England's advantage ; the English negotiators succeeded in reducing the Hanseatic demands for damages to a relatively small sum, and they even managed to create a serious cleavage in the Hanseatic ranks. Lübeck and the Wendish towns, when drawn into the conflict, had none of Danzig's economic motives for anti-English action ; now that the problem of peace was under discussion they had none of Danzig's economic motives for hurry and impatience. The consideration which in the first place decided their attitude to the English was the English piracies, and they consequently saw no reason now for concluding peace without adequate compensation for their losses at the hands of the pirates. Moreover, the Hanseatic factory in Bruges, with its interests in the Flemish cloth trade, was more perturbed by the prospects of peace than by the possible losses and dangers of war. It advised the Hanseatic towns to hold out against the English, and to force them to submission by tightening up the blockade.[33]

It was in spite of this advice, and in the face of the opposition of the Wendish and Saxon towns, that Prussia in the end concluded peace with England. And it was against the settled policy of Danzig that the treaty, which was finally concluded between Prussia and England, embodied a general recognition of the principle of " reciprocity ".[34] The English were confirmed in their right to come to Prussia, and there to *conversari, libere more mercatorio tam cum Prutensis quam aliis, cuiuscumque nacionis vel ritus fuerint, mercari, ibidemque morari et exiende ad lares et domicilia propria redire.*

Thus ended the second important clash, the first in the fifteenth century. It occurred over the same issues and brought out the same alignment of interests as the preceding clash of the fourteenth century. Like the preceding clash it ended in favour of the English, and the English gains were made more real still by the political situation in the years immediately following the conclusion of the treaty. A series of democratic revolutions in the Wendish towns in 1408 and 1410 disabled for a time the central section of the Hanse, and deprived the league as a whole of any effective leadership. At about the same time the Teutonic Order was overwhelmed by a disastrous war with Poland, and after the defeat of Tannenbeg (1410) was not in the mood or in the position to enforce the execution of England's obligations to Prussia. The English government made use of the opportunity to withhold the further instalments of the sum due to the Hanse under the treaty; delegation after delegation failed to extract full payment from England, and most of the sum was still unpaid in the thirties. In Prussia itself the High Master of the time, Henry of Plauen, who was no friend of Danzig's, helped the English to protect and consolidate the positions they had won in 1408. Thus favoured, the English developed their trade in Danzig to a remarkable extent. The English custom accounts record large and regular shipments to and from Prussia. In Danzig the English residents were taking a firm root.[35]

Yet, advantageous as the issue of this second clash was, the settlement was by no means permanent or secure. After a few years, events in England and Prussia began to move again towards another impasse, and the subsequent conflict was not to be settled till 1437. The treaty of 1408 itself contained the roots of the revived strife. From the English point of view it was at least as good as that of 1388, but not as good as the one for which they had clamoured. The general formula of reciprocity could not confer privileges as tangible and as valuable as those which the Hanseatics enjoyed under their charter in England. As long as full parity and reciprocity remained unrealized, the English programme could not satisfy English merchants in Prussia nor arrest the agitation of English merchants in England. It was not enough that they could come to Danzig, settle there, and trade wholesale and retail with Danzigers and foreigners. They also wanted to be admitted to the Livonian and West Russian markets, and to be given fiscal exemptions equivalent to those which the Hanseatics claimed in England; above all, they wanted an official permission to form a corporate body with a communal seat, a " Hanse " of their own. We have already seen them insisting upon their " right to a society " after the treaty of 1388, and the very fact that the treaty of 1408 contained no provision for a " society " made the English demand for one even more insistent than before. In some of their later petitions the English merchants justified their insistence by considerations of practical, and largely of social, convenience. The society was wanted, they argued, in order to keep their members out of taverns and the company of loose women. But the real value of a " society " lay elsewhere. The existence of a corporate body involved the right of jurisdiction over its members, and the power to enforce its own rules and regulations, or, in other words, the opportunity for escaping the jurisdiction of Danzig's courts and the rules and regulations of Danzig's municipality. A common " house " combined with English-owned lodgings and shops meant a virtual exemption from that oversight and control, which Danzig, like most mediaeval municipalities, exercised over its foreign residents through the machinery of licensed hosts and hostelries. The " society " was meant to be the English counterpart of the German Steelyard in London, an institutional embodiment and a guarantee of the exceptional position of the English in Danzig. Without the " society " the parity provided by the treaty was incomplete and unreal.[36]

The treaty was equally unsatisfactory to the Danzigers. The formula of the English " rights " was too vague to give complete satisfaction to the English, but it was sufficiently vague to alarm the Prussians. They were afraid that it might, after all, be construed into a body of privileges as extensive as those of the Steelyard in London. But what they feared most was the attempt to read into the treaty the " right to a society ". They feared it for the same reasons for which the English wanted it. In some of their memoranda to the English Government they tried to justify their opposition by the assertion that the English had used their communal house as a " prison ". On other occasions they alleged political motives. The English, they feared, were congenital Empire-builders; if allowed to settle and trade in Danzig, they would soon annex the country of Prussia, as they had annexed Bordeaux and Gascony.[37] But behind all these official motives, however genuine, there was the determination to prevent the English from developing their trade outside the control and jurisdiction of the town, and thus making the *Gastenrecht* impossible to enforce.

With both the English and the Prussians in this mood, the struggle was bound to break out anew, and in the thirties all the issues were again in the melting-pot. As on the previous two occasions the crisis followed after a long period of steadily accumulating friction; and friction began to accumulate before the ink was dry on the treaty. Some of that friction was undoubtedly due to the English refusal to

ANGLO-HANSEATIC ECONOMIC RELATIONS 113

honour the financial obligations of the treaty. Much ill-feeling was created by piracy and mutual commercial reprisals. Attacks on the high seas were more or less inevitable in the international commerce of the time, but the period between 1417 and 1430 received more than its rightful share of naval perturbations. Most of these were due to the war between Denmark and the Hanse in 1427, in the course of which the Hanse was compelled to close the Sund, and the English suffered equally from King Eric's agents and from the Hanseatic privateers.[38] But it was the revived dispute over the English position in Prussia and the Hanseatic position in England, that provided the main source of conflict.

The dispute revived first of all in Prussia. The Danzigers, who had never accepted the English interpretation of the treaty, tried to assert their point of view as early as 1410, when, according to an English complaint, the burgomaster proclaimed that the English should no longer traffic with foreigners, and sell their goods retail or possess a corporate organization. Fortunately for the English, Henry of Plauen was then the High Master of the Order, and through his intervention the English merchants obtained the revocation of the measure. But within a year of his intervention Henry of Plauen was deposed by a revolution, and his successors were not inclined to fight Danzig on behalf of the English. For another three years the position of the English apparently remained unchanged, and then, in 1414, the municipality of Danzig again re-enacted the order as to English trade, which the High Master had overriden in 1410.[39] But even this action had little immediate effect upon the trade and economic position of the English merchants, for the English trade to Danzig continued to flourish all through the second decade of the century. It is in 1418, after the failure of the Hanseatic appeal to the Emperor, that we observe the first signs of the English counter-agitation. In that year we find Henry V addressing to the High Master a complaint against the maltreatment of the English merchants in Danzig, reminding him of the maxim that "the English should be treated in the Hanse even as the Hanseatics are treated in England". This reminder was accompanied by an anti-Hanseatic offensive in London. In January, 1418, the merchants of the Steelyard complained before the Mayor's Court of the exactions of certain local dues, from which they considered themselves exempt under the terms of their charter. On this occasion the Mayor's Court decided for the Hanseatics, but two years later the sheriffs of London proclaimed their determination to collect the dues from the merchants of the Hanse and the King's Council overruled the verdict of the Mayor's Court. London's official attitude was underlined by the refusal of the Mayor and Corporation in 1419 to appoint an English alderman to the Steelyard: a refusal which went against an explicit provision in the Hanseatic charter and an established practice of the City. If we are to believe a later petition of the Steelyard of 1423, the fiscal "oppression" of the preceding few years had been prompted by the English merchants and above all by the merchants of London. Their agitation redoubled its vigour on the death of Henry V in 1422. With the accession of a new king the Hanseatic charter came up again for confirmation, and the whole machinery of organized pressure was now brought into play to prevent the renewal of the "privileges". The records of Lynn have preserved an illuminating account of a meeting of merchants, at which an impost was levied for the costs of the anti-Hanseatic campaign in Parliament; and the merchants of Lynn were no doubt well supported by merchants of other towns. A formal case against the Hanse was provided in the petition of merchants trading to Prussia, enumerating all their grievances against Prussia and Danzig. Within a few weeks of the petition, and while the question of the charter was still under consideration, the Government granted the Hanseatic merchants protection for a year. But during the same year a decision of the Council made the Hanseatics liable to the subsidy of tunnage and poundage, and the Steelyard had a grievous tale of "oppression", actual and threatened, to report to the Hanseatic towns.[40]

In the Hanseatic towns the events in England produced an immediate, though not a very violent, repercussion. The Danzig municipality continued that policy of curtailment of English rights which it had begun in 1414. It tried to prevent the permanent settlement of the English in the town, to stop their retail trade, and their intercourse with "foreigners". It was in vain that the English merchants complained at what they considered a breach of their rights and pressed their demands for an organization in a series of petitions and deputations to the High Master of the Order, for both their complaints and their demands remained unsatisfied. But at the same time the Order and the municipality of Danzig carefully avoided the violent courses advocated by others. When in 1423 the Hanseatic diet at Lübeck recommended that the English merchants resident in the Hanseatic towns should be imprisoned, and their goods confiscated, as reprisals and protest against the recent events in England, the Order and the Prussian towns refused to carry out the decision, and the English trade to Prussia continued uninterrupted.[41]

This moderation was temporarily successful, for neither party was at the time prepared to court the danger of a formal rupture. The English trade had been badly hit by the Dano-Wendish war and the closing of the Sund, and was threatened by the renewal of Flemish measures against the English cloth in 1428. Prussians, in their turn, were not over-anxious to bring about a complete cessation of their English trade. It is therefore no wonder that the counsel

ANGLO-HANSEATIC ECONOMIC RELATIONS 115

of moderation for a time prevailed on both sides, and during the four years between 1426 and 1430 the brewing trouble was somewhat allayed by a number of conciliatory measures. In February, 1426, the government, in response to a Hanseatic petition, appointed an English alderman to the Steelyard, thus overriding the decision taken by the City of London seven years before. For a few months the City tried to resist, but a repeated royal order in January, 1427, broke its opposition. Direct negotiations between the Steelyard and the City led to a general compromise, by virtue of which the City sanctioned the appointment of the English alderman. The same compromise also settled the outstanding question of municipal dues, and the merchants of the Hanse were exempt from the payment of most of the local imposts. As their part of the compromise, the merchants of the Steelyard undertook to intercede with the High Master and the town of Danzig on behalf of the English merchants there. When, a year later, the English merchants in Danzig tried again to draw attention to their unsatisfactory position in Prussia, the Steelyard addressed a carefully worded request to Danzig to respect the old customs of the English in Danzig for the sake of the position of the Hanse in England. Whether as a result of this intercession or for other reasons, the Order and the towns seemed for a time to modify their attitude to the English demands. In its reply to the Steelyard, Danzig expatiated on the exceptional favours which the English, in spite of their complaints, continued to enjoy there. At the same time, the Englishmen in Danzig obtained their first important concession on the question of corporate organization. In December, 1428, the High Master, while still refusing to recognize the formal claim of the English to exceptional treatment, conceded to them the right to have an elected governor to lead and rule over their members. In 1429 a Prussian delegation visited England to exact the payment of further instalments under the treaty of 1409 and to settle the outstanding differences. In its financial mission the delegation fared no better than the previous delegations, but it apparently obtained from the Government a confirmation of the Hanseatic freedom from all taxation not specified in the charter and the trade showed signs of revival after the ominous slump of the year before.[42]

Unfortunately, this spirit of moderation could not, and did not, endure for very long. The mutual concessions of the years 1426 to 1430 did a great deal to relieve the growing tension, but they left the important issues unsolved, and therefore could not prevent another change for the worse. The English in Danzig, in spite of the High Master's concession in 1428, continued to clamour for full parity and to protest against recent taxation. The English merchants in London and other towns, in spite of the compromise with the Steelyard in 1427, were preparing to renew their agitation against Hanseatic privileges. The slightest pretext was likely to lead to an outbreak, and the pretext was found in the ever unsettled problem of Hanseatic liability to tunnage and poundage. When in 1431 the subsidy of tunnage and poundage was granted to Henry VI for two years, the merchants of the Steelyard were made to put up sureties for the payment of an additional " increment " of 6d. for each pound worth of goods and 3s. for a tun of sweet wine, imposed upon foreigners. As might be expected, the imposition raised a storm in the Hanseatic towns, and the threat of reprisals in Prussia forced the English Government to suspend the collection of the additional " increment ", pending the decision of Parliament and Council. But by that time the damage had already been done, the agitation on both sides had been resumed, and was not to be stopped. The Prussians began to behave as if the day of reckoning had come at last. They forced the English merchants in Prussia to produce sureties to the sum of 1,200 nobles, to be forfeited if the " increment " were exacted in England. For his own part, the High Master resuscitated all his ancient financial claims, satisfied some of them by seizing English goods, and threatened to settle the others in a similar fashion. For a time, the position of the English became so difficult that it seemed as if they would have to leave the country altogether. Their deputation to the High Master did not help much, nor did the somewhat half-hearted intercession of the Steelyard. If anything the anti-English movement grew. In June, 1434, a Hanseatic diet in Lübeck elaborated a plan of action against the English; a delegation from the diet to the High Master extracted from him a promise to expel them from Prussia; and in fulfilment of his promise, he sent a letter to Henry VI, which was worded as a complaint, but conceived as an ultimatum. The extension of the campaign was probably due to simultaneous events in England. In spite of the fact that in December, 1433, the government extended the protection to the Hanseatics for another year, the goods of Wendish towns seem to have been arrested. This, and the new regulations as to the manner of valuation of goods for customs purposes, threatened to stop the entire flow of Hanseatic trade to England.[43] The breach was now as wide as it had ever been before; correspondence and mutual recriminations obviously could not heal it; and if a commercial war or, what was practically the same, ruinous reprisals on the high seas, were to be averted, the whole problem of Anglo-Hanseatic relations had to be resubmitted, as in 1388 and 1408, to a complete revision by a fully authorized peace conference.

It is doubtful whether a conference of this nature was intended when the Hanse sent out its great delegation of 1434–6. But the seriousness of the situation, the comprehensive scope of Hanseatic claims and grievances, and the English insistence on matters of justice and right, were bound to focus the negotiations on fundamental principles. The head of the delegation, Henrich Vorrath, the

Burgomaster of Danzig and probably the greatest statesman among contemporary leaders of the Hanse, soon realized the position, and was prepared to go considerably beyond his limited terms of reference. In the end the negotiations, however small their practical consequences proved to be, struck a balance of the events of the preceding twenty-five years, and wound up the third successive clash in the history of Anglo-Hanseatic relations.

Yet the debut of the delegation in England was far from auspicious. The Hanseatic memorandum contained an enormous claim for compensation, and the English were as yet in no haste to consider it. Moreover, the international situation on the eve of the conference of Arras was still too uncertain, and the English attitude to the Hanse could not be defined while war and peace hung in the balance in Flanders and Northern France. The Hanseatic address elicited from the government "vele soter wort na older Engelschen gewonheit", but beyond "sweet words" nothing of importance was done or said and the negotiations were adjourned, to be resumed in Flanders in the following spring. But even in the following spring the negotiations did not produce any material results. The peace conference with France and Burgundy was yet to take place, and the English delegates were probably relieved to find that the instructions of the Hanseatic delegates prevented them from the discussion of those subjects in which the English were most concerned, and in the first place the situation at Danzig. The negotiations were postponed again, and the delegation had to try and accelerate matters by pressure. In order to force England to immediate negotiations, and to safeguard the Steelyard from possible reprisals, the delegation ordered a formal cessation of trade with England. It commanded the Hanseatic merchants to leave England, warned them to avoid English waters, and urged the towns to expel the English merchants. In the meantime the Hanseatic towns were preparing materials, lists of grievances, and instructions to ambassadors for the coming negotiations.[44]

As these grievances and instructions show, the expectation of Prussian towns had run very high. Their representatives were to demand payment of all the old debts and damages for the attacks of pirates and breaches of privileges; they were to insist on the full and unequivocal restoration of the charter, and at the same time to refuse to concede to the English any definite privileges in Prussia. But even before the negotiations were due to begin the political and economic situation made the Prussian programme impossible to carry out. The political situation after the conference of Arras, with its formal breach with Burgundy, made the English anxious to restore economic relations with the Hanse, and weakened their position in the negotiations. But it also weakened the position of the Hanse and Prussia, for their relations with Flanders were almost as uncertain as their relation with England. When the news of the possible outbreak of war between England and Flanders reached Danzig, a letter went to Vorrath urging him to arrange a truce with England as soon as possible, and at any rate before the hostilities with Flanders began, so that at least one avenue of trade with England should remain open. Even more unfavourable was the economic position. The very measures Vorrath had taken and recommended in the spring rebounded against the Hanse. The embargo on English trade, like similar embargoes in the past, was impossible to enforce, and merely revealed the economic disunion of the Hanse and its dependence on English trade. As on previous occasions it provided an opening for neutrals and intermediaries, and above all for the Dutch. But there were men and towns within the Hanse itself only too willing to break the injunction. The Cologners treated the whole dispute as no concern of theirs, continued their trade with England, and, to make their position secure, contemplated separate negotiations with the English government. The Zuider Zee towns, and especially Campen, whose allegiance to the Hanse had always been loose and somewhat wayward, acted now in complete independence of the rest of the Hanse. The Bergen factory, in spite of its connections with the Wendish towns, issued permissions of trade to England. In the circumstances it is no wonder that in the winter of 1436 we find the Steelyard still functioning in London, and entries of Hanseatic imports reappearing over and over again in the customs accounts. It is equally no wonder that the Prussians themselves found it impossible to observe the embargo. Prussian goods were carried by land to Flanders in spite of prohibition, and some Prussian goods belonging to merchants of Danzig were shipped directly to England. In April, 1436, the High Master for a certain sum of money (*gegen Entgelt*) allowed a group of English merchants to come to Prussia with "six great ships". In the circumstances, Danzig had to confess its inability to make the prohibition effective. "We must let things go as best they can; we cannot do more than is in our power."[45]

Danzig was now obviously hard pressed. In July, 1436, it furnished its delegates with another set of instructions much more moderate than those of 1435. The tone of the dispatch was now distinctly troubled and anxious; Vorrath must use all the possible means to restore mutual traffic if the men and land of Prussia "are not to lose their livelihood". But moderate as the tone of the Hanseatic instructions now was, it was still impossible to carry them out without wrecking the negotiations. They still withheld from Vorrath the power to treat about the English privileges in Danzig, which were the central issue and the stumbling-block of the negotiations. In the conversations of autumn and winter of 1436, Vorrath's position was very difficult, almost tragic. He knew that the negotiations could not succeed as long as he adhered to the Danzig instructions, and the failure of the negotiations might mean the break-up of the Hanse. The non-Prussian parts of the Hanse were loth to lose their hard-won privileges in England for the sake of Danzig's monopoly over its local market. Their spokesman were careful to remind the Prussians that the towns had won the privileges for their merchants two hundred years previously, " while the Prussians were still pagans." Rather than suffer from Danzig's intransigeance, the Wendish towns, the leaders of the Hanse, would sooner have concluded a separate peace with England.[46] It was therefore obvious that if the old privileges and the unity of the Hanseatic policy were to be preserved, Vorrath would have to go beyond Danzig's instructions. After a great deal of hesitation he was forced to break his undertaking to his own town and negotiate about the position of the English in Danzig.

The concession made, Vorrath was able to report progress to the Hanseatic towns, and in the early winter of 1437 the treaty was in sight. The Hanseatics obtained the renewal of the privileges and the confirmation of their freedom from new taxation, including the tunnage and poundage. They also obtained from the English a promise to pay the outstanding instalments of the debt under the treaty of 1409. But they had to forgo all the financial claims of more recent date, and what was most important of all, had to include in the treaty a general clause defining and safeguarding the English position in the Hanseatic regions more exactly and fully than any similar formulas had done in the past. In addition to the general and conventional reciprocity clause restating the English right to enter Prussia, settle there (*morari*), and trade unrestricted with whomsoever they pleased, it gave the English fiscal exemptions as exceptional as those the Hanseatics possessed in England, for they were to be free of all taxes imposed in the course of the last hundred years and more.

Even these concessions fell short of the *maximum* of English demands, and might not have been accepted had it not been for the moderation of the lords and the open advocacy of Cardinal Beaufort. The English merchants tried to prevent the ratification of the treaty, or, as Vorrath believed, to postpone it so as to be first in the field with their cloth fleet.[47] Yet the treaty was an undoubted English triumph. It again demonstrated the strength of England's position, and it again concluded a period of violent disagreement by reasserting in favour of England those very principles about which England and the Hanse had in the first place disagreed. Vorrath tried to justify himself before the Hanse by insisting that his concessions did not involve a definite grant of privileges to the English. But the Danzigers themselves refused to accept his interpretation and regarded the treaty as a complete capitulation, while the English merchants, as soon as they reappeared in Danzig, spoke and behaved as if a charter of privilege had indeed been granted to them.

§ 3

THE FAILURE (1437 TO 1475)

The treaty of 1437, though never confirmed by Prussia or recognized by Danzig, attained the furthest limit of Hanseatic concessions to England. For the third time the Prussian resistance to English demands was broken and for the third time the Hanseatic league had to sacrifice the interests and prejudices of the Danzig merchants in order to save its political unity and its trade to England. After half a century of agitation, the English merchants trading to Prussia and the Baltic acquired the substance, if not the form, of the " privileges " which would serve as counterpart of the Hanseatic charter in England. Whether Vorrath actually delivered and sealed a grant of " privileges " apart from and in addition to the treaty can well be doubted. No traces of a grant of this kind have come down to us, and in spite of the repeated challenge from the Hanseatics, the English negotiators in the second half of the century were unable to produce any documentary evidence of the grant. But whether a document of this kind was ever issued or not, both the English and the Prussians were convinced that the treaty of 1437 embodied a concession of " full privileges ". On the strength of it the English merchants and official representatives in Prussia claimed full parity with the Hanse. They presented a formal statement to that effect to the High Master and the municipality of Danzig the moment they appeared again in Danzig, and repeated it over and over again in the negotiations which took place in the forties and the fifties. In these subsequent negotiations the English claims never went beyond the provisions of the treaty, and from 1437 till the end of our period their demands were all narrowed down to the contention that the treaty of 1437 be confirmed and observed. The treaty obviously gave a full, or at any rate the fullest possible, satisfaction to their fifty years' old claims, and marked the furthest point they had as yet attained in the offensive against the Hanse.[48]

This point was not to be passed or even reached again until the Tudor era. The English success of 1437 was the last success in the fifteenth century, and marked the end of one epoch and the beginning of another. Hitherto every clash had ended to the advantage of the English merchants ; with every successive peace treaty they were brought a step nearer to the coveted position of parity. But in the forties a reverse process set in. The same issues, interests, and ambitions continued to dominate the situation, and conflict broke out as frequently and as easily as before. But the results were no longer the same. The successive clashes brought the English merchants no advantage, real or fictitious ; most of them were disastrous to English shipping and trade ; and after thirty years of unrest they terminated in the Hanseatic triumph at the peace conference of Utrecht.

No single fact or group of facts will explain this reversal of fortune, but the student of the fifteenth century will find an easy and an obvious connection between the English position in the Baltic and the general political situation of England during the middle decades of the century. The late thirties saw the beginning of that disastrous period of Henry VI's reign which ended in the loss of Normandy and Aquitaine and the civil war at home. Of this general decline of English fortunes, the defeat of English ambitions in the Baltic was merely a part, and was due to the same set of causes as the other defeats of a mid-century: the disintegration of the Lancastrian government. The very year, 1437, in which the peace with the Hanse was concluded, witnessed the formal end of Henry's minority, and a new turn in English government and policy. The government of Henry VI's minority, however venal and inefficient, had been saved from complete subservience to a clique by the balance of parties on the Council. But Henry's quasi-personal government established the domination of a single baronial party, which was only more reckless and selfish for being shielded by the saintly figure of the King. The ruin of the government now proceeded by rapid and irretrievable steps. The retirement of Beaufort from active politics in 1443 and his death in 1447, the defeat of Gloucester in 1440 and his death in 1447, led to the brief but disastrous ascendancy of Suffolk. And then the assassination of Suffolk in 1450 delivered the deranged King and the distracted country into the incompetent hands of the Queen and the Beaufort litter.

The new regime was bound to affect the course of Anglo-Hanseatic relations. Its foreign policy, or rather the absence of it, destroyed the advantages of England's economic position. A great deal of England's strength in the first phase of the struggle was due to the fact that her direct commercial connections with the Hanse, however valuable, were not indispensable. There was no need for English cloth to remain unsold and for her imports of continental, or even Baltic, goods to cease, as long as the markets of Flanders, Zealand, and Brabant remained open to English merchants. These markets were kept open in the last quarter of the fourteenth and the first quarter of the fifteenth century by the policy of Burgundian alliance during the first phase of the Hundred Years War. Unfortunately, after the conference of Arras the relations between England and Burgundy were steadily getting worse. England's mismanagement of the war, and the French military successes, forced the shrewd Duke Philip to withdraw from the unprofitable entanglement. But the withdrawal would not have led to a definite breach or to war, had it not been for the faults of the English government: its incapacity to see and accept a reverse, its political inconsistency in relation to

France, and its bellicosity against the Burgundian "traitors". To these standing causes of friction, there were added difficulties arising from Philip's protective measures against English cloth, with the result that the two countries were constantly at loggerheads and the English trade to the great marts of Flanders, Zealand, and Brabant was repeatedly interrupted.[49] And whenever these interruptions occurred England had to maintain peace with the Hanse in order to keep at least one channel of North European trade open to the merchants. On these occasions the English government was forced into an attitude of anxious moderation, and was prepared to give in to the Hanse both in the question of privileges in England, and in that of the English position in the Baltic.

But it was the political situation at home that affected most the course of Anglo-Hanseatic rivalry. It is not that the domestic policy of Henry VI's "personal" government was inspired by any new and different principles. Its worst failing was that it ceased to be inspired by any principles whatsoever. The mercenary interests of the ruling magnates in, and out of, the King's council were allowed full licence. Matters of state policy were made to serve the private gains of party chieftains. And as there were easy and substantial gains to be derived from attacks on the Hanseatic commerce, the anti-Hanseatic piracy developed with every successive stage in the disruption of the English government. Persons with grievances, real and imaginary, found it easy to obtain letters of marque against the Hanse. With these letters and without them, attacks on Hanseatic shipping became more frequent than at any other period in the fifteenth century. And for the first time in the fifteenth century the attacks proceeded not only without opposition, but also with the assistance of the government. The ordinance for the keeping of the seas of 1442 established an organized system of privateering, free from the cumbersome restrictions of the earlier laws as to safe conducts and truce on the high seas. Thus freed, the English privateers were able in a short time to revolutionize the relations of England and the Hanse, and lead, through the great "coups" of 1449 and 1465, to the naval war and the Hanseatic triumph of the sixties and the early seventies.

The revolutionary effect of this privateering outburst is hard to over-estimate. In the first half of the century piracy had been an accompanying feature of the Anglo-Hanseatic rivalry, disturbing and annoying, but never sufficiently important to overshadow the economic and political issues. Now from being a mere incident piracy became, by its very magnitude and blatancy, the central issue in the relations of England and the Hanse. It was now the main subject of Hanseatic grievances, the main cause of conflict, and the main topic of negotiations. And with the change of issue there came a change in the grouping and the attitudes of the combatants.

As long as the issues were predominantly economic and related to the English demand for equal treatment in Danzig, the quarrel was very largely confined to England and Prussia. Lübeck and the central section of the Hanse remained largely unaffected, and their indifference to the Prussian point of view very largely explains the isolation and the defeat of Danzig in the successive clashes of the late fourteenth and early fifteenth centuries. But now that piracy was becoming the principal issue, Lübeck and the Wendish towns entered the fray, and eventually assumed the leadership against England. Lübeck was the principal victim of the successive attacks on the Hanseatic fleets, and was determined to wrest penalties and reparations. The very paucity of its direct trade to England, which explains its want of sympathy with Prussian intransigence in the first half of the century, enabled it now to adopt a radical policy. It had little to lose from the interruption of trade with England, and it might even benefit by a naval war involving the closing of the Sund and the diversion of all the west-to-east traffic to the old trans-Jutland route. If we are to believe a Prussian allegation, Lübeck's taste for naval war had been whetted by the conflict with Holland, when it diverted to itself the shipping and the profit of other towns.[50] Its action against England was thus bound to be more vigorous, and consequently more successful, than that of Prussia, and the vigour of this action, as well as the cohesion of the anti-English coalition, grew with every important capture of Hanseatic shipping. Under Lübeck's leadership the different groups in the Hanse, with the single exception of Cologne, succeeded in establishing a real unity of front against England, and found themselves in a position not only to wage a naval war, but also, for the first time, to enforce a really effective embargo on the direct trade between England and the Baltic.

Thus the combined effect of anarchy at home and slap-dash policy abroad was to weigh the scales heavily against England in her struggle with the Hanse. The whole situation, international and domestic, was unfavourable to the policy of expansion and reciprocity, but even on those few occasions on which the general situation happened to favour the English, unforeseen but inevitable events intervened against them. The clash of parties at home, the war abroad, and above all the piracies on the high seas, could always be relied upon to produce a catastrophic event of this kind and destroy again the revived hopes of success.

The first of these catastrophic events did not occur till the capture of the Bay fleet in 1449, but the twelve years which had elapsed since the conclusion of Vorrath's treaty were filled with rumblings of a gathering storm. Much of the unrest was due to the Prussian opposition to the Vorrath treaty, and more still to the agitation of the English merchants in Prussia. Yet the principal centre of disturbance was to be found not in Prussia, but in that confined world of English baronial politics from which most of the mid-century storms were to come.

The English complaints at the non-fulfilment of the treaty began almost as soon as the English merchants set foot again on Prussian soil. In 1439, they tried to obtain from the municipality of Danzig the recognition and concession of their rights under the treaty. In 1440 they approached the High Master with a similar request. In the same year, a petition was addressed to the English government complaining against the new taxation in Danzig, and the imprisonment of the boats and goods of several English merchants. In 1441 the merchants of England were petitioning the King and Parliament that the High Master should be called upon to seal the Vorrath treaty on pain of forfeiture of Hanseatic privileges. In 1442 another petition with a comprehensive list of English grievances against the Hanse was submitted to Parliament.[51] Nevertheless, the real position of the English in Danzig and their prospects there would not in themselves have created any serious difficulties with the Hanse. For one thing the Danzigers were completely isolated in their opposition to the treaty. The rest of the Hanse, including Lübeck, not only confirmed it themselves, but were urging Danzig to do the same. The Steelyard in writing to Danzig had to admit the justice of some of the English complaints. Even the other Prussian towns differed from Danzig, and were prepared to ratify the treaty. And the Danzigers themselves, in spite of all the show of obstinacy, were very anxious that the traffic with England should remain uninterrupted and undisturbed. They opposed the imposition of the pound-toll (*Pfundzoll*) by the High Master in 1442, on the plea that it kept the English merchants away. In reply to the English complaints of 1439, 1441, and 1442, they were careful to point out that the English enjoyed greater favours in Danzig, and traded there more than other foreigners. The official representatives of the English merchants in Danzig swore an affidavit in 1422, repudiating all responsibility for the complaint of the previous years, and denying its allegations against Danzig. This affidavit was no doubt extracted from the English merchants by a great deal of pressure, but the statements which it contained, whether voluntary or not, were not all fictitious. In their petitions of 1439 the English merchants themselves claimed that they were frequenting Danzig more than any other nation, and they apparently extended their trade during the war between the Hanse and Holland in 1440. In 1440 the Livonian towns complained of the unusual abundance of English cloth in Novgorod and Livonia, some of which must have come via Danzig; and at the end of the decade, after the capture of 1449, the Prussian authorities were able to lay their hands on an amount of English merchandise which they themselves described as very plentiful and exceeding in value their very considerable claims for compensation. All through these years the English maintained in Prussia a corporate organization which officially represented them in their negotiations with Prussia and Danzig.[52]

It was therefore not in Prussia that the real source of the unrest was to be sought. The real source was now in England, where a succession of events in the forties was slowly preparing the way for a rupture with the Hanse. The first harbinger of the coming trouble was the official revival of aggressive anti-foreign policy in the Parliament of Reading in 1440. By an act of that Parliament the foreign merchants in England were again subjected to the limitations and control of the municipal *Gastenrecht*. They were forced to reside in approved hostelries and to submit all their dealings to the registration and control of their hosts. Their freedom of trade was limited by the obligation to sell all their goods within a prescribed period of time, to employ all the proceeds on the purchase of English goods and confine their dealings to wholesale transactions with Englishmen. In short, the maximum of the anti-foreign demands of English towns, which had been checked and opposed by the early Lancastrian governments, was now carried into effect. Taken by itself this measure is somewhat hard to explain, but fitted into the political situation of the time it acquires its proper meaning as an attempt to draw the middle-classes into the struggle of the baronial parties. In some of his previous clashes with Beaufort's party, such as that of 1426, Gloucester had been able to mobilize a certain amount of middle-class support, at any rate among the burgesses of London. Whether his middle-class party was still alive by 1440 we do not know. What we do know is that throughout the intervening years the Beaufort party persisted in those very same policies and actions which had originally brought it into conflict with London opinion. Thus even if we are not entitled to assume the survival in London of the active pro-Gloucester sympathies, we can safely assume the survival of the anti-Beaufort antipathies. And, according to private reports to Germany, these antipathies descended to Suffolk and the younger Beauforts together with the rest of the Cardinal's heirloom. In the circumstances the anti-Council interests in the City, unless previously bribed and reconciled, could be expected to side with the Gloucester faction as soon as the conflict broke out anew. As the conflict broke out again with Gloucester's memorandum against Beaufort in 1440 and the counter-attack on Eleanor Cobham in 1441, it is natural to assume that the anti-foreign legislation in the Parliament of 1440 was something in the nature of a bribe. That the coincidence of the two events was no mere accident is further suggested by the recurrence of a similar situation in 1447. And if it was not an accident, then what it meant was that the economic interests of the merchant class were being exploited by the ruling party for its political ends, and the issues of commercial policy made a mere pawn in the inter-baronial struggle.[53]

The act was therefore bound to affect the future of Anglo-Hanseatic relations. The Hanseatic merchants were excluded from its provisions, but they could not be excluded from the changed atmosphere in Parliament and the City of London, or from the partisan manipulations of economic policy. It was the changed temper and the partisan politics at home rather than the position in Danzig that instigated the sequence of anti-Hanseatic petitions in 1440, 1441, and 1442, and determined the attitude of the Parliament of 1442. The petition which the English merchants in Danzig were made to disclaim apparently proceeded from individuals with personal grievances and claims against the Hanse. But at the Parliament of Westminster in January, 1442, a petition of the Commons demanded resolute action against Prussia and, in accordance with the demand, an ultimatum was issued to the High Master threatening the annulment of privileges in England if the Vorrath treaty were not ratified before Martinmas.[54]

Equally ominous were some of the other measures of the Westminster Parliament, and none of them more so than the so-called act for the safe-keeping of the seas. The act provided for the equipment and maintenance of a fleet of twenty-eight ships for the protection of English shipping from attacks at sea. Judged by its face value it was a genuine measure for the policing of the seas, not unlike similar provisions repeatedly made in the first half of the century. But judged in the light of some of its special clauses, and in conjunction with the other acts of the same Parliament, it was itself a menace to peace, more likely to extend piracy than to suppress it. The fleet had to be provided by private individuals, mostly powerful men like Sir William Bonville, Sir Philip Courteney, Lord Pons, John Howard, John Church, Hugh Taverner, and others who, as the subsequent events showed, were closely related to certain members of the King's Council. The distribution of prizes was arranged in a manner extremely generous and profitable for the masters and owners of boats. Legal obstacles to captures at sea were raised by several acts limiting the validity of safe-conducts and virtually revoking the earlier law against the breaking of truce, under which the English privateers had found it very difficult to "faire de guerre pur le sauf gard du mer". But whether the act was a genuine measure of national policy or a piece of mercenary legislation, it became in the end a cloak for extensive privateering and a source of anarchy on the high seas. And what the official privateering under an act of Parliament left undone, private captures and reprisals completed.[55]

The troubles, thus begun, were slowly mounting in the subsequent years, until in 1446 the political situation of 1440 and 1442 was re-enacted, and a second decisive action against the Hanse was taken. Gloucester, defeated over the trial of Eleanor Cobham, could still be expected to oppose Suffolk in the matter of the royal marriage and the cession of Maine, and was now to be annihilated. The ground

ANGLO-HANSEATIC ECONOMIC RELATIONS

had been prepared for his impeachment, and at the end of 1446 a Parliament was called at Bury St. Edmunds, "away from his friends the Londoners," to accomplish his destruction. At the same time the much-prorogued Parliament of 1445-1446 had shown its temper by refusing to vote new supplies until its final session in 1446. It was, therefore, not a mere coincidence that at that last session, and only a few months before the writs for the anti-Gloucester parliament were to be issued, the 1442 ultimatum to the High Master was recalled, and a similar ultimatum issued threatening the revocation of privileges if the treaty were not ratified.[56] As the Steelyard correctly observed, what the English wanted was not so much the confirmation of the treaty as the revocation of privileges and freedom of reprisals and piracy against the Hanse. All sorts of claimants were alleging damages and grievances as a pretext for letters of marque against Hanseatic shipping. The letters of the Steelyard to Lübeck, Cologne, and Danzig struck a note of real panic: there were no friends left in Parliament or Council. When in the summer of 1447 a Prussian delegation visited England, the government could not negotiate because the king and everybody else were "away in the country for the summer vacation". But in the opinion of the Steelyard the "vacation" was merely a subtle pretext for prolonging the state of indecision until the last day of August when, under the terms of the ultimatum, the Hanseatic privileges would lapse and "no end of letters of marque would be issued".[57]

Most of these fears came true, though not immediately. The charter was made to lapse, but the anti-Hanseatic move in England was too insincere, and the Hanse too pacific, for an immediate and final rupture. In March, 1449, after a year of manœuvring, a conference between the Hanse and the English took place in Lübeck, which very nearly succeeded in postponing a crisis. The beginning of the conference was not very promising. The English delegates, with Thomas Kent at their head, were uncompromising. They took a stand by the treaty of 1437, and demanded the exclusion of Prussia from the conference as a preliminary condition of negotiations. The Prussians on their part were equally determined not to recognize the treaty and to remain at the conference. Yet both sides were unwilling to close all the roads to peace. A new conference was arranged for 1451, and in the meantime private and separate conversations between the English and the Prussian delegates led to mutual promises of truce and toleration.[58] Thus a path was still open to a compromise, and a compromise might well have been attained in 1451 if, within two months of the closing of the Lübeck conference, the misgovernment in England had not culminated in the "great capture" of the Bay fleet. On 23rd May, 1449, a fleet of a 110 vessels, Flemish, Dutch, and Hanseatic, on its way from the Bay of Bourgneuf, was attacked and captured by the English privateers under Robert

Winnington. The boats were taken to the Isle of Wight, the vessels and the goods belonging to Flemish and Dutch merchants were released, but the bulk of the booty, which belonged to the Hanseatic merchants, was made a lawful prize of the privateers.[59]

The news of the capture burst upon the unsuspecting world like a bomb, and provided a turning-point in the relations of England and the Hanse. The effect was only partly due to the great number of ships and the high value of goods captured. Its real importance lay elsewhere. To begin with, it was the first important attack on the Bay fleets. Ever since the opening of the Hanseatic navigation to the saltworks in the Bay of Bourgneuf, large fleets had passed within a few miles of the English coast. The safety of the Bay route must have weighed heavily with the Hanse in their dealings with England. In the words of the *Libelle of Englyshe Polycye*, the Hanseatics, who "aventure full greatly into the Bay", were compelled to seek England's friendship, for "if they would not our friends be, we might lightly stop them in the sea". Now for the first time the peace of the Bay route was broken, and broken in a mere quest for booty, without direct cause or provocation. In the second place, the assailants were no mere pirates, outlaws of the sea, or merchants seeking revenge and compensation, but the king's privateers, a fleet maintained and equipped on the same vicious principles as that of 1442. What is more, its leaders were connected with an important party in the Council. At least some of Winnington's boats belonged to Thomas Daniell, an influential member of the Council, and it is quite probable that Winnington was merely Daniell's agent and representative at sea. Immediately on the capture of the fleet, Winnington wrote to John Trevelyan, a member of the Council and an active partisan of the Suffolk faction, informing him of the coup and asking for his good offices. The request obviously was not made in vain. Within a few days of the capture, the Steelyard had to report to the Hanse that the "lords" were making it known that the booty would not be restored to its owners. The names of the members of the Council in league with pirates were no secret to anybody. The merchants of the Steelyard and the popular opinion in London imputed the guilt to the whole of the Suffolk clique in the Council, and above all to Lord Say, Thomas Daniell, and John Trevelyan.[60] Finally, the capture had an immediate and disastrous reaction upon the position of the English merchants. On the morrow of the attack on the Bay fleet the country was filled with rumours of further and better exploits to come. And if the narrow seas were not at once plunged into the anarchy of mutual and general piracy, it was probably due to the fact that the English merchants were made to bear the cost of the capture. The Hanseatics promptly arrested the English goods in their territories, and the Prussians noted with satisfaction that the English merchandise in Danzig was sufficiently plentiful to cover all their losses. It goes without saying that the English government protested against the confiscations, and that the protest was not much more than a hollow formality. The Council threatened to compensate the English merchants out of Prussian and Lübeck goods in England, and the Steelyard was afraid that the English rulers might "rob Peter to pay Paul". Yet, in spite of the Steelyard's fears, Paul remained unpaid.[61]

It is in this abdication of all pretensions to state reasons that the real significance of the episode lay. By a single stroke the official policy divested itself of its connections with the interests or demands of the merchants. No sooner was the booty bagged than the government turned to the Hanseatic towns with pacific overtures. Its chieftains had had their fill, and it had every reason to feel friendly and satisfied.[62] Its concern for the merchants' programme and its bellicosity of 1449 were unsuited to the occasion, and quickly dropped. In their turn, the English merchants, deserted and betrayed by their fickle allies of 1442 and 1446, ceased to press for parity and reciprocity. They had suffered almost as much as the Hanse at the hands of the government. They saw the trade with the Hanse interrupted, and interrupted not for the sake of their economic demands, but for the private gains of well-connected adventurers. To them the present conflict was both senseless and unprofitable. It is, therefore, no wonder that a Prussian agent in London could report a short time after the capture that everybody was blaming the governing clique for the rupture with the Hanse, and that everybody wanted peace. One may or may not believe his report that the rebels of Kent had marched into London demanding the restoration of the Hanseatic trade, and the punishment of the pirates. But it was no mere accident that the men whose lives the rebels demanded were in the first place those very "statesmen" whom everybody thought responsible for the Bay capture.[63]

Equally striking were the repercussions in the Hanse. Only a few months previously at the conference of Lübeck, Prussia had, alone against the whole of the Hanse, resisted the English demands. But now a single stroke put Lübeck in Danzig's place as England's implacable foe. Lübeck was one of the chief sufferers in the attack of 1449, and Lübeck had always regarded itself as the guardian of the Hanseatic routes. But what counted most of all was the fact that unlike Danzig it had no English goods within its walls to cover its losses. As a result, the attitudes of Lübeck and of Prussia came to be completely reversed. Prussia, with all her losses made good, was not at all anxious to break with England. The High Master vetoed all the proposals for the cessation of English trade or prohibition of English cloth, refused to take any violent measures against the English, and readily agreed to the English proposal of separate negotiations. The arrangements for a conference at Deventer, made before the Bay capture, were now cancelled, and an English delegation with Thomas Kent at its head was sent to Prussia, there to negotiate a separate settlement. But this arrangement only stiffened Lübeck's attitude. Anxious to recover its damages, and enraged at what it considered the Prussian betrayal, Lübeck merely redoubled its demands for strong measures against the English.[64]

Unfortunately for the future of Anglo-Hanseatic relations, events soon provided Lübeck with an opening for " direct action ". The boat with the English ambassadors to Prussia was captured on 20th July, 1450, by the Lübeck *Bergenfahrer*, and brought to Lübeck together with a rich booty in cloth and no less a person than Thomas Kent on board. The goods were confiscated to cover Lübeck's losses, and the ambassadors put under arrest. Yet the capture, striking and profitable as it was, did not satisfy Lübeck's thirst for retaliation, and in the years immediately following Kent's imprisonment, accident and design combined to harden Lübeck's temper. To begin with, Thomas Kent, with some of the other prisoners, was let out on parole in order to go to England and obtain there compensations for Lübeck. But he broke the parole and stayed in England, to resume there his work on the Council and to remain for another fifteen years in charge of English policy in Northern Europe, and probably in command of the anti-Hanseatic forces in England.[65] Then, partly in retaliation for the capture of the ambassadors, and partly through the continued state of anarchy on the high seas, the English pirates redoubled their attacks on Hanseatic shipping, and especially on that of the Wendish towns. Finally in 1458, at the very time time when the epidemic of piracies seemed to have quieted down, there occurred the second capture of the Bay fleet, for which the Earl of Warwick himself was responsible. On the pretext that the Hanseatic boats refused to salute the English arms, Warwick engaged them in a battle from which he emerged with easy honours and an immense booty.[66]

It is, therefore, no wonder that throughout those years Lübeck persevered in its anti-English attitude, and refused to respond to the pacific invitations of England or the counsel of moderation from the rest of the Hanse. When in 1451 the English sent a delegation to a conference in Utrecht, Lübeck refused to negotiate with the head of the delegation, Thomas Kent, and the other " escaped prisoners ", and insisted on their return to captivity and the compensation for the Bay capture as a preliminary condition of negotiations. The expostulations of Prussia and Cologne were of no avail. Nor were the repressive measures against the Hanseatic merchants which the English government adopted a few months later. Lübeck meant war and prepared for it. By arrangement with Denmark it closed the Sund to English shipping, and prohibited the passage of English cloth to the East.[67] Several times during the subsequent years, in 1452, 1453, and 1454, the English made attempts to arrange another conference, and met with a willing response from every part of the Hanse, including Hamburg. But Lübeck still held out, kept the Sund closed to English shipping, and strained every effort, in the face of wholesale evasion on the part of Prussians and Cologners, to stop the trade in English cloth in Hanseatic regions.[68]

These relations between England and Lübeck were a direct result of a decade and more of misgovernment and piracy and the first step towards England's defeat in the late sixties and seventies. Yet during this first phase, in the fifties, the English position was far from hopeless. At times it even seemed as if, in spite of the political disorganization at home, and Lübeck's activities abroad, the clash might yet end again in a reaffirmation of England's claims in the Baltic. The English piracies had certainly succeeded in raising Lübeck's opposition, but the opposition was not formidable as long as Lübeck remained alone. And throughout this first phase of England's retreat Lübeck did remain alone. The other parts of the Hanse were showing every sign of an accommodating temper. The Prussians, ever since their abortive attempts at separate negotiations with England in 1451, were all tact and moderation. Danzig continued for a time to hug its old fears of English competition, but by 1453 even Danzig ceased to trouble about the English danger, for, as we have seen, the English seem to have dropped for the time being their old demands of parity and reciprocity. Under the protection of safe-conducts repeatedly issued to the English merchants during those years, the English trade to Prussia struggled on, and with Prussian assistance the English merchants sometimes succeeded in evading Lübeck's barrier across the Sund. Even for several years after the outbreak of war in Prussia between the Order and the Estates, the English merchants were still to be found in the Baltic East. The same is true in a still greater measure of the English trade with the western towns, and especially Cologne. There, Lübeck was powerless to interfere with the course of traffic, and the towns seldom considered themselves bound by the interests or decisions of the Hanse as a whole. But what must have completed the isolation of Lübeck was the attitude of Hamburg, its ancient ally and satellite, and now a determined advocate of peace with England. In the end, Lübeck was compelled to raise the embargo in 1454, and give a grudging consent to a peace conference, and although the civil war in Prussia prevented the conference from taking place, the trade could continue under the eight years' truce proclaimed early in 1456.[69]

Thus from the English point of view the prospects of the midfifties were not all black, and what made them rosier still was the fact that throughout those years the ports and the fairs of the Low Countries were open to the English. The situation continued to be promising until 1458, when the second capture of the Bay fleet by

Warwick raised new difficulties. Yet even this second capture did not alter the situation, or the issues, at all profoundly. Lübeck's interests and pride suffered again, and its wrath was as overwhelming now as it had been in 1449. But the other towns remained as anxious as ever to maintain the trade with England, and Danzig implored Lübeck not to do anything that might prevent the prolongation of the eight years' truce, due to expire in 1459.[70]

The isolation of Lübeck and the consequent strength of England's position were made still greater by the arrival of the Yorkists. The change of dynasty reopened the question of Hanseatic privileges, and at the same time revived the hopes and ambitions of the middle-class party. The demands of the English merchants, forgotten and neglected during the preceding period, were again resuscitated. The Council and the Parliament were again, as twenty years earlier, snowed under by petitions and complaints recalling the Vorrath treaty, and reasserting anew the programme of reciprocity. London resumed its anti-Hanseatic offensive, organized pressure on the Council and Parliament, and attempted to deprive the Steelyard of its constitutional position in the City. In deference to the pressure of the towns—and the Yorkist party apparently inherited the middle class policy, genuine or false, from the Gloucester faction—Edward announced to the Hanse his intention to revise the whole question of Hanseatic privileges. The government renewed the privileges by a number of temporary grants of 1461, 1463, and 1465, but pressed for a more permanent arrangement every time the temporary extensions expired.[71] If it continued at all to extend the privileges in this way, it was partly because the relations with Burgundy were much too uncertain for a definite breach with the Hanse, and partly because every successive year emphasized the isolation of Lübeck and seemed to prepare the way to its defeat. An abortive Hanseatic conference in 1465, at which English delegates were present, must have demonstrated to the Wendish towns the utter hopelessness of their position. At last, in 1467, Lübeck seemed to give way. In a manner as yet guarded and careful, its leaders notified the other Hanseatic towns that it would be prepared to waive the preliminary conditions on which it had insisted ever since 1451, and to enter into negotiations with England. With Lübeck thus humbled, and the other parts of the Hanse anxious to maintain peace and preserve their privileges, it looked as if the story of English penetration and political success were going to be resumed.[72]

It was at that moment that the arrests and the " verdict " of 1468 shattered the prospects of a renewed English offensive, and opened the second and final phase in the defeat of English expansion in northern seas. Already at the end of 1467, and the beginning of 1468, the Hanseatic observers began to notice a change in the Yorkist attitude to the Hanse. The truce for thirty years, which Edward concluded with Burgundy in the winter of 1467–1468, secured for England one channel of trade to the continent and the Parliament became less anxious to maintain good relations with the Hanseatics. And when in June, 1468, an English fleet bound for the Baltic was captured by the King of Denmark off the Sund, the government seized the Hanseatic goods in London as compensation for the English losses. A quasi-judicial verdict of the Council confirmed the seizure on the ground that a few Danzig boats were at the time serving in the Royal Navy of Denmark, though neither the Hanse nor Danzig had any part in the capture or any previous knowledge of it. The Danish government insisted that it was alone responsible, and that it was acting in retaliation for the English malpractices in Iceland. But whatever was the real rôle of the Hanse in the affair, all the Council wanted was formal ground for the seizure of Hanseatic goods in London. " They know that they cannot obtain any redress from the Danes, who do not trade to England, and have no goods in London and on the seas, and they have invented the accusation to cover their losses out of our possessions." Such was the Hanseatic complaint and such was apparently the actual position.[73]

The light-heartedness with which the Council acted on this occasion was doubtless due to the friendship with Burgundy, but it was also to a great extent due to the personal influence of certain men on the Council. The Hanseatics in their protests against the verdict alleged that the several members of the Council were themselves an interested party in the case they were judging. The contention was apparently well-founded. It was only through that personal influence in the Council that the claims of the fifteen Englishmen who had suffered at the hands of the Danes were given preference over the views and desires of the bulk of public opinion, including that of the merchant class. The Archbishop of Canterbury was reputed to have warned the government of the folly of the verdict; the clothworkers of Gloucestershire, mobilized for the purpose by the Steelyard and its well-paid friend the town clerk of Bristol, intervened on behalf of the German merchants, and so did also the Merchant Adventurers in the Low Countries in the person of their governor, William Caxton. But public opinion at home was no more effective than the pressure of almost all the princes and political powers of Northern Europe. The Emperor, the Pope, the Bishop of Utrecht, the Duke of Burgundy, the towns of Flanders, the feudal rulers of the Low Countries and Western Germany wrote to England to advocate the cause of the Hanseatic prisoners. But the Council remained adamant, the relations of England and the Hanse were thrown into confusion again, and the possibility of a peaceful solution of the Anglo-Hanseatic conflict favourable to England and advocated by the merchants was thrown away for the second time since 1449.[74]

The only compensation the English merchants could derive from the episode was the definite separation between the Hanse and Cologne. The Cologne merchants were at the time of the capture passing through a period of estrangement from the rest of the Hanse. The Hanseatic policy in Flanders at the time and Lübeck's irreconcilable attitude to questions of English policy had raised in Cologne a great deal of opposition to the Hanse. At the time of the "verdict" the separatist opinion dominated the town government in Cologne; the leader of the Cologners in London, Gerard von Wesel, was himself something of a separatist. So that when the verdict, however illegal and unjustified, made the goods of Cologne responsible for the reputed crimes of the other part of the Hanse, the Cologners decided to take the final step and break with the Hanse. The Council, where Thomas Kent was still active, did its best to help the split along, freed the arrested Cologners, exempted their goods from reprisals, and eventually reissued the privileges for the sole enjoyment of Cologne and the exclusion of the other towns.[75] The policy of splitting the Hanse, pursued since the middle of the century, thus seemed to triumph at last.

This triumph, however, was more than offset by its reactions on the rest of the Hanse. From the point of view of the Hanse as a whole the events of 1468 merely completed the reorganization of anti-English forces begun in 1449. If they succeeded in detaching Cologne from the Hanse, they also succeeded in restoring cohesion and unity among its other parts. Prior to 1449, Danzig had been alone and unaided in its opposition to England; between 1449 and 1468, Lübeck was similarly isolated in its struggle for compensations; but after the "verdict" the struggle against England became a joint concern of all the Hanseatic towns from Westphalia to Livonia. The moderate counsel was discredited, Lübeck's intransigeance stood vindicated; England indeed appeared the deadly foe and the menace to Hanseatic unity that Lübeck had made her out to be. The Danzigers now resuscitated their ancient anti-English attitude as suddenly as they had abandoned it in 1449, and events in Prussia facilitated their reconversion. The breach between the Prussian Estates and the Order had by now removed all extraneous restraints and moderating influences over Danzig's economic policy, while the continued state of civil war in Prussian territory made direct trade with England almost impossible. The Danzigers could now easily afford a naval war with England, for there was little that they could lose by a war of this kind which they had not already lost through the cessation of trade. The other Hanseatic towns merely followed the united lead of Danzig and Lübeck.[76]

The immediate result of the new alignment was the outbreak of the naval war which Lübeck had vainly tried to organize since 1450, and the war continued until well in the seventies. The varying fortunes of the combatants, the complications introduced by France and Flanders, the stalemate eventually reached, have all been faithfully chronicled by the German historians of the Hanse, and need not be repeated here. What requires stressing is the fact that although the war undoubtedly prepared the way for the triumph of the Hanse in 1473, it was not immediately and directly responsible for it. The fortunes on the high seas constantly fluctuated, and not always to England's disadvantage. In the first phase of the war the English had the worst of the struggle. But in the end the losses suffered by neutral shipping at the hands of Hanseatic and above all Danzig privateers provoked the hostility of Flanders, while the entry of France into the struggle created a state of triangular warfare equally damaging to the Hanse and to England. In the end the Yorkist government managed to equip a strong fleet under Howard's command, and to inflict great losses on the Hanseatic shipping. From this time onwards the contest was leading to a draw, with the odds slightly in England's favour.[77]

If the war was, nevertheless, disastrous to the interests of English trade and English merchants it was not through its unsuccessful issue on the high seas, but from other and more general causes. To begin with, war was disastrous because it was war; it preyed upon all shipping in the north seas, and thus intensified that state of anarchy which had prevailed there ever since the late forties. In the second place, it perpetuated the political relations and attitudes dangerous to the future of England's position and peace on the northern seas. Lübeck and Danzig were now cementing their friendship and unity, directed against England, while the separation of Cologne was not producing the good results expected from it. True, English cloth continued to be sold abroad throughout the war years; denied access to the old east to west channel, it went by the Southern route via Frankfort, Nuremburg, and Breslau. The Prussians themselves began to complain in 1471, as they had done in the previous blockades of England, that an embargo on English cloth could not be enforced. They were themselves accused of smuggling English cloth into the Hanseatic lands. It is also true that the cessation of direct traffic between England and the Baltic did not result in a serious shortage of Baltic goods in England. Timber, pitch, tar, ashes, and furs, both from the Baltic and from other parts of Europe, were obtainable in the neutral markets of Zealand and Brabant, and from there the Cologners, the Dutch, and the English regularly shipped them to England. Yet the new channels of cloth export and the new sources of Baltic goods were mere makeshifts, and not very satisfactory ones at that. The cloth exports of the Cologners after 1468, large as they now were, fell far behind the combined exports of the Hanse as a whole in the preceding period, and the decrease was not accompanied by a corresponding rise of the exports of the English merchants themselves. The customs returns of the principal cloth-exporting ports show a considerable decrease in the export of cloth during the middle decades of the century. This decrease may well have been exaggerated in the customs figures, for it is not unlikely that the collection of customs suffered during the years of anarchy, yet the decrease revealed by the figures is too regular to have been entirely due to the fault of the returns themselves. It must have been due to a variety of causes, of which the Anglo-Hanseatic war and the cessation of Hanseatic trade to this country, was certainly one. An examination of the particular customs accounts of London, Lynn, Boston, and Hull also reveals a decline in the importation of the Hanseatic commodities, while occasional references elsewhere would indicate a corresponding rise in their prices.[68] It is, therefore, no wonder that the country soon began to show signs of weariness and opposition to the struggle. The very "clothworkers of Gloucester", whose support the Cologners had mobilized in 1468, refused now to lend themselves to any further plans of Cologne against the Hanse. Apparently, the cloth producers, the general body of the consumers in the country, had all lost from the cessation of Hanseatic trade more than they had gained from the separate arrangement with Cologne. If the merchants of London and the East Coast continued to support the war party, the rest of the country was now anxious for peace.[79]

Still it can be doubted whether the peace would have come when it did, and would have been bought, as it was, at the price of English surrender, had it not been for the accompanying political developments. In the first place the War of the Roses was resumed in 1470 with the return of Margaret and the flight of Edward. The Hanse was drawn into the renewed struggle, and soon found itself in the position of *tertium gaudens*. Margaret, while planning her return, had approached the Hanse with requests of assistance, promising in return to restore the privileges in full and redress all the Hanseatic grievances. On that occasion the Hanse refused to commit itself, but when Edward in his turn began to plan an expedition to England, he was able to do so with the assistance of the Hanse. The Hanse may have acted on the advice of the Duke of Burgundy who sponsored Edward's enterprise, or it may itself have gauged the chances of the combatants and decided to back the winner. But whatever were its reasons, the fact remains that it was on Hanseatic boats and under Hanseatic escort that Edward sailed to England, there to resume the war, and to emerge victorious on the battlefield of Barnet. For these services he promised to satisfy the Hanseatic complaints and demands, and these services were alleged as the official motive for the far-reaching concessions made to the Hanse at the conference of Utrecht.[80]

An unofficial liaison was established between the English and the Hanseatic agents in 1472 in Bruges, and in 1474 the Conference

ANGLO-HANSEATIC ECONOMIC RELATIONS   137

met at Utrecht. From the very first, difficulties arose on which the negotiations very nearly broke. The Hanseatics demanded complete restoration of their old privileges, unequivocal exemption from all taxation not specified there, compensation for the losses suffered by their shippers and merchants, annulment of the "verdict" of 1468, and restoration of goods arrested on that occasion. They intended to obtain special guarantees from the principal towns as to the observation of the future treaty. Above all, they demanded the withdrawal of privileges from Cologne. The English negotiators took a stand against every one of these demands; on their part they recalled the Vorrath treaty, and insisted on the principle of reciprocity. But in the end they had to give way. After two adjournments, the conference ended in a peace treaty embodying almost all the Hanseatic demands. A formula of reciprocity was included in the treaty recalling that of 1408, but less definite and extensive than that of 1437. It promised in a general manner that the English should enjoy in the Hanseatic lands their old rights, but it did not contain the provision for the exemption from taxes. The point on which the English negotiators were most unyielding was that of Cologne's status, but even on this point they gave way in the end, and Cologne, deserted by the English and spurned by the Hanse, was deprived both of her privileges and of her position in the Hanse. It was only several years later that she was readmitted to the Hanse and the Steelyard.[81]

In 1475 the Hanseatic merchants returned to England in full possession of their ancient privileges, armed with the additional guarantees of London, Lynn, Boston, and Hull, and with their financial claims secured on their customs payments to the sum of £10,000. They immediately stepped into the place they had occupied in English economic life in the first half of the century, and this place they were to preserve until well into the Tudor era. Their share in English foreign trade soon passed the highest point it had reached before. While they exported on the average about 6,000 cloths annually between 1406 and 1427, and about 10,000 annually between 1438 and 1459, their exports rose to well above 13,500 between 1479 and 1482. Some of this rise may have been due to changes in the administration of the customs, yet it continued throughout the early Tudor reigns.[82]

The English derived whatever profit and comfort there was to be derived from the restoration of peace and the resumption of Hanseatic trade. But their attempts at direct relations with the markets of Central and Eastern Europe received a set-back from which they were not to recover until the age of Elizabeth. The formula of reciprocity would not have been of much avail to them now. Danzig under the sovereignty of Polish kings enjoyed almost a complete *Landeshoheit*, involving full autonomy in matters of government and economic policy. It refused to admit even the vague and shadowy claims to reciprocity in the new treaty. For some two years it refused

L

to confirm the treaty, in spite of the expostulation of all the other towns. When, in the end, it decided to confirm it, it did so on the understanding that the English were to be treated as all other foreigners. The English merchants themselves ceased to press for parity in the old and full sense of the term. According to the report of the Hanseatic delegates to Utrecht, all the English meant by " old rights " in Prussia were the " rights " actually exercised there on the eve of the war. But even these claims, modest as they were, ceased to be of great importance to English trade. The whole Baltic trade was no longer vitally important. Whether as a result of the continued friction with Denmark and consequent closing of the Sund, or as a result of the war-time rearrangements in the organization of English trade, the direct trade of English merchants to Danzig was dwindling very fast. While on several occasions in the first half of the century there were over thirty English boats anchored in the port of Danzig, only twelve boats arrived from England during the three years following the cessation of hostilities, and in 1497, when the registers of the Sund tolls begin, not a single English boat passed the Sund. As late as 1503 there were only twenty-one English boats passing the Sund and it was not until 1547 that the English shipping to the Baltic could again stand comparison with that of the Dutch.[83]

§ 4

The Trade

To pass from the story of the Anglo-Hanseatic rivalry to an account of the trade itself, its commodities, business routine, and corporate forms, is to exchange the shifting scene of politics and war for the enduring scheme of economic needs and habitudes. The needs which the trade with the Hanse served, and the forms which it took, were seemingly unaffected by the Anglo-Hanseatic conflict. Its economic basis was provided by the economic development and structure of Northern Europe, and could be neither easily destroyed nor fundamentally altered by the course of the struggle. Nor could the prevailing methods of trade and forms of commercial organization be affected, for these were determined by the transport, communications, and social structure of the later Middle Ages. Yet this constancy of economic facts can easily be exaggerated. Within the traditional channels of exchange, and the enduring framework of commercial organization, there was room for a certain number of variations, and some of these were undoubtedly due to the development

ANGLO-HANSEATIC ECONOMIC RELATIONS 139

of the Anglo-Hanseatic rivalry. It is not the object of this chapter to exhibit these variations to the exclusion of the other and the more static facts. But no student of the period will fail to note them, less in the account of the commodities and markets, more in the story of the business forms and the corporate organizations of the English merchants.

Occasional references in the previous chapters must have made it clear that the bulk of the commodities exchanged between England and the Hanseatic regions consisted of Baltic goods and English cloth. It goes without saying that the Baltic goods were by no means the only article of Hanseatic import. In the first place, some Hanseatic merchants took part in the trade between England and the great markets of the Low Countries, whence they imported all the miscellaneous commodities of Europe. In the earlier centuries, and as late as the middle of the fourteenth century, the trade to and from Flanders was one of the main Hanseatic activities in England.[84] In the late fourteenth and the fifteenth century the overwhelming bulk of that trade was already in English hands, yet even at this time there were to be found Hanseatic merchants, especially Cologners, who regularly exported cloth into the Low Countries and imported from there a most varied assortment of goods. In the second place, miscellaneous commodities other than those of Baltic origin were imported direct from the regions of the Hanse. Of these, canvas, linen, and linen yarn ("Cologne thread"), were probably the most important. Fish, chiefly the cured "white" herring of Skania, and fish oils, were imported by merchants of almost every region in the Hanse. Beer produced by Bremen and Hamburg, madder of Westfalian origin, a certain amount of woad, as well as metal goods from Cologne, Westfalia, the Harz mountains and Hungary, have also left a trace on the records of Hanseatic imports.[85]

But compared with the goods of Baltic origin, all these commodities were of only secondary importance in the Anglo-Hanseatic trade. They could be, and in part were, imported into England from lands outside the Hanseatic regions. In the linen trade important sources of supply were situated in certain districts of South Germany, Northern France, and the Low Countries, and from these large quantities of linen were imported into England, both directly and through the great continental fairs. Some of the English demand for linen was met by Irish production. The same in a still greater measure applied to woad and metal goods, of which by far the most important sources were situated in France, Spain, and Italy. Even the white herring could be, and often was, of Dutch origin, imported by English and Dutch merchants, and beer could also be brought from the recently established breweries of Holland. These commodities, therefore, would not have drawn the English merchants to the Hanseatic regions in the face of Hanseatic opposition, and would not have made the Hanseatic trade as important to England as it actually was.[86]

It was the goods of the Eastern Baltic that provided the basis of Hanseatic imports. One of these was corn. England's demand for corn considerably exceeded the immediate needs of her population. For the greater part of the century she had garrisons to feed in the marches of Calais, Guisnes, and Aquitaine. She supplied corn to Gascony in exchange for wine, and sometimes exported cereals to Iceland in exchange for fish. In years of plenty England had a surplus sufficient to cover all these needs, but in years of scarcity she was badly in need of supplementary imports, not only to meet outside liabilities, but also to feed her own population. The easiest and the most obvious sources of these supplementary supplies were the cornlands of the "colonial Germany" to the east of the Elbe and of Western Poland, with their natural geographical and commercial centre in Prussia. These Baltic sources were not directly tapped by industrial regions in their immediate vicinity, as were those of South Italy and Northern France, and they were above all plentiful and reliable. We consequently find the English turning to Prussia for supplies in years of dearth such as 1417 and 1439, and also carrying on a direct corn trade between Danzig and Gascony.[87]

Less urgent, but more regular and constant, was the demand for the sylvan products of the Baltic. The extent which the deforestation of England had reached by the fifteenth century is hard to estimate. But it is clear that already in the thirteenth and fourteenth centuries England depended on foreign and especially Norwegian supplies for the high-grade timber used in construction and ship-building. The opening up of Prussia in the fourteenth century introduced Western Europe to the untold reserves of forest possessed by the Baltic lands, Poland, and Russia; and from the beginning of the fifteenth century Prussia became the only important source of timber. The kinds most commonly imported were wainscot, bowstaves, masts, the so-called "clapholt", and "trenchours". But timber was also imported in the shape of manufactured wooden articles—boxes, coffers, furniture (counters) and, above all, boats.[88] Danzig, with its unlimited supplies of all the raw materials employed in the construction of boats, developed an important shipbuilding industry, of which the English merchant made wise use, and for obvious reasons. The nature of the return cargoes to England very often necessitated the employment of additional shipping. The English imports, chiefly cloth, were compact and valuable, while the Prussian exports, corn and sylvan products, were bulky and cheap. Thus the English merchants required larger shipping space for the westward than for the eastward journeys. Some of this additional freightage they obtained by hire. But some of it they bought, and as a great deal of Prussian exports into England consisted of materials for naval construction, there was every commercial reason for the importation of these materials " ready made up " into vessels. It is, therefore, no wonder that the Danzig shipbuilding industry attracted a great deal of English custom, and that the use the English made of it provoked alarm in the Hanseatic Councils. In 1428 we find the Hanseatic diet in Lübeck complaining that the sale of boats to the English and the Dutch was raising up harmful competition to Hanseatic shipping. One of the first measures of the municipality of Danzig against the English in Prussia was to prohibit the sale of boats to them. The frequent re-enactments of the prohibition suggest that it was by no means easy to enforce, but it automatically became effective with the general decline in the direct trade with England, to the great disadvantage and displeasure of the ship-building interests in Danzig.[89]

As important as timber, if not more so, were the other sylvan commodities: pitch, tar, and ashes. Ashes were one of the most important materials in the industrial chemistry of the Middle Ages, and were employed in England in the manufacture of cloth. Pitch and tar were chiefly used in shipbuilding. The same use was also served by some of the other commodities of East European origin, such as hemp and sail canvas. Two of the other typically Hanseatic commodities, wax and furs, were also of Russian and Polish origin; these, however, were also brought in by the merchants of other Hanseatic groups and from places other than Prussia. Hungarian copper, the high quality iron (osmund) of Sweden, and local varieties of ordinary iron formed also quite an important category among Prussian imports.[90]

The importance of all these Baltic goods will more than explain the special value which the English put on the Hanseatic, and above all on the Prussian trade. This importance was further enhanced by the extent and character of English cloth exports. Of course, cloth was not the only commodity habitually exported from England by the Hanseatics, or imported by the English into the lands of the Hanse. In the early part of the fourteenth century Hanseatic merchants had played an important part in the wool trade between England and the Low Countries, and wool formed the main basis of their exports.[91] But the consolidation of the staple system and the working of the preferential tariffs gave the English merchant the virtual monopoly of the wool trade to Northern Europe, and reduced the Hanseatic share in it almost to nothing. It is therefore only occasionally that we find Hanseatic merchants exporting small consignments of wool and wool-fells, chiefly of the kind that over the greater part of the century was exempt from the action of the Staple laws—thrums, shorlings, lamb-fells, etc. Equally irregular were the exports of other foodstuffs and raw materials, cheese, rabbit skins, tallow, red herring, and sometimes mineral coal. Somewhat more important were the exports of metals and metal goods. Tin from the West Country and pewter vessels manufactured in London were bought in large quantities by Hanseatic merchants, chiefly Cologners, and figure constantly in customs accounts and in the records of the English dealings with the Hanse merchants. A scrivener's book of 1442 shows that, in the course of a year's trade, the purchases of a group of Hanseatic merchants included tin and pewter vessels valued at £300. The other purchases of the same merchants included in the same book were valued at about £4,000.[92]

The English merchants trading to Prussia exported from England very much the same commodities; but in addition, they also brought into Prussia a certain amount of goods of foreign origin. The herring which they imported into Prussia was probably the red herring of Yarmouth, for it was salted and packed in England. But some of the other commodities undoubtedly came from those regions on the Atlantic seaboard of the Iberian Peninsula and France—especially Gascony—with which English merchants were in constant and close contact throughout the fourteenth and the greater part of the fifteenth century. We find them selling southern fruit ("figs and raisins"), and Gascon wine in Danzig, and some of the salt sold by them may well have come from the Bay of Bourgneuf.[93]

Yet both in the export trade of the Hanseatic merchants and in that of Englishmen trading to Prussia, cloth was overwhelmingly the most important commodity. The annual averages of Hanseatic cloth exports, exclusive of worsteds, varied from 6,000 in the years between 1406 and 1427, and 10,000 between 1438 and 1459, about equal to those of all the other foreigners and about half as large as those of English merchants. Compared with cloth, the other articles of Hanseatic exports fade almost to insignificance. Evaluated at the official rates adopted for the purposes of customs, the average annual value of the Hanseatic cloth exports between 1438 and 1459 was well above £20,000, while the value of their other exports could not much have exceeded the sum of £1,200.[94]

The cloth which the English themselves exported into the Hanseatic regions went almost invariably to the Baltic countries, and especially to Prussia. It has been shown that one of the motives of their penetration into the Hanseatic regions was their quest for Baltic goods. It was, therefore, in Danzig that the focus of the English-born cloth trade was to be found. At the end of the fourteenth, and the very beginning of the fifteenth, century, the herring markets of Skania attracted some of the English merchants with their cloth. As long as the English maintained these commercial relations with Scandinavia, and especially Norway, they also took their cloth there. But after the beginning of the fifteenth century direct references to English trade to Skania disappear from the records. As for the English trade in Norway, its history in the fifteenth century, when it is written, will reveal little more than a series of fitful and irregular endeavours by English merchants to resume the position they had occupied there in the previous century, and to penetrate into markets completely monopolized by the Hanseatics. In the second half of the century even these attempts came to an end, owing to the uninterrupted state of conflict with Denmark. Thus of all the regions of the Hanseatic *Verkehrsgebiet* Prussia stood out as the only important centre of the English-borne cloth trade.

On the other hand, the cloth exported by the Hanseatics was distributed on the continent through several channels. A small part of it, especially of that carried by the merchants of Cologne and the Zuider Zee towns, was taken to the great international marts of Northern Europe—Bruges, Antwerp, Bergen-op-Zoom, and Middleburgh—to be sold there, partly for further manipulation by Flemish and Brabantine cloth workers, but chiefly for distribution in the different parts of the continent. The bulk of the exports, however, went directly without the intermediary agency of the great fairs to the regions of the Hanseatic *Verkehrsgebiet*. In this direct distribution of English cloth there was a certain amount of territorial specialization between the different groups of Hanseatic merchants. The Cologners distributed the English cloth all along the valley of the Rhine; and from there, through the market of Frankfort-on-Main, it penetrated into Southern Germany as far east as the valley of the Danube and Galicia, with its great markets of Lemberg and Cracow. A certain amount of the cloth carried by the Cologners went east along the great Hanseatic route, but that was a secondary line of Cologne's trade, important only at the time when the other sections of the Hanse were prevented from direct trade with England. During the greater part of the late fourteenth and fifteenth centuries, the Rhine valley drew to itself the bulk of Cologne's trade, and Frankfort was the second seat of Cologne's *Englandfahrer*—the corporation of merchants trading to England.[95]

The merchants of Prussia, whose share in English exports was second only to that of the Cologners, distributed the bulk of their cloth in Prussia, Lithuania, and Poland, and took it as far east as Western Russia, Hungary, Wallachia (modern Roumania), and the north coast of the Black Sea. For a short time an attempt was made to establish a Staple for cloth in Elbing, but the continued economic growth of Danzig and its political importance defeated the project of the Staple. By the end of the first decade of the fifteenth century Danzig was the central market for English cloth in Prussia, with Thorn as a secondary outpost on the way to Poland and Western Russia. It was also from Danzig, and by Danzigers, that a great deal of English cloth came to Livonia for distribution there and further east in Novgorod. In the latter market the English cloth had become a serious competitor of the Flemish cloth in the first quarter of the century and the local demand for it was strong enough to raise serious alarm among the Hanseatic groups with vested interests in Bruges and the Flemish cloth trade.[96]

The other sections of the Hanse carried English cloth all over the Hanseatic *Verkehrsgebiet*, including Livonia and the lands beyond. The Wendish towns—Lübeck, Bremen, Wismar, and Rostock—dominating as they did trade with the Scandinavian countries, easily arrogated to themselves the bulk of the trade in English cloth in Norway, Denmark, and Sweden. In connection with that trade the Wendish towns founded an important intermediary station at Boston. Their boats commonly called at Boston on their way to Bergen, sometimes discharged there goods for the English market, and sometimes did not, but invariably took on board English commodities for sale in Scandinavia, partly victuals, but mostly cloth.[97]

It will be seen that the bulk of English cloth exported by the Hanseatics, or by Englishmen trading to Hanseatic regions, was distributed among the "ultimate" consumers of cloth. Most of the regions where the Hanseatics sold it belonged to the "flax and linen" areas of Europe, and did not possess important cloth industries of their own. A certain amount of cloth was produced in different parts of Germany, especially in the Rhineland, Brunswick, and Silesia, but most of this production was purely local, employed local wool and served local needs. Even in its principal centres the market was served by cloth of Flemish and English origin. Unlike Flanders, Brabant, or Holland the regions of Hanseatic trade took and demanded not so much wool, yarn, or unfinished cloth, as fabrics that could be sold directly to the consumers. Therefore the cloth imported there could be, and was, brought in a fully finished state, dyed, pulled, and shorn.[98]

The same fact emerges also from what we know of the English end of the trade. On the whole it will be true to say that the Hanseatic merchants drew their cloth from all the manufacturing regions in England, and exported all the varieties of cloth produced in this country. Although most of their shipping, and consequently the bulk of their trade, was concentrated in London and the ports on the sea-coast—Ipswich, Boston, Lynn, Yarmouth, Hull, and Newcastle—they did not confine their dealings to the production of the eastern cloth-producing regions, Essex, East Anglia, and Yorkshire. We find them buying and exporting large quantities of cloth of the western and southern counties, the Southampton broads, the Western says, the Welsh friezes. In the fourteenth and fifteenth centuries England was more of an economic unit than it is fashionable to imagine. The main branches of her trade were as much inter-local and inter-regional, as they were to be at any time before the arrival of the canal and the railway. The Hanseatics found it possible to concentrate their shipping in the ports on the East Coast only because they were not compelled thereby to confine their activities to the production of the near-lying Colchester, Norwich, or York. We find them dealing with cloth merchants and cloth producers all over the country, and those dealings were greatly facilitated by the part played by London as a national market of the cloth trade.[99] If the Hanseatic merchants sometimes concentrated on certain branches of cloth export, the concentration was largely fortuitous, and due to the accident of mediaeval taxation more than to any other cause. At the end of the fourteenth century the so-called kerseys and straits, cheaper and narrower fabrics than the standard cloth of assize, were not yet subjected to the payment of the general cloth custom and the Hanseatic merchants had every inducement for exporting them in large quantities. Apparently the same happened with worsteds. Judging by the indirect evidence in the customs accounts, worsted cloths of different varieties—cloths and beds, double, single, and semi-double—formed a greater share of Hanseatic cloth exports than they did of the cloth exports of other merchants, and the difference was apparently due to the fact that the Hanseatic exports of worsteds were taxed very lightly.[100] The only feature of the Hanseatic exports which cannot be put down to a fiscal cause, and which marked them off from the exports to the Low Countries at the end of the fifteenth, and in the sixteenth, century, was the fact that they were made up of finished cloth. This fact has already been stressed once, in the analysis of the cloth markets, and it will stand out again in its full significance in connection with the story of English commercial organization.

The business organization of the English trade to the Hanseatic lands and that of the Hanseatic trade to England possessed many features in common. Some of their similarity was doubtless due to the cosmopolitan origin and nature of merchant customs, for in Northern Europe the conventions of merchant law, the commercial terminology, and the business routine differed comparatively little from country to country. But a great deal of the similarity was due to the economic character of the trade between England and the Hanse, and above all to the nature of the commodities exchanged. It has been shown that the exchange between England and the Hanse was very largely confined to English cloth and Baltic goods. Both commodities had to be carried across long distances and disposed of in distant markets. The carriage and the disposal required longer and more continuous action than, to take an obvious example, the importation of onions from Flanders or the sale of pewter vessels to the Italians in London. Then, at both ends of the trade, in the purchase of cloth in England and its sale in Prussia, or in the purchase of timber in Poland and its sale in England, the transactions were based on credit.[101] This use of credit, coupled with the " reciprocal " character of the trade, called into being a complicated system of payments and assignments, and required constant and "continuous" activity on the part of the merchant. Finally, the trade in cloth and in Baltic goods lent itself very easily to that combination of wholesale and retail trade, which characterized big business in the Middle Ages. Recent discussions of the problem of wholesale trade in the mediaeval towns have established beyond dispute the fact that wholesale trade, i.e. purchase and sale in bulk between merchant and merchant, was very common, but that at the same time it was generally combined with dealings in retail. This relation of wholesale and retail prevailed also in the business of the Hanseatic merchants in England and in that of the English merchants in Danzig. The cloth brought by the English merchants was often sold in bulk to the local traders, but a great deal of it was retailed to consumers. It was this retail trade that provoked the opposition of the Danzigers, among whom the cloth merchants (*Gewantschneider*) were very influential. And it was this retail trade which formed the main, and at times the most disputable, point of the English programme of reciprocity. On their part the Hanseatic merchants in London had engaged in retail trade since their first appearance in England. In the fifteenth century the English records of debts show them selling Baltic goods not only to merchant intermediaries, but also directly to consumers.[102]

Now, the essential feature of an import trade combining wholesale with retail transactions is its "continuous" nature. The wholesale disposal of an imported cargo need not take more than a few days, or even a few hours, but its retail distribution is a matter of weeks and months. And if we remember that the Anglo-Hanseatic trade also involved a complicated machinery of payment and a difficult system of transport, we shall easily understand the comparative complexity of its commercial organization. This organization was even further removed from a "primitive mediaeval" type than the organization of some other branches of English trade. It can well be doubted whether the conventional picture of a vagrant trader, travelling with his goods to the foreign markets and bringing back his return cargo, ever represented the upper strata of the mediaeval merchant class. It certainly did not represent English merchants engaged in foreign trade in the fourteenth and fifteenth centuries. The buying and the preparing of goods in their country of origin, their transportation, their sale abroad and the management of credit and payments, were all activities of a "continuous" character requiring the constant attention, and often the simultaneous presence, of several persons in different places. The Merchant Adventurer of the old-fashioned textbooks, the artisan trader of Sombart's classification, a mere sea-going huckster, would have fared very badly in the trade between England and the Hanse. The trade was, and could only be, conducted by merchant firms, each employing a group of men, and each assisted by a well-developed system of commission trade.

It is not the object of this essay to describe the inner organization of the mediaeval firm or to trace the development of the mediaeval commission trade. The former has in part been done in connection with the English wool-trade in the previous essay, while the latter will have to be done by students specializing in the history of mediaeval partnerships. Both these subjects interest us here only in so far as they illustrate and explain some of the most significant features of Anglo-Hanseatic trade.

In theory, the " integral " firm, i.e. the business unit continually employing several persons, and the system of commission trade, were two alternative ways of serving the same economic ends. But in practice, both were used by the same merchants at the same time. The " integral " firm enabled the merchant to cope with the complexity of foreign trade by assigning the different members of his organization to the different departments or geographical centres of his trade. This system of " local branches " or " agencies " was common both among the Hanseatic merchants trading to England and the English merchants trading to Prussia. A merchant like Robert Garr, habitually trading to Prussia, employed a resident " servant " in Danzig, and apparently several other men in England. But he could also make use of persons occupying a position intermediate between that of a permanent member of a merchant firm and an independent commission agent. The agents or factors of the English merchants representing them in the different localities, especially abroad, were sometimes their servants and sometimes their partners. In itself the distinction was not of great importance, for junior partners commonly described themselves as the " servants " of their senior partners, while elements of partnership commonly entered into the ordinary contract of service. What is important is the fact that the designation of " partner ", " factor ", or " attorney " could also represent the relations of independent agents to their habitual clients overseas. A person representing a merchant in a distant place need not be a real member of his firm, his partner or servant. His services to the merchant could be temporary and occasional; they could be enlisted for individual transactions and relate to single consignments of goods. The records of mediaeval trade abound with instances of partnerships and associations concluded for the duration of single deals. Most of these were *commenda*-like arrangements (" depository partnerships ") by which merchants of Lynn or London could entrust their goods to merchants crossing over to Prussia for sale there. And from a *commenda*-like arrangement of this kind, it was only a short step to the equally common practice whereby merchants resident in England sent goods to merchants for the time being in Danzig, with a request and instructions to sell. This practice was widely used by the Hanseatic merchants in their foreign or inter-urban trade, and received a separate recognition in German law and language under the name of *sendeve*.

It was equally common, though it did not possess a separate name, among the English merchants trading to Prussia. The students of English records will be familiar with the merchant sending his goods to persons in other towns or abroad, with instructions to do their " best " to his " use and avail ". And with these requests to do their " best " we enter into the realm of commission trade pure and simple.[103]

There was thus no distinct line between the association of several persons within the framework of the " integral " firm and the conduct of trade by means of commission agents. The majority of mediaeval business firms combined both methods. They maintained permanent associates—partners or servants—in important centres of their trade, and sold or bought their goods through " commissionaires " in all those places where they did not at the time maintain agents of their own.

This organization of trade explains a great deal of what is otherwise unintelligible in the history of the commercial settlements and factories abroad. Above all it accounts for the conspicuous place which the problem of foreign factories occupied in the commercial policies of the time. The English settlement in Danzig and the Hanseatic settlement in England were largely composed of agents trading on behalf of merchant firms at home. These agents were—to use an expressive middle-German term—" liggers ". They were resident factors spending most of their time in the foreign centres. Their commercial activities were vitally affected by the condition of their residence and their rights of trade; these, in their turn, depended upon the organization and the status of the factory. Viewed in this light, the English and the Hanseatic claims on behalf of their respective settlements merely embodied the conditions required for the smooth functioning of the system of resident factors. It was because of that system that the commercial policies of the fifteenth century were so much concerned with the problems of corporate organizations and communal centres for the merchants abroad.

Of the actual organization and routine of the factories we know relatively little, though, thanks to the work of Lappenberg, Weinbaum, and Engel, we know more of the German settlements in England than we do of the English settlement in Danzig. At one time there was a whole chain of Hanseatic factories in England. The evidence of the thirteenth, and the early fifteenth, century suggests the existence of over twelve branches. In the fifteenth century, however, only four seem to have functioned—London, Lynn, Ipswich, and Boston, and these settlements were the only ones concerned in the transactions and land-transfers carried out under the treaty of 1475. In origin, and to some extent in behaviour, the provincial factories were independent of the Steelyard, but in theory the Steelyard was regarded as the headquarters of the Hanse in England, and successive measures in the fifteenth century strengthened its control over the provincial factories. The latter were dominated by merchants of the central and the eastern towns, while in London, at any rate prior to 1475, the majority of the members and the leading part in the government belonged to Cologne. In the fifteenth century the membership of the Steelyard was, for the purposes of government, divided into three parts—the western with Cologne at its head, the Westfalian-Saxon, and the Prusso-Livonian. The division was designed to prevent the domination of any separate group of towns in the government of the factory, for each part was to be represented by the same number of members in the governing court. But the method of election, by which the part under-represented among the members could have its places at the court filled by the other towns, gave Cologne much more than her constitutional share in the government of the Steelyard.[104]

The functions of the Steelyard government were manifold. It had to manage the finances of the settlement, to impose and collect the "schoss" payable into its treasury by the Hanseatic merchants trading to England, and to distribute the payments, both open and clandestine, to the national and municipal authorities in England. In the second place it represented the Hanseatic merchants in England before the English government and officials. This work of representation was done with the assistance of the English alderman of the Hanse, appointed to the government of the Steelyard under the Hanseatic Charter of 1303. The primary, though not the official, function of the English alderman was to serve as a liaison between the Steelyard and the English authorities, and in this he was assisted by a whole body of English intermediaries, mostly lawyers. But he also had extensive rights and powers in the exercise of jurisdiction in the mixed suits between the English and the Hanseatics, as well as the enforcement of internal discipline within the Steelyard. The maintenance of this discipline was the third important function of the government of the Steelyard. The Steelyard itself, with the houses rented in its immediate neighbourhood, formed the residential centre of the Hanseatic community. It was there that the goods were warehoused and the commercial transactions carried out, and that the bachelor merchants (the junior partners and factors were unmarried) resided.[105] It is therefore no wonder that the Ordinances of the Steelyard are filled with regulations concerning the morals and manners, both commercial and private, of the resident members of the factory, regulations which were sufficiently minute and sufficiently strict to suggest to an ingenuous and bewildered historian the theory that the Hanseatics in London were all knights of the Prussian order.[106]

Unfortunately no constitutional enactments comparable to the Ordinances of the Steelyard have survived for the English Association in Prussia, and we are consequently not in a position to reconstruct fully or coherently its fifteenth century organization. Some of its features, however, emerge clearly enough. Its government consisted of a governor and aldermen, and during the greater part of the century the post of governor was held by important merchants, heads of English firms trading to Prussia. Their functions were chiefly those of representation before the authorities in Prussia, and jurisdiction over matters arising between the English merchants themselves. When in 1428 the High Master finally gave his recognition to the corporate government of the English merchants, he did so " in order that the governour should keep order and hold court among the English ". The scope of that jurisdiction we do not know, but at a certain period it must have been very extensive. One of Danzig's replies to the English grievances mentions the prison in the English house—a statement which the English did not expressly deny or disprove. It was also alleged that the English society levied an impost from its members comparable to the " schoss ". But whatever the functions of the governing body, they certainly were less extensive than those of the government of the Steelyard. Unlike the Steelyard, the English factory in Danzig was not a communal settlement. Common residence was not enforced among the English in Danzig, nor is there any trace of common warehouses. Even at those times when the English possessed a " common house ", they also owned private lodgings and shops in the town, and the " house " was apparently nothing more than a meeting-place and the seat of the corporate government.[107] Hence the absence of evidence as to the regulation of the lives of individual Englishmen comparable to the disciplinary regulations of the Steelyard. The social and the business needs of the merchants and the activities of the governor and aldermen required something in the nature of a communal centre, and explain the agitation for the right to possess one. But neither the absence of a communal centre during a considerable part of the century, nor the want of official recognition, could prevent the government of the factory from functioning. We find " the governour and aldermen of the English merchants " addressed, or referred to, throughout the first half of the century and in those years during the second half in which trade between England and Prussia was maintained. It is only in the late sixties and the seventies, which saw the general decadence of the Anglo-Prussian trade, that references to the " governour and aldermen " became rare and cease altogether.

The eclipse of the society of the English merchants in Danzig throws a flood of light on the problem of the origin and the progress of the Merchant Adventurers. It is not the object of this essay to deal with this problem in its entirety. The early history of the Merchant Adventurers is closely related to certain important developments in the trading guilds at home, and will form the subject of a separate investigation. What interests us here is the connection which existed between that history, on the one hand, and the fortunes of the English in Prussia, on the other. That connection is clearly indicated in the very event with which historians commonly begin their accounts of the Merchant Adventurers in the fifteenth century. By a series of charters of between 1404 and 1408, a legal recognition and a corporate status were conferred upon three companies of English merchants trading abroad. One of these embraced merchants trading to the Low Countries, and the other two, merchants trading to Norway and the Baltic respectively. It was the Company of the merchants trading to the Low Countries that came in the end to be regarded and described as the Company of the Merchant Adventurers *par excellence*. The story of its origin is the story of its relative growth: the growth of one organization at the expense of the other two. The problem, therefore, is not to discover how the English merchants trading abroad came to form a company (there is nothing strange or difficult in that), but how they came to form a *single* company; it is essentially not a problem of origin, but one of concentration.[108]

To this problem an answer, albeit an indirect one, has already been given. The rise of a single company of Merchant Adventurers was merely the converse of the eclipse of the company in Prussia. If at the beginning of the century we find several companies all functioning, it is because in the beginning of the century the several channels of English trade were all active. Of these channels the one leading to the Low Countries was doubtless from the beginning the most important, but it was as yet not sufficiently important to embrace the overwhelming bulk of English trade and thus to overwhelm and overshadow the other channels and the other organizations. What happened between the beginning of the century and its last quarter was that trade in the Low Countries attracted to itself the bulk of English commercial enterprise. The English trade to the Low Countries was now the only branch of English foreign trade that mattered, and consequently the organization of the English merchants there was the only organization to function.

Why and how this happened we already know. The net result of the Anglo-Hanseatic rivalry was to interrupt the expansion of English trade in the east, and to sever its connections with the Scandinavian countries and Prussia. In Norway the Hanseatics had tightened their hold over the trade of Bergen and defeated all the attempts of the English merchants to restore their position. It was very largely the cessation of the Bergen trade that sent the English merchants to Iceland. But this new enterprise, however important in itself, only completed the ruin of the English trade in Scandinavia. It plunged England into a state of chronic conflict with Denmark and in the second half of the century definitely shut the Dano-Norwegian waters to English trade and navigation. Even more significant, and to the readers of this essay more familiar, was the

English defeat in the Baltic. In the second half of the century the English trade there was much reduced by recurrent conflict with the Hanse, by the civil war in Prussia, by the triumphant protectionism of Danzig, and by growing insecurity on the high seas. By the end of the eighties the direct trade to Prussia had been reduced to vanishing point. The traffic in Baltic goods had been taken out of English hands; some of it proceeded indirectly by way of the Brabantine fairs, and some of it was carried on by Dutch and Hanseatics. And with the end of the Baltic trade there came also the end of the Baltic trader. The English merchants were forced to restrict their maritime and commercial ventures in Northern Europe to the trade in the Low Countries, and the "Merchant Adventurers" absorbed the bulk of English trade and the mass of English merchants.[108a]

The story of this absorption emerges very clearly from the records of English foreign trade. The municipal records of the East Coast towns contain a number of references, mostly indirect, to the existence of distinct groups of merchants trading to the Baltic, Scandinavia, and the Low Countries. But these distinctions almost disappear from the records in the sixties and the seventies, while the references to piracy in the North Sea in the same period begin to abound with the names of merchants once active in the trade with the Hanse. More direct and conclusive is the evidence of the particular customs accounts. The customs accounts of London reveal the existence in the first half of the century of a specialization among merchants trading to foreign countries. Throughout the early part of the century the accounts record the regular shipments of a large group of merchants, mostly drapers, grocers, and mercers, and varying from 50 to 120 persons, exporting cloth to the Low Countries and importing miscellaneous commodities from the great fairs. These shipments are interspersed with those of a smaller group, which, judging by their cargoes and sometimes by their ships, must have traded with the Baltic lands. A few of the shippers in this group were grocers, mercers, or drapers, but most of them, and certainly those whose names recur most often together, are fishmongers and stockfishmongers. Similarly, some of them occasionally participate in the shipments of the Netherlands group, but the majority seems to keep away from the trade to the Low Countries. If there is any branch of trade which they combine with that to the Baltic lands, it is the trade to Spain and Portugal, or Gascony—a very natural combination, considering the connection between the Gascon wine trade and the Prussian corn trade, and the identity of some of the staple commodities of Iberian and German trade (iron, bowstaves, etc.). But whatever the lines of specialization in the southern trade, those in the English trade of Northern Europe ran clearly between the merchants trading to Prussia and the Baltic on the one hand, and the merchants trading to the Netherlands on the other. This differentiation, however, does not continue beyond the middle decades of the century. When at the beginning of Edward IV's reign a new and a very complete series of particular customs accounts begins, it has already lost almost all trace of the old demarcation. The shipments to the Low Countries are as regular as ever, but they now comprise the overwhelming bulk of English merchants active in the port of London. The shipments to Gascony follow an irregular curve corresponding to the fluctuations of peace and war with France. But the Baltic group has gone. Some of the erstwhile Baltic merchants have died in the meantime, some must have retired through old age or the cessation of the direct trade with Prussia, while others now ship regularly to the Low Countries together with the majority of English merchants. And, to accord with this tale of the exports, there is a remarkable change in the composition of the imports. The Baltic goods continue to be imported, but they are no longer brought by English merchants from Prussia. Some, especially after 1476, are imported by the Hanseatics. Most of them come in from the Low Countries as part of the general cargo from the great fairs.[109]

The predominance of the Netherland group, i.e. of the Merchant Adventurers *par excellence*, and of their trade to the fairs, is merely the other side of the English withdrawal from Prussia and the Baltic. In this light, the rise of the " Company of the Merchant Adventurers " loses a great deal of its conventional glory. It was not a " landmark in the history of English expansion ", for it occurred at a time when English trade was temporarily contracting. It did not open to the English trade any new " fields of enterprise ", though it may have adjusted it to the loss of the old ones. In the last quarter of the century, and in the Tudor era the Company may have enabled the English merchants to extend their trade beyond the highest peak it had ever reached before the treaty of 1475, but Unwin has argued that such growth of the English cloth trade as took place in the sixteenth century proceeded independently of the Company of the Merchant Adventurers, and in spite of its policy of restriction. Further research may add still more to Unwin's detractions. The historian of the wool-trade may find the Company helping to organize the premature demise of the wool-staple. The historian of the cloth industry may find a connection between the concentration of English trade in the Netherlands and the concentration of English production on undyed and unfinished cloth. But even if the conventional story of the Merchant Adventurers in the sixteenth century survive the onslaught of historical criticism, the story of its rise in the fifteenth century will have to be revised. It will have to be interpreted not as a victory, but as the by-product of a defeat; not as a stage in an inexorable growth, but as a sign of temporary concentration and contraction.

IV
THE ICELAND TRADE

"Of Yseland to wryte is lytill nede
Save of stokfische; yit for sothe in dede
Out of Bristow and costis many one
Men have practised by nedle and by stone
Thiderwardes wythine a lytel whylle,
Wythine xij yeres, and wythoute parille,
Gone and comen, as men were wonte of olde
Of Scarborowgh, unto the costes colde." [1]

§ 1
The Establishment of the Trade

To the Englishman at the close of the fourteenth century Iceland was a land of myth and fable, perilously poised on the outer edge of that "sea of darkness" which encircled the whole known world. He might perhaps read in monkish books, mere echoes of ancient geographers, of how "Iceland is an isle, having on the south Norway, on the north the sea congealed"; of "white bears breaking the frozen water to draw out fishes"; and of its people "short of language, covered with the skins of wild beasts, giving their labour to fishing". He might learn also that it was reputed distant from Britain "by the sailing of three days".[2] But such reports were scarcely to be relied upon; of first-hand information he had none; for certain knowledge he must go to Norway. There in the harbour of Bergen he might see Norwegian or German traders unloading cargoes of stockfish from Iceland's newly-exploited fisheries. There he might even see that excellent ship the "Bishop's Buss", bearing Bishop William, its builder, "of venerable memory," to his remote see of Skálholt.[3] Then he might realize that Skálholt was a yet longer journey from Norway than it was reputed to be from Britain, though no English sailors now put this matter to the proof.

Yet there had once been a time when Iceland, geographically nearer to Ireland than to Norway, was closely linked with our own islands. It was from Ireland in very early Christian days that saints and scholars had sailed to that larger but more remote Atlantic isle, seeking sanctuary from the tumults of a changing world. Rudely they had been driven forth when the fierce Norse rovers first appeared, and in their flight they had left behind them "books, bells, and croziers". The Norsemen themselves, it is said, were in some degree indebted to the Irish for their safe arrival in Iceland, for they traversed the ocean successfully with the aid of Irish captives who, by their long sea experience, saved the lives of their captors. Ere long evangelizing zeal prompted further voyages from Ireland to the Norse colonists in Iceland. Missionaries such as Bishop John the Irishman, together with some from Norway, won the north once again for Christendom, and Örlyg, trained by Bishop Patrick of the Hebrides, brought to Iceland timber for a church, a church bell, and some consecrated soil. Along with the missionaries went traders, and merchant ships plied to and fro, such as one from Dublin which anchored off Snaefellness in the year 1000. In this came an enterprising lady Thorgunna, proud possessor of a large chest with "bed clothes beautifully embroidered, English sheets, a silken quilt, and other valuable wares, the like of which were rare in Iceland". The Irish were indeed pioneers in voyaging across the ocean to Iceland, though ere long Englishmen also took their share. Seamen from the East Coast ports found their way thither, and it was from England that the light of the twelfth century Renaissance reached Iceland. St. Thorlak, from Iceland, then studied at Lincoln, and in England his compatriot Bishop Paul got great wisdom, and so "surpassed all other men in Iceland in courtliness and in his learning and in making of verse and in book lore". By this time Britain's horizon had widened even beyond Iceland to the far western shores of the Atlantic. Explorers of the lands of "forest and self-sown wheat" in North America had put in to Irish harbours; settlers in Greenland had traded with England. The detailed knowledge of Greenland in the thirteenth century is remarkable, and is a striking contrast to the darkness which shrouded it at the opening of the fifteenth century.[4]

For the promise of earlier days was not to be fulfilled. The bounds of the known world expanded no further but shrank. The "rich lands" beyond Greenland's barren wastes faded away into a myth. Soon the Greenland settlements also receded into outer darkness. Their settlers, isolated, struggling against the encroaching Eskimo, degenerated, lapsed into heathenism, and perhaps perished utterly. At any rate, voyages thither ceased almost completely during the latter half of the fourteenth century. Iceland herself was now losing touch with the outer world, and seems to have become completely estranged from Britain. The Icelandic annals, which carefully enumerate ships arriving from Norway, and in the next century record the visits of ships from England, are as silent as the English records of this period about any communication with our islands, save when a shipload of Scotsmen was driven inadvertently on to the coast of Iceland and "none understood their language". These annals show, also, that even between Norway and Iceland intercourse became more and more spasmodic in the later fourteenth century, until the annalist one year had sorrowfully to record "No news from Norway to Iceland", and the Icelanders made bitter complaints of this neglect.[5]

THE ICELAND TRADE

The isolation of Iceland at the close of the fourteenth century is very evident, and her decline is as marked in the economic as in the intellectual sphere. The reasons for such isolation are less obvious, and it has given rise to many conjectures. It is certainly clear that the great days of Viking venture were ended and that Scandinavian sea-power was waning. The Icelanders especially, ever ready to bewail their desertion by others, now showed little enterprise upon the sea. Had they indeed kept up the character of sea rovers in a land destitute of the raw materials for ships, theirs would have been a remarkable achievement. When, therefore, they agreed to the union with Norway in 1262 they stipulated that she should send them six ships annually. Their reiterated complaints that this promise was not kept indicate clearly that, left to themselves, they were helpless, even though a bishop or a " lawman " might occasionally fare forth across the sea in his own ship.[6]

The complaints that the Icelanders sent to Norway must, however, lead us there to seek further, in the policy of their rulers and in the eclipse of Norwegian shipping also, the cause of Iceland's isolation and detachment from the rest of Europe, and in particular of the severance of the link with England. Norway, regarding Iceland merely as a potential source of revenue, was quick to turn the union of 1262 to her own advantage. Before long Iceland was transformed into a complete dependency, whose commerce, existing solely for the benefit of the mother country, was strictly controlled by the Norwegian kings. To facilitate such control trade was concentrated at Bergen, which became the staple town for all dependencies and was forbidden to all but Norwegians. It finally became virtually a royal monopoly, hampered by excessive tolls, and permitted only through licence from the king, who himself owned a quarter of every ship concerned. Even the notable son of an Icelandic chieftain, named Jorsalafari on account of his adventurous travels to Jerusalem, was once arrested for voyaging to Greenland without the royal sanction.[7] Thus Iceland, destitute herself of ships, might look for assistance only from Norwegian merchants in Bergen. Had the Norwegians been still a great seafaring nation, the Icelandic trade now left in their hands might yet have prospered. But their shipping, too, was decaying, and its decline was hastened by the rise of a rival commercial power on the north coast of Germany, destined ere long to dominate the commerce of Scandinavia. The Hanseatic League already by the fourteenth century had driven the Norwegians from the southern coasts of the North Sea and the Baltic, thrusting them back upon their own dependencies. Hence, momentarily, trade with Iceland was stimulated, and so vigorously did the Norwegians develop it, that Iceland, alarmed at the vast cargoes of fish shipped from her harbours, was moved to remonstrate that she was left without sufficient for her own consumption.[8]

But the ever-encroaching Hanseatics, not content with expelling the Norwegians from the south, went on to challenge their monopoly even in Bergen, so that the restrictions on trade with the dependencies were from time to time relaxed in their favour. Slowly and steadily they undermined the naval power of Norway until her trade, even with her own colonies, languished and died. Iceland, already cut off from her former friends in Western Europe, could now look for scant succour even from Bergen, whence came no regular traffic, but only occasionally a German or Norwegian ship.[9] Thus we may seek a reason for Iceland's isolation and for her estrangement from Britain not only in the decay of the Icelanders' original spirit of enterprise, but in their political union with Norway, and in the restrictive policy which limited their trade, drew it all towards Bergen, and heavily taxed it, leaving them thus altogether stranded as Scandinavian shipping declined and was destroyed by the Hanse.

Iceland's plight was indeed pitiable when she was thus left to her own slight resources. "The desert in the ocean" is the apt description of the island by one monkish chronicler.[10] Far out to the north-west she lay, in the midst of the ocean, a solitary outpost of civilization. There, amidst a dreary waste of icy waters, rose this snow-capped volcanic tableland, girt on the north by ice-floes, veiled till far on into the summer by impenetrable mists. Even its meagre fringe of habitable coast, though rich in green pastures when the snow had vanished, yielded no corn. The Icelanders, therefore, like the Eskimo, clung to the shore. Fish was their staple food, and with this they were bountifully provided; some cattle were kept; their clothing was made from the rough *vaðmál* woven from their own sheep's wool, but for the supply of their other needs they looked out anxiously across the ocean. From earliest times corn came to them from other lands, drift wood was eagerly collected by the shore, and big timber for the building of churches was laboriously brought in long ships across the ocean.[11] Thus it was, when the days of their own sea-roving were over, that they depended so much upon the visits of foreigners, and lamented so loudly when the Norwegian ships failed to arrive, and the sorely needed provisions could not be obtained through Bergen. Their difficulties were aggravated at the close of the fourteenth century by a concurrence of natural calamities: violent volcanic eruptions, winters of exceptional severity, the Black Death and other widespread epidemics bringing famine and want in their train.

Still worse became Iceland's condition at this time, since she and Norway both came under the rule of far distant Danish sovereigns until finally these three countries, with Sweden, were formally united by the Union of Kalmar in 1397. Ere long her claims, like those of Norway and Sweden, were entirely subordinated to those of Denmark, the strongest and most populous partner in the union. Brought beneath the sway of self-centred, narrow-minded strangers with no interest in her welfare, anxious only to fill their own coffers and absorbed in their own concerns, she became a prey—albeit a restless one—to the extortion of governors (hirðstjórar) appointed by aliens, and to the selfish greed of foreign bishops who " travelled through the land collecting taxes from learned as well as from laymen, whatever they could get; and under the oppression of such burdens the people had to remain ". With complete indifference to her troubles, and contrary to the agreement of union, new and burdensome taxes were laid on the country and on any exports thence,[12] though no provision was made to ensure the stipulated visit of six ships annually. It was little wonder that when Bergen seemed unable to help, and the distant Danish government seemed deaf to their entreaties, the angry Icelanders were ready to ignore Bergen's monopoly, and to welcome eagerly the first foreign ships which came their way.

Not long were they to remain virtually deserted, dependent upon spasmodic visits from Bergen, and cut off from their old connections with the British Isles. For while famished Iceland was looking out anxiously for assistance, many circumstances were combining to bring about a renewal of English ventures thither, and to draw her once again within the orbit of England's trade. England, now rapidly developing as an industrial country, was seeking far and wide new markets not already captured by the clothmakers of the Netherlands, while to feed her own people there was an increasing demand for fish, and English fishers, growing ever more venturesome, were exploring every region profitable to them, no matter what the hindrance might be. Already during the fourteenth century, while the amount of cloth sent out of England grew steadily greater, more and more codfish came into England from Norway and more and more English merchantmen went to fetch it themselves. English fishers as well as English merchants sought the coasts of Norway for fish, like certain " fishers of salt fish of Cromer and Blakeney ", who carried on fishing " on the coasts of Norway and Denmark ".[13]

At the same time a striking advance was being made in English shipbuilding, rendering ocean trade practicable to an unprecedented degree. The single masted vessel with its one square sail, familiar from the days of the Vikings to the fourteenth century, had by the fifteenth century developed into a two or three masted vessel more adaptable to ocean gales, with high pointed bows to resist the buffetings of a strong head sea. Such an English ship was then carved on a pew end in the new church at Lynn, a church described in 1419 as " that most beautiful chapel of St. Nicholas newly built and constructed by the alms of the benevolent ". The ship has two masts; the mainmast is square rigged as of old, but the mizzen has the new three-cornered lateen sail, recently borrowed from the Mediterranean; this greatly facilitated the working of the ship by making it possible to sail nearer to the wind. The castles built up at stem and stern are now an integral part of the ship itself, the "forecastle" being noticeably the higher of the two. The mainmast has a stalwart fighting top, and is supported by elaborate rigging coming down abaft amidships; while there are many more forestays and backstays, for greater strength, than in earlier ships.[14]

This marked development in shipbuilding, which enabled the seaman to master his vessel as never before, was perhaps even more important than the contemporary improvement of the compass. For though at first men had fared perilously across the ocean to Iceland with the aid of birds, already by the twelfth century the principle of the compass was understood in Northern Europe, and when clouds obscured the Pole Star the pilot discovered the north by rubbing a needle with a lodestone, mounting it upon a piece of wood, and floating it on the water. Alexander Neckam, writing probably before 1200, described fully the sailor's use of this magnetized needle. A century later, Hauk Erlandsson, editing the ancient *Landnámabók*, commented on the striking contrast between the improved method of steering in his own day and that of the earliest Icelandic voyages when "the sailors of the north countries had not yet any lodestone". Such a primitive device, however, though it could be used occasionally to find the direction of the Pole Star, could not be used continuously for steering, since the rubbing had to be repeated every time the needle was consulted. The really practical mariner's compass with a pivoted needle and compass card, or "Rose of the Winds", was only commonly adopted by the Italians in the fourteenth century, and was not in general use in the north until the fifteenth century. Northern Europe, foremost in the use of the lodestone, lagged behind the south in superseding the lodestone and needle by the completed "compass". While the Mediterranean had with its aid been accurately mapped before the end of the fourteenth century, no comparable charts have been found for the northern seas dating before the sixteenth century. English ships were still purchasing "lodestones" in 1345, and the term was still as usual as that of "compass" was uncommon; no compass has been traced in a German ship's inventory until 1460. Fra Mauro, on his map made in 1458, wrote that the seamen of the Baltic sail "neither with chart nor with compass". The familiar reference in the *Libelle of Englyshe Polycye* (? 1436) to the needle and the stone by which men found their way to Iceland can indicate only the primitive instrument, and shows that even this was resorted to only for voyages across the deeps of the open ocean. Hence the latest improvements cannot have been generally adopted in England by the opening of the fifteenth century. The mariner's compass was not, therefore, an important factor in the reopening of communication with Iceland, though its increasing use during the century must greatly have facilitated and stimulated the trade.[15]

England's progress in the art of navigation, and the enterprise of her merchants and fishers in pushing her wares into new markets and striving to open new sources of supply, might alone have taken her ships to Iceland. A more direct impetus, however, came from Norway herself, in the many hindrances to the English traffic there at the opening of the fifteenth century. All fish caught off the coasts of Norway or any of its dependencies had to be brought before export to the Staple at Bergen, where heavy dues were exacted. This restriction, tiresome though it was, was nothing new, but it now became peculiarly obnoxious owing to the rapid advance of the Hanse in Bergen. Though their privileges there had for a time been cancelled on the death of King Haakon in 1380, and the English were then able to make much progress, by 1410 the Wendish group among the Hanseatics dominated the city; pursuing a policy of arrogant exclusiveness, they now did their utmost to oust all other foreigners, whether English or Hanseatic.[16] Thus while Bergen remained the Staple and the Hanse controlled Bergen, the English could have little recognized part in the trade and fisheries of Norway or her dependencies. They therefore boldly defied the law, opened up a direct trade with Iceland, and before long became so firmly established that they could not be dislodged, and the Bergen rules were perforce relaxed.

Where saints and scholars had once led the way across the ocean, braving monsters "passing dreadful", fishermen now opened anew the traffic between Iceland and the British Isles, thus re-establishing a connection older than that between Iceland and Norway. In the very year (1412) when the annalist had sorrowfully to record "No news from Norway to Iceland", a strange ship appeared off Dyrholm isle. Men rowed towards it, and there discovered "fishermen out from England". Henceforth more and more fishermen arrived. The next year "thirty or more" fishing doggers came from England to the Vestmann Isles off the south coast, and some of the crew rowed over to the mainland, twelve of them in a boat. There they sought to replenish their provisions, and because they were trafficking with a people whose language they knew not, they "put down money" and took from a farmer cattle in exchange. Some wandered far, to the north and to the east, and five lost sight of their ship and were stranded for the winter.[17]

Fishers were the forerunners of merchants. These at first succeeded in obtaining the necessary licence from the new king Eric, who, with his English wife, showed himself to be favourably disposed to the English.[18] For in this same year, besides thirty or more fishing doggers, there arrived in Iceland an English merchantman, whose captain carried letters from King Eric "to the effect that he might sail with his wares into the realm without toll". Taking oath to be faithful and loyal to the land, he called at many ports including

Hafnarfjördur and Horn, and rode inland to Skálholt, doing meanwhile a good trade. Thus both fishers and merchants began to desert the coasts of Norway, where so many hindrances beset them, and England and Iceland supplied each other's needs direct, ignoring the Staple at Bergen. But the next year King Eric, apprehensive perhaps of the proportions the trade was assuming, sent letters to Iceland forbidding all trade with the "outlandish men". The English, however, had already set out, armed with letters from their own king, who was himself tempted to risk a ship in the venture. This vessel, with four other merchantmen, arrived in the Vestmann Isles in the summer of 1414, bringing letters addressed by Henry V "to the people and chief men of Iceland, to the effect that licence should be given to transact business especially that relating to the king's own ship". The Icelanders, mindful of King Eric's letter, demurred at first and spoke, like dutiful subjects, of the Staple at Bergen. But, seeing that the English would have nothing to do with that, they swallowed their scruples and did business. The next summer six English ships rode at anchor in Hafnarfjördur. On their return voyage the *hirðstjóri* himself, Vigfus Ivarsson, embarked for England, taking with him fifty lasts of dried fish and silver of great price, that he might pay his vows at the shrine of St. Thomas of Canterbury. Fogs and snowstorms took their toll, once of no less than twenty-five English ships in a single day, but traders and fisherfolk, long bred to hardship on rough northern seas, persisted in the venture, flouting openly the monopoly of Bergen.[19]

So great was the sudden influx of fishermen, and so ungoverned were they, that in 1415 King Eric was moved to write to King Henry, complaining of the damage done by them in Iceland and the adjoining islands. His letter was answered during Henry's absence in France by the Duke of Bedford, who declared that for the next year none should sail to Iceland "except in accordance with ancient custom", thus prohibiting intercourse except through Bergen. Such a prohibition provoked an immediate petition to the English Parliament, expressing indignation that "certain of Norway and Denmark" should have been endeavouring to exclude the English fishermen. The Commons declared that since the fish had forsaken their former haunts, "as is well known", the fishers had searched elsewhere and found great plenty in Iceland, where they had fished six or seven years past. It is impossible now to judge whether the difficulty in procuring fish off Norway was due, as the petition alleged, to the migration or to the extermination of the fish, or merely to the Staple restrictions of the Norwegian kings, which made it a troublesome business. At any rate the protest proved ineffectual and the prohibition was proclaimed in sixteen ports throughout the East Coast of England.[20]

But the arbitrary decrees of distant kings, whether in London or in Copenhagen, could not actually put a stop to a business which in Iceland was equally opportune to both parties. Unable now to obtain letters from the King of Norway or from their own king, the English contented themselves with a licence procured in Iceland from the governor, and with his permission they engaged in the fisheries and bought and sold freely throughout the island. The Icelanders were not indeed particularly glad to see the English fishermen. None of them had much to offer; some of them were hardy ruffians, quick to take advantage of Iceland's lack of governance. But for the English merchants they had a ready welcome. Sorely stricken by famine and want, despairing of succour from Bergen, they cared little for the decrees of an alien king. "Our laws provide," they wrote to King Eric in 1419, " that six ships should come hither from Norway every year, which has not happened for a long time, a cause from which your Grace and our poor country has suffered most grievous harm. Therefore, trusting in God's grace and your help, we have traded with foreigners who have come hither peacefully on legitimate business, but we have punished those fishermen and owners of fishing smacks who have robbed and caused disturbance on the sea." Armed with this explanation of the licences he had granted, the *hirðstjóri* now set sail for Norway, and it is perhaps significant that he did not again appear as governor. Thus the Icelanders took matters into their own hands, recognizing gladly that trade with the English was an established fact. Instead of opposing it, they strove to control and to regulate it, checking the lawlessness of the more unprincipled fishermen, and calling to account those who exceeded their privileges.[21]

Encouraged by their readiness to trade, more and more English merchants forsook Bergen for Iceland. Ere long Lynn had its recognized body of " merchants of Iceland ", who in 1424 elected two of their number for taxing the merchants, as did " merchants of Norway ", " merchants of Prussia ", and " other merchants ". The owner of the " navis Roberti Holm ", which was in Iceland in 1420, was probably the notable citizen of Hull, Robert Holm, merchant and thrice mayor. Bristol men were not far behind those of Lynn and Hull, though they had no previous connection with Bergen. The earliest trace of them is in the *Libelle of Englyshe Polycye*, and if we put the date of this at 1436 we may infer that they too found their way to Iceland " by nedle and by stone " about 1424.[22]

This rapid development of the Icelandic trade and fisheries naturally roused the bitter resentment of those who controlled the staple market. The English had now to reckon not merely with the disapproval of the Danish king, who, after all, could collect his dues as well in Iceland as in Norway, but with the active hostility of the Hanse merchants in Bergen. These, despite their firm hold upon the city, now saw much of its business slipping from their grasp, as the direct Icelandic trade was vigorously exploited, and England ceased to demand fish from Norway. They therefore strenuously opposed all interlopers, whether English or German, and used all their influence to prevent any relaxation of the staple restrictions.

In 1420 there arrived from Denmark a new *hirðstjóri*, Hannes Pálsson, bringing with him many alien Danes. These were as unpopular as their grasping master who, with his companion Balthasar van Dammin, " made the most of the king's gift to them of that land in fief." " That," continues the annalist, " became a cause of little concord to themselves afterwards." Pálsson began not by stopping the trade, but by endeavouring to control it. He established a market in the Vestmann Islands, fixed prices, and brought to judgment those who exceeded their licences by wintering and building houses in the islands. But Danes and English were not the only strangers in Iceland. In this same year a German, one Stephen Schellendorp, was there spying out the land. Whether he was actually an agent of the Hanse is not clear, but he certainly served their interests well. Towards the end of the trading season he wrote to King Eric of Denmark an obsequious letter, fulsome in its protestations of disinterested service. Here he declared that English merchants and fishermen had acquired so firm a footing in Iceland that, unless their voyages were stopped, the land would certainly be lost to the Danish crown. Schellendorp's specious insinuations, however, perhaps assisted the cause of the Bergen merchants less than the high-handed behaviour of some of the English. Neglected Iceland offered a fair field to adventurers of every description, and among the fishermen especially were many rascals who, emboldened by the feebleness of the administration, defied all law and order, pillaging churches and carrying off flocks and herds. Both merchants and fishers, well aware that they were interlopers, came fully armed and, when hindered in their business, showed scant respect for royal decrees or for royal officials enforcing them. Crews landed in full battle array with trumpets and flying ensigns, governors were seized and obstructing officials slain, and when Pálsson and van Dammin, after five years of office, attempted to arrest the English ships in the Vestmann Islands, they were repelled with bows and arrows, captured, and carried off to England. Then in the heat of his indignation Pálsson composed a shattering indictment of the English, point by point at tedious length enumerating their crimes during his five years of office, to the number of thirty-seven.[23] It is to this almost interminable complaint of the deeply injured governor that we owe the whole of our evidence of the misdeeds of the English in Iceland during the first quarter of the century, misdeeds which have caused them without discrimination to be branded as the most unscrupulous of pirates.[24] Every recorded misdemeanour can be traced to this same source. It is therefore of interest to examine its allegations, with the help of the records of those English towns trading to Iceland, where the names of many of the delinquents may be found. At least half the complaints concern the same gang, many of whom prove to be mariners of Hull, where their leader, John Percy, figures not creditably in one of the unpublished Bench Books. Hull, carrying much of the merchandise of York, was itself predominantly a city of seamen rather than of merchants, as the lists of burgesses show; hence it was always more of a centre for piracy than cities such as Bristol and Lynn, with their influential bodies of responsible merchants.[25] No name which can be traced to either Bristol or Lynn figures once in the report. Most of the merchants therefore probably carried on a peaceful trade to the advantage of all concerned.

A further scrutiny of the complaints reveals the fact that out of twenty-nine specific accusations at least eighteen concern disputes with Danish officials and alleged " thefts " of fish from them. Thus it is clear that on the whole it was not the Icelanders whom the English attacked, but rather the Danish officials who endeavoured, if not to abolish the trade, to extort the exorbitant dues claimed in the name of their king. The English resistance to such alien officials, and even the kidnapping of one of them, would seem from the Icelandic annals to have been actually applauded by the Icelanders. For Hannes' voluble report may well be put side by side with the one act of violence recorded in these annals during these years. " The cloister of Helgafell despoiled and the church; the servants of Lord Hans did that." And when Hannes was carried away in an English ship the annalist laconically concludes: " Few were sorry at that." [26]

Icelanders evidently welcomed the English traders, if not the English fishermen, and bade joyful farewells to Pálsson, yet it was the Danish Pálsson and the German Schellendorp whom the king of Denmark heeded, rather than his neglected subjects. In the same year he issued orders that all sailing to Iceland without his permission were to be called to account. Meanwhile the " Consules Bergenses " had been diligently examining Pálsson's evidence with the aid of witnesses, and they now declared that the half had not been told, but that at present they would spare their readers and forbear to relate the many other wrongs perpetrated. King Eric's warnings reached the English ports, where, early next spring when the time came for the usual voyages, merchants and mayors took counsel together. At Lynn, in a Congregation of February, 1426, the decrees were read in an English translation, and the following week all the merchants frequenting Iceland were summoned to the Guildhall, and there forbidden to set sail under pain of forfeiture of their goods. Ten days later an ordinance forbidding the voyage was drawn up, sealed with the consent of the majority of the Congregation, and subsequently read out by the common clerk with the letters from the Danish king.[27]

Meanwhile the captive Pálsson had also lodged his voluminous indictment with the Council of England, and the Admiral, the Duke of Exeter, duly impressed, forbade the voyage to Iceland. His prohibition likewise was read out in a Congregation at Lynn, and the Mayor, acting upon it, a few days later arrested a boat which was about to sail for Iceland. Tense was the situation when, that autumn, a London boat put in at Lynn on its return from Iceland. John Vache, its captain, must have taunted the Lynn men for deserting Iceland so readily, for in solemn council privily held, the Mayor himself declared that Vache had called the Lynn merchants traitors, and Vache, before he was set free, was made to swear upon the gospels " that he never used those words ".[28]

The Congregation of merchants at Lynn, who thus by a majority banned the Iceland voyage, were no doubt actuated by a desire not to provoke the Danish king, because of the old-established connection with Bergen on which the prosperity of their city largely depended. And since King Eric was now on the point of war with the Hanse, they may have hoped, by falling in with his wishes, to secure from him greater favours for themselves.[29] At Bristol, on the contrary, which had no interest to maintain in other dominions of the Danish king, there is no trace of any action taken by the city itself to enforce the prohibition, nor is there at Hull, which, as we have seen, was a city of sailors rather than of merchants. At Bristol and Hull, however, no such complete minutes of the council meetings exist, though both have records of ordinances passed.

But if some of the English thought by abandoning Iceland to strengthen their position in Bergen, they were doomed to disappointment. For in 1428 and 1429 Bartholomew Voet and his fellow pirates, aided by the Hamburg *Bergenfahrer*, plundered the city of Bergen, so that the English fled in terror. Many therefore persisted in journeying to Iceland, so that in the spring of 1429 the sheriffs were again ordered to proclaim that the Staple was at Bergen. Then the Lynn council held further debates on the matter. Those who for some years had visited Iceland begged that they might sail just once again; those who frequented Bergen and Prussia, fearing that Danish reprisals might fall upon their heads, protested, reminding the council of the ordinance of 1425. The discussion continued while those principally concerned were sent out of the room, and finally the Icelandic merchants were compelled to abandon the venture on condition that they too might traffic in Bergen. The Lynn council not only did its best to stop the voyage to Iceland, but also tried to call to account those who had misbehaved there, particularly by carrying off young Icelanders. The fate of these children has given rise to much speculation. Behaim, writing of Iceland on his globe of 1492, declared that the famished Icelanders sold their children into servitude to secure bread for those that remained. At Lynn, five boys and three girls were found in 1429, and, whether they had been bought or stolen or lured away, their captors were ordered to restore them the following year. Many must nevertheless have remained to swell the number of England's foreign immigrants, such as those Icelandmen and Icelandwomen who now and again occur in the *Subsidy Rolls*, or those " born in Iceland " who take the oath of fealty.[30]

The King of England the next year, in conformity with the Danish ordinances, reinforced his proclamations by an act of Parliament to regulate the Icelandic trade. The statute of 1430, after reciting the Danish king's ordinance that " all strangers coming by ship to his dominions for fish or other goods shall come to Northbern ", forbade any " by the audacitie of their follie " to go elsewhere in the Danish king's dominions. A petition was immediately presented in Parliament against this " too grievous ordinance ", but the petitioners had to content themselves with the assurance that the King was sending ambassadors to Denmark to treat of the welfare of the merchants. The citizens of Lynn sent further ambassadors at their own expense to discuss their difficulties at Bergen, where they still hoped to retain their trade instead of resorting to Iceland. Many were the grievances to which the English ambassadors had to listen in Denmark; vast was the compensation demanded for " twenty years' " ravages in Iceland and other colonies, such as Finmark, which the English had frequented for fish. These tales had the desired effect on the English envoys, who meekly did as they were bid and promised that captives should be liberated, the plundered satisfied, the relatives of the slain compensated, and also that the merchants should peacefully visit one another's lands in places not prohibited. To give the treaty a simulated appearance of reciprocity, it was solemnly added that while the English might not go to Iceland or Finmark on pain of loss of life and goods, so Danish subjects on pain of similar penalties might not visit prohibited places in England. Accordingly once again proclamation was made of the Bergen Staple throughout the ports of England, and once again the English merchants replied by complaining of their maltreatment in Bergen. Lynn sent envoys to London, and Hull sent its Mayor and another, and a complaint was laid before Parliament asserting that the king's people " be greatly impoverished and undone and in part destroyed by the king of Denmark and his lieges, because they do daily take of the subjects their goods; of the merchants of York and Hull goods to the value of £5,000 within a year, and of other lieges and merchants of England to the value of £20,000, whereof they have no remedy because none of the subjects of the king of Denmark come to England or have anything in England ". The king promised to provide " convenable remedy ", but the way to Bergen, the one place they might go to in the parts of the north, was evidently still fraught with difficulty.[31]

Thus the direct road to Iceland was definitely closed to all legitimate English traffic. But the English venturers, who had beaten a path across the trackless ocean, were not to be daunted by the decrees of a distant Danish king. Scant respect had they also for the discredited English Council, and the liberty which they could not secure by diplomacy they were prepared to win by force if necessary. Scorning the royal prohibitions, they continued to voyage to Iceland, there loading their vessels " according to their own pleasure ", skilfully outwitting the royal officials whether Danish or English. Some flouted openly the monopoly of Bergen, trusting to their own wits to save them. Of such we hear only when disaster befell them. The official records of the years following 1430 are strewn with the relics of ships and their cargoes forfeited to the king, of warnings proclaimed, of commissions appointed, and of instructions to officials to imprison and forfeit. Cloth in the ship of a Coventry merchant was seized at Boston. Stockfish from Iceland was discovered at Bristol and Hull, at Cromer and Scarborough; more was probably smuggled into less obvious harbours, for commissions and proclamations concerned not only all East Coast ports from London to Newcastle, but also Devon and Cornwall, Somerset and Wales. Frequently offenders put in at Chepstow, while mariners of Fowey and of Saltash were fined for breach of the statute. Ships as well as fish were arrested, from doggers of Cromer worth £40 with fish worth nearly £100, to merchant ships of Hull or Bristol with cargoes worth from £200 to £300. Large rewards tempted stay-at-home seamen to prey upon the more adventurous. A Bristol ship home from Iceland fell a victim to two piratical ships of Newcastle, and while her cargo was handed over to the Danes, her sailors were thrown into Newgate prison, and the vessel herself was sold to the profit of the king and the men of Newcastle.[32]

A declaration of forfeiture, however, was not always effective, and a shrewd shipowner must often have outwitted a royal official. Such a one was the cunning and audacious John Wyche of Bristol, who, when himself a surveyor of customs, was evidently suspected of illegal practices, since a commission was appointed to inquire into his behaviour. His ship, the *Mary*, was arrested by his successor in office, John Maryot, on her return from Iceland laden with fish. The ingenious Wyche, however, forestalled the surveyor, promptly handed over all the fish to the Mayor in payment of certain debts to him, and sold the ship. The surveyor, nonplussed, appealed to Chancery.[33]

The immunity that craft and daring achieved for Wyche was won by others through wealth or influence. William Canynges, five times Mayor of Bristol, who lent large sums to the king, traded to Iceland in the *Katherine* of Bristol, owned jointly with Stephen Forster. Not only were he and Forster pardoned for this, but they were given permission to take the *Katherine* and the *Mary Redcliffe* to Iceland for four years, despite the statute.³⁴ Smuggling, after all, was risky. Kings, such as those of England and Denmark, were sorely in need of money. Privileges and immunities were therefore not difficult to procure, and were amply worth paying for when the return cargo from a single ship might be sold for £700 or more.³⁵ Thus, paradoxically, the English trade to Iceland increased rather than diminished in the years following its unsparing official condemnation by both parties. A flourishing licensed trade grew up, licensed by the King of England, the King of Denmark, or both. Fishing boats cannot be enumerated, but of actual merchant vessels there were for instance nineteen licensed in 1443, and fourteen in 1442 and 1444-5. It is improbable that so many actually sailed, but the particular customs accounts are too fragmentary to determine this. At any rate, the great bulk of the trade must have been in English hands, and Iceland, which had once begged for six ships annually, was now visited by from ten to twenty merchant ships, apart from the fishing boats. These licences, found scattered throughout the *Treaty Rolls*, were mainly granted to merchants of Bristol, often to merchants of Hull or of London, occasionally to shipowners of Newcastle, Dartmouth, Swansea, Cromer, while one was for a Sandwich boat equipped by London merchants. Some are specifically to fishmongers such as Napton of Coventry, and some to stock-fishmongers such as Robert Weston of London and Curteys of London.³⁶

The most singular, and the earliest, licences granted by the English king were those to certain of his own subjects, doomed to live in Iceland with neither bread, wine, beer, nor cloth fit to dress themselves and their servants.³⁷ For the Danish synod appointed at least two Englishmen as bishops, perhaps because they hoped they might keep their obstreperous countrymen in order, or because no Dane or Norwegian was eager to be thus ostracized; or was it that the Englishmen in question had sufficient influence to obtain a post with lucrative possibilities? Icelandic priests at this time were men of little education, and, with a few striking exceptions, the bishops, most of them foreigners, seem to have been more careful to supply themselves with beer than their flocks with instruction. English merchants were quick to take advantage of their need, and it was on the pretext of supplying the bishops that the first licensed trade, dating from 1427, was inaugurated. Between 1427 and 1440 four licences were given to Bishops of Hólar and three to Bishops of Skálholt. John Johnson, for instance, an Englishman by birth, was appointed bishop of the northern diocese of Hólar in 1427.³⁸ Before his departure for his see, he secured permission to buy in England 1,000 qrs. of wheat and 500 qrs. of malt or barley for his beer, and to transport them to Iceland from Lynn, Hull, or Newcastle. Accompanied by two priests he then set sail in an English ship, and duly arrived at Hafnarfjördur on the west coast. There the documents brought with him were read in a general council, but when he pursued his way northwards the inhabitants looked askance upon him, he quickly lost heart, and without even seeing his cathedral see, set sail again the same summer, after ordaining four priests and some deacons. The following year he paid one more flying visit, which seems to have been his last, and commended the bishopric to John Williamson, also probably an Englishman.[39] English venturers of the baser sort must have hailed with delight the arrival of such compatriots. Once when in difficulties they fled into the cathedral of Hólar; Bishop Williamson kept at bay their pursuers, declared them to be in sanctuary, and drew up a document to the effect that he had purchased half their ship, the *Bartholomew*, then lying off Skagafjörd, for twelve lasts of fish, so that she might now proceed to England under the solemn protection of the holy see. Bishop Williamson, when translated to Skálholt in 1435, continued his trading enterprises as a means of satisfying his creditors, and secured licences for this purpose both in 1436 and 1438. When his ventures failed ruin faced him, if we are to believe the story told in Chancery by John Richeman, citizen and stockfishmonger of London. The bishop, being in debt to the merchant, " gatte a licence " to send to Iceland wheat, wine, and other victuals and merchandise, and ordained Richeman his deputy so that the debts might be satisfied. But the ship, duly freighted, was taken treacherously by the pilot to Ireland instead. Richeman, in fear of his life, escaped thence to England, and the bishop " hearing of the disposition abovesaid sorrowed greatly, because he knew and well understood that he had not the wherewithal to live here. And he was taken in of alms into ' St. Thomas Spitell ' in Southwark, and there died."[40]

Other bishops were entirely non-resident, and lived on the profits of the see, paying their creditors with licences to trade to Iceland. Such was John Bloxwich, Williamson's English successor at Hólar. Declaring that he feared exceedingly to visit his diocese on account of the great perils by sea and by land, in 1436 he appointed a Hull merchant to bring him thence news—and no doubt wealth. In the following year he commissioned Robert Weston, stock-fishmonger of London, for the same purpose, and in 1438 he procured another licence to send two ships to Iceland with foodstuffs and to bring back the first-fruits, lest the papal bulls, held in pledge by certain London merchants, should be returned to Rome.[41]

Nor was it only bishops of English birth who were in close touch with England. John Geriksen, a former archbishop of Upsala, had been dispatched for his unlawful deeds to Skálholt, there to dwell in "a remote land among people well nigh barbarian". He wintered in England and started thence for his diocese in 1430. Two priests went with him, one of whom soon took to trading and returned to England in the same year with stockfish of the bishop's, " for he was a great gatherer of stockfish and other things ". With the bishop was also a retinue of thirty serving men; these pretended to be Danes, but were in reality Irishmen, so turbulent that the bishop " ruled them little or not at all ". These strange followers brought small credit to the Church. They seized the chief men of Iceland and put them in irons, and the bishop was further discredited by one Magnus who, as some said, was his son. Magnus wooed Margaret, sister of Ivar Vigfusson, and, receiving little encouragement, led a raid on Kirkjubaer and set fire to the town. In the skirmish Ivar was killed. Margaret declared that she would wed none but the man who avenged her brother, and the challenge was taken up by Thorvard Lopt. Riding with an army upon Skálholt, he followed the bishop into his cathedral, seized him as he stood clad in his vestments before the altar, dragged him to the river, and there drowned him with coils of ropes weighted with stones. Yet so accustomed were the Danes to attributing all harm to the English, that in the treaty signed a year earlier, the English had actually been made to promise amends for damages to this very bishop and his followers.[42]

§ 2

THE TRADE AT ITS HEIGHT

So the trade went on into the middle years of the fifteenth century, actively and profitably. Even the Danish king was compelled by its very magnitude to recognize it. And though he still strove to insist that each ship must have his licence, the matter of the Bergen Staple was tacitly ignored. Rivals as yet were few. The traces of other foreign competitors during the first half of the century are slight. The *Holy Ghost* of Schiedam sailed for Iceland in 1431, but she carried an English cargo from Hull; eight years later the *Marie Knight* of Amsterdam took fish from Iceland to Ireland. German merchants are first heard of in 1431, when the Althing forbade both English and Germans to winter in Iceland. But their advance was delayed by the exclusiveness of the Bergen merchants, who insisted in their own interests that the Hanse should forbid the direct voyage to Iceland from any of the German cities; not till the second half of the century is there evidence of great Hanseatic activity in the trade. Thus the commerce of Iceland came completely under English control, though there was no sign that they proposed, as Schellendorp insinuated, to follow it up by annexing the island. Indeed, the enfeebled English government was then more disposed to relinquish than to acquire overseas possessions, and merchants had to expect from the State not encouragement but obstruction.[43]

Great was the congregation of English off the coasts of Iceland every summer—big trading vessels perhaps bound for France during the following winter,[44] with merchants or their factors on board; little doggers with adventurous fishermen whose furthest goal had hitherto been Norway. Round the Vestmann Isles in particular they clustered, "where is the best fishing of all Iceland." There, it was reported to the Danish king, " they build houses, erect tents, dig up the ground, and carry on fishery as if it were their own property." [45]

The fishing doggers, small though they were, were greatly superior to those of the Icelanders, who had but " the smallest skiffs (*scaphas*) because there is scarcely any wood suitable for ships ". Hence before long the English had almost entirely wrested the fishing industry from the Icelanders. Early in the sixteenth century the Althing was moved to complain of this, explaining that with their larger boats the English could fish at a greater distance from the shore, with long lines and many hooks fastened upon them, and thus prevented the approach of the fish nearer in shore, so that the Icelanders waited in vain in their little boats. As to the exact size of the doggers, as of the amount which they caught, we have little information. The men of Cromer and Blakeney, it is true, had pleaded that their vessels were so small—" about 10 or 12 or at most 18 tuns "—that they could not carry horses across the channel for the king, but less biased corroboration of this small figure is not forthcoming. At any rate one dogger could carry 15 lasts of stock-fish valued at nearly £100. Whatever its size, every dogger had to take, besides from five to ten fishermen, a good store of provisions for the whole summer, since Iceland could scarcely be depended upon for these. Many a fifteenth century ship must have been equipped like that of Henry Tooley, which early in the sixteenth century was stocked with barrels of beer and meal, flitches of bacon, salt fish, a barrel of beef, a firkin of butter, and some herrings. The 18 weys of salt and the 3200 hooks which, besides warlike weapons, completed his equipment, tell much of the methods of the business. For the English were pre-eminently " fishers of salt fish ", and as the fishing continued, salting proceeded busily also, so that at the end of the season the mariners might hope to return with all their original cargo of salt absorbed into merchandise—salted codfish, ling, or keling, which found a ready sale at home in October and November.[46]

A case recorded in the Memoranda Rolls pictures vividly what must have been a possible if not an actual happening.[47] Thomas Erlyngham, accused of trading illegally with Iceland, tried to account for the quantity of salt fish in his ship by relating that he sent her under John Dickinson with eight other mariners, fishers, and servants, " on to the high seas towards the north for fishing and taking fish to salt." From 20th May till 4th September they were out on the sea fishing, and diverse fish " called lyng and kelyng " were taken " to the use of Thomas " and salted. Such, if not actual fact, was very likely the common custom of fishers of salt fish, very similar to that of the more recent Bretons, as vividly described in Pierre Loti's *Pêcheurs d'Island*. Erlyngham scarcely explains satisfactorily the presence of a large quantity of stockfish by an alleged transaction upon the high seas with certain famished foreigners, who bartered their stockfish for the Englishman's victuals. Evidently he had landed in Iceland and done business there. In fact the distinction between fishermen and merchants was often an impossible one. If the fishermen took more food than they actually needed, they could be sure of a ready sale for it in Iceland, in return for an addition to their own cargo of fish. Such a practice became so widespread that it had to be specifically prohibited by Henry VII. In attempting to regulate the fishing he insisted that the doggers should find surety " that they will only have grain for their victualing ".[48]

The fishing doggers which congregated off Iceland each summer were drawn from a wide area, but predominantly from the East Coast of England. A Cromer fisherman, Robert Bacon, is said to have " discovered Iceland " early in the fifteenth century,[49] and the assertion is not improbable. For fishers of Cromer and Blakeney were, as is shown above, among those who frequented the coasts of Norway, and a Cromer dogger certainly visited Iceland in 1439, though possibly not for fishing. Cromer mariners were also in Iceland in 1433, and in 1438 Roger Fouler of Cromer freighted for Iceland a ship of which he was the master, owned by Adam Horn of Cley. Cromer was closely linked with Cley and Blakeney, into whose harbours its boats frequently came, and shipmen of both these ports were acquainted with Iceland. Norfolk fishing doggers may also have gone thither from Burnham and Dersingham, for these then flourishing havens were included in a proclamation of 1415 against visiting Iceland for fishing. The same proclamation was made in sixteen East Coast ports from Newcastle to Orwell, including the fishing centres of Whitby, Grimsby, and Scarborough. At least one Scarborough boat, owned jointly by a Londoner and a Scarborough man, " went out of the Humber to Iceland " in 1437, and the *Libelle* implies that this was not the first time that Scarborough fishermen had visited Iceland. Suffolk also probably sent its doggers to Iceland. Such of its local records—account books of Dunwich, Southwold, and Walberswick—as Thomas Gardner discovered in private hands when he wrote his *Historical Account of Dunwich* in 1754, seem now to have vanished. But, if we may trust Gardner's quotation, Walberswick at any rate had " 13 barks trading to Iceland, Farra, and the North Seas " in 1451, and by 1509 William Godell of Southwold left in his will all his ships " that be in Iceland ".[50] Some of these fishermen visited other far northern dependencies of Denmark, such as the Faroë Islands and that most northerly of all Norway's domains, Finmark, where still to-day fishermen gather round the Lofoten Isles. Finmark is almost always mentioned with Iceland in decrees and prohibitions, and in 1439 four mariners were pardoned for sailing there in the *Nicholas* of Saltash.[51] Clearly the Cornish fishermen did not leave the exploitation of the Norwegian fisheries entirely to their more conveniently situated brethren on the East Coast of England.

The greater merchant vessels, taking English goods to barter in Iceland for stockfish, sailed usually from Bristol, Hull, or Lynn. East Coast ports, with old-established stockfishmongers and "stockfish rows",[52] hard hit by the collapse of business with Bergen, were naturally foremost in developing the possibilities of Iceland. Lynn, with its group of "merchants of Iceland", was already deeply involved in the first quarter of the century. And though later on its merchants were forbidden to traffic there, and never sought licences from the English king, it would seem from Danish accusations that they cannot have entirely abandoned the enterprise. Hull was a more active centre. Here the Iceland trade became a civic venture, and in the time of Edward IV the city regularly freighted three or four ships for Iceland in the name of "the mayor and burgesses". London merchants and stockfishmongers seem also to have preferred the shipping of Hull to their own, and it was seldom that a merchantman of London or of other eastern ports such as Newcastle sailed for Iceland. Merchants of inland cities, such as Thomas Napton, fishmonger of Coventry, traded likewise with Iceland, using the ships sometimes of East Coast ports, but sometimes of Bristol. For Bristol, though it had no previous dealings in stockfish, rapidly acquired an ascendancy in the Iceland trade. Its name is singled out for mention in the *Libelle of Englyshe Polycye*; its pilots were in demand for the voyage thither; Bristol men, it was persistently rumoured abroad, were responsible for subsequent outrages in Iceland; and an account of Iceland, said to have been written by Columbus after a visit there in 1477, describes how the English came with their merchandise, "especially those of Bristol".[53] The arrival of Bristol merchants is not surprising. For though, unlike the East Coast ports, Bristol had no previous connection with Bergen, Iceland was politically only, and not geographically, an appendage of Norway. Mediaeval cartographers might indeed depict it clinging close to Scandinavia, but in reality Iceland lies far out to the west in the North Atlantic, and it was Bristol, not Hull or Lynn, which looked out towards the Atlantic and was familiar with its coasts from the west of Ireland to the south of Spain. Like Ireland in early Christian days Bristol now became closely connected with Iceland, while Irish ships also revived their ancient trade to the north-west, taking goods not only of their own countrymen, but of Englishmen such as the merchants of Chester. Indeed, the voyage from Ireland to the chief havens of Iceland in the south-west was more direct than that from Hull, and Bristol sailors, in close touch with Ireland, could easily follow it. Most probably they took their customary way to the thriving ports of Western Ireland, and thence directed their course across the ocean to Iceland. It is unlikely that they chose the inner route by the Irish Sea, for here they would have to contend with the perplexing rocks and currents of that "*mare Hybernicum ferocissimum et periculosissimum*", as well as with the Scottish pirates who infested the narrow channel through which their heavily laden ships must pass. On the time spent in the journey no exact evidence is available. "Five days sail" was the mariner's reckoning from Iceland to Ireland in the thirteenth century, before the days of practical compasses. A Bristol ship of the fifteenth century, given a favourable wind, should certainly have reached Iceland within a week.[54]

The cargo carried by these merchant ships was rich and varied, and might be valued by the customers at as much as £500. Its contents appear not only from the customs accounts, but from the interesting edict made in Iceland in 1420, soon after the first coming of the English, regulating the "merchant meeting there by law established between English and Icelandic men who have come in good peace".[55] This gives a vivid picture of the market, for it determines the value of each of the wares in terms of fish. Food in plenty the English had brought to famished Iceland. Almost at the head of the list come barrels of wheat and meal, butter, honey, and wine, malt for the Icelanders' beer, and beer itself. Minerals also the Icelanders lacked; they had little iron, and that only of poor quality and, through lack of fuel, they possessed no smelting furnaces. Hardware was therefore as acceptable as food. Indeed certain Icelanders, like Pacific Islanders of a later date, were even accused of taking the nails from the boards of the English ships.[56] Now they might buy not only nails but iron and manufactured articles, such as swords and knives, pots and pans, or copper kettles. There were combs, probably for the weavers, while horseshoes must have met a crying need in a country so dependent on the horse. Wood could also be bought, which Iceland needed almost as much as iron, also pitch and tar, wax and salt. Articles of attire were there displayed for the delectation of both the men and the women of Iceland—hats and caps, shoes and cheaper shoes for the women, girdles, gloves, and purses. But the chief business of all was evidently done in lengths of cloth and linen. These take prior place in the list of commodities, and the customs show that usually not less than a third of the value of a ship's cargo was in English or Welsh cloth, and Irish, Breton or Flemish linen. From this it is evident that there was some degree of comfort among certain classes in Iceland, since her land already produced a coarser cloth of its own, called *vaðmál*. This had been exported in considerable quantities in earlier days, and had evidently been one of the country's chief sources of wealth, since money and taxes were estimated in it.[57] Amongst many "small wares", trifles whose price could be "according to agreement", were needles and thread, pins by the thousand, lacing points, yarn for the fishermen's nets, and at least one consignment of paper. Thus the English ships were almost universal providers for the Icelanders, and must have stocked many a pedlar's pack.

In contrast to such diversity the Englishman's demands were monotonous. It was fish that he had come to seek, and indeed Iceland had little else with which to tempt him. " For three fish " he would give a pair of women's shoes, " for fifteen fish " a firkin of honey. And though he might occasionally take back *vaðmál* or hides or oil, he left it to the Germans to develop later the export of these and of other lesser products such as falcons, sulphur, and eiderdown. Fish meant principally the hard dried codfish—" *piscis durus vocatus Stockfyssh* "—sometimes alluded to by the Latin *Strumulus*. For it was from the cod and his kindred in the extreme north of Europe that fishmongers supplemented their inadequate supplies from nearer waters, in days when, with a strict observance of Lent throughout Western Europe, fish was no luxury but a necessity. There came also in smaller quantities hake, pollack, and salmon, still plentiful in the rivers of Iceland, with herring and unspecified " saltfish ". The total value of these return cargoes of fish was, according to the customs valuation, anything up to £600, and, according to the prices they would fetch in England, anything up to £1,000 or more. Aptly does that merchant's handbook, *The Noumbre of Weyghtes*, sum up the variety of Iceland's imports and the sameness of her exports : " The cheffe merchaundyse in Iseland ys Stokefysch and Wodemole and oyle ; and good merchaundyse from hens thedyr the course Ynglysche clothe coloured, mele, malte, bere, wyne, Salettes, gauntlettes, longeswerdes, lynon cloth and botounes of sylver, ambyr bedes, knyves and poyntes, Glasses and Combys, etc." [58]

The Iceland trade, unlike most other English enterprise of the time, was closely defined by the seasons. In early spring, between February and April, ships usually left England. Throughout the summer they remained in Iceland while the market was open and goods were bought and sold. Between July and September they returned home, making but one voyage thither in the year. Thus John Gough, captain of the *Ive*, was laden ready to leave Bristol on 14th February, 1479, and on 18th July arrived home again with his cargo of fish. But this did not complete his work for the year. For as Autumn came on the *Ive* set sail again, this time through less inhospitable seas, to reach Bordeaux in time for the vintage. Some merchants attempted to remain in Iceland, thus setting up permanent places of business, but this was forbidden at the outset by the Icelandic authorities, and those who came " in the right merchant manner " disposed of their wares during the summer, and left before winter tempests came on. Now and again, however, when all the wares had not been sold, one or two factors were left behind with them until the following summer. Thus certain merchants from Drogheda left two of their number, Abbot and Wild, behind, promising to fetch them the next year. Abbot complained later in Chancery that no one had come to rescue him, that as a result he had become ill, his servant had died, and his goods had been forfeited " by the rule of that land ". It was little wonder that when certain Englishmen began to build themselves houses in the Vestmann Islands the Icelanders renewed their prohibitions against wintering in Iceland, intent on avoiding a permanent colony of such vigorous foreigners in their land.[59]

§ 3

THE DECLINE OF THE TRADE

The commercial dominance of England over Iceland was, however, to prove shortlived. The second half of the fifteenth century witnessed the loss of much that had been gained in the first half, until in the sixteenth century England was to lose her supremacy in the trade, though not in the fisheries.

The distracted condition of English politics, the dynastic struggles which made firm government impossible, proved almost as disastrous to merchants as to barons. Already before 1450 the liberty of sailing to Iceland had become the sport of factions, a mere pawn in the political game. Rival barons, struggling to maintain their ascendancy, used it as a bribe with which to make surer the allegiance of the wealthy middle-class. Just as in 1440 they abolished the privileges of foreigners in England, thus satisfying the clamour of the native merchants, so too they multiplied licences to sail to Iceland, " notwithstanding any Act to the contrary." The Iceland voyage became a reward for political services in the sordid strife at home, so that when in 1461 Edward IV had triumphed at Towton and had been crowned king in London, in the closing months of that year, he granted licences for no less than sixteen ships, a record for this century. One was to a servant of his ally the Earl of Warwick, and another for an exceptionally large ship " of 800 tuns or less ", to be equipped by supporters of his among the merchants of Bristol. A few years later, after the final victories of Hedgeley and Hexham in the north, Warwick's younger brother received, in addition to his title of Earl of Northumberland, a licence for one of the biggest ships of Hull.[60] Thus England's mercantile policy ceased to be directed by any definite principle, save that of political expediency, but was sporadically dictated by the immediate interests of the dominant party of the moment.

But civil strife in England was not the only foe of the Iceland merchants. For just when they were abandoning hope of support at home, their Hanseatic opponents overseas, intent on maintaining the Bergen Staple, were steadily strengthening their influence over

Iceland's rulers. Earlier in the century Denmark had been at war with the Hanse, and had been only too ready to grant privileges to the English in return for their aid, but since 1435 the two powers had been at peace. The Danish kings, destitute themselves of naval strength, henceforth came more and more to rely on the support of the Hanse, especially of the Wendish group which monopolized Bergen, until gradually they were mere pliant instruments in its hands.[61] So close were the connections between the two powers that a rupture with the one almost inevitably involved a rupture with the other, and it is often impossible to distinguish under whose immediate orders ships of the Hanse were acting. Yet the attitude of the Danish kings towards the Icelandic trade was directed not merely by their subservience to the Hanse. Their need of money was as great as their need of the Hanseatic fleet, and even prompted Christian I to pawn the Orkney and Shetland Islands. Hence the Bergen Staple was to them primarily a means of collecting their exorbitant dues, and when it proved impossible thus to confine the trade, their chief concern was to insist on the payment of the dues in Iceland itself. At the same time, like the English kings, they too were readily tempted to make capital out of licences for the evasion of the Staple.

The interaction of these various forces on the progress of the Icelandic trade is clearly apparent in the early years of Christian I's reign. Within a year of his accession in 1448 England resumed her war with France and, since Burgundy was now pro-French, the outlook for trade seemed dark. She was therefore particularly anxious to strengthen her position in Scandinavia and the Baltic, and accordingly in 1449 came to terms with Denmark. The Danish king insisted, in the interests of the Bergen Staple, that she should again prohibit the direct voyage to Iceland, as in the treaty of 1432, but promised in return a safe conduct to England's merchants throughout his realms. This truce, which was to last till 1451, was ratified in England in 1450, and commissions were set up to inquire into infractions of it. Christian I, on his part, gave effect to it by a decree at his coronation that "all Englishmen and Irishmen who sail to Iceland without our letter and seal shall be outlawed and their goods forfeited." At the same time, despite the Staple regulations, he granted licences to both John Wolffe and William Canynges (in 1449 and 1450) to trade freely to Iceland. That of Canynges at any rate was endorsed by the English king, in consideration of his "notable and faithful services especially when lately Mayor of Bristol, to his great labour and expense".[62]

The settlement, however, was of short duration. The truce was not renewed in 1451; already by a desperate act of piracy England had antagonized the Hanse and driven them to reprisals, and by 1452 Denmark had followed their lead, broken with England, and closed the Sound. With the opening of civil war in England, any attempt to control the trade was practically abandoned. Merchants seldom troubled to beg a licence from a king over whose custody rival barons were warring, for ships were seldom forfeited. The king of Denmark, meanwhile, was involved in a costly war with Sweden, and could do little beyond publishing a decree to control the affairs of his outlying provinces. The dues that should have been paid in Bergen were not collected in Iceland, and his resentment grew with his losses through the unlicensed trade. Angry with England, he made an alliance with France, and wrote to the king of Aragon of " new dissensions over Iceland with the king of England ".[63]

Nor was there much hope of regularizing the trade even when civil war in England was over. For Edward IV was fatally hampered in his action by his indebtedness to both English merchants and their rivals the Hanseatics, who had helped him to the throne. The Hanseatics and their subservient ally Denmark were not likely to consent to any abandonment of the claims of Bergen, while those English merchants who had been to Iceland would not readily submit to a curtailment of their freedom. Hence Edward prevaricated. Just as he renewed the privileges of the Hanseatics in England, so he made also a treaty with Denmark, like those of his predecessors, to the effect that " no English subject should go to Iceland without having asked and obtained the special licence of the king of Norway, on penalty of life and goods, nor to Halgoland or Finmark, unless driven thither by stress of weather ". But at the same time he placated the English merchants by granting licences abundantly for the evasion of the Staple. Likewise the Danish king forbade Iceland to English merchants generally, but furtively helped his depleted exchequer by selling licences to individuals to go there.[64]

The continuation of such an anomalous state of affairs, when trade was prohibited but permissible by special licences procured for a consideration from needy kings, inevitably stimulated smuggling. Smuggling, moreover, was comparatively easy in a country such as Ireland, languishing for lack of governance, particularly when the king's representative was waylaid on the high seas by pirates from Scotland, and for some years held prisoner. But so soon as the Danish king turned his attention seriously to Iceland itself and made a resolute effort to collect his dues and to bridle the interlopers, a clash was bound to come. In 1463 strict injunctions were sent to Iceland that, since the crown's rights had been much diminished, no trade was to be done with foreigners who did not pay the heavy dues levied on Icelandic goods imported into Norway. The governor, Björn Thorleifsson, now freed from captivity, arrived in Iceland determined to exert his authority. But his activity proved his ruin, and once again, in 1467 as in 1425, the position of the English was jeopardized and odium cast on all their merchants, legitimate or otherwise, by a flagrant act of piracy. For when Björn arrived with a large escort in Ríf, where the English were carrying on a brisk trade, there they fell upon him and " Björn the mighty was smitten to death ", his body cast into the sea, his house plundered and burnt, and his son taken prisoner and only ransomed for a large sum. But the English had reckoned without his wife. For when Mistress Olof heard of her husband's fate she cried, " There shall be no weeping but rather gather men." " That she did, and clad herself in a shirt of mail, and a woman's dress over it; so she set out with her men in array. Then they came with craft upon the English, and slew a great company of them, except the cook, who got his life very narrowly for that he had before helped their son." The game was now in the hands of Mistress Olof. Taking her son, she sailed to Norway, put their case before the king, and is said to have been complimented by him as " a woman pleasant to behold ". At last King Christian acted. Not only were the usual letters sent to the new governor, ordering him to outlaw all Englishmen without permits, but four English ships were seized in the Sound in 1468 and sequestered as compensation for the outrage.[65]

Great was the indignation in England. Edward IV wrote haughtily to the King of Denmark that if any offence had been committed he should have been informed, and asking for the restitution of those captured ships which were innocent of any connection with Iceland. But no further satisfaction was forthcoming save that in King Christian's letter to " the mayors and rulers of all cities and towns in England except those of Lynn ". Here he declared plainly that he was keeping certain ships of Lynn which " had fallen into his hands " to satisfy the relatives of the innocent dead; that, not wishing to penalise others, he granted a safe conduct for any that were not of Lynn; but that if any through Lynn's crime had lost their possessions, they must seek damages from Lynn itself. The English merchants, baffled in their appeal to Denmark, and unable to retaliate since no Danish goods came to England, turned to avenge themselves on the Hanse. And since Hanseatic ships had undeniably assisted in the capture, all the Hanseatic merchants in London were arrested and thrown into prison. Vainly King Christian wrote on their behalf to King Edward that he himself had ordered the sequestration because of the outrage in Iceland. Neither party would yield, and though in the spring of 1469 the Hansards were released, in that year a state of war broke out. The contest was but half-hearted, and within two years a truce was concluded. In 1473 it was followed by a second truce renewed in 1476 and in 1479. By these " mutual freedom of trade " was granted—a phrase signifying little, especially when with it was coupled the important exception that the English might still not visit Iceland without special permission.[66]

It was particularly unfortunate for England that she should again have alienated Denmark at this moment and failed to establish a lasting peace. For her prospects in Iceland were less bright than they had been at the opening of the century. At that time not only was the king of Denmark, with his English wife, disposed to be friendly to England and hostile to the Hanse, but in Iceland itself the English merchants were unchallenged by rivals. Now, however, when Denmark was estranged and obedient to the Hanse, to the point of excluding the English altogether from Bergen,[67] formidable competitors had appeared, striving to win for themselves the trade of the island. For with the intensification of the Bergen monopoly by the Wendish towns, those Hanseatics who were not of this group had come to follow the example of the English, and to sail direct to Iceland. As early as 1430 some few had broken through the restrictions, but, like the English, they had met with strong opposition, and their venture had been checked by the Hanse League itself. Little was heard of them during the next forty years, but from 1475 evidence of Hanseatic activity in Iceland becomes abundant. The voyage to Iceland was now a regular annual venture on the part of Hamburg, undertaken at the expense of the city. Ships were sent out which belonged wholly or partially to the State, and profits or losses were duly noted in its accounts. Danzigers also now joined the interlopers who, like the English, secured licences from the Danish king. So numerous did these become that the Bergen merchants were moved to make a vigorous protest. On their behalf the Norwegian Reichsrath wrote letters in 1481, and again in 1482, to the Meeting of the Hanseatic League at Lübeck. In these they complained that Hamburgers and others of the Hanse had been allowed, contrary to the laws of the realm, to voyage direct to Iceland to the detriment of Norway and the Staple of Bergen, and they asked that the League should prevail upon them to desist. At the same time they induced the new Danish king to forbid the voyage. Meanwhile so much grain was being sent out of Hamburg that the city became alarmed and prohibited the export altogether, though ships continued to load in other places.[68]

Such a rapid advance, when Hanseatics began to compete with the English even in fetching fish from Iceland to London, and the Wendish towns too joined in the trade, brought about intense rivalry and, inevitably, friction in Iceland itself where the trade was so little regulated. Clashes ensued both there and on the high seas. The Hanseatics were voluble in their complaints. Some reported how their ships had been robbed in Iceland by men of Bristol or Hull, who took from them much merchandise including fish, cloth, oil, tallow, skins, and feathers. Others told how they had been pillaged on the way to London when by ill-chance they ran aground off Hartlepool. The English similarly complained of their treatment at the hands of the Hanse, who were quite equally guilty of acts of violence. Thus Richard III wrote to Hamburg of the spoliation of three English ships in Iceland, and when certain eminent Bristol merchants were accused by Hanseatics, letters were written by high dignitaries in Iceland exonerating the English. The original conflict of Danish officials with lawless interlopers was now inextricably complicated by the conflict of Englishmen with rival Germans, and of Hanseatics lawfully trading from Bergen with other Hanseatics, daringly intruding. In so many-sided a struggle the various parties could with difficulty be discriminated, and coalitions must have been made and unmade with bewildering rapidity. When, for instance, the Danish king's lieutenant in Iceland set forth to attack English ships from Scarborough, Hanse merchants hastened to his assistance, sending him speedily by horse " 3 *armamenta vocata blankharneys in quadam baga* ". Ships of necessity were fully armed. Sea fights were frequent, and the rights of them it is impossible now to determine from the fragments of evidence in records and annals.[69]

Amid the turmoil and confusion of the 'eighties some of the Icelanders must have looked back almost regretfully to the time of isolation, even though it had also been a time of dearth. Seeing their harbours thronged with ships, great merchantmen and little fishing boats so active that they had quite outstripped the native fishers; ninety or more German craft challenging the old-established English ones—they must have heard almost incredulously of how early in the century not a single foreign vessel had come near their shores, and of how vainly they had petitioned for six ships from Norway. Now the Icelandic venture was so common a one that Iceland had become too popular a resort; its enfeebled administration was quite unable to cope with the influx of visitors, and to adjust the claims of the many disputants. The English had yet more reason to regret the past. Times had indeed changed since the days of those pioneer merchantmen, eagerly welcomed by the Icelanders, duly accredited by English and Danish kings, and unchallenged by rivals, whose advent was of such moment that each was fully recorded in the annals. Now the annals wrote only of tumults and disasters on the sea. Now competition was so keen that Iceland was unpleasantly crowded. Danish kings, dominated by the rival Hanse, were unfriendly if not actively hostile, and English kings, struggling to maintain their power, had long made Iceland the sport of political expediency. Certainly the outlook for the English was less favourable than it had been at the opening of the century. Hence it came about that the more enterprising of them once again sought new fishing grounds. Just as formerly, thrust forth by the Hanse, they had abandoned Bergen for Iceland, so now, when the Hanse had pursued them thither, they were eager to leave Iceland behind, and to push out yet further into the Atlantic, towards fisheries more distant but less frequented. And so it was that when the companions of Cabot, most of whom were from Bristol, returned triumphantly from their quest of the New Found Land, they reported with much satisfaction that " they could bring thence so many fish that they would have no further need of Iceland ".[70]

V

THE OVERSEAS TRADE OF BRISTOL

§ 1

The Port of Bristol

"There are scarcely any towns of importance in the kingdom excepting these two: Bristol, a seaport to the West, and Boraco, otherwise York, which is on the borders of Scotland; besides London to the South."

The Italian Relation, 1500.[1]

Fifteenth century Bristol, according to a shrewd Italian, was one of the three most important towns in England, and of the three, it may well be studied as the typical trading city; for York was not a port, though it traded far afield through Hull, and London, though a port, was so much else that its story is very complex. Moreover, Bristol is of peculiar interest as a centre of English enterprise, for the principal southern and eastern ports were strongholds of foreign influence, from which Bristol was singularly free. Looking out westwards, she concerned herself little with the spheres of the powerful Hanseatic or Italian merchants, but carved out routes of her own, neither in the North Sea nor in the Mediterranean, but on the eastern shores of the Atlantic Ocean. This independent outlook, foreshadowing a new orientation of trade in the future, gives her yet further interest, for it was her seamen who, intimately acquainted with the eastern coasts of the Atlantic from Iceland to Gibraltar, were the first to venture forth from England across the ocean towards its western shores.

The silver ship freighted with incense which swung to and fro in one of its oldest churches, the banner bearing a ship under which its soldiers fought at Towton, the ship on the city's seal and on the bells from its foundry, all proclaim that the greatness of Bristol was built on its commerce. It boasted no ancient reputation as a cathedral see, as a military station, or as a shire town, but from its geographical position it had unique advantages as a centre for overseas trade. "Bristow," as Speed wrote later, "is not so ancient as it is fair and wel seated." The great waterways of the Severn, close to which Bristol lay, flowed through one of the richest agricultural regions of England, rivalled only by the wide river basin drained by the Humber. And the Humber had no such port as the Severn, for the harbour of Hull on its exposed estuary was never so secure as

BRISTOL
circa 1480

a. Customs House
b. Shipward's House
c. Vyell Place
d. Guildhall
e. Sturmy's House
f. Canynge's House
1. St. John Baptist
2. St. Stephen
3. St. Leonard
4. St. Werburgh
5. St. Ewen
6. Christ Church
7. All Saints
8. St. Mary le Port
9. St. Peter
10. St. Nicholas
11. St. John's Chapel
12. St. Thomas

⚓ Cranes
⚐ Pillories

Based on map in W. Hunt, Bristol.

that of Bristol. Here the encircling Avon and the " lusty Frome " gave protection from attack by land, while the seven miles of narrow gorge through which the Avon winds its way to the Bristol Channel guarded against violation by sea ; Southampton and the Cinque ports must often have envied Bristol its immunity from foreign invasion and constant assaults by pirates. Just as the Avon gorge has not its like in England, so the long fiord-like estuary of the Severn has no parallel on England's softer eastern and southern coasts of smoothly rounded outline. This also has been of great service to Bristol. For the sudden contraction of the long estuary where the Avon joins it causes exceptional tides, rising to a height of thirty or forty feet, and by these sailing vessels, after waiting at low tide at Kingrode, were swiftly carried up as far as Bristol.

The junction of the Avon and the Frome thus provided a sheltered tidal harbour, capable of defence, where great inland waterways converged, and gave to Bristol a unique opportunity of commanding the commerce of a district noted for its fertility. Already in the days of King Stephen it was characterized as " nearly the richest of all cities of the country, receiving merchandise by sailing vessels from foreign countries ; placed in the most fruitful part of England, and by the very situation of the place the best defended of all the cities of England ". Not many years later the charter of John (1188) enumerated cloth, wool, leather, and corn as among the articles in which it dealt.[2] To its river defences Bristol now added a turreted wall, almost circular in plan, pierced by three gateways each crowned by a stately church. From these three gates, three streets led to the central High Cross ; round this stood three more venerable churches, and near them was the Guildhall. Such was the nucleus of the port of Bristol, entrenched within its natural moat, and destined in years to come to be the business centre of an ever widening city.

Already by the close of the fourteenth century Bristol had grown far beyond the circle of these first city walls. Across the picturesque bridge over the Avon with its shops and gabled houses, lay a busy industrial suburb, marking the fact that Bristol was now one of the leading manufacturing cities of England, no longer exporting the wool which came to her in such abundance, but converting it into the famous Bristol cloth. In this second quarter of the city, sheltered in a curve of the Avon, and with its own protecting wall, lived numbers of clothworkers. Down by the river in Touker Street the tuckers fulled the cloth and hung it on tenters to dry ; there also worked the dyers. Further off in Temple Street rose the Weavers' Hall ; nearby the new Weavers' Chapel was built on to the ancient Temple Church ; in St. Thomas' Street was a colony of linen workers.[3] Fronting the river in Redcliffe Street, spacious houses with lofty halls were designed for merchants, like William Canynges, who dealt in cloth and shipped it overseas. Bristol's export of wool had now

o

THE REGIONAL TRADE OF BRISTOL during the fifteenth century

The names are those of the principal towns with which merchants of Bristol dealt. The dotted lines indicate the general direction of trade, with the chief commodities brought in to Bristol.

The shading shows the immediate hinterland of cloth manufacture. Goods brought from London & Southampton were mainly of foreign origin. ※ These castles were provisioned from Bristol by command of Henry IV.

[*Page 186.*]

THE OVERSEAS TRADE OF BRISTOL

ceased entirely, but her cloth was being marketed in Ireland, Gascony, Spain, and Portugal.

Fifteenth century Bristol, port and manufacturing city, was therefore a great collecting and distributing centre not only for overseas but also for inland trade. Goods poured into its market from a wide circle on whose circumference lay Chester to the north, Milford Haven to the west, London to the east, and Plymouth to the south. From the north, down the waterways of the Severn and the Avon, came rivercraft with all manner of produce from the heart of England. Cloth was brought from Coventry, where many Bristol citizens were members of the Holy Trinity Guild, and Coventry merchants were free of toll in Bristol, whence they must have procured woad for making the famous " Coventry blue ". From Coventry also, or from Nottingham, came the sculptured alabaster for which English craftsmen were then famed throughout Europe; this provided a reredos for St. Ewen's in Bristol, and for many churches abroad, from Iceland to Portugal.[4] The Forest of Dean sent quantities of iron, timber, and coal; the larger timber, called " Berkeley wood ", was discharged in Bristol at the Quay, and the smaller wood at the Back, where there were supposed always to be pennyworths for sale. Down the Severn from Worcester, Tewkesbury and Gloucester, came trowes and other craft laden with wheat, malt, and barley to feed the industrial population in and around Bristol, and for shipment abroad. Yet further north in Shrewsbury Bristol merchants had their agents; some of the cloth they exported came no doubt from the many drapers of Ludlow, and the road from Bristol to Chester with its five stone bridges was evidently a well frequented one.[5] Supplies of wool for the clothmakers were brought by carrier from places as distant as Buckingham; from Coventry, where William Meryell, woolman, had constant dealings with Bristol, and probably from Hereford, near which at Leominster was some of the best wool of all England.[6] From the west, Wales and Monmouth sent up the Bristol Channel wool, hides, and cloth, in innumerable boats of Milford Haven, Tenby, Haverford West, " Lawgher Havyn " (Laugharne?), Llanstephan, Kidwelly, Newport, Usk, Caerleon, Chepstow, and Tintern. The Abbot of Tintern was himself a member of the Staple in Bristol, where he and his monks were exempted from tolls, as were the men of Tenby who carried on quite a flourishing trade of their own with the continent. Wool came from Carmarthen, and hides from Tenby and elsewhere, some of them perhaps for the Bristol parchment-maker who had dealings with Cardiff. Welsh cattle were indeed an indispensable source of raw material to the many tanners, whittawers, pouchmakers, pointmakers, girdlers, glovers, corvesers, and curriers who did a thriving business in Bristol, shipping much of their produce abroad. " Welsh cloth " from Kidwelly and elsewhere, was a cheap frieze and provided russet gowns for poor folk in Bristol, whence it was also exported.[7] From the south, from the coasts of Devon and Cornwall, came tin, and also great quantities of fish, mainly for home consumption. The fish arrived mostly in boats belonging to Padstow, St. Ives, and Ilfracombe, but also in those from further afield, from Plymouth to the south to the Isle of Man ("Insula Humana") in the north. Packs of cloth came also up the Channel, especially from Barnstaple, and occasionally from as far as Kendal.[8]

All these districts received through Bristol merchants a variety of foodstuffs, raw materials, and luxuries. A Welsh boat, for instance, which brought in fish, was reladen with iron, and corn was sent to the people of Wales as well as to the English garrisons there. The Cornishmen who arrived with fish or tin left with frieze and other cheap cloth; Barnstaple, itself a flourishing cloth manufacturing town, took woad for its dyers, with wax and wine. Much fish was sent inland up the Severn, with coal, wax, and iron, perhaps for Birmingham's nascent industry, and the rich regions in the heart of England depended largely on Bristol for their supplies of luxuries from the South of Europe. Wine, for instance, travelled constantly by river to Gloucester, Worcester, and Bewdley; thence it went on into Shropshire, and one Ludlow merchant, who shipped his cloth through Bristol to Portugal, himself imported both fruit and wine. From Worcester it was taken on, probably in carts, as a century earlier, up the Avon valley to Warwick and Coventry. So much was it in demand for the banquets at Warwick Castle, that the enterprising earl, Richard Beauchamp, once had a scheme for making the Avon navigable as far as his own gates. Coventry bought also iron and manufactured metal goods from Bristol, such as guns from the famous foundry which more than once supplied cannon to the king, besides wax, and, no doubt, raw materials such as alum and woad; and though Coventry merchants, situated in the very centre of England, naturally had some dealings with the East Coast, they often collaborated with Bristol. Thus while they once sent a ship to Iceland apparently from Boston, they sent several ships thither in partnership with Bristol merchants.[9]

With her immediate hinterland Bristol carried on a lively business, for she was in the midst of one of the most vigorous cloth producing regions of England. Innumerable villages at the foot of the Cotswolds and the Mendips and along the valleys of the Somerset Avon and its tributaries had their organized groups of weavers, dyers, and tuckers, making ample use of the water power from the hills to drive their fulling mills. These districts naturally marketed much of their cloth at Bristol and took thence much of their raw material, though in wool they were amply provided locally from their steadily increasing flocks of sheep. A Somerset clothier of Shirburn, for instance, in payment for cloth sold to a Bristol merchant, received partly money and partly woad.[10] From the wealth thus accumulated, such villages were beautified with spacious churches, and these reveal for us incidentally not only which were the most prosperous clothing districts, but also with which of them Bristol had the closest connections. For their lofty towers were furnished with bells, many of which bear the mark of the Bristol foundry, then, next to that of London, perhaps the most important in the kingdom. These bells may still be found in large numbers in Gloucestershire, East Somerset and North Wilts, as also in South Wales, Devon, and Cornwall.[11]

But it must not be supposed that Bristol dealt only with the West of England, Wales, and the Midlands. She was in constant communication also with both London and Southampton. The list of tolls paid at Southampton inscribed on the first page of Bristol's *Great Red Book* shows how close was the connection between the two, and merchants seem often to have passed to and fro. Bristol sent cloth thither to be laden on the Italian galleys when they called there on their way up channel, and received in return some of the luxuries they brought, such as silk for the attire of her wealthy burgesses.[12] Still closer was the link with London, whose Lord Mayor is said to have presented to Bristol a rich sword " embroidered with pearls ". Carriers plied between the two cities, and the journey, by way of Chippenham and Newbury, could be done on horseback in rather less than three days. Much Bristol cloth, therefore, went to the capital. A Bristol tucker once stated that he commissioned a weaver to take thither for him a violet and a plunket cloth, and John Henlove and Alice Richards of Bristol both sold broadcloths there to the " Easterlings ". Indeed, Bristol men seem to have carried on a lively business in London with these Hanse merchants who, so they said, offered them more favourable terms than did the English merchants there. The *Acts of Court* of the Mercers' Company in London record an interesting discussion on this subject in 1486, at an " Assembly of the Fellowship of Adventurers ". It was reported that the men of Bristol had complained to the king's council that if the Easterlings were banished from London they would be utterly undone. For while the Easterlings bought their cloth for ready money, the merchants of London " buy not but for days, and therefore do make payment in Cardes, tenys balles, fish hooks, bristills, tassells, and such other simple wares ". More useful than the tennis balls was the madder for dyeing, which Bristol merchants brought often from London, imported probably from Flanders. London merchants sometimes came themselves to Bristol to purchase cloth, and London ships called sometimes at Bristol to collect cloth on their way to Bordeaux, just as Bristol ships called at London on their occasional trips to Eastern Europe. At least one London fishmonger co-operated with Bristol. " Stephen Forster, citizen and fishmonger of London," was probably the same as he who owned the *Mary Redcliffe* and the *Katherine* with William Canynges and traded with them to Iceland for fish. At any rate he named William Canynges as one of his executors, and gave generous bequests to several Bristol churches, including St. Mary Redcliffe, and it was in his house in London that one of Canynges' sons died.[13]

Goods thus came into Bristol's market from all quarters for redistribution—by the Severn and its tributaries, up the Bristol Channel, and by road from south and east. On the "Welsh Back", close to the bridge over the Avon, were unloaded fish and tin, cloth, wool, and hides from Wales and the southern coasts of England, while coal, timber, and other goods that came down the Severn were landed on the "Key" by the Frome.[14] Many a greater port must have been put to shame by both these quays. For while every tide left a muddy deposit on the irregular and unpaved quay of Bordeaux, Bristol had not only paved its streets and piled its strands, but had bound its Key and its Back with freestone.[15] Truly might Drayton praise this city as one of the healthiest and most delectable of its day :—

> "The prospect of which place
> To her fair building adds an admirable grace ;
> Well fashioned as the best, and with a double wall,
> As brave as any town ; but yet excelling all
> For easement, that to health is requisite and meet ;
> Her piled shores, to keep her delicate and sweet ;
> Hereto, she hath her tides ; that when she is opprest
> With heat or drought, still pour their floods upon her breast."

Bristol's "double wall" was by the fifteenth century ornamental rather than useful, and the city spent more on its quays than on its fortifications, though one burgess left money for their repair. For its life was centred at the quays and the adjoining customs house. There, outside the small circle of the ancient town, distinct also from the wide industrial suburb with its fashionable residential quarter, had grown up a third distinctive district, that of the mariners. In the low-lying region between the two rivers, the Avon with its "Back" and the Frome with its "Key", seamen lived in Baldwin Street, and nearby in Marsh Street the Fraternity for Mariners was formed in 1445.[16] This was supported by a levy from each master mariner, who, on arrival in port, had to pay 4*d*. a tun on his cargo within two days of receiving his hire. Two wardens were elected by the "craft", and the Fraternity maintained a priest and twelve poor sailors whose duty it was to pray for all merchants and mariners "passing or labouring" on the sea, either outwards or homewards. These seamen who brought fame to Bristol have left little record behind them. From time to time they appeared in the Tolsey Court, and there the clerk on one ocasion relieved his feelings by inscribing, in the midst of a monotonous record of debts claimed, a fragment of one of their shanties :—

> "Hale and howe Rumbylowe
> Stire well the gode ship and lete the wynde blowe.
> Here commethe the Pryor of Prikkingham and his Convent
> But ye kepe þe ordoure well, ye shull be shent,
> With hale and howe etc." [17]

It was for men thus in peril on the sea, whether from the Prior or from the sea-bishops, sea-unicorns, and the like who enliven mediaeval maps and bestiaries, that yet another institution was founded in this century, also in the mariners' quarter. On the Welsh Back was the chapel of St. John the Evangelist, and here Thomas Knappe appointed a priest to say mass for all merchants and mariners every morning at five o'clock.[18]

While the Welsh Back received the goods which were brought into Bristol from Wales and the southern coasts of England, it was at the larger quay by the Frome that Bristol's great sea-faring ships were built and loaded. Thence they were dispatched with English cloth and other merchandise, down the Severn and far away to north, south and west. Thither they returned to drop anchor, freighted with rich and varied produce from other lands to be stored in roomy cellars beneath the houses on the quay. Some had sailed simply to Ireland and home again. Others had voyaged on a long and complex course, visiting first Bordeaux or Lisbon, and then Ireland; sailing via Ireland and Brittany to Flanders, and returning by London and Southampton; crossing the ocean to Iceland and back in the summer, and then setting out for Bordeaux in the winter; or penetrating the Baltic to Danzig, and calling on the way home at Grimsby, Hull, and Sandwich. But three main routes were habitually followed, each of about equal importance in the volume of trade which it brought to Bristol. These led to Ireland, to Gascony, and to the Iberian peninsula, and it was on them that the fortunes of the city were founded. All three led away from the traditional centres of European commerce, the Baltic, and the Mediterranean, for Bristol looked out on the Atlantic, then to all appearance the utmost bound of the earth, and on its shores her merchants marketed their goods, faring forth as yet unknowingly upon the future great highway of nations.

§ 2

IRELAND

Spenser, describing the beauties of Ireland, her "excellent comodityes", her ports and havens "opening upon England and Scotland as inviting us to come to them", wrote at the close of a century which had brought her many hardships; his words seem even more applicable to what was, for her, the prosperous fifteenth century. With her "havens, great and goodly bays" and her land "plenteous and rich above most", she was a country offering abundant spoil to the foreigner; merchants from far-off Lucca came to her spacious harbours; in them lay ships from Iceland, from Spain, from Lübeck, from Bordeaux, and above all from England's two great western ports on the Severn and the Dee.[19]

Bristol, of all English ports, was then the one most favoured for traffic to Ireland, just as in Hakluyt's day it was well known as "a commodious and safe receptacle" for all ships directing their course thither. It was through a Bristol merchant that the Prior of Christ Church Canterbury once sent his letters to Ireland; while Sir Stephen Scrope, going as deputy thither in 1406, accompanied by fifty men at arms and 300 archers, arranged for their transport from Bristol, Liverpool, and Chester.[20] But if Chester and its less important neighbour were well situated for trade with the more anglicized north, Bristol's position fitted her pre-eminently for intercourse with the more numerous and wealthier Irish ports of the south. Thence ships sailed frequently for Waterford, "Harbour of the Sun." Alongside its extensive quay of half a mile no less than sixty vessels could anchor, and to them river boats brought the wealth of the interior, at small expense, down three great rivers which watered seven counties. There in 1398 the *Trinity* of Bristol unloaded a cargo of wine, and thence cargoes of fish were dispatched constantly to Bristol. Close were the connections between ships and merchants of the two cities. The *John* of Waterford, attacked in her own harbour by a notorious Falmouth pirate, was said to be the property of a Bristol merchant; and when the militant Prior of Kilmainham, with 200 horsemen and 300 foot, had sailed from Waterford to serve under Henry V in France, Bristol masters and mariners received £91 for conveying them thither. Waterford merchants were free of toll in Bristol, and were apparently as friendly to its merchants as they were to Edward IV, who recognized their services by letters patent, conferring on them special franchises and liberties. So great was their confidence in a certain Bristol merchant (who had sometimes transacted business for them), that they left these letters in his hands, until on his death they were found to have been mislaid, and the Mayor of Waterford was moved to sue the merchant's executors in Chancery. Thus Waterford, nearest of all large Irish ports to Bristol, and "urbs intacta" that was never captured in the later Middle Ages by Irish chief or Norman earl, naturally absorbed much of the Irish trade. During one winter Bristol shipped more cloth in her merchantmen than in those of any other Irish port.[21]

But Southern Ireland abounds in "great and goodly bays", and along the rugged shores of Munster there was many another sheltered harbour where vessels from Bristol and the Continent found refuge. Ships of Cork and of Kinsale, of Ross and of Youghal, all visited Bristol, and Kinsale bade fair to rival Waterford both in the number of its boats and in the amount of cloth they shipped. Its record is not, however, altogether creditable. Freebooting made it notorious rather than famous. In 1449-50, for instance, the *Mary* of Bristol, with her master, mariners, and fishers, " in fishing fare " on the high seas, captured a ship of Spain, the *Carveule* of Vermewe of 55 tuns, freighted with wine, iron, and salt, to the value of £160. Then Philip Martyn, Patrick Martyn, Thomas (?) Hanyagh, and Patrick Galwey of Kinsale, with many others of the same town, manned divers vessels, overcame the *Mary*, killed three of her men, and " divers moo of them hurted and grevousely bet ", and led the Spanish ship triumphantly into Kinsale. Thus John Wyche, owner of the *Mary*, told the tale, when later on Thomas Hanyagh turned up in Bristol with a skiff of Kinsale and 6,000 hake of other Kinsale merchants. Hanyagh, the skiff and the hake were all promptly " arrested " and Wyche had the effrontery to claim £200 damages in the Court of Admiralty. The Mayor, evidently suspicious, dismissed the case and cancelled the jury list of eighteen men, but Wyche took the matter into Chancery, asking for a subpœna against the Mayor, and secured a commission to arrest and bring before the king seven of the Kinsale men.[22]

Far away to the west, remote from England, but in a more direct line for Lisbon and Seville than was Bristol, were flourishing ports whose traffic with England was probably but a fraction of their total trade in Europe. There lay Limerick, " a wonderous prosperous city ; it may be called Little London for the situation and the plenty." Ships of 200 tuns could shelter in its secluded harbour on the Shannon, and it had ships of its own as large as that which in one voyage took from Bristol as much cloth as seven Kinsale boats took in six months, besides iron and salt. Its church of St. Mary was enriched by merchants of Bristol such as John Bannebury, who bequeathed to it and to the Friars Minor there 33*s*. 4*d*. and eight marks of silver, and to his wife two water-mills and other landed property in and near the city.[23] Yet further north, beyond " Munster of the swift ships ", stood Galway, centre of the Irish pilgrim traffic to Compostella. Girt about with lakes, her streets lined with houses all of hewed stone, garnished with fair battlements in a uniform course as if the whole town were built upon one model, she was indeed a noble city. Loudly the Irish bewailed that they were in continual peril from their own countrymen and from English rebels who extorted ruinous tolls outside their city gates ; and by such laments they sometimes contrived to evade their taxes, as did Limerick for fifteen years. Yet some among them must have amassed considerable fortunes thus to beautify their cities, and trade with the Continent evidently throve. Galway, Burrishoole, and Sligo had constant dealings with Spain and Portugal, and the ships which brought them southern luxuries for sale in Ireland reloaded with Irish produce for the markets of England or the Low Countries. For these three ports " or any one of them " John Heyton, merchant of Bristol, arranged that the *Julian* of Bristol should be freighted in Lisbon with wine, honey, and salt, and that, when she had delivered her burden, she should be reloaded with hides and sail on to Plymouth and thence to Normandy, Brittany, or the Low Countries. Commercial intercourse led to other speculative English enterprises in Galway. When the city was seized in 1400 by the rebel Sir William de Burgh, one " loyal Englishman " came over to Bristol and persuaded four adventurers to take their ships and help him to recover the town; they went at their own expense, but the king, who had little time or money to give to Ireland, and who only maintained troops there by quartering them on the country, gave them permission to recoup themselves with all the goods of the rebels.[24]

In contrast to South and West Ireland, Ulster, and its ports opening upon Scotland and Northern England had little connection with Bristol, though ships from Carrickfergus sometimes came thither.[25] Their arrival was imperilled by the diligence of those inveterate tormentors of England, the Scots, who preyed constantly upon ships venturing through the North Channel—a passage more dangerously narrow than the Straits of Dover. In 1482, for instance, Richard Chapman, fishmonger, and John Quyrke, mariner, were sailing the seas in the *Flowre* of Minehead when there came upon them two Scottish ships commanded by John de Rumpyll (thus did the Englishman distort their captor's name Dalrymple). He seized the *Flowre*, took her into Ayr, and then, being a man of business, proposed to sell both ship and cargo to her crew. But how could the £70 he demanded be produced in ready money in a barren land seldom visited by English merchants? At last it was agreed that the *Flowre* must be sent to Minehead with her merchandise and her tragic tale, while Chapman and Quyrke must remain with de Rumpyll to be ransomed. Accordingly the trapped Englishmen decided that one of their " fellowship ", William Porter, should be master of the ship and her cargo, should take her to Minehead, and should sell as much as was necessary to pay the £70 and the " costs and other losses " sustained by Chapman and Quyrke during their imprisonment: " which to do the said William Porter faythfully promysed and agreed in all goodly haste." But Porter's promises were apparently better than his practices, for the £70 was not forthcoming, and Chapman and Quyrke, languishing in the Scottish prison, were fain to send a petition to the Chancellor.[26]

Bristol men certainly visited Ulster less often than the Pale, that ever-dwindling place, scarce thirty miles in length, into which the English were now penned and " out of which they durst not peep ". Thence Drogheda sometimes sent ships to Bristol and bought from Bristol merchants, though it was probably in more constant touch with the nearer port of Chester. One Drogheda merchant, for instance, owing 20 marks to Clement Bagot of Bristol, sent to Chester six butts of salmon, which were sold at Shrewsbury for Bagot's benefit. Dublin also must have been more closely connected with Chester. Henry II's charter had granted to Bristol men all the privileges which they enjoyed in their own city, and men of Bristol origin, perhaps the descendants of early settlers, were still living there. But the men who took a prominent part in founding, in 1479, the Guild of English merchants trading in Ireland, with its chapel on the bridge in Dublin, were none of them well-known citizens of Bristol. And though some business was carried on between the two cities, Dublin ships scarcely ever arrived in Bristol.[27] It was, above all, the ships of South Ireland which had dealings with Bristol, carrying many a cargo for prominent merchants there, and trafficking no doubt also with other Irish ports than their own.

Irish vessels, indeed, took a far larger share in the business than did those of Bristol, which concerned themselves mainly with more distant traffic. Sixteen Irish ships were engaged in it during the winter of 1403-4, as compared with six Bristol ones. Even Bristol's smaller neighbours, especially Minehead, were sometimes more actively engaged than Bristol itself. Nine Minehead vessels went to Ireland in 1465-6 (November to May), and the towns of Berkeley and Walton took a share, as did also Welsh ports such as Milford and Chepstow.

Irish merchants as well as Irish ships busied themselves in the trade, though a part of their own continental commerce was in the hands of Bristol merchants.[28] Many of them must have been to and fro in Bristol, some of them men of doubtful reputations among the English; John Bullok was said to be a common withdrawer of the king's custom and a deceiver of his liege people, and was sued in Chancery by John Bonyfaunt who had stood surety for the payment of his dues. The " Irish Mead " on the outskirts of Bristol indicates that Irishmen must also have settled in the city; certainly the Bristol merchants, Patrick Irishman and Henry May (perhaps a member of the well-known Waterford family) were Irish at least in origin, as were Patrick Lawless and John Gough, masters of Bristol ships. An interesting light is thrown on Bristol's Irish immigrants by the decree of 1413. In that year " for quiet and peace within this realm of England, and for the increase and filling of the realm of Ireland " all the " wylde " Irish, except those who had an honourable position as burgesses, men of law, and so forth, were ordered to leave England. Amongst those permitted to remain were Nicholas Devenysh, a merchant, Philip Faunt, a master tanner, John Stone and John Ayleward, all of Bristol. When in 1430 the exclusion decree was repeated, exemption was granted to Robert Londe, priest, who is depicted with paten and chalice on a brass dated 1460, in St. Peter's Church at Bristol. Complaint had already been made that the Bristol weavers were taking as apprentices children and young men born in Ireland who were taught for only one, two, or three years and then departed. A decree of 1439 imposed a penalty of £20 on any Mayor of Bristol who admitted to his Council a man born in Ireland of an Irish father and mother. The inference that these immigrants were both numerous and unacceptable is confirmed by a quaint entry in Ricart's Calendar. He records, under the date 1456, that the Irish burgesses began a suit against the mayor and council before the Lord Chancellor, Harry May being "vaunt parloure and chief labourer"; for which he and all his fellows were deprived of their freedom "til they bought it ayen with the blodde of theyre purses, and with weping Ien, knelyng on their knees, besought the Maire and his brothern of their grace".[29]

But if Irish people were not always welcome in Bristol, Irish merchandise, on which its fortunes had originally been founded, was eagerly sought after as one of its chief sources of wealth. "Heryng of Slegothe and salmon of Bame heis made in Brystowe many a ryche man." Thus ran a common proverb, quoted for the merchant's instruction in a fifteenth century commercial handbook, and fish was probably the product of Ireland that Bristol men valued most. They caught it themselves off her shores, though an act of 1465 forbade any stranger to fish without a licence; they chaffered for it in Ireland with fishermen, who sometimes promised to send it at least as far as Kingrode where the Bristol men might receive it and "convey it at their pleasure and liberty". John Mold, fisherman of Malahide, died in debt to a prominent Bristol merchant who exported fish to Spain; John Jonet owed 5s. to a Lusk fisherman's wife who possessed (besides sheep, cows, pigs, and a cart horse), one boat and fourteen sea-nets.[30]

Of the salt-water fish sent from Ireland the herring came first in quantity. For as the East of England supplied itself with herring from Norfolk and Suffolk, so "as for the west party of Ynglond, thei have ther herynge howe of Yrland". Herring was one of the fish most in demand among housewives of the period. As Margaret Paston's bailiff wrote to her one autumn: "Mastres, it were good to remember your stuffe of heryng nough this fisshyng tyme"; and in the regulations of the baronial breakfasts of the Percy family throughout Lent it is ordained that my lord Percy (aged 11) and master Thomas Percy shall breakfast daily on three white herrings or a dish of sprats besides a piece of salt-fish, bread and butter, and beer; similarly for the two younger folk in the "Nurcy" there is to be "a Manchet, a Quart of Bere, a Dysch of Butter, a Pece of Saltfisch, a Dysch of Sproitts or iij White Herryng". The same provision of sprats or herring is made for all, from my lady to her

THE OVERSEAS TRADE OF BRISTOL

"Gentyllwomen". These white herrings (fresh or salted as contrasted with smoked herrings) are priced in the Bristol customs accounts at £3 the last of 12,000 fish, and the same customs valuation is given to red herrings, that is herrings salted for about twenty-four hours and hung up to smoke. The Pastons expected to purchase half a last from the North Sea Fisheries for £2 in the fishing season of autumn, when the wise housewife replenished her stock for the following Lent, and it was at this time that boats came from Ireland with as much as £100 worth of herrings, whereas in the spring and summer they brought not more than two or three lasts. So the Paston's bailiff wrote, " Ye shal do more nough with xl*s*. then ye shal do at Cristemes with v marke." [31]

"Pecys of Saltfisch" similar to those provided for the Percy breakfasts came also to Bristol from Ireland in many varieties, chiefly of the cod family. Among these large fish (gadoids), the most highly priced were hake, pollack, scalpin (whiting), and milwell (cod). Inferior qualities of these and other species of the same family, such as haburden (cod used especially for salting) and ling, called grenefish when fresh, very likely went to make up the bulk of the unspecified "fish" and "dry fish". A diminutive shark, the hound fish, was also imported. More rarely seen in Bristol were seals, valued in the customs at 2*s*. 6*d*. each and reputed as fit only for the digestions of mariners; the royal fish, whale, at 2*s*. the barrel; and porpoise at 5*s*. the barrel—the "sea pig" whose tongue was considered such a delicacy that Henry I, in giving the Bishop of London the right to all those taken on his land, had excepted "the tongue, which I have retained for myself". Some of the fish certainly arrived fresh, for when in 1488 the old records of the town were searched at the request of the water-bailiff, it was found that the king was entitled to a prise of six fish from every boat with thirty or more fresh milwell, ling, hake, ray, conger, and of twelve fish from every boat with thirty or more fresh gurnard, haddock, whiting, bream, mackerel, plaice, or other small fresh fish. The king had also the right to a hundred fish from every boat with fresh herring not belonging to a Bristol burgess, but for fresh-water fish and fresh salmon there was no prise. Much of the fish must, however, have been cured since, even when it arrived in autumn, it was needed especially for Lent. Ling, indeed, would keep not only until Lent but for two years, if it were put into thick straw and covered with mats "close and dry". Salt was therefore much in demand. For a barrel of salt a man might have " a Barrell fylled full of new herynge nott a day " ; and many boats left Bristol for Ireland with salt and cloth, to buy salmon or herring there, salt them, and bring them back to England. Salmon was more highly priced than the salt-water fish, and was frequently imported. Bristol men often secured licences either to buy it or to catch it themselves. Perhaps the Bristol burgess with water-mills in Limerick set traps for it in the Shannon; at any rate it came often from those parts, and sometimes from merchants of Kilkenny, as well as from the river Bann in the north.[32]

Next in amount and value to fish came the hides exported in great quantities as the fishing season waned. For Ireland with its moist climate, " greate mountaynes and wast desartes full of grasse ", nourished many thousands of cattle " for the good of the whole realm ". Being only fed and not fattened, however, their value was in their hides. These provided shoes and gloves, saddle and harness, coffer and purses, girdles and jerkins, trimmings for the rich, writing materials for the scribe, and rugs for rich and poor alike. Almost every vessel arriving in Bristol brought its quota: shiploads also went in Bristol boats direct from Ireland to the ports of Southern England, France, and to Flanders, where they could be sold more profitably than anywhere else for £18 the last.[33] Skins of sheep, lambs and kids were very common, and the unspecified hides and salted hides must have included the ox-, cow-, and calf-hides, which are seldom entered separately. In the fastnesses of Irish bogs and mountains wild animals abounded, and from their skins the skilful hunter must have made good profit. Deer skins and rabbit skins were the most common. Less often appear hares, martens, foxes, otters, goats, and squirrels. Wolves also lurked in the forests and toll was once paid in Bristol for three dozen of their skins. The skins usually arrived raw in Bristol, where they were then worked up, often for re-export, by the many tanners, curriers, whittawers, and corvesers who did business there. Besides the skins of the animals there came tallow, lard, wax, and occasionally butter. But six " bacons " from Carrickfergus, and twelve carcases in a Drogheda boat are unique mentions of " beasts' flesh ", in striking contrast to present-day statistics of Irish produce. Other live-stock, however, appear in the accounts, for Ireland was even then famed for her horses, especially for those " gentyll horsys that be callyd hobbeys of Irelond ". Merchants of Drogheda once freighted a Flemish ship for Brittany with hides and thirty-four unfortunate horses, which were driven by tempests into Dartmouth, and there, so the owner averred, distributed by the bailiff.[34] The needs of sportsmen were further ministered to by the export of hawks, male and female, valued at 2s. 6d. each.

The " goodly woodes fitt for building of howses and shippes " proved also a valuable source of wealth. Irish timber, used freely in Ireland for herring casks, was even more prized abroad, in England, where Irish oak beautified many a church during the golden age of English woodwork, and in France, where it was considered specially fit for furniture, painting, and sculpture.[35] Ship-boards came constantly to Bristol, as did oars and occasionally bow-staves.

But Ireland was no mere cattle-run interspersed with forests. By the thirteenth century more land had been brought under the plough than was necessary to supply her own needs, especially in the east midlands, and the export of corn was a profitable business. In the early fifteenth century she was still known as a possible source of grain, and Bristol merchants shipped corn thence direct to the Continent. Later on, however, her supplies began to run short. By 1437 Bristol was shipping corn to Ireland; in 1475 the export of corn from Ireland was forbidden [36]; and in the last quarter of the century there were constant shipments from Bristol.

Skilled manufactures were now developing in Ireland, especially that of linen from her unrivalled flax, known by the middle of the century as far afield as the Netherlands and Italy.[37] Its abundance was graphically demonstrated by the Irishman's thick folded saffron shirt, his smock of thirty yards or more wound about him, with sleeves falling to the knees, and by the great linen rolls upon the women's heads. In vain the English passed laws, "impertinent and unnecessary," forbidding such "barbarous" Irish customs as these and the entertaining of bards and pipers, and setting a limit of seven yards to the shirt; the traditional Irish apparel was still in vogue in Elizabethan days. Consignments of this linen and of linen yarn reached Bristol constantly, and the industry evidently flourished in the fifteenth century, particularly towards its close. During one year the import of over 20,000 cloths was recorded, and the activity of Kilkenny merchants may perhaps indicate a manufacturing centre in that neighbourhood. According to the customs valuation the worth of the linen was $1\frac{1}{4}d.$ a yard. This linen manufacture, for which the Irish soil and climate was peculiarly fitted, tended to overtake the manufacture of that low-priced cloth which was, however, always popular in England. "Drap d'Irland" was one of the cheap cloths which Parliament asked might be exempted from the payment of cocket, provided the dozen (half a cloth) did not exceed in value 10*s.*[38] Forty yards of Irish frieze were valued in the customs at 20*s.*, and both this and faldynges (rough-napped cloth) was exported in considerable quantities to Bristol. Even more popular seem to have been the capacious ready-made mantles; these, for a cost of something over 3*s.* 4*d.*, could serve as garment, bed, or even tent when necessary and, as Spenser picturesquely paraphrased it, were "a fitt howse for an outlaw, a meete bedd for a rebell, and an apt cloke for a theif". Whittles also (shaggy blankets) were sent by the Irish at half the price, and also rugs. Finally, they shipped some of their wool as flock, suitable for bedding, at 5*d.* the stone. Amongst other manufactured articles are now and again exports of "oldware" and "newware"— a foreshadowing of the extensive trade in old pewter and brass of the following century.

Amply supplied for almost all ordinary needs, Ireland asked but two necessaries from outside—salt and iron. Salt often came to her direct from the Continent, sometimes in foreign ships *via* Bristol, and sometimes in Bristol ships, either for sale or for salting their own return cargo of fish. Shipments of salt from Bristol came almost invariably between January and October, so as to be in readiness for the autumn deep-sea fisheries, and for the salmon fishing which took place mainly from January to March and from July to August; it is in February and July that the largest imports of salmon are usually recorded. Iron went throughout the year in small quantities, but manufactured metal goods were still more acceptable—knives, nails, hauberks, basinets, and gorgets, or tools of the weaving trade such as cards, combs, or teagels. Leather goods, too, found a sale, for the tanning industry was further advanced in England than in Ireland— tanned hides, girdles, and points; also pots and pans ("battery") and pedlary ware. Alum, invaluable in the dyeing of cloth and the tanning of leather, was frequently sent. This was a re-export, as were pitch, oil, anise, soap, almonds, fruit, and wine. Ireland evidently depended for spices on Bristol as well as on her extensive direct trade with the Continent. Most of her wine, however, she probably received direct. At any rate that shipped from Bristol was usually labelled "corrupt", "old and undrinkable", or at least "not drinkable in England".[39] Possibly this sour wine was not even drinkable by the Irish, but was used for the extensive business of pickling fish. Drinks more usually exported from England to Ireland were perry and beer.

Salt and iron had in the thirteenth century, according to Higden, been the chief goods sought from England by the Irish. But by the fifteenth century neither these nor the luxuries of the south were Bristol's principal export. English cloth now held the premier place in the list, cloth more costly than that of Ireland, for prosperous Ireland, with her superfluity of necessities, was able to purchase luxuries. Coverlets of worsted, the usual ungrained cloth, and even the rich scarlet cloth were sent, and during one winter Bristol's export of cloth to Ireland amounted to one-third of her whole cloth export for that period. Yet even this, with the salt, iron, and other goods shipped, did not nearly equal the wealth of imports from Ireland, and the balance of trade seems to have been clearly in Ireland's favour.[40]

During this period Ireland, though "miserably tossed and turmoyled", enjoyed virtual independence. After Richard II's visit in 1394 no English sovereign set foot there until the fugitive James II arrived, and the general policy of her nominal rulers at the close of the Middle Ages was neglect rather than interference. Little but the ports and the restricted Pale remained steadfast in their allegiance, and the rest of Ireland was left to its own internecine feuds and private wars, with no firm central authority to keep the peace. Yet, despite the "tumultuous broils" which the English delight to record, there can be no doubt that, left to herself, Ireland was more prosperous than in most subsequent periods. Her dealings with Bristol alone, and her constant intercourse with the Continent, are an eloquent testimony to her flourishing trade and industry and to her great potential commercial value, which even to the present day has remained unrealized.

§ 3

Gascony

Bristol's close connection with Gascony had its origin in the wine trade, and on this trade her prosperity was in large measure based. Wine was then the one article of large daily consumption which England could not supply to the well-to-do Englishman. So, said the Italian Salimbene, " We must forgive the English if they are glad to drink good wine when they can, for they have but little wine in their own country." Naturally it was to Gascony that they turned in their need. This sunny province, with its sheltered valleys peculiarly suited to the vine, had been part of the king of England's realm ever since Henry II married Eleanor of Aquitaine, and on its vineyards its very existence depended. From the fertile dunes at the estuary of the Gironde to the eastern extremities of the great valleys which there converged, the rivers were fringed with vines which penetrated even into the heart of at least one large city. All ranks of society, from the mighty prelate to the humble shoemaker, possessed their vineyards; for the mass of the population their cultivation was the dominant interest in life; a bad harvest was a calamity to the community duly recorded in local annals.[41] To have sent their wines overland for sale would have been a task fraught with difficulty. Roads were so rudimentary and roving bands of freebooters so menacing that land transport was tedious and perilous; it was also costly because of the inordinate exactions of covetous seigneurs. They therefore shipped them to other shores by the two convenient natural outlets of the Gironde and the Adour—to Normandy and Brittany, to the Low Countries, to Spain, to Portugal, but above all to England; for with England, then part of the same realm, trade was assured, and England not only made the biggest demand but had the most to offer in return in her cloth and hides, corn and fish. " How," as a fourteenth century Bordeaux merchant remarked, " could our poor people subsist when they could not sell their wines or procure English merchandise? "

Thus ports owing their prosperity mainly to the wine trade grew up at the river estuaries, and among these Bordeaux and Bayonne rapidly gained the pre-eminence. These two cities had by the fifteenth century become the customary resort of the English merchants, and in both Bristol merchants were domiciled.

Bayonne's reputation as a port was the more transient. By the latter half of the century her decline was marked, and less than a quarter of the wine imported to Bristol from Gascony came from Bayonne. The chief reason for this decay was doubtless the silting up of the Adour. Choked with sand swept thither by wind and sea, it was driven to seek new and ever shifting channels along the low-lying coast. The obstacles to navigation became, therefore, well-nigh insurmountable. Further, her position as a southern outpost of the English territory exposed her to attack not only from Frenchmen but from Spaniards, who on more than one occasion laid waste the surrounding country, leaving ruin and desolation behind them.[42] Yet in spite of her decay as a port, the seafaring enterprise of her shipmen continued, and Bristol sometimes received more than half as many tuns of wine in Bayonne ships as in ships of her own.

In situation alone Bordeaux had extraordinary advantages. Protected seaward, unlike Bayonne, by wide landes and lagoons, this was the effective meeting-place of five great river valleys, built at the lowest point at which the largest of them could be bridged, a point where the tide might still be felt. So the city had unrivalled opportunities of monopolising the commerce of an extensive and highly productive area wherein the vine throve exceedingly. Through the great wealth they accumulated her citizens gained influence, and this they used to win for themselves special privileges, so that it was with these ambitious burghers that English merchants could most effectively deal. They strove, for example, to draw to their own city for export all the wines of the rich river valleys round about, to concentrate trade there, and to strangle all possible rivals. And so anxious were English kings to conciliate the leading towns of Gascony and to simplify the control of trade, that they frequently granted exclusive rights of trade to Bordeaux and Bayonne, even forbidding their English subjects to bargain for wines elsewhere in Gascony. Bordeaux also took advantage of being on the route by which most wine for export must reach the sea to enrich herself by levying heavy tolls on passing vessels. Such was the Issak or Petty Custom on all wines brought from the Haut Pays, except on those from vineyards owned by Bordeaux citizens. Possibly this had come to include the two small local customs of Mortagne and Montendre. This duty was granted to the city for its own use in 1442. Bordeaux further handicapped the wines of the Haut Pays by forbidding their import before St. Martin's day, so that by the time they arrived the Bordelais had already gathered his harvest and monopolized the first sale. Moreover, for her own citizens she secured exemption from the Great Custom due on all exported wines; this privilege was recognized by all English sovereigns, and confirmed in 1401, 1420 and 1441. Thus the wines from the estates of Bordeaux citizens—though not the wines bought by them from Gascons—could be brought to and dispatched from Bordeaux free of any tax. Further, the Bordelais gained complete immunity from all river tolls, including the multitudinous dues extorted by covetous seigneurs who were fortunate enough to live on the banks of the Gironde. These exactions had caused tedious delay and a serious addition to the expense of the voyage, and their remission benefited not only the Bordelais but also English and aliens, for their goods too could now sail unchecked down the Gironde and out into the open sea. One such toll had been paid to the lord of Cypressat, a small domain opposite Bordeaux, and in sign of payment a cypress branch used to be delivered to the captain of each ship. This due survived, but the branch was now delivered at the castle of l'Ombrière in Bordeaux by the Constable, who handed over part of the money to Cypressat, keeping part for the king. Finally, after an intense and prolonged conflict, and in spite of the hostility of the Londoners, the citizens of Bordeaux secured in 1388 complete freedom to come and go in England.[43]

Such comprehensive privileges raised Bordeaux to the rank of a commercial suzerain on the Gironde, and naturally evoked strong opposition from her neighbours, who succeeded to some extent in modifying them. Such river ports as could claim special consideration on account of their strategic value as well as of their wealth, made frequent complaint to the king against the arrogant encroachments of Bordeaux. Some of their petitions, with records of the subsequent relief granted, are preserved among the Archives of Bordeaux and in the Public Record Office in London. Such is the petition of Libourne to be free of customs, resulting in her admission to equal privileges. Later on a declaration of Henry IV specifically mentioned that the privileges of Bordeaux were not intended to prejudice Libourne, Bourg or St. Emilion. Likewise Blaye, a formidable fortress guarding the approach by water to Bordeaux, secured freedom to sell its wines there ; and when English rule in Gascony was ended its privileges were confirmed by the French king, as were those of Libourne. Besides these cities on the Dordogne and the Gironde, some of those on the Garonne, still more at the mercy of Bordeaux, won treaties assuring them freedom of trade. La Réole, for instance, had been allowed to take a toll of wines from which Bordeaux was exempt. Keenly jealous of this and of the restrictions imposed on her own wines in Bordeaux, she finally secured freedom to sell them there at any time and also won exemption from local duties there, as did her neighbour, St. Macaire. These six cities, and perhaps others, had with some degree of success challenged the supremacy of Bordeaux in Northern Gascony, securing for themselves reciprocal treaties, with freedom to sell their wines to the stranger. Yet Bordeaux still retained her virtual monopoly of the export trade, and she seems to have been the only one of the cities to possess sea-going ships.[44]

The pretensions of Bordeaux to control the trade aroused the hostility not only of her neighbours but also of the English, who resented both the increased cost of the Haut Pays wines through the high dues paid at Bordeaux, and the prohibition from time to time against purchasing them elsewhere. At times they combated the claims of Bordeaux with success. Thus in 1444 the Commons complained that they were now forbidden to " bye wynes of the growyng of the High Countr' in swich tyme as they wer wont to doo ", elsewhere than from Bordeaux or Bayonne. Their petition in Parliament won them liberty freely to buy and sell anywhere, as they had formerly been accustomed to do, while any officials who opposed them were liable to a fine of £20 with treble damages.[45] One privilege at least which the English were allowed throughout the first half of the fifteenth century was that of importing goods into Gascony free of duty.[46] There were thus two classes of privileged merchants in Bordeaux—the English and the merchants of specially favoured towns. Of them all, it was the citizens of Bordeaux whose long-established privileges never fluctuated whilst English rule lasted.

Bayonne, in contrast to Bordeaux, though enjoying some of the same privileges as a centre for export, was not sufficiently influential to insist on controlling the river traffic in her own interests. In 1409, for instance, to her intense but unavailing indignation, the king granted a toll to the redoubtable lord of the stronghold of Mauléon on all wines passing Guiche.[47]

Bordeaux was thus the paramount port for the dispatch of wines to England and elsewhere, with Bayonne as a keen competitor in the early part of the century. But the citizens of Bordeaux were far behind those of Bayonne in seamanship and relied upon strangers to fetch their wines and even to keep open the gates of their own port in time of danger. Of over 200 ships leaving their harbour in one year, only five were their own; and they were helpless before the threat of a foreign navy. Thus when the French ships lay between them and the open sea, besieging Blaye, the heavily laden merchantmen, ready to depart, dared not venture forth without a convoy. So the town council, meeting day after day to discuss the situation, could only advise immediate dispatch of a vessel to England to crave assistance. It was urged, however, that none of the four craft owned by the town of Bordeaux could with impunity venture across the high seas in November. An English ship had therefore to be persuaded to take the message, and another hired to go to the relief of Blaye.[48]

The constitutional aversion of the Bordelais to the risks of the open sea stands out in striking contrast to the enterprise of the men of Bayonne. Their vessels not only took wine from their own port, but provided as much freight for that of Bordeaux as she did herself. In 1409-10, for instance, Bordeaux provided five ships, and so did Bayonne. In the winter of 1403-4 no less than nine Bayonne ships brought wine to Bristol, seven of them sailing from Bayonne, and two from Bordeaux, while Bordeaux herself sent not one ship. These figures are typical and not exceptional.[49]

It was, however, the ships neither of Bordeaux nor of Bayonne, but of England, which carried the bulk of the wine exports from Bordeaux. The elaborate and interesting accounts of the Constable of Bordeaux noting the departure of the wine ships, record a few Flemish, Breton, and French vessels, but a multitude of English craft, coming from at least thirty-five English ports from Newcastle in the north to Plymouth, Fowey, and Bristol in the west, and from Welsh ports such as Chepstow, Tenby, and Milford Haven. Among the English ships, those of Dartmouth were the most numerous. During one year (1409-10), between December and March, over 200 ships left Bordeaux, and of these twenty-seven belonged to Dartmouth, thirteen to London, eleven to Hull, nine to Bristol, and nine each to Fowey and Plymouth. Their exact destination is not ascertainable, but amongst those bound for Bristol there must have been ships of Bayonne and Bristol and perhaps of Dartmouth, Plymouth, and Fowey.[50] Certainly more than half Bristol's imports of wine from Gascony came at this time in her own ships, and the rest almost entirely in ships of Bayonne, though occasionally in those of Lynn, St. Jean de Luz, or La Rochelle.

These 200 ships and more, which came each year to fetch wine at Bordeaux, arrived usually in the vintage season or in early spring, returning home in December or March. They set out in large companies for mutual safeguard, fifty of them sometimes leaving Bordeaux within a few days of each other. Royal protection had frequently been granted to these wine fleets in the fourteenth century, and again and again ships were warned not to venture singly. Richard II, for example, once ordered all vessels bound for Bordeaux to assemble at the Isle of Wight, in view of the alarming naval preparations of the French, and to put themselves under the command of the Constable of Bordeaux. Scorning such timorous counsels, Adam of York and his fellows returned alone and fell a prey to the pirates of Talmont and Rochelle. But such royal help was not regular, and became less frequent in the fifteenth century. Now merchants more often combined with each other for mutual protection on outward and homeward voyages, and made their agreements binding by solemn attestation before some public authority such as the Constable of Bordeaux. In 1415, for instance, when a fleet of English ships was laden with wine ready to depart, the chief merchants and masters elected an admiral for the voyage and swore before the Constable that nothing should separate them before their arrival in port. When, therefore, the *Christopher* of Hull was attacked and captured by Spanish pirates, and the others fled away in fear and left her to her fate, the deserters were ordered to make good the damage.[51]

The English ships which left Bordeaux were bound for many different destinations. Some put in at Channel ports such as Southampton, more at Bristol and Hull, and more still at London. The actual journey from London to Bordeaux took about ten days, and the whole expedition there and back usually occupied about two months.[52] At least a month must thus have been spent in Bordeaux, repairing the ships, disposing of their cargoes, and bargaining for wine, or purchasing it from the Haut Pays when this was allowed.

In late autumn and in spring these ships often carried no other merchandise but wine, but this was now by no means the only source of wealth in Gascony. In mid-winter and in summer there came a variety of produce not only from Gascony but from as far away as Brittany to the north and Spain to the south. Chief among these was woad. Casks of this blue dye, made up in the form of dry balls, frequently constituted the whole freight of a ship. Even in the month of March cargoes worth £690 once came to Bristol, and it seems likely that still more was brought in the summer when ships were no longer freighted with wine, and when the woad itself was harvested. How largely British merchants dealt in it may be inferred from the fact that it was a form of property they often bequeathed. Ludovic Mors left a quarter of woad to pay for his burial in St. Mary Redcliffe, and the only other property specified, besides his house in Old Corn Street and his shop on the quay, was twenty pipes of woad to be divided among his three sons; six of these were in his house, and fourteen in certain ships " returning by the Grace of God from parts beyond the sea ". Similarly, Edward Dawes left eight measures of woad towards buying a new pair of organs for St. Werburgh's church. The demand for this woad in the cloth manufacturing districts of the west, especially in Bristol itself, was very great, for though its cultivation in England had almost ceased, it was one of the commonest dyes, used not only for blue cloth, but as a mordant for other colours. Its importance is evident from the number of regulations made by the town council in Bristol insisting upon its preparation by special " porters "; these had to supervise the breaking up of the dry balls, the moistening with water, the subsequent fermentation and the storage. Other ordinances were passed regulating the actual dyeing processes, and arranging for the proper measurement and marking of each cask before its shipment. The import of woad was almost entirely in the hands of English merchants who, in the early fifteenth century, shipped it mainly from Bayonne though partly from Bordeaux. The plant from whose leaves it was prepared was grown around Toulouse, Albi, and Montauban, and had long since been used by the cloth manufacturers of Languedoc. They for a time had succeeded in prohibiting its export, but this had been permitted since 1359, subject to a toll. Before long, Languedoc's own cloth industry had almost vanished, and its harvest of woad was so potent a factor in the growth of England's industries that Bristol merchants might well speak of this trade as the "moost chieff, noblest and ponderoust merchaundys of good & able Wode, thencrece whereof in old tyme causyd, manteynyd and susteynyd the noble prosperous felicitee of this Worshipfull Town".[53]

Other less important raw materials for fixing the dyes included alum and *cineres*.[54] And from Bordeaux came also occasionally Breton linen, with wax and honey from the Landes and Narbonne.[55] Bayonne, however, sent a much more varied assortment of goods than did Bordeaux. For since she was situated close to one of the two land gateways into Spain, many goods came to her thence, and they were sometimes allowed through free of duty to increase her business. Iron was a very usual export, probably from the Cantabrian mountains. Steel came sometimes, but more often manufactured metal goods such as combs—another evidence of the growing importance of the cloth industry in England. Pitch and rosin, bowstaves, beaver, and cordovan (Spanish leather) were often included. For the housewife came many delicacies—honey and once sugar, almonds, licorice, and saffron, recommended in all good cookery books of the period to give colour and flavour to such dainties as fritters. If Bayonne sometimes wished that her hostile Spanish neighbours were further off, she must often have been glad to have them so conveniently near as sources of supply for such a variety of produce.

While Gascony throve by exporting her own produce of wine and woad, she became more and more dependent upon foreign lands for such necessaries as cloth, fish, and corn with which she could no longer provide herself. Cloth reached her from Flanders, from Ireland, but above all from England, and the cargoes unloaded by Bristol ships in Bordeaux or Bayonne consisted usually almost entirely of cloth. Gascony was now one of the principal markets for Bristol's cloth, which was sold not only in the wine-growing regions but also as far inland as the woad centre of Montauban.[56] Hides from Bristol were also an acceptable commodity though insignificant in comparison with cloth. Some of the coal brought by river craft to Bristol found its way to Gascony, and also small quantities of fish, white and red herring, and hake; but the big demand for fish in Gascony during Lent was met mainly by boats from other ports, especially of Cornwall; the Archbishop of Bordeaux once laid in a stock of 1,000 red herrings from Cornwall in exchange for his wines.[57] Foreign corn was often as much in demand as foreign fish, and for this England was said to be Gascony's chief source of supply. The civic books of Bordeaux record the arrival of corn by land or sea as an event of great moment; its import, unlike that of other goods, was always exempt from duty, and the city as a whole became responsible for ensuring the supply, sometimes borrowing the money with which to pay for it. On some occasions corn was so urgently needed that it was allowed through from the Haut Pays even when that region was in French hands, and thus nominally at war with the English, and sometimes it was stipulated that a certain proportion of corn must be included with every cargo of Haut Pays wine. The overseas supply from England seems, however, to have been intermittent, coming probably in times of famine, siege or other emergency. Thus during the great famine of 1403 permission was given to export grain to Bayonne, and again in 1419 when the Spaniards threatened to besiege Bayonne, and yet again in 1420. Big purchases from England are noted in the civic records of Bordeaux during a time of scarcity and high prices in 1406–7. The amount sent from Bristol it is impossible to ascertain, since corn was sometimes exempt from duty. That Bristol merchants took some share in provisioning Bordeaux and Bayonne is evident, however, not only from the customs accounts, but also from the licences granted when the export of corn was otherwise forbidden. Thus corn to the value of nearly £100 was shipped from Bristol to Bordeaux in 1442–3; and between 1449 and 1452, when Bordeaux was hemmed in by conquering French armies, Harry May and Patrick Davy of Bristol, with David Selly of Westminster, were commissioned to buy " grain, flesh, and fish " to victual Bordeaux.[58]

This traffic, in which England exchanged her cloth for the wealth of the Gascons, was indeed " gret plesur to all estatez and degreez, grete richesse and by the myght of such Nave, gret defence for all this lond ". Bordeaux and Bayonne likewise became through it exceedingly opulent. Firmer and firmer economic bonds strengthened their political union under the English crown, and judicious English rulers gave them every opportunity of managing their own affairs as they pleased, unfettered by interfering officials and mulcted of a minimum of taxation by the central authority. Truly had Froissart surmised in 1399 that Bordeaux and Bayonne " wyll never tourne Frenche, for they cannat lyve in their daunger nor they canne nat suffre the extorcyon and pollinge of the Frenchemen; for under us they lyve franke and free, and if the Frenchemen shulde be lordes over them they shulde be taxed and tayled and retayled two or thre tymes in a yere the whiche they are nat nowe accustomed unto, which shulde be a harde thyng nowe for them to begynne ". The lot of Gascon cities was indeed a striking contrast to the feudal oppression and the high taxation and official interference under which French towns languished, and eager was their desire to remain under the lenient rule of the English.[59]

The fortunes of the Gascon trade were, however, closely involved in the fortunes of the Hundred Years War and, as the French gradually reconquered Gascony until the link of allegiance to England which had endured for three centuries was snapped, marked changes took place in its volume and character. Trade had already suffered when at the opening of the fifteenth century the English dominion in Southern France had shrunk to little beyond Bordeaux and Bayonne. Goods were more expensive, for higher duties were levied on the inland enemy districts, and these retaliated by extorting duties on merchandise from English possessions. In 1406 La Réole, for instance, which had hitherto been exempt from customs at Bordeaux, became French. Bordeaux forthwith took 10 per cent on her wines and a tax on other goods; but a petition to the French king's lieutenant in Guienne secured for La Réole permission to exact precisely similar duties on all merchandise taken down the Garonne by the English. In 1435, however, she came again under English rule, and her privileges at Bordeaux were restored. Trade was now not only more costly, but also more precarious, both on account of the havoc wrought by war and epidemics on land and through assaults at sea. In spite of the nominal truce, Gascony was attacked in one place after another in the first decade of the century, and on at least one occasion all shipping was held up in the Garonne. Kings gave little help; messages of distress were sent in desperation to towns such as Bristol; the Archbishop lamented that he had cried out till he was hoarse, and that nothing could save the country but the feebleness of the French.[60] When at last English merchantmen had assisted in reopening the river and another truce had been signed in 1407, trade revived, and in 1409-10 nine Bristol ships left Bordeaux heavily laden with wine.

During the next fifteen years local levies raised at Bordeaux made a determined effort to recapture the wine districts, and won back strongholds such as St. Macaire and La Réole, which controlled the Garonne route. From that time until 1451 Gascony remained almost entirely outside the theatre of war, except for a Spanish raid on Bayonne, and for the sudden alarming incursions of the French in 1438, and again in 1443, when the great fortress of Dax capitulated.[61] In this period of virtual immunity from war, Gascony, though often tormented by *routiers*, enjoyed considerable prosperity. Her progress was in striking contrast to the fate of the once rich land between the Loire, the Seine, and the Somme; this lay overgrown with thorns and brambles, and even the very sheep and swine fled at the familiar sound of the alarm bell. But in Gascony trade flourished, and it is remarkable that in spite of the long and costly wars, of lawlessness on the sea, and of misgovernment in England, imports of wine to Bristol increased markedly during this period, reaching their maximum on the eve of England's final defeat, at a figure never exceeded throughout the Yorkist and Lancastrian period. This conclusion is suggested by an investigation of the enrolled customs accounts. Here it appears that the wine imports reached their highest figure between 1440 and 1448, and that exports of cloth were largest about the same time. It is impossible precisely to distinguish the origin of these imports, but the Bordeaux accounts confirm the inference that this expansion marks an increase especially in wine from Gascony. These show, for instance, that in the autumn only of 1443, six Bristol ships left Bordeaux with 1,614 tuns of wine [62]; this is almost as much as Bristol's total annual import of wine from all sources early in the century. Again, whereas in 1409-10, of over 200 ships of all nationalities leaving Bordeaux, only two had carried as much as 170 tuns, 170 was now the average cargo of Bristol's ships, while the *Marie de Wilshore* carried as much as 249 tuns, 40 per cent more than any ship in 1407-8. And these were no exceptional cargoes, as later accounts prove.

This remarkable expansion of Bristol's trade with Gascony in the last years of English rule was not, however, due solely to Gascony's immunity from war, nor to the increased size of Bristol's ships and the progressive enterprise of her merchants. It is surely no mere coincidence that the year 1444 saw the successful petition of the Commons that the English might buy wines freely in the Haut Pays, and also the signing of the five years' truce between England and France, a truce that was later on to cost the Duke of Suffolk his head. Ships were then no longer in peril from organized attacks of the enemy; no longer were they liable constantly to be diverted from their peaceful business by being commandeered for the king's service, as were the Bristol ships in the two years preceding the truce. Further, the elaborate scheme of 1443 for the safeguarding of the seas by a permanent naval force, to which Bristol contributed two ships,[63] may not have been without effect, even though these ships were not themselves of blameless reputation. Yet more welcome to the merchants, no doubt, was definite permission to take the law into their own hands. They had in vain petitioned for the repeal of the stringent statute of 1414 against breakers of truces and safe-conducts, but between 1435 and 1451 this was suspended and they were free to recoup themselves to any extent they thought fit by privateering.[64] This new privilege naturally brought about an increase in piracy, but it probably stimulated rather than discouraged enterprise.

This rapid progress of Bristol's merchants was shortly, however, to be checked by circumstances beyond their control. While England's political power in France had been waning gradually, her commercial collapse was to come with startling suddenness. In 1449 England and France went to war once more. On the conclusion of the rapid reconquest of Normandy in that year, the French took up with ardour the reconquest of Gascony, and her strongholds fell one after another before their advance. Finally, when Bourg and Blaye, Libourne and St. Emilion, and almost every Gascon fortress except Bayonne had capitulated, and when the Gironde was swept by French ships, Bordeaux, surrounded by 30,000 French troops, despairing of the help that the English continually promised and never sent, at last sued for peace with her own countrymen (12th June, 1451). Even then she did not humble herself. Full of consideration were her conquerors, eager to conciliate these proud and wealthy citizens, all that they required was that they should promise to be good and loyal Frenchmen. Their privileges were all confirmed, merchants were to pay only the accustomed dues, and those who wished to do so were free to depart under safe-conduct within six months.[65] Bayonne, however, suffered a worse fate. Her gates were still closed to the French, and a month later Bristol was ordered to provide ships and mariners for a relieving force. Once more the procrastinating English government was too late, for on 21st August Bayonne was compelled to surrender, all the goods of the English there were forfeited, and so were the privileges of the town.[66] But so much had the Bordelais come to depend upon England, and so firm was their allegiance to English rule, that they would not become good and loyal Frenchmen. Chafing beneath the yoke of their conquerors, who foolishly provoked them with levies of tribute and of soldiers, they opened their gates to the Earl of Shrewsbury in the following year, and before the year ended had chased the French from the rich valleys of the Garonne and the Dordogne. When their city was at last, after a spirited resistance, recaptured by the French in 1453, they were severely punished for their revolt. Their privileges were suspended, a crushing indemnity was imposed, and twenty of the leaders of the defence had to be surrendered. Six months later the harshness of the terms was in some degree mitigated, but a tax of 25 sous per tun was levied on all wines exported, and further duties on almost all other exports and imports; while instead of being virtually self-governing, Bordeaux became part of an increasingly centralized state with a council nominated largely by the king.[67]

Trade with the English now ceased, for English merchants were enemy aliens who could only with difficulty recover their own goods with the help of foreign ships.[68] Thus fell Bordeaux from her former greatness; poverty-stricken, oppressed with taxation, and threatened with famine, her vineyards lay desolate, and her houses empty.

Many of the Gascons came to England, preferring English to French rule, and the number of Bristol's merchants was increased by several of these immigrants. Such were Barnard Bensyn " late of Bordeaux, merchant "; Moses Conterayn, " Gascon and merchant of Bordeaux ", who became one of Bristol's most active merchants, and probably also William Lombard, " merchant of Bordeaux," who in 1488 was buried in St. Nicholas' church, Bristol, and whose will is inscribed in the *Great Red Book*. Many also of those who lost property in Gascony or were captured and had to find ransoms, took to trade to recoup themselves, and the *Great Red Book* abounds in copies of safe-conducts granted at their request; one is for Petronilla, wife of

Bertram de Montferrant, who lost all her goods in Bordeaux and came to England relying on the king; another is for John Ducastet who likewise lost his goods and came to England; another for John Freme, merchant of Bristol, who with others had fallen into the hands of the French and were " ad financiam ducentarum librarum sterling ultra les droitz positi ".[69]

Those merchants who remained in Gascony attempted to find outlets for their wares to England through other parts of France. Bristol's French trade had hitherto been almost exclusively with Gascony. Breton boats had sometimes visited her, from Penmarch, Vannes, Conquet, S. Pol de Léon, Quimper, Quimperle, Concarneau, Nantes, Crozon, and Guarande. But they were usually on their way from ports other than their own, and Bretons were known to Bristol men chiefly as pirates, plundering more ships than they loaded peacefully, and preying on those who passed their rocky coasts bound for the harbours of the south. Neither had Bristol in the past dealt much with Normandy or Flanders, though Bristol merchants were sometimes in Flanders on business, and sometimes shipped goods from Ireland thither. Occasionally a foreign ship called on its way to or from Flanders with hops, wainscot, tar, and madder, but Flanders was more in need of Irish produce such as hides which she could procure direct, and she and Bristol, each with their flourishing cloth industry, had little to give each other. But now, when the direct trade with Gascony was checked, new routes were explored. Wine was brought from ports in Brittany, which, profiting from the embarrassments of England and France, developed her shipping just as she developed her manufactures with the aid of skilled refugees from the English provinces. Even more interesting is the shipment of woad from Caen, the first clear indication of trade between Bristol and Normandy.[70]

These new routes, cumbrous and expensive as compared with the old, were, however, never extensively developed by Bristol. For in 1461, with the accession of Edward IV in England and Louis XI in France, there came an opportunity of recovering the more profitable trade with Gascony. Louis' predecessor, Charles VII, had rudely conquered and tried to crush the Gascons. But the astute Louis, " the greatest traveller to win a man that might do him service or harm," realized that in the struggle of the crown to build up a united nation the bourgeois were his strongest support against the nobles. He therefore won their favour by granting privileges to the towns, restoring to many of those in Gascony a large measure of the autonomy which they had enjoyed under English rule. Bordeaux recovered its privileges, foreigners were encouraged to occupy its empty houses, exiles were recalled and in 1463, on the petition of the town, trade with England was again permitted. Bristol merchants hastened to take advantage of the renewed opportunity, and went as of old in autumn or spring to seek Gascon wines. The fall in imports of wine was checked and recovery began. Tiresome restrictions, however, still hampered the merchant. Safe-conducts were compulsory; these had to be purchased for a large sum, and lasted only for a year or two. Customs dues were still heavy, and wines could only be purchased inland from Bordeaux cititzens and under French supervision. Every ship had to stop on the way to Bordeaux, first at Soulac to fetch her permit, then at Blaye to be certified as a genuine merchantman and to deposit all arms; in each case a fee had to be paid. At Bordeaux merchants had to obtain a special licence, lasting only a month, to dwell in the city; they might lodge only in specified houses, and might not emerge thence before 7 a.m. or after 5 p.m. These petty annoyances in Bordeaux itself had their counterpart in similar restrictions on foreigners in Bristol. No ship was allowed into port until it had forwarded its safe-conduct from Kingrode, had been inspected by officials in the city, and had deposited all its arms. Every Frenchman, merchant or mariner, must purchase a licence to be kept ever on his person; he must dwell in the lodgings assigned to him, and must always wear a white cross upon his shoulder. Intercourse therefore was still difficult and precarious. Moreover, England and France were not yet formally at peace. Each sought opportunity to strike a blow at his adversary, and, in spite of safe-conducts, many boats fell a victim to pirates or privateers.[71]

It was with the Treaty of Picquigny in 1475 that trade with Gascony made a further marked recovery. Then at last the long rivalry between the two nations was brought to a formal close, and the merchant was encouraged not only by the greater security thus given, but by the removal of many hindrances. Now, as of old, he might sail freely to Bordeaux, and there dwell where he pleased for as long as he pleased as freely as any of its citizens. Customs and dues were modified, and the only restrictions remaining were those on the purchase of wine.

Commines, true type of the diligent chronicler of the time, in describing this treaty details elaborately those articles touching the wars of kings and their unruly barons, adding but briefly—"Divers other trifling articles there were touching matters of entercourse, which I overpasse." The people of Bordeaux, however, rightly estimated the worth of this treaty's "trifling" commercial provisions, gratefully naming it the "paix marchande". For Louis XI saw further ahead than most of his contemporaries in insisting that political separation should not imply economic estrangement, and Edward IV had the shrewd sense to win the advantages of peace by the display of war, and thus to revive England's languishing commerce. Before long Bristol's imports of wine had risen to a level at least as high as at the beginning of the century, while her exports of cloth reached an average equal to that during their zenith before the loss of Gascony.

So much did the English profit from the removal of hindrances, that, thirty years after their expulsion, it was said that during the vintage season there were no less than 6,000 of them in the city of Bordeaux.[72]

§ 4

The Iberian Peninsula

The author of the *Libelle of Englyshe Polycye*, writing probably in 1436, calls the Englishman a donkey for not seizing his opportunities of trade with Spain. Why does he allow Spanish ships, laden with wine and other precious wares, to sail up the English Channel direct to Flanders, there to traffic with the Low Countries for cloth made of English wool? Why does he not detain them in English ports, and himself sell them cloth made in his own country:

> "Thanne may hit not synke in mannes brayne,
> But that hit most, this marchaundy of Spayne,
> Bothe oute and inne by oure coostes passe?
> He that seyth nay in wytte is lyche an asse." [73]

Bristol, however, hardly deserved the taunt. Her busy looms and mills were each year contributing about 6,000 pieces to that steadily increasing output of English cloth which was now rapidly replacing England's export of wool. Already a few Spanish ships were visiting Bristol and taking thence large quantities of cloth, while many Bristol ships were sailing each year to Spain, heavily laden, to exchange their cargoes of cloth for the luxuries of the south.

Spanish produce was particularly welcome in England as England's hold on Gascony weakened. Already at the opening of the century Spanish wines were supplementing those of France, though even at its close the amount imported to Bristol from Spain did not exceed a quarter of that which came from Gascony. The wine ships from Spain, like those from France, protected themselves by sailing together in a fleet during the vintage season and in spring, and on one occasion nine of them arrived together in Bristol.[74] But wine, though one of the chief, was by no means the only import from Spain, and the increasing variety of luxuries brought to Bristol points certainly to a rising standard of comfort in England. Foreign fruit such as figs, raisins, and dates, was especially welcome during the winter months, but in summer the expense of transport was not worth while. Thus when Moses Conterayn was shipping wheat at Bristol in the *John de la Passage*, he asked the master, Nicholas Palmer, to sail to Southern Spain, there to sell the wheat on his behalf and to reload with "certain tons of fruit called figs and raisins ".[75] Palmer did this, but because of great tempests and "lack of wind and weather" he had to put into so many ports on the way that he only reached England ɩat Easter. The season was then too far advanced for the fruit to be profitably sold, and Conterayn sued Palmer for damages in the Tolsey Court at Bristol.

Other southern delicacies came also for the housewife in increasing quantities during the century—honey, almonds, licorice, and saffron, with vinegar, lard, and occasionally tunny-fish and rice. But the Spanish trade was not merely one in luxuries. Valuable raw materials came also for England's industries. Iron (probably from the Cantabrian mountains) is scarcely mentioned in early Bristol accounts of the century, but it soon became one of Spain's chief exports to Bristol, and was usually shipped in the summer when the wine and fruit seasons were over, together with manufactured iron goods, from brigandines, crossbows, and anchors down to nails and combs, probably for the wool-combers. Southern Spain was one of the chief sources of supply for oil, so that "laden with wine and oil" was a common description of ships which had suffered shipwreck or piracy. Oil also came in the form of ready-made soap from Castile, and as "smigmates", a species of soap, as may be inferred from the fact that some was purchased at Durham for washing the linen of the lord prior. Other raw materials included wax, tallow, rosin, tar, white cork, beaver, boards, bowstaves, and grindstones, while the dyers obtained alum used in fixing the dyes, and sometimes the scarlet dye which came more often from Portugal. Woad came also now and again from the ports of North-East Spain, but this had probably found its way thither from Southern France, just as Spanish iron was sometimes shipped from Bayonne. Leather of Cordova had already given more than one word to the English language, for merchants dealt often in Cordovan, while kid skins, goat skins, and other "wild ware" were expecially useful for laces and such articles as demanded strong leather, so that cheap imitations were sometimes made in England to resemble the "Civill (i.e. Seville) and Spannish skynnes ".[76]

The entry most commonly met with after wine, oil, and fruit, is that of salt. The low sand dunes in the south-west of Spain, broken by lagoons, lent themselves to its production, and it was of great importance for England's fishing industry.

Variety was thus the conspicuous feature of imports from Spain :—

"fygues, raysyns, wyne, bastarde and dates,
And lycorys, Syvyle oyle and also grayne,
Whyte Castell sope and wax is not in vayne,
Iren, wolle, wadmole, gotefel, kydefel also,
(For poyntmakers full nedeful be the ij.)
Saffron, quicksilver." [77]

In comparison with these varied luxuries and raw materials the goods shipped from Bristol to Spain seem uninteresting, though significant, since vessels were usually laden almost entirely with cloth. Most of this was ungrained broadcloth, of which a ship on one occasion took over 200 pieces,[78] though sometimes cheaper qualities were sent. Thus Henry Vaughan alleged that he shipped 136 broad cloths, 32 narrow cloths, and 20 cloths of Welsh frieze in the *Mary* of Ipusco " whereof Ochoa Daramayo after God was master ".[79] In this same ship a Spanish merchant once took 18 broad cloths and 124 kersies. Freize of Kendal and Irish mantles went also occasionally. Thus it would appear that Spain was becoming more and more directly indebted to England for her cloth, and found less need to ship " full craftily " to Flanders figs, raisins, and the like, there to reload with Flemish cloth made of English wool. While cloth was the regular export from Bristol to Spain, fish such as herring and hake was sometimes included in the cargo, with tanned hides, lead, tin, and now and then carved alabaster. But the only considerable export after cloth was corn and beans, sent probably at times of superfluity in England and dearth in Spain. The *Mary* of Guetaria was once, except for five broad cloths, entirely charged with corn, and during three months in 1475 there were twelve shipments of corn from Bristol, valued in the customs at nearly £400. The arrival of these ships, perhaps as many as twenty in one summer, laden with cloth and corn, must have been of no little importance to the Spaniards, and to Bristol the trade was equally advantageous since Spain with its neighbour Portugal were the nearest lands whence such products as oil, figs, and raisins could be procured.

To the Bristol merchant Spain implied Castile ; with Aragon he had no dealings. Southwards his ships sailed to far-famed Seville, seeking wine, oil, or fruit, sometimes calling on the way at Saltes, Huelva, or S. Lucar Barrameda. Spanish ships and seamen ventured with them in the trade, but these came not from the south, but from those rocky northern shores which, like the coasts of Cornwall, bred a race of seamen as bold as they were unscrupulous. In Guipuscoa and its neighbouring provinces of Biscay and Santander there were at least twelve havens whose ships visited Bristol in the fifteenth century—Fuenterrabia, Passage, Renteria, San Sebastian, Guetaria, Deva, Motrico, Bilbao, Portugalete, Castro, La Redo, and Santander. Ambassadors of Guipuscoa came often to negotiate with Edward IV, and its merchants did much business with Bristol, where some, like Domingo de Fuenterrabia, were admitted to the liberties of the Staple. Their ships and their seamen were frequently used by Bristol merchants. Henry Vaughan, amongst others, shipped cloth in vessels of Guetaria, and the *S. Sebastien* of Guetaria, when in Flanders, was once freighted by Bristol merchants with madder, tar, wainscots, and hops, and brought to Bristol, where her Spanish captain took on board in his own name a cargo of English and Welsh cloth for the return voyage to Spain. This district especially was haunted by pirates, as may be gathered from Bristol's complaints, such as this typical one of about 1400 : four Biscay ships had captured the *Trinity* on her way from Seville, and another Biscay ship had captured the *Mary*; the *Katherine* had been seized by a ship of Motrico, and the *Alison* by four ships of Santander. Westwards, beyond Santander, the coast was a forbidding one, with only " verie naughty havens for great shippes " until Galicia was reached. There where the mountains, hitherto parallel to the shore, run out into the sea, deep sheltered gulfs are hidden between their ridges. Yet these really good ports in Galicia seem scarcely to have been used by Bristol, perhaps because of their distance from the chief wine and iron districts. Only one kind of traffic was carried on there, that in pilgrims for the shrine of St. James at Compostella. Bristol ships could carry a hundred or more of these wayfarers, and were often licensed to do so. It seems likely that they took some of their passengers on board at Plymouth, where they sometimes called on the way, and those unaccustomed to the sea would surely prefer the four days' voyage thence to the prolonged woes, so vividly pictured in a late mediaeval poem, of those who took the sea—

" At Sandwyche, or at Wynchylsee,
At Brystow, or where that hit bee." [80]

Some pilgrims certainly ventured the whole way from Bristol. Such were those who on their way stole some of the books for which the library of All Saints Church was renowned ; so highly prized were these volumes that two priests were sent after them, and a special iron cage was meanwhile made for their custody. The accounts of All Saints also contain entries of gifts from those on their way to St. James.

There is no record of pilgrims entrusting themselves to Spaniards, but in other branches of traffic Spaniards, little in evidence early in the century, took an increasingly active part. Sometimes they shipped in their own and sometimes in English vessels. Frequently, even when a Spanish ship carried mainly goods of English merchants, the Spanish captain himself took a share in the venture, as did John Renamond of the *James* of Guipuscoa, and at least one Spanish captain was admitted to the liberties of the Staple in Bristol. Prominent English merchants sometimes acted as factors for the foreigner, as did Jordan Spryng, " factor for John de Varrole merchant and owner of the *Marie* of Navarre," and throughout the century Englishmen and Spaniards, jointly or severally, seem entirely to have controlled the Spanish trade with Bristol in contrast to that with other ports. Italians, as the *Libelle* complains, had got into their hands much of the Spanish trade with London and Southampton, but Bristol, with its flourishing native trade, was singularly free from their influence. Its independence and its close co-operation with Spanish merchants, is illustrated by a petition from certain aggrieved Genoese, who had freighted the *Julian* in Spain with wine, oil, and other goods for London or Southampton. Since her master, Godfred de Sasiola, had taken her to Bristol instead, he had there been arrested at the suit of the Italian merchants. These complained, however, that the mayor and other great officers and merchants of Bristol owe the nation of Spain "so great love and affiance" that they propose to let the merchandise remain in Bristol, and to make the Genoese pay for its freight.[81]

Spanish ships, like Spanish merchants, increased noticeably in numbers during the century, and merchants of either country employed each other's ships and seamen as occasion served. Sometimes a partnership of Bristol merchants used almost the whole tunnage of a Spanish vessel, as when the *James* of Guipuscoa arrived at Bristol with goods of John Shipward and his associates, and left with cloth of William Canynges and his associates, in both cases in the charge of English factors. While early in the century a Spanish ship was seldom seen in Bristol, towards its close about the same number of Spanish as of Bristol ships seem to have been engaged in the trade. It is clear, therefore, that Spaniards were becoming more actively concerned in intercourse with Bristol during the century. No precise estimate, however, is possible of the general growth of the trade. For the detailed customs accounts survive only in fragments and even conclusions drawn from these may be very misleading, when in any one year as many as seven Spanish ships might fall a prey to pirates.[82]

This constant peril from pirates made the Spanish trade, profitable though it was, the most precarious of all Bristol's regular enterprises. Piracy was endemic owing to the doubtful relations between the rulers of England and of Castile. For during the Hundred Years War Castile had allowed herself, in spite of her goodwill towards England itself, to be drawn into an unusually prolonged alliance with France against the neighbouring English provinces. This alliance lasted almost without interruption for 130 years, and was renewed by each successive sovereign. Yet so anxious was Castile to live at peace with all men except the Moors, that France could scarcely persuade her to translate words into action, and even when she did make war upon the English she hastened to conclude peace at the earliest possible moment.[83] The English, not unnaturally, regarded this long-standing, though passive, ally of France as their "notorious enemy". Hence sea-rovers on either side plundered with impunity, knowing that merchants had slight chance of restitution. If indeed an interval of peace came, the successul pirate might be required to disgorge his gains. When, for instance, the truce of 1403 included England as an ally of both Portugal and Castile, there was a sudden increase not, as might appear, in piracy but in the number of commissions appointed to deal with it, and inquiries were set on foot concerning no less than seven Spanish ships, captured in October, 1403, by a gang under Thomas Norton of Bristol, and the notorious John Hawley. These efforts were of little avail, for Hawley at least was a man of considerable influence who would not lightly yield what he had won at the risk of his life. In fact, such prominent pirates as he were often themselves on the commissions, and even less redoubtable rovers, when alliances were being constantly made and unmade, could easily plead that they had not been present when the sheriff proclaimed the truce. Thus seldom and only with difficulty could Spanish or English merchants secure legal redress. Despairing of it, both were driven to reprisals, with or without the sanction of their governments. When William Skyrmot's ship the *Petre* of Bristol, bound with cloth for Bayonne in 1449, was captured by a ship of Motrico and taken to Spain, Skyrmot sued vainly before the king of Castile, and was finally permitted by the king of England to retain the *Marie* of Motrico, then lying at Bristol under arrest. The king of Castile once issued letters of marque against all English subjects, but the more cautious Edward IV, anxious to avoid any vigorous action, and to stand well with both parties, indemnified at the same time both Spanish and English merchants. Thus in 1476 he granted 3,000 crowns from the customs revenue as an indemnity to the men of Guipuscoa, and five years later 3,600 crowns to one of his own merchants, John Payn, who had fallen a victim to them. Payn, a merchant of Brisol, in spite of letters of safe-conduct bearing the seal of the province of Guipuscoa, had under letters of marque been seized at Deva with his partner John George and his ship and goods. Four times he secured letters from the king of England "for the reformation of his injuries", once to the king of Castile and thrice to the governors of Guipuscoa. These he delivered himself, crossing three times to Spain for the purpose, but no reply was vouchsafed. Then "by the advice of learned council in those parts following the law there" he protested to the king of Castile by writing placed on the doors of his chamber and those of his council. For this John George was killed and John Payn for fear of death "retreated to England". Remonstrances now and again passed to and fro between the governments, but they were often answered merely by counter remonstrances; when the king of England wrote in 1411, asking for the restitution of the *Marie* of Bristol, the queen of Castile wrote back that she could not reply to the request since she had not yet received an answer to her last letter.[84]

Gradually, however, after the Hundred Years War was over, and the English were no longer near neighbours of the Spaniards in Southern France, the two peoples came together and the bonds between Castile and France were loosed. In 1466 a formal treaty of peace was concluded. This new alliance was from time to time almost nullified, as when France renewed her alliance in 1470 and again in 1478; merchants still made frequent complaint of ill-treatment; and it was not until the advent of the Tudors that the new friendship was finally sealed by the marriage of Prince Arthur with Katherine of Aragon. By this time, however, the route from Bristol to Spain was considered so safe that letters of state were not even written in cipher. Bristol was now evidently one of the principal ports for Spain. The ambassador De Puebla, very likely on his way from Spain, wrote home in 1495 from Bristol. Two years later, Ferdinand and Isabella directed him to select a trustworthy person in Bristol to receive and forward their letters. It was through Bristol that the negotiations for the marriage of Katherine of Aragon were carried on, and Bristol was named as one of the fittest ports for her arrival.[85]

There is a marked contrast between the dealings of Bristol with Castile and with Portugal, since Portugal's relations with England were consistently friendly. These two states were naturally disposed to be allies, since neither of them was on good terms with Castile. There was also kinship between their dynasties, and the men of both countries were born seamen and adventurers. Prince Henry the Navigator was great-nephew to the Black Prince, and he and his successors made their little country the foremost maritime power in Europe. The friendship sealed by the Treaty of Windsor in 1386 between Richard II and John I of Portugal, lasted on in spite of temporary ruptures through acts of violence and changes of dynasty in England; and throughout the fifteenth century the provisions made in this charter of commerce were confirmed, and the kings of both countries were pledged to punish infractions of it. Privileges hitherto enjoyed by the merchants of Genoa and Pisa only were now extended to merchants of England, who were as secure in Lisbon or Oporto as were natives of Portugal. Portugal's desire to favour them showed itself also in the choice of a special proctor at Lisbon to ensure prompt payment for cloth sold; in the appointment of a single judge in place of a jury of foreigners to settle disputes between English and Portuguese; and in the greater security from the malpractices of customs officials afforded them in response to their petitions of 1454 and 1458.[86]

The Bristol merchant had thus exceptional opportunities of doing business unmolested in Lisbon and Oporto. Moreover, he found there goods specially acceptable in England. Although Portugal is in many places infertile, the vines grown in its sheltered valleys rivalled those of Gascony and competed favourably with those of Castile. When the Hundred Years War ended, it was only at exorbitant prices, by French favour and under French supervision, that English merchants could buy wine in Gascony, and trade with Castile, their other chief source of supply, was still precarious. Hence the demand grew for wine from Portugal. Whereas two Bristol customs accounts early in the century mention wines only from Gascony and Spain, in the winter and spring of 1465-6 six ships came from Portugal bringing nearly 500 tuns of wine, and from this time such entries recur in each account. Nor was wine the only import. For many years cork was obtainable only from Portugal and sugar from Portugal's first colony, Madeira. Sugar was a luxury unknown to the author of the *Libelle*, and occurs for the first time as an import to Bristol in a ledger of the time of Henry VI. From this time larger and larger consignments arrived, valued at £2 the cwt., till in 1479 one boat brought nearly 200 cwt. " Ther is also grete salt," as the merchants' handbook noted, and one summer a whole shipload of this came into Bristol, though there was never any very considerable import. Wax came also, and olive oil " wiche is most holswmyst for mannys mette and medicins ", and when old was used for wool oil. The sunny southern provinces yielded quantities of fruit, and Sir John Vasquez, who exported from England lances for the king of Portugal, once imported steel. Most valuable of all Portugal's products in England was perhaps the " grain " used in the dyeing of the precious scarlet cloth. The tiny insect—*kermes*—from which this dye was derived, grew in great plenty on a mountain in Portugal, which was England's chief source of supply.[87]

Thus, Portugal, as the *Libelle* observes, had many useful commodities to offer the English, in contrast to the " nifles, trifles " palmed off on them by some. Nor was Bristol at a loss for return cargoes. English cloth was in great demand in Portugal, and in 1482 the Portuguese even demanded that the wearing of garments of any other cloth should be forbidden. Ships often took nothing but cloth, though occasionally the monotony was varied by iron, lead, halyards, hats, barrel staves, or an alabaster reredos. Corn was sometimes sent, and ships occasionally took fish, calling perhaps in Brittany on the way home for salt for their next cargo from the bay of Bourgneuf.[88]

At first it had been the Portuguese who brought their own goods to England.[89] In the fifteenth century, however, England's seamen were overtaking those of Portugal, and the largest consignments of goods landed in Bristol were those of Bristol merchants in Bristol ships. Thus in 1479-80 only two Portuguese, but ten or eleven Bristol ships, were engaged in the trade, together with two or three ships of Brittany. The Portuguese were no doubt taken up more and more with their colonial ventures, but though they jealously tried to keep their colonial trade to themselves [90] at least one Breton ship, from Quimperle, took cloth of Bristol merchants to Madeira. Bristol seamen, even if they did not visit Madeira themselves, must have learnt much, through their constant contact with the Portuguese, of these isles in the Atlantic.

English ships seem to have carried only English goods, but Portuguese ships were often used by English merchants. Most of the well-known Bristol merchants took part in the Portuguese trade, and sixty-seven of them once contributed to the cargo of the *Mary Redcliffe* when she was bound for Portugal. Nor did the trade attract only English and Portuguese. Ever since King Diniz in 1317 had appointed a Genoese to be an Admiral in his navy, the Portuguese, with ambitions on the high seas, had availed themselves of the skill and initiative of foreigners, thus training themselves in the science of navigation. And even in the fifteenth century Italians were still in evidence in the Portuguese trade, and occasionally came to Bristol. Thus Jerome de Ozerio, merchant of Genoa, asked for a safe-conduct for himself, his factors, attorneys, and servants, and for diverse goods in the *James* of Bristol of which an Englishman, Richard William, was master.

The most frequented of all Portuguese harbours was Lisbon, whose spacious port at the outlet of the Tagus was safe from all gales except those of the west. Favoured at the expense of all other cities by royal decrees, the one place in which foreigners, by an ordinance of 1423, were permitted to buy merchandise, it had become (said one observer) as large as London. Its fine English church of San Domingo marked it out as the centre of our whole trade with Portugal—at any rate until the decree of 1451 permitted the purchase of fruit and wine in Algarve. Portuguese ships, however, sailed sometimes from Oporto, and this had one advantage over Lisbon, in that within easy reach of it grew some of the finest vines on the sunny northern slopes of the Douro valley, sheltered by the lofty Sierra de Marao. From Viana, further to the north, a cargo of steel came once in a Portuguese boat.

Though the progress of this peaceful trade between England and Portugal is in striking contrast to the story of our relations with Castile, it had perils of its own in the many pirates, Cornish, Breton, Gascon, or Castilian, who were often encountered during the long voyage involved. Especially was this the case during the disorders of the middle of the century, when Portuguese and English preyed equally upon each other's shipping in spite of royal injunctions that treaties should be kept; reprisals and counter reprisals were resorted to, and special protections applied for, as by William Canynges and John Alberton of Bristol.[91] One typical illustration may be found in documents preserved among the early chancery proceedings.[92] In 1443 the *Anthony* of Faro was laden in Algarve with fruit and wine belonging to four merchants who sailed with her—John Veilho, Gunsallo Gile, Vasqueannus, and Alfonso Gile. On her voyage she was taken captive by Hankyn Selander, one of the most notorious of west country pirates. Thereupon a ship of Henry May, the *Trinity* of Bristol, came to the rescue, and with the help of the Portuguese themselves, restored them to their ship, gave them armour for six men, and (so said the English) meat and drink for a day and a night for sixty men. In spite of his repulse, however, Hankyn again attacked the *Anthony*, captured her, put her master, merchants, and mariners on shore in Brittany, took the ship to Fowey, and there sold both her and her goods. Veilho in course of time made his way to Bristol and begged help from the mayor through Henry May. When no help was forthcoming, May wrote several letters for him " in friendly wise " to John Chirche, Stephen Stychemersh, and Piers Alfold of London, and through their good offices the case was finally brought into Chancery. Meanwhile Henry's brother, Richard May, merchant of London, was in Lisbon with goods of his own in the *George Heron*. The other merchants concerned in the *Anthony*, therefore, declaring that Henry was responsible for her fate and had acted in collusion with Hankyn, took action against Richard. All his property and his goods in the *George Heron* were seized, the ship was delayed five weeks in Lisbon so that her owners demanded heavy compensation, and finally Richard himself was cast into prison. Richard and Henry then appealed together to the Chancellor, begging him to consider the great " trouth, gode wille and favour " done by them to John Veilho and his fellow merchants of Portugal, and the " grete untrouth wrong and iniurie " done to them by John Veilho.

Veilho in his reply did not deny that Henry May brought him good cheer, though as to keeping sixty Portuguese in food and drink for a night and a day, that was impossible, since there were not more than twenty men on board, and they had " sufficience of vitailles " though " som of theym drank with them oo nyght ". He declared, however, that the English had soon wearied of well-doing, for that John Fleming, on learning that the pirate ship was English, said he would not for a great sum have done as he did, and that he would no more meddle in the matter because he had been given nothing for his pains. So the Portuguese had offered half of all the merchandise in their ship as the price of an escort to Bristol, and in spite of this the *Trinity* had left them to the mercy of Hankyn. Yet Veilho protested vigorously that had he been in Lisbon and not stranded in Brittany, Richard May should never have been molested. On the strength of this, though the *Trinity*'s men were entirely exonerated, each side had apparently to bear its own loss.

Such an incident illustrates not only the perils of the Portuguese trade, but the frequent collaboration between merchants of the two lands. One further instance may be added showing the close and friendly relations between the two in peace as well as in war. When English and Portuguese ships had together blockaded Rochelle in 1403, the men of Rochelle had retaliated by preying upon Portuguese as well as English commerce. They had captured a ship of Bristol laden with cloth and two other ships with produce of Portugal. So close was the alliance between Portugal and England that, it was said, the Portuguese were taken flying English colours, bearing the red cross on their banners in the English manner.[93]

5

The Mediterranean

The stately vessels of Venice and Genoa, bringing the luxuries of the Mediterranean and of the Far East to the shores of England, there to exchange them for her more homely wares—wool and tin and cloth—deigned not to visit Bristol. In London, in Southampton, and in Sandwich they unloaded silks and damasks, fruits and spices, finely wrought armour, delicate goldsmiths' work, and many another precious ware down to " apes and japes and marmasettes tailed ", and there they were privileged to ship staple English goods direct to southern Europe and the Levant.[94]

Yet Bristol was not quite unrepresented in this trade. Its riches were needed to minister to the growing luxury of her burghers, and therefore, when the Italian fleet lay at anchor off Southampton, Bristol cloth and other goods were dispatched thither overland, and there, no doubt, silks and spices were purchased. Thus in 1478, when the *Andrew* and the *Salva Deo* were in Southampton harbour, Petrus de Antina and Nicholas Nadale sent overland from Bristol for shipment in them a cargo of cloth and hides.[95]

But though the great fleets of the Mediterranean kept to the Channel, diverging thence for the Flemish or English ports, a stray vessel of Venice or Genoa, bound possibly for Ireland, found its way now and again into the Severn laden with goods of Spain and Portugal. Such wayfarers were more than once set upon, doubtless with joy, by Bristol mariners. A carrack of Venice in 1421 put in at Goldhap in Wales, and was there seized, with its raisins, figs, and almonds, by three ships of Bristol and a barge of Plymouth. Again a rich cargo of Balthasar Gentilis was, in 1458, brought into Bristol from a carrack wrecked near by.[96]

Great must have been the awe roused in the English mariners when their sturdy little boats met these portly Italian vessels; keen must have been their jealousy of the opulent foreigners who bore the merchandise not merely of their own states and of the East, but also of Spain, Portugal, and France; eager their desire to snatch from them the carrying trade to their own ports, and to challenge their virtual monopoly of the Mediterranean. But whereas in the vast spaces of the North Sea the claims of the Hanse might be flouted at times with impunity, the Mediterranean was an enclosed lake where traps for the intruder could easily be set at Gibraltar, Malta, or elsewhere, and from the Pillars of Hercules to the gateways of the East, where caravans discharged their precious burdens, the merchants of Venice and Genoa still reigned supreme in the early fifteenth century. In vain the English petitioned against the lavish privileges obtained with a great sum by these merchants from needy kings whose financiers they had become, begging that they might be restricted to bringing goods of their own manufacture; unable to vie with the mighty Italian cities in wealth, the little English towns received scant attention.

Nevertheless the men of Bristol, Hull, and other rising ports were not content to ply their trade only with lands where no powerful interests contested their authority. Away in the far north, as is elsewhere related, they had already recklessly ignored the monopoly of Bergen and the privileges of the Hanse, opening across uncharted seas a new route to the shadowy realm of Iceland. Now the same intrepid spirit of daring impelled them also to seek new highways for their ships in waters frequented from the dawn of history. Boldly they pushed through the Straits of Marrok to fetch for themselves the spices which they had hitherto meekly received from foreigners. The history of Bristol's earliest attempt to penetrate the Mediterranean is inseparably bound up with the name of the great pioneer Robert Sturmy, one of the most notable but least known of Bristol's citizens. His last ill-fated expedition arrested the attention of more than one fifteenth century chronicler, but the allusions to him in modern histories (like those to John Taverner of Hull, and other pioneers beyond the straits) are slight and misleading.[97] It may therefore be of interest here to set down what evidence has come to light of one commemorated in Bristol as a " ful notable worshipful marchaunt ".[98]

Little is known of his early career. In contrast to William Canynges and his distinguished family he stands out as a solitary figure of obscure origin. During the two decades in which he must have traded most actively, one year only appears in the detailed customs accounts. Hence there is no means of knowing in what goods he trafficked or with what lands he had dealings in an ordinary way. Almost his only recorded transactions are those exceptional enough to need licences; his only known ventures those which came to a tragic end. His experience as a merchant was gained in part through provisioning the king's forces in France, whither he sent corn in 1441-2, and by this time he possessed at any rate a share in a ship.[99]

By 1444 he was sufficiently well known in Bristol to be chosen bailiff. In the following year the Venetians were driven out of Egypt, and the monopoly of the Italians in the Levant was threatened. Not long after, with shrewd insight, Sturmy was planning his first recorded expedition to the Mediterranean, and procuring for it the *Cog Anne* and a special licence enabling him to share the privilege of shipping staple goods elsewhere than to Calais. Three English commodities were certain of a Mediterranean sale—wool, tin, and cloth. For cloth he needed no permit, so the licence was made out on 3rd November, 1446, for him to ship forty sacks of wool and 100 pieces of tin (26,000 lb. in weight) by his attorneys or deputies, " by way of the Straits of Morocco " to Pisa.[100] By sending to Pisa he designed to avoid Venice and Genoa, and to deal with a now humbler rival in commerce, namely Florence. But the *Cog Anne*'s journey was not to end at Pisa. For she was on her way to fetch from the gateways of the East the spices—pepper, ginger, and the like—which were the most coveted of the infidels' goods. For this, what outward freight could be better than pilgrims for the Holy Sepulchre?

In 1446, then, the *Cog Anne*, with 160 pilgrims and a crew of thirty-seven, charged with 20½ sacks and 12 cloves of wool, and probably other goods too, set sail from Kingrode for Pisa. Tin may have been taken on board at some Cornish or Devon port. Who was the luckless captain, and who went as Sturmey's representative to parley with the Turks, is unknown. Calling at Seville, she passed the ill-omened straits, defiantly entered the Mediterranean, and, perhaps because she was quite an unexpected apparition, arrived safely at Joppa, her goal, and landed her pilgrims. These travellers very likely returned by the overland route, then often preferred to the long journey by sea. At any rate, the *Cog Anne* did her business and set out for home without them. It is not known whether she had secured her spices, for on a dark and gloomy night in mid-winter (23rd December), as she sailed along the rugged coast of southern Greece, there arose a sudden tempest and a mighty wind; the *Cog Anne* was driven onto the rocks off the island of Modon and dashed to pieces, and there her whole crew perished " to the extreme grief of their wives and their friends at Bristol ". Then came a certain faithful bishop of Modon, who gave honourable burial to the thirty-seven bodies, and built and consecrated a chapel from which prayers might arise for the souls of these ill-fated adventurers. Such is the story, as given in two places by William of Worcester. How great a sensation the calamity made is apparent from the stress laid on it in his usually terse and unemotional pages.[101]

Sturmy seems to have been neither ruined nor daunted by so melancholy a shattering of his hopes—he had at least not fallen into the clutches of the grasping Italians, whom his petty traffickers must have dreaded more than the elements. During the next ten years he figures as a prosperous and respected (*venerabilis*) citizen, doing his duty in such civic offices as only a man of wealth could afford to fill. We find him attending a meeting of the town council (in 1450) to arrange for the spending of money bequeathed by a fellow merchant for the repair of the town walls; being chosen (in 1451) as sheriff; assisting (in 1452) to pass a decree degrading from office an unworthy steward; and finally elected by his fellow-councillors as their mayor for 1453-4. More councils had now to be attended, ordinances for the welfare of the town passed, elections presided over, industrial disputes between masters and men settled; courts held constantly— the Tolsey court sat at least three times a week; quarrels heard between natives and aliens, customs officer and refractory shipowner, and judgment given sometimes under threat of vengeance from the loser. Royal mandates, too, had to be carried out, such as that to Sturmy and three others to levy £150 in Bristol for the wages of certain lords and others associated with them for the keeping of the sea. A special effort had been made this year under the new Protectorate to remedy the chronic state of piracy on the seas, and it had been ordained in Parliament that money should be collected promptly from the chief ports. Bristol's allotted share was more than that of any city except London, yet so public-spirited was Sturmy, or so thoughtful for royal favours to come, that he further assisted matters himself by making " new at Brystow ... a stately vessell, only for the warre ". Prominent in private as in public life, he was long remembered for his liberal hospitality and his generosity to fellow-merchants whether foreign or otherwise. We can well imagine him in his fur-trimmed gown of rich scarlet and his golden girdle, with the help of Mistress Ellen his wife sumptuously entertaining in his hall some distinguished visitors from foreign parts, and keenly questioning them on the distant lands which he purposed to visit.[102]

In these years of strenuous public duty, Sturmy can have had little time for business enterprises out of the usual, but as soon as his mayoralty was over, new ventures claimed him. Again in 1456 he procured a licence to take pilgrims, this time to Compostella, to the number of sixty in his own ship the *Katharine Sturmy*. Very likely this was the one from Bristol which joined company with five others at Plymouth.[103] This voyage was for the *Katharine* but a prelude to a far more daring one the following year. By 1457, when English merchants, shut out from Gascony, must have had much cloth on their hands, the Italian merchants were losing their grip on the Levant as the tide of Ottoman invasion steadily advanced. When Constantinople at last fell in 1453, Genoa lost her rich colony at Pera, and her merchants were becoming more and more exhausted by the struggle to protect their Black Sea colonies from the Turks as well as their western possessions from the growing menace of the Catalan fleet. Venice, with greater influence in the Near East by reason of her situation and her superior naval strength, was still able to conclude a treaty with the Sultan preserving her rights of free trade and of self-government in Constantinople. Such a time of upheaval must have seemed opportune to Sturmy, who had the vigour and initiative to adapt old resources to changing needs. Once again he resolved that an English ship should fetch spices from the Levant, venturing not alone, but with two attendant caravels, and that he himself would go with them. Once again, on 8th February, 1457, a licence was procured. Its figures give some idea of the magnitude of the venture conceived by Sturmy. For even if he sold a part of the licence to other merchants, it indicates an English Mediterranean enterprise of an altogether exceptional character. He had permission to ship 100 fothers of lead, 10,000 pieces of tin, 600 sarplers of wool, and 6,000 pieces of cloth—that is cloth then worth at least £20,000. Security to the extent of 500 marks was to be left with the customers that the goods were to be sent " beyond the mountains by the straits of Marrok " and nowhere else, and a certificate of their unloading was to be delivered within one year. A month later Sturmy procured a further licence for 40 quarters of wheat to be carried to Italy with other goods. Three months more must have been spent with John Eyton, who provided one of the ships, in repairing and victualling them, and in collecting cargo. At last on 27th June Sturmy made his will, beginning as follows :—" In the name of God, Amen. The 27 day of June in the yere of our Lord m^{l}cccc^{mo} lvii, I, Robert Sturmy, Burgeys and marchant of Bristowe, make my Testament in this wise. First I bequethe my soule to God and to our Lady Seint Mary, and to alle þe seintes of hevyn, and for as much as I am now passinge over the see under the mercy of god I bequethe my body to be buryed ther as is moost plesing to God." He must have been hoping for considerable profits from this voyage, for the legacies to his family and to his servants were to be doubled if his ship returned in safety, many more masses were to be sung for his soul, and further sums of money were to be given to the overseers of his will, the Vicar of St. Nicholas and a Ludlow draper.[104]

There is no clue as to the date of embarkation or as to the precise cargo, though it seems most probable that the *Katharine* set out in 1457. Safely she sailed into the Mediterranean and on into " divers parts of the Levant " (" hetheness ", as the London chronicler expresses it), " and other parts of the East ". Of this stage of the trip only hearsay reached the chronicler, though official documents amply corroborate the main facts. Then, continues Fabyan, " for so much as the fame ran upon him, that he had gotten some green pepper and other spices to have set and sown in England (as the fame went)," the Genoese determined that the *Katharine* should never reach home. So they lay in wait for Sturmy near Malta, and there they spoiled his ship and another.[105]

Thus provokingly brief are State records and chronicles alike, but, whatever the damage done, the outrage roused the wrath of the English. All the Genoese in London (their chief English depot) were arrested and incarcerated in the Fleet, and their goods were confiscated. Relations between England and Genoa were further complicated at this time, since in 1458 Genoa, desperately seeking aid against the Turks and against Alfonso of Naples with his troublesome Catalan fleet, had persuaded Charles VII of France to become her overlord. In that year, therefore, French soldiers were assisting to defend the harbour of Genoa against the Catalans. Moreover, French ships had in the previous year been responsible for the sacking of Sandwich and the burning of Fowey, and were now being vigorously chastised with those of their allies the Castilians by the Earl of Warwick. It is therefore highly probable that the French instigated the seizure of Sturmy's ships by the Genoese. Indeed, it has even been suggested that the arrest of their ships and goods in England in that year was merely the natural sequel to their accepting the French as overlords;[106] it seems, however, more likely that, as the Chronicles relate, the attack on Sturmy immediately prompted such drastic action, especially in view of the magnitude of the damages extorted for it before the Genoese could be delivered. For there now began a great lawsuit when Philip Mede, Mayor of Bristol, "sewid byfore the kyng and his counseile al the Lumbards Januevs at that time in Englande, bicause of the takyng of Robert Sturmy and of his shippes. Which Janueys, after long sewte of the same, were judged and condempned to pay the saide maire and his brothern the some of 9,000 marcs, to be paide at certein termes." In due time, on 25th July, 1459, Sir John Stourton, Philip Mede, John Eyton, William Canynges, Richard Chok, and William Coder were commissioned to receive from the Treasurer £6,000 to be distributed among those involved in the venture, and the Genoese were delivered from prison. The fate of Sturmy himself is an unsolved mystery. But at least it is clear that he perished in the very year of the disaster, for his will was proved on 12th December, 1458. Its administration was entrusted to his wife, who lived on in Bristol, renting a house in Baldwin Street, and leaving the princely mansion on the Back to become the meeting-place of the first society of Merchant Venturers in Bristol.[107]

The tragedy of Sturmy is but an episode in the story of Bristol's trade at the close of the Middle Ages. No other record has come to light of similar Mediterranean ventures thence before the time of the Tudors. In the south, even more than in Iceland, the English were sharply rebuffed in their attempt to penetrate the spheres of their formidable rivals. It was not until the middle of the sixteenth century that the monopoly of the Mediterranean was wrested from the Italians, and even then the tradition of their ascendancy over the "petty traffickers" died hard. Yet already by the time of Henry VII England had a consul at Pisa, whither Sturmy had taken wool, and by 1511 "divers tall ships of London" with ships of Southampton and Bristol were voyaging still further to Candia, Cyprus, and even to

Beyrout. Thus Sturmy was but a little before his time in sailing with his three English ships past the Straits of Marrok into " so jeopardous and far parts ".

§ 6

THE MERCHANT OF BRISTOL

Merchandise rather than merchants has hitherto been the subject of this essay. The routes have been traced by which the wares of Bristol were carried over almost the whole of Europe; reckoning has been made of the rich and varied imports unloaded at her quays. What of the persons who trafficked in these things? Were they Englishmen or strangers? What was their status in society and what their influence over the city's government? Did they build and own the ships to which they committed their precious freights? Who helped them at home and transacted their business abroad? How large were the fortunes they amassed, and how did they spend their wealth when they had won it? Such are a few of the innumerable questions whose answers might well fill a bulky book, had letters or private papers of the merchants survived. But the absence of these is so complete that it is now only possible to catch an occasional glimpse into their manner of life through their legal transactions, their civic activities, their contact with the customs officers and other officials, and their dealings with the church. Through these they may be pictured resplendent in robes of scarlet, violet, blue, green, and murrey, edged with the finest of costly furs, girdled with gold and silver, and adorned with chains of gold and rings of great price; proud mayors past and present, in black velvet hoods with scarlet trains borne behind them, entertaining the highest in the land in their lofty timbered and tapestried halls.[108] Right royal was the reception given by these opulent burghers to the ill-fated Margaret of Anjou, to Henry VI, and, in happier circumstances, to Edward IV. Brilliant was the pageant prepared for the new sovereign in 1461. " First atte the comyng ynne atte Temple Gate there stode Wylliam Conquerour with iij lordis, and these were his wordis :—

> ' Well come Edwarde, oure son of high degre,
> Many yeeris hast þou lakkyd owte of this londe,
> I am thy fore fader, Wylliam of Normandye,
> To see thy welefare here thrugh goddys sond.'

Over the same gate stondyng a great Gyaunt delyveryng the keyes. The Receyving atte Temple Crosse next folowyng. There was seynt George on horsbakke upon a tent fyghtyng with a dragon, and þe kyng and þe quene on hygh in a castell, and his doughter beneathe with a lambe. And atte the sleying of the dragon ther was a great melody of aungellys." [109]

The merchants' houses were indeed not unworthy to shelter kings, built as they were with great attention to comfort and, with the increasing use of glass, to a novel craving for light and air. Of no mean proportions were those in the fashionable and less congested quarter of Redcliffe, set among gardens and meadows stretching down to the brink of the river. Pre-eminent among them was the mansion of William Canynges the younger, five times mayor of Bristol. Its central feature was the great hall, probably older than the fifteenth century, with its steep-pitched timbered roof, whose mutilated and much obscured remains may still be seen. Such an apartment had probably originally been at once hall, dining-room, and parlour. But later on more rooms had been added, and down by the river had been built a " tower " of great beauty, with many chambers and four of the new-fashioned " Bay-wyndowes ", the whole nearly fifty feet long.[110] No doubt there was also a solar besides the bed-chambers and kitchens and other offices quite adequate to produce a feast for the king himself. William of Worcester does not make clear whether these were grouped round a courtyard, as in a country house of the period, with the hall under its own roof on one side, and the tower on the other, nor whether this tower was built (as seems probable) of stone, with delicately mullioned stone bays like those of the George Inn at Glastonbury. " A mansion of great stones " is Worcester's description of another luxurious house nearby, called Vyell Place after its owner, and many a merchant lodged in a stone tower upon the city wall onto which chambers had been built out. But a stone house remained a landmark, though many another possessed ample accommodation with hall, parlour, kitchen, and chambers. In the more constricted central thoroughfares of Old Bristol the wealthy burgher's house could not stand in grounds of its own, and was chiefly distinguished by its superior height or adornment. The High Street, with its buzzing market, boasted the house of more than one important merchant, jostled by the shops of tailors, goldsmiths, drapers, and saddlers. Here dwelt Clement Wiltshire at " le Cok in the Hope " ; near by John Compton might be found at " le Grene Latyce " ; and here the widow Alice Chester, who traded in cloth with Spain and Flanders, rebuilt her house between " the Bull " and the dwelling of John de Cork, corvesor. Her agreement with the Welsh carpenter, Stephen Morgan, is preserved among the archives of All Saints, and is of some interest, since the planning of mediaeval town houses is very much a matter of conjecture. Stephen was to build it of good timber and boards ; it was to be only 10 ft. 5 in. wide, but nearly 20 feet in length ; on the ground floor was to be a shop, over it a hall with an oriel window, above this a chamber, also with an oriel, and on the fourth floor yet another chamber. Such oriel windows are rarely depicted in manuscripts of the period, so that Alice Chester's house must have been a distinctive one. The windows were probably leaded, for the lattices were to be completed by another hand; the timber walls were later to be covered with lath and plaster; but the whole framework of this compact but lofty house, with floors, doors, and partitions, was to be Morgan's work, and he was to receive for it £6 13s. 4d. (paid in instalments) with all the timber of the old building.

Thus some of these narrow houses in the busy highways of Bristol were four stories high, with shops below open to the street and projecting upper stories nodding to their neighbours on the other side. Equally important, however, were the one or more stories below the ground, dark vaults burrowed out even under the street for the storage of casks of wine, woad, salt, and other bulky merchandise. The letting of these underground cellars apart from the house above must surely have given cause for strife unless they were all very soundly made, like those which were finely vaulted in stone. Behind the house were stables, for many a merchant possessed his own horse, while others hired them—once at a cost of 4d. a day—when going on a journey. To ride to Salisbury and back, one merchant paid 3s. 4d. for his mount.[111]

In such wise were the houses of the merchants designed on the outside. Within they were partitioned into sundry rooms, each often hung with its distinctive tapestry or brightly coloured cloth, or perhaps lined with English oak or with wainscotting imported from eastern lands. Their furniture was scanty. A "joined" table had seldom superseded the customary trestles; John Gaywode mentions one in his will, of wainscot with four feet and "a beast carved therein", but then Gaywode was a prince among merchants, a partner with Canynges, owning a mansion not far from him in Redcliffe Street, in the height of luxury as then understood. Tapestries enriched his hall and parlour, and to match each set were "bankers"—covers for the wainscotted benches, and cushions to make snug seats in them and in the embrasures of the windows. In his hall hung a candelabra of laten; since candles were still a costly indulgence, to judge by the price paid by Elizabeth Stonor, this may have been reserved for special occasions, as were the two great andirons for the yule-log. The rapidly rising standard of comfort can be even more clearly perceived in the bed-chamber fittings of the merchant's house. Richly garnished with coverlets of tapestry or brightly patterned cloth, in blue and white, or green and yellow, the beds were canopied by testers to match, and screened with curtains. So elaborate were these fittings that the bequest of a "bed" often meant that of a coverlet and tester. Even at the close of the fourteenth century a house in Redcliffe Street had three such beds, one white embroidered, one blue embroidered with an eagle, and one red embroidered with a hawk. The ten beds bequeathed by John Hunt, including the one "wherein I have lain for the last two weeks", can scarcely all of them have been so complex. Feather beds and pillows were highly prized at a time when many a man thought himself fortunate to be able to purchase a flock bed and "thereto a sack of chaff to rest his head upon". Already known at the end of the fourteenth century, they were more usual, though not common, a century later, when Edward Kyte left his "optimum ffethirbedde" to his daughter Joan, and John Esterfeld a featherbed and bolster and "ij pylowes garnesshed", such as were then, if we are to believe Harrison, thought "meet only for sick women". Sheets were also sufficiently valuable to be sometimes specified in wills, and of these one merchant's widow left four pairs with a towel. Blankets, as was natural in Bristol, were well known. Little else besides the bed can there have been in the chambers except shining basins, ewers, and the ubiquitous wooden chest, serving, amongst other functions, that of a "press for my clothes". In chambers, hall, and parlour the sparseness of the furniture must have given full value to the rich glow from the brightly coloured hangings and cushions, and, on state occasions, the gleam of plate. John Gaywode possessed a Parisian cup with a coloured design in enamels; James Cokkes' great silver cup weighed over two pounds; and William Bird had to adorn his table five cups with covers, two flat cups, two gilt bell cups, and two gilt standing cups, also two dishes, one of them covered, for the precious spices that flavoured the food, and two and a half dozen spoons, and, as principal ornament, one silver salt cellar and two of the best gilt salt cellars. Clearly there was a "great amendment of lodging" during this century among the wealthier burghers, as during the succeeding one when bequests become still more rich and varied. The average standard of comfort of the merchant of the fifteenth century must have been very much that of the farmers and lesser artificers of a century later, who, according to Harrison, had learned " to garnish their cupboards with plate, their joined beds with tapestry and silk hangings, and their tables with carpets and fine nappery, whereby the wealth of our country (God be praised therefore, and give us grace to employ it well) doth infinitely appear ".[112]

Moreover few ambitious merchants were content if they had not laid up enough by their trafficking to purchase land, then almost the only practicable form of investment, procuring on a long lease at any rate a tenement here and there in the city or the suburbs or perchance beyond. Clement Wiltshire, mayor of Bristol, purchased his own house " le Cok in the Hope " and two other tenements in High Street, two tenements in Temple Street and Wine Street, and two cellars near the Welsh Back. John Shipward, another famous mayor, possessed at his death four tenements and a stable in High Street, with cellars and a tenement in St. Nicholas' Street, seven acres of meadow in Redcliffe Mead, five gardens and a tower with a large garden at Llafford's Gate. William Canynges the younger held, besides fourteen shops, at least seventeen tenements, a close and two gardens in Bristol, and lands in Wells, the hundred of Wells and Westbury on Trym. Similarly Philip Mede, mayor, owned lands in the counties of Somerset and Bristol; Hugh Withiford, mayor, left lands in Shropshire in Oswestry and round about; and another mayor, Robert Jakes, had extensive property in various parts of Leicestershire. Which of these worthies were squires' sons who had taken to trade, and which were traders destined to become landed gentry it is difficult to determine. Clearly, however, the aristocrats among the merchants were accepted then as readily as now in county society. Philip Mede married his daughter to Sir Maurice Berkeley, lord of Beverston; and the famous Canynges' son and heir, John, was considered an eligible match for Elizabeth, daughter of Thomas Middleton, Esq., of Stanton Drewe. When Canynges drew up the marriage agreement he promised that he would "competently find" John and Elizabeth in meat, drink and clothing, and all things necessary to their degrees during his life, and would leave his son as well off as any man left his son in Bristol within a hundred years, "saving only Robert Cheddar." [113]

At any rate traders in Bristol wares were recruited from many quarters, and its population became more and more cosmopolitan. Englishmen from neighbouring counties—Malmesburys, Ludlowes, and Devonshires—sometimes, like Philip Excestre, founded a family of merchants. Irishmen such as "Harry May" and "Patrick Irishman" were too numerous to be welcome; and Welshmen, more readily absorbed than the Irish, were almost as common as Englishmen, as is shown by the notable array of Vaughans, Goughs, Lloyds, ap Ryses, ap Meryks, and so forth. Frenchmen such as Barnard Bensyn;[114] Spaniards like Simon Aragon; Genoese, and perhaps Venetians, such as John Lombard and the more renowned Cabots, made Bristol their headquarters, and the Gascon, Moses Conterayn, who became a Bristol merchant, must have been of Jewish origin. While, however, some foreigners sought admission to the liberties of the Staple at Bristol, the evidence of many living there is slight. In Bristol there was no parallel to the foreign colony of Englishmen in Lisbon, nor to the Hanseatic colony in London. Detailed records of Bristol's dealings with her various customers prove that her trade was mainly in English hands, and reveal a rich and powerful group of native merchants, controlling all the affairs of her city.

Sometimes a commercial enterprise was carried on from generation to generation, as was the case in the Canynges family. William Canynges, burgess and merchant, who died in 1396, left his share in the ship *Rodecog* to his son Simon, and the rest of his property (after his wife's death) to his son John. This John traded with the talents committed to him, continued like his father to deal in cloth, shipped it to Spain and Bayonne, imported thence woad and iron, and in 1399 was elected mayor. He survived his father barely nine years, and died in 1405, possessed of three halls and five gardens, six tenements, twenty-two shops, and other lands and "void places" in Bristol, leaving six young children under age. His wife thereupon was married again to a prosperous merchant, Thomas Yonge, and three of her children distinguished themselves. One, Thomas Yonge, deserted trade for the law and became the well-known judge and member of Parliament who in 1451, for petitioning that the Duke of York should be declared heir to the throne, was cast into the Tower. Another, Thomas Canynges, made his way in London as a grocer, until in 1456 he was elected mayor there; and a third, William Canynges, followed his father's profession in Bristol, sent his ships to Iceland, the Baltic, Spain and Portugal, France, and the Netherlands, increased the family property, and was mayor five times. He outlived both his childless sons; at his death the family vanished from Bristol, though his great-nephew and heir occasionally imported goods thither, and it was from the mayor of London that the nineteenth century statesman, George Canning, was descended.[115]

Many another merchant's son or grandson chose thus to follow him, acted as his father's representative, and then launched out on his own. For the outsider, apprenticeship for seven or eight years was normally the first rung on the ladder. Thus the "Childe of Bristow", somewhat priggishly declining to perjure his soul by amassing wealth through the law, resolved to take himself to Bristol and bind himself to a respected merchant there.

> "Hit hath ever be myn avise
> to lede my lyf by marchandise,
> to lerne to bye and selle;
> that good getyn by marchantye,
> it is truthe, as thynketh me,
> there with will I melle.
>
> "Here at Bristow dwelleth on
> is held right a juste trew man,
> as y here now telle;
> his prentice will y be vii yer,
> his science truly for to lere,
> and with hym will y dwelle."

In like manner a Worcestershire lad, Richard Denton, was apprenticed by his father to Robert Gaynard and his wife for seven years. On Gaynard's death his wife married a second husband, John Gawge, who did business with Bordeaux and Bayonne. Then the young Richard, giving as his excuse an outbreak of plague in the city and a slump in business, "when Gawge kepith noon occupation and they die dayly in Bristowe," ran away to his father in Worcestershire. Evidently heavy penalties could be imposed on refractory apprentices, for when the father sent him back, as he alleged, Gawge refused to receive him and won £100 damages. Part of their training was to do business for the merchant abroad, until they had sufficiently learned the science of commerce to become, like the exemplary "Childe", the more responsible factor, trusted agent, and finally perhaps heir to the merchant.[116]

The position of factor was normally the next step taken by the ambitious apprentice when he was no longer a "Childe", though still young and ready to see the world before marrying and settling down in Bristol. This would probably mean living abroad, for the merchant usually kept a resident factor in towns with which he dealt constantly, with fuller powers of transacting business than his apprentices. Often the factor was a younger member of his family like John Canynges who seems to have been factor for his father, William Canynges. Much loss must have been suffered through the dishonesty of some of these agents, who had to be trusted to carry on business abroad with little supervision from home. Robert Russell once had occasion to complain of his factor, Thomas Hoper, in Bayonne. Cloth and other goods had been sent to him, but Hoper had converted these to his own use, married a woman of Bayonne, and was so " meintenuz et sustenuz par les Cosyns et alliez de sa dite femme " that Russell could not secure legal redress. The best that he could apparently do was to appoint one William Roger, a merchant, as his attorney beneath the great seal of Bristol, to sue Hoper on his behalf, a journey abroad being then a tedious and difficult enterprise for a busy man.[117]

The attorney was usually, as in the case of William Roger, an agent appointed to transact a particular piece of business, though the words "factor" and "attorney" were sometimes used indiscriminately, and not in the strict legal sense in which the attorney, with more complete powers than the factor, would have fuller authority to act for another. Thus the master of a ship or a merchant trading abroad on his own account would take charge of a consignment of goods for another merchant or group of merchants. When the word is used, however, in connection with customs payments, it has sometimes a peculiar significance. For if a merchant shipped goods in virtue of a special licence granted to another, having perhaps purchased a share in the licence, he would enter the goods in the name of the licencee, naming himself as the attorney. From the customs, for instance, it would appear as though Canynges, Shipward, Gaywode, and Baron, in partnership, once during four months (1465–6) shipped goods through no less than seventy-one attorneys, monopolizing almost the whole of the native trade of Bristol. But the fact that Canynges and his associates then had a licence to ship

THE OVERSEAS TRADE OF BRISTOL

customs free [118] makes it plain that the attorneys were the real owners of the goods, and succeeded in shipping them under the name of this influential partnership in order to benefit by their privileges. Indeed, the customs accounts themselves disprove the inference that such a partnership ever dominated the trade of Bristol. For the group makes its first appearance simultaneously with the granting of the licence and vanishes again later.

It is further remarkable that the other extant customs accounts at this time not only yield no evidence of such a partnership, but scarcely even mention the name of Canynges. Now this period was the very climax of Canynges' career, and it seems at first strange that he, traditionally the greatest Bristol merchant of the century, should appear to be taking so little active part in foreign trade. The story of Canynges, however, marks a new stage in the evolution of Bristol's trade. For one of the most notable features of the time is the emergence of the shipowner as a still more wealthy and influential citizen of Bristol than the merchant.

The shipowner on a large scale, as distinct from the merchant, was a new phenomenon in Bristol's history, and had developed probably from that newly emerged class of merchants making their fortunes entirely by foreign trade. It was in fact the latest of a series of changes in mercantile organization which accompanied the rapid expansion of England's foreign trade, each change tending towards greater specialization.

Early in the century there were few " merchants " concerning themselves primarily with foreign trade in a variety of commodities. Ship-masters took goods abroad on their own account; others concerned in the production of cloth were themselves responsible for its shipment abroad.[119] Thus William Symondes of Bristol, shearman, commissioned Richard Davy who was setting out for Bordeaux, to take thither for him twelve broad murrey cloths to deliver to John Essey of Bordeaux.[120] Out of fifty-nine burgesses making their wills between 1380 and 1400, only five, including William Canynges the elder, were designated " merchant ", though the epithet is a common one later. Rapid changes were, however, taking place in both industry and transport, and the significance of many terms connected with them changed also. The drapers, originally identical with the fullers or finishers, had already by the middle of the fourteenth century been divided into " manufacturing " and " trading " drapers. But now still further specialization took place. As the towns abandoned their original attempt to confine the industry within their walls, and it grew with ever-increasing speed beyond them in the country districts, a new class of " clothiers " emerged who arranged for every stage of its manufacture and sold the finished product to the drapers. So William Lewys bought of Philip Coke, clothier, three broad woollen cloths.[121] Not only in its manufacture, but also in its export, there were marked changes, as the English cloth trade expanded and the drapers, who purchased the cloth in England from the clothiers, ceased gradually to concern themselves with its sale abroad. In the second half of the century, while those concerned in its production still occasionally shipped it overseas themselves, most of those who exported cloth were not merely drapers but merchants, for they dealt in many other things. Thus developed a distinctive merchant class, specializing in foreign trade, no matter in what commodity, not always ceasing to be concerned in production, but more and more exclusively mercantile. Since these middlemen, doing business in many commodities, seem often to have been connected with the production of cloth,[122] it may possibly have been from among the drapers that this distinctive mercantile class arose. The fortunes of the Canynges family were very likely typical. In Richard II's reign John Canynges and William the elder were concerned both in the production and in the export of cloth.[123] But in a list of over 240 people accounting to the ulnager for over a thousand cloths early in the reign of Henry VI, and in all later accounts, the name of Canynges never appears. William Canynges the younger was therefore probably in the first instance purely a foreign merchant, procuring the cloth which he exported from drapers or clothiers. Just as the cloth producers and cloth dealers in England were thus ceasing to trade abroad on their own account, giving place to the foreign merchant, so the ship-master now seldom entered goods in his own name, but, leaving them in the charge of the foreign merchant, became more exclusively concerned with navigation.

But now in this new group of foreign merchants itself yet further specialization took place. Early in the century many merchants were themselves ship-owners, having perhaps a share in a ship with five or six others. Such shares were a form of property often bequeathed. Walter Derby left to his servant Nicholas half of the *Nicholas* and half of the balinger called the *Trinity*, and to his servants William and John half of the *Marie* and *Nicholas* respectively. Ships sometimes came into the hands of women. Thomas Sampson left the whole of the *Cog Joan* to his wife Joan, and William Spaynell left three-quarters of his " barge " to his wife Soneta and his two sons, bequeathing also money to " old John Wynne of the balinger " of whom we should like to know more.[124] Later in the century, however, while some merchants still had shares in ships, many more owned the whole of a ship, and gradually a wealthy class of ship-owners appeared possessing small private fleets of ten or more vessels. These great ship-owners, employers of several hundreds of men, fully occupied with the building, equipment, and management of their craft, concerned themselves little, if at all, with the buying and selling of goods, but made their profits on the freights paid by merchants whose goods they carried.

Pre-eminent among such ship-owners was William Canynges the younger, himself once a foreign merchant. According to his contemporary and fellow-citizen, William of Worcester, he kept 800 men for eight years employed in his ships, and had workmen, carpenters, masons, etc. to the number of a hundred men. Worcester enumerates ten ships as his, including one lost in Iceland, and says that six years after his death, in 1480, Thomas Strange possessed about twelve ships and John Godeman several more, while there were ten other ships belonging to Bristol in that year (*naves Bristolliae pertinentes*). This figure is corroborated by the customs records, which mention at least twenty Bristol ships, many of which can be identified in Worcester's list. These Bristol ships account for rather more than half the total trade of Bristol, leaving out of account Ireland, where the Irish ships were in the majority. Canynges, therefore, controlled about a quarter of all the shipping at the port of Bristol, owning nearly half of Bristol's ships, and amassed his wealth not by dealing in cloth or in other wares, but by carrying the merchandise of others who paid freight on the goods they entrusted to his ships. These freights were usually paid on the safe delivery of the cargo, a very small sum being sometimes paid in advance. Thus when the *Marie* came into port from Bayonne, her master received from Bristol merchants with goods in the ship over £100 *in plenam solucionem tocius affretamenti predicte navis* for the owners of the ship or for whoever else might claim it. Similarly John Heyton, merchant of Bristol, made an agreement with Clement Bagot, owner of the *Julian*. Bagot was to freight his ship for Lisbon at the pleasure of Heyton, reserving to himself only ten "tontight". The rate of payment was high, since risks were considerable; for wine it was usually at least a sixth of its price in England. Heyton was to pay £1 for every tun of wine brought from Lisbon to Ireland, and out of the total, twenty marks were to be paid to the mariners within six weeks of their arrival. Another merchant, shipping wine from Bordeaux to England, agreed to pay 21*s.* a tun within three weeks of its discharge, and handed over in advance in the church of St. Peter at Bordeaux the small sum of 3*s.* 4*d.*[125]

The appearance of the specialised ship-owner was accompanied by a marked development in Bristol's ships. These differed widely in size and character. Some were little "crayers", a term often applied to river boats. Others, used commonly as fishing boats and in trade with Ireland, were "picards", named often in the Tolsey Court books as pledges for debts, and worth about £8. For larger vessels the terms ship, barge, balinger, cog, and caravel, are often used indiscriminately, nor is there any clear distinction between the two most usual expressions "navis" and "batella". The "ship" usually designates one of the larger trading vessels, the cog or the caravel. The broadly built cog, evolved during the thirteenth century, was pre-eminently a cargo ship. At the opening of the fifteenth century it could carry about 200 tuns, and was the commonest type of merchant ship, though before long England began to imitate the Portuguese caravel, built with planks edge to edge instead of clinker fashion with overlapping edges. Sturmy, for instance, sent the *Cog Anne* on his first expedition to the Mediterranean, and the second time had two attendant caravels. The barge was, strictly speaking, smaller than the " ship ", and the balinger smaller than the barge. Both had originally oars, but the barge had by the fifteenth century been built up into a high vessel of the sailing type, while the balinger was then the typical pirate ship.[126]

Early in the century few of Bristol's ocean vessels can have carried more than 100 tuns, and the average cargo of the Bordeaux wine ships was 88 tuns, though one ship loaded 179 tuns. By the middle of the century, however, ships from Bordeaux were bringing on an average 150 tuns and some carried as many as 250 tuns. This may be compared with the figures for French and Spanish ships visiting Bristol, given in the lists of safe-conducts for this period in the *Great Red Book*. These vary from 80 to 250 tuns, occasionally reaching 300 tuns. Such figures are more likely to be purely formal than those given in the customs account of amounts actually carried; but it is clear that by the middle of the century Bristol boats had considerably increased in size, that 200 tuns of wine was no unusual cargo, and that they compared favourably in size with those of France and Spain. This marked increase tends also to confirm William of Worcester's oft-criticized figures for the last quarter of the century, the time of the great ship-builders, Canynges and Strange. Worcester puts four of Canynges' ships at under 200 tuns, three more between 200 and 250 tuns, the *Mary Canynges* at 400 tuns, and the *Mary Redcliffe* at 500 tuns, the size of the largest of Warwick's ships in 1464. The most difficult figure to believe is that of 900 tuns for the *Mary and John*. Worcester, however, was scrupulous in those measurements of his which we can check to-day in Bristol; he was cautious, for he admits that he does not know the exact tunnage of the ship lost in Iceland, stating it to be " about 160 tuns "; and it is evident that the *Mary and John* was quite exceptional, for he states that she cost Canynges the great sum of 4,000 marks to build. Why should not Canynges, like John Taverner of Hull, have built a ship " as large as a carrack or larger " ?[127]

The total tunnage of Canynges' ships must thus have amounted to close on 3,000. Each ship usually made one of the longer voyages twice a year, and thus if we estimate on the basis of the freights paid on wine, Canynges might have received in freights during one year over £10,000, though it is impossible to judge how much of this would be profit. With such a large scale shipping enterprise Canynges must have been remarkable as an employer of labour alone. Crews then were much larger than in sailing ships of the nineteenth century. In the safe-conducts in the *Great Red Book* ships of about 300 tuns are described as having crews of from sixty to eighty, and ships of about 80 tuns from twenty to thirty men, though these figures no doubt include convoys as well as actual crews. According to this, Canynges' ships would have employed 600–800 men, and since this last figure exactly coincides with that given by Worcester, apart from those engaged in building the ships, such an estimate of Canynges' employees may be roughly correct.[128]

Canynges was not the only Bristol owner who built his ships at home, though some purchased them abroad, for example in Prussia. The tower beside which was built the famous *Nicholas de la Tour*, in whose boat Suffolk's head was smitten off with a rusty sword by " oon of the lewdeste of the shippe ", was for long pointed out in Bristol; and when Edward IV visited the town in October, 1474, he promised a reward to any who would build a ship of considerable value. Perhaps as a result of this, ten Bristol merchants in the following November were licensed, " for the continuance and increase of shipping in the port of Bristol," to take their four ships to Spain or Portugal and back, customs free; while the following May similar permission was given to William de la Founte, because he had " fully made and apparelled a ship of the portage of 200 tuns or under ".[129]

Large and valuable cargoes went in these new ships in the latter part of the century. The *George,* for instance, probably the one enumerated by Worcester as of 511 tuns, was freighted, in the very year in which he wrote, with the goods of sixty-three merchants worth altogether over £1,000. Such a multifarious division of the cargo was very common when merchants preferred not to risk too large a consignment in one vessel. Each merchant distinguished his particular goods by a " mark " of his own, and this was legally recognized as establishing at least prima facie evidence of ownership in case of shipwreck, piracy, or other mishap.[130]

Risks indeed were great. Although laws of the sea existed, lawlessness had become a habit. Losses from piracy, from wrecks and the plundering of wrecks, legalized or arbitrary, were constantly recorded, and ships were in peril even at Kingrode; there in 1488 " a grete ship," the *Antony,* was lost; there, four years earlier, she and a ship of Bilbao had run aground, and other boats and cogs had been sunk in a fierce storm, whose effects had been felt even in Bristol where the cellars had been flooded and much merchandise spoilt. Many a ship, like Canynges', must have perished in the fogs off Iceland, and others by fire through carelessness.[131] Little wonder was it that merchants sought heaven's protection against the elements; and that parish accounts contain such entries as " Item of John Foster, merchant, at his going to sea, 4*d* ". Against piracy and the risks of war the only and very ineffectual protection, beyond their own armed resistance, was a safe-conduct. This lasted usually only for a year or two, and was purchased for a great price from their own or a foreign monarch. Some foreigners who once procured a safe-conduct through Bristol merchants offered in payment £12 for every voyage made. John Wylly, a Bristol brewer, and his son-in-law promised to pay forty marks for a safe-conduct from the French king. Their petition to Chancery illustrates yet another menace at a time when there was scarcely any royal navy, that of the commandeering of their vessels in time of war. Their ship, the *Julian* of Fowey, fell in with the Earl of Warwick on his way to Ireland " in his grete wrongfull trouble " to bring the Duke of York to England. It was seized by the Earl and detained for six months, and by this time the safe-conduct had expired and was worthless. Meanwhile the merchants shipping in the *Julian* had taken action against Wylly at Bristol for not delivering their goods. On occasions such as these the goods seem often to have been landed at the nearest port, and the merchant had to profit by them or not as he could. The ship-owner's compensation for the use of his ship was, when obtainable, 3s. 4d. per tun per quarter from the crown. There were usually three or four merchants travelling in each ship, and when one of these was captured the pirates made a goodly profit. For Thomas Canynges, sent overseas on business by his father (nephew of the great William), the Bretons asked £100, and to pay this land had to be mortgaged in Bristol. John Wode, factor of Thomas Wode, was of a less distinguished family, and for him and his ship and goods in Zealand the Scots asked only £28. John Wode was unable to pay, and so the factor of one John Seglysthorn lent him the money.[132]

Merchants must often have helped each other thus abroad, in days before consuls and permanent ambassadors existed. One John Pavy with goods worth £500 or more in France charged two fellow citizens, as he lay dying at Bayonne, to restore his property to his wife and children in Bristol. William Rowley, junior, who died in Bordeaux in 1478, entrusted to John Chester the return of the ship and goods for which he was responsible. The following year his uncle, William Rowley, senior, died in the Netherlands at Damme, in the house of " the honourable Roger of Dam ", and was buried in the ambulatory of St. Mary's there, only a few months after his elder brother, Thomas, had died in Bristol.[133]

When a merchant's business was thus suddenly cut short, his wife frequently wound it up for him. Thus Joanna, widow of William Rowley senior, received sugar from Lisbon in 1479, and in the following year oil and wax from Lisbon and woad and wine from Spain. Similarly in the name of Margaret, widow of Thomas Rowley, came three shipments of wine from Bordeaux and one of oil from Seville. Often when the husband was away the wife had to receive

THE OVERSEAS TRADE OF BRISTOL

the goods or money due to him, though sometimes she refused to take the responsibility of handing over the bond.[134]

Some able and energetic women ventured into foreign trade on their own account, though not often to such an extent as Margery Russell of Coventry, who was robbed of goods worth £800 by the men of Santander.[135] The customs accounts of the reign of Edward IV name seven women merchants who were probably widows, and eight others who made a few small shipments, all of them imports. Elizabeth Jakes, wife of a merchant and mayor, three years after her husband's death exported cloth and an alabaster reredos to Lisbon. Still more enterprising was the wealthy widow of Henry Chester who died in 1470. Alice lived on in High Street, and two years later arranged for the building of her new and elegant house there. Both she and her son carried on a varied business, importing iron from Spain, sending cloth to Lisbon, to Flanders, and so forth. Meanwhile she earned the gratitude of both citizens and strangers by making a crane on the Back by Marsh Gate, where there had been none before, at a cost of £41, "for the saving of merchants' goods of the town and of strangers." The accounts of All Saints record also a number of munificent benefactions made by her and her husband and their son John, "also a well-wisher in all this business." These show that she must have amassed a considerable fortune, as does the mention of her loan of £20 to the Prior of Taunton, when he was in great poverty and could neither repair his house nor pay his debts. Seven years after the building of the crane, "being in good prosperity and health of body, considering that the rood loft of the church was but single and nothing of beauty," Alice took counsel with the "worshipful of the parish and with others having the best understanding and sights in carving". Then she had made a new rood loft resting on two pillars, each with four saints in carved niches, with three principal images of the Trinity, St. Christopher and St. Michael, twenty-two images in all. Alice also had a new front carved for the altar in the south aisle, gilded the altar of Our Lady, and made an elaborate tabernacle there; and besides many vestments, altar cloths and ornaments, she gave "a cross of silver gilt enamelled with Mary and John", costing £20 and weighing sixty ounces, for hitherto the best cross had always to be used. On 16th December, 1485, concludes the All Saints record, "the soul of this blessed woman departed out of this world." [136]

Alice Chester's work is to-day but a tradition hidden among the archives of All Saints, for the excellent carved work of the fifteenth century has long been broken down. Others have left more enduring memorials. The stately tower of St. Stephen's, whose pinnacles rise high above all others in the old city, was erected at the sole expense of the merchant and mayor, John Shipward, whose house stood near by. William Canynges, his yet more renowned partner in trade, ship-owner, ship-builder, and five times mayor of Bristol, splendidly completed the work of his father and grandfather beyond the city walls, earning the title of " renovator et quasi alter fundator ac inter ceteros specialissimus benefactor ecclesie de Redeclif",[137] and leaving behind him one of the last and greatest achievements of English Gothic. With no son to succeed him, since both had died young, he roused the wrath of his daughter-in-law's family by bestowing more and more of his great wealth upon the church.[138] Like the merchant saint, Godric, he " began to yearn for solitude and to hold his merchandise in less esteem than heretofore ", until finally he purposed to give himself also to the church, and retired at the close of his fifth mayoral year, to become first presbyter and then dean of Westbury-on-Trym. There, in 1474, he died—" ditissimus et sapientissimus mercator villae Bristolliae."

The Bristol merchant was no doubt a hard-headed business man, yet the grace and perfect proportions of his buildings show that he was not lacking in appreciation of other than mere monetary values. He cared for learning and collected books, as the *Book of Wills* testifies. John Esterfield, merchant and mayor, left two matins books, a mass book, and a psalter; William Pavy possessed more than one missal besides a " good psalter " and legends of the saints; William Coder had many Latin books in a chest in his house, and others which he had lent to a kinsman; several merchants presented missals and psalters to their parish churches. Probably their brothers, who became men of law, acquired more secular books and read more widely, as did Thomas Yonge who borrowed from William of Worcester a book on ethics and " le Myrrour de dames " covered in red leather. And some of the merchants must have sent their sons to college as the Bristol glover sent his son, William of Worcester.

The merchants' local patriotism prompted them not only to endow noble churches but to appropriate a large share of the burdens of office. The government of the town was almost entirely in their hands, and all except five of the mayors between 1450 and 1490 were well-known merchants. That their duties were arduous is evident from the list of functions that had to be attended,[139] from the almost daily session of the Tolsey Court to such celebrations as those of St. Katherine's eve, when there were " drynkyngs with Spysid Cake brede " in the Weavers' Hall, and performances by the St. Katherine's players at the doors of the civic dignitaries.

Now and then they took part in the public affairs of the nation, serving in Parliament, lending ships, money or men. But only grudgingly did they contribute to the Exchequer, and in dynastic struggles they interfered little. Their loans were usually in direct relation to favours expected,[140] and on the whole they were more concerned with the ordinances of their city than with the laws of their country, which gave them little protection at home or abroad. Scant support could they look for from sovereigns, who, unlike their cousins of Portugal, preferred adventures in France to adventures on the sea, or who, in contrast to the rulers of Spain, encouraged pioneers only after they had proved successful.

The peace and prosperity of the city which they governed stands out in striking contrast to the disorder and misery occasioned by partisan strife elsewhere. For while the barons were wearing themselves out in the elaborately recorded Wars of the Roses, such vigorous and self-reliant men as these merchants were quietly amassing wealth and worldly wisdom. Despite England's lack of governance at home, her defeats abroad and her failure to keep the sea, these citizens, refusing to be intimidated by marauding foreigner, "overmighty subject," or Yorkist or Lancastrian army, were steadily extending their trade and commerce.

Though the volume of their trade was as yet comparatively small, their knowledge of the seas was now wider than that of either of the traditional sea-powers of Europe, who so stubbornly resisted their intrusion. For while the trade of the Italians extended from the Levant to the English Channel, and that of the Hanseatics from thence to the Baltic, and so to Norway and Iceland, the men of Bristol were acquainted with all these routes, from southern Joppa to the frozen north. Nor had they merely groped darkly round the coasts of Europe, for in sailing to Iceland they had launched out boldly across the ocean, thereby spanning a distance nearly half as great as that to the still undiscovered New World.

Their main business throughout was on the Atlantic. For Bristol's reputation as the second port in the kingdom was built up, not in a perilous and uncertain competition with Italians or Hanseatics in the Baltic or the Mediterranean, not in the traditional marts of the Netherlands, nor in the ancient wool trade with Flanders, soon doomed to extinction, but in a steady and mainly uneventful traffic on the western shores of Europe, less chronicled since less disputed. Rebuffed in the north by the arrogance of the Hanse, in the south by the exclusiveness of the long-established Italians, inevitably they concentrated more and more on this Atlantic trade and pushed out towards the west. Not only did they rebuild successfully their ancient trade with Gascony, but, turning their backs upon Europe, they sought new outlets for their enterprise in those fabled isles lying beyond Ireland, far out in the unknown Western Ocean. In the summer of 1480 two ships, the *George* and the *Trinity*, were laden in the port of Bristol "not for the purpose of trading, but to seek and discover a certain island called the *Ile of Brasile*". The venture was a joint one, in which several Bristol merchants co-operated, amongst them being John Jay, who apparently provided one of the ships, and Thomas Croft, whose share was one-eighth in each ship. The navigation was entrusted to a Welshman, one Lloyd, "the most scientific mariner of all

England." On 15th July the ships set sail, under the protection of the Virgin (*fulcando Maria*), towards the " Island of Brasylle in the western part of Ireland ". For two months they sought it, till, tossed by the sea, they were driven into port in Ireland, and the news of their failure reached Bristol on the 18th September.[141]

Baffled though the Bristol merchants seemed at this moment, their failure was but the prelude to adventures of undreamed of magnitude. For the foundations they had well and truly laid of a purely English trade upon the Atlantic, based on a flourishing industrial hinterland, and their proved readiness to venture their wealth in search of new lands, had prepared the way for achievements more notable than those of their rivals, the Italians or the Hanseatics. They had already staked out a claim on the highway of the future, and it was with a true instinct that the Venetian citizen Cabot now departed from Italy and made his home in Bristol, there to find among its merchants support for his ventures across uncharted seas to the wide lands of the New World.

VI

THE GROCERS OF LONDON: A STUDY OF DISTRIBUTIVE TRADE

§ 1

INTRODUCTION

Although much has been written on the subject of the London livery companies, they have been strangely neglected by the modern English economic historian. They have been discussed chiefly in their capacity as social and religious clubs and benevolent societies; the question of their economic functions at the time when they were vital business institutions has attracted little attention.

In the case of the industrial crafts, of course, it will be agreed that they met the need for standardization of manufactures, for technical education, and for regulation of wages and the conditions of labour in each industry. But the functions of the different merchant companies are not so readily apparent. It is true that the name of each was derived from an occupation characteristic of its members. Thus their charters and by-laws show that the fishmongers sold fish, the drapers cloth, the vintners wine, and so on. Yet it is common knowledge that in course of time the companies ceased to have any real connection with the trades after which they were named, and so much still remains obscure about their original character, that the full implications of membership in the mediaeval period have never been made clear.

The problem is most easily approached through a specialized study of a single group. Most of the merchant companies, it will be seen, ranged over the whole field of the import and export trade. A detailed analysis of the undertakings of any one is therefore sufficient to make the general situation clear, for it necessarily involves a definition of the position of each of the others.

On account of the fullness of its records the grocers' company has been selected for the purpose. After a brief sketch of its early history, its constitution and membership, the business of its members is examined in order to see how far they specialized, and, hence, what division of functions existed among the companies. The aim is to illustrate the practical working of the craft system with regard to trade.

§ 2

Early History and Constitution of the London Grocers' Company

1. *Early History of the Grocers' Company*

Of the organization of the London crafts or companies in the early Middle Ages, practically nothing is known. But from the period of their earliest records, the fourteenth century, until the days of their decline, they were in constant process of reorganization and rearrangement, groups alternately amalgamating and separating. One of the greater companies known to have been formed by the amalgamation of smaller groups is the grocers' company.

The initiative in this movement was taken by the pepperers. Their own craft was one of the oldest in the city, occurring among the adulterine guilds of 1180, and had numbered many leading citizens among its members. But in 1345, it was entirely reorganised. A new fraternity was formed by a body of twenty-one pepperers of Sopers Lane, who laid down the rule that no one should be eligible to join " sil ne soit de bones condiciouns et de lour mestier Cest assavoir Poyverer de Soperslane canevacer del Roperie ou Espicer de Chepe ou autre homme de lour mestier quel part qil demoerge ".[1] The description is a little vague. What was the " mestier " or trade common to the pepperers, the canvas-dealers, and the spicers, and what were these allied groups ?

An intimation of the general nature of their trade is given on the occasion, in 1312, when representatives of the pepperers, corders, ironmongers, apothecaries, and of other trades not named " qui se intromittunt de averio ponderis," met to appoint a weigher for the king's beam.[2] This term, " averium ponderis " or " avers de poys ", embraced all sorts of merchandise sold by weight with the exception of those important enough to be placed in a class by themselves, such as wool or victuals. Thus it included metals, dyes, wax, drugs, and spices. The latter formed a large and very valuable class of goods. The mediaeval craving for pepper made it one of the most profitable articles of commerce. There were, besides, many other condiments in use, and sugar, rice, almonds, and dried fruits were also classed as spices. The pepperers, as their name would suggest, were especially interested in this type of merchandise. In 1316 they drew up a set of regulations aiming at the prevention of fraud in the sale of spice, both wholesale and retail. It is probable that they were the most important of the groups into which the London dealers in goods of " avers de poys " were split.

THE GROCERS OF LONDON

Their allies the "canevacers" of the Ropery must have been a group of the ropers or corders after whom that quarter of Thames Street was named. It is usually surmised that these were makers of rope, but it is evident that there was a trading element amongst them. This appears, in the first instance, from their employment of brokers. The broker was a wholesale agent whose function was to bring together buyer and seller. For the better enforcement of trading regulations the office was kept under strict supervision, and the holders were sworn to honesty. The fact that the corders had in 1293 appointed three brokers suggests, therefore, that there were wholesale dealers in the craft. A part of their stock-in-trade apparently consisted of canvas or other cloth, for in 1315 they were concerned in the framing of a protest against the king's action in appointing an alnager to measure all canvas, linen, and English cloth sold in London. Some of them were wealthy and influential men, five corders rising to the rank of alderman during the fourteenth century. One of these is described both as pepperer and corder, and two corders held office as wardens of the pepperers. This wealthy trading element merged with the pepperers into the company of grocers. The corders, their ranks thus depleted, counted henceforth as one of the minor crafts.[3]

The other group joining with the pepperers, the spicers of Cheap, was in all probability identical with the craft of apothecaries. This had been a flourishing and well-organized craft, as one may judge from its election of four brokers in 1293, and seven governors in 1328. But there is no later evidence of its separate existence, and proof of amalgamation is afforded in 1365, when twelve surveyors of the "Mistery of Grossers, Pepperers and Apothecaries" were elected.[4] Spicer was the general name applied to anyone connected with the spice trade in any capacity, from great London merchants to poor shopkeepers and country chapmen, and was a common surname throughout the kingdom. It was used indiscriminately of both pepperers and apothecaries. As a matter of fact, there was little distinction between their occupations. John de Grantham, one of the most prominent of the pepperers, can be found described as "ipothecarius".[5] The word may signify a wholesale merchant, a shopkeeper, or a dispenser of drugs. In London the apothecaries followed all three lines. They sold medicines, but they did not restrict themselves to this. William de Stanes, one of the apothecaries to Edward III, was able to make himself useful as a general merchant trading on behalf of the great wardrobe.[6] Both apothecaries and pepperers, therefore, were merchants, and there is no reason to suppose that the former had any monopoly of the trade in drugs. The preparation and sale of medicines was nowhere a specialized occupation until the use of non-vegetable drugs became more common, in the sixteenth century. Before that time it was merely a profitable

s

sideline for any dealer in spices. Many popular remedies were very simple prescriptions. Ginger and honey, for instance, were the main ingredients of cough mixtures. Medicated treacle was imported from Genoa, and many other drugs. The vogue of foreign medicines, to the neglect of good home-grown English herbs, was one of the signs of degeneracy lamented by the author of *The Libelle of Englyshe Polycye*.[7] There was nothing to prevent the apothecary from dabbling in medical practice beyond the fact that if his treatment failed, he would be condemned by a jury of physicians. In Geneva the apothecaries are said to have combined the functions of spice-merchants and doctors; but in England the healing art was mainly in the hands of physicians and surgeons, and the apothecaries merely dispensed their prescriptions. They dealt, besides, in cosmetics and confections. A file of bills presented by the queen's apothecary in 1393-4, discloses the names of forty preparations that had been supplied—syrups, electuaries, ointments, simples, and perfumes.[8]

The grocers' company, then, was formed of these three elements—pepperers, or merchants trading largely in spice, corders trading, for one thing, in canvas, and apothecaries, who were merchants having a retail business in drugs and confections. For some time the separate designations of pepperer, corder, and apothecary were retained, but they were gradually superseded by the name of grocer. There has been some difference of opinion as to the derivation of this word, but it would seem most probable that it was suggested by transactions in bulk, or *en gros*. It occurs as a surname early in the fourteenth century, and as the name of an occupation as early as 1210.[9] That the meaning attached to it in London was that of a dealer in goods of avoirdupois is made clear by a case in the Mayors' Court in 1298, when certain German merchants were declared to have been acting at the same time as " grossores " of avoirdupois, as drapers, and as woolmen. The officers of the pepperers were in 1328 registered as " grossarii ", and in 1373 the new group adopted the name of " Compaygnie des Grossers ".[10]

The company was clearly composed of wealthy merchants, men " de bones condiciouns ". John Hamond, for example, and Andrew Aubrey would import £2,000 worth of merchandise at a time. Though not all of their fellows would have had so much capital afloat as this, yet all were merchants of the better sort. They co-operated in foreign trade, shipping in the same fleets from Flanders, and pooling the costs of defensive measures against pirates.[11]

Its enrolment steadily increasing, the company pushed its way to the fore in city politics. During the fourteenth century forty-four aldermen were chosen from the ranks of the grocers and pepperers, a record equalled only by the mercers.[12] The latter afterwards took the lead, the grocers ranking second.

2. *Constitution and Membership*

The foundation of the grocers' constitution was laid down by the small exclusive fraternity of 1345. Additions to it were made later, but no radical alterations. In essentials it was typical of the constitution of any other of the merchant companies. Each had its own individual customs and peculiarities, but variations from the type were on minor points. Similar needs produced similar rules, and the main features, the mingling of democratic and autocratic elements, were common to all.

Executive control was vested in two wardens, with, in the fifteenth century, a master, or upper master, set over them. They served for a year, and, on retiring, appointed their own successors. During their term of office they exercised very wide powers over their fellows, and were treated with great respect. Every dispute was to be brought to them, and submitted to arbitration as they directed. They had powers of distraint in collecting fines and dues from the refractory and the careless, and could, on complaint to the mayor's court, cause rebellious members to be committed to prison for as long a term as forty days.[13]

But the master and wardens were not the entire governing body. In all important matters they acted with the advice of a standing committee. This institution, in course of time adopted by all the companies, appears among the grocers very early, dating from at least 1365. In 1376 there is reference to the six associates of the wardens, and in 1418 it was ordained that six or ten men should be chosen annually to help the new officers. Later the number was set at ten or twelve, usually referred to as the "feliship associed". The committee was large enough to serve the threefold purpose of retaining the retiring officers and the benefit of their experience for an extra term, to give future wardens some practical training, and to include representatives of that class of member which did not attain the dignity of warden.[14]

The wardens had no legislative authority. Although their disciplinary powers appear to have been somewhat arbitrary, they could be exercised only in enforcing obedience to rules that had been drawn up with the assent of the whole livery. The constitution was thus thoroughly democratic. If the wardens wished to act hurriedly in an emergency, they obtained the assent of as many members as possible, for they were expected to call full meetings of the company to discuss important matters as they arose. Moreover, there were four regular assemblies during the year, "to treat of the common necessities of the mistery," to which every liveryman was summoned, and in which he had both voice and vote.[15]

But, since elections were not open, there was room for the

dominance of a certain clique. The founders of the company, however, had frankly regarded the duties of warden as a burden.[16] They had provided that no one should be made to serve a second term until an interval of seven years had elapsed, and by forbidding any man to refuse election on pain of fine and expulsion, had arranged that the less public-spirited among them should not shirk their turn. A free livery was issued in reward for the warden's services, but no payment. During the thirty-one years of the fourteenth century for which the names of the wardens are available, only five men held office a second time, and then only after an interval of five years or more. In the fifteenth century, though new blood was regularly admitted, the office was not so widely shared, partly because of a tendency to allow terms to run concurrently for two years, partly because of the appointment of a third officer, the upper master. Among the wardens themselves there were only eight men who served more than twice. But the upper master's was a much more exclusive position. It was filled usually, and after 1470 always, from among the aldermen in the company. Thus the aldermen exerted a preponderating influence, one man presiding as often as five, six, or seven times. And since the wardens were commonly chosen from the more substantial members, there was clearly a predominance of wealth in office.

The grocers were not legally incorporated before 1428, and could not before that time employ a common seal nor hold landed property. But from the very beginning they had maintained a corporate fund. The administration of this fund was really the chief function of the wardens, and their greatest responsibility. There was a number of minor expenses incidental to the organization of any craft—the rent or upkeep of a meeting-place, the salary of a beadle to summon members to assemblies, and of the priest who sang for the souls of the brotherhood. These were normally met from the fees charged at the entrance of new members, and on the enrolment of apprentices, and from the fines collected on the infringement of rules. Such receipts rarely did more than balance the expenditure. Yet the grocers, and the other merchant companies, steadily accumulated larger and larger funds. These were increased partly by legacies from wealthy members, partly, again, through investing the money in trade.

This corporate trading was highly successful. The company itself bore no risks; the risk was the personal concern of the wardens. The mercers made their officers find surety that they would render an account at the end of the year. The grocers made the wardens sign a bond for the amount entrusted to them, and expected them to show a profit in their accounts through trading. As much as £41 might be made on deals in pepper in a single year. Between 1450 and 1479 the rate of profit ranged from 6 to 19 per cent, averaging about 10 per cent. The gain was regularly turned back into the general funds.[17]

The grocers had the more money available for trading, since they did not, like some of the other companies, invest large sums in land. Their charter, authorizing the acquisition of property to the annual value of twenty marks, was not obtained until 1428. A house and land in Conyhopelane, recently bought from Lord Fitz-Walter and held by trustees, was then formally transferred to the wardens. In 1436 the company was taxed on lands worth £10 a year; in 1450-51 the valuation was £20, in 1496 it was £34. The increase must have been due to property being left to the company, as no further purchase of land is recorded until 1503.[18]

If there were no distribution of profits, and no investment in lands, one wonders what the grocers did with their money, and why they were so anxious to augment it. Their only great outlay was on the building and decoration of their hall, which cost them about £600. But the greater part of this was raised by means of levies on the members, who were assessed according to their means. All surplus funds were swallowed up for several years, but recuperation, through borrowing and trading, was rapid, and by 1450 the company had a balance of £500; by 1488 this had been doubled. Once this point was reached, however, its policy lost energy and, although there was no extraordinary expense, the capital had by the end of the century fallen to £900. During the last twenty-two years there is no record of any corporate trading. Instead of the regular entries of trading profit, the accounts contain notes to the effect that the wardens have given a certain sum out of their goodwill; but their goodwill realized only about 2 per cent on the capital in hand. It can hardly be supposed that the money was allowed to lie idle. Even the sums required to pay the salaries of chantry priests were not kept as loose cash; it is several times mentioned that the total assets included "goods leyde into this place to keep obits with and for priests' wages". It can only be assumed that the money was circulating on loan. About the middle of the century several loans were advanced both to members of the company and to outsiders. In some cases the charge is noted. Three merchants of the staple borrowing £477 paid 8½ per cent, and a group of eight merchants of the Staple, including several grocers, paid 12 per cent on a loan of £300. In the latter part of the century only one loan is recorded, of £200. Obviously there is something to be read between the lines of the accounts. During the period when the capital sum was allowed to diminish, it may have happened that money was advanced to privileged members and their friends without interest, or at a very low rate.[19]

This control and power of disposal of the common funds must have placed more power in the hands of the governors of the company than is explicit in the constitution. Men already wealthy above the average, they must have enjoyed a very marked ascendency. At the same time, each man had his vote in the mass meetings and his chance of serving a turn on the governing body. But these privileges belonged only to the fraternity in the livery. The democratic element is overshadowed on the one hand by the dominance of the aldermen and the wealthier men in the fraternity, and on the other hand by the exclusion from its ranks of some half the freemen of the company.

It is thought that the members of a company were originally all on the same level, wearing a common livery and sharing in the same privileges. But it is evident that the grocers did not contemplate receiving all their apprentices into their fraternity without question when they had served their time, for the ordinances of 1345 set the entrance fee at 40s., and provided that the candidate should be examined to see whether he were " de bone condicioun ". By the fifteenth century a subordinate class of poorer members, who wore no livery and did not belong to the inner fraternity, was a conspicuous feature of the crafts. The distinction between the two classes was entirely a matter of money. If a man engaged in the trade could afford to buy his livery and pay the fees of the fraternity, he was under an obligation to join, and if he wished to withdraw he would have to pay a fine. The grocers' livery was at its strongest in 1386, when it numbered 135. After this the number rapidly dwindled. By 1397 it had shrunk to 103, by 1433 to 61. The latest lists are for the year 1470, when there were 75 in the livery and 102 out of it.[20]

In the early fifteenth century the line between the two classes was less sharply drawn than later. Until 1433 there was an intermediate class wearing the hood of the livery alone. Until 1464 the freemen not of the livery were allowed to attend the quarterly assemblies and listen to the proceedings. But one may distinguish three groups among these subordinate freemen. There was, first, a number of men serving under contract variously called servants, bachelors, lowys, vallets, and covenant men. It is possible, however, that men described as servants were sometimes in reality junior partners in a firm. There was, then, a second group of these junior partners and of men who had started an independent career in a small way. Of fifty householders and bachelors not in the livery in 1428, eighteen were in the service of others, the rest presumably keeping shops of their own. Finally, there was a small group on the fringe of the livery, made up of young men looking forward to enter it, and of older men who had withdrawn. Of the forty-two " howsholders and schoppholders " listed in 1431, about a third shortly entered the livery. In the fifteenth century the non-livery men, the " Bacheleris of the Grocery ", had their own organization, elected their own masters, whose authority was upheld by the wardens of the company, and had their separate social life.[21]

THE GROCERS OF LONDON

A few of these bachelors, subscribing as much as forty and fifty shillings towards the building of the company's hall, must have been fairly prosperous. As servants they might receive as much as £10 a year, but they could add to their income by a little trading as they found opportunity. The mercers tried to prevent this, but the grocers were not nearly so strict. Whereas the mercers made it a rule that no one should set up a shop unless he had £100 of capital, the grocers in 1480 set the minimum at £40, and later dropped even this restriction.[22]

By far the majority of the company's servants was composed of boys and young men serving an apprenticeship. In common with other crafts, the grocers deliberately limited the number of these. In 1496, " to the entent that covenaunt servants myght the better be sett a work when they come out of their terms and have the better wagis," it was ordained that apprentices should serve at least ten years, and should not be presented to the freedom before the age of 25 or 26. One effect of this policy was to enhance the value of apprentices' labour. In the last few years of their terms they were frequently bought and sold, the term of service being regarded as a chattel of the master. The last three years' service of a certain young goldsmith, for instance, sold for £4.[23]

Mediaeval apprenticeship has been many times described, but usually only in terms of the ordinary indenture. The indenture, however, does not tell the whole story of the conditions of the contract. In the familiar form the master engaged to provide food and clothing for the boy and to maintain him suitably during his term. But it does not necessarily follow that he engaged to do so at his own expense, and there is unmistakeable evidence that the boy frequently had to pay for the food and clothing thus provided for him. A certain citizen makes provision for the maintenance of his grandson during his apprenticeship with a goldsmith; a guardian's accounts show an expenditure of 40*s*. on bedding, clothing, shoes, and other necessaries for a boy who had been apprenticed for a year to a grocer; a grocer mentions in his will that one of his apprentices owed him money for his bread.[24]

In the grocer's company there were two classes of apprentices, those who paid a premium and those who were accepted free. This distinction is clearly drawn in the earliest of the ordinances, the fee demanded on enrolment of a moneyed apprentice being higher than that due in other cases: " Et quant asun del fraternite desore en avant prigne apprentiz ove ascun sume dargent il paiera xl*s* al commun boiste dedeinz le utisme jour qil resceive lapprenticiante et sil ne paiera maintenance Et si ascun apprentiz soit pris saunz argent or autre avoir rienz ne paiera iii*s* iiii*d*."

In 1418 this was restated as a rule that any member taking an apprentice " w*t* any summe of goods or moneye w*t* hym" should pay 6s. 8d., otherwise the fee was only half this. But the records do not enable one to judge what proportion of the apprentices had money, as soon after the complete register becomes available, that is by 1466, the fee paid by the master was in all cases 20s., rising in 1500 to 40s.[25]

Premiums were exacted in other companies besides the grocers, and in other towns besides London, the sum varying from £2 to £10. In one instance a grocer took as much as £22, apparently the whole amount of an orphan's patrimony; this was perhaps entrusted to him as a loan, after the custom prevailing in Ypres.[26]

That it was a matter of course to make some charge for instruction appears from Bishop Peacock's discussion of the ideal relations between master and apprentice, in which he declared that the master should draw up a reasonable contract " without [taking] over mych reward for teching of his craft ". In practice there might be an additional charge for board—a certain fishmonger who had failed to look after his apprentice was ordered to return the 60s. premium paid, less a deduction for board.[27]

In the circumstances it is of no small interest to find that a company in the position of the grocers should have left the door open to recruits who could pay neither for board nor instruction. The question arises whether such apprentices were really on the same footing in the company as those who had paid. Surely they must have been required to work harder or for a longer term; another possibility is that they formed an inferior class of servants not destined for the freedom at all.

Some colour is lent to the latter supposition by the fact that barely half the apprentices enrolled ever became freemen. No doubt some boys died before their term was finished, or proved unsuited to the business and dropped out, but death and desertion could hardly account for so large a proportion. Yet there are no grounds for assuming that the requirement of a premium necessarily barred the poor boy from the freedom of the company. If an apprentice had served the term specified in his indenture, and was ready to pay the fee for enfranchisement, the custom of the city compelled his master to present him.[28]

One may fall back on the hypothesis that by serving for a longer term, or submitting to more menial labour, the poorer boy might, provided he could pay the fee for enfranchisement, attain the status of a freeman and the right to set up a shop of his own. Des Marez notes that the fishmongers of Brussels excused an apprentice from paying a premium if he would serve two years instead of one.[29] But there is no means of judging whether the grocers followed a similar plan.

It is unlikely that there was any rigid rule in the matter. One can only point to the probability that the majority of the freemen

THE GROCERS OF LONDON

in the company had been able to pay both for their training and their enfranchisement and suggest that the company employed a class of servants below the rank of citizen.

3. *Civic Functions*

Each of the merchant companies undertook some public function in connection with trade. Early in their career the grocers acquired the privilege of nominating two important public officers, the weigher of the king's beam and the garbeller of spices.

The maintenance of standard weights, one of the primary requirements of trade, could be entrusted only to highly responsible officers. The apothecaries, pepperers, and corders seem originally to have shared this responsibility. The earliest record of the appointment of a keeper for the king's beam is that of Silvester de Farnham, an apothecary and broker, in 1294. Three years later a committee of woolmen, pepperers, and corders was appointed to test the standards in use. In 1309 the weigher was a pepperer. A reform in the manner of weighing was carried through in that year at the king's demand, and with the assent of a group of foreign merchants, and of representatives of the pepperers and corders. The Londoners were compelled to abandon their custom of allowing a draught to the customer, a practice which had evidently been used as a means of discrimination against foreigners.[30]

Nothing more is heard of the keepers of the great beam until the appointments made in 1365 and 1376, both at the nomination of the grocers. But their enjoyment of this privilege was not secure against royal interference. In 1392 a writ was sent to the warden of the city, ordering him to deliver the custody of the common beam to one John Spencer for life. This name is not to be found on the grocers' lists. A month later a writ of *supersedeas* delayed the delivery of the beam until further notice. That the grocers had intervened and obtained the appointment for their own nominee may be inferred from the mention of William Culham as "commune poysour" in their memoranda the following year. Thenceforward they were left in uninterrupted possession of their privilege, though its apparent security was obtained at some expense. The accounts for 1452-4 note several payments to scriveners for writing bills to parliament " for the bem ", and the sum of £56 13s. 4d. was paid to John Yonge, grocer, " for safe garde of the Beem." [31]

The usual custom was to farm the beam from the city. In 1426 the weigher paid 40 marks for his office. But there was some dissatisfaction with the system, and in 1441 the experiment was tried of placing the official on a salary of £26 13s. 4d. with a controller paid 10 marks, neither to weigh except in the presence of the other or his deputy. This plan proved even less satisfactory than the other, and in 1442 the weigher was taken off his salary, and made to pay £40 a year for his office. In 1458 the composition was raised to £50.[32]

Although thus disposed by the city, the common beam was the king's, and he received a part of its revenues. The traditional fee was a penny for the sheriffs for every thousandweight, and a farthing to the weigher for every hundredweight. The grocers charged the weigher 40s. a year for his office, and further made him pay rent for the weigh-house. What further profit they made does not appear. But, apart from the question of its profits, the possession of the beam was a great asset to the grocers in that it kept them informed of all attempts at competition in their trade. Theoretically, at least, every wholesale transaction had to pass under the scrutiny of the weigher.[33]

The king's beam was used only for the so-called goods of avoirdupois, and must be distinguished from the instrument used for weighing wool, usually called the "tron". With the latter the grocers had no connection. Statements to the contrary have been based upon the fact that it was a grocer, John Churcheman, who in 1382 leased a building on the "Wollewharf" to the king to be used as a custom-house and for the tronage of wool. But neither he nor his company had anything to do with the actual office of tronage, which belonged at the time to one Richard Filongley, and in 1399 Churcheman's interests in the custom-house were transferred to a mercer, John Shadworth. The beam managed by the grocers was in 1392 kept in the house known as "le Herber", in Walbrook, later being moved to Cornhill, where it remained in Stow's time.[34]

A second important public service which the grocers undertook was that of the cleaning or garbling of spices. That this service should be efficient was as much in their own interests as in those of their customers, and their anxiety was prompted further by a desire to gain the upper hand of their Italian competitors. In 1393 they represented to the mayor that alien merchants were in the habit of selling them bales that contained as much as from twelve to twenty pounds of rubbish. The unsuspecting grocer who then resold them would afterwards be accused of cheating. They prayed accordingly that no spice or wax should be sold until it had first been cleansed by an officer elected for that purpose by themselves. Their petition was granted, one of their nominees appointed, and his authority linked with that of the weigher of the great beam, the latter being forbidden to weigh any wax or spice that did not bear the garbler's stamp.[35]

That the duties of garbler were well performed is indicated by a petition presented to the commons in 1439, desiring that in every port of the realm where spices were sold, they should be garbelled "in godemanere and trewe fourme as hit is used in the Porte and Citee of London". Accordingly in 1447 the grocers' wardens were granted the right to garble spices and drugs in Southampton, Sandwich, and in all other places in the realm where it might be necessary. One half of any forfeitures they made was to be kept to the use of the company, and an annual account was to be presented to the Exchequer. But it is uncertain whether this right was ever systematically exercised. Three of the annual reports, which have been preserved, declare that there was no profit to be shown, and there is no mention in the grocers' own books of any confiscation made outside London. In 1480 it was stated that, owing to the greater strictness in London, much spice was taken to Southampton and Sandwich to be sold there, and the right of garbling in these towns was subsequently vested in the London garbler.[36]

Until 1442 the grocers had retained the right of nominating candidates for the office of city garbler, claiming £2 a year from its revenues, and a further fee for the use of their seal. In that year the king took the office into his hands, and sold it to Richard Hakeday, his apothecary and clerk of the chandlery, and William Aunsell, one of his serjeants. Hakeday was a member of the grocer's company, but, much to the general displeasure, had negotiated for the office without consent.[37] It was not until 1484 that the grocers were able to resume their right of nomination.[38]

There can be no doubt that these privileges in connection with the offices of weigher and garbler were of very great advantage to the grocers in their business. As will be shown later, the possession of the beam was used as a means of discrimination against competitors, and influence over the garbler was perhaps equally useful. In the city itself the prestige of the company was such that no other body could challenge its rights; but the interference of the king, it has been seen, could at times upset the balance of power in the city.

4. *The Fourteenth Century*

In the fourteenth century there was provoked a good deal of discussion upon the proper regulation of trade. The rapid rise of the native class of merchants, and their prosperity during the difficult years following the Black Death, a period of rising prices, drew upon them no small degree of odium. A petition on the rolls of parliament for 1363 represents that, all through the country, dealers in foodstuffs—innkeepers and merchants alike—were in the habit of conspiring to buy at a low figure and sell at a high, making profits of 200 per cent and more. In a further petition charges of "cornering" all sorts of merchandise were levelled against guilds and fraternities in general, and in particular against the grocers, the success of whose organization had brought them into the limelight. Wyclif illustrated a sermon against the principle of trade combines, with their disregard of the fair price, by special reference to the grocers. But he included all victuallers, and it is clear that the complaints in parliament were not a partisan attack upon the grocers' company, but reflected upon the merchant class as a whole. The remedy proposed, and promptly embodied in statute form, was that merchants should be compelled to select one kind of merchandise and to trade in that alone. But it was found that the enforcement of this measure would have involved an insufferable amount of interference with vested interests both in London and the provinces, and within a year it had to be withdrawn.[39]

This act of 1363 has been the subject of much comment, but neither of the two views adopted is altogether correct. Unwin, seeing no logic in the remedy, attributed the act entirely to influences behind the scenes, mainly to certain London interests seeking monopoly rights.[40] That these were factors in the situation can hardly be denied. Nevertheless, they obviously worked in conjunction with other interests. The petition of the commons shows open annoyance at the intrusion of the native middleman between the consumer and the foreign merchant. Moreover, their remedy, though it proved impracticable, was under the conditions of the time not without a certain logic. To force merchants to deal in one commodity alone meant to force their organizations into the channels of monopoly, and to eliminate the moderating effect of competition on price levels. But the mediaeval theorist did not consciously think of competition as modifying prices. Prices—at least of victuals—were a question of law. The commons may well have been honestly convinced that it would be easier to regulate prices when the dealers in each commodity could be distinguished, than when merchants like the grocers, for instance, were free to manipulate the supplies of all sorts of commodities.

This experimental cure for high prices, then, must be regarded as the product in part of the impatience of the consumers, in part of the influence of those London groups which stood to gain through monopoly. In the circumstances it is scarcely correct to refer to its provisions as though they were typical of English trade legislation and policy. Yet it has more than once been so described, even without mention of the fact that it was never enforced and was quickly repealed. Recently it has again been adduced in support of the theory of " the mediaeval passion for division of function ".[41] On the contrary, its repeal bears witness to the exact opposite of this—to the fact that minute division of function was incompatible with the organization of mediaeval English trade.

The only permanent results of the legislation of 1363 were three charters, which under cover of its terms granted monopoly rights to the fishmongers, the drapers, and the vintners of London. Even in theory, however, these monopoly rights were not absolute—they referred chiefly to retail trade. The fishmongers' charter begins with the declaration that none shall meddle in their trade except only those who belong to the mistery, but it goes on to say that " every man may sell his fish in gross, as he will to any one for his own use but not to retail". The vintners were granted a monopoly of the wine trade with Gascony, in so far as no other native merchants were to be licensed to export cloth to be exchanged there for wine; but the Gascon merchants retained their footing in the wholesale trade, and nothing was said of the import of German wines. The grant to the drapers was aimed specifically at the weavers, fullers, and dyers, who were evidently their chief competitors. It was intended to exclude them from both the wholesale and the retail trade; it was complained that their intervention in the trade was unnecessary and harmful, since, as the cloth had in any case to be retailed by a draper, their profit on a wholesale deal only tended to raise the price. Yet there was no general wholesale monopoly, for anyone bringing cloth to the city was allowed to sell it to consumers who would buy wholesale.[42]

The feeling in the city was that monopoly rights should be strictly limited to retail trade, and that wholesale trade should be entirely free. The formulation of this theory was doubtless prompted by a fear that the newly chartered companies would try to press their rights too far. In December 1364, directly after the grant of the last charter, the common council petitioned the mayor to take up a definite stand on the matter, declaring that " it seems right that everyone who is enfranchised ought to buy and sell wholesale, within the city and without, any manner of merchandise on which he can make a profit, but he may keep a shop and sell by retail only those goods which belong to his particular mistery, which he ought to support whenever necessary. This they believe to have been the intention of their ancestors of old, but these ancient usages had been allowed to lapse, whereby the good misteries which used to maintain the City are likely to be hopelessly destroyed, unless speedy steps be taken to guard against it". Receiving no immediate reply, they again pressed the point, describing their request as for restitution of " the articles of the franchise which had been taken from the good folk of London without gainsaying ". But the mayor delayed his decision, and it was not until October 1365, that an official statement was issued, allowing, " that if any one has been admitted to the freedom of the City in some one mistery, and afterwards wish to pursue some other mistery he shall be allowed to do so, and to trade in all kinds of merchandise at his will without any hindrance." [43]

The interpretation of this ordinance is of the highest importance. Two distinct and separate rights are implied, first, the right to transfer from one mistery to another, and second, the right of freedom of trade. A man who had served an apprenticeship in any one craft was presumably to be allowed to transfer himself to any other. He was not necessarily licensed to carry on more than one industrial occupation at the same time.[44] Trade, however, was a different matter, and the citizen was to enjoy the privilege of trading in whatever kind of merchandise he pleased. It does not follow from this that craft distinctions and powers were to be obliterated. The previous petitions bear witness so plainly to customary restrictions in retail trade along craft lines, that it can scarcely be doubted that the ordinance was interpreted with reference to wholesale trade alone.

Thus the official theory current in fourteenth century London strictly limited the functions of the mercantile crafts to supervision of the different branches of retail trade. But the crafts themselves do not seem to have shared this view. To the principle of freedom in wholesale trade they opposed the principle of group monopoly and exclusive privileges, as appears most plainly in the charters obtained by the drapers and the vintners. These contradictions must be our guide in seeking to ascertain the true position of the crafts in the fifteenth century. Since there is no record of serious conflict over craft privileges, there must have existed some sort of peaceful compromise between the two extremes.

The actual situation must be read in the records of trade. In the following pages the activities of the grocers are traced in all directions. in order to see where their interests were concentrated, what were their relations with other merchant groups, and what were the distinctive functions of their own company. The theories of the fifteenth century as to the place of the companies can then be better interpreted.

§ 3

The Main Branches of the Grocers' Trade

1. *The Wool and Cloth Trades*

Theoretically, wholesale dealing was free in all trades. Actually, the degree of freedom depended on the importance of the trade. Wholesale dealing was most open in the great staple commodities—wool and cloth, foodstuffs, wine, timber, metals, dyes. No single craft could control the supplies of any necessities or of articles in very general demand.

Chief among these staple commodities were wool and cloth. Both gave rise to flourishing trades in which there was unrestricted freedom of enterprise, merchants of all descriptions taking part. With many this constituted simply one side of a varied business, but the evidence does not altogether preclude the possibility of a small amount of specialization in wool and cloth. In the study of any particular craft the extent of its members' interests in wool and cloth is therefore a most important factor to determine. Since by the custom of the city every citizen had to belong to one of the crafts,[45] it follows that if any merchants dealt solely in wool, or if anyone but a draper put all his money in the cloth trade, then craft membership was in so many cases a mere formality.

In order to discover the functions of the grocers' company, it is accordingly necessary to consider the undertakings of its members in wool and cloth. For if any were occupied solely with these, they could obviously have had no further motive in joining the company than to obtain the privileges of citizenship, and the appellation of "grocer" would in such cases have signified nothing.

The grocers played a prominent part in the wool trade, yet the number who may have been occupied in this alone can be narrowed down to a very few. Unfortunately there is no means of drawing up a complete list of those who were merchants of the Staple; one has to depend on the broken series of customs accounts, supplemented by a few scattered references. In this way the names of between forty and fifty wool merchants in the company for the fifteenth century can be collected. Nearly a third of these names appear also in the customs accounts as importers of grocery; the absence of the others, however, is of no significance, for the majority of he craft bought supplies from foreign importers. Four were described as woolmen, including William Lynne, a man of outstanding wealth, and Sir John Crosby, who was one of the members serving as mayor of the Staple of Calais.[46] If there had been any tendency for London merchants to concentrate all their capital in the wool trade, one would certainly expect to find it exemplified in the case of these rich woolmen. Yet Crosby, for instance, dealt in mercery, wine, fruit, and general groceries as well as in wool[47]; similarly other wealthy Staplers of the grocers' company dealt in imports. If men of the aldermanic, the richest class, found that it paid to supplement their wool business by a regular trade in imported goods, it seems more than likely that the rest of the group of Staplers among the grocers followed the same plan. Besides the Staplers, there were probably many lesser men in the company who handled wool. As a useful medium of exchange both with foreign merchants and with anyone connected with the cloth industry, it doubtless figured in many miscellaneous bargains.

The cloth trade, far from being monopolized by the drapers, was a wide-open field of enterprise. Merchants of all kinds were engaged in collecting cloth from the manufacturers, in selling it to the great exporters, or in exporting on a smaller scale themselves. The grocers' company was one of seven leading companies participating in regular export trade as the Merchant Adventurers, under the presidency of the mercers.[48] The lines of craft grouping were retained in the larger organization, but this did not mean that all the members of these companies were engaged in the trade. There was simply a small group from each.

But the extent of the grocers' interests in the cloth trade cannot be judged merely from their export business, for some of the largest dealers sold cloth to Italian firms. Their part in the collection of cloth for export by the latter may be fairly estimated from a file of accounts kept by citizens appointed as official hosts to supervise the business of foreign merchants in London during the years 1439-44.[49] Though incomplete, these files are representative, for they contain the names of sixty grocers buying Italian imports wholesale, and it is unlikely that there were any more than this number in a position to buy goods by the bale. Out of the sixty there were eleven selling cloth. Customs accounts for the decade provide us with the names of five more who exported on their own account, making a total of sixteen. Raised to twenty-five—to make a generous allowance for omissions—it represents about a third of the livery.

Though this number always included some very large dealers, there seems to have been little or no specialization in the trade. Almost all the grocers whose names occur in the customs accounts as exporters of cloth are known to have dealt also in imported goods. A few additional names can be found in the London records of the Merchant Adventurers for the last twenty years of the century— names of members who served on business committees of the company. Amongst these were eleven grocers. Seven of the number were dealers in imported goods as well as in cloth, but of the rest nothing can be discovered save that one was a Stapler as well as an Adventurer.

Thus there is a margin of possibility that a few grocers were entirely absorbed in the cloth and wool trades, though a very small margin. But it is clear that there was a group which combined one or both of these forms of trade with a business in foreign goods, and it is important for our purpose to see which side of their business was the more valuable and regular.

It is difficult to base any general conclusions upon the evidence of the customs accounts alone, since a man's actual exports and imports did not necessarily represent all his dealings; moreover, the valuation is unreliable. In one year, however, two grocers imported an unusually large amount of stock. In 1390 Geoffrey Broke and Walter Newenton imported merchandise valued at £2,330 and £1,738 respectively.[50] Their exports of cloth, even if one doubles the customs valuation, amounted in value to only a sixth and a third of these sums. But in some years their exports were much higher; in 1398, for example, Broke exported over 165 sacks of wool.[51] It is probably safe to conclude that their interests in cloth and wool were roughly equivalent to their interests in imported goods. Further evidence is available in the case of the eleven grocers selling cloth between the years 1439-44. Even if probable exports be taken into consideration, there is only one instance in which the interests in cloth exceeded those in other merchandise, four in which they were roughly equal, but in the rest the sales of cloth amounted to only a trifling amount of the total business.

The extent to which the grocers were involved in the wool and cloth trades cannot be judged with any exactitude. The companies of merchants of the Staple and Merchant Adventurers, engaged in exporting, attracted perhaps half the members in the livery, but this does not necessarily include all who had interests in these trades. There was a small group of wealthy men who were equally interested in wool and cloth on the one hand, and imported goods on the other. But the majority of the company were probably mainly concerned with the distribution of imported goods.

2. *The Victualling and Mercery Trades*

The distinctive functions of the grocers' company must be sought in the nature of their import trade. How did it differ from that of other companies? According to the mediaeval classification there were but four main branches of the import trade—grocery, mercery, wine and fish, with which last one might class other victuals, such as fruit and vegetables. But all the leading companies had a stake in foreign trade—not only the grocers, mercers, fishmongers, and vintners, but also the drapers, the tailors, skinners, goldsmiths, ironmongers, salters, and haberdashers. It is obvious that the different branches of trade could not have been neatly monopolized by the appropriate crafts, but were somehow divided amongst them all. The principle that every citizen merchant could trade in what he pleased must have had fairly free play. What, then, was the function of the crafts? Had they none beyond the control of retail trade? The answer in each case depends upon the degree of specialization characterizing their trade. An investigation of the business of the grocers, however, in a measure makes clear the position of all, for it requires a study of the whole field. In order to tell how far the grocers were specialists one must know how far they were able to trespass on trades connected with other crafts, and it is therefore necessary to make a brief survey of the situation in the victualling and mercery trades.

Participation in the victualling trades was very general. Indeed, it was the policy of the city to preserve them from monopoly. This is particularly apparent in the fish trade. An ordinance of 1382 made it legal for any citizen to engage in coastal fishing ventures, provided that he did so at his own expense, and not in partnership with " foreigners ", that is, non-Londoners.[52] That members of other crafts frequented the fish fairs in the country is one of the complaints recited in the fishmongers' charter of 1364. Their objection that the competition of these outside buyers at the fairs tended to raise prices is also set forth, but the charter did not make such competition definitely illegal, and there is no reason to suppose that the fishmongers ever succeeded in effectively reducing it. To judge from another charter, issued thirty-five years later, which reiterated many of the old complaints and prohibited secrecy in shipping and selling, the position had altered very little in the intervening time.[53] In the import and general wholesale trade in the fifteenth century there was a good deal of competition on the part of merchants of other crafts —grocers, mercers, drapers, ironmongers, tailors, and salters.

But with none of these merchants was fish the mainstay of their trade; rather it was a casual incident as opportunity offered. The grocers' interest in the fish trade was of this casual nature. Less than a fifth of their shipments from the continent included fish, and it was seldom represented in large quantities. As exceptions to the rule there were a few grocers trading to Iceland, which meant importing stockfish by the shipload.[54] But very few indeed would have traded regularly in fish on so large a scale as this.

Trade in other foodstuffs was even more open than that in fish, for no other of the victualling crafts was so strong as the fishmongers. Neither the cornmongers nor the fruiterers were wealthy men; they did not import on their own account. Yet local supplies were not sufficient to feed London. There was a keen demand for fruit and vegetables, and a thriving trade in French and Flemish garlic, cabbages, onions, apples, oranges, and other fruits. Of this the grocers seem to have taken the lion's share, though fishmongers, mercers, vintners, drapers and foreign merchants all played a part. But nearly all the fruit coming to London through Southampton was in the hands of grocers,[55] and both fruit and vegetables figured in their shipments from Flanders; again, imported onion-seed was one of the articles of their stock-in-trade.

The import of corn was an emergency trade, necessary only when harvests were a failure; hence it was under no regular organization. Any Londoner might handle local grain. For example, one meets a case of a weaver selling 600 quarters to a draper. Fishmongers handled a good deal of it, but they were not in a position to cope with famine situations. It was a grocer, Stephen Brown, who during his mayoralty in 1438 organized the aldermen into a ring of importers to bring corn from Prussia to alleviate a famine in London.[56] Probably he himself was no stranger to the trade; possibly none of the aldermen were. But there is no means of judging whether in the ordinary course of events the grocers took any considerable part in the corn trade.

By far the most important of the London victualling trades, so far as foreign trade was concerned, was that in wine. To all but the poorest classes wine was one of the prime necessities of life. A little was made in England, but the home-made product was early neglected for the far superior wines of Gascony, Spain, Italy, and the Rhine, which were proffered by visiting merchants. Until the fourteenth century the country was dependent upon foreign merchants for the greater portion of its supply, mainly upon the Gascon vintners. The king, however, and nobles and ecclesiastics faced with the problems of catering for a large household, found it cheaper to employ agents and import for themselves. As for its distribution among the ordinary population, wine was so universally in demand that any man would deal in it who had a chance; even though, according to the taste of the time, it was a perishable article, it was always a safe bargain. It could readily be bartered; it could be offered in satisfaction of fines; in short, as Unwin remarked, in the thirteenth century wine was almost a form of currency.[57]

In the fifteenth century, in spite of the much greater volume of trade passing through English hands, and the emergence of a group of specialized wine merchants, the situation was essentially the same. Dealings in wine were common among all classes of merchants. The market was never controlled by the vintners. Their own charter of 1364, extending to Gascon merchants the privilege of exchanging their wine for cloth, shows that the foreign importer was still regarded as an indispensable agent. Likewise there was room for many more native importers outside the ranks of the vintners' company. Anybody trading abroad would be likely to bring back wine, whether he were grocer, mercer, draper, ironmonger, goldsmith, or tailor. Vintners predominated among the Londoners trading to Gascony, but here their monopoly rights could not have been taken very seriously, for other merchants were allowed to ship in company with them. The work of distribution was as widely shared as that of importing. Not only did merchants other than vintners have their own imported wines to dispose of, but they also bought largely from the foreign importers. A great deal of wine was taken up from the Italians by the cloth merchants who dealt with them. A wealthy draper, for example, might take over £300 in wine in exchange for cloth. In 1504 the vintners complained of the " greete numbre of persones of several felaushippes . . . of the Citee daily usyng the occupation of Vynteners for their most pryncipall lyvyng ".[58] Besides this general dealing among all classes of merchants, nobles and gentry, who were accustomed to buy their household supplies of wine wholesale, often bought with an eye to resale at a profit. Knights, esquires, and gentlemen bought and sold with London merchants. For instance, a knight comes in from Hertfordshire, buys £48 worth of wine from an ironmonger, and stores it till be can find a buyer. A knight's wife passes on a quantity of wine to a merchant to sell to their common profit. A gentleman accepts wine in payment of a debt, and promptly sells it. It was, perhaps, more freely bought and sold than any other imported article.[59]

In view of this freedom in the trade, it is not surprising that wealthy grocers sometimes dealt in wine on a very large scale. They would import forty or fifty casks at a time; one man had a hundred casks of Greek wine sent over in a Genoese carrack; the chattels of a certain bankrupt grocer consisted entirely of wine, and another who failed for a debt of £600 had sixteen casks in his possession. They would find markets not only in London but also in he provinces; one man shipped wine from London to Lynn, others had it carted from Southampton into the country. Yet, in spite of the opportunities, the company as a whole had not a great stake in the wine trade. Less than a quarter of their shipments from abroad contained wine, and only 10 per cent of their number included it in their purchases from Italian importers in London.[60]

In addition to the victualling trades, there was another valuable branch of the import trade which lay outside the grocers' own province. This consisted in mercery—fine fabrics such as cloth of gold, velvet, satin, damask, silks, tapestries, quilts, and linen; canvas, a term applied both to coarse sacking and the finest linen,[61] was also classified as mercery, and oddments such as thread, hats, amber, ivory, and mirrors, which were sometimes counted haberdashery. In contrast to commodities like fish and wine, these were mainly luxuries, and as such they did not circulate so freely among merchants in general. They formed the peculiar stock-in-trade of the mercers. The only articles on the list which attracted other importing merchants were canvas, linen, and sometimes hats.

Grocers imported canvas and linen, and occasionally a little haberdashery, but they seldom attempted to handle the richer stuffs of mercery. The explanation lies mainly in the strong organization of the mercers. Without any chartered rights in their trade, they were able to maintain a virtual monopoly of the sale of all fine fabrics. Their chief weapon was their control of the overseas branch of the Merchant Adventurers, which placed them in a particularly advantageous position for bargaining with Flemish merchants, and enabled them to bring pressure to bear upon any who sold mercery to members of other companies. This policy is revealed in certain proceedings recorded for the year 1477: "Where as divers Camerik men ben nowe here & have had & yitt have grete plente of lawn to sell, It is agreed that the Wardens shall send for them & to cause their reformacion for that they sell their lawne to other felishipps & to Straungers as in Southwerk & other places etc. And if they will not be therto comfortable that than we to make ordenaunce in banysshyng the same & alle suche of their disposicion oute & from oure ffelishipp bothe here & by yonde the see & ellis to cause a letter to be made & sent unto the towne of Cameryk for a reformacion." Apparently the Cambrai lawn merchants remained obdurate, for a letter was shortly dispatched to the governor of the Merchant

Adventurers in Bruges, directing him to warn the " dekons of lawenmen " or the " Rulers and Guyders of the towne of Cameryk " that unless their merchants sold exclusively to the mercers, the latter would have no further dealings with them.[62]

This monopolistic policy of the mercers was the only check to the free enterprise of the grocers as general importers and dealers. Neither in the wine nor fish trades were there any effective restrictions to curtail their liberty. Yet they were not deeply committed in either of these, and in the fruit trade, equally open, it was only the wealthier men who were engaged to any extent. The value of their business in all these lines could not have amounted to a very large proportion of their total undertakings. If one accepts as representative the business of the two wealthiest grocers importing in 1390, who among other things handled fish, wine, thread, quilts, and skins, the value of such commodities came at most to about 14 per cent of the total imports.[63]

3. *The Trade in Grocery*

The foregoing sketch has roughly outlined the grocers' position. Apart from their interests in wool and cloth, at least 80 per cent of their business was in grocery. This was a comprehensive term, covering three different types of merchandise—metals, dye, with which one might class such things as alum and soap, and spices. Let us define the grocers' position with reference to each of these branches, seeing what competition they met, and whether their situation was in any respect comparable to that which the mercers occupied in the mercery trade.

Although metals were technically classed as grocery the trade was never regarded as pertaining especially to the grocers. Consisting as it did chiefly in the import of iron and steel and the marketing of Devon and Cornwall tin, it concerned the ironmongers and the pewterers more nearly than any other group. But it is doubtful whether the ironmongers by themselves could have imported enough to supply the market. At any rate, all the great merchants trading to Gascony, Spain and the Baltic would import iron and steel or buy it from foreigners for distribution. The tin trade, too, attracted a number of London merchants; there was always a group from the four leading companies engaged in the business, sending tin along the coast to Southampton to be reshipped for export or carted to London. Besides these the pewterers took an active part, the company being anxious to obtain its supplies directly from the mines without the intervention of outside middlemen. There was an obvious clash of interests with the exporting merchants, who tried to control the market. In 1441 seven of the chief dealers, including two grocers, two drapers, a fishmonger, a salter, and a pewterer, were accused of combining to buy up all the tin coming to London for a year. After this the interests of the pewterers were protected by an ordinance reserving to the wardens the right to take a quarter of the supply at the current price.[64]

In the dye trade the grocers played a more conspicuous part, but it was by no means their private preserve. The demand for dyestuffs was so great that no single company of merchants could have satisfied the needs of London and the surrounding neighbourhood. In the form of woad, madder, scarlet grains, saffron, and brasil, dye was one of the principal imports of the country. Great quantities of woad were distributed from Southampton to Salisbury, Winchester, London, Romsey, Coventry, and to villages in the cloth-producing areas. From about the middle of the fifteenth century the grocers took an exceedingly active part in this Southampton trade. The drapers and mercers had a certain share of it, and fishmongers and ironmongers were represented, but the grocers were the most numerous group.[65] But it is not clear that they sold the greater part of the dye that was distributed from London. Woad was of all commodities the most useful for exchange in the cloth trade, and it is probable that most cloth merchants had some dealings in it.

There was a further miscellaneous class of articles—alum, soap, wax and oil, subject to much the same conditions as dye; that is to say, they were handled indiscriminately by all merchants. Grocers handled them in large quantities, especially soap, for in addition to selling both the fine Castile soap and the coarser " black soap " that were imported, they engaged in the manufacture of the coarser grades.[66]

Finally, there was the spice trade. To this the grocers laid claim as their peculiar province; here lay their most characteristic business and their common interests. For some time they managed to exercise a virtual monopoly in spice. In 1411 it was said that, together with the Italians, and other foreign merchants, they held all the stocks of pepper in the country.[67]

The right of search which the wardens of the company possessed pertained only to spice. In 1386 they had assumed jurisdiction over the entire retail spice trade, asserting that everyone who kept a shop of spicery should be under the rule of their masters, whether or not he wore the livery of the company. Their authority was perhaps hardly consolidated before 1400, the date of their first recorded prosecution for the possession of adulterated spice, but during the first half of the fifteenth century a determined effort was made to set up standards of purity of wares. Fraudulent dealers were punished by fines running up to £10, the penalty for a third offence being expulsion from the company. The favourite form of deceit was to mix with the pepper the dust extracted from it by the garbeller. Apparently the dust had enough market value to warrant its export for sale abroad, but this was allowed only under strict supervision. Special officers were sworn in to take charge of the powdering of spices, and there was an effort to ensure that confectionery should be made of unadulterated sugar. Most difficult of all must have been the regulation of the sale of medicines. In 1424 the common council arranged that two apothecaries should be appointed every year as inspectors of drugs and medicines exposed for sale. Occasional confiscations were made by the grocers, but there is no record of the regular appointment of these inspectors, and prosecutions were sometimes initiated from the Guildhall.[68]

It was not a complete monopoly which the grocers exercised. Probably there was always some intermittent poaching in their field on the part of other merchants. The mercers entered spices on their list of brokerage rates, and would buy them from Italians, or even import them, and fishmongers would do the same. The accounts kept by the hosts of Italian merchants in London between 1439–44 show that a draper, Simon Eyre, bought nearly £1,000 of spice during these years, and that the largest purchase of pepper made by any single merchant at one time was that of a fishmonger, Stephen Forster, who took twenty-two bales, worth £529. Even so the greater part of the spice sold by the Italians was taken up by grocers.[69]

But after the middle of the century there seems to have been an increasing pressure of competition. Such, at least, is the inference to be drawn from the nature of the efforts made to reduce it. There was an attempt to penalize all individual dealing with outside native merchants. In 1455 it was prescribed that no member should buy any " sotill war[e] ", that is, spice, from anyone outside the company except " atte firste hande of the merchaunte straunger ", upon pain of forfeiting half the value of his purchase. By 1471 this had to be modified into a prohibition of buying spice outside the company whilst it could be obtained as cheaply within, and by special exemption the trade in imported saffron was allowed to be free. At the same time there was an attempt to mobilize the brokers of the company as trade spies. Their numbers were reduced to four, who were required to take an oath requiring, in addition to the usual vow of secrecy and obedience, that " Also ye shall sell no maner of Grocerieware to no maner person owte of the feliship of the Grocerie wt owte frawde or collucion but ye have licence of the wardens for the tyme beynge. Also ye shall geve knowleche unto the wardens of all maner sotill waris beynge in any mannis handes owte of the feliship wt ynne as goodly hast as ye can ". They were strictly watched, and one was dismissed a few years later for breach of his oath. Every member of the company was placed under the same obligation as the brokers, that is, he was bound to inform the wardens if he heard that " ony quantite of any merchandise whiche the feliship have nede of be in any merchauntis handis deneseyn . . . and Yei to see a Remedy Yeroff bi the advise of the feliship associatt". The remedy, presumably, was for the company to buy these competitors out, a measure indicated by an ordinance of 1479, a final desperate effort to make the company present a united front to its trade enemies; "yt no man of this feliship Bye no maner of Grocerie Waris as well Sotyll Waris as othir of no maner person or persones ow$_3$t of the seid feliship w^t ow$_3$t a licence of the Wardens. . . . Excepte of Merchauntes Strayngers and the said ware or waris to be Bowght by the advice of the wardens to the use and by hofe of the hole feliship." But the company was fighting a losing battle. It was impossible to adhere to such a policy, and by the end of the century all these ordinances were cancelled.[70]

A further indication of the grocers' loss of grip on the spice trade is found in their abandonment of attempts to fix selling prices. In earlier years this had apparently been one of the routine functions of the wardens, and members were often fined for the offence of underselling their fellows. But an ordinance of 1470 merely forbade members to sell cheaper than they bought unless they were forced to do so in an emergency, ordering them then to sell into the company. Recently the mayor had taken over the office of setting the price of figs and raisins, for this purpose classing them as victuals. The grocers still clung to their right to search in the trade. But after the close of the century even this was challenged. In 1523 their rights were curtailed, wholesale spice-dealers outside the company being exempted from inspection.[71]

Thus it appears that the bulk of the grocers' trade was in grocery, but that the field was far from being exclusively theirs. Trade in the staple commodities of this class—metals, dye, alum, soap, wax, oil, etc.—was fairly well distributed among the different merchant groups of the city; it was only the luxury trade, in spices, in which the grocers for a time, in the early part of the fifteenth century, approached monopoly.

§ 4

WHOLESALE AND RETAIL TRADE

1. *Wholesale Trade*

It has usually been assumed, from their connection with the great beam for weighing goods in large quantities, that the grocers were wholesalers. The mercers, on the other hand, have been described as retailers.[72] But the view that wholesalers and retailers were thus differentiated and organized in separate companies is totally unfounded.

Continental historians have carried on an interesting controversy over the existence of the wholesale merchant in the Middle Ages. It has been urged by one school that the mediaeval merchant was essentially a retailer, that there was no regular organization of wholesale trade. As Bücher put it, "wholesale trade was exclusively itinerant and market or fair trade," and there was no such thing as a resident class of wholesale merchants carrying on business in the towns. Von Below, too, took pains to point out that the typical foreign trader of Germany was in his own town merely a retail shopkeeper. From the universal jealousy with which mediaeval townsmen prevented outsiders from retailing within their walls, he argued that it was at that time the most profitable form of trade. His conclusions had to be qualified, however, by the admission that the leading merchants of Augsburg were chiefly engaged in wholesale trade. Again, Des Marez proved the existence of a superior class of wholesale cloth merchants in Ypres.[73]

Parallel conditions existed in England. As on the continent, the right to sell by retail was so highly prized that in nearly every town it was reserved to citizens. Neither aliens nor outsiders were to buy to sell again, nor might they sell in small quantities save on specified market days. But it does not necesarily follow that retailing was the typical form of business with the generality of merchants. A fifteenth century commercial handbook observes that "in every good towne suche men as sell by grose schall wyn more to sell aftre ii*d*. in schelyng by grete, than they that retayle and sell aftre iiii*d*. encrasse in the schelynge for that dele with grete summes and many small mak a grete ".[74]

There was undoubtedly a class of merchants mainly engaged in wholesale trade, that is, in distributing goods to a poorer class of retailers—town shopkeepers and country chapmen. In London its members were to be found not only among the grocers but in all the leading companies. Ample and unmistakable evidence of their activities is to be found in records of debt.

In their petition for the appointment of a garbler in 1393, the grocers stated that they sold pepper by the bale as well to lords as to " gentz paissantz ".[75] Since the Mediterranean trade was largely centred in London, the rest of the kingdom was practically dependent on the capital for the luxuries of Southern Europe and the Levant, and the companies which handled these luxuries, the grocers and the mercers, were therefore bodies of national importance. An analysis of the wholesale country trade of one of these groups, and of the manner in which it was conducted, forms a significant chapter in the economic history of London.

In the early Middle Ages fairs had been the chief means of distribution; later they became relatively less important. It is evident that the provincial trade of London merchants in the fourteenth century was by no means confined to the great fairs; they were constantly trading all over the country.[76] But towards the end of that century the fairs must have suffered from a concentration of trade in London. It became increasingly common for the country chapmen to come to London to buy their supplies.

The reason for this is to be found in the policy of the two chief distributing crafts. Originally they had been content to undertake the transportation of their wares into the country, but with growing prosperity they felt secure enough to abandon the old-fashioned custom, and to compel the country merchant to come to their headquarters. The mercers had always despised people who peddled in the country; in a ruling of 1347 they classed them together with boys of servile birth as ineligible for apprenticeship in the company. In 1376 they went so far as to forbid any of their members to attend fairs or markets outside the city, or to entrust goods to a country agent unless they had first been sold in London, on pain of ostracism; no one was to eat or drink, buy or sell, or ship from Flanders with a disobedient brother.[77]

Later the grocers adopted the same policy. Their first step, in 1420, was to forbid the selling of spice in the country except at fairs— ". . . no maner off Manne off the Felloschippe schall sende no malys (do sende ne make ne karyge) nor none horslodys Off no sotylle ware Inne to countre yere to proffre hit to sale ne To Reteylle hit Inne smalle But at Feyrys uppon payne off Forbedynge off his Felloschippe." The words "But at Feyrys" were shortly afterwards struck out, and the ordinance was interpreted as a prohibition of going to fairs or markets of any kind. From the year 1423 fines rising up to £4 were collected from members who disregarded the rule by going to the fairs at Oxford, Wye, Winchester, Salisbury, or, as was most often the case, to Stourbridge. Among the offenders were magnates such as Nicholas Wyfold, Thomas Catworth, Richard Lee, Robert Marshall, and other men who were prominent enough to serve as wardens of the company.[78]

The new rule cannot be considered a device for raising money by selling licences to trade at fairs. The whole subject was evidently the cause of much discussion. On one occasion the grocers gave a dinner to Carpenter, the town clerk, and others, to ask their advice in the matter. It was doubtless felt that fairs took away trade that would otherwise come to London, and perhaps that they offered too much opportunity for breaking of agreements as to selling price. In 1455 the grocers restated their rule more emphatically, " yt no maner of person w^t ynne the seid feliship of what degre yt he be shall take upon hym self be no maner Color nor means to send any maner of sotill ware nor grose ware into the Cuntry upon the peyne of lesyng V*li.* sterling." [79]

The grocers' books record no further discussion on the matter. But, so far as the mercers were concerned, the plan was obviously working much less satisfactorily as the century wore on. By 1477 they were beginning to doubt the wisdom of adhering to it any longer. They found that the haberdashers were taking advantage of their absence from fairs to go into the country and cut off much of their trade, and they decided that, unless they could persuade the rest of the crafts in the city to ban fairs, they would have to drop their own restrictions, and set their members free to trade where they pleased. They succeeded in getting the mayor to appoint a committee to make inquiries, but they failed to bring all the crafts into line. Seventeen were found to be willing to remain away from fairs, if there were a general agreement for all to do the same, but eleven others definitely refused. Thereupon the mercers gave way and abandoned their traditional policy—" Forasmoche as that alle or the more parte of all felyshipps in this Citie be at theyre libertie and many of them accustumed and gretely use fayres and markethes owt of this Citie thurgh which many persones abydyng at hom be gretely hurt in losyng of their Custumers that used and cam unto this Citie and here bought their Ware that nowe be served of the haberdisshers and other hauntyng such ffayres and markethes etc. and no remedy therfor Wherfor many and in speciall yonge men in oure felyshipp that be ther w^t gretely greved and as they say sorely hurte by the mean of non comyng of their Custumers and other Chapemen to towne mony a day have desyred to be at libertie the which wolde in no wise be graunted trustyng alway to have a generall Restraynt and for asmuche as it can not be don therfor nowe in this present Courte it is agreed to disolve oure Ordenaunce etc. . . . and to sett every person at libertie to go to fayre and marketh where as shall pleas them." It was complained, however, that this led to " grete inconveniences ", and they resumed their efforts to reach a general agreement among all the crafts.[80]

By February 1487 they prevailed on the common council to issue an ordinance forbidding freemen of the city to send wares to any outside fairs or markets for seven years. Owing to difficulties in the way its execution was deferred until Michaelmas, and in November it was annulled by parliament. The mercers continued to agitate, but the vested interests in fairs had won the day. The statute of repeal suggests that the fairs were at that time largely dependent upon the London merchants, declaring that the enforcement of the ordinance would have ruined them, and mentioning particularly those at Salisbury, Bristol, Oxford, Cambridge, Ely, Nottingham, and Coventry.[81]

There is no means of discovering who were the allies of the mercers in this movement. Probably their strongest supporters were the grocers, their chief opponents the haberdashers. They must have worked through the influence of the richer masters in each craft, those who could afford to make a temporary sacrifice for the sake of the greater gain which they hoped would accrue from the diversion of the trade of the fairs to London.

The grocers, not suffering from such organized competition as the mercers experienced from the haberdashers, perhaps did not feel the loss of country trade in quite the same way. Perhaps, too, they were not quite so hampered by their rule respecting fairs. At the time when they first decided upon it, they had several members in provincial towns, in Banbury, Shrewsbury, Coventry, Cambridge, and Ipswich.[82] These may have acted as important distributing agents. It is possible that some of these had served an apprenticeship in London, and had returned to the town of their origin to set up in independent business. It was unusual for a London company to have country members—the mercers did not record any—and these affiliations of the grocers reflect the importance of their provincial trade. Again, they effected a certain amount of distribution direct from Southampton. Although they carted straight to London most of the goods which they imported here, some were sent on to other towns, presumably to be sold there by agents. Several grocers seem to have had connections in Salisbury; fruit and wine, but chiefly dye, were sent here, and to Guildford, Newbery, Bristol, Northampton, Coventry, Reading, Oxford, Gloucester, and Tewkesbury.[83]

But they succeeded in concentrating a great deal of country business in London. The outlines of this can be traced in records of debt. Piecing the evidence together, one can form some idea of the grocers' trade. A number of spicers and apothecaries, in Bristol, Gloucester, Leicester, Oxfordshire, Dunstable, York, and Maidstone, failed in the payment of sums varying from two to twenty pounds. Dyers, too, were prominent among their country customers. A certain grocer by his will released three dyers of York, one of Beverley, and one of Ripon, from the payment of small remnants of debts. There were others who failed to pay in Northampton, Chichester, Shropshire, and Hertfordshire. Trade in wine is reflected by debts owing from taverners and hostillers of Beverley, Bury St. Edmunds, and Hertfordshire, and a vintner of Lincoln. The occupations of other debtors suggest further sides to the grocers' business—a waxchandler of Northampton, a jeweller of Plymouth, a glover of Somerset, fishmongers of York and of Bedford, and " naylers " of Lancashire and Staffordshire. In other cases there is no clue as to the nature of the transaction, the debtor being simply described as a mercer, merchant, chapman, or husbandman. Sometimes he was merely an itinerant merchant, a pedlar in fact, calling himself " chapman of Westmoreland ", or of Oxfordshire, Staffordshire, Essex, or Somerset. Others had more definite addresses—Exeter, Salisbury, Southampton, Sandwich, Boston, Lincoln, Coventry, York, or Bridport. A pepperer dying in 1391 had bad debts owing him by men of Shrewsbury, Hertford, Beckington, Lynn, and the Isle of Wight, while he himself owed money to men of Winchester, Hull, Whaddon, and Waterford.[84]

In the same way the mercers had customers from all parts of the country. Among the assets left by a certain mercer were debts owing by men of Salisbury, Shaftesbury, Glastonbury, St. Albans, Dunstable, Buckingham, Coventry, Manchester—dyers, glovers, and others.[85] Merchants of other companies, too, shared in this wholesale distribution of general merchandise to provincial merchants.

2. *Retail Trade*

It is clear that among the grocers and the other leading London merchants there was a class of wealthy merchants mainly engaged in wholesale trade. At the same time, there was no line of demarcation between the wholesaler and the retailer; retail trade formed a regular part of the business of the greater men.

The chief object of the charters issued in 1364 to the drapers, the vintners, and the fishmongers was to confer retail monopolies. How highly even the importers among the fishmongers valued the right to sell by retail is shown by a quarrel between the men who lived on the Fish Wharf, and the rest of the company.[86] The former shipped directly to the wharf and sold their fish on the spot to all comers, regardless of the rule that it should be retailed only in the three regular market-places. The rancour that was aroused testifies to the profits at stake. In the wine trade, a proclamation of 1311 attempted to draw a line between the functions of the wholesale merchant and the retailing taverner. But the taverner would sometimes contract to sell the wines of a certain vintner, who thus became the virtual owner of his business. Moreover, there is evidence that vintners themselves openly retailed from their houses, or kept taverns.[87]

Turning to the grocers, one finds that connection with retail trade was typical of the livery, the upper section of the company, both in the fourteenth and fifteenth centuries. In the first place, a considerable number of members kept apothecaries' shops. Among these apothecaries were substantial and respected citizens such as John Chichele, prominent for many years as chamberlain of the city. They may not have included all the great merchants whose business connections reached beyond London, but it is obvious that the latter were not above selling by retail. For example, John Aubrey, one of the wealthiest grocers of the late fourteenth century, retailed through an agent in Southampton, and it can scarcely be doubted that he also kept a shop in London. No description of his London establishment is available, but a number of other prominent grocers mention their shops in their wills. Some possessed warehouses in addition; others evidently used the shop for serving customers both wholesale and retail, furnishing it with a great beam for weighing hundred-weights, as well as with small balances and with mortar and pestle for pounding small quantities of spice. At least two of the great cloth merchants among the grocers are known to have kept shops—William Burton and Robert Marshall. That the latter's shop was not merely a warehouse is shown by the record of a dispute with a customer, to whom he had sold a small piece of wax adulterated with tallow.[88]

Retail trade being of importance even to the greater merchants, any record of its management must throw valuable light upon the working of the craft system, upon the powers of the crafts and the degree of freedom allowed the individual. Were the grocers free to retail everything they imported, or had they to specialize? What were their relations with the victualling crafts, with the industrial crafts affected by the trade in foreign wares, with other importers? And what principle guided the city authorities in their regulation of retail trade?

In the victualling trades, it has already been seen that there were no wholesale monopolies, that the grocers and other merchants had a certain share of the business. For the same reasons that the wholesale trade was left open to them they were also given opportunities for retailing. The powers of the victualling crafts themselves were limited. More than any others, they were under the strict supervision of the mayor and aldermen, one of whose chief responsibilities was the maintenance of an adequate supply of food for the city at a reasonable price. Their ruling idea was to ensure the direct contact of the country farmer with the town consumer. To this end certain localities were reserved for open market every morning, where all comers might sell their goods.[89] The intention was to reduce to a minimum the part played by the London middleman, and particularly, in the late fourteenth century, to curb the power of the fishmongers. Various experiments were tried at that time in the way of minute regulation of the trade in provisions. For example, the fishmongers were forbidden to buy for resale any fish, garlic, onions, or other victuals brought to town until they had been exposed in the market for three whole days. Other tiresome disabilities were imposed on them, but this plan was finally abandoned in favour of a general control to be exercised at the discretion of the mayor. The markets were maintained, where those who wished could buy directly from the country vendor, the fishmongers competed from their shops and stalls, and there were also street hawkers. The sale of salt fish was supposed to pertain to a separate mystery of stockfishmongers. This, however, does not necessarily indicate all the sources where fish might be bought. That it was sold all over the city was one of the regular complaints of the fishmongers, and it may be doubted whether they ever succeeded in consolidating the retail monopoly conferred by their charter. In Lent they were not always able to keep up with the increased demand, and the salters and chandlers were then sometimes licensed to sell fish.[90] Probably they hovered on the borders of the trade at all times. Of other competition there is little direct evidence. But there is a case of a mercer discovered with a supply of rotten eels, which he proposed to sell.[91] These were confiscated at the instance of the fishmongers, and duly buried, but there is no hint in the record of the proceedings that the mercer was censured by the mayor for trespassing on the trade of another craft, nor any implication that he could not have sold his fish if it had been fit to eat. There is therefore some reason to believe that grocers importing fish may have been allowed to sell it in their shops without interference. Those receiving shipments of stockfish from Iceland no doubt disposed of it on the wholesale market, but smaller quantities, especially during Lent, may have been retailed directly by the importer. In the absence of any strong organization in the trade in other provisions, it is even more likely that the grocers were free to retail the fruit and vegetables which they imported.

Next to the sale of fish, the most regulated trade in the city was the retailing of wine. In this it cannot be discerned that the mayor and aldermen, in their capacity as controllers of the trade, showed any anxiety to champion the monopoly of the vintners. Their concern was to see that the legal price, which was set by statute and advertised in the city by frequent proclamation, should not be exceeded, that new and old wine should not be mixed, and that no fraudulent colouring matter should be used. The function of the vintners was to assist them in their task. They undertook most of the burden of inspection, and in particular the oversight of the taverners. This was no easy task, since the taverners were not organized, and the city allowed people of any craft—armourers, for instance—to sell wine. The vintners' own records testify to the disregard of their monopoly rights. " It is ordained, that no maner of person of whatever craft soever he be, occupying the said craft of Vintners and retailing of wines within the City of London . . ." so ran their by-laws in 1507.[92]

There was therefore nothing to prevent a grocer from selling wine by the pint if he pleased. There is an instance of a spicer doing so in 1350,[93] and it is likely that all apothecaries sold wine for use with their medicines. It is probable, however, that the retailing of wine and other victuals played but a very casual and minor part in the business of the average grocer.

A further question arising out of the miscellaneous nature of the grocers' trade is whether they had the right to retail the manufactured goods which they imported—their pots and pans and odds and ends of haberdashery. Had the native manufacturing crafts no right to supervise the sale of such things ? Were the grocers on account of their wealth in a privileged position, above the law ? The answer obviously depends upon how general was the obligation to specialize.

We may briefly consider the organization of industry and the system of marketing manufactures from this point of view.

In the work of the minor crafts there were some remarkable instances of specialization. There was the distinction between the bakers of white and brown bread, between the cordwainers, or workers in new leather, and the cobblers, or workers in old leather, and the rule that the skinners must use only one kind of fur or skin at a time. Such distinctions were drawn in the interests of the public, in order to ensure that sound materials were used in all products for sale. Yet another motive for division of function was sometimes advanced by the crafts themselves, who hoped by simplifying the processes to be carried out in one workshop to be able to keep a sharper watch on the type of labour employed, and so to keep up their standard of living. The ironwiredrawers and the cardmakers, for example, desired in 1425 to be separated from the pinners, on the grounds that some members of each trade had been surreptitiously employing " foreigners " on the work of the other, thus depriving freemen of a livelihood. But this minute division of function was not carried into all branches of industry. Nor, even when specialization prevailed, was it enforced by the law for its own sake. Anybody, for instance, might make caps, provided they came up to the standard set by the regular manufacturers. Among offenders arraigned by the hurers in 1394 for making and selling " false " caps were two spicers and a pinner, but the charge against them was not that of infringing upon the rights of the hurers, but simply concerned defects in the method of fulling. In general the only principle that could be invoked against competitors in industry was that of the necessity of conforming to accepted standards of good work.[94]

The same principle governed the system of marketing manufactures. For these there were three classes of salesmen—members of the manufacturing crafts themselves, itinerant pedlars, and the haberdashers. None of these was under an obligation to specialize in one class of wares; all that was demanded of them was that they should not cheat the public.

Craftsmen sold goods from their own workshops and from stands allotted to them in Cheap and Cornhill, where open market was held every morning.[95] In addition to the working members there was probably a distinct merchant element in every craft. Sometimes it had the upper hand, as among the brasiers, who, petitioning for the right to elect two or four wardens annually, stipulated that one of these was to be a workman, and the rest chapmen.[96] But neither workmen nor chapmen were restricted to selling the product of their own craft. In the first place, they sold articles of foreign manufacture if they chose. Cappers, for example, sold German caps as well as their own.[97] Secondly, they were not restricted to selling the single type of article in the manufacture of which their craft ostensibly

THE GROCERS OF LONDON

specialized. The inventory of a certain bankrupt glover's shop mentions points, silk purses, and painted cloths as well as gloves.[98] Some of these he may have bought from foreign merchants, some may have been made in his own shop. Again, they were possibly made by poorer workers outside the craft altogether. The craftsmen with shops were nowhere near the bottom of the social scale. There was probably a large class of poor workers unattached to any particular craft, making miscellaneous small wares to be sold through glovers, pursers, haberdashers, or whatever other shopkeepers would take them.

A good deal of marketing was done through pedlars who carried packs of mixed wares. " Men as march with fote packes . . . owe to buy al maner of peny ware, also pursys, knyvys, gyrdlys, glassys, hattes, or odyr peny ware . . . and farthyng ware," says a handbook of the time.[99] There must have been countless numbers of these wandering about the countryside and coming to London to buy their stock. In London itself they constituted such a nuisance that in 1347 a large committee of citizens was appointed to see that they were kept out of the highway of Cheap. On feast days they were allowed to congregate at special markets held in Cheap and Cornhill, the latter traditionally devoted to hardware, the former a general market. There was much opposition to these " evechepynges " as they were called, on the grounds that they gave occasion for cheating and vice and general disorder, but they were finally allowed to continue, subject to the oversight of the wardens of the various crafts. These were appointed as official inspectors, with powers to confiscate gimcrack wares on suspicion.[100]

The London haberdashers were in a different category from the obscure pedlars of the street markets, but they performed the same function of marketing for the crafts. They were an organized body of shopkeepers, increasing in size and importance through the fifteenth century. Manufacturing nothing themselves, they may be regarded as an amalgamation of merchant elements from a number of the minor crafts. So far from being specialists they kept a stock essentially miscellaneous. Their largest single line consisted in hats, chiefly the coarse woollen caps worn by the working people. These were eked out with odds and ends such as girdles, purses, buttons, points, babies' boots, bells, straps, spurs, chains and bow-strings, dishes, boxes and gaming-tables, probably all obtained from local workshops, and with other things picked up from foreign merchants—paper, linen thread, plaster images, beads, ivory combs, and spectacles.[101]

Only in the case of cloth was the retail trade in a native manufacture supposed to appertain to a single specialized merchant craft. But the very charter which conferred this monopoly upon the drapers bears striking testimony to the competition to which they were exposed, stating that " one can scarce find a shop in the city which has not

U

some drapery, less or more, set to sale ".[102] One should, perhaps, allow for slight exaggeration in a document of this kind. The real aim of the drapers was to subordinate the weavers, dyers, and fullers, and almost no one else was ever prosecuted for competing. But in view of the general buying and selling of cloth, it is not unlikely that the statement was correct. Certainly, the mercers competed, and there were grocers who laid out pieces of cloth among their spices.[103] In practice, the situation was probably the same in regard to cloth as in regard to all other manufactures; that is, there was complete freedom in the marketing, and no one could interfere with a merchant whose wares were of standard quality.

The grocers, then, must have been at liberty to sell native manufactures, including cloth, whenever they chose, and in doing so would not have been assuming any extraordinary privileges. Undoubtedly they were also free to retail what manufactures they imported. The industrial crafts would naturally have liked to check the activities of the importers, but they were powerless to do so. This point was settled in the time of Edward II, when the cappers waged a campaign against importers and were defeated. They managed to obtain parliamentary sanction for an ordinance that caps should be made out of pure wool, and on the strength of this began to destroy all the imported caps they could find. The latter were made of inferior material—" flock "—and, though less durable than the London product, were cheaper and in wide demand. They were handled chiefly by German merchants and by the London mercers, whose combined influence eventually prevailed against that of the cappers. The foreign caps were declared to be " good and sufficient ", and as such were admitted on the market. The manufacturing interests, however, were not reduced to silence. By 1464 the flood of foreign trifles brought into the country had become such a grievance that they were able to obtain legislation forbidding all imports of the kind. Yet the repetition of the act, and the evidence of the customs accounts, show that the prohibition was of no avail.[104]

The only effectual check which the grocers might have encountered in the retailing of their foreign wares would have been the claims of other great importers, particularly the mercers. Yet both grocers and drapers sold canvas, linen and thread[105]; articles in such common demand the mercers could not keep to themselves. Nor, in view of the interests of the haberdashers, could they have objected to competition in miscellaneous small wares. But in the more costly articles of their trade it has already been seen that the mercers enjoyed a virtual monopoly, and there was therefore no question of retail competition on the part of the grocers. There may have been a certain amount of intimidation. A haberdasher who had bought a mercer's shop and stock complained to the chancellor that he had been robbed by two mercers " havyng dispyte and malice that yor besecher beyng a haberdasher shuld medill w^t mercery ware ".[106] Technically, however, there was no barrier. The only power which a craft could exercise over casual competitors was the power of inspection and confiscation of low quality goods. The wardens of a craft had the power to search any shop in the city for this purpose. It is not likely, of course, that the importing crafts would have submitted to search by minor crafts such as the pinners, particularly after the act of 1464, since the only legal object of such a search then would have been confiscation. But the mercers, for instance, submitted to search by the skinners for inspection of the furs they sometimes imported.[107] Subject to search by the wardens of the mercers or other crafts, therefore, the grocers could legally have sold mercery or anything else they pleased.

Actual evidence of the degree of freedom that prevailed in the retail trade of the importing crafts is confined mainly to a number of inventories of the time of Richard II. These show that the grocer's shop contained a remarkable diversity of wares—honey, licorice, dyes, alum, castile soap and the coarser product made on the premises, brimstone, paper, copperas, gall, and gum arabic for making ink, vermilion and turpentine for colouring wax, pieces of prepared coloured wax, lamp oil, painters' oil, garden seeds, vinegar, salt, varnish, red lead, arsenic, even books and firewood. One man sold spices, canvas, Breton linen, blanket cloth and coloured woollen cloth from Bristol, kersey, quilts, and furs, varnish and vinegar, balances, candelabra, washing basins and pot brass in bulk. In another shop there was no spice, but simply a miscellaneous stock of pitch, tar, charcoal, wainscot, and "rygoll" steel, wine, bowstaves and flax, and a barrel of fish. In nearly every case, however, there was a large stock of spices—pepper, ginger, saffron, anise, cummin, cinnamon, cloves, nutmegs, mace, almonds, raisins, figs and dates, sugar, rice, flour of rice, confectionary, musk and incense. To these an apothecary would add ointments and medicated syrups, sal-ammoniac, mastic, borax, cubebs, herbs, mercury and a great number of other drugs. But even an apothecary would supplement his medicines and spices with a variety of general merchandise. One, for example, sold cotton-wool and sponges, pots from Genoa, painted boxes, pyxes, leather bags, and the coarse cloth known as wadmol, and another sold banners, Prussian canvas, cotton thread, flax, silver spoons, and lead in bulk.[108]

The typical grocer, then, was a general merchant, but one who could usually be relied on to keep spices. In this line there is no evidence that in the earlier part of the period he encountered any retail competition beyond that of the chandlers in selling mustard, and of the treacle-mongers and surgeons, who sold drugs and possibly other spices as well.[109] At the same time, any merchant who chose could have sold spices, subject to search by the grocers' wardens.

The grocers had no official grant of monopoly, no right to coerce competitors.

One must conclude that such specialization as existed was in the main a natural development, arising from the advantage of expert knowledge in each trade, an advantage that was greatest in the luxury trades. It is significant that when the grocers' company wanted fine cloth for its liveries, it bought from drapers, and fine linen for its banqueting table was bought from a mercer; presumably the grocers themselves handled only inferior grades.[110] Obviously there was no strict obligation to specialize. Public regulation of retail trade was entirely in the consumers' interests, and its sole guiding principle was apparently the enforcement of standards of purity in the goods sold and honesty in dealing.

§ 5

THE DIVISION OF FUNCTIONS AMONG THE COMPANIES

1. *The London Companies*

It has been seen that the custom of London allowed citizens to deal wholesale as they pleased, and investigation shows that in practice there was also a large measure of freedom in retail trade. Nevertheless the companies were recognized as having certain definite powers. Each presided over a particular branch of trade through exercise of the right of search, and although this did not carry with it any direct power to suppress competition, organization undoubtedly tended to emphasize the specialization natural to trade. Without being pushed to its logical extreme—group monopoly—there was a rough division of function among the mercantile companies.

Yet, as has been pointed out, all alike dealt in wool and cloth, metals and dye, and there was a further pool of miscellaneous business, in such things as imported bowstaves, armour, pitch, tar, rosin, metal pots and pans, timber and tiles, in which all engaged indifferently, and which pertained to no particular one of the greater crafts. Consequently it is often difficult to tell, from stray notices of his dealings, to what company a man belonged. For example, William Coventry, a mercer and cloth merchant, imported hats, mirrors, paper, soap, wax, fish and iron; Alan Johnson, grocer and merchant of the Staple, ship-owner, while exporting cloth and wool, dealt also in wine and sugar, and sent two ships annually to Iceland for stockfish; Stephen Forster, fishmonger, trading to Iceland for stockfish, bought all that Venice could offer him in the way of silks and spice in exchange for Cornish tin; Philip Malpas, draper, handled spice, wine, dye, and tin, as well as cloth.[111]

In the circumstances it is not surprising to find that common business interests led to the formation of partnerships between men of different crafts. In the wool and cloth trades this hardly calls for comment, but one finds further that a grocer might associate with a pewterer, or with mercers in the purchase of pepper, or with a salter in importing fruit. Grocers and mercers fitted out ships for trade and privateering together, and fishmongers and salters co-operated in the fruit trade.[112]

Furthermore, it appears that there was nothing to prevent a man from joining two companies if he wished. The earliest instance found is that of John Otteley, who in one of his two wills, both dated the 12th of October, 1404, describes himself as citizen and grocer, and in the other as citizen and mercer. His name is on the grocers' lists, though not on the mercers', yet he is the only native merchant in the London customs account for 1390 noted as importing both spice and mercery, and he sold mercery to the great wardrobe. One of the largest establishments of the pewterers was maintained by a mercer, Thomas Dounton. Thomas Bataill, mercer, in his will left £10 " to the boxe of my Bretherin of mercery ", and another £2 to " the Almesboxe of my bretherin of Taylors ". Stephen Forster, fishmonger, traded with a group of grocers, besides buying grocery on his own account, subscribed to a fund to meet expenses concerning the common beam in the grocers' charge, and at his death left money both to the grocers and to the fishmongers.[113] Sometimes the second connection was in the nature of an honorary membership, or one with only partial privileges. Two fishmongers who subscribed to the building of grocers' hall were given the right to " by and sel wt us . . . wt owty any oyer fredome Imong us "; this perhaps referred to wholesale trade alone. Others received a hood of the livery, but the exact standing which this signified is not explained. In 1428 three mercers wore hoods of the grocers' livery, and a grocer at the same date was paying £2 to join the mercers' livery.[114] Again, at the beginning of the fifteenth century civic officials were in the habit of accepting liveries from a number of different crafts. In 1415 this was made illegal, perhaps merely with the intention of keeping craft influence out of city politics as much as possible. Yet at least two of the offenders had apparently been practising two trades. William Cambridge, alderman and grocer, was declared to have been practising the trade of an ironmonger as well as his own, and Richard Merlawe, another alderman, had been trading with both the fishmongers and the ironmongers. He was shortly afterwards formally admitted to the fishmongers' company, but he continued to be described as an ironmonger.[115]

Evidently there was a certain solidarity of business interests among the wealthier citizens, the great cloth and wool merchants, general importers and wholesale dealers, besides which their differing craft affiliations were of small significance. Moreover, they could buy their way at will into the exclusive privileges of more than one craft. With the middle and lower merchant classes, on the other hand, craft distinctions may have been of more consequence.

But among all classes it was understood that certain definite obligations were attached to craft membership. The custom of the city upheld the principle that a citizen must contribute to the funds of whatever craft was connected with the chief trade he practised.

This principle was adopted at the instance of the great mercantile crafts. Anxious to draw into their ranks all who engaged in their special trades, they yet erected a barrier of high entrance fees. Country merchants settling in the city and admitted to the freedom by redemption, that is, by payment of a sum of money instead of by apprenticeship, therefore tended to seek admission through minor crafts in which the fees were more reasonable. To discourage this it was provided in 1384 that every man received into the freedom by redemption should find six citizens of the craft in which he was admitted " to testify to his fitness ", and also " as to his ability to pay ". In the following year two men from Barking were deprived of the freedom for having obtained admission to the company of haberdashers under false pretences, most of their trade being in mercery. The plea that they sold haberdashery as well did not excuse their action. The haberdashers had charged them only twenty shillings, whereas the mercers claimed that one of them, being worth over £200, should have paid £20 or even £40. The drapers, as well as the mercers, kept a jealous watch upon the lesser crafts. A weaver, forced to confess that " he never used the mistery of *Webbes* as a common workman, but only for the cloth his wife made ", and a tailor, " his mistery being drapery and no other," were both deprived of the freedom. So also was a man who had obtained the freedom through the fishmongers' company with the intention of trading only in cloth and grocery. But there were many offenders, obtaining the freedom through crafts with which they had no real connection, who were too influential to be prosecuted. Hence in 1433 the system of admission by redemption was brought under more rigorous control, and it was decreed that no one should be so admitted into any craft without a guarantee that such admission was not prejudicial to any other craft. The guarantee took the form of a bond of 100 marks ; in addition there had to be three or four sureties each bound in £20, the money to be forfeited if at any time it should be proved that an entry into the grocers' company, for instance, had been made " sub colore ad utendum aliqua arte seu mistere dicte Civitatis et non vel minime dicta mistera de Grocers etc . . ." This did not mean that a man was obliged to restrict himself to a single line of trade, for it was specifically declared " that it be leefull to every man that be redemption herafter truly without disceite shalbe made free in any felishp of suche craft as he hath verrily used to use for the seid craft after and such other occupacions as god & fortune for the tyme will avaunce and able hym too ". His bond was forfeit only if it could be shown that he had no serious business connections with his original craft.[116]

It cannot be assumed that these precautions entirely achieved their purpose. Indeed, in so far as it was directed against wealthy country merchants who had bought the freedom of the city too cheaply and escaped contributing to the funds of the greater crafts, the law was perhaps little more than a gesture. A man who was wealthy enough to provoke prosecution would be able to bribe his way out of it. The common council several times decided to prosecute people with their sureties " for not exercising the mistery in which they were admitted ", but the only proceedings on record concern a merchant who had joined the fishmongers, and who, on offering the chamberlain £20, was given leave to trade as he pleased. On the other hand, ordinary people would not be able to protect themselves in this way. But, again, jealousies among the crafts themselves stood in the way of a consistent enforcement of the law, for none cared to lose the fees of a member. To lessen the disputes that arose over the question of these translations from one craft to another, it was a rule that none should take place without the consent of the mayor. In the interests of peace this consent was sometimes withheld when it should legally have been granted. When Robert Goodeer, a mercer who had married a grocer's widow and taken over her shop, applied for permission to join the grocers, the mercers would not allow him to change, and though he continued to agitate and appeal for two years, the mayor declined to interfere.[118]

Yet the great number of translations that took place during the century is an indication that the law was by no means a dead letter, and that the trading element in the industrial crafts was at least to some extent absorbed by the mercantile crafts.[119] At the same time, the circumstances show that there was no great vigilance in enforcing the obligation to join these crafts in order to carry on their trade. For example, a man who had obtained his freedom through the chandlers traded with the vintners for six years before applying for formal translation to their craft. A young ironmonger desiring to become a grocer declared that he and his master " had always used the mistery of grocers ". More curious is the case of Simon Eyre, who served as an apprentice for seven years before discovering that his master was an upholder (upholsterer), and not, as he had imagined, a draper. Yet, though obviously an upholsterer must have been able to trade in cloth, Eyre was anxious to begin his own career in the drapers' company. Again, a tailor's apprentice who declared he had always dealt in mercery was allowed to join the mercers.[120]

There were unmistakable advantages in setting up in trade under the auspices of the proper craft. Robert Goodeer, the mercer who had acquired a grocery business by marriage, explained that he wanted to change his craft because he would not be allowed " to have knowlege of the Secretts of that occupacion ne any avauntage to have at the beme oon'es he were a grocer or a brothir sworne unto the Grocers ". As an outsider he could get no help in learning the business, could not ask advice from more experienced dealers nor draw upon their information as to prices and supplies, for every freeman grocer was sworn to " geve no Informacion nor Instruction yat touchith the occupacion to noñ other persone owte of the felishipe " and to " kepe secrete all leefull cowncels of the felishipe ".[121] In the second place, the grocers' possession of the beam gave them opportunity to discriminate against competitors; they had their goods carried for less by the porters of the weigh-house,[122] and possibly arranged a reduction of other fees. The mercers were in a similar strategic position through their control of the weighing of silk and the measuring of linen, and likewise other companies could turn the control of trade appointments to their own advantage. Finally, it appears that the companies acted to some extent as co-operative buying concerns, members having the right to share in occasional common purchases. In the grocers' books there is but one record of the practice, mention being made of payment to a Venetian, an honorary member of the company, for merchandise " pertable Imoinge all ye craft ". The company of fishmongers, on the other hand, was authorized to buy up all the fish sent to the city by strangers, and to divide it amongst the members. In this case there was an obvious advantage to the retailer in belonging to the company.[123]

The system of grouping among the London merchants was therefore based upon a division of functions. According to the common council of 1364, this division was supposed originally to have pertained to retail trade alone. The companies then had powers simply in the nature of police authority—theirs was the responsibility of ensuring that pure goods were sold in honest measure. In the fifteenth century their authority was extended. They were recognized as having vested interests each in a certain branch of trade, and the right to assess contributions from all who proposed to make their livelihood in that line. The division of function was not imposed by outside authority, nor was it carried to such extremes as seriously to interfere with the liberty of the individual. So long as he remained an active supporter of his company, a merchant was free to undertake any other form of enterprise he pleased. Thus a satisfactory compromise was reached between freedom of trade and monopoly.

2. *Provincial Merchant Companies*

In thus providing for a certain degree of specialization in trade, the custom of London was unique. As a rule the merchants of a provincial town were organized in a single body which regulated trade without reference to specialization among its members.

There was nowhere any counterpart of the London mercantile companies. For example, there was no other company of grocers. It is true that grocers, or spicers, or apothecaries, are mentioned in the records of most provincial towns, but they were nowhere numerous enough to form any organization of their own. Not until the sixteenth and seventeenth centuries do they appear in groups, and then they are always found in amalgamation with other small groups.[124] Again, merchants are often described as drapers, but they formed no separate organizations as such until the close of the fifteenth century. Vintners, too, are mentioned; in 1364 licences were granted to a number of vintners from York, Kingston, Sandwich, Rye, Hastings, and other ports to take money and cloth across to Gascony with which to buy wines. These men called themselves vintners on this occasion in order to qualify for admission to the privileges which had just been granted to the London craft, and extended to the vintners of other towns. The wording of the grant implies the absence of any specific organization among the latter; merchants were forbidden to meddle in the wine trade, " to wit, in London, except only those free of the vintners' craft; and in other cities, boroughs and towns those who have knowledge of the craft (ceux qui sont sachantz et conuz de mesme la mestier)."[125] Fishmongers, tailors, skinners, goldsmiths, and salters, who in London engaged in foreign trade, ranked elsewhere among the minor craftsmen. The leading group in the town often went by the name of mercers. They were not, however, in any way analogous to the mercers of London. It was only in London that the name had the special connotation of a dealer in costly fabrics. Elsewhere it was synonymous with "merchant".

On the eastern coast the main imports were fish and wine. To these could be added a long list of miscellaneous commodities, none of which, however, nor any group of which, appear in sufficient quantity to suggest specialized dealing. Nor is there conclusive evidence of specialisation in fish or wine. On the contrary, merchants of Kingston can be found combining the import of both of these with shipments of fruit, beer, butter, honey, soap, dye, horseshoes and iron, bonnets, linen cloth, and thread.[126] The customs accounts for Newcastle suggest that there, too, the merchants were general dealers. It is true that grocers and others in London imported a great variety of merchandise. But there could have been no groups of merchants in the northern towns resembling either the grocers or mercers of London. Spice, the characteristic stock-in-trade of the grocer, was barely represented among the imports of the north. Even pepper was brought over only in tiny lots worth a few shillings each, not by the bale, and the quantity of mercery, in the sense in which the word was used in London, was hardly more considerable.

Some canvas, linen, " spinall," a few of the popular continental felt hats, and a little thread, were sometimes contained in a shipment, but never enough to stock a shop.

The customs accounts for Bristol point to the same conclusion, that the merchants there were general dealers. For Southampton there is a more satisfying amount of evidence. A long series of customs accounts, and a record of goods sent overland, show that the chief trade was in wine, woad, fish and iron, and that the average merchant dealt in all of these commodities. In the latter half of the century he might have added a few deals in fruit and spice; formerly most of the spice entering the port had been conveyed directly to London by the Genoese shippers. Wine heads the list in value, dye running a close second, but it is only in wine that one can observe any tendency to specialize. The only outstanding instance is that of Robert Bluett, a prominent merchant who happened to be affiliated with the London grocers. Though he sold every other article on the market, the greater part of his imports consisted of wine. The Salisbury and Winchester merchants using the port conducted business on much the same lines as the Southampton men. So far as one can judge from these sources alone, wine was their chief stock-in-trade, though dealings in fish, salt, dye, alum, soap, spice, fruit, oil and wax make it impossible to call them specialized wine merchants.[127]

It is apparent that in the provinces there were no distinctions within the general calling of a merchant. In Northampton, for instance, the son of a freeman took his oath as a burgess "as sone as that he will marchaundizen". In Bristol no further credentials were demanded of a new citizen joining the general group of " merchants and drapers " save that he be " marchaund conu homme de bone fame et honeste conversacion ". In York the mercers or Merchant Adventurers claimed a complete trade monopoly in the city; market-day visitors excepted, no one but a member of the company could ever buy for resale or retail any goods brought to York. Anyone desiring to set " a shop of mercery or merchaundise " had to belong to the " craft of mercerie ". There is no indication of any subdivision of the area thus staked out. The suspension of the Sunday-closing act during Lent with regard to the sale of " vitayle and lentynstore " suggests that the fish trade, for example, was more probably open to all than restricted to any special group. Moreover, there was no arrangement for supervision of the sale of different kinds of wares, the only official form of inspection being the testing of weights and measures. In Newcastle the situation was much the same.[128]

The liberty enjoyed by the provincial merchant is the more striking when contrasted with the meticulous care shown in the organization of the minor crafts. In York there were over fifty different crafts, but the most remarkable instance is that of Norwich, with a population only about one-third that of York, and one-sixth that of London. For convenience it was provided that similar crafts should be grouped together; for instance, the misteries of bladesmiths, locksmiths, and lorimers were to form the craft of smiths, the right of search for inspection of their work being vested, however, not in the warden of this general craft, but in a separate warden for each little group. If it contained as many as seven people, they were to hold " a general assemble " to elect the official; if there were less than seven, he was to be appointed by the mayor. Yet the merchants of Norwich seem to have been of one denomination only; all the principal citizens, we are told, enrolled themselves as mercers.[129] This example of the tiny crafts of Norwich shows how absurd it would have been for the merchants of any small town to trouble to organize themselves with a view to the separate supervision of each branch of trade. Constituting as they did the ruling class, they served no compulsion but their own interests, and they found that the central machinery of their craft or of the town could impose as much honesty as was necessary.

Granted, then, that the provincial trading organizations did not allow for it, there yet remains the possibility of individual specialization, particularly in wine. But, as Unwin remarked, the localization of certain trades had the effect of hindering specialization in provincial centres. For instance, every merchant in Newcastle, whatever his other interests, was attracted to the coal trade, and everyone in Yarmouth went to the herring fair; similarly, everyone in Reading seems to have traded in tiles.[130]

The typical provincial mercer, or merchant, was undoubtedly a general dealer. In a single shipment through Southampton one finds a Salisbury merchant importing fish, garlic, madder, soap, onion seed, tar, hemp, steel, nails, timber, tables, brushes, points, hats, teazles, and tapestry covers.[131] Still more comprehensive is the inventory of the shop of a Leicester mercer, which has been preserved among bankruptcy records.[132] This man was at the same time draper, haberdasher, jeweller, grocer, ironmonger, saddler, and dealer in timber, furniture and hardware. Even this does not describe him adequately, for he had a small stock of wool, wool-fells and skins on hand, and he could have offered you ready-made gowns in taffeta or silk, daggers, bowstrings, harpstrings, writing-paper, materials for making ink, and seeds for the vegetable garden. His resources were greatest in the drapery department, which comprised twenty different kinds of British and imported cloth; he was also well stocked with small wares, notably purses of gold cloth, belts, ribbons, skeins of Paris silk, children's stockings, silk coifs, and kerchiefs for nuns. In the way of hardware he had everything from cutlery and candelabra to coal-scuttles and horse-shoes. Provisions he had none beyond honey, raisins and salt; but the absence of any note of perishable foods from a document of this kind does not prove that they had not been included in the original stock.

In short, business opportunities in the smaller towns were naturally limited as compared with the scope offered in London. The greater population of the capital—by the fifteenth century three and four times the size of the largest provincial towns—attracted a greater volume and variety of trade. Consequently there was a greater subdivision of occupations.

VII
THE RELATIONS BETWEEN THE LANCASTRIAN GOVERNMENT AND THE MERCHANTS OF THE STAPLE FROM 1449 TO 1461

§ 1
The Loans from the Merchants of the Staple and their Repayment

One of the most interesting and least studied problems in the history of the Wars of the Roses is the part played in that struggle by economic forces. The relations between the contending parties and the towns offer one important line of investigation, which has been partly pursued elsewhere;[1] another is offered by their relations with the Company of the Staple, a body powerful by reason of the large financial resources of its members and the influence which it exercised at Calais, the centre of the wool trade and the surest foothold of the English on the Continent. The purpose of this study is to trace the general history of the dealings of the Company with the government during the last years of Henry VI's reign (1449 to 1461), with the special object of determining whether the Company was inclined to champion the cause of either Lancaster or York, and whether it exerted any influence on the political situation at that critical juncture.

Reference has already been made in a preceding study to the importance of the Staple as an instrument of royal finance, by which the Crown was able to obtain large sums of money on credit. During the first half of the fifteenth century, loans had been frequently made by the merchants of the Staple, and had been repaid either from the proceeds of the customs, or from direct taxation. This had given to the Staplers an opportunity of urging upon the Crown a policy favourable to their interests. The chief items in their programme comprised the relaxation of the bullion laws, by which they were compelled to receive from their foreign customers a large proportion of ready money, the maintenance of an efficient customs system, and the enforcement of a strict monopoly for Calais as the market for staple goods, other than those sent by the Mediterranean. This was the demand most keenly pressed, and it implied a restriction on the royal power, which was freely used to grant licences releasing the recipient from the observance of staple regulations. Until 1449, in spite of repeated protests, the Company had achieved a very limited measure of success. The bullion laws had been occasionally suspended, but the Crown had succeeded in maintaining its power to grant licences modifying staple regulations, and there was good reason to complain of the way in which the customs system was administered.

In 1449 matters reached a crisis. The renewal of the French attack on Normandy and Guienne, the last remaining English possessions in France, greatly increased the financial difficulties of Henry VI's government. Money was needed for the military expeditions to France, and to meet the exceedingly heavy cost of keeping the defences of Calais in a state of efficiency. At first, the government attempted to raise this money by increased taxation. The parliament which met at Leicester in 1449 imposed a subsidy on the country, and granted tonnage, poundage, and the subsidy on merchandise for a period of five years. The latter grant was accompanied by unusual stipulations; many of the assignments on the subsidy were to be revoked; and persons obtaining exemption from the obligation to ship to Calais, or from the payment of subsidy, were to forfeit half the goods so shipped.[2] This was an attempt to clear away some of the claims which had been established upon the customs. A considerable proportion of the proceeds—a rough estimate would suggest between one-third or a half—was never received by the Exchequer, but was paid over by the collectors to persons who had been granted assignments on the customs. Other persons had received the privilege of shipping goods wholly or partially free of duty. These alienated sources of revenue were now to be rescued for the Crown, while at the same time the monopoly of Calais was to be more strictly enforced.

An attempt was also made to set the finances of Calais on a more satisfactory basis. Since 1437 twenty shillings of the subsidy on every sack of wool had been reserved for Calais, and additional sums were transmitted from the Exchequer from time to time, but in spite of this the wages of the garrison were continually in arrears, and the soldiers remained in a state of perpetual discontent and of occasional mutiny. Now it was proposed to devote five shillings of each twenty shillings to paying off arrears, ten shillings to present wages, and five shillings for victuals, a proportion changed by the king to 13s. 4d. for wages past and present, and 6s. 8d. for victuals.[3]

Later in the year a still more stringent statute was passed. This was based on a petition presented by the merchants of the Staple in which they complained that, in spite of Staple regulations, the customs had been reduced from £68,000 to £12,000, to the damage both of the merchants and of the soldiers of Calais. This was due, they asserted, to the " divers and many licences given by Letters Patent, and by misusing of the said Licence, buying of wools and wool-fell in other places than their licence containeth, shipping more number and weight and colouring, by new faned names ", to the sale in Brabant of wool that should have been taken overland to Italy, and to the " great stealing of wool not customed out of the kingdom, oftimes by consent and means of untrue officers ". They demanded, therefore, that their privileges should be confirmed; that no licences should be granted, and that if any were, they should have an action for the recovery of the goods; and that anyone should be allowed to seize the goods of offenders shipping elsewhere than to the Staple. Exemptions were only to be granted in the case of the recognized trade to Italy by the Straits of Morocco, which had always been free from the Staple regulations, and of privileges already granted to the Duke of Suffolk and to Queen Margaret. The king granted the petition, though he added four other exemptions, and it was embodied in a statute which was to continue in force for five years. Next year, an act of Resumption was passed, and though its force was weakened by many exemptions in favour of officials of the Royal Household and others, the claims of a host of petty pensioners to commercial and other privileges were set aside.[4]

The withdrawal of the licences, against which they had been protesting for so long, was a signal triumph for the merchants of the Staple.[5] It is clear that their success was the outcome of the financial difficulties of the government. In spite of the efforts made to increase the revenue, the proceeds of taxation were insufficient to meet the increased expenses of the war. In 1450 the receivers of the subsidy voted at Leicester in 1449 were informed that, as the money could not be collected speedily enough, " the King has borrowed divers notable sums for lack thereof, to be applied to the defence, and intends to borrow still greater sums."[6] It was necessary to obtain loans, and the government turned, as it had often turned before, to the merchants of the Staple, who were likely to be exceptionally accommodating where the safety of Calais was concerned.

On 20th October, 1449, an agreement was made with seventy-nine merchants of the Staple, who received letters patent authorizing them to recoup themselves for a loan of £10,700 which they had made to the king at divers times, by exporting from London, Boston, Hull, and Ipswich, within the next four years, sufficient wool and wool-fells to enable them to repay themselves by retaining 13*s*. 4*d*. out of the subsidy of 33*s*. 4*d*. paid by denizens on the sack. This was an attempt to clear off a debt which had been accumulating for some years. According to the Receipt Rolls the Exchequer had received nothing from the merchants of the Staple since a payment of £6,666 13*s*. 4*d*. which had been made on 7th December, 1447. There is in the Treaty Rolls for 1447-8, however, an entry to the effect that Robert White, the present mayor, and his predecessors, had lent at divers times the sum of £10,366 13*s*. 4*d*., but had received no repayment. It was therefore to be repaid by the collectors of the lay and clerical tenths and fifteenths, and for " speedier repayment " the Treasurer was directed to issue warrants for the making of tallies. There is no record in the Issue Rolls that this sum was ever repaid. In the previous year, Robert White, the mayor of the Staple, is noted as having lent 500 marks (£333 6s. 8d.) for which he was to ship five hundred sacks of wool from London, retaining all the dues except 20s. of subsidy.[7] These two sums make up a total of £10,700, of which £6,666 13s. 4d. must have been contracted before 7th December, 1447.

Arrangements having been made for the repayment of old debts, the government proceeded to contract a series of new ones. On 27th February, 1451, £5,866 13s. 4d. was received by the Exchequer from the merchants of the Staple, for which they were to have repayment " in divers ports of England ". Most of this was immediately applied to the upkeep of Calais, for on the same day large sums were issued to the Treasurer and Victualler of Calais, which included a loan of £4,533 6s. 8d. received from the merchants of the Staple " at divers times ", £2,000 of which had been handed over by Lord Sudeley. Provision had already been made for the repayment of the latter sum, for on 20th March, 1450, a group of merchants, some of whom had been concerned in the previous loan, were directed to recoup themselves for a loan of £2,000 which they had advanced to Lord Bourchier and Lord Sudeley for the safekeeping of Calais and Rysbank by retaining 13s. 4d. the sack on wool exported by them.[8] No provision was made for paying off the rest of the loan.

On 7th June, 1451, the Exchequer received from the merchants of the Staple loans of £2,666 13s. 4d., £2,000, and £666 13s. 4d., which were to be repaid by the shipping of wool from London, Boston, Hull and Ipswich. The purpose for which these loans were made can also be identified. On the day that they were made, a group of twenty-six merchants was directed to ship from Ipswich wool sufficient to enable them to recover 1,000 marks which they had forwarded for the Royal Household. The same group was also directed to recover a further 1,000 marks there as part of an indemnity of 4,000 marks which had been paid to the Duke of Burgundy to secure the release of merchandise which he had seized by way of reprisals. The rest was to be recovered in London, Boston or Hull. A further £2,000, paid as compensation for the plunderings of an English pirate, was to be recovered in Boston by another group. This was the price that the English had to pay for the renewal of the truce with Burgundy, and ten days before, the money had been paid to Adrian Skyvile, the Duke's agent, by the merchants of the Staple. Most of the money advanced, therefore, was connected directly or indirectly, with the safeguard of Calais, inevitably a matter of great importance to the merchants of the Staple. That year they not only provided large sums of money, but they co-operated with the commonalty of London in raising a contingent of men-at-arms for its defence.[9]

The negotiations for the repayment of the £10,700 were carried out through William Cantelowe, who " at the speciall request of the seid Marchauntes was Solicitor to sue for the assignment to be hadde for theire repayement".[10] He had already had much experience in such dealings on his own account, and was making an independent loan of £800 at this time, besides joining with Alan Johnson and Thomas Cantelowe to make the most considerable contribution to this one.

The whole loan was divided into thirty unequal shares, which were described as the joint contributions usually of three, but sometimes of one or two persons. Each group of partners was responsible for recovering either in London, Boston, Hull or Ipswich, one quarter yearly for the following four years of its own share of the loan. In the case of the other loans, the contributors were arranged in larger groups, embracing all those who were entitled to repayment in a particular port, but the customs accounts show that the shipping was carried out by small groups of partners, who retained for themselves sums due on their own shipments. As the first debt had been accumulating for several years, it is not likely that all those to whom repayment was now assigned had themselves advanced the money in the first place. The debt must have been treated as the joint concern of the Company, and a share in the arrangements for repayment must have been taken over by members of the Company as a piece of speculation. Some merchants participated in more than one of the loans, and a few in all. Some of the partnerships must have been temporary associations, formed specially for the purpose of contributing jointly to a loan, and of co-operating to secure its repayment, for members of one group often joined with entirely different partners for different loans; sometimes one new member joined two original partners. A few groups, such as that formed by Feld, Cely, and Bowell acted permanently together.[11]

A sidelight on the proceedings is given in a petition presented to the Chancellor by John Levyng, merchant of the Staple, who complained that he had been defrauded of his share. He explained that the arrangements had been made by William Cantelowe; "by vertue of which graunte oon Robert Horne of London aldemann in absence of youre seid Besecher made such instaunce to the seid Cantlowe that he had lettres patentes made unto hym and only as well of the money that hymself hadde apprested to the seid some as of the seid some of £65 19s. 10d. that youre seid Besecher hadde apprested," and had retained to his own use the whole sum, "utterly refusing" to satisfy Levyng.[12] The letters patent bear this out, for Horne is there represented as having made an unusually large individual contribution of £447 18s. 8d.[13]

The repayment of these four loans can be followed from the customs accounts.

The loan of £2,000 made to Lord Bourchier is easy to trace. By comparing the various dates for which the accounts run in the four ports, London, Boston, Hull, and Ipswich, it appears that the whole quantity required to produce the sum of £2,000 was shipped in the summer and autumn of 1450, and the money duly retained.[14]

The loan of £10,700 was not so satisfactorily cleared. All went well for the first year. The whole quantity of wool due from each port was exported during the autumn of 1450. In the second year, the London group did not export quite their full share, and were able to recover only £1,049 15s. 4½d. of the £1,133 7s. 4d. that was due to them yearly. The delay may have been due to the fact that the king was "preferred" in £20,000 from the customs on all goods in London and on Staple goods in Southampton (that is, he was to receive that sum before other claims were paid), a provision from which it was necessary to exempt the Staplers shipping to recover their share of the loan.[15] The second year's shipping is entered in the names of one or more representatives from each group, so that it is impossible to tell on whom the loss of £83 11s. 11½d. fell, but the Memoranda Rolls supply the information that White, Walden, and Pyrton failed to ship the whole of their share. Pyrton's reason is given at length; that he, as lieutenant of Guines "was so occupied the second yere . . . about Reparations and fortifying of oure said Castell of Guisnes considered the malice of oure ennymyes and lyklyhode of Siege . . . that he might not in any wyse that yere attend to shipping of Wolles as other merchauntes did after the contynne of oure graunte", wherefore, "considering the premisses and the good and notable service of many and long yeres unto us by the said William," he was directed to ship the following year instead, as also were White and Walden. In the third year, £748 2s. 4½d. was recovered by a joint shipping, but additional sums were recovered by groups of partners shipping independently, and by joint shipping in the names of partners belonging to several groups. The whole amount recovered this year was £1,406 12s. 0¼d., leaving a balance of £189 12s. 7¾d. after the previous year's deficit had been made good. The changing personnel of the exporting groups makes it impossible to determine how the profits were shared, though William Cantelowe recovered his share by shipping independently of the others, in addition to the common shipping which is headed by his name. The fourth year's share had not been recovered when the last year expired. £524 13s. 10¼d. was recovered in 1452-3, and £127 15s. 5½d. probably between April and July 1454, leaving a deficit of £450 18s. 0¾d. on the year, and of £291 5s. 4½d. on the whole transaction.[16]

In Boston during the second year, the fortunes of the different groups varied; in one case only was the exact sum retained; in six cases the amount was rather more, and in one case rather less than the real share, making a total excess of £42 0s. 10½d. The third year's shipping was entered in the names of the whole group, and the exact amount due, £531 14s. 4½d. was retained.[17] No further shipping took place in 1454, leaving the Boston group with a deficit of £488 13s. 6d.

In Hull, during the second year, difficulties arose with the customs officials, who refused to deliver the " cockets " unless the merchants surrendered the " obligations of subsidy " which served as the title for their retention of the subsidy, until an order was sent from the Exchequer directing them to do so. It was not until the summer of 1453 that a number of merchants belonging to all groups received collectively the sum of £270 16s. 9½d. for the second year, and £118 5s. 6¾d. for the third. Between October, 1453 and the following April, they received £179 15s. 1¾d. for the second year, bringing that up to £450 11s. 7½d. and £332 7s. 11¼d. which exactly cleared off the third year's debt.[18] This left them with £450 18s. 9d., the fourth year's instalment, unpaid, and 2s. 1½d. short on the rest.

In Ipswich, the whole group received £343 13s. 5½d. instead of the £517 7s. 5½d. due to them for the second year; for the third year the whole share was recovered.[19] But they, too, had still to recover the fourth year's share when the time expired.

Thus, according to the customs accounts, the amount outstanding from the whole loan was £2,111 12s. 10¼d. A still smaller proportion of the other loans had been recovered, £200 of the £2,000 due in Boston, and £193 15s. 5½d. of the three thousand marks in Hull.[20]

The meeting of Parliament in 1454 gave the Staplers an opportunity of restating the financial position. They claimed that though assignments had been made to them for " grete notable sommes ", about 12,000 marks remained unpaid, and the assignments were now about to expire. The government acted justly. On 16th October, the day on which the assignments for the £10,700 were due to expire, an account was made out of all sums still outstanding, and of the position of each merchant. According to this, £2,113 0s. 1¾d. was still due on the first loan, £1,800 of the £2,000 from Boston, £2,472 2s. 2½d. of the four thousand marks, and the whole of the thousand marks for the Household in Ipswich.[21] Fresh assignments were made out, directing the Staplers to continue their shipping until the whole amount was recovered. But the king refused to continue to suspend the granting of licences to export elsewhere than to Calais, and so circumstances were not quite so favourable in this respect.

The renewal of the assignments was followed by a revival of shipping. This time, the merchants did not confine themselves closely to the ports for which their privileges had originally been given. The London merchants appear to have taken over the business of export from some of the provincial merchants. Thus the whole of the loan of one thousand marks which was to have been recovered in Ipswich was ultimately recovered by shipping from London, together with a large proportion of the other loans. Even within the London group a small number of merchants appear to have taken over the business of obtaining a final settlement.

A large quantity of wool was exported between the spring of 1455 and the autumn of 1456. As a result, £1,662 4s. 10d. was recovered towards the loan of £10,700; £1,263 16s. 4¾d. towards that of four thousand marks; £418 11s. 6¾d. towards that of £2,000; £393 15s. 8¼d. in Ipswich towards one of the loans of a thousand marks, and £681 18s. 7¾d. in London for a like sum. In Boston, no distinction was made between the various loans, but £2,176 18s. 5¾d. from the subsidy on wool was retained " by denizens with the knowledge of the Exchequer ", which could be no other than that retained by the Staplers.[22] Taking all the loans together, this would leave £980 19s. 7½d. still unpaid.

The repayment of the final instalments was long delayed. From November, 1457 to August, 1460, a few of the original London group, Feld, Walden, Brewes and Pyrton, received occasionally small sums amounting in all to £92 18s. 0¼d.[23]

By this time, however, a new situation had developed. In May, 1458, John Thrysk, who was then mayor of the Staple, Robert White and six others, had been directed to ship wool to Calais in order to recover £843 6s. 8d. for the expenses of an embassy to the Duke of Burgundy. In December, the merchants of the Staple collectively were directed to ship from any port in the kingdom wool on which they were to retain the subsidy above 33s. 4d. the sack in order to recover a loan of £1,000 a quarter which they had just undertaken to lend to the king.[24]

The former loan was more than recovered, £946 17s. 5½d. being retained.[25] The repayment of the latter one, and indeed the whole Staple trade, was disorganized by the outbreak of civil war, and the seizure of Calais by the Yorkist leaders. Payment was never recovered in Henry VI's reign, and may have been an item in the settlement between Edward IV and the merchants of the Staple. This was probably the fate of the loans that have been traced. A small amount was still outstanding when the Lancastrian government collapsed, and may have been honoured by its successor.

One remarkable conclusion suggested by the history of these loans is the fact that no interest was apparently reckoned on these debts. Provision was always made for the repayment of the exact sum received by the Exchequer. Payment for the use of money was so general among private traders that it is almost incredible that the weak Lancastrian government could have obtained gratuitous loans, especially when the means of repayment were so uncertain. The only instance of direct remuneration, in addition to trifling concessions in Calais, is a grant of £80 made to the mayor and company in 1454 by the advice of the Council, " as a gift for their great labour and expenses touching the King's business." Sometimes the exporters were able to retain rather more than the amount due, as they did with the loan of one thousand marks, with the money advanced to the Duke of Burgundy in 1458, and with some instalments of the loan of £10,700, but they had no legal justification for it, and the matter must have been arranged informally with the customs officers or the Exchequer. Their advantage must have consisted chiefly of the concessions which they were able to extract from the government in return for loans; the withdrawal of the licences to export elsewhere than to Calais in 1449 and 1458, and possibly, the limitation, though not the withdrawal of privileges in 1457.[26]

On the whole, the merchants stood rather to lose than to gain on these transactions. Repayment was long delayed. They were unable to complete their shipping within the four years agreed upon in 1449. The reason for this was, probably, not the state of the market, but the entirely unforeseen circumstance that between May and July, 1454, a mutiny broke out in the garrison at Calais, and the soldiers laid hands on the wool in the market.[27] This must have disturbed trade and hindered the recovery of the loans. Most of the money was recovered by the end of 1456, but the repayment of the remainder lingered on indefinitely. The speculation could not have been regarded as entirely unprofitable, for in 1458 the merchants of the Staple undertook again to make large advances which were to be repaid in the same way. But, for in 1454, political disturbances again intervened to hinder the carrying out of the arrangements. It was only after the fall of the Lancastrian government that the Staplers began to recover the security that was needed for their trade and their financial operations.

§ 2

THE FINANCING OF CALAIS BY THE MERCHANTS OF THE STAPLE

Between May and July, 1454, when part of the last instalment of the wool due to be shipped for the loan of £10,700 was on the market at Calais, there took place an event which greatly disturbed that arrangement and which led to a series of new advances by the merchants of the Staple. This was the mutiny of the garrison at Calais. In order to understand why this happened it is necessary to consider the method by which the garrison was paid.

The financing of the garrison at Calais can be traced from the Issue Rolls of the Exchequer, and from such accounts of the Treasurer and Victualler as remain.[28] The expense was exceedingly heavy, and has been estimated at more than one half of the whole income of the English Crown during this period.[29] Important as Calais was for the English wool trade, it may be questioned whether its retention after the loss of the other possessions in France was really worth while from the point of view of the government. The first charge of maintaining the garrison was borne by the subsidy on wool, 20*s.* on the sack being reserved for the purpose, of which 13*s*. 4*d*. went to the Treasurer and 6*s*. 8*d*. to the Victualler. The proceeds of the subsidy were paid to the Exchequer by the customers in the ports, and the Exchequer remitted to Calais the proportions due. Large sums were also paid to the Treasurer and Victualler out of general funds, but all these sources were insufficient. The wages of the garrison were continually in arrears, and the soldiers remained in a state of perpetual discontent, which had led to the outbreak of mutinies in 1431 and 1441.[30] They had then seized the wool which they found on the market, and had retained for themselves the proceeds of its sale. Like the officials of the Royal Household, the officials at Calais were obliged to pledge their own account to defray the expenses of their office, and their indebtedness to others was treated as a loan made by them to the government. In 1450, when the Duke of Buckingham resigned his post as Captain, the government acknowledged itself indebted to him for a "loan" of £19,395.[31] This, then, included the expenses incurred by him and his predecessors, which had not yet been paid off by the government.

The first reference to the intervention of the Staplers in the affairs of Calais since their loans of 1451 was in a petition presented on 2nd July, 1454, in the second session of Parliament. This was a comprehensive document "for the suertee and saufgard of the seid Staple, Towns and Marches of the same". The old complaints about the licences were repeated, and fresh assignments were demanded for the 12,000 marks still unpaid from the shipping of wool, and a protest was made against the raising of the subsidy on denizens' wool from 33*s*. 4*d*. to 43*s*. 4*d*. a sack. A new item was included; that "sufficient purveance be made for the saufgard of the seid Towne . . . and that the seid Merchantz may have fro hensforth, fre issue of alle theire . . . Merchaundises . . . without any restraint or impediment", which premisses being fulfilled, the Company undertook to advance to the soldiers at Calais 40*s*. on each sarpler of wool they sold there to the sum of 10,000 marks, to be repaid from the clerical subsidy.[32] Only the clauses relating to the withdrawal of restraints and to the fresh issue of assignments for the debt still outstanding were accepted outright; the subsidy on wool was suspended for a period of five years. The victory rested with the king in the matter of the licences, for by tacitly ignoring the demand for their withdrawal he resumed the right to grant them, now that the five years' respite had expired.

In spite of the partial nature of the concessions, the financial arrangements were carried out. Between 24th May and 6th June, £2,000 and £4,666 13*s*. 4*d*.—making 10,000 marks in all—was received by the Exchequer, and the whole amount was repaid out of the tenths and fifteenths on 12th July, with an additional £80, the nature of which is not explained, and £80 to the Mayor and Company " by the advice of the Council for all their great labours and expenses in certain matters " as a gift from the king.[33]

Further light on these financial transactions comes from the accounts of Sir Gervase Clyfton, the Treasurer of Calais, which cover the years 1453 to 1456. These were evidently made up after 1456,[34] and though they are arranged in years the division is plainly artificial, and relates to subjects rather than to chronology. The accounts show that between 1453 and 1454, the Treasurer received about £3,000 from the Exchequer, and nearly £21,000 in four " indentures " from the subsidy on wool, that is, in tallies drawn on the collectors of customs in four ports. Then came a loan of £40,943 9s. 9¾d. advanced by the Company of the Staple to the Duke of Somerset for wages from 1451 to 1455, and a loan of £2,530 15s. 8d. to the Earl of Warwick for one quarter's wages in 1455. The expenses included £34,832 17s. for wages, together with additional sums for ships, messengers, and the payment of old debts. £5,315 10s. 3½d. was handed over to the Company of the Staple in " obligations of the subsidy of wools ". The result of the financial year was to leave the Treasurer with a balance of £21,748 7s. 1¾d. During the next two years the receipts consisted only of advances and receipts from the Exchequer, with payments from the collectors of customs in various ports, and the regular receipts from Calais. The expenditure included sums for wages, labourers, messengers, " works," and the repayment of old debts, leaving a deficit of £15,002 12s. 2¾d. for the two years, which, when subtracted from the surplus of the first year, left a balance of £6,742 14s. 11d. for the whole period.

In the winter of 1454, another petition was presented to Parliament relating to these transactions; here it was stated that the merchants of the Staple had undertaken to provide 23,000 marks (£15,333 6s. 8d.) for the soldiers, for which they had been promised obligations of 12,000 marks from the Treasurer, and 2,000 marks from the Victualler. The first part of their petition contained a request that the Exchequer should " discharge " Sir John Cheyne, the Victualler, " ayenst you, as ayenst the said Soudeours," of the 2,000 marks, which he had received from them; that is, that their payment should be acknowledged by the Exchequer. We learn from a petition presented to the Chancellor that they had had some difficulty in getting the Victualler to perform his part of the contract. It is remarkable that they made no complaint against the Treasurer, although they had advanced much larger sums to him. The second part of the petition refers to the general situation. It was stated that " for grete sommes of money by hym (Sir John Cheyne) due . . . there hath been taken by the seid Souldeoures of money " 26,000 marks (£17,333 6s. 8d.), " growyng of the sale of Wolles and Wolfells there, of the Maire and Merchauntes of the Staple," and as a further £2,530 15s. 8d. was needed for the garrison and £66 13s. 4d. for the wages of commissioners sent by the king, " which in no wise can be purveyed but by way of a prest (loan)," the Company had agreed to forward these sums as well. For their repayment, they were to have the proceeds of all the customs in Southampton from the following Christmas, and 6s. 8d. on every sack of wool after 1st March, 1455, together with obligations to the value of 7,703 marks—3s. 7½d. from the Treasurer, and 2,000 marks from the Victualler.[35]

By the winter of 1454, therefore, the loan had risen from 10,000 marks to £17,333 6s. 8d., and further sums were still needed. The advance of £2,530 15s. 8d. to the soldiers under Warwick can be seen as a separate item in the Treasurer's account. The wages of the commissioners appear to have been entered along with the general expenses. Ten thousand marks had already been repaid out of taxation, but the later loans were to be repaid partly from the customs, and partly from " obligations " or tallies secured on the customs on wool.[36] This arrangement was duly carried out, for £5,135 10s. 3½d. (which is in fact 7,703 marks 3s. 7½d.) is entered in the account as having been handed over in obligations to the Mayor of the Staple. The Victualler's account has not been preserved, so that we cannot check the delivery of the 2,000 marks.

There is an entry in the Memoranda Rolls which recites in almost identical terms the second part of the petition; and adds the detail that the Staplers have agreed to " satisfy and content . . . the residue of their wages and rewards at days and times to be appointed . . . though it be to their grievous and unportable charge ".[37] There is here a hint of dissatisfaction which does not appear in the earlier accounts. This is the only indication in an official document of the fact that the arrangement had been the result of a serious mutiny which had taken place between May and July, 1454, and which was the immediate cause of all these negotiations.

A dramatic version is given in a petition presented to the Chancellor in 1527: " May it please your Grace to understand when and how the said staplers entered into the firste acts of reteignour . . . soe it was, that in the convention and warre betweene kinge Henry the 6th and kinge Edward the 4(th), the retynue of Caleis beinge unpaide of their wages by the space of three yeares, in a great rage and fury for want of money fell upon the stapull and closed them in a house and would not suffer them to be at large unto such tyme as they had promised to content and pay them all their said wages beign behinde and unpaide, so that at length they did so to their greate damage, hurt and dekay of many of the said stapulle for the tyme "—after which the retinue were paid by the Staplers out of the customs on Staple merchandise.[38]

Contemporary references to the mutiny are casual and fragmentary, but they leave no doubt as to its occurrence. In 1456 Sir Thomas Kirkeby received a licence to ship wool, fells, and tin to Calais,

THE GOVERNMENT AND STAPLE MERCHANTS

retaining £200 of duties, because the execution of an earlier grant had been hindered by reason of the "great disturbance"—*ob magnam perturbacionem*—of the soldiers in Calais. In 1454 directions were given to John Wodehouse and to Richard Whetehill, alderman of Calais, that they "shal mowe selle . . . wolles and wollefell amountyng to the summe of £4,100 6s. 8d. afore any other wolles and wollefelles beyng at Caleis aftre the price of the staple, And that letters be directed to the Meire Constable and feliship of the Marchantes of oure said Estaple at Cales to suffre the seid souldeours to haue and reioisse the seid preferrement and other letters to be directed to the said John Wodehous squier and Richard Whetehill to take upon them thexecucion of the seid graunte". Then follows the entry, "That the said preferrement hath in no wise been put in execucion by cause that other meanes were founde more easy for redy payment of the seid somme, in so muche as the said preferrement was thought preiudiciall and hurt to oure Estaple at Caleis." Wherefore the king "reuoketh annulleth and casseth the acte a boue rehersed".[39]

This does not tally exactly with the account of the attack on the Staplers given above, nor with the story of the seizure of the wools, but all the accounts could be reconciled with an interpretation such as this : the failure to pay their wages caused the garrison to get out of hand ; at first they attempted to lay hands on the wool in the market, and to organize a "restraint", that is, to limit the amount of wool in the market in order to sell at a high price, but the attempt had to be given up in the face of opposition from the merchants of the Staple. But although they managed to defeat this "restraint", the Staplers were compelled, under duress, physical or otherwise, to forward to the soldiers the ready money received from the sale of their wool. Ten thousand marks had been received by 6th June, and was repaid out of taxation by 12th July, but the Treasurer's accounts show that they continued to advance money for wages, although in the first place they had undertaken only to forward 10,000 marks.

We are still without an explanation of the chronic shortness of money to pay the wages of the garrison. It is the more strange because the Issue Rolls of the Exchequer show that £15,256 1s. 8d., exclusive of loans from the Staplers, was paid to the Treasurer and Victualler of Calais between 25th May, 1450 and 25th July, 1453.[40] Mere dishonesty would hardly account for the insufficiency of these sums. The only explanation which seems to fit the facts is that these sums were transferred to the officials at Calais not in money, but in tallies such as the creditors of the government usually received. This was quite plainly the case with the proceeds of the subsidy on wool, which were handed over in the form of "indentures", or "obligations", tallies or written promises to pay drawn on the local customs officials. These obligations passed from hand to hand in the commercial world without being realized, but in that form they were useless for the payment of the soldiers. These at last laid hands on the wool in the market, in order to sell it for the ready money they needed. After the mutiny the merchants of the Staple undertook to forward to the garrison the ready money arising from the sale of wool. Their first advances were repaid out of taxation, but after that they proceeded to take over from the Treasurer and Victualler some of the obligations of subsidy, which they were in a much better position to use.

Even these advances did not satisfy the garrison,[41] and it was not until 1456 that a final settlement took place. In that year, "at the request of the Mayor and Company of the Staple," a commission was appointed which included John Williamson of Louth, a prominent member of the Company, the Mayor of Calais, Lord Fauconberg, and the leaders of the garrison, with very wide powers to investigate the financial position, and to make arrangements for completely paying off the garrison.[42] The Earl of Warwick had just gone to take up the captaincy there, and he may have pressed for a settlement in order to strengthen his position.[43] The Commission presented a report which summed up the financial position from 28th September, 1451 to 20th April, 1456.[44] According to this, £17,333 6s. 8d. had been received before 1st March, 1456 from the proceeds of the sale of wool. It was not until 1456 that fresh advances were made. Between 1st and 25th March, Robert White had forwarded £2,253 11s. 9¾d., and between 25th March and 20th April his successor, John Thrysk, had forwarded £20,498 5s. 6½d., leaving as yet unpaid a further sum of £444 19s. 7½d. which had been promised. This makes a total of £40,530 3s. 7½d. According to the Treasurer's account, £40,943 11s. 9¾d. had been received for wages up to the end of 1455. As to chronology, the report of the commission and the petitions of 1454 must be accepted, rather than the artificially neat arrangement of the account. They establish the fact that, after the payment of £17,333 6s. 8d., and the taking over of the obligations of subsidy in 1454, it was not until 1456 that the garrison was finally satisfied of its wages. The discrepancy of about £400 between the two statements may be due to the fact a small sum was received after the commissioners report was drawn up, but in time to be included in the Treasurer's account.

After the end of 1456, it is impossible to be sure how the garrison was paid. The Treasurer's accounts have not been preserved, and the records of the Exchequer become more and more scanty, a telling witness to the confusion into which the government was falling. According to the Issue Rolls, £1,131 was paid in 1456, and £500 in 1457, sums quite insufficient to meet the bill for wages.[45] The proceeds of the subsidy on wool must have been diminished by many grants to ship free of duty. Lack of funds may have accounted for this somewhat indiscriminate piracy in which Warwick allowed his men to indulge.

The mutiny of 1454 must have brought home to the merchants of the Staple the manifest inability of the government to provide for the garrison at Calais. They had already become accustomed to make advances for extraordinary expenses. The mutiny had forced upon them for a time the responsibility of financing the garrison, and while they continued to pay they were free from fears of further upheavals, although they had not complete responsibility. In 1465 Edward IV completed the process, when he made the Company responsible not only for providing the funds, but for the entire financial administration of Calais.[46]

§ 3

INCREASING DIFFICULTIES: 1454 TO 1459

In October, 1454, the king had resumed his right to grant licences to export elsewhere than to Calais, and had succeeded in defending these licences against repeated attacks in the Parliaments of 1454 and 1455. Within the following five years the results of his success became evident. Urged on by the increasingly serious financial situation, the government tried to meet its obligations by a distribution of commercial privileges on an increasingly lavish scale, only to be driven back in 1458 to the merchants of the Staple, and on their terms. But again the necessity of obtaining other supplies made imperative the renewed distribution of commercial privileges. An extremely difficult economic situation was finally brought to an end by the collapse of the government.

At first, the government proceeded cautiously, and for two years the only important grant was to Simon Nori, the agent of the Medici, doubtless in return for a loan, to export 1,200 sacks of wool without subsidies overland to Italy.[47] From the end of 1456, there was a large increase. Many officials of the Royal Household and magnates holding important offices were compensated for money owed by the Crown by being allowed to export wool overland to Italy at reduced rates of subsidy, or by being appointed factors for shipping the king's wool. Only a trifling proportion of wool, however, was exempted from Staple regulations;[48] the government must have realized that these grants were specially obnoxious to the merchants of the Staple. The grants recorded are very much more extensive than those made in 1456-7, which had provoked the protest of 1449, but their number is deceptive, as many of them were cancelled by a later arrangement. In 1457[49] the Council drew up an ordinance, which was described as having been made " for the weal of the land and especially for the weal of the Company of the Staple ", that the king would ship " but 2,000 sacks of woll over the mountaignes and that in his own name of the wolles of Cotteswold marches or lymster or such wolles as of old tyme hath bene accustomed to be draped beyond the mountaignes yereyly " for three years, to be sent from London and Chichester; "And that the factours and attourneys of the kyng ... that shall execute the shipping ... shall fynde sufficient suerty in the Chauncerie that the seid wolles shall passe the mountaignes withoute fraude or malengyne," unless they went by the Straits of Morocco. Writs were to be issued to the customers and packers that no other wool was to be sent except to Calais, and the Mayor of the Staple was to be informed of sureties taken; "And that the merchauntes fo the seide estaple of Caleys shall shippe in alle godely haste yerely during the seide three yeares as moche wolles or wolfelles ... as is or shall be to theym possible but if there be a Restraynte at Caleys ... or the town be beseged or any wolles or wolfelles passe by way of licence ... that myght be to the hurte of the seide estaple." [50]

Although the fact does not appear in the ordinance, its effect was to set aside in favour of the king the claims of persons exporting elsewhere than to Calais by royal licence. This is the point upon which a petition presented to the Chancellor turns. Richard Bole and Robert Horsle of Chichester relate that "Oon Thomas Hoo that tyme beyng deputee to Herry Percy Erll of Northumberland to shippe in the seid Poort xl sarplers Wolle ... for to haue passed owte of this lande by vertu of the kynges letters patent of licence yeven unto the seid Erle. And at the delyuerance and shippyng of the seid Wolle the Custumers than ther beyng ... wold not suffre the same woll to passe by the seid licence ... but that it shuld passe under letters patentz made for the kyng by vertu of a speciall acte of Counceill late made to be shipped in his name to John Coppuldike the kynges factor in that behalf ffor wiche variaunce of licence to be avoided a direction was taken ... for the spede of the shippyng of the seid wolle for the kynges avayle ", by which Bole and Horsle entered into bonds for the payment of the duties on wool, one of which was delivered to the controller in Chichester, and two others to Thomas Hoo for the payment of the dues : " upon condicion that if the Erll of Shrowesbury Tresorer of England awarded the licence of the Erll of Northumberland to be no sufficient warant to your seid orators to shippe theer seid Wolles by then the seid obligacions soo delyvered to the seid Thomas Hoo to be delyvered to youre seid oratours. And in cas he awarded the seid licence to be good then the seid obligacions to be good and effectuall. After whiche tyme the seid Tresorer of Englond by the advise of the Barons of the kynges Exschequer" decided that the Earl of Northumberland's licence was not sufficient warrant.[51] The rest of the case does not concern us. The obligation which was now invalid was passed on to a mercer

THE GOVERNMENT AND STAPLE MERCHANTS

by Thomas Hoo in payment of a debt, and the petitioners found themselves sued for payment.

The Earl of Northumberland had been granted permission in 1456 to export wool, fells and tin, and cloth to Italy by sea or by the mountains, retaining dues to the sum of £6,000.[52] The incident shows that these grants made a short time before were set aside in favour of the king by the Council's decree. It could thus be described as a concession to the Staplers, since it turned an unlimited right into a definite agreement, and, in theory at least, prevented the export of wool to "any parts abroad", a common euphemism for Flanders, for the next three years. This accounts for the "godely haste" which the Staplers were urged to use in their shipping. Money still remained overdue from the loans of 1449 to 1451, which they had a better chance of recovering with a monopoly of the market.

The king's wool was distributed as before among a number of his creditors, English and Italian. The English factors included Henry Fylongley, the Keeper of the Great Wardrobe, William Beaufitz, the Clerk of the Cellars, and Thomas Fynderne, who had been Lieutenant of Calais under Somerset. John Coppuldyke, who had succeeded in seizing the wool from the Earl of Northumberland's factor, had shared a grant of 600 sacks with Richard Glover, "for notable causes concerning our good and the defence of our kingdom." The Earl of Northumberland was granted 375 sacks, perhaps as compensation for his former loss, but this time his factor was an Italian, Roger Gentile. The Earl of Shrewsbury was granted 545 sacks. Three Italian firms took over between them the shipping of 2,000 sacks.[53]

Several grants were made in 1457-8 for the export of Staple goods at reduced rates of customs; the largest was one made to the Duke of York to recover 10,000 marks due to him as Lieutenant of Ireland, by shipping Staple goods to Calais, or by sea to Italy.[54] As before, none of these grants infringed the monopoly of Calais, although the overland route to Italy was only a lesser evil in the eyes of the merchants of the Staple. But about two-thirds of all the wool concerned was to be shipped by Italian firms.

This fact helps to account for a strong anti-Italian movement which developed in London in 1456. It was not the only cause, but it may have brought the already strong prejudice against them to a head. The traditional hostility was apt to break out into open violence when the authority of the government was weak. In the disorders which follows the fall of Suffolk in 1450, there had been an anti-alien element, which had manifested itself chiefly against the Italians during Cade's rising, and which had led the Venetian Senate to decree that the galleys should not visit London that year if the disturbances continued. There had been spasmodic acts of violence such as that which led Peter Gentile, the Earl of Northumberland's

Italian factor, to complain to the Chancellor in 1454 that " where he was wythyn the Cytie of London in the paryssh of Seynt Petyr in Cornhyll . . . in goddes peace and the kynges of England . . . usyng the fete and occupacon of merchandise . . . there came oon John Mulso Squyer violently with force and armys agaynes the kynges peace, And your seid bysecher thenne and there beyng toke and imprysoned, And soo hym in pryson kept vn to such tyme that hit pleased your gode lordship " to release him on bail. Several petitions were presented to the Chancellor by aliens, both Flemish and Italian, on the ground that it was impossible to get justice from an English jury.[55]

In 1453 the tax on aliens had been raised from 16d. to 40s. a head, and the subsidy on their wool from 53s. 4d. to 100s., and in the last Parliament of 1455 economic jealousy had inspired petitions against " merchants strangers Italians " who bought up wool outside their ports of call.[56] The favour shown to them by the government, and the suspicions of their commercial misdoings, which subsequent events proved to be thoroughly well-founded, must have stimulated their unpopularity still further.

The riots of 1456 broke out as the result of a chance insult offered by a mercer's servant to a Lombard, which led to a general attack in which the mercers' men played a leading part. According to Gregory's Chronicle, the city authorities and the company of mercers were definitely connected with the riot: " This year was the rising and wanton rule of the mayor and mercers of London against the Lombards." In 1457 the royal family withdrew from the city. Fabyan states that " This yere, and begynnynge of the same, the quene suspectynge the cytie of London, and demyd it to be more fauourable vnto the duke of Yorkys partye than hyrs, causyd the king to remoue from London vnto Couentre ". The absence of the court gave a fresh impetus to the anti-Italian movement. There was a fresh " hurlynge " between a mob in which the mercers' men were well to the fore and the Italians, but it was more promptly and effectively suppressed by the Mayor than that of the year before. However, the Italians decided to leave London for Winchester. The Venetian Senate ordered its citizens to withdraw for ten years.[57] This order was never strictly enforced, but for two years the galleys ceased to call at London, and some of the Italians left the city for a time.

The Londoners had some hand in an attack by sea. In 1457 English ships from Sandwich and Calais seized certain vessels of Zealand at Tilbury, which were loaded with cloth, wool, and other merchandise belonging to merchants of Italy. The king addressed a stern letter to the Mayor of London, ordering him to release the vessels, " letting you wit for certain, if ye be remiss or negligent in the punishing of their misgovernance and executing this our commandment, as we think ye have been in other before this, ye shall run into the pain provided by our laws as well in your franchise as otherwise "; [58] but, with or without his connivance the malefactors had disappeared, and the king had to confine himself to an injunction to arrest them, if they should appear in the city. Part of the cargo carried in these ships consisted of wool that was being carried to the Netherlands by Lorenzo Barbarigo and Homobone Griti, two of the king's factors, in order to be sent overland to Italy according to the king's licence, and its capture must have been particularly gratifying to the merchants of the Staple. The official explanation cast the guilt upon the soldiers of the garrison at Calais. It recited that Barbarigo and Griti, factors of John Walcomstraso, merchants of Venice, by virtue of letters patent had loaded about 273 sacks of wool in three ships of Zealand, having faithfully paid the subsidy, as appears in the books, intending to have taken the wool to Zealand, and from thence over the mountains, when " certain soldiers of Calais, together with a great force of others of our subjects in certain ships of Calais furnished and arrayed in manner of war . . . violently seized (them) at Tilbury in our river of Thames, and led them to our town of Calais, and disposed of it at their own pleasure, in manifest contempt of us ", inflicting losses of £3,200 upon Barbarigo and Griti.[59]

The attack on the Italians could not have been displeasing to the merchants of the Staple, and they may have given it some encouragement. The mercers, who, according to Fabyan, were foremost in the attack, were closely connected with the Staplers and a number of merchants, including Cantelowe himself, belonged to both. Cantelowe was not above suspicion. The attack at Tilbury was directed against the very persons whose privileges the Staplers had most reason to resent. For the most part, however, the more influential citizens seem to have been moved as much by dislike of disorder as by hatred of the Italians. Fabyan's statement that in 1457 the supporters of the Duke of York gained the upper hand is interesting, but apart from the fact that both had reason to distrust the party dominant at court, there is no evidence to show that the merchants of the Staple can be described as partisans of York.

After the court had withdrawn to Coventry, the more responsible elements in the city joined with the Mayor of the Staple to institute a great inquiry at the Guildhall into all kinds of offences against commercial regulations. The inquiry went on through 1458 and 1459. It was directed against both aliens and denizens, but in its early stages most of the delinquents were Italians, which suggests that the inquiry grew out of the preceding riots. Many of the accusations were presented by John Thrysk, who had succeeded Robert White as Mayor of the Staple, and by the Earl of Shrewsbury, who was then Treasurer.[60]

The amount of fraud revealed was enormous and varied; it included the buying of goods on credit instead of for ready money, the corruption of the wool-packers in London, especially by Italians, and, above all, the sending of Staple merchandise to places other than Calais. A most notorious offender was Simon Nori, who was accused of shipping some 1,100 sacks of wool elsewhere than to Calais, and of having induced the wool-packers to beard some of it. In this case the Mayor of the Staple is stated to have come in person to ask for process against him. Next year Nori was again accused of buying bearded wool from two Italians. Such was the record of one of the most favoured of the king's factors, and it is borne out by a number of cases of fraud for which he was summoned to answer in Bruges. Another group of hardened offenders included Barbarigo, Griti, and Walcomstraso, the king's factors whose goods had been seized by the soldiers of Calais early in the year. Information was given against them by the Mayor of the Staple and the Earl of Shrewsbury for shipping the enormous quantity of 2,230 sacks of wool to Zealand and other parts abroad.[61]

The Guildhall inquiry leaves no room for doubt that commercial privileges had been granted to persons who were certain to make a most unscrupulous use of them, and it provides a vivid justification for the repeated complaints in Parliament of the frauds connected with the shipping of the king's wool and the licences. It proved impossible, however, to bring the offenders to account. Everyone of any importance, including all the Italians, proceeded to bar further proceedings by producing letters of general pardon, and the government seems to have tried to stifle further proceedings. On 23rd August, 1458, a commission had been issued to Geoffrey Boleyn, Mayor of London, and others, to enter the dwellings, houses, "warehouses," chests, and cellars of any merchant of Genoa in London, and to search all goods and merchandise, to take an inventory, and to sequestrate them. A note is added, " vacated, because nothing was done thereof by command of the Lords." [62]

The Guildhall inquiry went on through 1459, but it was confined chiefly to goods other than Staple merchandise. It was followed by a "round-up" of offenders by the justice William Nottingham. A great number of offences committed by Englishmen were revealed, including some on the part of London merchants who had hitherto escaped prosecution,[63] but an even greater number were committed by Italians. As before, most of the offenders protected themselves by obtaining a general pardon.

It is impossible to resist the conclusion that the Italian merchants generally showed an almost wholesale contempt for English commercial regulations, but the anti-Italian movement had ended in an irritating anti-climax. The Crown had again intervened to rescue its protégés from the consequences of their misdeeds.

It was not long before financial necessity drove the government to seek for new accommodation from the merchants of the Staple, with promises of concessions more valuable than before. This time it was the problem of providing for the payment of the Royal Household. In 1457, John Stourton, the Treasurer of the Household, threw up his post, leaving the Exchequer to pay off his creditors.[64] The government turned again to the merchants of the Staple. On 11th December, 1458, an agreement was embodied in letters patent by which the Company undertook to forward £1,000 a quarter for four years for the expenses of the Household. Repayment was to be had from the export of wool, on which they were to retain 6s. 8d. of the subsidy in London and Hull, and 13s. 4d. elsewhere. But the agreement was accompanied by large concessions; that the king " considering that for the good of this realm . . . divers ordinances have been made . . . for the entire repair of wool and woolfells to Calais . . . and considering that much substance of wools and woolfells has been carried to Holand, Seland and Flanders . . . by colour of licences and shippings in the king's name to the impoverishment of the growers of such wool . . . to the insecurity of the said town . . . and to the destruction of the merchants of the Staple of Calais ", granted to the Mayor and Company that for four years he would refrain from granting such licences and permissions to ship, the losers receiving compensation, that a commission should be appointed to negotiate with the Duke of Burgundy for the sale of wool only at Calais, and that means should be found to restrict transport without the payment of customs or subsidies.

On the same day, a commission consisting of Master William Sharp, Doctor of Laws, and six merchants of the Staple, was appointed to treat with the Duke of Burgundy on the ground that the king had been credibly informed that wool and wool-fells had been conveyed from his dominions " furtive et occulti ", without having paid customs, to the great loss of the Staple of Calais, and they were directed to make arrangements with the Duke of Burgundy and with the representatives of the Flemish towns for the buying and selling of wool and fells at the Staple, for the method of payment and the regulation of bullion, and to prevent Staple goods being taken to the Netherlands without having first been sent to the Staple.[65]

This was the greatest length to which the government had yet gone in providing for the observance of Staple regulations. The loan which they received in return was a comparatively small one, considerably smaller than the advances made to the garrison at Calais from 1454 to 1456. It suggests that their credit was on the wane. The first instalment was duly paid into the Exchequer on 28th December, 1458, and three days after the Mayor of the Staple received a licence directing him to ship in accordance with the agreement. The further history of the loan is very difficult to trace. It was not until 15th May, 1459, that £843 6s. 8d. was received. After that there are no entries in the Receipt Rolls acknowledging the payment of further instalments, but from other sources it appears that the government continued to receive advances for some time. In March, 1460, directions were issued for the continuance of the Stapler's shipping in which it is definitely stated that an instalment had been received at Michaelmas, 1459.[66] The financial history of the last years of Lancastrian rule is so obscure that it is impossible to determine whether the Staplers continued to make their payments until the end of the reign.

There was no difficulty in receiving the money paid to the Duke of Burgundy. Within a year, £946 17s. 5½d. was recovered from the subsidy on wool exported in London,[67] £103 10s. 7½d. more than had been originally advanced. The surplus appears to have been retained without question. The recovery of the loan for the Household was less satisfactory. By August, 1460, only £497 19s. 6d. had been retained. The times were unpropitious, and political disturbances had unforeseen reactions on the Staple trade. Calais fell into the hands of the Yorkists, and the government proceeded to forbid all trade with the town. The Staplers were directed to export to other parts abroad until it had returned to its obedience. There was also a large export of wool by the king's factors. The debt had not been cleared by the end of the reign, and may have been included in the settlement made by Edward IV.

Early in 1459 the Mediterranean trade was also modified in favour of another group of royal creditors. On 16th March, a licence was issued for shipping in the name of the king. It laid down that, in order that the Crown might meet various obligations, in particular those incurred for the expenses of the Household, all the wool and cloth in every port should be shipped only by factors in the king's name, and all shipping in the name of other persons should cease for the period of one year. Furthermore, with the advice of the Council, " we depute and ordain . . . Thomas Founde, John Whityngham, and Simon Nori, Lodowic Strosse and Angelo Aldebrand, merchants of Florence, Bartholomew Schiates of Lucca, Homobone Grete and John de Pounte of Venice merchants, jointly and severally as our attorns to ship all such wools and woollen cloths from Southampton or other ports . . . and to take them to parts abroad by the Straits of Morocco to the west during the term of one year, without rendering any account, and without any hindrance whether the wool belongs to them or not, notwithstanding any statutes to the contrary."[68]

Strictly interpreted, this ordinance would have confined all trade in wool and cloth to the small group of royal factors. The customs accounts show, however, that it applied only to the Mediterranean trade, for wool and cloth continued to be exported in the ordinary way from many ports on the East and South Coasts. In Southampton, however, Pounte and Aldebrand monopolized the shipping.[69] The king's factors enjoyed a twofold privilege. In the first place they had a monopoly of the Mediterranean trade for one year, and they also retained the whole of the customs and subsidy, in repayment of their advances. They were thus better off than the Staplers, who retained part only of the subsidy. Their monopoly was not likely to be popular, for among them were included the notorious Simon Nori and many more of the Italian merchants whose frauds had lately been exposed, and whom the merchants of the Staple had vainly tried to bring to justice.

Most of the Mediterranean trade was thus placed under the control of a group of the king's Italian creditors and their associates. The trade from London was also falling into the hands of privileged persons. After the end of 1457 the names of private traders almost disappeared from the accounts. Wool was exported by the Staplers in order to recover debts, by individual holders of licences, and by factors shipping in the king's name.[70] The small merchant was becoming confined more and more to the provincial ports, while the trade of the two principal ports was passing into the hands of specially privileged persons and of the great mercantile groups.

§ 4

The Struggle for the Throne: 1459 to 1461

After 1456 Calais became the headquarters of the Earl of Warwick. It has been pointed out that he probably found it difficult to provide for the payment of the garrison, and this may have been the motive that led him to turn its indiscriminate piracy into more systematic though no more legitimate attacks on Genoese ships, a policy which had the advantage of being popular in the country, and of relieving him from the possibility of embarrassments with Flanders.[71]

At the same time, he was careful to cultivate a good understanding with the Duke of Burgundy. In 1457 he met the Burgundian envoys to discuss the project of an alliance with the Dauphin against the king of France, and in June, 1458, the Duke of Burgundy came to Calais in person.[72] In this policy he had the goodwill of the merchants of the Staple, who had their own reasons for wishing to keep on good terms, since fresh disputes had broken out with the Duke's subjects. The government appointed a commission to treat with him which included the Earl of Warwick, John Thrysk, the Mayor of the Staple, and three other members. What arrangements they made is not recorded, but the merchants of the Staple succeeded in getting a favourable decision on another matter of great moment to them. The perennial dispute over the jurisdiction which was claimed by both the Staplers and the Merchant Adventurers over merchants of the Staple travelling in the Netherlands reached a crisis in 1455, when Thomas Wymark, the factor of Robert White, then Mayor of the Staple, was arrested and thrown into prison by the orders of the governor of the " English nation " in the Netherlands. The Council intervened and sent a protest to the Duchess of Burgundy, but the affair was not settled until 1458. The Duke then gave a decision entirely in favour of the Staplers, with whom jurisdiction over members of their company in Flanders, Brabant, Holland, and Zealand was declared to rest.[73]

Warwick's tenure of the captaincy of Calais must have been considered a distinct success from the Staplers' point of view. In the struggle which was about to develop, a question of great importance was whether these friendly relations were sufficient to become the basis of an alliance with Warwick and his party against the bankrupt Lancastrian government at whose hands the Staplers had suffered much.

In September 1459 the political situation reached a climax. The Yorkist lords finally joined forces to attack the Queen and her party. Warwick came over to England with " all the chefe Sowdiours of Calaies "[74] under the command of Andrew Trollope and Sir Walter Blount. The combined forces of York, Salisbury and Warwick were brought face to face with the royal army at Ludlow. Before any engagement took place, Trollope deserted to the king. The effect of his action was decisive. The Yorkist lords realized that they could not rely on their professional troops, and immediately broke up their camp. The Duke of York made his way to Ireland; Warwick, Salisbury and the Earl of March fled to Calais. The town now became the headquarters of the Yorkist party. The Duke of Somerset was sent over to supersede Warwick as governor, but he was driven into Guines. In January Warwick's men made a surprise attack on Sandwich, capturing Lord Rivers and his son, and in May they captured a force sent to relieve Somerset. An encounter at sea with the Duke of Exeter revealed the untrustworthiness of the Lancastrian fleet.

The fact that Calais was in the hands of the enemy placed the government in a very difficult position. They were at least relieved from the responsibility of having to provide for the payment of the garrison, but they could not willingly countenance any trade with Calais. They had good reason to know that the ready money arising from the sales of wool was a temptation almost irresistible to an impecunious commander. Consequently the Parliament that met at Coventry after the Yorkist rout took the momentous step of prohibiting all trade with Calais, " until the town and Castle of Calais shall be under the rule of captains whom we have sent or shall send." It is extremely doubtful whether this injunction was ever obeyed. The Staplers could afford to disregard the government, for they must have been aware that it would be unwilling to incur their hostility. Fabyan states that it was ignored; at Coventry it had been ordained that " no merchaunt passynge into the costys of Flaunders, shulde passe or goo by Calays, for fere that any shulde come to the ayde of the sayde lordys. But this prouysyon not withstandynge, comfort to them was sent daylye out of Englonde ". Perhaps by way of compensation for the dislocation of the Staple trade, arrangements were made at Coventry for payment of the debt that still remained over from the loans contracted before 1458 by granting to the merchants of the Staple a further 6s. 8d. on wool exported from all ports but Southampton, Sandwich, Hull and Boston, including that shipped in the name of the king.[75]

Having established themselves in Calais, the Yorkist lords began to prepare for another attack on England. They had the ships of Calais at their disposal, and Warwick was in touch with the burgesses of the Cinque Ports. The Duke of Exeter's fleet could not be relied on to defend the Channel against them, and in its extremity the government sought for friends who could. Its obvious allies for the purpose were the Italians, whom it had courted and protected for so long. On 13th February a treaty of amity and commerce was made with Genoa for four years, each power undertaking not to aid the enemies of the other, and the Genoese to assist with ships.[76]

On 20th March the government proceeded to take a most unwise step, which can only be justified at all by supposing that it was dictated by panic at the prospect of an immediate Yorkist descent. Orders were given to arrest the Venetian galleys which were then at Southampton, and to requisition them for the king, only allowing the merchants time to unload their goods. Either the order was neglected, or they left Southampton in time to escape, whereupon the king ordered the arrest of all the Venetian merchants, and compelled them to ransom themselves by giving security for the payment of 36,000 ducats.[77] Thus the alliance of the Italians, who had most reason to support the government, was rashly thrown away without any benefit being gained. A belated attempt to secure the alliance of the Duke of Burgundy also miscarried. Commissioners were appointed for the renewal of the truce, but the Duke had already entered into a friendly understanding with Warwick.[78]

The attack on the Venetians might be expected to react unfavourably upon the king's credit with his Italian financiers. The monopoly enjoyed in Southampton by Nori, Griti, and their associates expired in March, 1460. In May a fresh monopoly was established, for it was ordained that until Michaelmas, all Staple goods and cloth exported from London, Southampton and Sandwich should be shipped only " in the king's name or otherwise for the king's benefit ", and eight persons were appointed to take over the shipping.[79] This time only two were Italians, and both Nori and Griti were omitted, which makes it likely that the original group had refused further accommodation, forcing the king to turn to other sources. The arrangement had no chance of being carried out, for in June, 1460, Warwick, Salisbury, and the Earl of March crossed from Calais without meeting with any opposition, and began the struggle which ended only with the fall of the Lancastrian government.

During these critical events, the merchants of the Staple had played no outstanding part. They had obviously maintained friendly relations with the government, for a mandate authorizing them to continue shipping for the recovery of their loan for the Household had been issued on 20th March, 1460.[80] On the other hand, they must also have been on good terms with Warwick, or the Yorkist lords would hardly have their headquarters at Calais. In this desire to avoid taking any definite side in the struggle, they shared the attitude of the whole bourgeois class.

Fabyan, however, definitely states that they gave very important financial assistance to the Yorkists. He relates that while the Earl of Warwick was at Calais, " They daylye came so thycke to them out of dyuerse partyes of Englande, . . . so that they wanted no men, but money to meynteyne theyr dayly charge with. For remedy whereof they shyfted with the staple of Calays for xviii.M.*li.* (£18,000) whiche summes of money whan they had receyued, the sayd lordys of one assent made ouer ye forenamyd maister John Dynham with a stronge companye, and sent hym un to Sandwyche, to wynne there the kynges nauye ", an enterprise which resulted in the capture of Rivers, and an expedition to concert measures with the Duke of York in Ireland. Later, he goes on to state that " whan kyng Edwarde was thus stablysshed in this realme, great sute and labour was made to hym for the repayment of the forsayd xviii.M.*li.* to hym and other delyuered by the stapelers . . . Where it by the agrement of ye sayde stapelers, or otherwyse, one named Richarde Heyron, a marchaunt of pregnaunt wytte, and of good maner and speche, for them shewyd. To whom at lengthe was answeryd by ye kynges counceyll, that the sayd M.*li.* with moche more, ye which was couertly kept from ye kynges knowledge, belonged of ryght vnto the erle of Wylshyre ", then High Treasurer, and had been forfeited on account of his treason, " wherefore the kyng reteynyd ye sayd £18,000 as parceyll of his forfayture and wold reteyne as his owne. Vpon whiche answere, this Heyron seynge yt of the kyng he myght have no remedy, and for somoch, as moch of the sayd good belongyd to his charge, he then resortyd vnto ye stapelers, for contentacion of the sayd money. But how it was that there he founde no comfort, he fynallye suyd the mayer of the staple and his company, and put them vnto great vexation and trouble," eventually getting a favourable verdict in the Papal court ; " howe be it, that soone after they purchasyd an absolucyon, and he in conclusyon, after longe beynge in Westmynster as a seyntwary man, without recouery of his costys or duties, dyed there, beynge greatly endetted vnto many parsonys." [81]

If Fabyan's account is to be relied upon, therefore, the merchants of the Staple had committed themselves very definitely to the Yorkist cause by making a loan larger than any they had made to the

Lancastrian government within the last twenty years, and the sequel reflects very unfavourably upon the honesty of Edward IV.

Fabyan's account, however, is not entirely borne out by an examination of the case. At Christmas, 1460, Richard Heyron brought an action before the King's Council against John Thrysk, John Walden, the Mayor of the Staple, and a number of prominent members of the Company, for losses to the sum of 13,000 marks which he claimed to have suffered by reason of a "restraint" on the sale of wool imposed by them in 1459. The defendants replied by denying the fact of the restraint.[82] Shortly afterwards Heyron fled from Calais to Bruges, and proceeded to bring an action against them for the recovery of goods which he valued at £24,000. His opponents managed to get the case evoked before the Council of the Duke of Burgundy, where judgment was given in their favour. Heyron, however, taking advantage of the fact that the king of France was attempting to emphasize his authority as overlord of the Duke of Burgundy by encouraging appeals from the ducal court to the Parlement of Paris, appealed to the latter court. Here, the defendants did not merely deny the fact of the restraint, but put forward a very different story, and one which they could not have revealed before the Lancastrian King's Council. According to this, when the Yorkist lords came to Calais in 1460 they attempted to raise money for the descent on England. "Heron offered to lend them 2,000 marks and 300 sarplers of wool. They learned, however, that the merchandise in Heron's possession belonged not to him but to the Treasurer of England, who was of the opposite political faction: they therefore confiscated the merchandise and imprisoned Heron. Later, a servant of Heron's, one Richard Copin, was arrested and letters found upon him. Learning of this, Heron effected his escape and joined his master the Treasurer in Holland. Thence he made his way to the Duke of Burgundy to whom he offered 10,000 crowns for letters of marque, but this request was refused."[83] According to the defence, therefore, the money which was taken from Heyron was not his own, but belonged to the Earl of Wiltshire; the confiscation was caused by political motives, and not by the commercial policy of the Staplers. Heyron evidently wished to recoup himself, and, as he was not likely to get the money from the harassed government, sued the Staplers on the irrelevant charge of a restraint, a claim which was likely to gain him favour in a foreign court, where its imposition would be resented. But Louis XI, not very securely established on the throne, was anxious not to give offence to the new Yorkist king. The jurisdiction of the Parlement was doubtful and the case was therefore discharged. Heyron thereupon reopened the prosecution in England, but getting no satisfaction, he appealed to the Papal court, where, after a preliminary failure, he succeeded at last in 1480 in getting a favourable verdict. By this time the English government had intervened to put an end to the long-drawn dispute. In 1478 the sheriffs of London were directed to make proclamation that " the seid Richard shall surcease of alle suts and actions determinable in eny of the Kynges Courts, whiche he hathe or may have ayenst the seid Maire and Marchants ... oute of the Reame of Englonde ",[84] and in 1482 the Council drew up a final repudiation of his claims. After which he may well have ended his life in sanctuary, " greatly endetted vnto many parsonys."

For our purpose, it is important to try and discover what measure of truth there is in Fabyan's statement that the merchants of the Staple advanced to the Yorkists the large sum of £18,000, or whether the inference to be drawn from their own account is to be preferred, viz. that Heyron, along with individual members, advanced comparatively small sums, and that the bulk of the money was obtained by the seizure of the funds of the Earl of Wiltshire.

There are strong reasons for doubting Fabyan's version. He himself, writing in the Tudor period, would eagerly adopt an interpretation which cast an aspersion on the honesty of the Yorkist king. His insinuation that Edward IV did not repay his debts to the merchants of the Staple has been disproved by Miss Scofield, who has demonstrated that Edward repaid his own borrowings, together with sums which remained outstanding from the reign of his predecessor.[85] Moreover, the good relations which existed between the merchants of the Staple and the Crown would hardly have been possible if they had had such a grievance. Fabyan's statement, therefore, does not warrant the assumption that the merchants of the Staple really gave such invaluable support to the Yorkists at this critical juncture. It seems probable, however, that individuals made contributions, but whether voluntarily or because of the uncomfortable proximity of the Yorkist forces it is impossible to determine. There is no reason to suppose that they were any more eager to do so than they were when they made their advances to the garrison in 1454.

Thus, at the most critical stage in the period which we have been examining, we have no better guide to the activities of the merchants of the Staple than the intricacies of a lawsuit. The balance of probability points to the same conclusion as that which must be drawn from the history of the previous years; that is to say, that, throughout the rivalry of parties the merchants of the Staple maintained their detachment from the political and dynastic issues, and continued to carry on their commercial and financial ventures, willing to deal with either party, if impelled by necessity or by the chance of gain. The difficulties and losses which they had undergone in the later years of Lancastrian rule did not induce them to alter their attitude. Their political indifference and absorption in commercial and financial interests they shared with the commercial classes throughout the country.

VIII

TABLES OF ENROLLED CUSTOMS AND SUBSIDY ACCOUNTS: 1399 TO 1482

§ 1

INTRODUCTION

The following digests are an attempt to make available from the fifteenth century such information as Schanz published almost fifty years ago for the reign of Henry VIII.[1] It is the information contained in the " Enrolled " Customs Accounts [2] relative to English foreign trade. Schanz has described the aspect of the accounts and has noted the injuries which some of them have suffered. Written on both sides of membranes five or six feet long, some fifty of which are sewed together at one end to form cumbrous rolls, the accounts are none the less written in the admirable hand characteristic of English government documents to which final form has been given. In this and in general aspect they differ from the " Particular " accounts from which they have been compiled; for, when the collectors and the controller of customs at any port periodically rendered their accounts, their port book or small roll [3] might or might not be well written, systematic or balanced. The labour of exchequer clerks in balancing, summarizing, co-ordinating and condensing these numerous returns was not inconsiderable. If they had not done the work, we of to-day in search of knowledge about early English trade should have had to do so, could we find courage.

Even with courage the results would be fragmentary. Relatively few of the port books survive, and many of those which do are injured or extend over periods briefer than a year. It would probably be impossible to reconstruct from them the trade of all English ports for any single year of the fourteenth, the fifteenth, or the sixteenth century, to say nothing of a series of years. Gras has published a few of these " Particular " accounts, but has necessarily selected those of the briefer sort.[4] The tunnage and poundage accounts of a single year for London and Southampton would be nearly as long as all of his texts together. These detailed accounts are of the highest value in supplying what the " Enrolled " accounts omit—names, quantities

---

[1] G. Schanz, *Englische Handelspolitik gegen Ende des Mittelalters*, vol. ii.
[2] L.T.R. Cust. Accts.
[3] K.R. Cust. Accts.
[4] N. S. B. Gras, *The Early English Customs System*.

and values of commodities, names and nationalities of shippers, dates of shipment and often names of ships and of their owners. Information about the volume of trade in all ports, however, and about the fluctuation of this from year to year they do not furnish. For such we must turn to the " Enrolled " accounts and it is the surpassing service of the latter that in these matters they are surprisingly complete and comprehensive.

Apart from Schanz's meticulous compilation, they have been little used except in a fragmentary way and for particular subjects. The neglect is probably due to the labour involved in transcribing, adapting and combining them, as well as to the space which would be required to publish a long series of them as fully as Schanz has done. His tables for the thirty-eight years of Henry VIII's reign fill more than one hundred pages, his introduction and comment thirty-six pages more. The very fullness of the tables renders their use a little difficult except in the summaries, and, since tables and summaries are grouped on the basis of ports and type of custom or subsidy, it is not possible to envisage the total trade of any year except by further computation.

For the purpose of this volume, which is to give a summary view of English foreign trade in the fifteenth century, the information garnered from the " Enrolled " accounts is presented in a manner different from that of Schanz and in simplified form. In the first place, fractions of the units involved, whether pounds sterling, sacks of wool, tuns of wine, broadcloths or worsteds are not entered as such. If the fraction is greater than one-half, it is treated as an additional unit; if it is smaller than one-half, it is disregarded. The sacrifice of accuracy is slight, much slighter than that sometimes forced upon us by incomplete data, and conclusions will in no way be vitiated because they are drawn from round numbers.

In the second place the revenues accruing to the exchequer in customs and subsidies are not tabulated at all. To the compilers of the accounts, such an elimination would have taken from them all value; for it was precisely the income from the customs and the responsibility of various collectors for it that made the record indispensable for immediate and future consultation. The advantage of recording revenues, still considerable for modern scholars as it was for the exchequer of the moment, would to-day accrue to students of finance. Since, however, the theme of this volume is the trade of the fifteenth-century England, the finance of the customs and subsidies, itself an intricate subject with wide ramifications, may be disregarded. The completeness of the data relative to trade is in no way thereby affected. The only occasion on which commodity figures might be modified by reference to revenues collected is an occasional slip in the transcription of the former. It is a type of error to be corrected by noting the corresponding pounds, shillings and pence, which in turn can be tested in totals and in expense accounts. At times the commodity figures of the following tables have been so corrected.

In a much more comprehensive way, however, the figures presented are dominated by the finance of the customs and subsidies.[1] Commodities singled out for specific and quantitative enumeration, as contrasted with others not so recorded, depended for the distinction upon their being the object of a special tax. Sacks of exported wool had been subject to custom from the time of Edward I, and to subsidy from the time of Edward III. English cloths, too, had paid export duty at certain rates per cloth since 1347. From the middle of the fourteenth century wine had been subject to the subsidy of tunnage upon each tun imported. These were the three commodities exported or imported in large quantities upon which a customs tax was levied per unit, or, in modern phrase, as a "specific" duty. Other commodities traded in far less extensively, but also subject to specific duty, were hides and wax. Of five commodities, therefore, it is possible to ascertain from the enrolled accounts the quantity exported or imported annually. Other commodities, both exported and imported, were subject to an *ad valorem* tax of 12*d*. in the £ called poundage and also, if exported or imported by aliens, to one of 3*d*. in the £ called the petty custom.[2] With reference to them we have to be content with values rather than quantities, and we shall further not be able to segregate the commodities upon which they were imposed one from another.

In the presentation of this information the tables which follow depart further from the method of Schanz. Whereas he has special tables for hides, wax, pewter vessels and tin, port by port, the traffic in these commodities, being small in the fifteenth century, is not here separately tabulated. Exportation of hides in the fifteenth century was unimportant, seldom amounting to ten lasts (of 200 hides each) annually; whereas under Henry VIII the annual export was nearly fifty lasts.[3] During the earlier period the ports shipping hides were principally London, Sandwich, Southampton, Bristol, and Hull, and the share of each in a total so small is of little consequence. Wax, on the other hand, was imported almost wholly through the ports of London, Southampton, Sandwich, and Ipswich, with small amounts occasionally coming into other East Coast ports. Though the quantity involved was relatively greater than the quantity of hides, it was yet far below the relative quantities and value of the other commodities on which specific duties were levied and which have here been separately indicated. For tin and pewter vessels, the fifteenth

---

[1] Gras (op. cit.) traces the imposition of customs and subsidies and changes in rates.
[2] Imposed in 1350 and 1303 respectively (A. Beardwood, "Alien Merchants and the English Crown in the Later Fourteenth Century," in *Econ. Hist. Review*, ii, 244).
[3] Schanz, op. cit., ii, 116.

century accounts do not indicate, as do those of the sixteenth century, the value of these commodities when shipped by denizens and aliens respectively. In the fifteenth century the rate for aliens was 2s. in the £ *ad valorem*, whereas that for denizens was 1s. Since the latter was the rate for all commodities liable to the subsidy of poundage and since the subsidy on tin and pewter vessels was only a form of poundage, always appearing as such in the accounts, the fifteenth century record usually incorporates the value of these vessels exported by denizens into the poundage total. Only one part of the exportation of tin and pewter vessels is therefore ascertainable, the part exported by aliens. This not very satisfactory figure has consequently not been given a separate column in the tables.

Liberties have also been taken in the selection of data for English cloths recorded in the enrolled accounts. The record of the collector at each port embraced the number of cloths exported by denizens, Hansards, and other aliens respectively, a valuable differentiation, which is, of course, retained and which reverts to the different rate of duty paid by each group. The record also embraced a distinction between kinds of cloth exported by each group. This arose when in 1347 the rates upon cloths exported were different not only for the above-named groups but also for the grade of cloth exported. Highest was the rate for scarlets or cloths of "full grain", next that for cloths of "demi-grain", next that for cloths "without grain" or cloths of assize. All these were broadcloths. Much smaller were the rates on four sorts of worsteds—singles, doubles, single beds and double beds.[1] At the end of the century, when kerseys came to be exported in large numbers, no new category was introduced, but the new variety was rated for purposes of the subsidy at three kerseys to the cloth "without grain". Thenceforth kerseys were not differentiated from broadcloths, although the less important worsteds continued to be.

The exports of each sort of broadcloth (including the undifferentiated kerseys) by denizens, Hansards and other aliens Schanz retained, although he disposed of worsteds as a single item. It would, of course, be desirable to enumerate the cloths exported in the fifteenth century in the same precise manner. The distinction between cloths of full-grain, half-grain, and no grain had, however, a significance curious rather than commercially important. The scarlets and cloths of half-grain exported yearly were very few in number, seldom amounting to more than 200 annually; the cloths "of assize" or "without grain", on the other hand, were many thousands. The former thus did not constitute 1 per cent of the total exportation and for the wider aspects of trade a differentiation of them has little importance. They have therefore not been tabulated here. For the first half of the century down to 1446 they have been

[1] Gras, op. cit., p. 72.

omitted altogether, for the second half they have been incorporated with the almost universal broadcloths, as indeed the kerseys must perforce be incorporated.

The record of worsteds exported has also been omitted. Worsteds shipped from English ports in the fifteenth century were not numerous and not widely distributed. Nearly all passed through London or Yarmouth, with sometimes a few from Ipswich, Sandwich and Southampton. Their separate entry in the customs record was reminiscent of a time when they actually rivalled broadcloths, and it was destined to have future interest when the manufacture of these stuffs in the sixteenth century was widely extended. For fifteenth century trade worsteds were of little significance.

So far it has been implied that the " Enrolled " accounts extend neatly over periods of a year each and that the compiler has only to set these in order. While such systematic balancing does often prevail, there are certain periods during which the accounts do not extend, as could be wished, from Michaelmas to Michaelmas. Schanz notes that such irregularity is more characteristic of the accounts of the reign of Henry VII than it is of those of the reign of Henry VIII. Similarly it is more characteristic of the third quarter of the fifteenth century than of the earlier decades. Schanz solved what was for him a minor problem by striking an average for years not separated in the accounts, and he thus presented all periods as extending from Michaelmas to Michaelmas. The method has its disadvantage in concealing from scholars who may wish to use the record for their own ends the precise character of the data furnished by the accounts. It might, for instance, be of considerable interest to know that certain collectors of customs were changed, say after the battle of St. Albans in May, 1455, that new accounts were begun in June, and that trade moved in greater volume after than before the battle.

It has seemed best, therefore, to present the record of the accounts, not indeed in all its fragmentariness, but at least without its averages. For each year, when the account or accounts do not extend from Michaelmas to Michaelmas, the date nearest Michaelmas is selected and made the point of division between years. If, for instance, eight accounts constitute the record of a port over a period of three years, but none of them end at the two intervening feasts of Michaelmas, they are here so combined that the years are divided, say, in August and December. Within these divisions the trade is accurately indicated. Any student concerning himself with precisely these three years may, if he prefers the average, readily ascertain it. If, however, his concern should be with only one of the three years, he may prefer the precise record of the accounts.

Apart from the general method of presenting the record of the " Enrolled " accounts, there arise certain perplexities originating in the nature of the tax imposed or in exemptions from it which at one time were granted. Both attend upon the record of exported wool. With regard to the differentiation between shorn wool shipped in sacks and wool shipped as fells, however, no difficulty arises. The rate per sack or per 240 fells was always the same. Since the accounts usually note for the fells the equivalent in sacks, it is this equivalent which is here recorded. Comparison between amounts of wool shipped at one time or another is thereby facilitated.

Variations in rates and exemptions from paying custom or subsidy on wool applied particularly to the distinction between denizens and aliens and to the place to which the wool was to be shipped. Denizens usually and normally shipped wool to Calais. On such wool the rate was practically unchanged during the period covered by these accounts. The custom was 6s. 8d. the sack, the subsidy 33s. 4d.[1]

The second general category for exported wool was that sold to aliens. Upon this the custom was always 10s. the sack, while the subsidy varied during the fifteenth century from 43s. 4d. to 100s. The discrimination against aliens might thus become severe, and when the subsidy reached 100s., they usually secured a remission, often amounting to the added 56s. 8d. Yet the cost of this along with the total custom and subsidy must at times have put aliens at a heavy disadvantage as exporters of wool. With the exception of rather small quantities shipped during the fourteenth century and during the early fifteenth, aliens seldom took their wool to the Low Countries. They transported it instead in galleys and carracks *ad partes exteras ultra strictus de Marrok* or *ultra montana*, i.e. to the Mediterranean. For Southampton these shipments were constant enough to deserve separate columns in these tables, but in most ports they were exceptional, and have been noted as such in the footnotes.

So far there is little difficulty in arrangement. The high rate of duty which aliens were willing to pay upon their exports of wool suggests, however, that the profits to be got from shipments to the Mediterranean would be tempting to denizens or to a needy king. Hence we find as marks of royal favour in the fifteenth century numerous concessions to persons standing close to the king or to merchants to whom he was under obligations conceding the shipment of a stated number of sacks of wool to the Mediterranean. Sometimes the king himself undertook enterprises of this sort. Though the collectors of customs and subsidies at the ports entered all such shipments and entered them usually at the higher rates, eventually a part or all of the subsidy was remitted, this being the essence of the royal concession. In the case of the king we are usually told that the shipment was through alien deputies or factors and often the same statement is made relative to the king's licencees. It has seemed best to enter all such shipments as alien ones, although it is quite

---

[1] The subsidy was nominally increased to 43s. 4d. in 1453, but the additional 10s. was never actually paid.

TABLES OF ENROLLED CUSTOMS

possible that denizens may at times have been not only beneficiaries but the principal beneficiaries, actually reaping the profits from sale in a Mediterranean market.[1] Still nearer the dividing line between denizen and alien shipments are those cases in which denizen grantees sent wool to the Mediterranean without mention of alien factors. Since, however, the actual transportation and sale must have involved the co-operation of alien factors, these transactions too have been entered as alien shipments. To distinguish the last two types of shipment, many of the instances which occur have been noted as *rex* or *indigenae per factores alienos* and *indigenae ad partes exteras* (i.e. *ultra strictus de Marrok*). To determine the precise character of these transactions, the Memoranda Rolls should be consulted for each case.

A perplexity of classification, not unlike that just described, sometimes arises regarding English cloths. The king, and occasionally a favoured licencee, is recorded as exporting these at the rate paid by aliens, i.e. 2s. 9d. on the cloth without grain, in contrast with the denizen rate of 14d. Usually the shipment is by alien factors and the high duty is wholly or in part remitted. The situation differed from that affecting wool, since no act of parliament penalized shipment of cloth to foreign parts other than Calais. A denizen might himself send cloths to any port and pay only 14d. the cloth. Hence the shipments in question must have been looked upon as made by aliens. The king's connection with them, or his licencees', was probably that aliens bought from him the privilege of a certain remission at the exchequer instead of paying there the usual rate. It was a royal device

---

[1] An instance of royal shipment of wool to the Mediterranean by alien factors, there to be sold for the king's profit, is recorded in *L.T.R. Memoranda Roll*, Mich., 1453, to Mich., 1454, Status et Visus Comp., Pasch., ro. 15. The barons of the exchequer discharge the collectors of the *antiqua custuma* at London from an entry on their account of 27th Oct. 31 Henry VI to 3rd Apr. *seq.* amounting to £91 8s. 7¼d. This is the custom, subsidy and Calais pence (8d. the sack) accruing from 44¾ sacks 11 cloves of the king's wool (*lane domini regis*) shipped by William Bert, his factor, an alien merchant of Florence, in various ships *versus partes exteras ultra montana*. The remission is granted "eo quod Rex, considerans certas provisiones pro expensis hospicii sui et aliis stuffuris suis multipliciter necessarias in proximo fieri et haberi debere nonnullas pecuniarum summas pro huiusmodi provisionibus necessarias esse et oportunas, disposuit idcirco certam quantitatum lanae suae de crescencia huius regni sui Angliae prout necessitas sua exigit et requirit ad partes exteras ultra montana de amicitia Regis existentes ad quas sibi melius et utilius videbitur ad amploires ac promptiores pecuniarum summas pro huiusmodi lana habendas transmitti et traduci facere ad effectum quod Rex pecuniarum summas pro huiusmodi lana recipiendas circa provisiones predictas exponi facere valeat".

The enrolled accounts show that along with the 45 sacks were shipped under the same conditions 134½ sacks more by another alien factor of the king, Henry de Monte, merchant of Liguria. In these transactions the emphasis is clearly put upon the profit to be derived by the king from sale in southern marts rather than upon any privilege granted to foreign merchants. Such an interpretation is borne out by the rates of custom and subsidy imposed, these being denizen rates. The instance, however, is not normal in this, since the rates on so-called royal shipments by alien factors were usually alien rates. The entering of cases like the above as alien shipments, although not altogether accurate, is perhaps preferable to grouping them with denizen shipments. Investigators concerned with royal shipments by alien factors will trace each shipment further and will probably see fit to make within the group further differentiation.

for getting money without mediation of the exchequer and in advance of the normal time of payment. Doubtless the alien purchaser of the license saved himself something by getting it. At least it is clear that cloths paying 2s. 9d. should be entered as alien shipments, although ownership ascribed to the king may well be indicated in a note. In other respects the tables of the exports of cloth tell their own story, the adaptations noted above always being kept in mind.

The tunnage figures for wine do not distinguish denizen from alien trade. Since the rate upon Rhenish and Gascon wine, red or white, was 3s. the tun for both denizens and aliens, the "Enrolled" accounts, interested in income only, give the total importation at this rate. On sweet or Malmsey wine, however, the rate was 6s. and the tuns paying this are noted.

In these tables however the distinction has not been observed in spite of the fact that for some ports and for several years it offers important data for a distinction between native and alien imports, otherwise lacking.

A distinction between shippers, much to be desired, is likewise lacking in the record of the petty custom of 3d. per £ imposed on the value of all alien exports or imports save wool, hides, and wine. Since all aliens paid the same rate, the "Enrolled" accounts have no occasion for differentiation. No more have they for differentiating between exports and imports. While, therefore, it is of some value to have the total value of foreign trade (with the exceptions noted) and to observe its fluctuations from year to year, the figures from a statistical point of view are somewhat disappointing. Thus only during the last eight years of the reign of Edward IV is the Hansard trade separated from the total.

The item of the accounts which is most subject to exclusions and combinations is the poundage of 12d. in the £ on most merchandise exported and imported. The exclusion of wool, hides, and wine, causes, of course, no trouble, though it should be noted that inferior wool, known as "shorlings and morlings", was subject to poundage. Cloths were not treated so simply. Owing to privileges granted to the merchants of the Hanse, English broadcloths exported by them, as all their other exports and imports, were usually exempt from poundage. For long periods of time the collectors did not trouble to mention their shipments of cloth in connection with this subsidy. Brief periods, however, intervened when the privileges of the Hansards were threatened with cancellation or were subject to negotiations. During such intervals the collectors usually entered broadcloths exported by Hansards as subject to poundage and included in their totals the revenues payable. The expense account shows that this impost was practically always remitted. To make the record uniform, therefore, whenever the poundage total included a levy on Hansards' cloths, the amount of this has been deducted and the total brought into conformity with other poundage tables. Cloths exported by denizens require the same occasional readjustment. For the most part exempt from poundage, they were at rare intervals subjected to it by act of parliament; and until denizen merchants had once more secured exemption the collectors entered a charge for poundage. Such entries, few in number, should of course be deducted from any totals in which they figure. Unlike Hansard and denizen shipments, English cloths exported by aliens other than Hansards, were subject to poundage, and the poundage totals always include sums so paid, the amounts being computed at the rate of 12d. in the £ on the value of the cloths in question. Since the practice is uniform and since we are seldom told what value was put upon these broadcloths, it is best to leave the totals with this item always included. Cloths exported by aliens other than Hansards thus appear twice in our tables, once in the cloth custom which gives the number of them and once in the poundage totals which include the value of them. On worsteds poundage was paid if they were exported by non-Hanseatic aliens, otherwise not.

Two other commodities are to a considerable degree incorporated in the poundage figures. They are tin, often called block tin, valued by the hundredweight, and pewter vessels entered with their weight and value. Here again the distinction between denizen and alien intrudes. Hansards paid nothing, of course, being exempt from poundage, and their exports were not noted. Other aliens, however, paid not merely the denizen rate of 12d. but an additional 12d. in the £ on the value of tin and pewter vessels exported. The "Enrolled" accounts naturally make note of these alien payments and consequently of the value of tin and pewter vessels exported by aliens. We can, therefore, record these values year by year and have done so; but the items lose much of their significance through the want of the corresponding figures which would indicate the value of denizen exports of tin and pewter vessels. The latter are indistinguishably embedded in the poundage totals.

These poundage totals as they are presented in the tables are subject, therefore, to the following exclusions and incorporations. They do not include the value of any Hansard shipments whatever; they do not include the value of wool (except shorlings) or of exported hides or of imported wine; they do not include the value of English broadcloths or worsteds exported, save those exported by aliens other than Hansards; they do include the value of all other exports and imports shipped by denizens and non-Hanseatic aliens, including tin and pewter vessels (though at a higher rate for aliens), wax, and shorlings. They constitute the part of the record which most overlaps other parts. In them are included some, but not all, of the values of exported cloths, some but not all wax, which itself sometimes paid a petty custom, and even an occasional item from the wool subsidy known as shorlings. Such complications make it difficult to extricate the valuable ingredients from the totals and students will have to evolve their own devices for doing so. The poundage figures, however, round out what the "Enrolled" accounts concede us as their contribution to our knowledge of English trade.

Tables of Enrolled Customs and Subsidy Accounts

[The ports of Berwick and Cumberland (Carlisle) are omitted]

1. Boston

Date.	Wool Exported. Sacks. (Wool.)	Sacks. (Fells.)	Broadcloths Exported by Denizens.	Hansards.	Other Aliens.	Value in £ of Alien Mdse. paying the Petty Custom of 3d. in the £.	Value in £ of Mdse. paying Poundage.	Tunnage. Tuns of Wine.
Mich. 1399–Mich. 1400	2951	120	678	1801	12	1258	—	—
,, 1400–2.10.1401	2961	66	936	2089	10	8312	—	—
2.10.1401–2.10.1402	2890	128	834	2934	13	6538[1]	—	—
2.10.1402–Mich. 1403	948	82	827	1808	28	6136	6493[2]	40[2]
Mich. 1403– ,, 1404	1477	29	160	1533	9	4784	10019	303
,, 1404– ,, 1405	2731	14	277	1643	5	4434	8545	113
,, 1405–3.10.1406	2051	58	409[3]	1368[3]	4[3]	6231[3]	—[5]	—[5]
3.10.1406–Mich. 1407	2119	82	300[4]	1812[4]	3[4]	6792[4]	7271	44
Mich. 1407– ,, 1408	1851	94	323	1452	32	3633	9607	224
,, 1408– ,, 1409	2623	277[6]	462	1419	40	4301	10636	269
,, 1409– ,, 1410	1976	193	276	1315	13	4785	10247	327
,, 1410– ,, 1411	1670	79	234	1004	10	4391	8758	338
,, 1411– ,, 1412	2515	68	144	1041	2	3800	1490	268
,, 1412– ,, 1413	2535	63	184	1793	3	5220	11365	354
,, 1413– ,, 1414	1874	69	525	95	25	350	4608	463
,, 1414– ,, 1415	2471	85	246	12	5	139	2486	348
,, 1415– ,, 1416	1943	78	311	348	9	1027	4913	246
,, 1416– ,, 1417	2282	100	55	1481	9	4847	9368	327
,, 1417– ,, 1418	2499	138	335	1462	36	4020	9751	319
,, 1418– ,, 1419	1962	274	314	1484	15	4149	9150	191
,, 1419–10.10.1420	1927	171	348	1882	37	3917	10488	169
10.10.1420–Mich. 1421	1635	69	481	2179	20	4757	11043	101
Mich. 1421–30.8.1422	1805	180	233	2409	6	4068	10409	73
1.9.1422–Mich. 1423	1572	250	497	1643	20	5874	5874[8]	36[8]
Mich. 1423– ,, 1424	1727	171	772	2150	—[7]	3227	6401[8]	4[8]
,, 1424– ,, 1425	1837	194	909	1801	17	3309	5979[9]	4[9]
,, 1425– ,, 1426	2425	11	606	1463	12	2645	5614	138
,, 1426– ,, 1427	3487	227	585	1051	8	2515	6718	177
,, 1427– ,, 1428	2631	42	831	—	5	129	2383[10]	11[10]
,, 1428–1.11.1429	2315	251	1686	3	57	411	1527	207
1.11.1429–1.11.1430	697	198	1650	17	32	154	3891	289
1.11.1430–2.10.1431	1490	203	384	—	30	89	1345	181
2.10.1431–Mich. 1432	1382	85	697	41	20	283	1660	152

[1] Including £145 of exports.
[2] Subsidy from 3.4.1403.
[3] To 8.9.1406.
[4] From 8.9.1406.
[5] Account missing.
[6] Includes 19 alien.
[7] Figure illegible.
[8] Alien only.
[9] Alien only; the English tunnage and poundage from 1.8.1425, the value of merchandise being £128.
[10] No English subsidy between 11.11.1427 and 4.4.1428.

TABLES OF ENROLLED CUSTOMS 331

Date.	Wool Exported. Sacks. (Wool.)	Sacks. (Fells.)	Denizens.	Broadcloths Exported by Hansards.	Other Aliens.	Value in £ of Alien Mdse. paying the Petty Custom of 3d. in the £.	Value in £ of Mdse. paying Poundage.	Tunnage. Tuns of Wine.
Mich. 1432–Mich. 1433	1894	15	394	47	12	230	1874	40
,, 1433– ,, 1434	—	—	507	521	2	1264	2921	57
,, 1434– ,, 1435	2833	324	651	593	—	1098	4015	143
,, 1435–10.10.1436	—	—	96	3	—	1147	1801	2
10.10.1436–11.11.1437	—	—	394	1176	21	922	686	—
11.11.1437–Mich. 1438	—	—	396	1393	33	3248	838	13
Mich. 1438– ,, 1439	—	—	501	1197	44	2514	778	2
,, 1439– ,, 1440	3406	487	343	915	—	1923	980	1
,, 1440–31.6.1441	1008	41	142	53	—	1105	618	8
31.6.1441–Mich. 1442	—	—	277	836	—	1305	913	11
Mich. 1442–12.8.1443	2730	125	203	889	1	1275	665	55
12.8.1443–12.10.1444	1908	570	360	957	23	1615	1346	11
12.10.1444–12.10.1445	—	—	351	129	4	2429	1107	22
12.10.1445–24.6.1446	3444	149	339	753	10	2702	538	16
24.6.1446–18.7.1447	17	—	382	1164	1	1941	1764	7
18.7.1447–21.11.1448	2101	189 [1]	465	506	—	1242	863	6
21.11.1448–21.11.1449	—	—	102	1463	2	2815	609	92
21.11.1449–Mich. 1450	4233	332	465	100	11	333	960	8
Mich. 1450–3.2.1452	994	106	498	—	12	228	1129	5
3.2.1452–Mich. 1452	2503	274	240	—	—	138	483	—
Mich. 1452– ,, 1453	—	—	53	—	13	178	980	35
,, 1453– ,, 1454	61	—	317	—	2	9	62	7
,, 1454–10.10.1455	4635	526 [2]	207	138	—	568	196	—
10.10.1455–10.10.1456	—	—	91	535	—	846	344	2
10.10.1456–Mich. 1457	—	—	185	81	52	1520	127	—
Mich. 1457– ,, 1458 [3]	2092	212	5	112	—	1023	455	3
5.12.1459–1.9.1460	—	—	55	948	3	1182	82	—
1.9.1460–Mich. 1461	2200	571	188	346	—	563	50	1
Mich. 1461– ,, 1462	54	—	125	636	—	1042	277	10
,, 1462–22.7.1463	939	177	189	—	—	1593	364	3
22.7.1463–25.2.1465	941	160	278	279	9	1002	164	2
25.2.1465–Mich. 1465	1984	181	54	450	4	281	293	38
Mich. 1465–25.3.1467	1987	145	387	95	144	1340	1100	9
25.3.1467–21.10.1467	1749	200	185	42	1	452	372	18
21.10.1467–25.12.1468	36	117	576	56	—	228	408	24
25.12.1468–Mich. 1469	2179	258	497	5	166	313	567	5
Mich. 1469–13.11.1470	1384	566	623	—	4	100	255	8
3.11.1470–Mich. 1471 [4]	1	2	273	—	30	166	266	1
Mich. 1471–8.10.1472	2667	988	372	—	43	160	341	4
8.10.1472–8.10.1473	1410	125	479	—	149	237	481	4
8.10.1473–2.11.1474	941	127	337	—	206	444	58	1
2.11.1474–Mich. 1475	1191	182	169	31	170	553	80	—
Mich. 1475– ,, 1476	1718	503	12	283	4	998	449	18
,, 1476– ,, 1477	—	—	84	—	6	543	489	15
,, 1477– ,, 1478	1624	667	107	548	6	1100	336	23
,, 1478– ,, 1479	1060	318	204	195	21	596	407	1
,, 1479– ,, 1480	1082	144	68	265	—	439	546	6
,, 1480– ,, 1481	1210	396	41	241	—	535	502	37
,, 1481– ,, 1482	1210	396	152	62	7	948	550	1

[1] Includes 2 alien.
[2] Includes 198 alien.
[3] Gap.
[4] Overlap.

2. BRIDGEWATER

Date.	Broadcloths Exported by Denizens.	Aliens.	Value in £ of Alien Mdse. paying the Petty Custom of 3d. in the £.	Value in £ of Mdse. paying Poundage.	Tunnage. Tuns of Wine.
Mich. 1399–Mich. 1400 [1]	—	—	—	—	—
,, 1400– ,, 1401	—	—	—	—	—
,, 1401– ,, 1402	—	—	—	—	—
,, 1402– ,, 1403	—	—	—	—	—
,, 1403–18.12.1404	31	—	—	—	—
18.12.1404–8.10.1405	91	—	—	144 [2]	80 [2]
8.10.1405–1.5.1406	97	—	—	—	—
1.5.1406–1.3.1407	131	—	—	373 [2]	99 [2]
1.3.1407–Mich. 1408	52	—	—	118 [2]	71 [2]
Mich. 1408– ,, 1409	17	—	—	269 [2]	232 [2]
,, 1409– ,, 1410	103	—	—	165	176
,, 1410– ,, 1411	60	—	19	199	91
,, 1411– ,, 1412	116	5	—	411	207
,, 1412– ,, 1413	57	—	—	222 [3]	84 [3]
,, 1413– ,, 1414	123	—	—	139 [4]	— [4]
,, 1414– ,, 1415	115	—	—	277	379
,, 1415– ,, 1416	201	18	17	730	397
,, 1416– ,, 1417	32	—	—	387	201
,, 1417– ,, 1418	37	—	—	227	259
,, 1418– ,, 1419	11	—	11	471	80
,, 1419– ,, 1420	93	3	14	358	111
,, 1420–12.7.1421	94	—	—	216	16
12.7.1421–31.8.1422	32	3	14	144 [5]	45 [5]
31.8.1422–13.1.1423 [8]	255	—	10	16 [6]	—
13.1.1424–7.3.1425	32	—	1	—	—
7.3.1425–22.8.1426	96	—	81	207	61 [7]
22.8.1426–Mich. 1427	51	—	—	275	168
Mich. 1427– ,, 1428	93	18	27	136	53
,, 1428– ,, 1429	46	—	15	130	120
,, 1429– ,, 1430	14	—	—	919	93
,, 1430– ,, 1431	66	—	10	317	193
,, 1431– ,, 1432	10	15	46	278	101
,, 1432– ,, 1433	36	—	—	329	135
,, 1433– ,, 1434	98	—	—	437	69
,, 1434– ,, 1435	42	—	—	485	104
,, 1435– ,, 1436	108	11	7	689	216
,, 1436– ,, 1437	50	—	—	470	6
,, 1437– ,, 1438	181	—	—	276	40
,, 1438– ,, 1439	60	—	—	390	36
,, 1439– ,, 1440	68	—	14	230	98
,, 1440–26.7.1441	44	—	26	527	166
26.7.1441–Mich. 1442	63	—	11	346	68
Mich. 1442– ,, 1443	91	—	12	283	105
,, 1443– ,, 1444	89	—	—	317	39
,, 1444– ,, 1445	53	31	143	483	43
,, 1445–11.11.1446	59	4	48	465	101
11.11.1446–Mich. 1447	111	16	50	424	67

[1] At the beginning of the reign, the accounts of Bridgewater are included under Bristol.
[2] The respective dates of the first four entries of the subsidies of tunnage and poundage are:—Mich. 1404 to 18.12.1404, 1.12.1406 to 1.1.1407, 1.1.1407 to 15.8.1408, 15.8.1409 to Mich. 1409.
[3] Accounts missing from 14.11.1412 to 21.5.1413.
[4] Accounts missing from 20.11.1413 to Mich. 1414.
[5] Subsidy to 31.8.1422.   [6] Subsidy to 13.1.1424.
[7] English subsidy levied from 1.8.1425 only.   [8] Gap.

TABLES OF ENROLLED CUSTOMS

Date.	Broadcloths Exported by Denizens.	Aliens.	Value in £ of Alien Mdse. paying the Petty Custom of 3d. in the £.	Value in £ of Mdse. paying Poundage.	Tunnage. Tuns of Wine.
Mich. 1447–Mich. 1448	162	4	17	377	—
,, 1448– ,, 1449	71	—	—	469	118
,, 1449– ,, 1450	74	—	—	219	67
,, 1450– ,, 1451	39	—	—	174	28
,, 1451– ,, 1452	62	—	26	352	35
,, 1452– ,, 1453	25	16	116	509	70
,, 1453– ,, 1454 [1]	71	—	27	399	103
28.12.1455–Mich. 1456	48	6	11	343	24
Mich. 1456– ,, 1457	221	10	4	573	9
,, 1457– ,, 1458	259	11	32	809	136
,, 1458– ,, 1459 [1]	114	10	47	394	33
21.8.1460–Mich. 1461	72	—	—	215	5
Mich. 1461–17.7.1463 [1]	31	13	102	367	69
12.2.1465–18.3.1466	—	19	152	435	187
18.3.1466–Mich. 1466	10	28	29	294	157
Mich. 1466–18.12.1467	50	32	228	436	53
18.12.1467–6.5.1468 [1]	12	—	—	120	20
15.11.1469–24.10.1470 [1]	75	—	7	127	—
11.6.1471–1.10.1472	51	34	109	692	174
1.10.1472–Mich. 1473	112	5	95	740	115
Mich. 1473–25.12.1474	164	10	178	668	44
25.12.1474–25.12.1475	203	52	50	688	74
25.12.1475–25.12.1476	95	140	42	690	121
25.12.1476–30.12.1477	494	—	—	1,090	171
30.12.1477–Mich. 1478 [1]	377	49	—	1,016	63
23.11.1478– ,, 1479	154	—	—	1,154	114
Mich. 1479– ,, 1480	266	90	—	1,179	142
,, 1480– ,, 1481	401	227	7	1,587	133
,, 1481– ,, 1482	889	75	34	4,095	170

3. BRISTOL

Date.	Broadcloths Exported by Denizens.	Aliens.	Value in £ of Alien Mdse. paying the Petty Custom of 3d. in the £.	Value in £ of Mdse. paying Poundage.	Tunnage. Tuns of Wine.
Mich. 1399–Mich. 1400	3471	28	98	—	—
,, 1400–8.7.1401	6228	78	148	—	—
8.7.1401–10.10.1402	6267	20	321	—	—
10.10.1402–16.10.1403	2753	—	144	5433 [2]	139 [2]
16.10.1403–25.3.1404	2119	25	8	9366 [3]	152 [3]
25.3.1404–16.5.1405	3848	18	—	13087	1385
16.5.1405–Mich. 1406	4041	95	—	17067	991
Mich. 1406– ,, 1407	2067	1	—	7533	594
,, 1407– ,, 1408	1688	34	34	7790	1459
,, 1408– ,, 1409	2661	91	—	13177	1751
,, 1409– ,, 1410	2532	14	—	3204 [4]	1148 [4]
,, 1410– ,, 1411	1978	22	149	8101	1094
,, 1411– ,, 1412	2137	10	22	7599	814

[1] Gap.
[2] Subsidy from 3.4.1403.
[3] Taken from *K.R. Cust. Acct.* 18/13.
[4] No account from 16.2.1410 to Mich. 1410.

334 ENGLISH TRADE IN FIFTEENTH CENTURY

Date.	Broadcloths Exported by Denizens.	Aliens.	Value in £ of Alien Mdse. paying the Petty Custom of 3d. in the £.	Value in £ of Mdse. paying Poundage.	Tunnage. Tuns of Wine.
Mich. 1412–Mich. 1413	2195	32	102	9958	939
,, 1413– ,, 1414	1523	21	101	7170	1535
,, 1414– ,, 1415	1914	11	—	6336	1338
,, 1415– ,, 1416	1844	2	11	11146	1293
,, 1416– ,, 1417	3338	—	290	14329	1795
,, 1417– ,, 1418	2718	40	495	16172	1690
,, 1418– ,, 1419	2123	27	481	10921 [1]	891
,, 1419– ,, 1420	2926	34	179	14541	1119
,, 1420– ,, 1421	3644	35	97	16558	1892
,, 1421–31.8.1422	3725	10	10	15207	1025
1.9.1422–Mich. 1423	6115	20	99	138	27
Mich. 1423– ,, 1424	4994	37	156	242	41
,, 1424– ,, 1425	4955	37	3.5	1156	76
,, 1425– ,, 1426	2607	60	47	10237	970
,, 1426– ,, 1427	4318	78 [2]	365	10297	1966
,, 1427– ,, 1428	4225	44	154	3364	219
,, 1428– ,, 1429	6609	9	38	2501	889
,, 1429– ,, 1430	2751	—	93	10280	452
,, 1430–14.11.1431	5825	4	198	7664	1306
14.11.1431–19.10.1432	3224	1	731	10126 [4]	736
19.10.1432–28.8.1433 [3]	1976	18	25	6998	875
2.9.1433–Mich. 1434	4889	—	6	14976 [5]	1718
Mich. 1434– ,, 1435	2025	—	—	13294 [6]	1659
,, 1435– ,, 1436	2529	—	127	10830	1631
,, 1436– ,, 1437	2742	10	—	5356	42
,, 1437–15.10.1438	6831	—	382	10192	882
15.10.1438–30.9.1439	5118	35 [7]	12	7135	882
30.9.1439–Mich. 1440	5637	—	52	10479	1625
Mich. 1440– ,, 1441	5658	119	310	11023	3075
,, 1441– ,, 1442	4045	62	265	1215	2070
,, 1442– ,, 1443	5560	12	815	11703	2383
,, 1443– ,, 1444	5112	122	282	14627	2364
,, 1444– ,, 1445	6088	358	827	12272	2457
,, 1445–11.11.1446	5440	43	143	12722	2190
11.11.1446–Mich. 1447	5292	1	26	10512	1587
Mich. 1447– ,, 1448	7534	12	69	9851	2197
,, 1448– ,, 1449	3254	—	361	9144	2500
,, 1449– ,, 1450	2338	11	25	6453	1139
,, 1450– ,, 1451	4763	28	86	7408	1812
,, 1451– ,, 1452	3952	53	254	10861	1377
,, 1452– ,, 1453	3089	56	246	8404	2413
,, 1453– ,, 1454	5124	77	88	8294	1692
,, 1454– ,, 1455	1864	11	25	8051	1670
,, 1455–2.11.1456	3689	47	254	7975	1046
2.11.1456–Mich. 1457	2754	38	193	7296	760
Mich. 1457–24.11.1458	3427	22	180	8169	755
24.11.1458–Mich. 1459	1827	51	418	6607	645
Mich. 1459– ,, 1460	2732	128 [8]	245	6537	874

[1] Does not include £13 6s. 8d. received by the Controller in subsidy at Gloucester, Newnham and "Berkley".
[2] Includes 36 cloths exported by Hanseatics.
[3] Gap.
[4] Does not include Welsh cloth exported by the English to the value of £198.
[5] Does not include Welsh cloth exported by the English to the value of £248.
[6] Does not include a small quantity of miscellaneous goods, for which no account rendered.
[7] Exported by Hanseatics.
[8] Includes 67 cloths exported by Hanseatics.

TABLES OF ENROLLED CUSTOMS

Date.	Broadcloths Exported by Denizens.	Aliens.	Value in £ of Alien Mdse. paying the Petty Custom of 3d. in the £.	Value in £ of Mdse. paying Poundage.	Tunnage. Tuns of Wine.
Mich. 1460–Mich. 1461	1173	41 [1]	240	2777	274
,, 1461– ,, 1462	2628	77	307	6985	574
,, 1462– ,, 1463	2012	59	112	4383	1156
,, 1463– ,, 1464	1604	10	124	7482	848
,, 1464– ,, 1465	2476	169	507	7114	1433
,, 1465– ,, 1466	3711	113	473	7751	1042
,, 1466–8.2.1467 [2]	539	4	24	933	18
,, 1467–26.8.1469	3968	63 [3]	671	11970	2403
26.8.1469–14.11.1469	736	9	120	1475	3
14.11.1469–4.11.1470	344	5	159	7532	850
4.11.1470–Mich. 1471 [2]	2074	—	30	3905	765
20.11.1472–14.12.1472 [4]	161	41	109	704	60
Mich. 1477–Mich. 1478	7343	192	—	12052	1679
,, 1478– ,, 1479	5827	35	205	13333	1671
,, 1479– ,, 1480	4690	46	380	15439	1297
,, 1480– ,, 1481	5825	472	333	14205	1603
,, 1481– ,, 1482	4498	610	14	15998	1070

4. CHICHESTER

Date.	Wool Exported. Sacks. (Wool.)	Sacks. (Fells.)	Broadcloths Exported by Denizens.	Aliens.	Value in £ of Alien Mdse. paying the Petty Custom of 3d. in the £.	Value in £ of Mdse. paying Poundage.	Tunnage. Tuns of Wine.
Mich. 1399–Mich. 1400	303	1	—	—	—	—	—
,, 1400– ,, 1401	341	1	—	—	262	—	—
,, 1401–16.10.1402	1284	1	—	—	257	—	—
16.10.1402–Mich. 1403	1018	5	—	—	65	30 [5]	18 [5]
Mich. 1403– ,, 1404	889	—	—	—	25	192 [5]	105 [5]
,, 1404– ,, 1405 [7]	717	—	20	—	89	533	—
1.10.1405– ,, 1406	418	—	—	—	—	26 [5]	7 [5]
Mich. 1406– ,, 1407	827	—	—	—	44	—	—
,, 1407–19.10.1408	573	3	—	—	251 [6]	692 [5]	194 [5]
19.10.1408–Mich. 1409	387	3	—	—	281	415	294
Mich. 1409– ,, 1410	177	—	—	2	228	342	271
,, 1410– ,, 1411 [7]	216	—	2	4	237	434	99
11.2.1412–20.3.1413	93	16	—	—	216	371	101
20.3.1413–Mich. 1413	—	—	—	—	80	211	—
Mich. 1413–12.4.1414	255	—	—	—	66	137	86
12.4.1414–Mich. 1415	76	17	—	3	196	454	558
Mich. 1415– ,, 1416	—	1	—	1	70	184	175
,, 1416– ,, 1417	256	—	18	7	348	904	240

[1] Exported by Hanseatics.
[2] Gap.
[3] Includes 7 cloths exported by Hanseatics.
[4] Gap. Some of the trade is recorded in the Particular Customs Accounts, but totals are unavailable.
[5] The dates of the accounts of subsidy are as follows : 3.4.1403 to 16.10.1403 ; 16.10.1403 to Mich. 1404 ; Mich. 1404 to Mich. 1405 ; Mich. 1405 to 1.4.1406 ; 20.2.1408 to 19.10.1408.
[6] The account of petty custom is missing from Mich. 1407 to 20.2.1408.
[7] Gap.

ENGLISH TRADE IN FIFTEENTH CENTURY

Date.	Wool Exported. Sacks. (Wool.)	Sacks. (Fells.)	Broadcloths Exported by Denizens.	Aliens.	Value in £ of Alien Mdse. paying the Petty Custom of 3d. in the £.	Value in £ of Mdse. paying Poundage.	Tunnage. Tuns of Wine.
Mich. 1417–Mich. 1418	—	1	—	—	61	156	363
,, 1418– ,, 1420	25	4	30	12	231	613	261
,, 1420–17.10.1421	—	3	19	5	452	762	35
17.10.1421–31.8.1422	112	9	3	—	241	1016	28
1.9.1422–22.11.1423	232	—	6	7	47	86	—
19.11.1423 [1]–26.7.1424	18	12	—	—	119	135 [2]	48 [2]
26.7.1424–19.4.1426	151	1	37	22	177	195 [2]	28 [2]
19.4.1426–Mich. 1426 [3]	36	2	34	—	23	551 [4]	198 [4]
25.10.1426–10.10.1427	272	19	60	—	35	975	175
10.10.1427–Mich. 1428	29	2	60	1	146	712	42
Mich. 1428– ,, 1429	21	1	66	6	202	437 [5]	119 [5]
,, 1429– ,, 1430	7	4	58	2	170	622 [6]	7 [6]
,, 1430– ,, 1431	34	3	34	6	122	570	208
,, 1431– ,, 1432	—	—	10	4	112	593	98
,, 1432–10.11.1433	21	2	8	—	173	150 [7]	1 [7]
10.11.1433–Mich. 1434	16	—	13	17	177	768	94
Mich. 1434– ,, 1435	12	2	90	2	633	1611	224
,, 1435– ,, 1436	---	3	20	—	481	818	226
,, 1436– ,, 1437	--	---	57	9	343	568	41
,, 1437– ,, 1438	—	--	76	31 [8]	325	1102	43
,, 1438– ,, 1439	87	—	91	12 [9]	224	828	56
,, 1439– ,, 1440	156	—	116	28	252	825	291
,, 1440– ,, 1441	56	—	49	21	252	685	270
,, 1441– ,, 1442	73	---	17	63	178	541	324
,, 1442– ,, 1443	—	—	42	49	198	829	400
,, 1443– ,, 1444	—	---	89	31	634	1470	223
,, 1444– ,, 1445	132	2	123	43	822	1989	382
,, 1445– ,, 1446	452 [10]	1	168	33 [11]	683	1629	283
,, 1446– ,, 1447	—	17	193	7	763	1397	211
,, 1447–27.10.1448	41	---	237	51	429	1487	276
27.10.1448–Mich. 1449	—	---	54	—	599	1002	232
Mich. 1449– ,, 1450	---	---	53	4	190	343	64
,, 1450– ,, 1451	--	---	102	—	350	451	20
,, 1451– ,, 1452	—	—	98	3	242	715	34
,, 1452– ,, 1453	—	1	105	—	416	671	137
,, 1453– ,, 1454	—	—	48	1	232	363	38
,, 1454–7.6.1455	—	—	78	—	271	482	13
7.6.1455–19.11.1456 [3]	—	—	64	1	546	813	3
27.10.1457–4.12.1458 [3]	8 [12]	—	188	50	244	534	36
15.12.1458–12.1.1460	—	—	418	5	233	279	4
12.1.1460–12.8.1460	51	—	—	—	70	101	14
12.8.1460–22.6.1461	—	---	12	12	135	166	11
22.6.1461–4.6.1462	5	---	55	32	229	378	36
4.6.1462–24.9.1463	—	—	10	10	262	292	16
24.9.1463–30.10.1464	—	---	21	3	270	300	42
30.10.1464–Mich. 1465	—	—	53	56	194	361	149
Mich. 1465–3.10.1466	—	—	22	41	475	780	41
3.10.1466–Mich. 1467	—	—	36	38	609	928	152
Mich. 1467– ,, 1468	—	---	54	19	517	789	118
,, 1468–14.11.1469	—	—	92	22	591	1063	84

[1] Overlapping 3 days.   [2] Aliens only.
[3] Gap.
[4] English only to 29.4.1426; English and alien from that date.
[5] English to 4.4.1429 only.   [6] English from 6.12.1429 only.
[7] From 18.8.1433 only.   [8] Includes 1 cloth exported by Hanseatics.
[9] Includes 1 cloth exported by Hanseatics.   [10] Includes 37 alien.
[11] Includes ½ cloth exported by Hanseatics.   [12] Alien.

TABLES OF ENROLLED CUSTOMS 337

Date.	Wool Exported. Sacks. (Wool.)	Sacks. (Fells.)	Broadcloths Exported by Denizens.	Aliens.	Value in £ of Alien Mdse. paying the Petty Custom of 3d. in the £.	Value in £ of Mdse. paying Poundage.	Tunnage. Tuns of Wine.
14.11.1469–24.10.1470 [1]	—	—	50	64	513	944	42
3.6.1471–30.9.1471	—	—	2	46	545	598	14
30.9.1471–30.9.1472	—	—	121	29	433	885	115
30.9.1472–30.9.1473 [1]	—	—	20	17	859	1479	165
Mich. 1473–Mich. 1474	—	—	7	6	569	842	—
,, 1474– ,, 1475	2	—	18	25	408	792	78
,, 1475– ,, 1476	—	—	94	13	893	1336	104
,, 1476– ,, 1477	—	—	37	24	699	1258	117
,, 1477– ,, 1478	1	—	23	—	377	1275	97
,, 1478– ,, 1479	4	1	16	16	341	1763	126
,, 1479– ,, 1480	—	—	24	—	407	1585	126
,, 1480–20.10.1481	—	9	28	—	1085	2010	120
20.10.1481–Mich. 1482	28	—	12	2	1115	1952	109

5. EXETER AND DARTMOUTH

Date.	Wool Exported. Sacks. (Wool.)	Broadcloths Exported by Denizens.	Aliens.	Value in £ of Alien Mdse. paying the Petty Custom of 3d. in the £.	Value in £ of Mdse. paying Poundage.	Tunnage. Tuns of Wine.
Mich. 1399–21.11.1400 [2]	—	249	—	253	—	—
21.11.1400–10.2.1402	—	291	6	291	—	—
10.2.1402–17.10.1402	—	190	—	217	—	—
17.10.1402–Mich. 1403	—	77	—	19	—[3]	—[3]
Mich. 1403– ,, 1404 [1]	—	584	36	268	1728[4]	337[4]
18.12.1404– ,, 1405	—	37	—	110	679[4]	183[4]
Mich. 1405–11.3.1407	—	579	229	147	2276[5]	291[5]
11.3.1407–11.8.1407	—	100	34	554	2501[6]	108[6]
11.8.1408–Mich. 1408	—	107	—	—	5373[7]	793[7]
Mich. 1408– ,, 1409	—	226	140	108	1974	666
,, 1409–18.11.1410	—	206	20	142	1406[8]	737[8]
18.11.1410–Mich. 1411	—	170	19	156	1956	433
Mich. 1411–22.1.1413	—	380	43	292	414	265
22.1.1413–Mich. 1413	—	506	46	130	1422[9]	595[9]
Mich. 1413– ,, 1414	—	622[10]	156[10]	389[10]	1067[11]	16[11]
,, 1414– ,, 1415	—	410	49	144	2298	653
,, 1415– ,, 1416	—	208	14	42	1605	989
,, 1416–18.7.1417	—	563	3	90	1245	855
18.7.1417–Mich. 1418	—	600	143	315	2051	663

[1] Gap.
[2] Few accounts for Plymouth have been found enrolled separately during the early years nd the accounts of Exeter suggest that the Plymouth trade was probably included here. See nder Plymouth (Table 12).
[3] Account missing.
[4] Dartmouth subsidy of tunnage and poundage to 18.12.1404 and from that date only.
[5] Subsidy to 25.10.1405 includes Plymouth, but from Mich. 1405 to 1.4.1406 does not clude Exeter.
[6] Subsidy from 25.10.1406 includes Plymouth.
[7] Subsidy includes Plymouth to 4.8.1408.
[8] Subsidy from 18.11.1409 to 18.11.1410.
[9] Subsidy from 22.1.1413 to 22.1.1414.
[10] Accounts missing from 21.3.1414 to 15.4.1414.
[11] Subsidy from 22.1.1414.

ENGLISH TRADE IN FIFTEENTH CENTURY

Date.	Wool Exported. Sacks. (Wool.)	Broadcloths Exported by Denizens.	Aliens.	Value in £ of Alien Mdse. paying the Petty Custom of 3d. in the £.	Value in £ of Mdse. paying Poundage.	Tunnage. Tuns of Wine.
Mich. 1418–Mich. 1419	—	372	61	191	2865	629
,, 1419– ,, 1420	—	342	28	98	1911	417
,, 1420– ,, 1421	—	246	108	221	1683	488
,, 1421–31.8.1422	4[1]	390	—	18	1741	421
1.9.1422–Mich. 1423	—	442	43	122	1364	227
Mich. 1423–14.11.1423	—	—	—	—	181[2]	7[2]
14.11.1423–22.5.1425	—	449	63	89	180[2]	196[2]
25.5.1425–Mich. 1426	—	406	58	106	415[3]	90[3]
Mich. 1426– ,, 1427	—	244	37	109	67	—
,, 1427– ,, 1428	—	273	66	184	834[4]	5[4]
,, 1428– ,, 1429	—	332	39	123	508	352[5]
,, 1429– ,, 1430	1	143	26	130	1673	153[6]
,, 1430– ,, 1431	—	704	85	403	2296	827
,, 1431– ,, 1432	—	712	107	177	1213	443
,, 1432–25.8.1433	—	756	121	177	747	85
25.8.1433–25.8.1434	—	1276	63	166	1542	481
25.8.1434–Mich. 1435	—	812	9	77	3728	575
Mich. 1435– ,, 1436	—	818	66	119	2975	477
,, 1436–26.10.1437	—	1059	109	238	2366	49
26.10.1437–Mich. 1438	—	820	61	115	1355	267
Mich. 1438–30.9.1439	—	1638	97	33	1761	252
30.9.1439–Mich. 1440	—	1767	40	63	1938	473
Mich. 1440– ,, 1441	—	1495	62	129	1785	620
,, 1441– ,, 1442	—	974	32	75	1480	468
,, 1442– ,, 1443	4	860	34	59	1528	481
,, 1443– ,, 1444	4	1889	71[7]	83	3026	637
,, 1444– ,, 1445	—	2046	126	248	2460	671
,, 1445– ,, 1446	—	1809	68	108	2224	764
,, 1446– ,, 1447	—	2554	29	53	2191	742
,, 1447– ,, 1448	—	3076	23	22	2602	563
,, 1448– ,, 1449	—	1721	4	8	578	567
,, 1449–28.7.1450	—	410	—	—	816	363
28.7.1450–Mich. 1451	—	1279	4	17	1059	318
Mich. 1451– ,, 1452	—	1083	47	79	1541	292
,, 1452– ,, 1453	—	1904	16	134	1521	274
,, 1453– ,, 1454	—	748	12	359	1261	246
,, 1454– ,, 1455	—	1252	22	124	2080	318
,, 1455– ,, 1456	—	1345	12	106	1072	136
,, 1456– ,, 1457	—	1094	6	15	1029	45
,, 1457– ,, 1458	—	1142	1	173	1358	141
,, 1458– ,, 1459	—	1075	6	448	1659	198
,, 1459– ,, 1460	—	1536	—	223	1055	148
,, 1460– ,, 1461	—	944	8	101	1459	134
,, 1461– ,, 1462	—	987	21	462	1484	113
,, 1462– ,, 1463	—	1328	29	279	1789	252
,, 1463– ,, 1464	—	1126	10	125	1229	153
,, 1464– ,, 1465	—	575	212	554	1732	552
,, 1465– ,, 1466	—	843	19	292	1032	113
,, 1466– ,, 1467	—	732	36	535	1448	223
,, 1467– ,, 1468	—	805	37	628	1657	423
,, 1468–14.9.1469	—	783	135	582	1789	332

[1] Including 1 alien.
[2] Alien subsidy only.
[3] Alien subsidy from 22.5.1425 and English subsidy from 1.8.1425.
[4] No English subsidy between 16.11.1427 and 16.4.1428.
[5] English subsidy to 4.4.1429 only.
[6] English subsidy from 17.1.1430.
[7] Includes 2 cloths exported by Hanseatic merchants.

TABLES OF ENROLLED CUSTOMS

Date.	Wool Exported. Sacks. (Wool.)	Broadcloths Exported by Denizens.	Broadcloths Exported by Aliens.	Value in £ of Alien Mdse. paying the Petty Custom of 3d. in the £.	Value in £ of Mdse. paying Poundage.	Tunnage. Tuns of Wine.
14.9.1469–13.9.1470	—	801	121	584	1613	250
13.9.1470–Mich. 1471	—	717	109	406	1182	164
Mich. 1471– ,, 1472	—	462	119	185	2243	228
,, 1472– ,, 1473	—	660	47	378	1267	237
,, 1473– ,, 1474	—	796	80	134	1446	180
,, 1474–17.10.1475 [1]	—	377	50	67	966	157
6.6.1476–Mich. 1477 [1]	—	3046	296	409	4607	452
Mich. 1478– ,, 1479	—	1862	76	304	3418	415
,, 1479– ,, 1480	—	1956	242	239	3655	597
,, 1480– ,, 1481	—	2472	770 [2]	1397	6437	14
,, 1481–25.10.1482	—	4149	2165 [3]	406	9481	450

6. Ipswich

Date.	Wool Exported. Sacks. (Wool.)	Wool Exported. Sacks. (Fells.)	Broadcloths Exported by Denizens.	Broadcloths Exported by Hansards.	Broadcloths Exported by Other Aliens.	Value in £ of Alien Mdse. paying the Petty Custom of 3d. in the £.	Value in £ of Mdse. paying Poundage.	Tunnage. Tuns of Wine.
1.10.1399–Mich. 1400	444	3	926	185	125	1139	—	—
Mich. 1400– ,, 1401	481	27	681	398	128	529	—	—
,, 1401–21.9.1402	840	45	23	55	1	415	—	—
21.9.1402–Mich. 1403	1142	12	423	141	46	1274	1010 [4]	— [4]
Mich. 1403– ,, 1404	1007	37	84	4	19	158	2438 [5]	257 [5]
,, 1404– ,, 1405	465	22	— [6]	— [6]	— [6]	— [6]	1093	140
,, 1405– ,, 1406	1200	53	— [6]	— [6]	— [6]	— [6]	3941	115
,, 1406– ,, 1407	1648	7	667	315	47	931	4324	37
,, 1407– ,, 1408	—	—	428	206	81	1471	4108	359
,, 1408– ,, 1409	2038	68	597	153	30	1306	2039	328
,, 1409– ,, 1410	1151	106	378	41	142	649	2277	261
,, 1410– ,, 1411	604 [7]	23	278	231	22	431	1414	298
,, 1411– ,, 1412	618 [8]	13	404	334	36	632	2634	227
,, 1412– ,, 1413	1641	—	454	348	30	431	2321	208
,, 1413– ,, 1414	1461	87	1089	204	18	361	2699	223
,, 1414– ,, 1415	7	40	573	737	33	1148	3157	314
,, 1415– ,, 1416	660	57	407	1090	51	1143	3619	300
,, 1416–17.10.1417 [9]	434	34	1018	677	6	808	3896	253
,, 1417–Mich. 1418	576	38	773	598	4	826	4003	312
,, 1418– ,, 1419	1375	363	1098	45	5	1033	3895	159
,, 1419– ,, 1420	1144	76	1014	765	3	696	3342	125
,, 1420– ,, 1421	1265	39	1716	590	36	1363	6372	185
,, 1421–31.8.1422	1160	49	593	657	7 [10]	1003	4005	118
1.9.1422–Mich. 1423	1515	90	1249	550	5	365	1098	—
Mich. 1423– ,, 1424	1971	93	1496	836	49	1490	2681	7
,, 1424– ,, 1425	967	95	2391	1190	14	909	3606 [11]	53 [11]
,, 1425– ,, 1426	1549	28	1291	923	12	1455	5989	318

[1] Gap. [2] Includes 2 cloths exported by Hanseatic merchants.
[3] Includes 23 cloths exported by Hanseatic merchants. [4] Subsidy from 3.4.1403.
[5] Subsidy to 12.5.1404 only. [6] Account missing. [7] Includes 98 alien.
[8] Includes 9 alien. [9] Overlap of 18 days.
[10] Computed from the sum yielded by customs.
[11] From the beginning of the reign to 1.8.1425, subsidy was paid by aliens only; the English subsidy levied from 1.8.1425.

Date.	Wool Exported. Sacks. (Wool.)	Sacks. (Fells.)	Broadcloths Exported by Denizens.	Hansards.	Other Aliens.	Value in £ of Alien Mdse. paying the Petty Custom of 3d. in the £.	Value in £ of Mdse. paying Poundage.	Tunnage. Tuns of Wine.
Mich. 1426–Mich. 1427	1887	63	965	279	7	671	2570	231
,, 1427– ,, 1428	2179	76	1704	375	13	878	2223	2
,, 1428– ,, 1429	784	5	1074	884	10	1238	2797	132
,, 1429– ,, 1430	626	52	1251	338	6	1012	3760	171
,, 1430– ,, 1431	1178	119	2142	804	7	727	3395	282
,, 1431– ,, 1432	1454	31	632	152	4	120	685	29
,, 1432–18.10.1433	1291	8	1851	281	8	409	1953	146
18.10.1433–Mich. 1434	—	—	1962	1224	57	1042	6977	555
Mich. 1434–4.10.1435	1850	63	2266	929	61	310	7293	271
4.10.1435–30.9.1436 [1]	—	—	761	417	105	139	2057	212
Mich. 1436–Mich. 1437	—	—	2018	3569	141	3669	1871	86
,, 1437– ,, 1438	—	—	2076	3113	118	4009	2410	168
,, 1438– ,, 1439	—	—	2170	1353	103	3144	2689	91
,, 1439– ,, 1440	2870	367	3556	3638	39	1917	2275	351
,, 1440– ,, 1441	658	55	2322	1243	22	918	2978	372
,, 1441– ,, 1442	—	—	1732	2233	12	2424	1887	263
,, 1442– ,, 1443	971	111	2347	974	10	1119	1420	306
,, 1443– ,, 1444	899	492	1962	2930	11	2481	1089	205
,, 1444– ,, 1445	—	—	2107	3618	40	2823	2326	207
,, 1445– ,, 1446	1429	210	754	2961	47	4559	2690	233
,, 1446– ,, 1447	—	—	2884	5105	8	4500	3250	202
,, 1447–16.10.1448	1233	160	1257	1728	19	789	1988	155
16.10.1448–2.7.1449	31	—	391	168	14	2139	646	137
2.7.1449–Mich. 1450	1092	390	2578	2590	24	714	817	108
Mich. 1450– ,, 1451	—	—	1357	372	13	312	1094	—
,, 1451– ,, 1452	713	101	645	254	—	577	620	105
,, 1452– ,, 1453	1378	345	760	1823	—	2142	1029	91
,, 1453–29.11.1454	—	—	384	1072	3	3131	937	165
29.11.1454–Mich. 1455	1295	632	250	2024	—	4241	726	—
Mich. 1455–22.10.1456	—	—	385	1883	—	3548	1362	52
22.10.1456–Mich. 1457	741	352	622	1079	8	1849	946	107
Mich. 1457–29.11.1458	—	—	1009	2721	3	4483	1590	1
29.11.1458–Mich. 1459	—	—	599	1237	—	1375	751	16
Mich. 1459– ,, 1460	—	—	116	1112	1	1930	656	468
,, 1460– ,, 1461	689	749	313	1844	2	3934	1092	61
,, 1461–16.10.1462	33	85	313	1372	1	2443	926	5
16.10.1462–10.7.1463	14	35	105	1032	51	1184	616	67
10.7.1463–31.8.1464	470	343	118	501	31	1738	1041	95
31.8.1464–Mich. 1465	90	3	63	1167	82	1561	697	166
Mich. 1465– ,, 1466	180	34	159	4525	43	3148	704	38
,, 1466– ,, 1467	372	79	520	606	115	1494	1095	73
,, 1467– ,, 1468	1873	216	460	852	63	1300	1199	687
,, 1468–2.4.1469 [1]	—	—	476	132	16	513	945	68
1.9.1469–9.10.1470	911	334	388	—	—	238	648	6
9.10.1470–30.9.1471	245	83	595	184	20	352	741	7
30.9.1471–Mich. 1472	88	15	287	242	18	775	855	66
Mich. 1472– ,, 1473	1076	94	328	50	35	668	1074	80
,, 1473– ,, 1474	780	47	337	—	1	491	2063	81
,, 1474–8.11.1475	825	93	114	349	5	1968	1508	22
8.11.1475–8.11.1476	890	144	460	851	30	786	1152	20
8.11.1476–8.11.1477	132	51	648	40	8	632	1329	89
8.11.1477–7.10.1478	560	165	355	159	6	249	1238	114
8.10.1478–14.10.1479	535	113	458	155	2	339	1322	47
14.10.1479–14.10.1480	428	59	532	194	5	497	1363	44
14.10.1480–Mich. 1481	550	146	514	146	16	2061	3172	44
Mich. 1481– ,, 1482	477	273	391	228	12	778	1810	45

[1] Gap.

TABLES OF ENROLLED CUSTOMS

7. Kingston-upon-Hull

Date.	Wool Exported. Sacks. (Wool.)	Sacks. (Fells.)	Broadcloths Exported by Denizens.	Hansards.	Other Aliens.	Value in £ of Alien Mdse. paying the Petty Custom of 3d. in the £.	Value in £ of Mdse. paying Poundage.	Tunnage. Tuns of Wine.
Mich. 1399–Mich. 1400 [1]	2952	199	1883	683	20	2075	—	—
,, 1400– ,, 1401 [2]	2616	122 [5]	3068	369	84	2844	—	—
,, 1401– ,, 1402 [3]	3387	118	2485	693	95	3609	—	—
,, 1402– ,, 1403 [3]	2345	96	2427	326	123	1988	5484 [6]	1 [6]
,, 1403– ,, 1404 [4]	3317	70	1494	135	45	406	6164 [7]	1210 [7]
,, 1404– ,, 1405	3100	79	1130	288	115	1108	7411	1066
,, 1405– ,, 1406	4178	146	1370	690	166	2529	14368	869
,, 1406– ,, 1407	3423	109	1056	564	111	1893	12442	420
,, 1407–21.8.1408	3406	133	911	517	60	1490	11203	1209
21.8.1409–Mich. 1409	3842	268 [8]	1653	390	74	1706	12267	836
Mich. 1409– ,, 1410	2540	141	1397	406	49	1906	11641	1617
,, 1410– ,, 1411	2976	120	1104	377	21	1235	9408	1621
,, 1411– ,, 1412	2044	158	1521	297	67	1532	10265	1215
,, 1412–30.9.1413	4291	231	2061	258	34	822	9131	1194
30.9.1413–Mich. 1414	3541	229	1845	950	54	4252	14855	1838
Mich. 1414– ,, 1415	2525	198	1254	1174	16	3387	11392	1816
,, 1415– ,, 1416 [9]	3581	246	901	1540	47	3721	12502	1634
,, 1416– ,, 1417	4091	331	2456	192	68	1450	10305	1287
,, 1417– ,, 1418	4497	244	1826	875	51	1846	12822	1208
,, 1418– ,, 1419 [10]	4376	295	1045	329	37	1615	9682	690
,, 1419– ,, 1420	3495	315	1683	488	47	2394	11588	899
,, 1420– ,, 1421	3874	190	82	1610	26	1172	11723	1087
,, 1421–31.8.1422	3806	201	—	35	—	465	9746 [11]	730
1.9.1422–Mich. 1423	5641	443	2598	242	40	827	1240 [11]	34 [11]
Mich. 1423– ,, 1424	4792	329	2802	40	17	557	619	7 [11]
,, 1424– ,, 1425	2973	149	3101	58	26	688	2217 [12]	29 [12]
,, 1425– ,, 1426	3458	147	3005	13	13	526	9897	187
,, 1426– ,, 1427	3933	140	2242	4	12	763	9191	1335
,, 1427– ,, 1428	4832	101	2986	—	1	733	6789	8
,, 1428–28.10.1429	3496	380	6505	66	8	1386	14819 [13]	864 [13]
28.10.1429–Mich. 1430	1573	207	3122	122	9	988	11402 [14]	312 [14]
Mich. 1430– ,, 1431	2885	346	2935	61	1	734	6543 [15]	984
,, 1431– ,, 1432	3801	145	3077	13	1	657	1630	583
,, 1432– ,, 1433	1106	7	3535	90	32	1133	7568	727
,, 1433– ,, 1434	—	262	2890	59	28	410	7727	1240
,, 1434– ,, 1435	3105	259	1140	38	3	651	6627	1256
,, 1435– ,, 1436	658	9	828	—	20	323	3611	1408

[1] Including Scarborough from Easter 1399 to 30.11.1400, accounted for separately.
[2] Including Scarborough from 30.11.1400 to Mich. 1401, accounted for separately.
[3] Including Scarborough, accounted for separately.
[4] Including Scarborough to 16.11.1404, accounted for separately.
[5] Includes 12 alien.
[6] Subsidy from 3.4.1403.
[7] Including Scarborough, accounted for separately.
[8] Includes 8 alien.
[9] Without Scarborough. The customs at Scarborough between Mich. 1415 and 6.4.1416 were paid on 20 broadcloths exported by Englishmen, £103 of alien merchandise and subsidy was paid on £560 of merchandise
[10] Including Scarborough.
[11] Aliens only.
[12] English subsidy from 1.8.1425 only.
[13] English subsidy to 4.4.1429 only.
[14] English subsidy from 6.12.1429 only.
[15] Aliens paid 18d. poundage from 18.3.1431.

Date.	Wool Exported. Sacks. (Wool.)	Wool Exported. Sacks. (Fells.)	Broadcloths Exported by Denizens.	Broadcloths Exported by Hansards.	Broadcloths Exported by Other Aliens.	Value in £ of Alien Mdse. paying the Petty Custom of 3d. in the £.	Value in £ of Mdse. paying Poundage.	Tunnage. Tuns of Wine.
Mich. 1436–Mich. 1437	62	4	887	803	66	2125	8368 [1]	13 [1]
,, 1437– ,, 1438	—	—	4961	171	312	1491	8351	635
,, 1438– ,, 1439	—	70	3784	312	22	1502	6180	448
,, 1439– ,, 1440	5410	342	2927	106	8	918	7032	829
,, 1440– ,, 1441	1885	40	2077	17	13	592	5507	1207
,, 1441– ,, 1442	154	3	3245	352	2	933	5553	1184
,, 1442– ,, 1443	4986	216	2664	74	7	872	4185	1102
,, 1443– ,, 1444	2472	754	2731	44	3	641	7013	879
,, 1444– ,, 1445	—	—	3180	23	2	632	4606	1288
,, 1445–26.8.1446	2019	196	3561	37	2	1093	3722	1193
26.8.1446–Mich. 1447	—	—	4106	60	8	1606	9610	912
Mich. 1447–29.12.1448	2280 [2]	232	4338	—	33	1182	8146	1444
29.12.1448–Mich. 1449 [3]	29 [4]	—	925	—	14	183	2264	1487
21.12.1449–Mich. 1450	2410	453	2447	—	—	385	5792	708
Mich. 1450–3.11.1451	1828	111	2608	—	6	728	6192	770
3.11.1451–2.10.1452	1475	190	1243	53	6	794	5360	295
2.10.1452–Mich. 1453	1730	289	2545	396	31	1439	4617	945
Mich. 1453– ,, 1454	237	6	1516	352	—	2212	5914	370
,, 1454–1.10.1455	3159	481	2766	28	26	545	5604	1050
1.10.1455–19.10.1456	61	7	2162	118	—	1265	7747	550
19.10.1456–Mich. 1457	—	—	1929	313	2	911	4523	184
Mich. 1457–31.12.1458	1198	110	1758	176	2	1330	1263	3
31.12.1458–1.1.1460	587	118	1129	—	—	404	— [5]	— [5]
1.1.1460–12.8.1460 [3]	—	—	722	30	—	308	1803	298
11.4.1461–Mich. 1461	502	138	628	114	16	716	1709	301
Mich. 1461– ,, 1462	165	33	2065	101	—	997	4204	252
,, 1462–6.10.1463	173	70	1616	252	—	1990	5515	168
6.10.1463–Mich. 1464	389	17	928	487	21	1102	3904	392
Mich. 1464– ,, 1465	190	37	730	93	75	1027	3359	672
,, 1465– ,, 1466	—	19	125	134	4	1365	4431	281
,, 1466– ,, 1467	896	96	326	31	16	1026	3210	300
,, 1467– ,, 1468	998	84	1449	189	25	1415	3654	704
,, 1468– ,, 1469	842	141	738	30	3	651	2935	322
,, 1469–5.11.1470	253	114	480	—	—	50	1504	294
5.11.1470–Mich. 1471	16	7	577	—	—	431	2485	386
Mich. 1471– ,, 1472	462	204	839	—	1	606	3771	633
,, 1472– ,, 1473	639	74	699	—	91	1357	5591	389
,, 1473–24.8.1474	167	43	699	—	16	1353	4268	157
23.8.1474–8.8.1475	739	41	784	444	22	2674	5049	225
8.8.1475–Mich. 1476	1012	220	2074	438	102	2578	5134	116
Mich. 1476– ,, 1477	51	5	1938	435	79	2431	5552	621
,, 1477– ,, 1478	—	699	2623	208	21	1026	5305	474
,, 1478– ,, 1479	327	129	1872	232	44	2396	4956	795
,, 1479– ,, 1480	454	144	2354	791	67	2228	5335	714
,, 1480– ,, 1481	173	80	2724	915	70	3055	4055	558
,, 1481– ,, 1482	301	182	2069	690	14	4256	4687	288

[1] Subsidy of tunnage and poundage was payable from 1.4.1437; none was paid between 11.11.1436 and 1.4.1437; English cloth paid poundage before 11.11.1436 but was exempt until 1.4.1437.
[2] Includes 30 ind. ad p.e.
[3] Gap.
[4] Ind. ad p.e.
[5] Subsidy account missing.

TABLES OF ENROLLED CUSTOMS

8. LONDON

Date.	Wool Exported. Sacks. (Wool.)	Sacks. (Fells.)	Date.[21]	Broadcloths Exported by Denizens.	Han- sards.	Other Aliens.	Value in £ of Alien Mdse. paying the Petty Custom of 3d. in the £.	Date.[21]	Value in £ of Mdse. paying Poundage.	Tunnage. Tuns of Wine.
12.10.1399–Mich. 1400	4495 [2]	72	6.10.1399–Mich. 1400	—	[1] 3359	—	[1] 41361		—	791
Mich. 1400–6.10. 1401	4605 [3]	838	Mich. 1400– ,, 1401	—	[1] 3407	—	[1] 30514		—	5310
6.10.1401–Mich. 1402	3379 [4]	820	,, 1401– ,, 1402	8004	3524	5726	12930		—	2450
Mich. 1402– ,, 1403	2346 [5]	604		6877	3866	409	20344	3.4.1403–Mich. 1404	19784	1889
,, 1403– ,, 1404	3227 [7]	521		7062	3672	6490	21365		92009	1663
,, 1404– ,, 1405	2207	483 [8]		5701	1641	243	8854		49360	1923
,, 1405– ,, 1406	5166 [9]	723		7643	3130	5238	38851		115555	6292
,, 1406– ,, 1407	2411 [10]	513		4058	5104	5062	29490		88427	6911
,, 1407– ,, 1408	4682 [11]	700		3737	3393	442	23788	Mich. 1407–28.9.1408	77876	3906
,, 1408– ,, 1409	4553	611		4555	2633	7298	27489	28.9.1408–Mich. 1409	67755	4258
,, 1409– ,, 1410	5030 [12]	808		4384	2747	11709	24550		73466	4906
,, 1410– ,, 1411	2843 [13]	885		3200	1927	7271	19226		50066	8205
,, 1411– ,, 1412	4051 [14]	676		3550	2479	4280	22792		57170	7393
,, 1412– ,, 1413	4845 [15]	1169		5501	2539	10807	20430		73806	8790
,, 1413– ,, 1414	3987 [16]	1097		6142	3128	947	19018		64176	6136
,, 1414– ,, 1415	5058 [17]	739		2836	2056	15472	7770		77421	5264
,, 1415– ,, 1416	3902 [18]	988		3454	1316	8634	22794		74491	
,, 1416– ,, 1417	4812 [19]	938		4184	1828	6253	18847		64393	
,, 1417– ,, 1418	5418 [20]	626		4036	2907	3826	21446		66435	

[1] No account.
[2] Includes 410 alien.
[3] Includes 584 alien, of which 482 ad p.e.
[4] Includes 257 alien, of which 185 ad p.e.
[5] Includes 54 alien.
[6] Wool account missing from 25th March to Easter (30th March).
[7] Includes 217 alien, of which 124 ad p.e.
[8] Includes 5 alien.
[9] Includes 429 alien ad p.e.
[10] Includes 351 alien ad p.e.
[11] Includes 472 alien ad p.e.
[12] Includes 960 alien, of which 865 ad p.e.
[13] Includes 626 alien ad p.e.
[14] Includes 962 alien, of which 938 ad p.e.
[15] Includes 393 alien, of which 386 ad p.e.
[16] Includes 2 alien ad p.e.
[17] Includes 920 alien, of which 895 ad p.e.
[18] Includes 281 alien, of which 241 ad p.e.
[19] Includes 420 alien ad p.e.
[20] Includes 578 alien ad p.e.
[21] Throughout the London tables dates in these columns are the same as in the first column, unless otherwise stated.

ENGLISH TRADE IN FIFTEENTH CENTURY

Date.	Wool Exported. Sacks. (Wool.)	Sacks. (Fells.)	Broadcloths Exported by Denizens.	Hansards.	Other Aliens.	Value in £ of Alien Mdse. paying the Petty Custom of 3d. in the £.	Date.	Value in £ of Mdse. paying Poundage.	Tunnage. Tuns of Wine.
Mich. 1418–Mich. 1419	4709[1]	1394	3854	3943	6051	24737			3834
,, 1419–28.9.1420	3810[2]	571	4751	4311	4989	27494	Mich. 1319–Mich. 1420	72814	4679
,, 28.9.1420–Mich. 1421	3422[3]	1122	2705	4796	1069	20164	1420– ,, 1421	73581	582
Mich. 1421–31.8.1422	3303[4]	872	3839	2205	7583	21936		67746	3045
1.9.1422–Mich. 1423	4712[5]	972	7263	4866	12896	31387		81536	3588
Mich. 1423– ,, 1424	5332[6]	977	8193	3534	1611	24429		53873	644
,, 1424–9.10.1425	4164[7]	890[8]	8240	3880	10112	22549	Mich. 1424–Mich. 1425	36451	1032[9]
9.10.1425–5.11.1426	4532[10]	462	4208	3503	11572	30940	,, 1425– ,, 1426	47634	3015
5.11.1426–5.11.1427	5891[11]	1113	3819	3991	7248	24394	,, 1426– ,, 1427	74946	4419
5.11.1427–24.1.1429	5017[12]	948	3620	1071	8329	18833	,, 1427– ,, 1428	74327	552[13]
24.1.1429–18.10.1429	2277[14]	467	6177	3757	7375	29932	,, 1428– ,, 1429	60746[13]	3248
18.10.1429–Mich. 1430	1987	740	6919	3650	8036	26018	,, 1429– ,, 1430	67491	4482
Mich. 1430–8.12.1431	3545[15]	1194	10488	2138	5048	13137	,, 1430– ,, 1431	73038	3962[16]
8.12.1431–Mich. 1432	2090	451	13315	2030	945	9071	,, 1431–30.9.1432	48095[16]	3899
Mich. 1432– ,, 1433	3066	481	12671	3141	494	15557	30.9.1432–16.8.1433	43959	3287
,, 1433– ,, 1434	393[17]	411	9860	3268	4480	12665	16.8.1433–Mich. 1434	32894	4258
,, 1434– ,, 1435	3278[18]	1087	8670	4208	4321	27958		77522	3732
,, 1435– ,, 1436	1630[19]	263	2073	1901	4542	10069		79247	3498
,, 1436– ,, 1437	526[17]	—	3422	5553	5547	17569		38133	510
,, 1437– ,, 1438	836[20]		8839	6152	4579	17474		33506	2071
								41674	

[1] Includes 221 alien, of which 194 ad p.e.
[2] Includes 564 alien, of which 497 ad p.e.
[3] Includes 316 alien, of which 244 ad p.e.
[4] Includes 14 alien.
[5] Includes 740 alien, of which 420 ad p.e.
[6] Includes 349 alien, of which 218 ad p.e.
[7] Includes 776 alien, of which 692 ad p.e.
[8] Does not include 3 alien.
[9] English subsidy from 1.8.1425.
[10] Includes 577 alien, of which 486 ad p.e.
[11] Includes 1081 alien ad p.e.
[12] Includes 230 alien, of which 22 ad p.e.
[13] No English subsidy between 11.11.1427 and 4.4.1428.
[14] Includes 564 alien, of which 531 ad p.e.
[15] Includes 366 alien ad p.e.
[16] Includes Hanseatic subsidy until 22.3.1431.
[17] Alien ad p.e.
[18] Includes 225 alien ad p.e. and 13 ind. ad p.e.
[19] Includes 325 alien ad p.e.
[20] Includes 709 alien ad p.e.

TABLES OF ENROLLED CUSTOMS

Date.	Wool Exported. Sacks. (Wool.)	Sacks. (Fells.)	Date.	Broadcloths Exported by Denizens.	Hansards.	Other Aliens.	Value in £ of Alien Mdse. paying the Petty Custom of 3d. in the £.	Date.	Value in £ of Mdse. paying Poundage.	Tonnage. Tuns of Wine.
Mich. 1438–Mich. 1439	342[1]	322		8773	5826	9073	23073		46201	2016
„ 1439– „ 1440	3374[3]	1387		9065	5703	9089	21263		51770	3618
„ 1440– „ 1441	1944[3]	383		8353	6873	7620	20201		47884	6110
„ 1441–22.11.1442	625[4]	—		9849	9222	7995	26289		50846	5248
22.11.1442–8.7.1443	2920[5]	676	Mich. 1441–Mich. 1442	10774	8952	5048	27570	Mich. 1441–Mich. 1442	49467	2845
8.7.1443–Mich. 1444	2928[6]	1094	„ 1442– „ 1443	8114	6946	6808	28154[7]	„ 1442– „ 1443	47659	3060
Mich. 1444– „ 1445	479	—	„ 1443– „ 1444	13125	7192	2536	23624	„ 1443– „ 1444	38885	4572
„ 1445– „ 1446	4668[8]	1076		6827	7847	1374	25575		31872	3517
„ 1446–3.7.1447	685[10]	50	Mich. 1446–21.7.1447	7827	6531	4165	25059	Mich. 1446–17.7.1447	43909	3299
3.7.1447–1.1.1449	2147[11]	1197	21.7.1447–21.7.1448	4413	6785	1447	22914	17.7.1447–22.10.1448	39858	3979
1.1.1449–Mich. 1449	726[12]	—	21.7.1448–10.3.1450	8444	4761	3661	29431	22.10.1448–10.6.1449	22233[13]	3676[13]
Mich. 1449–20.12.1450	3594	1737	10.3.1450–Mich. 1450	4249	2658	100	8221	10.6.1449–Mich. 1450	34754[15]	1691[15]
20.12.1450–16.5.1452	2442[14]	640	Mich. 1450– „ 1451	8048	6938	2501	20712	Mich. 1450– „ 1451	34558[15]	1799[15]
16.5.1452–27.10.1452	1447[16]	934	„ 1451–6.5.1452	3519	2972	42	9430	„ 1451–19.5.1452	15907	2208
27.10.1452–3.4.1453	1521[17]	354	6.5.1452–Mich. 1453	16132	9191	1616	35105	19.5.1452–Mich. 1453	43764	3180
3.4.1453–2.10.1454	3133[18]	163	Mich. 1453– „ 1454	4113	7136	512	27803	Mich. 1453–3.4.1454	17375	1466
2.10.1454–30.3.1455	898[19]	43	„ 1454–8.6.1455	8160	5238	850	18594	3.4.1454–13.6.1455	31866	4610
30.3.1455–8.11.1456	5905[20]	2207	8.6.1455–22.10.1456	10848	10078	1810	30938	13.6.1455–20.10.1456	41139	1745
8.11.1456–8.11.1457	6017[21]	311	22.10.1456–Mich. 1457	4983	5996	626	14229	20.10.1456–Mich. 1457	18014[22]	834
8.11.1457–16.1.1459	3074[22]	847	Mich. 1457–2.9.1458	9887	9209	533	14362	Mich. 1457– „ 1458	16796	1782

[1] Includes 342 alien ad p.c.
[2] Includes 387 alien ad p.c. and 65 ind. ad p.c.
[3] Includes 412 alien ad p.c.
[4] Includes 562 alien ad p.c. and 99 ind. ad p.c.
[5] Includes 848 alien and 100 ind. ad p.e.
[6] Includes 831 alien and 100 ind. ad p.e.
[7] Does not include a consignment of Spanish goods to the approximate value of £600.
[8] Includes 305 alien and 90 ind. ad p.e.
[9] Includes 203 alien ad p.e.
[10] Includes 576 alien and 100 ind. ad p.e.
[11] Includes 620 alien and 336 ind. ad p.e.
[12] Includes 93 alien and 633 ind. ad p.e.
[13] Includes Hanseatic subsidy imposed in 1448.
[14] Includes 376 alien and 112 ind. ad p.e.
[15] Hanseatic subsidy suspended in 1450.
[16] Includes 101 rex ad p.e.
[17] Includes 180 rex ad p.e.
[18] Includes 135 alien ; 988 rex ad p.c. ; 138 rex f.a. ; 1794 ind. ad p.e.
[19] Includes 180 rex ad p.c. ; 456 ind. ad p.e.
[20] Includes 1578 alien ; 90 rex per f.a. ; 179 ind. per f.a.
[21] Includes 1481 alien ; 334 rex per f.a. ; 742 ind. per f.a.
[22] Includes 20 alien ; 1484 rex per f.a. ; 170 ind. per f.a.

2A

346 ENGLISH TRADE IN FIFTEENTH CENTURY

Date.	Wool Exported. Sacks. (Wool.)	Sacks. (Fells.)	Date.	Broadcloths Exported by Denizens.	Hansards.	Other Aliens.	Value in £ of Alien Mdse. paying the Petty Custom of 3d. in the £.	Date.	Value in £ of Mdse. paying Poundage.	Tunnage. Tuns of Wine.
16.1.1459–6.8.1460	2270[1]	1024	2.9.1458–Mich. 1459	10739	9033	462	25958	Mich. 1458–13.11.1459	25177	1916
			Mich. 1459–31.7.1460	4000	4985	290	10333	13.11.1459–1.8.1460	8774	1635
6.8.1460–1.8.1461	2126[2]	1969	31.7.1460–Mich. 1461	7962	8317	993	19849	1.8.1460–Mich. 1461	32809	1575
1.8.1461–Mich. 1462	990[3]	413	Mich. 1461–16.10.1462	13553	9050	804	19040	Mich. 1461– ,, 1462	32744	1932
Mich. 1462–16.7.1463	587[4]	707	16.10.1462–Mich. 1463	9300	4274	453	17599	,, 1462– ,, 1463	28718	2136
16.7.1463–23.7.1464	2004	1429	Mich. 1463–5.12.1464	14389	8734	223	18100	,, 1463–5.12.1464	30263	3776
23.7.1464–Mich. 1465	1964[5]	1162	5.12.1464–Mich. 1465	776	2850	1012	22154	1465–5.12.1464	26442	2167
Mich. 1465– ,, 1466	2633[6]	946		8131	3816	5338	34091	16.11.1465–Mich. 1466	42899	1519
,, 1466– ,, 1467	3805	961		8134	6437	2171	27990		43134	2178
1467–25.12.1468	4325[7]	1050	Mich. 1467–Mich. 1468	15052	6877	3986	27859	Mich. 1467–Mich. 1468	39911	2361
25.12.1468–10.11.1469	4120[8]	1382	1468–6.11.1469	24260	697	3192	26196	1468–6.11.1469	45341	2784
10.11.1469–Mich. 1470	4264[9]	1651	,, 6.11.1469–9.10.1470	10679	3898	1033	19293	8.11.1469–24.10.1470	31053	1502
			6.11.1469–9.10.1470	13383	3158	690	11639	24.10.1470–Mich. 1471	18267	660
3.6.1471–3.8.1471	243	204[10]	Mich. 1471–4.8.1472	8657	2960	1670	28835	Mich. 1471– ,, 1472	68563	2602
3.8.1471–Mich. 1472	4332	2239	4.8.1472–Mich. 1473	17917	4037	7035	35591	,, 1472– ,, 1473	74380	3133
Mich. 1472– ,, 1473	3072[11]	754	Mich. 1473– ,, 1474	16432	1949	5913	20758	,, 1473– ,, 1474	91108	2986
,, 1473–7.4.1474[10]	4143	809	,, 1474– ,, 1475	11959	3095	7341	22789	,, 1474– ,, 1475	57714	645
13.5.1474–4.6.1475	3877[12]	577	,, 1475– ,, 1476	19239	8272	6782	26385	,, 1475– ,, 1476	59639	2413
4.6.1475–Mich. 1476	4088[13]	2609	1476–20.11.1477	15305	8305	10925	33464	,, 1476– ,, 1477	76775	2433
Mich. 1476– ,, 1477	694[14]	17	20.11.1477–9.7.1478	12923	5264	3333	33268	,, 1477– ,, 1478	75943	2532
1477–4.7.1478	3139[15]	1657	9.7.1478–Mich. 1479	28724	11450	9827	33867	,, 1478– ,, 1479	80421	2880
5.7.1478–Mich. 1479	4640[16]	2417		20748	10068	9694	24235		96050	3105
Mich. 1479– ,, 1480	4334	1108		23115	14079	7558	43857		124246	3870
,, 1480– ,, 1481	4878[17]	2338		20558	13386	7254	38411		107819	3310
,, 1481– ,, 1482	1710	2423								

[1] Includes 120 alien to Calais; 800 rex ad p.e.; 254 ind. ad p.e.
[2] Includes 173 alien, and 169 ind. per f.a.
[3] Includes 99 alien and 596 rex per f.a.
[4] Includes 252 rex per f.a., and 22 ind. per f.a.
[5] Includes 274 rex per f.a.
[6] Includes 345 rex per f.a. and 254 rex per ind. ad p.e.
[7] Includes 393 alien and 180 ind. per f.a.
[8] Includes 599 alien.
[9] Includes 244 alien.
[10] Gap.
[11] Includes 598 alien.
[12] Includes 89 alien.
[13] Includes 338 ind. per f.a.
[14] Includes 217 alien.
[15] Includes 17 alien.
[16] Includes 282 alien.
[17] Includes 64 alien.

TABLES OF ENROLLED CUSTOMS

9. LYNN (BISHOP'S LYNN, NOW KING'S LYNN)

Date.	Wool Exported. Sacks. (Wool.)	Sacks. (Fells.)	Broadcloths Exported by Denizens.	Han-sards.	Other Aliens.	Value in £ of Alien Mdse. paying the Petty Custom of 3d. in the £.	Value in £ of Mdse. paying Poundage.	Tunnage. Tuns of Wine.
Mich. 1399–12.10.1400 [1]	1625 [2]	79	—	—	—	—	—	—
12.10.1400–Mich. 1401	332	63	—	—	—	—	—	—
Mich. 1401–6.11.1402	1039	190	—	—	—	—	—	—
6.11.1402–Mich. 1403	416	102	—	—	—	—	6568 [3]	4 [3]
Mich. 1403–8.10.1404	—	—	—	—	—	—	6370	578
8.10.1404–Mich. 1405	—	—	—	—	—	—	3751	210
Mich. 1405– ,, 1406	—	—	— [4]	364 [4]	— [4]	564 [4]	10602	360
,, 1406– ,, 1407	324	—	2385	405	9	1063	12378	156
,, 1407– ,, 1408	—	—	2061	23	16	1197	10746	408
,, 1408– ,, 1409	278	65	881	—	12	525	7776	402
,, 1409– ,, 1410	334	94	1200	75	23	523	8176	417
,, 1410– ,, 1411	708	34 [5]	1219	45	—	193	6360	435
,, 1411– ,, 1412	1133	67	1113	209	—	473	5702	320
,, 1412– ,, 1413	681	78	1427	305	8	171	7991	390
,, 1413– ,, 1414	1232 [6]	4	1500	170	43	438	7372	736
,, 1414– ,, 1415	1156	54	1891	271	18	699	8077	353
,, 1415– ,, 1416	788	39	1616	88	2	1157	8221	437
,, 1416– ,, 1417	334	26	1389	176	2	376	6040	449
,, 1417– ,, 1418	321	56	1455	104	8	304	5563	410
,, 1418– ,, 1419	190	70	1506	184	2	417	6468	200
,, 1419– ,, 1420	—	—	1347	141	6	432	7862	226
,, 1420– ,, 1421	—	—	1859	206	9	724	8933	152
,, 1421–31.8.1422	—	—	1210	10	3	511	7629	173
1.9.1422–Mich. 1423	—	1	1589	160	1	487	773 [7]	—
Mich. 1423– ,, 1424	—	35	2014	173	2	447	737 [7]	—
,, 1424–30.7.1425	—	—	1879	—	—	194	1986 [7]	23 [7]
30.7.1425–Mich. 1426 [10]	—	—	1908	179	4	562	5982 [8]	280 [8]
20.10.1426– ,, 1427	—	5	538	116	—	488	2753 [9]	370 [9]
,, 1427– ,, 1428	—	5	2012	143	1	688	1084 [11]	8 [11]
,, 1428– ,, 1429	501	89	1002	—	—	169	862 [12]	154 [12]
,, 1429– ,, 1430	—	25	1006	95	2	361	3354	210
,, 1430– ,, 1431	—	40	624	59	—	245	1699	245
,, 1431– ,, 1432	—	—	439	72	—	271	2190	93
,, 1432– ,, 1433	—	11 [13]	559	79	—	489	626	230
,, 1433– ,, 1434	—	—	1775	182	7	564	5793 [14]	315
,, 1434– ,, 1435	—	156	874	89	13	349	3878	206
,, 1435– ,, 1436	—	—	569	27	3	261	2107	395
,, 1436–11.11.1437	—	—	3262	1089	38	1889	2001 [15]	3

[1] The petty custom was farmed until 5.4.1406.
[2] Including 23 alien.
[3] Subsidy from 3.4.1403.
[4] Petty custom is accounted for from 5.4.1406; a total of £8 5s. was paid on broadcloths and worsteds exported by denizens and aliens.
[5] Including 11 alien.
[6] Including 80 alien.
[7] Alien subsidy only.
[8] English subsidy included from 1.8.1425 to Mich. 1425.
[9] Subsidy from 23.10.1426.
[10] Gap.
[11] No English subsidy from 11.11.1427 to 4.4.1428.
[12] English subsidy to 4.4.1429 only.
[13] Lambskins and shorlings; including 6 alien.
[14] Including poundage on English cloth from 13.1.1434.
[15] Poundage on English cloth ceased on 11.11.1436.

ENGLISH TRADE IN FIFTEENTH CENTURY

Date.	Wool Exported. Sacks. (Wool.)	Sacks. (Fells.)	Broadcloths Exported by Denizens.	Hansards.	Other Aliens.	Value in £ of Alien Mdse. paying the Petty Custom of 3d. in the £.	Value in £ of Mdse. paying Poundage.	Tunnage. Tuns of Wine.
11.11.1437–16.2.1438 [1]	—	· ·	49	6	4	704	1324	188
Mich. 1438–Mich. 1439	—	—	1439	454	2	1103	1548	171
,, 1439– ,, 1440	—	58 [2]	1353	30	—	278	1468	31
,, 1440– ,, 1441	—	—	1778	260	12	465	1804	398
,, 1441– ,, 1442	—	—	1615	268	2	903	1905	177
,, 1442– ,, 1443	—	—	1754	323	—	240	1823	155
,, 1443– ,, 1444	—	—	936	295	3	524	1208	33
,, 1444– ,, 1445	—	—	1854	568	—	1197	1401	290
,, 1445– ,, 1446	1148	—	2401	379	6	1437	2750	237
,, 1446– ,, 1447	—	—	2129	247	5	2235	334	319
,, 1447–30.4.1449	788	86	694	337	3	1212	2325	697
30.4.1449–Mich. 1449	—	—	235	78	3	98	429	7
Mich. 1449– ,, 1450	20	10	1188	39	1	490	1023	251
,, 1450–12.7.1451	—	1	579	39	2	424	1639	9
12.7.1451–12.5.1452	—	9	853	—	9	920	1560	147
12.5.1452–1.6.1453	—	—	724	212	—	793	1729	10
1.6.1453–3.4.1454	—	—	264	93	—	642	436	156
3.4.1454–13.6.1455	40 [3]	—	687	—	—	231	754	152
13.6.1455–24.1.1457	—	—	523	186	—	1687	1684	127
24.1.1457–Mich. 1457	8 [4]	—	344	191	—	959	1402	5
Mich. 1457– ,, 1458	182 [5]	25	435	315	—	740	1736	20
,, 1458– ,, 1459	757	481	146	261	—	599	603	112
,, 1459–6.8.1460	39 [6]	—	235	66	—	992	961	53
6.8.1460–24.11.1461	—	—	330	47	—	1026	768 [7]	15
24.11.1461–29.8.1462	—	—	180	31	—	467	1355 [8]	215 [8]
29.8.1462–12.7.1463	—	—	297	27	—	296	57 [9]	— [9]
12.7.1463–19.11.1464	—	—	561	72	—	954	1652	102
19.11.1464–19.11.1465	—	—	125	502	—	742	832	126
19.11.1465–2.11.1466	—	—	277	150	—	979	1160	21
2.11.1466–2.11.1467	—	—	217	145	—	748	1225	116
2.11.1467–2.11.1468	—	—	911	52	—	497	476	182
2.11.1468–17.8.1469	—	—	63	—	—	508	876	66
17.8.1469–16.5.1470 [1]	—	—	19	—	—	260	588	44
3.11.1470–13.11.1471	—	—	29	—	—	214	270	28
13.11.1471–13.11.1472	—	—	56	—	—	271	504	46
13.11.1472–13.11.1473	—	—	92	—	—	325	1054	13
13.11.1473–13.11.1474	—	—	6	—	—	646	1223	79
13.11.1474–13.11.1475	—	—	25	270	1	929	853	79
13.11.1475–13.11.1476	—	—	108	308	24	1259	871	80
13.11.1476–13.11.1477	—	—	250	83	—	615	753	49
13.11.1477–13.11.1478	—	—	432	129	—	821	917	112
13.11.1478–13.11.1479	—	—	471	187	—	556	646	103
13.11.1479–13.11.1480	—	—	132	183	1	588	1163	68
13.11.1480–Mich. 1481	—	—	183	184	35	997	1317	61
Mich. 1481– ,, 1482	—	—	217	181	—	1247	566	67

[1] Gap. [2] Morlings.
[3] Ind. ad p.e. [4] Ind. ad p.e.
[5] Including 83 ind. ad p.e. [6] Rex ad p.e. by native factor.
[7] Account missing 3.12.1460 to 4.3.1461. [8] Subsidy to 2.2.1463.
[9] Subsidy from 23.2.1463.

TABLES OF ENROLLED CUSTOMS 349

10. Melcombe and Poole

Date.	Wool Exported. Sacks. (Wool.)	Sacks. (Fells.)	Broadcloths Exported by Denizens.	Aliens.	Value in £ of Alien Mdse. paying the Petty Custom of 3d. in the £.	Value in £ of Mdse. paying Poundage.	Tunnage. Tuns of Wine.
Mich. 1399–24.3.1401 [1]	243	—	185	22	98	—	—
24.3.1401–24.6.1401 [1]	—	—	17	3	43	—	—
24.6.1401–18.11.1403	214	—	382	30	77	—	—
18.11.1403–30.9.1404	328	—	135	17	103	223 [2]	56 [2]
30.9.1404–Mich. 1404	273	—	247	—	—	662 [3]	16 [3]
Mich. 1404– ,, 1405 [4]	177	—	73 [5]	—	—	502	12
9.11.1405–4.10.1406	274	—	26	—	—	73	40
4.10.1406–Mich. 1407	60	—	91	6	11	255	12
Mich. 1407– ,, 1408	215	—	97 [6]	10 [6]	116 [6]	261	247
,, 1408– ,, 1409	149	—	251 [7]	2 [7]	60 [7]	844	273
,, 1409– ,, 1410	90	—	371	30	40	1306	351
,, 1410– ,, 1411	84	—	143	—	37	480	309
,, 1411– ,, 1412 [8]	108	—	91	28	122	576	128
,, 1412– ,, 1413	247	—	93	—	10	388	117
,, 1413– ,, 1414	122	—	94	14	59	382	180
,, 1414– ,, 1415	144	—	47	3	67	415	342
,, 1415– ,, 1416	110	—	407	—	—	824	228
,, 1416– ,, 1417	112	—	362	4	—	978	443
,, 1417– ,, 1418	69	—	718	5	—	1801	293
,, 1418– ,, 1419	171	—	327	4	43	1353	133
,, 1419– ,, 1420	126	—	457	6	98	1458	164
,, 1420– ,, 1420	100	—	398	18	75	1193	169
,, 1421–31.8.1422	47	5	191	7	53	851	100
1.9.1422–Mich. 1423	207	7	339	—	40	47	37
Mich. 1423– ,, 1424	233	18	352	4	30	34	—
,, 1424– ,, 1425	164	10	246	4	6	11 [9]	—
,, 1425– ,, 1426	100	3	460	—	—	751 [10]	170 [10]
,, 1426– ,, 1427	—	3	318	—	—	497	179
,, 1427– ,, 1428	243	—	216	42	53	423 [11]	2 [11]
,, 1428– ,, 1429	—	18	532	9	30	219	148
,, 1429– ,, 1430	106	—	749	—	20	884	101
,, 1430– ,, 1431	30	—	703	8	15	667	279
,, 1431– ,, 1432	188	—	556	9	10	166	136
,, 1432– ,, 1433	165	17	555	26	—	582	238
,, 1433– ,, 1434	11 [12]	6	634	18	19	1237	295
,, 1434– ,, 1435	224 [12]	—	584	123	53	1834	264
,, 1435– ,, 1436	—	—	521	37	46	1332	273
,, 1436– ,, 1437	—	—	1305	41	30	1485	7
,, 1437– ,, 1438	—	—	894	42	70	1294	133
,, 1438– ,, 1439	—	—	1020 [13]	10 [13]	20 [13]	822	119
,, 1439– ,, 1440	144	—	853	6	159	1018	187
,, 1440– ,, 1441	—	—	1331	6	106	419	396
,, 1441– ,, 1442	—	14	955	40	64	1170	288

[1] Without Poole; for these years Poole was included with Southampton, *vide infra*, also C.P.R. 1401–5, p. 2.
[2] Subsidy from 3.4.1403 to 30.9.1403.   [3] Subsidy from 30.9.1403.
[4] Gap; see also note 1.   [5] To 19.11.1405.
[6] To 7.4.1409.   [7] From 7.4.1409.
[8] Account missing from 18.12.1411 to 21.1.1412.
[9] Alien subsidy only.   [10] English subsidy only.
[11] Alien subsidy from 24.11.1427 to Mich. 1428, English from Mich. 1427 to 24.11.1427 and then from 14.4.1428 to Mich. 1428.
[12] Alien.
[13] Account missing from 14.3.1439 to 9.5.1439.

350 ENGLISH TRADE IN FIFTEENTH CENTURY

Date.	Wool Exported. Sacks. (Wool.)	Sacks. (Fells.)	Broadcloths Exported by Denizens.	Aliens.	Value in £ of Alien Mdse. paying the Petty Custom of 3d. in the £.	Value in £ of Mdse. paying Poundage.	Tunnage. Tuns of Wine.
Mich. 1442–Mich. 1443	42	34	1020	5	65	847	368
,, 1443– ,, 1444	59	46[1]	1038	9	22	702	317
,, 1444– ,, 1445	19	65[2]	1749	34	138	1584	269
,, 1445– ,, 1446	16[3]	15[2]	648	48	59	735	321
,, 1446– ,, 1447	71[4]	—	2091	55	150	1156	314
,, 1447– ,, 1448	73[5]	36	1623	13	30	1252	222
,, 1448– ,, 1449	24[6]	—	953	36	61	691	163
,, 1449– ,, 1450	—	—	919	47	30	699	63
,, 1450– ,, 1451	—	—	725	28	2	1533	13
,, 1451– ,, 1452	75	29	971	23	34	942	162
,, 1452– ,, 1453	—	—	959	—	52	182	123
,, 1453–8.1.1455	40	—	709	5	—	217	91
8.1.1455–Mich. 1455	39	—	381	27	41	121	20
Mich. 1455–23.11.1456	17	10[3]	1094	3	69	1193	77
23.11.1456–13.8.1457	—	9[3]	734	—	25	1313	40
13.8.1457–Mich. 1458	—	5	1139	—	—	1349	37
Mich. 1458– ,, 1459[7]	—	—	989	—	—	492	99
26.8.1460–Mich. 1461	—	—	622	—	—	627	55
Mich. 1461– ,, 1462	—	8	453	28	6	1013	15
,, 1462–12.7.1463	—	—	194	149	35	467	61
12.7.1463–25.6.1464	—	—	1065	77	46	613	240
25.6.1464–18.7.1465	13	—	466	165	288	1008	249
18.7.1465–12.2.1467	—	11	794	389	610	2756	393
12.2.1467–1.8.1468	—	724	1761	435	1258	3681	114
1.8.1468–19.12.1468	—	—	273	52	107	575	21
19.12.1468–3.9.1469	—	—	1037	283	585	2662	343
3.9.1469–13.10.1470[7]	—	2	:324	273	628	2799	169
11.6.1471–Mich. 1471	—	—	501	113	276	1429	26
Mich. 1471–20.10.1472	—	—	916	381	150	2713	284
20.10.1472–1.8.1473	—	—	435	88	215	1151	64
1.8.1473–Mich. 1474	—	—	963	233	524	2848	105
Mich. 1474–20.7.1475	2	—	391	240	345	1767	153
20.7.1475–Mich. 1476	—	25[8]	861	130	315	1902	216
Mich. 1476– ,, 1477	—	12	900	139	392	2126	231
,, 1477– ,, 1478	—	25	1152	641	547	2435	146
,, 1478– ,, 1479	—	6	1253	214	247	2250	180
,, 1479– ,, 1480	—	8	1332	205	427	2692	214
,, 1480–16.7.1481	—	—	1389	759	1262	5157	188
17.7.1481–Mich. 1482	—	—	3226	2364	1838	11932	91

11. NEWCASTLE-UPON-TYNE.

Date.	Wool Exported. Sacks. (Wool.)	Sacks. (Fells.)	Broadcloths Exported by Denizens.	Hansards.	Other Aliens.	Value in £ of Alien Mdse. paying the Petty Custom of 3d. in the £.	Value in £ of Mdse. paying Poundage.	Tunnage. Tuns of Wine.
15.4.1398–Mich. 1400	586	8	182	24	72	2422	—	—
Mich. 1400– ,, 1401	161	14	151	15	20	1629	—	—
,, 1401– ,, 1402	282	12	126	52	20	2183	—	—

[1] Includes 42 sacks of morlings.   [2] Morlings.   [3] Alien.
[4] Includes 41 alien.   [5] Includes 51 alien.   [6] Ind. ad p.e.
[7] Gap.   [8] Includes 17 alien.

TABLES OF ENROLLED CUSTOMS

Date.	Wool Exported. Sacks. (Wool.)	Sacks. (Fells.)	Broadcloths Exported by Denizens.	Hansards.	Other Aliens.	Value in £ of Alien Mdse. paying the Petty Custom of 3d. in the £.	Value in £ of Mdse. paying Poundage.	Tunnage. Tuns of Wine.
Mich. 1402–Mich. 1403	20	2	72	25	21	1261	502 [1]	2 [1]
,, 1403– ,, 1404	5	1	24	5	11	611	892	138
,, 1404– ,, 1405	97	5	33	—	11	512	1003	2
,, 1405– ,, 1406	188	13	15	1	11	316	856	1
,, 1406– ,, 1407	—	—	8 [2]	25 [2]	17 [2]	579 [2]	943 [3]	—
,, 1407–7.9.1408	—	—	54	23	33	793	1750	147
7.9.1408–Mich. 1409	403	44	—	36	—	803	1992	56
Mich. 1409– ,, 1410	214	6	86 [4]	5 [4]	27 [4]	617 [4]	1824	126
,, 1410– ,, 1411	181	3	48 [5]	2 [5]	5 [5]	315 [5]	1079	126
,, 1411– ,, 1412 [6]	—	—	7	9	15	213	825	83
,, 1412– ,, 1413 [7]	—	—	47	1	12	149	725	24
,, 1413– ,, 1414	—	—	36	18	23	359	1173	139
,, 1414– ,, 1415	209	20	19	19	3	161	705	117
,, 1415– ,, 1416	86	20	2	19	11	279	1163	86
,, 1416– ,, 1417	—	—	30	5	9	195	574	130
,, 1417– ,, 1418	—	—	7	21	20	611	1014	139
,, 1418– ,, 1419	—	—	29	4	12	330	968	9
,, 1419– ,, 1420	—	—	3	12	17	385	928	48
,, 1420–12.9.1421	—	—	48	3	12	285	821	16
12.9.1421–31.8.1422	149	10	13	13	28	242	913	5
1.9.1422–Mich. 1423	218	12	14	17	11	175	203	1
Mich. 1423– ,, 1424	339	16	—	24	11	244	279	—
,, 1424– ,, 1425	221	18	17	5	—	127	615 [8]	4 [8]
,, 1425– ,, 1426	196	12	32	32	4	185	729	91
,, 1426– ,, 1427	191	5	—	8	—	284	880	121
,, 1427– ,, 1428	286	44	42	4	10	401	998	7
,, 1428– ,, 1429	288	65	75	25	39	728	1090	113
,, 1429– ,, 1430	—	—	137	30	29	621	1519	141
,, 1430– ,, 1431	—	—	34	14	7	384	915	164
,, 1431–15.7.1432	—	—	21	—	9	186	557	148
15.7.1432–Mich. 1433 [9]	441	71	190	57	15	351	1117	2
3.11.1433–12.5.1434	33	26	1	—	6	65	354	63
12.5.1434–Mich. 1435	201	11	72	2	12	446	1483	7
Mich. 1435– ,, 1436	—	—	6	—	12	127	427	137
,, 1436–25.12.1437	—	—	37	12	27	352	1246 [10]	8
25.12.1437–Mich. 1438	—	—	75	16	6	243	872 [11]	80
Mich. 1438– ,, 1439	—	—	17	14	2	183	839	3
,, 1439– ,, 1440	—	—	47	—	1	132	1082	2
,, 1440– ,, 1441	144	7	45	—	2	161	1011	44
,, 1441– ,, 1442	346	23	15	—	1	245	1534	87
,, 1442–31.9.1443	216	35	8	3	4	265	1091	5
31.9.1443–Mich. 1444	343	39	22	—	4	322	1568	6
Mich. 1444– ,, 1455	609	69	70	7	1	114	755	47
,, 1445– ,, 1446	693	97	87	1	1	140	809	110
,, 1446– ,, 1447	393 [12]	127	120	44	5	396	568	89
,, 1447– ,, 1448	643	59	60	3	2	149	821	124

[1] Subsidy from 3.4.1403.
[2] Account missing from 25.12.1406 to 20.2.1407.
[3] Account for 1.4.1407 to 22.12.1407 is entered on the roll of customs accounts and not on that of subsidy accounts.
[4] Account ends 27.9.1410.   [5] Account begins 27.9.1410.
[6] Customs account missing 4.12.1411 to 19.12.1411.
[7] Customs account missing 2.2.1413 to 3.4.1413.
[8] English subsidy from 30.7.1425 only.   [9] Gap.
[10] Does not include £14 3s. 4d. of Hanseatic goods ; no Hanseatic subsidy after 1st April.
[11] Does not include £48 13s. 4d. of Hanseatic goods ; no Hanseatic subsidy after 1st April.
[12] Includes 17 alien.

352 ENGLISH TRADE IN FIFTEENTH CENTURY

Date.	Wool Exported. Sacks. (Wool.)	Sacks. (Fells.)	Broadcloths Exported by Denizens.	Hansards.	Other Aliens.	Value in £ of Alien Mdse. paying the Petty Custom of 3d. in the £.	Value in £ of Mdse. paying Poundage.	Tunnage. Tuns of Wine.
Mich. 1448–22.12.1449	59	42	51	—	4	122	544	213
22.12.1449–Mich. 1450	—	20	21	—	2	32	277	47
Mich. 1450– ,, 1451	—	35	20	—	—	4	28	—
,, 1451– ,, 1452	11	3	14	—	—	107	1012	—
,, 1452–30.8.1453	186	127	16	4	2	305	430	192
30.8.1453–29.4.1455	343	292	50	—	—	230	982	200
29.4.1455–13.6.1455	—	—	—	—	—	5	26	—
13.6.1455–23.10.1456	299	176	39	—	—	58	875	—
23.10.1456–10.3.1458	213	106[1]	66	—	—	46	501	1
10.3.1458–21.12.1458	247	19[2]	18	—	1	95	715	44
21.12.1458–24.12.1459	228	127	10	—	—	122	632	42
24.12.1459–20.9.1460[3]	—	—	—	—	—	27	172	27
10.5.1461–18.2.1462	225	169	11	—	—	85	739	—
18.2.1462–1.8.1463	157	258	—	—	6	416	1582	227
1.8.1463–3.5.1464	128	66	—	—	—	111	844	69
3.5.1464–4.3.1465	133[4]	11	2	—	—	342	897	66
4.3.1465–11.4.1466[3]	50	124	16	—	11	590	1487	173
18.3.1467–28.3.1468[3]	100	18	11	—	—	521	1347	402
19.7.1468–19.7.1469[3]	105	98	15	—	—	239	560	153
30.3.1476–17.6.1476	5	17	—	—	—	24	24	58
17.6.1476–1.6.1477	113	96	—	2	—	65	193	74
1.6.1477–1.6.1478[3]	—	—	28	8	—	110	530	9
1.11.1478–Mich. 1480	8	6	3	—	—	—	792	—

12. PLYMOUTH AND FOWEY

Date.	Broadcloths Exported by Denizens.	Aliens.	Value in £ of Alien Mdse. paying the Petty Custom of 3d. in the £.	Value in £ of Mdse. paying Poundage.	Tunnage. Tuns of Wine.
Mich. 1399–Mich. 1400[5]	—	—	—	—	—
,, 1400– ,, 1401	—	—	—	—	—
,, 1401– ,, 1402	—	—	—	—	—
,, 1403– ,, 1403	—	—	—	1374[6]	37[6]
,, 1403– ,, 1404	—	—	—	1893	69
,, 1404– ,, 1405	—	—	—	1174	236
,, 1405– ,, 1406	—	—	—	556[7]	141[7]
,, 1406– ,, 1407	—	—	—	—	—
,, 1407– ,, 1408	—	—	—	1[8]	134[8]

[1] Includes 79 alien.   [2] Includes 5 alien.
[3] Gap.   [4] Includes 89 alien.
[5] The only accounts found enrolled separately for Plymouth for this and the eight subsequent years are those for 16.12.1404–Mich. 1405 (67 broadcloths by denizens and £4 mdse. paying petty custom) and Mich. 1405-Mich. 1406 (20 broadcloths by aliens). The enrolled accounts of Exeter suggest that for a number of years the trade of Plymouth was included there. See under Exeter (Table 5).
[6] Subsidy from 3.4.1403.
[7] To 1.4.1406; between that date and 11.8.1408 the subsidies of tunnage and poundage were also included with Exeter.
[8] From 11.8.1408.

TABLES OF ENROLLED CUSTOMS

Date.	Broadcloths Exported by Denizens.	Aliens.	Value in £ of Alien Mdse. paying the Petty Custom of 3d. in the £.	Value in £ of Mdse. paying Poundage.	Tunnage. Tuns of Wine.
11.8.1408–Mich. 1409	106	14	44	2165	403
Mich. 1409– ,, 1410	116	11	62	2601	439
,, 1410– ,, 1411	109	—	16	2049	293
,, 1411– ,, 1412	55	10	55	1184	227
,, 1412– ,, 1413	147	—	60	1937	198
,, 1413– ,, 1414	152	—	3	1598	205
,, 1414– ,, 1415	180	—	—	1244	548
,, 1415– ,, 1416	68	8	310	1171	494
,, 1416–16.12.1417	187	3	20	1577 [1]	399 [1]
16.12.1417–Mich. 1418	204	23	88	1887	349
Mich. 1418– ,, 1419	822	6	16	3002	219
,, 1419– ,, 1420	330 [2]	79 [2]	151 [2]	1680	494
,, 1420– ,, 1421	217	2	88	1710	617
,, 1421–31.8.1422	141	1	35	1830	319
1.9.1422– ,, 1423	221	8	34	373	59
Mich. 1423– ,, 1424	452	30	74	142	58
,, 1424– ,, 1425	335	39	47	336 [3]	72 [3]
,, 1425– ,, 1426	211	6	28	1426	151
,, 1426– ,, 1427	220	39	29	1531	452
,, 1427– ,, 1428	241	45	147	998 [4]	11 [4]
,, 1428– ,, 1429	283	58	226	524	119
,, 1429– ,, 1430	344	10	104	2109	129
,, 1430– ,, 1431	419	74	294	2479	564
,, 1431– ,, 1432	373	57	101	2730	584
,, 1432–16.9.1433	488	41	101	1612	611
16.9.1433–28.9.1434	859	23	66	4343	883
28.9.1434–Mich. 1435	776	81	133	3637 [5]	765
Mich. 1435– ,, 1436	1061	17	60 [6]	3314	898
,, 1436– ,, 1437	865	52	98	1527	97
,, 1437– ,, 1438	928	7	131	2200	387
,, 1438–30.9.1439	829	99	170	3637	352
30.9.1439–Mich. 1440	919	12	220	2405	569
Mich. 1440– ,, 1441	842	95	118	1568	982
,, 1441– ,, 1442	844	63	58	1108	749
,, 1442– ,, 1443	619	73	87	1328	902
,, 1443– ,, 1444	1090	—	107	2005	586
,, 1444– ,, 1445	961	60 [7]	118	2814	729
,, 1445– ,, 1446	1163	7	106	1825	493
,, 1446– ,, 1447	1059	20 [8]	59	2184	582
,, 1447– ,, 1448	1372	38	96	2287	574
,, 1448– ,, 1449	401	20	83	828	798
,, 1449– ,, 1450	742	17	63	1608	336
,, 1450– ,, 1451	444	79	200	1291	101
,, 1451– ,, 1452	311	17	100	851	205
,, 1452– ,, 1453	343	61	118	777	672
,, 1453– ,, 1454	546	155	149	1239	336
,, 1454– ,, 1455	396	48	153	1281	353
,, 1455– ,, 1456	375	37	166	999	177

[1] Subsidy to Mich. 1417.
[2] Includes the customs for the Duchy of Cornwall, accounted for separately.
[3] English subsidy from 1.8.1425 only.
[4] No account of subsidy from 2.11.1427 to 4.4.1428.
[5] Does not include the value of 2,000 lb. of tin.
[6] Does not include 5 sacks of Spanish wool.
[7] Includes 1 cloth exported by a Hanseatic merchant.
[8] Includes 4 cloths exported by Hanseatic merchants.

354 ENGLISH TRADE IN FIFTEENTH CENTURY

Date.	Broadcloths Exported by Denizens.	Aliens.	Value in £ of Alien Mdse. paying the Petty Custom of 3d. in the £.	Value in £ of Mdse. paying Poundage.	Tunnage. Tuns of Wine.
Mich. 1456–Mich. 1457	379	202	383	1274	101
,, 1457– ,, 1458	290	68	122	532	149
,, 1458– ,, 1459	289	24	137	764	172
,, 1459– ,, 1460	305	57 [1]	47	556	344
,, 1460–30.9.1461	137	25	126	578	48
30.9.1461–Mich. 1462	325	25	290	938	104
Mich. 1462– ,, 1463	33	11	143	702	176
,, 1463– ,, 1464	29	10	96	777	305
,, 1464– ,, 1465	81	142	272	1000	698
,, 1465–25.5.1466	106	5	33	356	58
25.5.1466– ,, 1467	204	149	484	2692	252
Mich. 1467– ,, 1468	200	22	175	1480	267
,, 1468– ,, 1469	310	1	158	1332	147
,, 1469–5.11.1470 [2]	277	—	543	1444	159
29.5.1471–27.11.1471	225	—	357	774	59
27.11.1471–Mich. 1472	352	180	672	1618	170
Mich. 1472– ,, 1473	141	14	418	896	212
,, 1473– ,, 1474	90	—	186	666	230
,, 1474– ,, 1475	103	15	70	447	76
,, 1475– ,, 1476	389	52	242	927	438
,, 1476–30.11.1477	267	70	162	1679	496
30.11.1477–Mich. 1478	375	18	128	2028	140
Mich. 1478– ,, 1479	236	142	104	1525	308
,, 1479– ,, 1480	168	80	85	1936	326
,, 1480– ,, 1481	205	221	188	2277	436
,, 1481– ,, 1482	659	395	92	4133	156

13. SANDWICH

Date.	Wool Exported. Sacks. (Wool.)	Sacks. (Fells.)	Broadcloths Exported by Denizens.	Hansards.	Other Aliens.	Value in £ of Alien Mdse. paying the Petty Custom of 3d. in the £.	Value in £ of Mdse. paying Poundage.	Tunnage. Tuns of Wine.
30.10.1399–Mich. 1400	10 [3]	4	308	—	60	1592	—	—
Mich. 1400– ,, 1401	122	5	133	—	47	1047	—	—
,, 1401– ,, 1402	283	5	225	—	109	1321	—	—
,, 1402– ,, 1403	247	17	233	—	3	815	414 [4]	177 [4]
,, 1403– ,, 1404	166	26	38	—	2	1797	3696	406
,, 1404–1.10.1405	258	22	360	—	—	1969	4291	395
1.10.1405–Mich. 1406	239	16 [5]	290	—	22	4430	2837 [6]	224 [6]
Mich. 1406– ,, 1407	13	35	329	14	39	3516	5291 [7]	149 [7]
,, 1407–28.7.1408	105	22	306	—	15	3389	4719	525
28.7.1408–Mich. 1409	389	20	373	—	5	1034	3025	386
Mich. 1409– ,, 1410	161	12	231	—	12	3216	4884	393
30.9.1410– ,, 1411	119	32	252	11	24	4231	5543	825
Mich. 1411– ,, 1412	246 [8]	27	262	—	11	2059	3520	278

[1] Includes 6 cloths exported by Hanseatic merchants.   [2] Gap.
[3] Includes 1½ alien.   [4] Subsidy from 3.4.1403.   [5] Includes 2 alien.
[6] Subsidy to 1.4.1406.   [7] Subsidy from 22.12.1406.   [8] Includes 80 alien.

TABLES OF ENROLLED CUSTOMS

Date.			Wool Exported. Sacks. (Wool.)	Sacks. (Fells.)	Broadcloths Exported by Deni-zens.	Han-sards.	Other Aliens.	Value in £ of Alien Mdse. paying the Petty Custom of 3d. in the £.	Value in £ of Mdse. paying Poundage.	Tunnage. Tuns of Wine.
Mich.	1412–Mich.	1413	344	20	507	1	339	7179	12408	221
,,	1413–	,, 1414	107 [1]	12	332	29	88	8854	9567	706
,,	1414–	,, 1415	97 [2]	25	325	—	785	3659	7308	951
,,	1415–	,, 1416	207 [3]	13	498	10	4	5037	7445	579
,,	1416–	,, 1417	152	38	538	—	1654	3339	8186	477
,,	1417–	,, 1418	136	21	521	4	896	1584	4757	170
,,	1418–	,, 1419	23	6	337	—	8	2146	3584	305
,,	1419–	,, 1420	234	18	650	2	584	3644	7179 [4]	558
,,	1420–	,, 1421	112	31	465	—	1853	4081	8182	376
,,	1421–31.8.1422		117	13	627	—	1241	2587	6111	186
	1.9.1422–Mich. 1423		155	12	784	—	2590	2774	6192	409
Mich.	1423–	,, 1424	127 [5]	14	589	—	92	3117	3370 [6]	431 [6]
,,	1424–	,, 1425	96 [7]	6	584	—	1326	2785	4674 [6]	343 [6]
,,	1425–	,, 1426	164 [8]	5	339	1	355	4312	7664	309
,,	1426–	,, 1427	164 [9]	6	541	14	434	3992	9739	427
,,	1427–	,, 1428	95 [10]	6	729	—	1099	3597	9185	338
,,	1428–	,, 1429	168	—	364	—	1275	4667	8862 [11]	400 [11]
,,	1429–	,, 1430	194 [13]	1	613	—	760	3643	6354 [12]	521 [12]
,,	1430–	,, 1431	201 [14]	2	305	—	1695	3837	10169	480
,,	1431–28.3.1432 [16]		—	—	206	1	3	132	1966 [15]	575 [15]
Mich.	1433–Mich. 1434		15	1	405	4	190	10870	17210	665
,,	1434–	,, 1435	—	—	280	4	50	9550	14129	982
,,	1435–	,, 1436	194	1	161	1	18	5957	7854	462
,,	1436–	,, 1437	—	—	178	29	1159	7838	8640	320
,,	1437–	,, 1438	—	—	297	3	183	12856	11763	417
,,	1438–	,, 1439	—	2 [17]	217	—	1454	13276	14703	580
,,	1439–	,, 1440	111	6	210	143	123	20075	20234	970
,,	1440–	,, 1441	37	9 [18]	333	127	31	7423	6426	631
,,	1441–	,, 1442	100	9 [19]	450	—	4451	14540	21282	1292
,,	1442–	,, 1443	339	10 [20]	202	36	6664	14308	22441	895
,,	1443–	,, 1444	116	8	637	138	2515	17221	22715	862
,,	1444–	,, 1445	48	9	445	—	76	10767	12299	613
,,	1445–	,, 1446	63	14	438	—	134	10336	9005	673
,,	1446–	,, 1447	14 [6]	6	613	—	850	12628	15564	710
,,	1447–	,, 1448	7	27	400	—	269	10722	9900	341
,,	1448–	,, 1449	169 [21]	13	871	—	1207	16262	20449	1042
,,	1449–28.8.1450		6	19	228	—	9	8948	10543	271
	28.8.1450–Mich. 1451		281 [22]	13	525	—	256	7957	13308	514
Mich.	1451–	,, 1452	423 [23]	3	778	—	3139	2408	8247	762
,,	1452–	,, 1453	437 [24]	10	839	—	653	8938	12308	620
,,	1453–	,, 1454	—	6	547	39	175	4937	6773	958
,,	1454–	,, 1455	639 [6]	3	570	—	2984	4812	11580	529
,,	1455–	,, 1456	369 [25]	15	1058	—	2022	8082	13098	413
,,	1456–	,, 1457	135	5	324	—	99	5425	6964	357
,,	1457–	,, 1458	1490 [26]	2	118	—	58	2736	3594	135
,,	1458–	,, 1459	1092 [27]	15	466	—	1	4139	4703	235

[1] Includes 12 alien. [2] Includes 4½ alien. [3] Includes 80 alien.
[4] Does not include 105 sheep, valued at £52 10s. 0d. [5] Includes 8 alien.
[6] Alien. [7] Includes 37 alien. [8] Includes 49 alien.
[9] Includes 5 alien. [10] Includes 64 alien. [11] English subsidy to 4.4.1429.
[12] English subsidy from 6.12.1429. [13] Includes 3 alien.
[14] Includes 47 alien. [15] Subsidy levied on Hanseatic goods to 2.4.1432.
[16] Gap. [17] Includes 1 alien. [18] Includes 5 alien.
[19] Includes 4 alien. [20] Includes 3 alien. [21] Includes 133 alien.
[22] Includes 5 alien. [23] Includes 326 alien.
[24] Includes 305 alien and 50 ind. per f.a. [25] Includes 286 alien.
[26] Includes 36 alien. [27] Includes 13 alien.

356   ENGLISH TRADE IN FIFTEENTH CENTURY

	Wool Exported.		Broadcloths Exported by			Value in £ of Alien Mdse. paying the Petty Custom of 3d. in the £.	Value in £ of Mdse. paying Poundage.	Tunnage. Tuns of Wine.
Date.	Sacks. (Wool.)	Sacks. (Fells.)	Deni- zens.	Han- sards.	Other Aliens.			
Mich. 1459–5.8.1460	38	1	64	—	12	2746	3473	402
5.8.1460–27.7.1461	579	4	140	—	—	3151	4777	369
27.7.1461–Mich. 1462	1169 [1]	16	212	208	223	6894	8727	168
Mich. 1462– ,, 1463	2173 [2]	26	1176	469	129	2447	3986	283
,, 1463–13.11.1464	2500 [3]	21	20	—	34	1678	3498	1658
13.11.1464–16.11.1465	1574 [4]	29 [5]	700	34	1609	3253	3948	13
16.11.1465–Mich. 1466	1986 [6]	—	287	—	2250	2813	8760	166
Mich. 1466–18.8.1467 [7]	793 [8]	—	264	—	11	9264	8758	155
28.8.1467–29.9.1468	13	3	209	—	30	5912	4441	655
29.9.1468–8.11.1469	233 [9]	6	201	—	3426	6645	12447	724
8.11.1469–8.11.1470	48 [10]	6	81	—	2171	6692	8841	183
8.11.1470–8.6.1471	—	—	6	—	—	1014	1140	14
8.6.1471–6.8.1472	125 [11]	5	35	—	808	19688	20565	346
6.8.1472–Mich. 1473	51 [12]	4	120	—	121	10991	13615	163
Mich. 1473–17.11.1474	84 [13]	5	128	—	7	7959	10065	167
17.11.1474–17.11.1475	23	85	91	1	19	6883	10126	647
17.11.1475–Mich. 1476	194 [14]	61	241	—	6	1776	3210	241
Mich. 1476– ,, 1477	132 [15]	25	158	—	20	10021	10240	203
,, 1477– ,, 1478	151 [16]	80	148	—	45	6930	7263	104
,, 1478– ,, 1479	148 [17]	45	292	—	12	3649	5268	612
,, 1479– ,, 1480	214 [18]	37	321	—	5	11428	14558	286
,, 1480– ,, 1481	110	33	491	—	2	6385	14948	178
,, 1481– ,, 1482	300 [19]	60	343	—	—	7269	13470	105

14. SOUTHAMPTON

	Sacks of Wool Exported by		Broadcloths Exported by			Value in £ of Alien Mdse. paying the Petty Custom of 3d. in the £.	Value in £ of Mdse. paying Poundage.	Tunnage. Tuns of Wine.
Date.	Denizens.	Aliens.	Deni- zens.	Han- sards.	Other Aliens.			
Mich. 1399–Mich. 1400 [20]	115	1484	1462	—	5341	8812	—	—
,, 1400–1.10.1401	517	391	1993	144	5321	8516	—	—
1.10.1401–1.10.1402	363	1206	— [21]	— [21]	— [21]	11256	—	—
1.10.1402–Mich. 1403	61	412	755	4	2396	8940	8204 [22]	202 [22]
Mich. 1403– ,, 1404	129	876	1284	5	3263	4031	15813	1177
,, 1404– ,, 1405	—	1488	325	—	3799	5314	15238	615
,, 1405– ,, 1406	66	1662	155	4	7059	15220	35397 [23]	808 [23]
,, 1406– ,, 1407	254	1259	252	—	3612	13620	26082	405
,, 1407– ,, 1408	250	974	532	9	7667	15445	39577	1359
,, 1408– ,, 1409	404	1400	542	—	5751	12211	30560	1848

[1] Includes 9 alien. [2] Includes 71 alien.
[3] Includes 39 alien and 64 rex per f.a.
[4] Includes 99 alien and 225 rex per f.a. [5] Includes 22 ind. ad p.e.
[6] Includes 64 alien. [7] Gap. [8] Includes 24 alien.
[9] Includes 218 alien. [10] Includes 17 alien. [11] Includes 69 alien.
[12] Includes 40 alien. [13] Includes 49 alien. [14] Includes 1 alien.
[15] Includes 130 alien. [16] Alien. [17] Includes 148 alien.
[18] Includes 214 alien. [19] Includes 207 alien.
[20] Customs account includes Poole to 5.7.1401. [21] Account missing.
[22] Subsidy from 3.4.1403. [23] Subsidy from 1.4.1406 to 22.12.1406.

TABLES OF ENROLLED CUSTOMS

Date.	Sacks of Wool Exported by Denizens.	Aliens.	Broadcloths Exported by Denizens.	Hansards.	Other Aliens.	Value in £ of Alien Mdse. paying the Petty Custom of 3d. in the £.	Value in £ of Mdse. paying Poundage.	Tunnage. Tuns of Wine.
Mich. 1409–Mich. 1410	501	240	735	—	4551	16760	33292 [1]	1921
,, 1410– ,, 1411	88	514	644	—	4493	12999	28826	1463
,, 1411– ,, 1412	59	82	345	—	960	2635	8284	1349
,, 1412– ,, 1413	122	351	850	—	511	997	4685	855
,, 1413– ,, 1414	126	341	767	—	672	2046	6098	1449
,, 1414– ,, 1415	141	802	378	—	1366	2136	8291	2016
,, 1415– ,, 1416	77	899	986	—	1591	2727	8977	1668
,, 1416– ,, 1417	78	264	942	—	807	3792	7296	2530
,, 1417– ,, 1418	533	788	1006	3	1910	5295	13059	2415
,, 1418– ,, 1419	128	667	934	11	2127	6890	15256	713
,, 1419– ,, 1420	86	261	818 [2]	33 [2]	132 [2]	3838	7050	1176
,, 1420– ,, 1421	107 [3]	375	—	7	1823	1959	8271	830
,, 1421–31.8.1422	77 [4]	784	742	52	3138	4436	14689	860
1.9.1422–Mich. 1423	382	181	2332	—	3502	9287	18926	255
Mich. 1423– ,, 1424	27	259	2583	7	5607	2301	15828	505
,, 1424– ,, 1425	226	44	1763	21	3748	16062	27565 [5]	424 [5]
,, 1425– ,, 1426	—	124	1570	4	3997	7044	32693	461
,, 1426– ,, 1427	67	233	1808	1	5055	8929	23226 [6]	993 [6]
,, 1427– ,, 1428	30 [7]	302	1118	—	3892	8803	21419	354
,, 1428– ,, 1429	—	550	2697	48	5156	12628	26889	867
,, 1429– ,, 1430	36	834	1868	37	7861	11975	35781	552
,, 1430– ,, 1431	261	316	2242	5	4296	3067	17213	909
,, 1431– ,, 1432	—	343	1913	—	7682	6445	25387	551
,, 1432– ,, 1433	20	264	1071	—	7205	7380	20283	378
,, 1433– ,, 1434	—	523	813	—	6243	8879	27830	440
,, 1434– ,, 1435	25	801	1366	—	7813	8245	29261 [8]	1131
,, 1435– ,, 1436	—	1046	1161	—	7110	6680	27245	579
,, 1436– ,, 1437	—	1045 [9]	753	55	4134	14278	26999	562
,, 1437– ,, 1438	29	683	2679	14	9132	21605	48863	611
,, 1438– ,, 1439	25	728	595	1	5436	12752	27766	830
,, 1439– ,, 1440	62	48	787	—	11272	9470	33267	178
,, 1440– ,, 1441	530	602	1374	—	14225	14019	44297	2042
,, 1441–6.11.1442	191	880	726	—	6737	11846	30666	1122
6.11.1442–Mich. 1443	210	732 [10]	857	—	6097	8841	26691	1196
Mich. 1443– ,, 1444	175	1252	1579	—	5626	11038	26064	1240
,, 1444– ,, 1445	305	1233	2332	—	5661	12014	28195	1351
,, 1445–28.9.1446	672	375	2091	—	8193	8338	29431	1402
28.9.1446–17.7.1447	6 [11]	945 [12]	1482	—	5141	8180	22701	836
17.7.1447–Mich. 1448	—	1078 [13]	4623	—	13207	8236	38674	1068
Mich. 1448– ,, 1449	—	769 [14]	1971	—	4639	8141	20077	2166
,, 1449–6.10.1450	35	601 [15]	1947	—	10865	9208	36736	496
6.10.1450–Mich. 1451	—	745 [16]	863	—	7087	14198	33076	460

[1] Does not include the poundage on 36 cloths and a small quantity of other merchandise exempted from payment.
[2] From *K.R. Cust. Acct.*, 140/25.
[3] Does not include 373 pockets of Spanish wool exported by William Soper by royal licence.
[4] Does not include 24 sacks of Spanish wool, exported.
[5] English subsidy from 1.8.1425 only.
[6] Account missing from Mich. to 1.12.1426.
[7] Does not include 91 " sacks " of lambfells.
[8] Does not include the value of 21 tuns of iron, imported by the Bishop of Winchester.
[9] Does not include 274 pokes of Spanish wool, exported to Rouen.
[10] Including 1 sacks of fells. [11] Sacks of fells.
[12] Including 184 ind. ad p.e. [13] Including 708 ind. ad p.e.
[14] Including 714 ind. ad p.e. [15] Including 597 ind. ad p.e.
[16] Including 32 ind. ad p.e.

358 ENGLISH TRADE IN FIFTEENTH CENTURY

Date.	Sacks of Wool Exported by Denizens.	Aliens.	Broadcloths Exported by Denizens.	Hansards.	Other Aliens.	Value in £ of Alien Mdse. paying the Petty Custom of 3d. in the £.	Value in £ of Mdse. paying Poundage.	Tunnage. Tuns of Wine.
Mich. 1451–Mich. 1452	5	1120[1]	1715	—	9391	8429	28059	1253
,, 1452– ,, 1453	—	392	555	—	1774	7318	11312	919
,, 1453– ,, 1454	—	861[2]	1309	29	5402	3906	16310	480
,, 1454–23.8.1455	—	4	611	—	243	10455	11922	738
23.8.1455–25.12.1456	—	1242[3]	1713	—	11499	7512	28727	310
25.12.1456–Mich. 1457	—	213	1471	61	3316	10538	17041	420
Mich. 1457– ,, 1458	—	139	1566	25	5743	7321	17458	890
,, 1458– ,, 1459	—	535[4]	4211[5]	—	3407[6]	5631	13349	1717[7]
,, 1459–28.8.1460	—	641[8]	945[9]	—	7591[10]	12899	27693[11]	692
28.8.1460–24.7.1461	—	629[12]	1002	—	5469	3736	14121	246
24.7.1461–Mich. 1462	—	91[13]	2086	84	2780	12353	18970	660
Mich. 1462–16.7.1463	—	387[1]	1695[14]	202	187	2228	2365	400
16.7.1463–26.12.1464	—	—	621	19	4765[15]	4122	15232[16]	1402
26.12.1464–Mich. 1465	—	—	319	—	411	1421	3475	747
Mich. 1465–1.5.1466	—	114[1]	519	—	1480	11434	15831	400
1.5.1466–Mich. 1467	139	628	680	—	18164	10478	46567	706
Mich. 1467– ,, 1468	—	523[17]	—	—	6132	5822	19285	1088
,, 1468–7.11.1469	—	365	600	—	2247	4099	9390	607
7.11.1469–26.10.1470	—	67	79	—	3002	2063	6628	322
26.10.1470–Mich. 1471	—	739[18]	341	—	5224[19]	4351	9537	864
Mich. 1471– ,, 1472	—	1150[20]	1639	—	13584	4652	33452	1095
,, 1472–22.5.1473	—	150	887	—	4363	6023	11647	990
22.5.1473–Mich. 1474	—	1365[21]	1182	—	3879	6372	22006	568
Mich. 1474–2.11.1476	—	1285	1773	27	2933	16573	26488	2424
3.11.1476–22.6.1478	5[22]	1754	1016	—	1248	7875	13476	1840
22.6.1478–Mich. 1479	12[22]	926	1332	—	1638	5006	10409	1182
Mich. 1479– ,, 1480	10	819[23]	641	—	1033	7925	10989	415
,, 1480–28.7.1481	—	1465	480	—	431	2594	5521	—
28.7.1481–Mich. 1482	—	1762[24]	1082	—	932	6332	10202	192

[1] Ind. per f.a.
[2] Including 9 ind. ad p.e.
[3] Including 37 ind. ad p.e.
[4] Rex per f.a.
[5] Including 2875 by the king.
[6] Including 2598 rex per f.a.
[7] The account gives 717 but the charge for tunnage shows that 1000 tuns have been omitted.
[8] Including 49 ind. ad p.e.; 592 rex per f.a.
[9] Including 771 by the king.
[10] Including 6903 rex per f.a.; 54 ind. per f.a.
[11] Including £12,211 poundage on the cloth of the king and of W. Burgh.
[12] Including 83 rex ad p.e.
[13] Including 50 ind. per f.a.
[14] Including 1368 by the king.
[15] Including 3000 rex per f.a.
[16] Including £6,690 poundage on the king's cloths.
[17] Including 418 rex per f.a.
[18] Including 620 rex per f.a.
[19] Including 3911 rex per f.a.
[20] Including 100 rex per f.a. and 275 ind. per f.a.
[21] Including 300 ind. per f.a.
[22] Sacks of fells.
[23] Including 259 by the Duchess of York per f.a.
[24] Including 135 by the Duchess of York per f.a. and 198 ind. ad p.e.

TABLES OF ENROLLED CUSTOMS

15. YARMOUTH

Date.	Wool Exported. Sacks. (Wool.)	Sacks. (Fells.)	Broadcloths [1] Exported by Deni- zens.	Han- sards.	Other Aliens.	Value in £ of Alien Mdse. paying the Petty Custom of 3d. in the £	Value in £ of Mdse. paying Poundage.	Tunnage. Tuns of Wine.
Mich. 1399–Mich. 1400	—	—	970	398	90	1644	—	—
,, 1400–7.11.1401	—	—	761	786	117	3063	—	—
7.11.1401–13.11.1402	—	—	780	771	103	1749	—	—
13.11.1402–Mich. 1403	—	—	494	145	76	1900	2719 [2]	2 [2]
Mich. 1403– ,, 1404	61	—	42 [3]	938 [3]	1 [3]	42 [3]	6873	130
,, 1404– ,, 1405	48	49	—	—	—	—	3926	136
,, 1405– ,, 1406	93 [4]	27 [5]	—	—	—	—	8343	73
,, 1406– ,, 1407	—	—	251 [6]	477 [6]	14 [6]	1255	1123 [7]	2
,, 1407– ,, 1408	—	—	529	687	51	2228	7659	120
,, 1408– ,, 1409	12	8	202	198	61	1923	5225	197
,, 1409– ,, 1410	—	9 [8]	348	1382	50	1261	5698	222
,, 1410– ,, 1411	—	—	595	729	37	1446	5757	208
,, 1411– ,, 1412	—	1	211	617	49	1662	4459	218
,, 1412– ,, 1413	—	5	664	802	56	1571	5159	223
,, 1413– ,, 1414	—	12 [9]	400	35	34	1850	4994	209
,, 1414– ,, 1415	—	3 [10]	580	642	38	1589	3869	443
,, 1415– ,, 1416	—	15 [9]	543	10	70	955	4789	446
,, 1416– ,, 1417	—	19 [9]	595	31	35	1268	5045	341
,, 1417– ,, 1418	—	40 [4]	826	38	91	1191	5529	189
,, 1418– ,, 1419	—	35 [4]	605	56	25	961	2672	87
,, 1419– ,, 1420	—	7 [5]	660	14	88	1365	4676	310
,, 1420– ,, 1421	—	15 [11]	957	8	87	949	6411	78
,, 1421–31.8.1422	—	5 [10]	766	—	65	1949	9128	30
1.9.1422–Mich. 1423	18	6	1183	12	79	831	1133	44
Mich. 1423– ,, 1424	—	12	1193	51	52	828	1076	4
,, 1424– ,, 1425	4	18 [12]	842	135	48	824	1524 [13]	148 [13]
,, 1425– ,, 1426	2	1 [8]	770	85	43	1080	4152	140
,, 1426– ,, 1427	53	10 [14]	491	24	8	936	2259	108
,, 1427– ,, 1428	—	1 [15]	492	91	4	1032	1579 [16]	5 [16]
,, 1428– ,, 1429	—	5 [9]	434	52	3	717	1440 [17]	—
,, 1429– ,, 1430	43	3	381	63	2	345	2107	21
,, 1430– ,, 1431	9	16	591	49	13	648	1682	59

[1] The cloth exported from Yarmouth included a much larger quantity of worsteds than that from most of the other ports, being some 12,000 for the year 1400–1401. These exports fell off considerably later and varied from a few hundreds to one thousand. In accordance with the plan adopted for these tables, the exports of worsteds have been omitted altogether.
[2] The accounts of tunnage and poundage begin at 3.4.1403.
[3] From Mich. to 24.11.1403 only. For the remainder of the year and the two subsequent years the accounts for cloth and alien merchandise paying 3d. in the £ are missing.
[4] Includes 12 alien.
[5] Includes 4 alien.
[6] From 11.3.1407 only.
[7] From Mich. 1406 to 20.2.1407 only.
[8] Alien.
[9] Includes 3 alien.
[10] Includes 2 alien.
[11] Includes 11 alien.
[12] Includes 9 alien.
[13] English subsidy levied from 1.8.1425 only.
[14] Includes 6 alien.
[15] Includes 1 alien, but does not include 12 sacks of alien shorlings and morlings.
[16] No English subsidy between 11.11.1427 and 4.4.1428.
[17] English subsidy of poundage levied to 4.4.1429 only.

Date	Wool Exported. Sacks. (Wool.)	Wool Exported. Sacks. (Fells.)	Broadcloths Exported by Denizens.	Broadcloths Exported by Hansards.	Broadcloths Exported by Other Aliens.	Value in £ of Alien Mdse. paying the Petty Custom of 3d. in the £.	Value in £ of Mdse. paying Poundage.	Tunnage. Tuns of Wine.
Mich. 1431–Mich. 1432	—	—	806	—	11	314	600	113
„ 1432–17.9.1433	4	9	953	1	15	597	2315	—
17.9.1433–Mich. 1434	16	5	726	24	5	298	2629 [1]	72
Mich. 1434–31.10.1435	33	5	1055	8	1	349	2959	246
31.10.1435–Mich. 1436	74	—	118	—	39	272	1195	48
Mich. 1436– „ 1437	—	—	578	7	41	2065	3009	1
„ 1437– „ 1438	—	—	387	53	65	2351	3741	44
„ 1438– „ 1439	—	7 [2]	448	52	23	728	2132	3
„ 1439– „ 1440	61	25 [2]	343	30	25	502	1557	58
„ 1440–5.9.1441	15	—	125	—	3	433	1166	88
5.9.1441–Mich. 1442	—	—	987	43	4	440	1118	52
Mich. 1442– „ 1443	—	—	465	6	9	647	1902	48
„ 1443– „ 1444	—	—	776	20	6	906	1846	133
„ 1444– „ 1445	—	—	635	21	—	787	1914	61
„ 1445– „ 1446	—	—	464	51	—	971	1576	18
„ 1446–1.9.1447	61	—	458	2	2	1627	1042	38
1.9.1447–8.4.1449	479	40 [3]	711	62	46	2584	3595	311
8.4.1449–20.7.1449 [4]	—	—	72	—	—	69	265	61
28.11.1449–Mich. 1450	—	—	374	—	35	894	1644	17
Mich. 1450–16.7.1451	—	—	1026	—	6	733	1515	17
16.7.1451–29.5.1452	—	—	485	—	7	724	2014	11
29.5.1452–Mich. 1453	—	—	629	8	3	794	1967	119
Mich. 1453– „ 1454	—	25	319	—	—	357	1031	6
„ 1454– „ 1455	—	—	901	—	—	484	1138	47
„ 1455– „ 1456	—	—	651	—	—	1463	2807	3
„ 1456– „ 1457	—	—	547	30	—	1118	2660	—
„ 1457– „ 1458	—	—	281	—	—	536	959	12
„ 1458– „ 1459	—	—	305	29	—	336	877	21
„ 1459–1.9.1460 [4]	100 [5]	—	266	—	—	443	836	8
4.3.1461–16.5.1462	32 [6]	—	341	—	—	918	1962	122
16.5.1462–3.9.1462	—	—	133	—	—	245	702	24
3.9.1462–11.7.1463	—	—	153	—	—	183	499	2
11.7.1463–Mich. 1464	—	—	269	18	5	748	2183	32
Mich. 1464–20.8.1465	—	—	276	10	28	710	1820	120
20.8.1465–Mich. 1466	—	—	145	—	10	929	2454	27
Mich. 1466– „ 1467	—	—	266	—	18	826	2135	39
„ 1467– „ 1468	—	—	300	—	3	581	1706	38
„ 1468–4.9.1469	—	—	229	—	14	758	2513	16
4.9.1469–9.10.1470	—	—	325	—	5	635	1330	4
9.10.1470–24.6.1471	—	—	6	—	—	166	223	—
24.6.1471–Mich. 1472	—	—	217	—	—	605	1360	47
Mich. 1472– „ 1473	—	—	37	—	3	609	1434	21
„ 1473–10.11.1474	—	—	89	—	3	1716	2514	26
10.11.1474–Mich. 1475	—	—	124	—	—	678	1126	2
Mich. 1475– „ 1476	—	—	109	—	—	434	1585	58
„ 1476– „ 1477	—	—	176	—	—	342	1364	29
„ 1477– „ 1478	—	—	555	—	—	323	1769	—
„ 1478– „ 1479	—	—	304	—	—	409	1351	26
„ 1479– „ 1480	—	—	300	80	8	327	2446	49
„ 1480– „ 1481	—	—	221	—	—	1969	4350	39
„ 1481– „ 1482	—	—	319	3	11	649	2605	43

[1] English poundage includes the value of cloth.   [2] Shorlings and morlings.
[3] Includes 18 alien.   [4] Gap.
[5] Ind. ad p.c.   [6] Alien.

NOTES TO THE TEXT
I
ENGLISH FOREIGN TRADE FROM 1446 TO 1482

[1] In the second half of the fourteenth century, annual shipments of English woollens had expanded until the average for the years Mich., 1392 to Mich., 1395, amounted to 43,072 broadcloths. H. L. Gray, "The Production and Exportation of English Woollens in the Fourteenth Century," in *E.H.R.*, vol. xxxix (1924), p. 35. With the reign of Henry IV came a sharp contraction, the average annual exportation from Mich., 1410 to Mich., 1415, being only 26,958 cloths (computed from *L.T.R. Cust. Accts.* 19). Recovery attended the substitution of victorious foreign war for the civil disorders which had followed the coming of the new dynasty. Exports rose until from Mich., 1437 to Mich., 1440, they averaged 56,317 cloths (ibid.). The two movements thus suggested, viz. the decline of trade in the first quarter of the century, and the recovery in the second, were to recur, as will appear in the last half of the century.

[2] *Rot. Parl.*, vol. v, p. 74.

[3] The average exportation of these years was 53,699 broadcloths; from Mich., 1437 to Mich., 1440, it was 56,317.

[4] Occasionally this is not true, as it would not be with the record of a year of revolution, valuable for its own implications. There might, for example, be ground for isolating the year Mich., 1470, to Mich., 1471, in order to see what were some of the economic effects of the six months' restoration of Henry VI.

[5] Cf. below, pp. 321–330.

[6] During the thirty-six years under consideration 150 lasts of hides were exported. Of the total, thirty-five were shipped in 1446 to 1455, nine in 1455 to 1470, and 116 in 1470 to 1482. The average annual exportation of the last twelve years was, therefore, nearly ten lasts. Hides were worth from 20 marks to £20 the last. A Sandwich customs account of Mich., 1439, to Mich., 1440, values them at 13s. 6d. to 20s. the dicker; *K.R. Cust. Acct.* 127/18, ff. 13-15.

[7] The enrolled accounts record exports of worsteds by denizens and aliens. During 1446 to 1464, denizen exports of doubles averaged 459 yearly, and of singles 78; alien exports of doubles averaged 59, and of singles 62. During 1468 to 1482, denizen exports of doubles averaged 1,291 yearly, and of singles 152; alien exports of doubles averaged 58, and of singles 36. The "aliens" in question, however, did not include Hansards who, as the accounts show, paid on exported worsteds only the petty custom of 3d. in the £. Hanseatic shipments of worsteds, therefore, are discernible only in the particulars of accounts. The record for London, Mich., 1438 to Mich., 1439, enters such shipments, which add up to 278 doubles; the one for Yarmouth, 1st Sept., 1447 to Mich., 1448, shipments amounting to 260 doubles (*K.R. Cust. Accts.* 73/12 and 194/9). Since Hansards exported scarcely any worsteds from other ports, their annual exports may be estimated at about 500 doubles. In the London and Yarmouth particulars of account just cited, double worsteds were valued at from 20s. to 30s. each; in the Yarmouth account three single worsteds at 4s. 6d. each. But in a Southampton account of Mich., 1443 to Mich., 1444, three singles were worth 10s. each; in an Ipswich account of 19th March, 1466, to Mich., 1466, five singles 14s. each; and in an enrolled account for Southampton for 1st May, 1466 to Mich., 1467, forty-five singles, 15s. each. (*K.R. Cust. Accts.* 140/62, f. 40 and 52/49; *L.T.R. Cust. Accts.* 21.) The maximum values may be adopted.

[8] The household accounts call it "wine of Tire, Rumney, and Malves" (*Var. Accts.: Wardrobe and Household*, 409/16).

[9] *L.T.R. Cust. Accts.* 16 and 22.

[10] A late fifteenth century enumeration of the commodities which paid customs and subsidies implies that wine imported by Hansards paid only the butlerage of 2s., but not the subsidy of 3s. paid by other aliens and by denizens. (N. S. B. Gras, *The Early English Customs System*, p. 692.) Schanz has doubted the accuracy of this document (G. Schanz, *Englische Handelspolitik*, vol. ii, p. 7), and he was right. The particulars of accounts show that Hansards paid the tunnage of 3s. One from Sandwich of Mich., 1439 to Mich., 1440, records such payment on 64 tuns by John Norrell, alien of the Hanse (*K.R. Cust. Acct.* 127/18, f. 8); one from Yarmouth of 1.9.1448 to 8.4.1449, notes 5s., paid on 1¾ tuns by Godefry Hase of the Hanse (*K.R. Cust. Acct.* 194/9, m. 4); and one from Hull of Mich., 1464 to 18th March, 1465, records payment on 12 tuns by Nicholas Molyner, Hansard (*K.R. Cust. Accts.* 62/6, f. 22v). In still another way it can be seen that exemption from tunnage was not one of the privileges of the Hansards. When for various reasons these privileges became temporarily inoperative, poundage and the full cloth custom were charged against Hansards in the customs accounts, but later these charges were remitted *per processum* in the court of the exchequer. Since tunnage was never treated in this

way, it must have been a charge always borne. Hansards, however, imported little wine, instances in the particulars of accounts being rare.

[11] Schanz, op. cit., vol. ii, p. 73.

[12] F. Schulz, *Die Hanse und England*, chap. 7, especially pp. 123-5, 129-30; *Foedera*, vol. v, 2, p. 37. With the Hansards should be grouped the merchants of Veer and Weston Stowe, similarly privileged.

[13] Cf. below, pp. 27, 34.

[14] This trade of the Hansards, like their trade in cloth, was confined to certain ports. Such were the ports of the East Coast, save Yarmouth, where they bought little besides worsteds. Rarely did they touch upon the South Coast. In the ports which they visited their share in alien shipments of merchandise subject to the custom of 3d. in the £ varied considerably. In Newcastle, Hull, Boston, Lynn, and Ipswich, it averaged from Mich., 1475, to Mich., 1478, about one-half of all such shipments, but in the following four years came to average nearly three-fourths of them. In London the corresponding averages were at first one-fourth, and then rather more than one-half; in Sandwich at first one-twelfth, then upwards of one-eighth.

[15] During the last nine years of the reign of Henry VIII (1538-47) the accounts once more make a similar distinction. Then the average share of the Hanse was 25 per cent (Schanz, op. cit., vol. ii, pp. 62-3).

[16] In their ratings the collectors may have been following a book of rates in which different values for stuffs of different quality may have been set down. A book of rates seems to have been drawn up shortly before our period begins.

[17] K.R. *Cust. Accts.* 73/23 and 140/62.

[18] Kerseys were frequently so equated from the time of Richard II. In the Southampton account just quoted, 230 pieces of Essex straits, probably "dozens", are said to be equivalent to 57¼ broadcloths (f. 28 v). In Cornwall six dozen straits were the equivalent of a cloth of assize and the value of each dozen was usually 6s. For example in 1446 " xvi duodene panni lanei albi et russeti stricti quarum . . . sex duodene faciunt unum pannum de assisa " were valued each dozen at 6s. (K.R. *Memo. Roll*, Mich. 26 Hen. VI).

[19] L.T.R. *Cust. Accts.* 21:—Lynn, 2.11.1466, to 2.11.1468, 197 cloths valued at £262 13s. 4d.; Ipswich, 5.11.1466 to Mich., 1467, 605¼ cloths valued at £807 14s. 8d.; Boston, 4.3.1461 to Mich., 1461, 338¼ cloths valued at £225 10s.

[20] Schanz, op. cit., vol. ii, p. 31, n. 1. He supports his suggestion by a questionable interpretation of certain acts of Parliament.

[21] K.R *Accts. Var.*, 341/12, 13 14, 16, 18, and 19. Normally the *pannus* was equivalent to two dozens, being so rated in ulnagers' accounts, and it consisted of 28 yards unshrunken or 24 yards shrunken (*Stat*. 27 Edw. III, i, c. 4; 47 Edw. III, c. 1; 12 Ric. II, c. 14; 7 Hen. IV, c. 10). But occasionally the length of a cloth increased to 36 yards or dropped to 20 yards. The width, too, was a complicating factor. By statute it should have been five quarters, but many cloths were straits, being only three-quarters wide. In consequence, a strait cloth, like the dozen, was equivalent to about one-half of a *pannus*, and a " dozen straits " equivalent to one-fourth, or even one-sixth, of a *pannus*.

[22] A *pannus de Murrey granatus*, containing 28 yards, was valued in court at £7 4s. 8d., or 5s. 2d. the yard, but cloths "in grain" were confessedly rare and costly. Smaller pieces of murrey, not said to be in grain, brought respectively, 3s., 18½d., and 17d. the yard (*Var. Accts.*: Ulnage, 341/16 and 12). A piece of *nigri coloris vocatus puke*, containing 19½ yards, was sold for £5 17s., or 6s. the yard, the highest price recorded in these London accounts (*Var. Accts.*: Ulnage, 341/19). Of the *panni lanei coloris de mustre villers*, one containing 30 yards was worth 110s. and two and one-half, containing respectively 36, 32, and 15¼ yards, were worth together £13 17s. 6d., or 39d. the yard. Elsewhere "mustered vylers" were sold for 24d. and 28d. the yard. Finally, a *pannus* described merely as *coloris marble* was worth £3 10s.

[23] *Stat.* 4 Edw. IV, c. 1.

[24] 5s. 9d.; 5s. 9d.; 13s. 4d.; 18s.; 20s.; 22s. 6d.; 33s. 4d.; 46s. 8d.

[25] A. Schaube, *Die Wollausfuhr Englands*; Gray, op. cit., pp. 15, 25, 32.

[26] By years, 11,383, 12,074, 16,385, 14,368, and 13,901 sacks respectively, L.T.R. *Cust. Accts.* 17.

[27] A memorandum of the time of Edward VI allows "for every cloth iii Todde", *Tudor Econ. Docs.*, ed. Tawney and Power, vol. i, p. 180. Since a sack of wool contains 13 tods it seems that about 4¼ cloths were manufactured from every sack.

[28] Just after the middle of the fourteenth century about two-thirds of all wool manufactured for sale seems to have been exported. Gray, op. cit., p. 2.

[29] E. Power, "The English Wool Trade in the Reign of Edward IV," in *Camb. Hist. Journ.*, vol. ii, p. 21. Cf. below, pp. 44, 48.

[30] The volume of these shipments was not maintained.

[31] *Rot. Parl.*, vol. v, p. 274.

[32] *Cely Papers*, ed. H. E. Malden, pp. 10, 11, 31, 45, 64, 121.
[33] That the average price of exported wool at the beginning of the fifteenth century lay somewhere between the extremes of four marks and sixteen marks and hence was perhaps about £7 is to be inferred from a petition presented in Parliament about 1400. It is a protest against "another bill" of the Commons, which asked that all wool be shipped to Calais. The protest came from merchants of certain counties which are said to produce coarse wool (*grosses leins*) and which are enumerated as Northumberland, Cumberland, Durham, Westmoreland, Norfolk, Kent, Sussex, Devon, Cornwall, Suffolk, Surrey, Cambridgeshire, Essex, Wiltshire, and Dorset. The argument is that wool similar to the coarse wool of these counties is brought to the marts of Flanders from Scotland, paying only a half-mark custom, and from Normandy, Picardy, and Flanders, paying nothing. If shipment of the coarse wool of England to Calais is made obligatory, no Flemish merchant will trouble to go there to buy it, especially at a higher price. Hence not only English merchants who traffic in such wool, but also lords who grow it will be ruined, and the king will lose his customs. Inasmuch as the same custom and subsidy is collected from a sack of coarse wool which is not worth more than four or five marks as from a sack which is worth fifteen or sixteen marks, it is more advantageous that coarse wools should go where they can be sold than that they should go to Calais (". . . pur quoi semble qe desicome homme paie a tant du custume et subside pur une sak de grosse leine qe ne vaut outre iiii marcz ou v marcz comme homme fait pur une sak qe vaut xv marcz ou xvi qe greignour proffait est al roialme qe les grosses leins irroient la ou els meuth purroient estre venduz . . . qe daler a Caleys . . ."; *Parliamentary and Council Proceedings, Chancery*, 13/1). Professor Power would adopt a higher average valuation for the sack of wool delivered at Calais (below p. 71). But in arriving at such a valuation regard should be had to the large quantities of wool shipped from East Coast ports, much of which must have been of midland growth and of medium quality. Moreover, to set a higher average value on the sack would be to increase the already extremely favourable balance of trade enjoyed by England in 1446-8 (below p. 20). The same awkward result would follow the adoption of values for broadcloths higher than those accepted in the text.
[34] Cf. above, p. 4.
[35] How far wool merchants traded in other commodities is discussed below, pp. 15–17.
[36] *L.T.R. Cust. Accts.* 22.
[37] Successively, £3½, £3, £3, £4½, £4, £4½, £3½. Var. Accts.: *Wardrobe and Household*, 16 and 20. Cf. Gras, op. cit., pp. 41–3.
[38] *C.P.R.*, 1476–85, p. 145.
[39] Schanz adopted the average values of £4 for non-sweet wine, of £10 for Malmsey wine, and of £6 for other sweet wine (Schanz, op. cit., vol. ii, p. 33). Fifteenth century enrolled accounts make no distinction between Malmsey and other sweet wines.
[40] £6,800 as the value of 1,700 tuns of red wine, and £6,100 as the value of 762 tuns of sweet wine.
[41] *K.R. Cust. Acct.* 76/39. The account is in places damaged or illegible. The number of sacks and fells which can be assigned to shippers amounts to about 3,900 sacks. Since the enrolled account of the wool custom records that denizens shipped 4,309 sacks during the year (*L.T.R. Cust. Acct.* 16), 400 sacks are unaccounted for. The entries, however, are numerous, exceeding 300, and it is not likely that anyone who shipped wool on a considerable scale is unrecorded.
[42] The enrolled customs accounts at times distinguish denizens shipping wool to Calais as Staplers or non-Staplers.
[43] *C.P.R.*, 1446–52, pp. 315–16, 323. *K.R. Cust. Acct.* 73/12 and 77/4.
[44] This conclusion is confirmed by the London tunnage and poundage accounts of 10th June, 1449 to 10th June, 1450, which fortunately survive (*K.R. Cust. Accts.* 73/23 and 25). Of the fifty-eight men who were trading in wool in 1439 or in 1450, or at both times, eleven appear as importers of miscellaneous commodities, although none of them exported such. Five had imported or exported miscellaneous commodities in 1442–3, viz. Bolle, Felde, Johnson, Malverne, and Holt. Now in 1449–50 their combined imports were 49 tuns of wine and miscellaneous commodities worth £200. Two others, John Michell and John Pulter, were merchants who in 1439 traded only in wool, but who now in 1449–50 imported respectively 3 tuns of wine and iron worth £381. The four remaining traders, Walter Brewes, William Bere, John Grafton, and John Matlok, imported commodities worth £165. Altogether the imports of the eleven wool traders were 52 tuns of wine and miscellaneous commodities worth £746. The total was a little smaller than that of 1438 to 1443.
[45] Cf. below pp. 68–70. M. Postan, "Credit in Medieval Trade," in *Econ. Hist. Review*, vol. i, pp. 238–44. *Cely Papers*, p. 64.
[46] Presumably for a good return, which, however, might be concealed in the mechanism of exchange.

[47] Cf. above, p. 5. Since Italians exported considerable tin, their export trade may be valued at relatively more than that of denizens or Hansards.
[48] Including worsteds valued at £500.
[49] Including worsteds valued at £700.
[50] Estimated, although the total value of exports and imports in each instance is known.
[51] In the particular customs accounts wax is valued at £2 the quintal (*K.R. Cust. Acct.* 77/4, mm. 4*v*., 6).
[52] Perhaps this is true for the Hanseatic balance through over-valuation of cloths exported. Otherwise it must be assumed that Hansards adjusted the balance in their continental trade. They paid little in customs.
[53] Shipments of this sort during the six years averaged about 1,400 annually, twice what they had been in the five preceding years.
[54] Only 870 sacks were shipped during the ten months; 10,636 sacks were sent abroad during the next year.
[55] *Rot. Parl.*, vol. v, pp. 613–16. The enrolled customs accounts show the Exchequer acting henceforth merely as recorder of the transaction, and the accounts of the treasurer and victualler of Calais confirm our knowledge of the new procedure. See below, pp. 74 ff.
[56] It is doubtful whether there was further improvement under Henry VII. During the first twelve years of Henry VIII's reign, the average annual exportation of wool was still 8,624 sacks; but during the remainder of the reign it fell below 5,000 sacks (Schanz, op. cit., vol. ii, p. 15).
[57] Including an estimate for Bristol, from which port the accounts are missing in these years.
[58] See below, pp. 127–31.
[59] See below, pp. 132–3.
[60] The importation of English cloth into Hanseatic cities was forbidden, but the prohibition was not entirely effective (ibid., pp. 116, 119).
[61] *Rot. Parl.*, vol. v, pp. 150, 201. The Burgundian ordinance which forbade the importation of English cloth and yarn was dated 16th January, 1447 (Schanz, op. cit., vol. ii, p. 660).
[62] *L.T.R. Cust. Accts.* 19, Boston, 31.5.1452 to Mich., 1452.
[63] W. Stein, "Die Merchant Adventurers in Utrecht (1464–7), in *Hans. Gbl.*, vol. ix (1900), pp. 179–89.
[64] *Foedera*, vol. v, ii, pp. 149–53.
[65] Ibid., p. 166.
[66] For 1446 to 1450, 88 per cent.; for 1450 to 1454, 76 per cent; for 1454 to 1458, 86 per cent. For March, 1461 to Michaelmas, 1462, about 80 per cent; for successive two-year periods, 66 per cent, 44 per cent, and 77 per cent, respectively.
[67] From 1471 to 1477 the accounts for Bristol are missing. Since for the years 1471 to 1476 all red wine imported elsewhere averaged 4,178 tuns annually, the share of denizens would have been about 2,800 tuns. To this should be added, as imported into Bristol, perhaps 1,000 tuns, 800 of them by denizens. Since the butlerage accounts for the last year of the reign are missing, denizen wine imports cannot be exactly ascertained. They seem to have dropped to about 5,000 tuns.
[68] In the time of Henry VIII the denizen wine trade was only slightly greater, imports throughout the thirty-eight years of the reign averaging 7,143 tuns of non-sweet wine a year. Alien imports of non-sweet wine during the same period averaged 1,646 tuns yearly. Denizens, however, now did what they had not done from 1446 to 1482; they imported sweet wine, their annual shipments averaging 720 tuns. Alien shipments of sweet wine still averaged 550 tuns (Schanz, op. cit., vol. ii, pp. 146–8).
[69] The butlerage accounts for 1456 to 1458, extending over a period five months short of two years, record alien imports of both red and sweet wine amounting to 2,355 tuns. During the full two years alien imports of sweet wine alone were 875 tuns. The 600 tuns for the years 1458 to 1462 is derived from the estimate made above, p. 14, that the share of denizens in imports of red wine during these years was 85 per cent of the total. Since the total for the four years averaged 3,835 tuns, the 15 per cent assigned to aliens was 575 tuns.
[70] Under Henry VIII the average annual importation of sweet wine was 1,270 tuns; but only 550 tuns of it was still imported by aliens. Cf. n. 68.
[71] Cf. above, p. 30.
[72] Cf. above, pp. 5–6.
[73] Cf. above, p. 18.
[74] Including worsteds valued at £2,000.
[75] Including worsteds valued at £800.
[76] Estimated, the total of exports and imports being known. See above, n. 50.

II

THE ENGLISH WOOL TRADE IN THE FIFTEENTH CENTURY

[1] See, for instance, the complaint of certain Leyden merchants in 1445, that the Burgomaster and sixteen merchants came to Calais in August, 1444, to make the town's purchases of wool, and were persuaded by bad advice to purchase none at that time, with the result that " withyn a while therafter ther voidede out of the same towne of Leythe mor than 2000 personnes for lakke of werke of wolle and wolfelle . . . and have sette hem in labour of lande and otherwise " ; they add that if they are delayed in the receipt of certain money which they claim, they will be unable to buy wool at Calais " to fynde werke by mene of that merchaundize to the multitude of the people of the seide towne of Leythe to erne withe their lyvyng, for whiche cause, yf other remedie may not for hem be purveyede, the saide multitude of peple must nedes voide the saide towne of Leythe and put hem in other labour, to win in other wise thair lyvyng to grete disolacionne of the same towne in that partie ", *Letters and Papers illustrative of the Wars of the English in France during the Reign of Henry VI*, ed. J. Stevenson, vol. i, pp. 466, 668. Compare the decree of the Venetian Senate in November, 1485, when the Flanders Galleys had been intercepted, and the supply of English wool cut off, " and on this account little work can be put in hand by the drapers, who have come into the presence of the signory, earnestly requesting that proper provision may be made and setting forth the great detriment incurred both from lack of purchasers exporting Venetian cloths . . . as also because the great part of the poor of this city was maintained by the manufacture of woollens, which manufacture failing, their supply of food fails and they perish of hunger." *C. St. P. Ven.*, vol. i, p. 157.

[2] Gower, " Mirour de l'Omme," in *Complete Works*, ed. G. C. Macaulay (Oxford, 1899), vol. i, pp. 280–1. He is intent to show the rule of Trickery in this, as in other trades, but he waxes eloquent about wool, " noble lady, goddess of the merchants," in the process.

[3] See his debate between " Horse, Goose and Sheep ", written some time after 1421, in *Political, Religious and Love Poems*, ed. F. J. Furnivall (E.E.T.S., 1866, re-edited, 1903), p. 15 ff.

[4] *The Libelle of Englyshe Polycye*, ed. Sir George Warner (1926). The author, probably Adam Moleyns, afterwards Bishop of Chichester, writing in 1436, saw clearly the dependence of Flanders upon English wool:—

> By draperinge of oure wolle in substaunce
> Lyvene here comons, this is here governaunce,
> Wythoughten whyche they may not leve at ease ;
> Thus moste hem sterve or wyth us most have peasse.

He declares that Spanish wool is useless unless mixed with that of England, l.c., pp. 5–7.

[5] Lydgate, l.c. p. 30.

[6] A. Schaube, " Die Wollausfuhr Englands vom Jahre 1273," in *V.S.W.G.* (1908), vol. vi, p. 68.

[7] G. Schanz, *Englische Handelspolitik gegen Ende des Mittelalters* (1881), vol. i, p. 351.

[8] Richard Cely senior writes to his son George on 26th June, 1477, to tell him that Robert (another son) is coming with his (Richard's) apprentice, Thomas Folboune, to make him free of the Staple. *Ancient Correspondence*, 59/46. Sometimes persons with no connection with the trade were made free of the Company. See the reference in William Cely's letter of Lady Day, 1484, reporting an assembly of the Fellowship including Lord Denham and other members of the Council " that be free made of the Staple now late," *The Cely Papers*, ed. H. E. Malden, pp. 145–6. See also the will of John Barton of Holme, Stapler (1490), " Volo quod Thomas filius meus Johannem Tamworth fieri faciat liberum hominem stapulæ Calisiæ, si possit cum x li ; vel dat ei x li," *Testamenta Eboracensia*, ed. Raine (Surtees Soc., 1869), iv, p. 62. The hanse or entrance fee of the Fellowship was 100 marks (£66 13s. 4d.) in Henry VIII's day. Schanz, op. cit., ii, p. 560. A document of 1558 (hostile to the Staplers) puts it at £150. *S.P.D., Mary*, vol. xiii, No. 49.

[9] See above, p. 12.

[10] Schanz, op. cit., vol. ii, p. 567.

[11] *Test. Ebor.*, vol. iv, p. 61.

[12] *Var. Accts.*: *France*, 197/11.
[13] *K.R. Cust. Acct.* 73/40.
[14] Ibid., 10/7 and 52/54.
[15] *Bronnen tot de Geschiedenis van de Leidsche Textielnijverheid*, ed. N. W. Posthumus, vol. i, pp. 48-9, 74-5, 133-4 (etc.). There were similar regulations at Douai, *Rec. de documents rel. à l'hist. de l'industrie drapière en Flandre*, ed. G. Espinas and H. Pirenne (Brussels, 1906), vol. ii, pp. 322-3, and at Haarlem, *Kuerboch der Stadt Haerlem*, ed. A. J. Enschedé and C. J. Gonnet (Haarlem and the Hague, 1882-7), pp. 85, 88, 90, and at Amsterdam, *Rechtsbronnen der Stad Amsterdam*, ed. J. C. Breen (The Hague, 1902), p. 39.
[16] *Rot. Parl.*, vol. v, p. 564, vol. vi, pp. 157, 164.
[17] Uzzano, a Florentine merchant who compiled a handbook for traders at the beginning of the fifteenth century, describes the transport of four sarplers of wool bought at Calais in April, 1417, and carried to Bruges and thence to Sluys and by sea to Milan. Pagnini, *Della Decima* [etc.] (Lucca, 1766), vol. iv, pp. 186-7.
[18] For the history of this toll in the late fourteenth and early fifteenth centuries, when it was farmed to various financiers, see Georges Bigwood, *Le Régime juridique et économique du commerce de l'argent dans la Belgique du moyen âge* (Académie Royal de Belgique, Classe des lettres [etc.], Mém. Sér. ii, Tom. xiv, 1ʳᵉ Partie (Brussels, 1921), pp. 657-9, 661.
[19] G. Daumet, *Calais sous la domination anglaise*, p. 125.
[20] *Proc. and Ord. P.C.*, vol. iii, p. 65, vol. v, p. 280; H. J. Smit, *Bronnen tot de Geschiedenis van den Handel mit England* [etc.], vol. ii, p. 717.
[21] *Rot. Parl.*, vol. v, p. 149.
[22] *Cartulaire de l'ancienne estaple de Bruges*, ed. L. Gilliodts van Severen, vol. ii, pp. 10, 36, 63.
[23] See below, p. 47.
[24] On the Flanders Galleys, see *C. St. P., Ven.*, vol. i, introduction and Nos. 21, 23, 32, 34, 37, 138, 194, 230, 238, 263, 334, 339, 440, 479, 480.
[25] His career has been sketched by Miss C. L. Scofield, *Life and Reign of Edw. IV* (1923), ii, pp. 420-8.
[26] *C. St. P., Ven.*, vol. i, p. 130.
[27] *K.R. Cust. Acct.*, 73/40; *L.T.R. Cust. Accts.* 22, m. 71d. On the royal shipment in the *Mary de la Towre*, see Richard Cely's letter of 29th March, 1482, *Cely Papers*, p. 87, quoted below, p. 57.
[28] "The Noumbre of Weyghts," *MS. Cott. Vesp. E IX*, ff., 107d-108d.
[29] *Proc. and Ord. P.C.*, vol. ii, pp. 165-6.
[30] *Foedera*, vol. iv, pp. 131, 136, 148.
[31] *C. St. P., Ven.*, vol. i, pp. 72, 83.
[32] *Libelle*, ed. Warner, p. 24.
[33] *Cely Papers*, pp. 45, 48.
[34] *E.C.P.*, 59/69. A group of Cotswold dealers (including Bryddok and Fortey, concerning whom, see below, p. 54), sued Caniziani's widow for £884 13s. 4d. worth of wool supplied to him for shipment from Southampton. *E.C.P.* 59/60; and see below, pp. 54-5.
[35] See below, p. 58.
[36] *C. St. P., Ven.*, vol. i, p. 83.
[37] *Rot. Parl.*, vol. iv, p. 509.
[38] Op. cit., p. 24.
[39] For example, Henry IV granted one of these licences to Richard Whittington, *C.P.R.*, 1408-13, p. 289, who obtained another from Henry V, ibid., 1416-22, p. 233; Edward IV granted one to Sir John Crosby, William Heryot, and Sir William Stokker, ibid., 1467-77, p. 153, and ibid., 1476-85, p. 1. All of these were prominent Staplers; but they were general merchants doing an import trade as well.
[40] For a clear case of the sale of a licence to ship 600 sacks of wool through the Straits of Marrock by one Godfrey Wolleman of London to one John Maldon, grocer, see Guildhall, *Plea and Memo. Rolls*, A 73, m. 6. The phrase used is that Godfrey " desired John to be his factor and attorney" for the purpose.
[41] On Edward IV as a trader, see Scofield, l.c., vol. ii, pp. 84 ff.
[42] *Rot. Parl.*, vol. iv, p. 251.
[43] Ibid., vol. iv, p. 360.
[44] See a case in *Select Cases before the King's Council*, ed. Leadam and Baldwin, pp. 103-4.
[45] Many cases of smuggling to Holland have been collected from the Memoranda Rolls by Smit, *Bronnen*, *passim*. For an analysis of the modification of Staple regulations by royal licence and of the smuggling of Staple goods between 1444 and 1461, see

W. Haward, *The Transactions between the Merchants of the Staple and the Lancastrian Government*. Thesis presented for the degree of Ph.D. in the University of London (1931), chapters iii and iv. (Deposited in the University of London Library.)

[46] The most interesting of these are published in *The Cely Papers*, ed. Malden, but it is essential also to study the business memoranda of the firm, which remain unprinted among the *Chancery Miscellanea*. Another collection of fifteenth century letters, *The Stonor Letters and Papers*. ed. C. H. Kingsford, affords some supplementary information of the same sort.

[47] *Rot. Parl.*, vol. v, p. 275. See above, p. 12.

[48] C. L. Kingsford, *Prejudice and Promise in Fifteenth Century England*, p. 126.

[49] A sixteenth century (c. 1582) document says that Cornish wools " nowe ar verye good and moch bettere and plenty fullere then in tymes past, when yt boere the naeme of Cornyssh heare, then beynge so herye & cores by the wylldnes of the Contre and evell chessynge & myssarderynge and tymynge thear sepe [? shepe] and land." *S.P.D.*, *Eliz.*, vol. clvii, No. 3, quoted in *Tudor Econ. Doc.*, vol. i, p. 194. Cornish wools are mentioned with other coarse wools in a document relating to export early in the fifteenth century ; see below, note 56.

[50] See above, p. 45, note 28. This treatise (*MS. Cott. Vesp. E IX*, ff. 86–110) is a sort of merchant's handbook. It may have been drawn up by a Stapler, because it contains a great deal of detailed information about prices, expenses, and methods of reckoning in the wool trade. That part of it which deals with weights and measures has been printed in *Select Tracts and Table Books relating to English Weights and Measures* (1100–1742), ed. Hall and Nicholas, pp. 12–20.

[51] *MS. Cott. Vesp. E IX*, ff. 106d–107.

[52] A Leyden ordinance of 1415 (Posthumus, *Bronnen*, vol. i, p. 93) orders merchants to buy wool of high value such as Colswout, Braeschier, Lindzade, Kesteven, Lindza-Mersch, Notegham, Werverieschier, Noort Hollant, and other wools of high price, which are priced highest by the Staple " ; and among the ordinances of the Leyden weavers in 1436–7, is a regulation that the finest cloth called *puyken* should be made only from " Mersch " wool. Ibid., vol. i, p. 156. In *Rot. Parl.*, iv, p. 126 (1420), Cotswold, Kesteven, Lindsey, and the wools of the Welsh March are classed as the best.

[53] *L.T.R. Cust. Accts.*, 22 ff., 70–2, *passim*.

[54] *Rot. Parl.*, vol. iii, pp. 323–4.

[55] *Rot. Parl.*, iv, p. 251.

[56] *Parliamentary and Council Proceedings*, Chancery, 13. This document gives a useful list of the counties producing coarse wools ; Northumberland, Cumberland, the Bishopric of Durham, Westmoreland, Norfolk, Kent, Sussex, Devonshire, Cornwall, Suffolk, Surrey, Cambridge, Essex, Wilts, and Dorset. It is undated, but belongs to the end of the fourteenth or the beginning of the fifteenth century.

[57] In *E.C.P.* 194/19, reference is made to a bargain for " certeyn sakks of Wolle of the growyng of Banbury Contre, every sakk for xi marcs, and it was covenaunted and agreed that the same wolle shuld rise ij sakks of good wolle and one of myddell woll ". Another kind of arrangement is found in a contract between Richard Cely and the wool-dealer John Busshe of Northleach in 1476, for " xl sacke of good cottys wolle woll, good woll and midde wolle of the same pryse, the sacke of bothe good and midde xii markes xxd. The refuse woll for the cost to John busche". *Chanc. Misc. B.* 37/11, f. 19. The difference in value of good and middle wool may be calculated from a note of a sale made by Cely to a Dutch merchant on 18th September, 1480, where " good cotes " is rated at 19 marks the sack and " midde cotes " at 13 marks. Ibid., 37/12, f. 3. Stonor's apprentice, Henham, writing to inform his master of the safe arrival of their wool at Calais (1st May, 1476), says : " Yeff hyt plesse your maysterschipe ffor to understone of your wollys houne maney I have resayvid : Summa xxx sarplers ffyne Cottes wolle, and of M[iddle] Cottes x Sarplers and off ffyne yonge Cottes wolle vij sarplers and of M[iddle] yonge Cottes iiij sarplers and a sarpler of Refuse, Summa ij sarplers." *Stonor Letters*, ii, p. 4.

[58] See the *Cely Papers*, *passim* ; Schanz, *Englische Handelspolitik gegen Ende des Mittelalters*, ii, pp. 320, 331 ; *E.C.P.* 84/585 ; Smit, *Bronnen*, vol. i, 615 (distinction between " Endewolt " and " Cliftwolt ").

[59] Thus 3,880 woolfells arrested on a Poole boat for non-payment of customs were classed as " somer ware ", valued at 35*s*. per 100, " wynter ware ", 26*s*. 8*d*. per 100, and " shorlyng and morlyng " 10*s*. per 100. *K.R. Memo. Roll.*, Mich., 34, Hen. VI, m. 25.

[60] How careful the grading was may be seen from some of the valuations of wool arrested for non-payment of customs or some other breach of the law. These valuations

were made on oath by wool merchants or wool packers; for example, a consignment of "12 pokes of wool and a fardel of woolfells and 8 small bundles of woolfells", found in a barn at Barking, ready for smuggling to Holland, were valued by four wool merchants in the port of London. They had the wool and woolfells sorted according to quality and repacked into a sarpler of " good wool of the March of Wales ", valued at £8 the sack, a sarpler of " Midelwolle " also of the March of Wales, valued at 8 marks the sack, a sarpler of " Refuse flees ", valued at 4 marks the sack, a sarpler of " Clift wolle of divers counties ", valued at the same, two sarplers of wool called " lokes ", valued at 4 marks the sack, a fardel and 8 bundles of woolfells called " Mordyns ", of which 150 were valued at 60s. and 151 at 30s. *K.R. Memo Roll.*, Mich., 23, Hen. VI, m. 9.

[61] See Smit, *Bronnen*, vol. ii, pp. 716, 721, 740, 742, 803, 807, 810-11, 830, 889, 891.

[62] *Rot. Parl.*, vol v, p. 149, and compare *C.P.R.*, 1436-41, pp. 384, 409, 412, the former 1449 and the latter 1440.

[63] See Smit, *Bronnen*, ii, pp. 964-6, for the account of exports from Newcastle-on-Tyne from 10th May, 1461 to 18th Feb., 1462. From Sandwich between 17th Nov., 1475 and 17th Nov., 1476, there were exported, besides some twenty-two sacks of wool and 8,220 woolfells, " 3110 quarters of *lambwoll* and *pelwool*, each qr. weighing 5 lbs. wool, where of 500 called *lamfele* and *mortkyns* and 645 called *milkfell* and 900 lbs. of wool called *lamwol* and 14 dozen woolfells called *mortkyns* and *mesanz*, containing 168 fells [in all equal to 50¼ sacks 10 cloves and 53 fells] " all exported by native merchants to the Staple. *L.T.R. Cust. Acct.* 22, f. 68r.

[64] " Item, lambe fells is good merchaundyse yf thei be Perschelettes, that is to say the slauuter from Ester to Myghelmas, so that thei be parckyd, that is to say well dryed and spred owe the legges and the necke, as they owe to be. The Lumberdes have bowght of thame for 1jd. ob j pece, that is ij s vj d the dossyn and xxvs the C., etc. Also the Schrofftyde slawter of lambefells ys worth xs, xij s and marke itt ys well sold the C, and the Lumberdes by theym and haue them with galeys and Carykks att Sandwyche." *MS. Cott. Vesp. E IX.*, f. 104.

[65] See *Chan. Misc.* 37/12.

[66] *Test. Ebor.*, vol. ii, p. 56. In *E.C.P.* 16/592 is a petition from John Russell's executors relating to Lindsey wool bought in partnership by Russell and a York merchant, John Bolton.

[67] *K.R. Var. Accts.*: *Foreign Merchants*, 128/30, mm. 2 and 10.

[68] *Rot. Parl.*, vol. iv, p. 359, and *Stats. of the Realm*, vol. ii, p. 254. For the great Guildhall inquiry of 1458-9, into breaches of commercial regulations, see below, pp. 311-12.

[69] *K R. Memo. Roll.*, Trin. 33, Hen. VI, m. 16.

[70] Ibid., Hil. 36, Hen. VI, m. 17; ibid., Trin. 38, Hen. VI, m. 4.

[71] Ibid., Hil. 36, Hen. VI, m. 27.

[72] Ibid., Trin. 36, Hen. VI, mm. 40, 64, 66; ibid., Mich. 38, Hen. VI, m. 58, Hil. 38, Hen. VI, m. 7.

[73] Ibid., Mich. 38, Hen. VI, m. 32d.

[74] Ibid., Mich. 38, Hen. VI, m. 41.

[75] Ibid., Mich. 38, Hen. VI, m. 51. This is a prosecution for illegal sale of cloth.

[76] Ibid., Trin. 38, Hen. VI, m. 7.

[77] See F. Holt, " The Tames of Fairford," in *Journ. of Brit. Archæol. Assoc.*, vol. 27 (1871), pp. 110-48.

[78] John Fortey, dyer, of Cirencester, and Peter Draper, citizen and ironmonger, executors of John Fortey, late of Northleach, woolman, bring an action against Simon Nory of Florence, 6th Oct., 1460. Guildhall, *Plea and Memo. Rolls*, A 84, m. 5.

[79] *P.C.C.*, Stokton, 25.

[80] *P.C.C. Moore* 16 (William Midwinter), *Wattys* 29 (John Busshe), and *Bodfelde* 38 (Thomas Busshe).

[81] *Chanc. Misc.*, 37/10, f. 12 v, and 37/14, f. 13.

[82] *Stonor Letters*, vol. ii, pp. 18, 22.

[83] *K.R. Memo. Roll*, Trin. 38, Hen. VI, m. 7.

[84] Ibid., Hil. 36, Hen. VI, m. 18.

[85] *C.P.R.*, 1441-6, pp. 80, 150.

[86] *K.R. Memo. Roll*, Trin., 3, Hen. VI, m. 118, John Yong, grocer (26½ sacks); m. 14, John Forster, *pelliparius* (22 sacks 18 nails); mm. 15 and 62, Geoffrey Feldyng, alderman of London (44½ sacks 5 nails); m. 16, Henry Waver, *pannarius* (23 sacks); m. 77, John Worsop, *pannarius* (20 sacks). Ibid., No. 236, m. 26, Thomas Culgreve, *civis et aldermannus Londonie* (34 sacks); m. 30, Hugh Wych, mercer (40 sacks 19 nails); m. 48, John Claymond, draper (50 sacks); m. 59, John Wykes, draper (11 sacks 23 nails);

m. 61d, John Hygdon, grocer (7½ sacks 7 nails); m. 6d, Thomas Keseby, brasier (20 sacks); m. 63, John Bolt, tailor (32 sacks); m. 64, Reginald Langdon, girdler (25 sacks 18 nails); m. 65, Henry Turner, grocer (10 sacks 5 nails); m. 67, William Bray, draper, (17 sacks); m. 68, Thomas Muschangs, mercer (17 sacks); m. 70, Thomas Rede, draper (20 sacks); m. 71, William Lemyng, grocer (20 sacks); m. 76, John Salman, mercer (29½ sacks).

[87] See, for example, the indenture between John Elys, citizen and mercer of London, and Robert Warner of Watlington (Oxon.), woolman, for the purchase of wool (12th Sept., 1478), Camden Misc., xiii, *Suppl. Stonor Letters*, ed. Kingsford, pp. 12-13, and the receipt by Richard Gardener, mercer and alderman of London, and the same John Elys for wool received from the same Robert Warner, 24th Jan., 1476, *Stonor Letters*, ed. Kingsford, vol. ii, p. 1.

[88] A petition in Chancery relates that in February, 1468, John Chester, citizen and woolman of London and Merchant of the Staple of Calais, and Robert Stone, mercer of London, " covenaunted and agreed to marchandize to geder and tobe partners to geder either with oder of such wynnyng and losyng as shuld happe tobe and growe of suche stokke as they both shuld to geder putte forth and occupie." E.C.P., 64/1038.

[89] See the general pardon to a group of London mercers, ten of whom are also merchants of the Staple. C.P.R., 1476-85, p. 243. The famous mercer, Richard Whittington " thrice Lord Mayor of London ", was likewise Mayor of the Staple.

[90] Camden, Misc., xiii, *Suppl. Stonor Letters*, pp. 12-13, and compare a similar indenture between Richard Cely (senior) and William Midwinter of Northleach (24th Nov., 1478), *Cely Papers*, p. 11.

[91] *Chanc. Misc.*, 37/11, f. 19; *Cely Papers*, p. 11.

[92] For example, John Townsend of Lechlade on 14th March, 1456, sold to two Italians wool worth £1,078, of which £356 was to be paid down on that date, £361 at the following Candlemas (2nd Feb., 1457), and £361 at the Candlemas after (2nd Feb., 1458). K.R. *Memo. Roll*, Hil., 36 Hen. VI, m. 18 ; John Lenard of Campden sold John de Ponte 50 sacks 6 cl. on 10th Oct., 1457, payable £111 8s. 10d. at Easter next, and £111 8s. 11d. at each of the following Easters ; John Elmes of Henley-on-Thames, sold to another Italian, 120 sacks on 12th May, 1456, payable by sums of £280 on St. John's Day (27th Dec.) 1458, 1459, and 1460. Ibid., Trin., 38 Hen. VI, mm. 4 and 7. Many other illustrations might be cited.

[93] Ibid., Mich., 38, Hen. VI, m. 43.

[94] Ibid., m. 48.

[95] *Rot. Parl.*, vol. v, pp. 503-4.

[96] Ibid., vol. iv, p. 360. Compare *Cely Papers*, p. 102.

[97] *Rot. Parl.*, vol. iii, p. 270.

[98] Ibid., vol. iv, p. 360, vol. v, p. 277. Special commissioners and scrutineers were from time to time appointed to detect wool clacked and bearded contrary to the statutes ; see e.g. C.P.R., 1436-41, pp. 265, 372, 373, 439, 440, 554, 563, ibid., 1441-6, pp. 52-3, ibid., 1461-7, pp. 209, 230. On 24th July, 1448, the Queen received letters patent especially authorising her to export wools clacked and bearded. Ibid., 1446-52, p. 171, and on 6th June, 1475, a group of Florentine merchants, who had lent the king £5,000, received a similar licence, *Fœdera*, vol. v, iii, pp. 62-4.

[99] C.P.R., 1476-85, p. 321 ; *Fœdera*, vol. v, iii, p. 91.

[100] Cal. L. Bk. L., p. 259.

[101] E.C.P. 66/442. Subsequently Croke refused the wool. For other cases of wool alleged not to be up to sample on delivery, see ibid., 20/48, 27/137, and 64/311.

[102] *Cely Papers*, pp. 66, 87, 102. See other references to Breton, ibid., pp. 90, 92; payments to him are occasionally recorded in the unprinted Cely accounts.

[103] K.R. *Memo. Roll*, Hil., 36 Hen. VI, mm. 21, 22, 23.

[104] *Rot. Parl.*, vol. v, pp. 331-2.

[105] Ibid., vol. vi, p. 59.

[106] It is interesting to find John Bolle described as servant to a woolpacker, for about this time he, or a relative of the same name, was engaged in the export of wool. Compare K.R. *Cust. Acct.*, 73/26.

[107] K.R. *Memo. Rolls*, Easter, 33 Hen. VI, mm. 7, 15 ; Hil., 36 Hen. VI, m. 15. For a fuller account of the first of these cases see also K.R. *Cust. Acct.* 83/14.

[108] Ibid., Hil., 33 Hen. VI, m. 27.

[109] Ibid., Hil., 36 Hen. VI, m. 33.

[110] C.P.R., 1476-85, p. 277.

[111] C.P.R., 1476-85, p. 300. Grant for life to Henry Uvedale of the occupation

called "le pressing" or "steuyng" (stowing) of wools within ships at the port of Southampton.

[112] See *Chanc. Misc.*, 36/10, ff. 29-30, and compare the charges noted in *Stonor Letters*, vol. ii, p. 5, and "The Noumbre of Weyghtes", *MS. Cott. Vesp. E IX*, f. 107d, and by Pegolotti in the fourteenth century, Pagnini, *Della Decima*, vol. iii, pp. 260-1.

[113] *Cely Papers*, pp. 160, 162.

[114] *Fædera*, vol. v, iii, pp. 91-2.

[115] *Cely Papers*, p. 146.

[116] The numbers are as follows (1449 signifies November, 1448 to November, 1449, and so for each year) : 199,197 (1449); 254636 (1452); 292,704 (1460); 311,300 (1461); 336,662 (1462), 349,922 (1463), 182,080 (1464), 235,068 (1465), 256,972 (1466), 174,031 (1467), missing (1468), 312,058 (1469), 408,291 (1470), 148,299 (1471), 540,524 (1472), 288,201 (1473), missing (1474), 336,373½ (1475), 404,364½ (1476), 326,433 (1477), 508,721 (1484), 199,396 (1485), 340,324 (1486), 267,378½ (1487). Posthumus, *Bronnen, etc., passim*; and see N. W. Posthumus, *De Geschiedenis van de Leidsche Lakensindustrie* (The Hague, 1908), vol. i, pp. 422 ff. For most years the fells imported from places other than Calais are noted, but the numbers are much smaller. The names of purchasers are given. No wool was registered, but there was a regulation that one sack of wool should be imported for every 300 nobles worth of fells.

[117] See Posthumus, *Bronnen*, vol. i, pp. 46, 72, 74, 92-3, 148-52, 189, 299-306.

[118] See *Cely Papers*, " Sir, here came none Hollanders since you went, but one fellowship of Delft, the which I could sell none fleeces " (Jan., 1482), p. 83. " Sold . . . unto Jacob Tymanson and his fellowship of Leyden 2300 of my new summer fells " (April, 1482) p. 90 ; " I have sold all your fells that lie in the house next Bondman's to master John Johnson and his fellows of Delft for 14 nobles the 100 and half ready money in hand, the rest at Cold mart and Pask next ensuing ; they be not yet delivered. Sir, they desire to borrow £10 or £12 thereof till Balyng [Balms] mart but I would not grant them " (July, 1482), p. 107 ; " I have sold your 3200 and odd fells of Cotswold which came with the last fleet for 14 nobles the 100 to Claysse Peterson and William Ardson of Delft " (Feb., 1483), p. 138 and cp. p. 142 ; " Sold . . . to Adryan Wylliamson, Deryck Deryckson, Garrad Laurencon, Garrad Stevenson, Henryck Ottson, Clarysse Doo and Gyesbryght Moresson of Laythe 1500 Cottes pelts, price le 100, 14 nobles " (April, 1484), p. 151 ; " Vendz the 4th day of Feb. unto Peter Johnson of Delft and his fellowship . . . 3971 Cotswold fells " . . . Vendz the 4th day of Feb. unto Peter Johnson and his fellowship of William Maryon 2624 pells (pp. 171-2) ; " Jacob Williamson and his fellou[ship] of Delft £14 19s. 8d. flemish, John Williamson and his fellow[ship] of Leyden £8 19s." (p. 204).

[119] See, e.g. *Cely Papers*, pp. 172-3, *Chanc. Misc.*, 37/12, ff. 6, 10.

[120] *Cely Papers*, p. 172.

[121] See Posthumus, *Bronnen*, vol. i, pp. 352-3, 425-61, *passim*, 562-9 *passim*, vol. ii, pp. 8-10, 42, and compare pp. 23-4. See also Posthumus, *De Geschiedenis*, etc., ch. iv, for the relations between Leyden and the Staple.

[122] Rymer, *Fædera*, vol. v, pp. 85 ff.

[123] Posthumus, *Bronnen*, vol. i, pp. 568-9.

[124] The process has recently been described by Mr. M. Postan in an article on " Credit in Medieval Trade," in *Econ. Hist. Review*, vol. i (1928), pp. 240-4, 255.

[125] *Cely Papers*, pp. 9, 16, 32-3, 73-81, *passim*.

[126] Ibid., pp. 121-2.

[127] Ibid., pp. 124, 128.

[128] *Le Cotton MS. Galba B.* 1, ed. Scott and Gilliodts van Severen, No. 135. Compare the complaint of the English merchants in 1410, that on the strength of the treaty with Flanders renewed that year, they " surent communicacion en fait des merchandises ouesques les enhabitans du dit paijs de Flandres, en leur apprestans selom la cours de la monde leur leins et marchandises, queux ne purroient ne ne purront estre delivrerez a la verray value pour commune prouffit du toute le Roialme, sans ce que eulx soient apprestez en parcelle." Ibid., No. 127.

[129] Posthumus, *Bronnen*, vol. i, p. 184. Cantelowe's will is in *P.C.C.*, Godyn, 4.

[130] See an excellent example in *Cely Papers*, pp. 147-8.

[131] *Libelle*, ed. Warner, p. 23. Compare the trick mentioned amongst the complaints of the Staplers at the meeting of English and Burgundian envoys to discuss grievances at Lille on 12th July, 1478. In some towns if one Fleming owed another a sum of money it was asserted that the creditor lent the debtor another £20 or £30 or more, the debtor went to Calais and purchased wool partly with the cash thus obtained, and partly on

credit, and took it back; the creditor then had the whole of the wool arrested. *Fœdera*, vol. v, iii, pp. 89-90.

[132] *Chanc. Misc.* 37/11, f. 30, and compare similar transactions printed in *Cely Papers*, pp. 12-13, and *Stonor Letters*, ii, pp. 62-3.

[133] *Cely Papers*, p. 5.

[134] Posthumus, *Bronnen*, vol. i, pp. 46-8, 151, 185, 193-4. Cf. p. 466.

[135] John Feld and Lowes Lyncham often occur in documents of the time; cf. the Staple debenture for £334 1s. 2d., in favour of John (7th May, 1446), in *Chanc. Misc.*, 25/9/17. A letter from Lowes Lyncham written from Calais in 1465 states that he is shipping " 3 barrels of March beer, a pot of butter and a little quiver with shooting tackle for the king ". G. A. C. Sandeman, *Calais under English Rule* (Oxford, 1908), p. 82.

[136] *E.C.P.* 16/369 and 24/247. A Colard de May was a well-known Bruges money changer; the name occurs thirty years later in the Cely accounts (1478): " Item I made with Gilbard Pallman c li. at viiis viiid, summa cxxx li. fl., to be paid May [and] Jowne at eache tyme l li sterling. I writ hym uppon Collard day may l li viiis vid fl. [etc.] " (*Chanc. Misc.* 37/11, f. 3). He seems to have gone bankrupt in 1482: " En 1482 Jean Mettenye, caution de Colard de May, rembourse la ville, qui avait paye quelques creanciers privilégies ". G. Bigwood, op. cit., 1re Partie, p. 421.

[137] Posthumus, *Bronnen*, vol. i, p. 68.

[138] Posthumus, *Bronnen*, vol. i, p. 613.

[139] Ibid., vol. i, p. 614. " Mercatores tam nostri quam vestri super solucionem promptam in manibus habendam ex empcione pellium lanutarum, inter se ut eis placuerit inde ipsos disponant. Sed solomodo et presertim super emptionem lanarum volumus quod veluti desuper ordinavimus in manibus hic in stapula recipiatur."

[140] Ibid., vol. i, p. 615.

[141] Ibid., vol. ii, p. 24.

[142] " Car les Merchauntz de l'Estaple de Calais . . . ne sount comenes achateurs des Marchandises de Flaundres " (1423). *Rot. Parl.*, vol. iv, p. 252; and see above, pp. 16-17.

[143] See above, p. 65.

[144] *Cely Papers*, p. 159. Diego de Castro, " Spanyerd " also occurs, ibid., pp. 161, 163,

[145] Ibid., p. 165.

[146] Ibid., p. 169.

[147] Reprinted from Pauli's edition in *Tudor Econ. Doc.*, vol. iii, pp. 90-114.

[148] *Cely Papers*, pp. 194-6. On another occasion they paid freight for woolfells at 20d. per 100. *Chanc. Misc.*, 37/11, f. 26.

[149] *Chanc. Misc.*, 37/11, f. 19. Elizabeth Stonor writes on 7th November of this year that Betson is loath to forego Elmes' wool, " never the less he thynkithe that xiij markes and a d [i . . .] pryse for to bye lx saks; after that pryce it wold draw myche m[oney] and lytell gettyng suld be therin." *Stonor Letters*, vol. ii, p. 18.

[150] Schanz, *Englische Handelspolitik*, vol. ii, pp. 569-71 (No. 130). For other copies or variants of this document, see *S.P.D.*, Edw. VI, vol. ii, No. 15, and *Var. Accts. : France*, 207/12 and 14.

[151] Schanz, l.c., vol. ii, p. 566 (from a Staplers' petition, c. 1527).

[152] Daumet, op. cit., pp. 134, 167-8.

[153] See *Rot. Parl.*, vol. v, pp. 550-1 (1464).

[154] Daumet, l.c., pp. 141-2. In the Public Record Office there are a number of audited accounts, with particulars relating thereto, of the administration of these revenues of the company under the arrangement of 6 Edward IV. See P. R. O., *Lists and Indexes*, No. xxxv, *List of various accounts and documents connected therewith* (1912), under " France ". Good examples are *Var. Accts.*, France, 196/18, 197/3, 11 and 13, 198/17 and 20.

[155] The cost of the convoy varied. From 14th April, Edw. IV to 15th April Edw. IV it amounted to £331 5s. 7d. *Var. Accts.*: France, 198/8.

[156] *Rot. Parl.*, vol. vi, pp. 55-61, 100-3.

[157] Ibid., vol. vi, p. 59.

[158] See the petition of Richard Conton, merchant of the Staple of Calais, " that where as it was so that a reule and an ordynaunce was made amonge all the hole felaship of the merchaunts of the said Staple that eny merchaunt which had at that tyme any merchaundys ther shuld lende and ley ynto the said Staple the xth peny of the valewe of the samd merchandise to be repeyed of suche money as shuld after that growe of the said Staple. Wherapon your said oratour leyd unto the seid Staple xiij li. xviij s. vijd. for the xth peny of such merchaundises as he had than ther. And thereof had a bill of debentur under the seall of the seid Staple." *E.C.P.*, 59/105 (between 1475 and 1485).

[159] M. Postan, "Private Financial Instruments in Medieval England," *VSWG*. (1930), vol. xxiii, pp. 55-6. For an excellent example of a Staple debenture, see *Chanc. Misc.*, 299, f. 17. For the negotiability of these instruments, see *Cely Papers, passim*. Sir John Sturgeon of Hitchin, citizen and mercer of the Staple of Calais, bequeaths by will (1509), " to the generaltie of the Staple of Calais to be deducted upon my debenters due to me by the said company 40*s*." *P.C.C.*, Bennett, 22.

[160] *MS. Cott. Vesp. E IX*, f. 104.
[161] *Cely Papers*, pp. 36-7 (No. 35).
[162] *Chanc. Misc.*, 37/11, f. 21.
[163] *Cely Papers*, p. 98 (No. 86).
[164] Ibid., pp. 99-100 (No. 87).
[165] Ibid., pp. 100-1 (No. 88). He had already on 23rd April, tried to get payment for these warrants or else to have them written on the bills of custom and subsidy, but the Lieutenant had refused because " there is more to do than may be performed, for the which they shall bring in sterling money into the collectors again and have their payment out of the Treasury ", ibid., p. 96 (No. 84). The " partition of 15*s*. in the pound " had apparently been declared in the previous August, 1481. Ibid., p. 65 (No. 60).
[166] Ibid., pp. 111-12 (No. 96). Compare George Cely's complaint at having to pay the soldiers in sterling in the summer of 1478, when " money is still at Calais 2*s*. 2*d*. lower than it is in Flanders and now sterling money at that. It is too great a loss ; we must suffer it—we may not choose ". Ibid., p. 6 (No. 6).
[167] Ibid., pp. 113-14 (No. 98).
[168] Ibid., pp. 115-16 (No. 100).
[169] Ibid., pp. 118-19 (No. 102).
[170] Ibid., p. 123 (No. 107).
[171] On this subject see Schanz, *Englische Handelspolitik*, vol. i, pp. 481-540, and W. van Ochenkowski, *Englands wirtschaftliche Entwickelung im Ausgange des Mittelalters*, pp. 187-217.
[172] *Rot. Parl.*, vol. iii, pp. 340. There had been previous enactments in 1379 (for every pound's worth of wool sold merchants were to bring 2*s*. in bullion to the mint in the Tower within a year of export), and in 1391 (for each sack of wool the merchants were to bring an ounce of gold to the mint at Calais). *Rot. Parl.*, vol. iii, pp. 66, 285.
[173] Ibid., vol. iii, pp. 369-70.
[174] Ibid., vol. iii, p. 429. See *Treaty Roll*, 1 Hen. IV, m. 16.
[175] *Rot. Parl.*, vol. iii, p. 470.
[176] *Rot. Parl.*, vol. iii, pp. 510, 553-4.
[177] Ibid., vol. iv, pp. 125-6 ; *Stat.* 8 Hen. V, c. 2.
[178] *Rot. Parl.*, vol. iv, p. 146 ; *Stat.* 9 Hen. V, c. 6.
[179] *Le Cotton MS. Galba B* 1, transcribed and ed. E. Scott and L. Gilliodts-van Severen, p. 412 (No. 169) ; date corrected by Smit, *Bronnen*, vol. i, p. 602.
[180] *Rot. Parl.*, vol. iv, p. 252 ; *Stat.* 2 Hen. VI, c. 6.
[181] *Rot. Parl.*, vol. iv, p. 359.
[182] Smit, *Bronnen*, vol. ii, pp. 697-8 (No. 1126).
[183] Ibid., vol. ii, p. 698 (No. 1127).
[184] *Cartulaire de l'ancienne Estaple de Bruges*, ed. L. Gilliodts-van Severen, vol. i, pp. 569, 582-3,
[185] *Foedera*, vol. v, i, pp. 16, 21.
[186] Smit, *Bronnen*, vol. ii, pp. 698-9 (No. 1128).
[187] *Rot. Parl.*, vol. iv, p. 490 ; *Stat.* 14 Hen. VI, c. 2.
[188] Ibid., vol. iv, pp. 485*a*-486*a*.
[189] *E.C.P.*, 112/89. The petition is translated in *English Economic History, Select Documents*, ed. A. E. Bland, F. A. Brown, and R. H. Tawney (1914), pp. 185-6.
[190] *Proc. and Ord. P.C.*, p. 168.
[191] *Rot. Parl.*, vol. iv, p. 508.
[192] Ibid., vol. v, p. 64.
[193] *Treaty Roll*, 22 Hen. VI, m. 13.
[194] *Proc. and Ord. P.C.*, vol. v, pp. 215-17, 219-20.
[195] *Rot. Parl.*, vol. v, pp. 256, 276, 503 ; *Stat.* 20 Hen. vi, c. 12.
[196] E. Varenbergh, *Hist. des relations diplomatiques entre le Compté de Flandre et l'Angleterre au moyen âge*, pp. 521-2.
[197] *Rot. Parl.*, vol. vi, p. 60.
[198] *Fœdera*, vol. v, iii, p. 90.

III

THE ECONOMIC AND POLITICAL RELATIONS OF ENGLAND AND THE HANSE (1400-85)

[1] The references to the Hanse in Chapter I are, when not otherwise stated, based on the accounts in E. R. Daenell, *Die Blütezeit der deutschen Hanse*, W. Vogel, *Geschichte der deutschen Seeschiffahrt*, and D. Schäfer, *Die Hanse*.

[2] W. Stein, *Die Hansestädte*, in Hans. Gbl. (1913-15), Jahrgang, 1913: Erstes Heft, pp. 233-94, Zweites Heft, pp. 519-60; Jahrgang, 1914: Erstes Heft, pp. 257-89; Jahrgang, 1915: Erstes Heft, pp. 119-78.

[3] C. Bahr, *Handel und Verkehr der deutschen Hanse in Flandern*, pp. 57-111; L. K. Goetz, *Deutsch-Russische Handelsgeschichte des Mittelalters* (Hans. Geschichtsquellen, Neue Folge, Band v; Ver. f. Hans. Geschichte; Lübeck, 1922), pp. 30-74; F. Schulz, *Die Hanse und England*, pp. 9-12; A. Schück, *Die deutsche Einwanderung in das mittelalterliche Schweden und ihre kommerziellen und sozialen Folgen*, in Hans. Gbl., Jahrgang, 1930 (1931), pp. 78-89; Bugge, *Der Untergang der Norwegischen Seeschiffahrt* (VSWG, 1904); *Die Lübecker Bergenfahrer*, ed. Bruns (1900), pp. iii-vii.

[4] *Aussenpolitische und innerpolitische Wandlungen in der Hanse nach dem Stralsunder Frieden*, pp. 149, 144-6, and *Die Hanse und die nordischen Länder* in F. Rörig, *Hansische Beiträge zur deutschen Wirtschaftsgeschichte* (Breslau, 1928); E. Daenell, *Holland und die Hanse im 15. Jahrhundert* in Hans. Gbl., Jahrgang, 1903 (1904), pp. 3-41; H. J. Smit, *De Opkomst van den handel van Amsterdam. Onderzoekingen naar de economische ontwikkeling der stad tot 1441.* (Amsterdam, 1914.)

[5] F. Rörig, *Die Hanse und die nordischen Länder*, op. cit., pp. 162-5.

[6] F. Rörig, *Aussenpolitische und innerpolitische Wandlungen*, op. cit., pp. 150-3; W. Stein, *Über die ältesten Privilegien der deutschen Hanse in Flandern und die ältere Handelspolitik Lübecks*, pp. 113-22, in Hans. Gbl., Jahrgang, 1902, pp. 51-133 (1903).

[7] For the growth of the English cloth exports in the fourteenth century, see H. L. Gray, *The Production and Exportation of English Woollens in the Fourteenth Century*.

[8] A. Bugge, *Handelen mellem England og Norge*; idem, *Den Norske Traelasthandels Historie*, pp. 165-6; H.R., 1, viii, Nos. 1167 and 1168; Schulz, op. cit., pp. 13-14; D. Schäfer, *Das Buch des Lübeckischen Vogts auf Schonen* (Hansische Geschichtsquellen, vol. iv) Halle a. S., 1887), p. 93, par. 58; H.R. 1, i, No. 51, par. 11 (p. 470), No. 522, par. 7; U.B. ii, No. 206 (Stralsund, 1312), iii, No. 507; T. Hirsch, *Danzigs Handels- und Gewerbsgeschichte*, pp. 98-100. In 1385, the goods of at least eighty-five English merchants were arrested in Danzig: H.R., 1, iii, No. 404 A, par. 1 (cf. list in B, par. 1).

[9] According to Dr. M. Weinbaum, *Stalhof und Deutsche Gildhalle zu London*, in Hans. Gbl., Jahrgang, 1928 (Lübeck, 1929), pp. 45-65, there were originally two separate settlements in London, that of Cologne and that of the other North German towns.

[10] See below, sections 2 and 3. The customs rates on cloth were: 1s. 2d. per cloth (English), 12d. (Hanse), and 2s. 4d. (other aliens).

[11] See below, p. 152. H.R. 2, iii, No. 669; K.R. Cust. Accts., passim; cf. the lists in H.R. 1, iii, No. 404 A, par. 1, and B, par. 1. Among the London aldermen in the fifteenth century there were thirteen fishmongers as against forty-one mercers, thirty-three drapers, thirty-one grocers, sixteen goldsmiths, thirteen skinners, seven ironmongers, and three vintners; in the fourteenth century there were forty fishmongers. A. B. Beaven, *The Aldermen of the City of London*, vol. i, pp. 329-30.

[12] *Libelle*, ed. Warner, line 420; the Hanseatic trade " is encrese ful grete unto thys londe ". Cotton MSS., Nero, 27; see below, p. 133.

[13] A statement of the claim to reciprocity was already contained in the English complaints of 1379; H.R., 1, ii, No. 212, par. 1.

[14] *Finance and Trade under Edward III*, ed. G. Unwin, *Introduction*.

[15] *Letters and Papers Illustrative of the Wars of the English in France*, ed. J. Stevenson (R. S.), vol. ii, part 2, p. 724, par. 7; *Johannis Capgrave Liber de Illustribus Henricis*, ed. F. C. Hingeston (R.S., 1858), p. 155; *Libelle*, ed. Warner, lines 6-7: " Cheryshe marchandyse, kepe thamiralté, that we be maysteres of the narowe see "; *Political Poems and Songs*

relating to English History (R.S., 2 vols., 1859-61), vol. i, part 2, pp. 282-7. The policy underlying the phraseology of legislation in the late fourteenth and fifteenth centuries is too vast a subject to be treated *en passant*. But a few things may be noted. To begin with, economic legislation is commonly justified by reference to the " bien universelle " of the kingdom (e.g. *Stat.* 14 Hen. VI, c. 2). That the notion of " common wealth " could have an economic meaning is shown by the constant reference to " profit ", " lencrece ", " la prosperité ", " encrece de riches ", " grande richesse " as the subject of legislation. It is also clear that the underlying concept of the " roialme " was national : " Engleterre," " cest terre " (e.g. *Stat.* 4 Edw. IV, c. 2) ; Englishmen rather than king's lieges, " natifs engloys " contrasted to the " persones dautri lange et destranges terres et nacions " (*Stats.* 18 Hen. VI, c. 1, 3 Ric. II, c. 3). It is also clear that the concept of national " wealth " was sometimes linked up with the abundance and prosperity of merchants (" lors esteantz plusours en nombre et de grande richesse ", *Stat.* 27 Hen. VI, c. 2), the accumulation of treasure and, above all, the growth of the navy (*Stats.* 3 Ric. II, c. 3, 4 Hen. V, 2, c. 7, 14 Hen. VI, c. 8, 15 Hen. VI, c. 2-c. 4, 18 Hen. VI, c. 2). In other words, the mercantilism of the fifteenth century, however tongue-tied, knew its text : " the navie and merchandises of this realm " (*Rot. Parl.*, vol. v, p. 31).

[16] *H.R.* 1, vii, No. 594, 2, v, No. 173, 2, ii, No. 65, 2, iii, No. 283, 2, v, Nos. 206 and 263 par. 7 ; *U.B.* viii, No. 285.

[17] The career of Thomas Kent will, it is hoped, soon form the subject of another study ; cf. W. Stein, *Die Hanse und England*, pp. 83-4. Hatcliff began to play a very conspicuous part in the Anglo-Hanseatic relations after the " verdict " of 1468, see below, pp. 132 ff.

[18] *H.R.* 2, ii, No. 65 : " dat de oversten herren namlik de prelaten dis landes nicht willen des dutschen copmans ut dem lande entberen " ; ibid., 2, v, Nos. 206 and 263 par. 7, contain a clear indication of the council's attempts to circumvent the anti-Hanseatic policy of the Commons. For commercial activities of nobles see *L.T.R. Cust. Accts.*, *passim*. Beaufort : Sir J. H. Ramsay, *Lancaster and York*. (Oxford, 1892), vol. ii, p. 34, Hall's Chronicle (1809) : " he standing the chief merchant of wools " (Gloucester's allegation) ; Suffolk : W. J. Haward, *Economic Aspects of the Wars of the Roses in East Anglia, passim* ; Buckingham : *H.R.* 2, iv, No. 25 ; the Yorkist nobles : C. L. Scofield, *The Life and Reign of Edward the Fourth*, vol. ii, pp. 417-20. Not all the noble recipients of export licences necessarily traded on their own account, yet Warwick, Fauconberg, Howard, Northumberland, and Hastings took a hand in trade. Cf. the Hanseatic allegations in *H.R.* 2, vi, No. 97.

[19] *H.R.* 2, i, No. 147 (p. 99), 2, iii, No. 283 : " wy hebben weynich vrende manck den heren unde der gemenheyt " ; *Proc. and Ord. P.C.*, vol. v, pp. 167, 170, 177, 228, 233.

[20] Cf. Stein, op. cit., p. 32.

[21] *H.R.* i, iii, Nos. 317, 318 (Norway). 319 (Skania) ; *U.B.* iv, No. 600 ; *H.R.* 1, ii, Nos. 210, 211, 212, iii, Nos. 102, 103.

[22] *H.R.* 1, ii, No. 212.

[23] *H.R.* 1, ii, Nos. 102, 210, 211 ; *U.B.*, iv, Nos. 645, 647, 674 ; *H.R.* 1, ii, Nos. 224, 225 (1380, not 1381 ?), cf. F. Schulz, op. cit., p. 33.

[24] Ibid., pp. 34-5 ; *H.R.* 1, ii, No. 236 ; iii, Nos. 142, 143 ; *U.B.* iv, Nos. 753, 759, 761, 762, 806, 835, 910, 1054 ; *Hanseakten aus England*, 1275 *bis* 1412, ed. K. Kunze, No. 327 pars. 1-2.

[25] *H.R.* 1, iii, No. 204, § 3, ii, Nos. 309, 329 ; iii, Nos. 197, 404 ; *U.B.* iv, Nos. 849, 850, 888, 933, 934 ; C.C.R., 1385-9, p. 535.

[26] *H.R.* 1, ii, No. 236 ; *U.B.* iv, No. 888. The negotiations took place in Prussia. *H.R.* 1, ii, Nos. 402-6 : " quod ligei mercatores Anglie quicumque liberam habeant facultatem se applicandi cum navibus bonis etc. ad quemcunque partem terre Prussie . . . transferendi ibique cum quaecumque persona libere contrahere et mercari, sicut antiquitus et ab antiquo extitit usitatum ; quod quidem in omnibus et per omnia Pruthenis concessum est in Anglia." The rest of the treaty is devoted to the subjects of claims and jurisdiction bearing directly on the immediate causes of the conflict.

[27] *H.R.* 1, iv, Nos. 124 par. 2, 192 par. 3 ; ibid., Nos. 360 par. 4 (" dat se alle lande mit erem wande vorvullen "), 397 par. 8 (retailing cloth in fairs), v, No. 101 pars. 2 and 3 ; Daenell, op. cit., vol. i, p. 64 ; ibid., n. 1 ; *H.R.* 1, iv, No. 5 : the corporate organization in 1391. The right was not provided in the treaty in spite of the English demands : *H.R.* 1, iii, No. 403 par. 4, cf. F. Schulz, op. cit., p. 51, n. 1 ; *H.R.* 1, iv, Nos. 397 par. 8, 537 pars. 3-6, 100 par. 4, 101 pars. 2 and 3 ; *Hanseakten*, ed. Kunze, No. 322 par. 9 ; F. Schulz, op. cit., p. 45, n. 2 (J. Beby, Governor of the English in 1391).

NOTES TO ENGLAND AND THE HANSE

[28] *U.B.* v, Nos. 386, 387, 391; *H.R.* 1, iv, Nos. 433, 345 par. 2, v, No. 101 pars. 2 and 3.

[29] *H.R.* 1, iv, Nos. 397 par. 19, 413 par. 7, 503 par. 11, 539 par. 6, 541 par. 23, 559 par. 11 (" blibet steende czu gutir geduld "); ibid., v, Nos. 74 par. 2, 83; *Hanseakten*, ed. Kunze, Nos. 317, 326, 329, 334-7, 345, 357, 359, 361; *H.R.* 1, v, Nos. 100 par. 1, 130; *C.C.R.*, 1402-5, pp. 101, 337, 419; *U.B.* v, Nos. 542, 569, 570, 597, 603, 613, 615, 618, 620, 621, 633, 634; *H.R.* 1, v, Nos. 211, 212, 225 pars. 3-5, 15.

[30] *H.R.* 1, v, Nos. 274, 302 pars. 1-15, 308 pars. 1-10, 20, 24, 25, 27, 311 par. 12, 255 par. 5, 262, 275, 659. But the same factory wrote in 1405 that the imports of Hanseatic goods into England and the Low Countries was, in spite of the embargo, so abundant that no shortage was felt (" neyn ghebrek en is "); *H.R.* 1, v, No. 274.

[31] *H.R.* 1, v, Nos. 255 par. 8, 256, 257, 271, 272, 390, 392, 404.

[32] *H.R.* 1, v, Nos. 265-9, 276 par. 4, 296 par. 7, 339 pars. 16-17, 343, 348, 350, 351.

[33] *H.R.* 1, v, Nos. 484, 525, 526, 537; cf. No. 319. That the English tried to sow dissent from the very beginning is clear from *H.R.* 1, viii, No. 1061. The attitude of the Bruges factory was the same all through the period; *H.R.* 1, v, Nos. 313, 392 par. 6, 659.

[34] *U.B.* v, No. 830; *H.R.* 1, v, Nos. 525, 633.

[35] Both sides were influenced by the bad harvest and the high prices for corn in England in 1409: *H.R.* 1, v, Nos. 547, 548, 643; Daenell, op. cit., vol. i, pp. 162-8, 174; *H.R.* 1, v, No. 620; vi, Nos. 24, 114, 195, 304, 500. *K.R. Cust. Accts.*, *passim*.

[36] *H.R.* 2, ii, Nos. 169 par. 3, 318 par. 3.

[37] *H.R.* 1, vii, Nos. 708, 649, 821; viii, Nos. 454, 668; *H.R.* 2, ii, No. 76 par. 25; *H.R.* 1, vii, No. 708 pars. 2-6.

[38] The attempt of the Hanse to enlist the support of the Emperor Sigismund at the Council of Constance ended in a fiasco: *H.R.* 1, vi, Nos. 186, 187, 381, 446 pars. 7-10. Having engineered the appeal to the Emperor, the Bruges contor found it almost impossible to extract from the towns a definite statement of grievances against England: ibid., Nos. 400 par. 21, 450, 451; *U.B.* vi, Nos. 661, 694, 712; *H.R.* 1, viii, Nos. 218, 240 par. 3, 414, 507, 508 A, 775, 777, 784, 794, 1167; *H.R.* 2, i, Nos. 53, 105. Until the outbreak of the Dano-Wendish war in 1427, the mutual attacks and arrests were not as frequent or important as alleged in the English and Hanseatic complaints at the time, e.g. *U.B.* vi, Nos. 187, 418, 447, 635, 934. The most important were: the arrest of the Hanseatic boats in 1417 (*H.R.* 1, vi, No. 451, where it is much exaggerated) and the arrest of the English in Greifswald in a dispute twenty years old: *H.R.* 1, vi, Nos. 556 A par. 57, 581, 582, vii, No. 592 par. 7.

[39] *H.R.* 1, v, Nos. 655, 674; vii, Nos. 592 pars. 1-6, 593; viii, No. 452 pars. 1-2; ibid., 2, ii, Nos. 76 par. 20, 169 pars. 2-3.

[40] *H.R.* 1, vii, Nos. 87, 88; *U.B.* vi, No. 238; *H.R.* 1, vii, Nos. 592-4; *U.B.* vi, No. 528, and *Entry Book*, ii, f. 3 (Archives of the Corporation of King's Lynn); *U.B.* vi, Nos. 474, 475, 479, 482, 613, 643, 611, 612, 651, 504, *Proc. and Ord. P.C.*, vol. iii, pp. 110-11; *H.R.* 1, vii, Nos. 609 par. 6, 671.

[41] *H.R.* 1, vii, Nos. 461 pars. 1 and 19, 708, 746, 773 pars. 7-8, 800, 821; ibid., Nos. 609 par. 6, 611, 623, 624 par. 5.

[42] *H.R.* 1, viii, p. 358 n. 5; *U.B.* vi, No. 767, n. 1; Smit, *Bronnen*, vol. i, No. 1012, p. 627, n. 1; *U.B.* vi, Nos. 533, 764, 767; cf. *H.R.* 1, viii, Nos. 451, 611, 777, 784, 794; *Rot. Parl.*, iv, p. 303 (27); *C.P.R.*, 1422-9, p. 346; *U.B.* vi, Nos. 651, 658; *L. Bk. K.*, f. 33 (MS.); *U.B.* vi, No. 723; *H.R.* 1, viii, Nos. 32, 433 par. 10, 453 par. 2, 546 par. 7; *U.B.* vi, No. 888; cf. the Danzig account of the active trade and privileged position of the English in Prussia; *H.R.* 1, viii, Nos. 454, 668.

[43] *Rot. Parl.*, iv, pp. 366, 389, 426, 503; *U.B.* vi, Nos. 942, 991, 992, 1005, 1011, 1021, 1046, 1061; *H.R.* 2, i, Nos. 146, 147, 168, 319; *U.B.* vi, No. 1065; *H.R.* 2, i, Nos. 146, 147, 168, 319; *U.B.* vi, No. 1065; *H.R.* 2, i, Nos. 169, 241, 192, 321 pars. 1-3, 324, 355 pars. 1-7, 356, 357; *U.B.* vi, No. 1099; *H.R.* 2, i, Nos. 319, 320; *Rot. Parl.*, vol. vi, p. 493.

[44] *H.R.* 2, i, Nos. 383-5, 406, 407, 421, 429-32, 435, 437.

[45] *H.R.* 2, i, No. 436, Ramsay, op. cit., vol. i, pp. 475-80; *H.R.* 2, i, No. 522. The problem of English cloth trade in Flanders had become acute again in 1433 and 1434; *H.R.* 2, i, Nos. 191, 192, 215, 268 par. 13, Smit, *Bronnen*, vol. ii, p. 668, footnote 2; *H.R.* 2, i, No. 567: " up date men yo von hynnen eyne side vrii hadde to besoken ", cf. Daenell, op. cit., vol. i, pp. 376-8; *H.R.* 2, i, Nos. 501, 568, 563, 577; ii, Nos. 4, 19, 25-8, 31, 37, 65, 70.

[46] *H.R.* 2, ii, No. 16, 4: " Doch hadden de stede vor 200 jaren, eer dat lant to Prusen

cristen was, in vel enden vryheit unde privileje von den kopman vorworven, de hope se wol to beholden, al moten se darumme lyden"; *H.R.* 2, ii, No. 53, and p. 14.

[47] *H.R.* 2, ii, Nos. 29, 46, 63, 65-8, 70, 73, 79, 84. According to the Hanseatic version, the opposition to the ratification was led by the merchants of the "nortcost" anxious " ere laken dar . . . bringen und allene den markt holden"; *H.R.* 2, ii, No. 71, also Nos. 67 and 73. On Beaufort's action, see *H.R.* 2, ii, p. 15; *H.R.* 2, ii, Nos. 220, 224, 226.

[48] *H.R.* 2, ii, Nos. 539 par. 2, 540 par. 1, 647 par. 1. The documentary evidence of a separate agreement regarding the status of the English in Prussia, if it existed, would have been seized by the "Bergenfahrer" together with the other documents of the English delegation; *H.R.* 2, iii, No. 687. *The Antient Kalendars and Inventories of the Treasury of His Majesty's Exchequer*, ed. Sir F. Palgrave (1836), vol. ii, pp. 213 and 221, refers to the original of the Anglo-Prussian *appunctamentum* in the hands of the delegation. Cf. the instructions to the English delegation to Utrecht in 1473: *H.R.* 2, vii, No. 22 par 11.

[49] It is hardly possible to speak, as Professor Pirenne does, of the continued economic peace between England and Burgundy from 1439 onwards: H. Pirenne, *Histoire de Belgique* (Brussels, 1903), vol. ii, p. 233. Yet it remains broadly true that from the mid-fifties onwards the English trade to Brabantine fairs and to Middelburgh was rarely interrupted. See below, footnotes 70, 72, 108.

[50] *H.R.* 2, iii, Nos. 647, 669 : "so schiffet man abir di gutir kyn lubeke, dormete krigen si di fart und gedeyen."

[51] *H.R.* 2, ii, Nos. 318, 346, 380, 539, 644 ; *Proc. and Ord. P.C.*, vol. v, pp. 167, 170, 177 ; *Rot. Parl.*, vol. v, pp. 64-5.

[52] *H.R.* 2, ii, Nos. 314, 570 par. 2, 318 par. 3; 638, 639, 647, 655, 682; ibid., Nos. 434 (date ?), 458, 325, 329 ; ibid., iii, No. 536.

[53] *Rot. Parl.*, vol. v, p. 24. Most of the English chronicles stress the anti-foreign legislation of the parliament.: *Chronicles of London*, ed. C. L. Kingsford, p. 146 ; Caxton, *Polychronicon*, chap. 22. The chronicles abound with stray references to Gloucester's party in the City in connection with the disorders of 1425 : *Incerti Scriptoris Chronicon Angliæ de Regnis Trium Regum Lancestrensium, Henrici IV, Henrici V, et Henrici VI*, ed. J. A. Giles (1848), p. 7, " cives Londonie favebant parti ducis," *Chronicles of London*, op. cit., p. 76, " to stande by the Duke of Gloucestre . . . and . . . agent the Byshop of Winchestre " ; cf. also p. 83 (Gloucester organizing military protection for himself in the City), and p. 81 (popular opposition to Beaufort). Direct evidence of the existence of a definite Gloucester party in the City at the time of the Cobham trial is lacking, yet the events of that year combined in a significant manner ; cf. Caxton's assortment : Eleanor Cobham's trial, the affray between the Court and the men of London, the struggle of parties in the City, and the distribution of titles among Suffolk's followers.

[54] Of the sponsors of the petition of 1441 (*Proc. and Ord. P.C.*, vol. v, pp. 167, 170, 177), two at least, Thomas Kymberley and John Hatterby, had personal claims against the Hanse : *H.R.* 2, ii, Nos. 539 par. 7, and 644 par. 42.

[55] *Rot. Parl.*, vol. v, p. 59. At the same time the Parliament definitely swept away the older legislation for the keeping of truce on the high seas : *Stats.* 2 Hen. V, 4 Hen. V, 14 Hen. VI, c. 8, 15 Hen. VI, c. 2-c. 4, 20 Hen. VI, c. 11.

[56] Caxton, *Polychronicon*, chap. 24 ; *Rot. Parl.*, vol. v, p. 65. Cp. Suffolk's speech in *Proc. and Ord. P.C.*, vol. vi, p. 33 : " language is sowen upon me in London." *HR*, 2, iii, p. 150, footnote 1, Nos. 265, 267, 283.

[57] *H.R.* 2, iii, Nos. 283, 286, 287, 294, 295 ; ibid., p. 164, n. 1 ; ibid., Nos. 479, 289, 317 par. 2.

[58] *H.R.* 2, iii, Nos. 479, 460, 464 ; ibid., Nos. 288, 289, 293, 308, 317-19, 353, 402 ; ibid., Nos. 480-7 ; ibid., Nos. 475, 488 ; ibid., 503-5 ; cf. Stein, op. cit., pp. 27-37 and p. 37, n. 2.

[59] *H.R.* 2, iii, Nos. 530, 531, 533, 535 ; *Paston Letters*, No. 68 ; Stein, op. cit., pp. 48-51. Winnington's commission for the guarding of the seas was dated 3.4.1449 (*Letters and Papers illustrative of the Wars of the English in France*, vol. i, p. 489), but his fleet was not a new venture but a direct descendant of the fleets equipped under the act of 1442.

[60] *Libelle*, ed. Warner, lines 326-7 ; cf. A. Agats, *Der hansische Baienhandel* (Heidelberg, 1904), pp. 25-6, 38 ; his assertion that Lübeck's trade was relatively unimportant is not borne out by the evidence ; *H.R.* 2, iii, Nos. 531, 638, 647, 669, 670. Very characteristically Hans Winter associates Thomas Kent with the party on the council accused of the capture. The same party, he thinks, was responsible for all the

NOTES TO ENGLAND AND THE HANSE

ills of the time. The king himself was not to blame, considering that he " is very young and inexperienced and watched over as a Carthusian "; cf. Stein, op. cit., p. 47, n. 1.

[61] *H.R.* 2, iii, Nos. 531, 535 (postscript), 570, 626; ibid., Nos. 533, 536, 555 par. 2, 557, 559. The English merchants in the Low Countries had to shoulder the responsibility for the capture of the Flemish and Dutch boats; *H.R.* 2, iii, No .560; Caxton, *Polychronicon*, chapters 25 and 26.

[62] *H.R.* 2, iii, Nos. 591, 563, 569, 570, 572; iv., No. 103; *U.B.*, viii, No. 100. According to *H.R.* 2, iii, No. 569, the privileges were restored to the Hanse, though not in full, in the early autumn. The exclusion of Danzig, unlike that of Lübeck, from the grant proved to be a mere formality, as the subsequent negotiations with Prussia and the safe-conducts clearly indicate; cf. below, n. 68.

[63] *H.R.* 2, iii, Nos. 638, 647, 669, 670. Winter was working hard to embroil Prussia with Lübeck and may well have been in the English pay. He himself constantly paraded his connections with high English functionaries.

[64] *H.R.* 2, iii, No. 555, par. 1, alleges the pressure of " other estates ", but cf. the attitude of Prussian towns themselves in ibid., Nos. 607, 574, 608, 651; cf. ibid., Nos. 638, 647, 669, 670; Stein, op. cit., pp. 54-8.

[65] *Die Lübecker Bergenfahrer*, ed. Bruns, p. 352, par. 18; *H.R.* 2, iii, No. 638; *U.B.*, viii, Nos. 1, 6. On Kent's and Stocker's flight, cf. Stein's version, Stein, op. cit., p. 76.

[66] *U.B.*, viii, Nos. 20, 21, 84 (especially pars. 1-50), 215, 780; *Three Fifteenth-century Chronicles*, ed. J. Gairdner (Camden Society, new series, 28, 1880), p. 71. See below, n. 70.

[67] *H.R.* 2, iii, No. 709, especially par. 8; *U.B.*, viii, Nos. 40, 47; *H.R.* 2, iii, Nos. 636, 654; iv, Nos. 19, 21, 41, 46; *U.B.*, viii, No. 87; ibid., No. 79; *H.R.* 2, iii, No. 662; ibid., No. 663; iv, Nos. 14, 20, 23, 24, 51 par. 3, 80; *U.B.*, viii, Nos. 261, 264.

[68] *H.R.* 2, iv, Nos. 55, 78 par. 3, 100, 102, 114, 122, 135, 168, 176, 127, 196 par. 32; 235, 248 par. 8, 263, 304; *U.B.* viii, Nos. 180, 280, 281 (p. 117) n. 1, 285; Stein, op. cit., pp. 79-89; *H.R.* 2, iv, Nos. 69-71, 80, 87, 101, 105, 106, 159, 160, 174, 176, etc.; *U.B.*, viii, Nos. 137, 140, 149, 171, 174, 178, 249, 261, 264, 305.

[69] *H.R.* 2, iii, No. 693 par. 1: 694 par. 1: 695 par. 1: ibid., No. 694 par. 12: iv, Nos. 16, 51 par. 3, 101, 133, 236, 354, 355; *U.B.*, viii, Nos. 27, 46; *H.R.* 2, iii, Nos. 567, 697; iv, Nos. 235, 236, 238, 399, 400, 401, 450-2; *U.B.* viii, Nos. 574, 754. The proclamation of truce (*H.R.* 2, iv, No. 452) did not involve the restoration of privileges but even the suspension of the privileges could not stop the Hanseatic merchants from coming to England: *U.B.*, viii, No. 100 (1451). On all these problems, cf. Stein, op. cit., pp. 89-90 and 109-25; his explanation of Lübeck's change of attitude is hard to check, and a different hypothesis is suggested by the evidence in *H.R.* and *U.B.*, e.g. *H.R.* 2, iv, Nos. 101, 105, 106. The same applies to Stein's explanation of the Prussian attitude, which was Danzig's as well as the Order's (cf. above, n. 64). What counted a great deal with the Prussians was the fear, freely admitted, that they could not afford to quarrel with both Burgundy and England at the same time: *H.R.* 2, iv, Nos. 693 pars. 2-3, 694 pars. 2-4.

[70] The political truce of four years concluded in 1447, was not interrupted by Philip's measures against English cloth. It was very nearly broken by the Bay capture, but was saved by the payment of compensation and renewed in 1451. *H.R.* 2, iv, Nos. 666-9; *U.B.*, viii, Nos. 769, 780. Prussian attitude: Smit, *Bronnen*, vol. ii, pp. 849 (footnote 1), 883 (footnote 1). The relations up to 1464: ibid., No. 1412, p. 903, footnote 1, No. 1541, p. 981, footnote 1. *H.R.*, 2, iv, No. 670; *U.B.* viii, No. 772.

[71] *H.R.* 2, v, Nos. 146, 117, 147, 173, 263 pars. 3, 10, and 32, 712 par. 8. The English programme went even beyond the treaty of 1437, and included the demand that the Hanseatics should not be allowed to import goods from the Bay and the Low Countries; *U.B.* viii, No. 1067; *H.R.* 2, v, Nos. 161, 165, 167, 168, 169, 176-9, 206; *H.R.* 2, v, Nos. 179, 263, 284, 537, 646, 647, 649, 655, 769, 770; *U.B.*, viii, Nos. 1110, 1116, 1117; ix, Nos. 71, 211, 212.

[72] *H.R.* 2, v, Nos. 176, 177, 218, 285, 327, 318, 542, 543, 548, 568, 583, 643, 644, 659-66, 693, 712 pars. 7, 9-12, and 36, 713-16, 719, 720, 731; *U.B.* ix, Nos. 253, 387; *H.R.* 2, vi, Nos. 53-5, 87; *U.B.* ix, Nos. 415, 433. A good measure of Hanseatic anxiety is given in the letters of the Bruges factory and of Hamburg: *U.B.* viii, No. 1190, and *H.R.* 2, v, No. 719. Relations with Burgundy in 1464-5 were upset by the tightening up of the anti-English cloth regulation and the migration of the Merchant Adventurers to Utrecht: Stein, *Die Merchant Adventurers in Utrecht* Hans Gbl. 1899; Smit, *Bronnen*, vol. ii, No. 1543; *U.B.*, ix, p. 91, footnote 4. But the trade to the Low Countries was not really interrupted for more than nine months.

[73] *H.R.* 2, vi, No. 87, " de sake nu kortes met deme selven heren konynge und deme heren hertogen van Burgundien in sunderlinges bestant und vruntschop gestalt

syn und dagelik mer gestalt werden, so dat de Engelschen deshalven den copman van der hense des de myn achten sullen"; *Fædera*, vol. xi, pp. 591-9; *H.R.* 2, vi, Nos. 97, 99, 103, 111, 119, 162, 165, 185; *U.B.*, ix, No. 467, 482, 526, 527, 530; *H.R.* 2, vi, No. 111; *U.B.*, ix, Nos. 468, 471, 476, 521, 524, 570; *U.B.*, ix, No. 467 pars. 1-4.

[74] *H.R.* 2, vi, No. 97, gives the names of Warwick, Northumberland, Fogge, and the Archbishop of York among those involved in the Danish capture, and further investigation would reveal names of other nobles. Thus Richard Outlaw, the nominal owner of the "James" and the "Mary" of Lynn (*U.B.*, ix, No. 478) captured by the Danes, was closely connected with Howard: Haward, op. cit.; *U.B.*, ix, No. 478; ibid., Nos. 431, 490, 497, 501-7, 511, 549, 554; ibid., No. 525 (clothworkers).

[75] *H.R.* 2, vi, Nos. 114, 115, 164, 182, 222, 356 par. 74, 106, 114, 115, 358; *U.B.*, ix, Nos. 479, 603, 698, 699. Cologne cultivated the friendship of the pro-Hanseatic party: the Bishop of York, the Privy Seal (the Bishop of Rochester), Master Lamport and Master Hatcliff. The latter was to play an important part in preparing the peace of 1474. Cf. *H.R.* 2, vi, Nos. 219 and 592, 223; *U.B.*, ix, No. 699.

[76] *H.R.* 2, vi, Nos. 161, 184 pars. 47-74, 185 pars. 11 and 22; 202, 221 pars. 21, 24, and 25, 283. Once the breach had become inevitable, it was to Danzig's interest to make the stoppage of trade as complete as possible. *H.R.* 2, vi, Nos. 356 pars. 61, 62, 58, 72, 73; ibid., No. 360; ibid., Nos. 418-20.

[77] *H.R.* 2, vi, Nos. 283, 321, 322-4, 316, 316a, 347; *U.B.*, ix, Nos. 691, 692; *H.R.* 2, vi, Nos. 317, 331 pars. 2-4; 352, 362, 371. It is interesting to note the fluctuations of the Burgundian policy on the Anglo-Hanseatic issue with the ups and downs of the Yorkist fortunes in England. *H.R.* 2, vi, Nos. 418, 420, 434, 444, 509, 531. The naval war definitely turned to England's favour in the late summer of 1472: *H.R.* 2, vi, No. 558; *U.B.*, x, p. 83; cf. Schulz, op. cit., p. 120.

[78] *H.R.* 2, vi, Nos. 547, 481 par. 1, 589. On the development of the southern route, see Daenell, op. cit., vol. ii, pp. 111, 112, 145. Prussian goods had been imported from Flanders during the previous conflicts: *H.R.* 2, ii, No. 4, *K.R. Cust. Acct.*, 73/25. For Prussian goods so imported, see *K.R. Cust. Accts., passim*. *U.B.*, ix, No. 541 contains a Prussian complaint that at the time of the 1468 conflict there came to England "eyn floet van schipen ut Selant mit onsen nacien gueder tegen onseen wyllen". In the following year it was alleged that the English traded freely in the Low Countries "und dar allerley ware glik hir bynnen landes kopen und vorkopen", *H.R.* 2, vi, No. 283; Smit, *Bronnen*, vol. ii, No. 1628. Yet of Baltic goods thus brought in, there was bound to be "a dearth and a shortage"; e.g. bowstaves, *Stat.* 4 Edw. IV, c. 2. A similar situation had arisen in 1450, when, during the interruption of trade following the capture of the Bay fleet, Prussian goods were imported from the Low Countries and rose in price: *H.R.* 2, iii, No. 670, cf. below, n. 109.

[79] *H.R.* 2, vi, Nos. 547, 594. The English representatives in the preliminary peace negotiations of 1472, made it clear that on the question of peace "sze in Engelant in twen partien ryden": *H.R.* 2, vi, n. 550. In May, 1472, London was still against peace, but "de anderen van den Engelschen begeren vrede": ibid., No. 547. A month later the report was that "in Engelant begheren se al pays to hebben myt den Duitschen": ibid., No. 594. On the attitude of the towns, see ibid., vii, No. 103.

[80] *H.R.* 2, vi, Nos. 315, 331 pars. 2-4, 434, p. 399, n. 1; ibid., vii, No. 22 par. 7, "because divers persones of their nation and company have acquitted themselves thankfully towards his highness at the time of his great business." From the very beginning of his reign Edward tried to obtain political support from the Hanse in exchange for the confirmation of their privileges: *H.R.* 2, v, No. 147. To what extent Edward's attitude was affected by the fear of an understanding between the Hanse and France it is difficult to say; cf. Daenell, op. cit., vol. ii, p. 124.

[81] *H.R.* 2, vi, Nos. 547, 548, 550, 592, 593, 595, 596, 608, 638, 639, 651. In these negotiations an outstanding part was played by William Hatcliff, who, according to *H.R.* 2, vii, No. 259, "der sake eyn procurator alle tiid gewest isz"; cf. n. 75, *H.R.* 2, vii, No. 103; *U.B.* x, No. 241; *H.R.* 2, vii, No. 22, 30, 34, 37, 43, 103, 105, 106, 259.

[82] *L.T.R. Cust. Accts.* (See App. iii); Schanz, op. cit., vol. ii, p. 28, footnote 1.

[83] *H.R.* 2, vii, Nos. 63, 65, 66, 131, 132, 161, 188, 189, 288, 151, 325 par. 14. Lauffer, *Danzigs Schiffs- und Warenverkehr*, in Zeitschrift des Westpreussischen Geschichtsverein, part xxxiii, tables i and iii; N. Ellinger Bang, *Tabeller over Skibsfart, etc.*, vol. i, pp. 1-50; *H.R.* 2, ii, No. 36, par. 26 (36 boats arrested in 1429).

[84] R. Häpke, *Brügges Entwicklung zum Mittelalterlichen Weltmarkt* (Abhandlungen zur Verkehrs- und Seegeschichte. Band I. Berlin, 1908), p. 63; A. Schaube, *Die*

NOTES TO ENGLAND AND THE HANSE

Wollausfuhr Englands vom Jahre 1273; *Hanseakten,* ed. Kunze, Nos. 365-75 ; Bahr, op. cit. p. 134.
[85] *K.R. Cust. Accts.,* e.g. 76/17, 203/1, 194/19. Commodities : *K.R. Cust. Accts.,* e.g. 73/5, 73/10 (beer, madder), 76/11 (thread), 8/21 (fish). For their countries of origin, see J. B. Hurry, *The Woad Plant and its Dye,* pp. 120-1, 127-31 ; K. Hoyer, *Das Bremer Brauereigewerbe,* p. 194, in Hans. Gbl., Jahrgang, 1913 : Erstes Heft (1913), pp. 193-232 ; G. Bens, *Der deutsche Warenfernhandel im Mittelalter,* p. 63 (madder) ; Bahr, op. cit., pp. 135-6, *Das Buch des Lübeckischen Vogt auf Schonen,* ed. D. Schäfer, pp. xix-lv ; B. Kuske, *Der Kölner Fischhandel vom 14-17. Jahrhundert,* pp. 230-2, in Westdeutsche Zeitschrift für Geschichte und Kunst, Jahrgang 24, Drittes Heft (Treves, 1905), pp. 227-313 ; L. Beck, *Die Geschichte des Eisens in technischer und kulturgeschichtlicher Beziehung* (5 vols., Brunswick, 1884-1903), vol. i, pp. 829-30 ; *Handelsrechnungen des Deutschen Ordens,* ed. C. Sattler (Verein für die Geschichte von Ost- und Westpreussen, 1887), pp. 258, 321, 353 and *passim* (copper).
[86] *K.R. Cust. Accts., passim.* An early fifteenth-century account (51/39) enumerates among the imports the linen of Westphalia, Hainault, Brunswick, and Brabant ; cf. A. Schulte, *Geschichte der grossen Ravensburger Gesellschaft,* vol. iii, pp. 73-86. Hurry, op. cit., pp. 94-104, 176-82 ; *Libelle,* ed. Warner, p. 18 ; Kuske, op. cit., p. 232 ff. ; Smit, *Bronnen, passim*; J. G. van Dillen, *Het economisch Karakter der middeleeuwsche Stad,* (Amsterdam, 1914), pp. 190-3. Smit, *Bronnen,* passim.
[87] *H.R.* 2, iii, Nos. 386, 390, 644 par. 9 ; *K.R. Cust. Accts., passim,* e.g. 76/32, 73/10 ; Sattler, op. cit., pp. 21, 77, 165 ff. ; Hirsch, op. cit., pp. 116, 181, 186 ; *U.B.,* vi, No. 111 ; Caxton, *Polychronicon,* chap. 21 ; *H.R.* 2, vi, No. 26 par. 21 ; Bens, op. cit., pp. 15-16.
[88] *K.R. Cust. Accts.,* e.g. 76/17, 62/4, 10/7 and 8 ; Bugge, *Den Norske Traelasthandels Historie,* p. 27 ; Hirsch, op. cit., p. 116.
[89] Vogel, op. cit., pp. 538-9 ; E. Baasch, *Beiträge zur Geschichte des deutschen Seeschiffbaues und der Schiffbaupolitik* (Hamburg, 1899), pp. 5-7, 197-8 ; *H.R.* 2, ii, Nos. 421, 434 ; *U.B.,* viii, No. 225.
[90] *K.R. Cust. Accts.,* e.g. 10/7 and 8, 96/37 (Reval wax), 62/4, 76/11 ; Hurry, op. cit., pp. 32, 177 nn.
[91] See n. 84 ; Schaube, op. cit. ; Häpke, op. cit., pp. 63-4.
[92] *K.R. Cust. Accts., passim* ; *K.R. Var. Accts.,* 123/37.
[93] *H.R.* 1, viii, Nos. 578 par. 3, 579, 583 ; ibid. 2, ii, Nos. 318 par. 2, 644 pars. 14-15.
[94] *L.T.R. Cust. Accts.*
[95] See n. 8. For Cologners in cloth fleets to the Low Countries, see *K.R. Cust. Accts., passim, H.R.* 2, i, No. 192. Cologners carrying cloth eastwards : *Quellen zur Geschichte des Kölner Handels und Verkehrs im Mittelalter,* ed. B. Kuske, vol. ii, Nos. 23, 24, 30, 69. The Cologners in Frankfurt : ibid., *passim* ; *U.B.,* viii, Nos. 87, 93 ; A. Dietz, *Frankfurter Handelsgeschichte* (4 vols. Frankfurt a. M., 1910-25), vol. i, pp. 60-1, vol. ii, pp. 313-14 ; J. Müller, *Geleitswesen und Güterverkehr zwischen Nürnberg und Frankfurt a. M. im 15. Jahrhundert,* pp. 192-4, in VSWG. Band 5, pp. 173-96 and 361-400. Stein, *Die Hansebruderschaft der Kölner England-Fahrer,* in Hans. Gbl, Jahrg. 1908 ; Smit, *Bronnen,* vol. ii, No. 1076.
[96] Schulz, op. cit., pp. 16, 46 ; Goetz, op. cit., p. 516 ; Hirsch, op. cit., pp. 165, 182, 186, 198 ; *H.R.* 2, ii, Nos. 325 and 329 (Novgorod), *U.B.,* viii, No. 514 (Wilno).
[97] *Die Lübecker Bergenfahrer,* ed. Bruns, pp. xc, xl-lix, xi-xii, 302 (" Englandvarer von Bergen uth Norwegen to Busten vorkerende ") ; *H.R.* 2, ii, No. 354.
[98] *K.R. Accts. Var.* 102/128/37. *Libelle,* ed. Warner, lines 321-3 ; *Quellen,* ed. Kuske, op. cit., vol. i, No. 1160 ; vol. ii, Nos. 264, 265 ; Schulte, op. cit., vol. iii, p. 111 ; *Die Lübecker Bergenfahrer,* ed. Bruns, pp. 131, 150 ; cf. Bens, op. cit., p. 46 ; van Dillen, op. cit., pp. 77-8, 82-4.
[99] *Quellen,* ed. Kuske, op. cit., vol. ii, No. 1160 ; Schulte, op. cit., vol. iii, p. 111,
[100] *L.T.R. Cust. Accts., passim* ; *Hanseakten,* ed. Kunze, p. xxxix, *H.R.* 1, viii. Nos. 909, 921 par. 7 ; *U.B.,* iv, Nos. 998, 1054, 1074 ; *Rot. Parl.,* vol. iii, pp. 272, 281, 294.
[101] *Chancery Brevia Regia or Files :* Tower Series. G. (*Statute Merchant and Statute Staple Certificates), passim* ; *K.R. Accts. Var., passim* ; M. Postan, *Credit in Medieval Trade.* For advances on corn and timber in Prussia and Poland, see Hirsch, op. cit., pp. 232-4.
[102] G. von Below, " Grosshandel und Kleinhandel," in his *Probleme der Wirtschaftsgeschichte* ; see below, p. .
[103] *H.R.* 2, ii, No. 644 pars. 27, 28, 45 ; *U.B.,* viii, Nos. 122-3 ; W. Schmidt-Rimpler, *Geschichte des Kommissionsgeschäfts in Deutschland.* Band I. (Hall a. d. S., 1915), *passim* and pp. 57-61.

[104] K. Engel, *Die Organisation der deutsch-hansischen Kaufleute in England im 14. und 15. Jahrhundert*, pp. 173-7, 199-212.
[105] Ibid., pp. 177-9, 192-6, 221-5.
[106] Walford,
[107] Hirsch, op. cit., p. 100; *H.R.* 2, ii, No. 655 (taxation and jurisdiction); ibid., No. 655 ("prison"). *U.B.*, viii, No. 45; *H.R.* 2, iv, No. 25 (aldermen). Some kind of oath is implied in *U.B.*, viii, No. 76. *H.R.* 1, vii, No. 593 par. 4, presupposes the possession of a coat of arms and a "bannere". In 1428, the English in Danzig describe themselves as a "cumpenye": *U.B.*, viii, No. 451. "Good stone houses," *H.R.* 2, ii, Nos. 380, 539 par. 2.
[108] *Foedera*, vol. iv, i, pp. 67, 107, 125; G. S. van Brakel, Gz., *Die Entwicklung und Organisation der Merchant-Adventurers* in VSWG., Band V (1907), pp. 401-32; Edward III's charter of 1353 contains the earliest reference to an organization of English merchants abroad (Cunningham, *Growth of English Industry and Commerce*, vol. i, p. 623), but the charter of 1407 is the first definite grant to an organization in the Low Countries distinct from the Staple. The charter of 1462 is characteristically restricted to the Merchant Adventurers in the Low Countries, and a petition of 1497 refers to the Brabantine marts as the only important ones. The trade to Brabantine fairs suffered only one severe interruption, that of 1464-5; see above, notes 70, 72. For the earliest reference to the organisation in Prussia, see above, note 27.
[109] *K.R. Cust. Accts.*, *passim*, e.g. London, 76/11 (Barr, Pelican, Swan), 77/3 (Saxby, Coke, Church, etc.; the same to Portugal), 77/1 (Gervoys, Pelican, Green, Barry); Hull: 62/4 and 16.

IV

THE ICELAND TRADE

[1] *The Libelle of Englyshe Polycye*, ed. Sir G. Warner, p. 41.
[2] *Polychronicon Ranulphi Higden Monachi Cestrensis*, ed. C. Babington (2 vols., R.S., 1869), vol. i, p. 322; cf. *Willelmi Malmesbiriensis Monachi Gesta Regum Anglorum, atque Historia Novella*, ed. T. D. Hardy (2 vols., English Historical Society, 1840).
[3] *Ice. Sagas*, p. 426.
[4] Dicuil, *De Mensura Orbis Terræ*, vii (see C. R. Beazley, *The Dawn of Modern Geography*, 3 vols., 1897-1906, vol. i, p. 227). A. S. Green, *Irish History Studies*, first series (1927), p. 10. *Origines Islandicæ*, ed. and trans. G. Vigfusson and F. Y. Powell (Oxford, 1905), vol. i, p. 431. K. Gjerset, *History of Iceland*, p. 26. A. Walsh, *Scandinavian Relations with Ireland during the Viking Period* (Dublin, 1922), p. 31. *Dipl. Island.*, vol. i, p. 481 n.; cf. ibid., vol. ii, pp. 439, 435, 453; *Rotuli Litterarum Clausarum*, ed. T. D. Hardy (Record Commission, 1833), vol. i, pp. 617*b*, 642*b*. *Origines Islandicæ*, op. cit., vol. i, pp. 463, 503. Gjerset, op. cit., pp. 100, 108. A. E. Nordenskiöld, *Facsimile-Atlas till Kartografiens Äddsta Historia*, pp. 52-4, ibid., *Periplus*, p. 92, cf. sailing directions from Iceland to Greenland and to Ireland in Olaf Tryggvason's Saga (thirteenth century), ibid., p. 101.
[5] Beazley, op. cit., vol. iii, pp. 455-6, 495; Gjerset, op. cit., p. 115; H. J. Shepstone, *Solving Greenland's Historic Mystery*, p. 415 in *Discovery*, vol. 6, No. 71 (November, 1925), pp. 411-15. There seems no foundation for the assertion in R. Hakluyt, *The Principal Navigations*, vol. i, p. 303, that Blakeney men fished off Iceland *temp*. Edw. III, though they certainly fished off Norway. G. Storm, *Islandske Annales*, p. 207.
[6] *Dipl. Island.*, vol. i, No. 152. Gjerset, op. cit., pp. 230, 235; T. Thoroddsen, *Landfraðissaga Islands* (Hinu íslenzka bókmenntafjelagi; vol. i, Reykjavík, 1892-6), vol. i, p. 101 ff.
[7] A. Bugge, *Studier over de norske byers selvstyre og handel før Hanseaternes tid*, p. 115. (Supplement to Historisk Tidsskrift; No. 16. Norsk Historisk Forening. Oslo, 1899). *Dipl. Island.*, vol. ii, No. 176; *Norges gamle Love*, vol. iii, p. 134. Ibid., vol. iii, pp. 118, 119. *Dipl. Island.*, vol. iv, No. 381. Gjerset, op. cit., p. 257.
[8] A. Bugge, *Den Norske Traelasthandels Historie*, p. 186 ff. Gjerset, op. cit., p. 236; cf. *Dipl. Norv.*, vol. ii, 1, p. 235.
[9] Gjerset, op. cit., p. 243 (i.e. 1343-8, 1361, 1376-80); Bugge, op. cit., p. 194 ff. There is no evidence that the Hanseatics actively developed the Icelandic trade at that time.
[10] *Adamnani, Vita S. Columbae*, ed. J. T. Fowler (1920) p. 156.
[11] Beazley, op. cit., vol. ii, p. 109. e.g. Gjerset, op. cit., p. 26.
[12] *Norges gamle Love*, vol. iii, pp. 118, 119.
[13] Ancient Petition 5100 (? 1383); A. Bugge, *Handelen mellem England og Norge*, pp. 56, 83, 88.
[14] The carving, once sold by the churchwardens, is now to be seen in the Victoria and Albert Museum. Cf. E. M. Beloe, *Our Borough: Our Churches: King's Lynn, Norfolk* (Cambridge, 1899), pp. 82-3.
[15] P. Benjamin, *The Intellectual Rise in Electricity* (1895), p. 113. Ibid., p. 129. Nordenskiöld, *Periplus*, p. 50. W. Vogel, *Geschichte der deutschen Seeschiffahrt*, pp. 520-1. *Libelle*, ed. Warner, p. 41. The fifteenth century "Sea-books" of northern Europe (see e.g. *Sailing Directions for the Circumnavigation of England, and for a voyage to the Straits of Gibraltar*, ed. J. Gairdner, appended to *Tractatus de Globis, et eorum usu. Robert Hues*, ed. C. R. Markham; Hakluyt Society, No. 79, 1889; and *Das Seebuch*, ed. K. Koppmann, Niederdeutsche Denkmäler, vol. i, Bremen, 1876; Verein für niederdeutsche Sprachforschung, Hamburg) show that in the shallow North and Baltic Seas sailors made extensive use of soundings, as Fra Mauro says; cf. Vogel, op. cit., and Nordenskiöld, *ut supra*. Some compasses were supplied to Henry V's warships, but their use seems exceptional; see L. F. Salzman, *English Trade in the Middle Ages* (Oxford, 1931), p. 242.
[16] Bugge, *Handelen mellem England og Norge*, pp. 89-90; E. R. Daenell, *Die Blütezeit der deutschen Hanse*, vol. i, p. 151 ff.

[17] *Ice. Sagas,* pp. 430, 431.
[18] See Daenell, op. cit., vol. i, p. 228.
[19] *Ice. Sagas,* pp. 431, 432, 433, 434. *Literæ Cantuarienses,* ed. J. B. Sheppard (3 vols., R.S., 1887-9), vol. 3, p. 137. *Inventaire-Sommaire des Archives Départementales antérieures à* 1790. *Nord. Archives Civiles. Série B. Chambre des Comptes de Lille, nos.* 1 *à* 1241, ed. A. Le Glay (Lille, 1863), vol. i, p. 329.
[20] *Dipl. Norv.,* vol. xx, part 1, Nos. 733, 755. *Rot. Parl.,* iv, p. 796. *Fœdera,* vol. iv, ii, p. 150.
[21] *Dipl. Norv.,* vol. xx, part 1, No. 749. *Dipl. Island.,* vol. iv, No. 330.
[22] *Congregation Book,* i, f. 84 (Archives of the Corporation of King's Lynn). *Bench Book,* iii, f. 95 (Archives of the Corporation of Kingston-upon-Hull); *Dipl. Island.,* vol. iv, No. 381. See above, p. 155.
[23] *Ice. Sagas,* pp. 435, 436. *Dipl. Norv.,* vol. xx, part 1, Nos. 753, 749. *Dipl. Island.,* vol. iv, Nos. 343, 381.
[24] See, e.g. F. Magnusen, *Om de Engelskes Handel og Færd paa Island i det* 15 *de Aarhundrede,* p. 119. J. Espolin, *Islands Arbaekur í sögu-formi* (Islendska Bókmentafélag, 2 vols., Copenhagen, 1823), vol. ii, chaps. 13, 14.
[25] *Bench Book,* ii, f. 246 ff. (Archives of the Corporation of Kingston-upon-Hull): Raulyn de Bek, Robert Thorkill, J. Pasdale, etc., admitted burgesses.
[26] *Ice. Sagas,* p. 437.
[27] *Dipl. Island.,* vol. iv, Nos. 380, 386. *Congregation Book,* i, ff. 111, 114, 115 (King's Lynn).
[28] *Dipl. Island.,* vol. iv, No. 386. *Congregation Book,* i, ff. 99, 103 (King's Lynn).
[29] Daenell, op. cit., vol. i, p. 231.
[30] Ibid., vol. i, p. 234; but the English did not entirely abandon the trade to Bergen as suggested here. *Congregation Book,* i, ff. 200-1, 247 (King's Lynn), (incorrectly quoted in *Dipl. Norv.*), ibid., ff. 147, 262. Nordenskiöld, *Periplus,* p. 92. *C.P.R.,* 1476-1485, p. 242; cf. p. 178, *Subsidy Rolls, Lay Series,* 192/99, 217/67.
[31] Hakluyt, *The Principal Navigations,* vol. i, p. 111. *Rot. Parl.,* iv, p. 378, *Treaty Roll,* 9 Hen. VI, m. 11. *Congregation Book,* ii, ff. 1, 2, 5, 6, 7, 9, 20 (King's Lynn). Gjerset, op. cit., p. 263. *Dipl. Norv.,* vol. xx, part 1, No. 800. *Fœdera,* vol. iv, p. 177. *Chamberlain's Account Roll,* 11 Hen. VI (Archives of the Corporation of Kingston-upon-Hull). *Stat.* 10 Hen. VI, c. 3.
[32] *Foedera,* vol. v, i, p. 132; *C.P.R.,* 1436-41, p. 315, 1446-52, pp. 137, 474; *Proc. and Ord. P.C.,* vol. iv, p. 208; *K.R. Memo. Roll,* Mich., 9 Hen. VI, m. 19. Ibid. Mich., 13 Hen. VI, m. 5; Mich., 15 Hen. VI, m. 20; Mich., 12 Hen. VI, m. 14; Mich., 18 Hen. VI, m. 19; Trin., 18 Hen. VI, m. 9; Mich., 19 Hen. VI, m. 27; Hil., 19 Hen. VI, m. 82; Mich., 13 Hen. VI, m. 5; Hil., 13 Hen. VI, m. 17 ff.; Easter, 26 Hen. VI, m. 6; Easter, 28 Hen. VI, m. 4; *C.P.R.,* 1436-41, pp. 232, 234, 235; *K.R. Memo. Roll,* Hil., 18 Hen. VI, m. 82; ibid., Hil., 28 Hen. VI, m. 18; Hil., 17 Hen. VI, m. 20; *C.P.R.,* 1446-52, pp. 156, 175; *Exchequer K.R., Extents and Inquisitions, General Series,* 143/22. *K.R. Memo. Roll,* Hil., 14 Hen. VI, m. 12.
[33] *C.P.R.,* 1436-41, p. 572; 1441-6, p. 274. *E.C.P.,* 19/316.
[34] *C.P.R.,* 1441-6, p. 81.
[35] See below, p. 176.
[36] *Treaty Rolls, passim*; for Sandwich, see ibid., 36 Hen. VI, m. 6, for Coventry, ibid., 38 Hen. VI, m. 12; 1 Edw. IV, m. 10; *C.P.R.,* 1436-41, p. 58.
[38] *Foedera,* vol. v, i, p. 75.
[39] C. Eubel, *Hierarchia Catholica medii ævi* (Librariæ Regensbergianiæ, Monasterii, 1901), vol. ii, p. 183. *C.P.R.,* 1422-9, p. 394. *Ice. Sagas,* pp. 437, 439. Magnusen, op. cit., p. 119.
[40] *Dipl. Norv.,* vol. xx, part 1, No. 790. Eubel, op. cit., vol. ii, p. 255. *C.P.R.,* 1436-41, p. 32. *E.C.P.,* 43/278.
[41] *Calendar of the Entries in the Papal Registers relating to Great Britain and Ireland. Papal Letters,* vol. viii, A.D. 1427-47, ed. J. A. Twemlow (1909), p. 499. *Treaty Roll,* 14 Hen. VI, m. 9. *C.P.R.,* 1436-41, p. 58. Ibid., pp. 140, 224.
[42] Eubel, op. cit., vol. i, p. 479 (1913). *Island. Ann.,* pp. 441-3; F. Jónsson, *Historia Ecclesiastica Islandiæ* (2 vols., Havniæ, 1772-4), vol. ii, p. 471 ff. *Dipl. Norv.,* vol. xx, part 1, p. 800.
[43] *K.R. Cust. Acct.,* 61/32. *C.P.R.,* 1436-41, p. 270. *Dipl. Norv.,* vol. xx, part 1, No. 789. *H.R.,* 2, i, p. 318. E. Baasch, *Die Islandfahrt der Deutschen, namentlich der Hamburger, vom* 15. *bis* 17. *Jahrhundert* (Forschungen zur hamburgischen Handelsgeschichte, No. 1, Hamburg, 1889), pp. 6-8.

[44] *K.R. Cust. Acct.*, 19/10.
[45] *Dipl. Island.*, vol. iv, No. 381.
[46] Ibid. Baasch, op. cit., p. 58. *Ancient Petition*, 5,100. *K.R. Memo. Roll*, Mich., 19 Hen. VI, m. 27. *Henry Tooley's Account Book*, f. 99 (Archives of the Corporation of Ipswich. Transcript lent by V. B. Redstone, Esq.). *Rot. Parl.*, iv, p. 79; for the number of men carried, see below, and cf. many refs. in *Ice. Sagas*, *K.R. Memo. Rolls*, etc.
[47] *K.R. Memo. Roll*, Easter, 9 Hen. VI, m. 13.
[48] *Paston Letters*, No. 367.
[49] F. Blomefield, *An Essay towards a Topographical History of the County of Norfolk*, vol. 8, by C. Parkin, p. 104; no authority is given.
[50] For Cromer, see *K.R. Memo. Rolls*, Mich., 19 Hen. VI, m. 27; Mich., 12 Hen. VI, m. 14; Hil., 18 Hen. VI, m. 82; for Cley and Blakeney, see e.g. ibid., Mich., 19 Hen. VI, m. 27, and *Exchequer K.R., Extents and Inquisitions, General Series*, 143/22; for Burnham and Dersingham, *Foedera*, vol. iv, ii, p. 150; for Scarborough, *K.R. Memo. Roll*, 25 Hen. VI, m. 38; for Suffolk, T. Gardner, *An historical account of Dunwich, anciently a city* (1754), p. 145, ibid., p. 248; cf. E. R. Cooper, *A Brief History of Southwold Haven* (Southwold, 1907), p. 4.
[51] Gardner, op. cit., p. 145, "Farra"; *Dipl. Island.*, vol. iv, No. 381. *C.P.R.*, 1436-41, pp. 232, 234, 235.
[52] *The Heart of Lynn*, ed. H. Ingleby, (1925), p. xvi.
[53] *K.R. Cust. Acct.*, 62/7. *Treaty Roll*, 1 Edw. IV, m. 10; *K.R. Memo. Roll*, Mich., 9 Hen. VI, m. 19; *E.C.P.*, 43/278. *U.B.*, vol. ix, p. 467 ff. B. F. De Costa, *Inventio Fortunata. Arctic Exploration with an account of Nicholas of Lynn* (Bulletin of the American Geographical Society, pp. 1-36, New York, 1881), p. 14; cf. *Itineraria Symonis Simeonis et Willelmi de Worcestre*, ed. J. Nasmith, p. 262.
[54] *Stats., Ireland*, vol. i, p. 697. Nasmith, op. cit., p. 4. Nordenskiöld, *Periplus*, p. 101.
[55] *Dipl. Island.*, vol. iv, No. 337.
[56] *Dipl. Norv.*, vol. xx, part i, No. 784.
[57] Gjerset, op. cit., p. 206.
[58] Baasch, op. cit., p. 78 ff. See *E.C.P.*, 43/278, and J. E. Thorold Rogers, *A History of Agriculture and Prices in England* (4 vols., Oxford, 1866-82), vol. iii, p. 310, vol. iv, p. 540 ff. 'The Noumbre of Weyghtes', *MS. Cott. Vesp. E ix*, f 99.
[59] *K.R. Cust. Acct.*, 19/13. *Stats., Ireland*, vol. i, p. 697. *Dipl. Norv.*, vol. xx, part i, No. 789.
[60] *Treaty Roll*, 1 Edw. IV, mm. 15, 27. Ibid., 4 Edw. IV, m. 2.
[61] W. Stein, *Die Hanse und England*, pp. 94-6.
[62] *Foedera*, vol. v, ii, pp. 23, 26; *Treaty Roll*, 28 Hen. VI, m. 2. W. D. Macray, *Report on the Royal Archives of Denmark*, etc., p. 5. *C.P.R.*, 1446-52, pp. 479, 528. *Dipl. Island.*, vol. v, No. 142. *Treaty Roll*, 29 Hen. VI, mm. 12, 14. Ibid., m. 12.
[63] F. Schulz, *Die Hanse und England*, p. 98. *Dipl. Island.*, vol. v, No. 142.
[64] Macray, op. cit., p. 5; *Treaty Roll*, 6 Edw. IV, m. 13. Ibid., 4 Edw. IV, mm. 2, 4, 24; 5 Edw. IV, mm. 4, 7, 8, 19; 6 Edw. IV, mm. 3, 15 ff.
[65] *Annalar Biorns a Skardsa* (2 vols., Hrappseyal, 1774-5), vol. i, p. 50. *Icelandic Sagas*, vol. iv, *The Saga of Hacon, and a fragment of the Saga of Magnus*, trans. Sir G. W. Dasent (R.S., 1894), p. 446, *Caspar Weinreich's Danziger Chronik*, ed. T. Hirsch and F. A. Vossberg (Berlin, 1885), p. 4, *U.B.*, vol. ix, pp. 468, 584. Gjerset, op. cit., p. 266. *U.B.*, vol. ix, p. 467 ff., *H.R.*, 2, vi, p. 97.
[66] *U.B.*, vol. ix, p. 476. Ibid., p. 468. Ibid., pp. 478-82. *H.R.*, 2, vi, p. 111. Macray, op. cit., p. 5.
[67] *Die Lübecker Bergenfahrer*, ed. Bruns, p. 240.
[68] See above, p. 171. Baasch, op. cit., pp. 8, 9, 16. *H.R.*, 3, i, pp. 350-1, 365. Gjerset, op. cit., p. 273.
[69] *C.P.R.*, 1476-85, p. 23. *Dipl. Island.*, vol. vi, p. 66. *H.R.*, 2, vii, p. 348. *C.P.R.*, 1476-85, p. 23. Baasch, op. cit., p. 6. *U.B.*, vol. x, pp. 470, 1201, 489.
[70] *The Reign of Henry VII from contemporary sources*, ed. A. F. Pollard, vol. 2, p. 333.

V

THE OVERSEAS TRADE OF BRISTOL

[1] *Italian Relation of England; A Relation or rather a true account, of the Island of England,* ed. C. A. Sneyd (Camden Society Publications, No. 37, 1847).
[2] W. Hunt, *Bristol*, p. 18. *Bristol Charters*, ed. N. Dermott Harding (Bristol Record Society Publications, vol. i, Bristol, 1930), p. 11, cf. p. 31.
[3] *Notes or Abstracts of the Wills contained in . . . The Great Orphan Book and Book of Wills*, ed. T. P. Wadley, *passim*. *The Great White Book*, f. 80. (Archives of the Corporation of Bristol). See map opposite p. 185.
[4] *The Coventry Leet Book*, ed. M. D. Harris, part 2, pp. 549-50. *Churchwardens' Account Book*, Church of St. Ewen, Bristol, f. 1, W. H. St. John Hope, *On the Early Working of Alabaster in England*, p. 239. (Archæological Journal, second series, vol. 2, 1904, pp. 221-40); cf. L. F. Salzman, *English Industries of the Middle Ages* (Oxford, 1928), pp. 96-7. *The Great White Book*, f. 57 (Bristol).
[5] *G.R.B.*, ff. 18, 23, 210; *The Victoria History of the County of Gloucester*, ed. W. Page, vol. 2 (1907), pp. 219-23; cf. Salzman, op. cit., pp. 4, 37. *Ricart's Kalendar*, pp. 82-3, *G.R.B.*, f. 18; *Rot. Parl.*, iv, p. 346 and cf. ibid., pp. 332, 351, iii, p. 665, cf. *C.P.R.*, 1361-4, p. 909, and *C.C.R.*, 1374-7, p. 324. *Eighth Report of the Royal Commission on Historical Manuscripts. Report and Appendix*, part 1, p. 367. *Itineraria Symonis Simeonis et Willelmi de Worcestre*, ed. J. Nasmith, p. 263; *Wills*, ed. Wadley, pp. 138, 149, 169; *Tolzey Court Books, passim* (Archives of the Corporation of Bristol).
[6] *E.C.P.*, 61/499, 27/201, *Tolzey Court Book*, 1480-1, f. 32 ff. (Bristol).
[7] *Escheat. Acct.*, 238/2; *Antiquities of Bristow*, ed. J. Dallaway, p. 111. *Tolzey Court Book*, 1487-97 (Bristol). *The Little Red Book of Bristol*, ed. F. B. Bickley, vol. ii, p. 199. *K.R. Memo. Roll*, Mich., 12 Hen. VI, m. 34. *Escheat. Acct.*, 238/2. *Tolzey Court Books* and *Wills*, ed. Wadley, *passim*. *Rot. Parl.*, ii, pp. 437, 541.
[8] *Escheat. Acct.*, 238/2, *E.C.P.*, 18/189, *Antiquities*, ed. Dallaway, op. cit., p. 111. Cf. *G.R.B.*, f. 96; see map for Summary of Regional Trade.
[9] *C.P.R.*, 1405-8, p. 163. *Escheat. Acct.*, 238/2. *E.C.P.*, 61/489, 45/58, *The Charters and Letters Patent . . . Bristol*, ed. S. Seyer, p. 220; *The Coventry Leet Book*, ed. Harris, part iii, p. 594. *K.R. Cust. Accts.*, 19/3 and 4, and see *Escheat. Acct.*, 238/2 for import of herring by a Bridgenorth merchant *via* Bristol. *The Victoria History of the County of Warwick*, ed. W. Page, vol. ii, p. 138. *The Coventry Leet Book*, ed. Harris, part iii, pp. 594, 260, cf. F. Devon, *Issue Roll of Thomas de Brantingham*, p. 332. *K.R. Memo. Roll*, Mich., 9 Hen. VI, m. 19. *Treaty Roll*, 1 Ed. IV, m. 10.
[10] *E.C.P.*, 48/85, cf. ibid., 49/33.
[11] H. B. Walters, *The Church Bells of Wiltshire, Their Inscriptions and History, passim* (3 parts; issued with the Wiltshire Archæological and Natural History Magazine, vol. 44, Nos. 147, 149, and 151, December, 1927, 1928, and 1929; Wiltshire Archæological and Natural History Society, Devizes), *Church Bells of England*, pp. 179 ff. (1912), see *Wills*, ed. Wadley, p. 133 for will of a Bristol bell founder.
[12] *K.R. Cust. Accts.*, 19/11 and 13, *E.C.P.*, 67/187; *G.R.B.*, f. 1; *Brokage Book*, 1439, p. 26 (Archives of the Corporation of Southampton).
[13] *Bodleian MSS. Gough, Somerset*, 2, App. 33. *Bristol Charters* (unpaged). (Archives of the Corporation of Bristol), *E.C.P.*, 32/314, 60/251; *Wills*, ed. Wadley, p. 172. *E.C.P.*, 66/354. *Acts of Court*, vol. i, f. 151. *E.C.P.*, 64/435. *K.R. Cust. Accts.* 19/1 and 2, 73/10 and 20. *P.C.C.*, Stokton, 15, 14; *C.P.R.*, 1441-6, p. 81.
[14] *Antiquities*, ed. Dallaway, p. 111. *Ricart's Kalendar*, pp. 83-4, *Antiquities*, ed. Dallaway, p. 69, *G.R.B.*, p. 18.
[15] *Adam's Chronicle of Bristol*, ed. F. F. Fox, p. 66, *C.P.R.*, 1429-36, p. 497, contrast T. Malvézin, *Histoire du commerce de Bordeaux* (Bordeaux, 1892), vol. ii, p. 184.
[16] *The Little Red Book*, ed. Bickley, vol. ii, pp. 186-9.
[17] *Tolzey Court Book*, 1487-97, p. 158 (Bristol). No other extant shanty apparently throws any light on the identity of the Prior.
[18] *Antiquities*, ed. Dallaway, p. 111, *Wills*, ed. Wadley, p. 68.

[19] A. S. Green, *The Making of Ireland and its Undoing*, 1200-1600 (1908), pp. 13, 25; *Stats., Ireland*, vol. i, p. 697 (1459-60). *The Reign of Henry VII from contemporary sources* ed. A. F. Pollard, vol. iii, p. 279; *E.C.P.*, 24/211 and 217.
[20] *Fifth Report of the Royal Commission on Historical Manuscripts*, Part I, *Appendix*, p. 446. *C.P.R.*, 1405-8, p. 237.
[21] Green, op. cit., pp. 10, 28. *Select Cases in Chancery*, A.D. 1364 to 1471, ed. W. P. Baildon (Selden Soc., vol. x, 1896), No. 34. *C.P.R.*, 1452-62, p. 119. *Issue Roll*, ed. Devon, p. 356. *E.C.P.*, 65/215, cf. ibid. 65/242. *K.R. Cust. Acct.*, 17/8-12.
[22] *E.C.P.*, 19/122, 24/221; *C.P.R.*, 1452-61, p. 60.
[23] *Wills*, ed. Wadley, p. 70.
[24] E. Curtis, *A History of Mediaeval Ireland from* 1110 to 1513 (1923), pp, 362-3. A. K. Longfield, *Anglo-Irish Trade in the Sixteenth Century*, p. 25. Green, op. cit., pp. 19-22. *E.C.P.*, 24/211 and 217. J. H. Wylie, *History of England under Henry the Fourth* (4 vols., 1884-98), vol. i, p. 226, *C.P.R.*, 1399-1401, p. 254, cf. R. Dunlop, *Ireland, from the earliest times* (1922), p. 51.
[25] *Escheat. Acct.*, 238/2.
[26] *E.C.P.*, 59/88.
[27] *Eighth Report of the Royal Commission on Historical Manuscripts, Report and Appendix*. Part i, pp. 367-8; cf. p. 372 for Chester's trade with Ireland. J. T. Gilbert, *History of Dublin* (Dublin, 1854-9), vol. ii, pp. 1, 240. *Register of Wills and Inventories of the Diocese of Dublin*, 1457-83, ed. H. F. Berry, p. 175, D. A. Chart, *An Economic History of Ireland* (Dublin, 1920), p. 19. *Wills and Inventories*, ed. Berry, pp. 28, 83; *K.R. Cust. Accts.*, 17/8 and 10, 19/14.
[28] *E.C.P.*, 26/274, 24/211 and 217.
[29] *E.C.P.*, 15/237 and 238. For names, cf. *Wills and Inventories*, ed. Berry, pp. 38, 144. Curtis, op. cit., p. 330, *C.P.R.*, 1413-16, p. 122, and see *The Little Red Book*, ed. Bickley, vol. ii, p. 110, *K.R. Cust. Acct.*, 17/37. *C.P.R.*, 1429-36, p. 64. *The Little Red Book*, ed. Bickley, vol. ii, p. 123. *Ricart's Kalendar*, p. 41.
[30] " The Noumbre of Weyghtes," *MS. Cott. Vesp. E IX*, f. 100d. *E.C.P.*, 19/122. Green, op. cit., p. 46. *Tolzey Court Book*, 1480-1, f. 23 (Bristol). *E.C.P.*, 64/591. *Wills and Inventories*, ed. Berry, pp. 83, 144.
[31] " The Noumbre of Weyghtes," *MS. Cott. Vesp. E IX*, f. 94. *Paston Letters*, No. 839, *The Northumberland Household Book*, quoted in *Social Life in Britain from the Conquest to the Reformation*, ed. G. C. Coulton (Cambridge, 1918), p. 383.
[32] *The Babees Book*, p. 171, in *Manners and Meals in Olden Time*, ed. F. J. Furnivall (E.E.T.S., No. 32, 1868), " The Noumbre of Weyghtes," op. cit., f. 94, 94d, cf. the inventory of Sir John Fastolf's goods, *Paston Letters*, No. 336. E.g. *C.P.R.*, 1399-1401, p. 248. *Escheat. Acct.*, 238/2.
[33] " The Noumbre of Weyghtes," op. cit., f. 101, *E.C.P.*, 24/211 and 217.
[34] *E.C.P.*, 71/54.
[35] Green, op. cit., p. 46.
[36] D. A. Chart, op. cit., p. 16. *C.P.R.*, 1413-16, p. 94. *K.R. Cust. Acct.*, 18/39; cf. N. S. B. Gras, *The Evolution of the English Corn Market from the twelfth to the eighteenth century* (Harvard Economic Studies, vol. xiii, Cambridge, Mass., 1926), p. 111. Green, op. cit., p. 94.
[37] Ibid., p. 50.
[38] *Rot. Parl.*, iii, p. 643.
[39] *E.C.P.*, 71/54. Salzman, op. cit., p. 272. *K.R. Cust. Accts.*, passim. *C.P.R.* 1399-1401, pp. 425, 503.
[40] *Polychronicon Ranulphi Higden*, quoted in Coulton, op. cit., p. 2. " Flaundres, loveth the wolle of this lond . . . Irlond the ore and the salt." *K.R. Memo. Roll*, Mich., 12 Hen. VI, m. 22, *K.R. Cust. Accts., passim*.
[41] *Inv. Som. Gironde*, vol. ii, p. 3.
[42] E.g. J. Balasque, *Etudes historiques sur la ville de Bayonne*, vol. iii, p. 480.
[43] *Rot. Parl.*, ii, p. 114. Malvézin, op. cit., vol. i, pp. 262, 280, 323, 332. C. Jullian, *Histoire de Bordeaux*, pp. 212-14, cf. *Arch. Hist., Gironde*, vol. i, p. 119.
[44] Ibid., vol. i, pp. 173, 305, vol. ii, p. 139. *Inv. Som. Gironde*, vol. ii, pp. 56, 3, 263, 346, vol. iii, p. 44. *Catalogue des Rolles Gascons, Normans et François* ed. T. Carte (2 vols., 1743), vol. ii, pp. 222, 207.
[45] *Rot. Parl.*, v, pp. 113-17.
[46] Malvézin, op. cit., vol. i, p. 299.
[47] Balasque, op. cit., vol. iii, p. 439.
[48] *Var. Accts.: France*, 184/19. Malvézin, op. cit., vol. i, p. 275.

NOTES TO OVERSEAS TRADE OF BRISTOL 387

[49] *Var. Accts.: France*, 184/19. *K.R. Cust. Accts.*, 17/8 and 10.
[50] *Var. Accts.: France*, 184/19. Cf. *K.R. Cust. Accts.*, 17/37.
[51] Malvézin, op. cit., vol. i, pp. 278-9. F. Michel, *Histoire du Commerce et de la Navigation à Bordeaux, principalement sous l'administration anglaise* (2 vols., Bordeaux, 1867-70), vol. i, p. 54. *Rot. Parl.*, iv, p. 85.
[52] *K.R.Cust. Accts.*, 17/8 and 12, 19/14.
[53] *K.R. Cust. Acct.*, 17/10. Salzman, op. cit., pp. 211-12, 214 n. *Wills*, ed. Wadley, pp. 138-9, 169. *The Little Red Book*, ed. Bickley, vol. ii, pp. 39, 81-90, *G.R.B.*, f. 231. Malvézin, op. cit., pp. 310-11, cf. F. Sargeant, *The Wine Trade with Gascony*, p. 260, in *Finance and Trade under Edward III*, ed. G. Unwin. *G.R.B.*, f. 231.
[54] Possibly a kind of carbonate of soda, see Salzman, op. cit., p. 208.
[55] Cf. Malvézin, op. cit., vol. i, p. 309.
[56] Jullian, op. cit., p. 218. E.g. *K.R. Cust. Acct.*, 17/10. Malvézin, op. cit., vol. i, p. 199.
[57] Jullian, op. cit., p. 219.
[58] Ibid. Malvézin, op. cit., vol. i, pp. 297, 298, 191, 297, 293. Carte, op. cit., vol. i, pp. 198, 200-3. Balasque, op. cit., p. 462. *L.T.R. Cust. Acct.*, 19, m. 6d. *E.C.P.* 19/409.
[59] *Rot. Parl.*, v, p. 113. E. Troplong, *De la Fidélité des Gascons aux Anglais*, p. 52. L. D. Brissaud, *L'administration anglaise et le mouvement communal dans le Bordelais. Les Anglais en Guyenne* (Paris, 1875), p. 234. *The Chronicle of Froissart translated out of French by Sir John Bourchier, Lord Berners, Annis 1523-5*, ed. W. P. Ker (6 vols., The Tudor Translations, 27-32, ed. W. E. Henley, 1901-3), vol. ii, p. 164.
[60] *Arch. Hist., Gironde*, vol. ii, p. 243, vol. i, p. 310, vol. ii, p. 139. Troplong, op. cit., p. 487.
[61] Balasque, op. cit., p. 462. Jullian, op. cit., p. 292. L. Puech, *Histoire de la Gascogne* (La Société Archéologique du Gers, Auch, 1914), p. 272.
[62] *Var. Accts.: France*, 194/3.
[63] *Rot. Parl.*, v, p. 59.
[64] C. L. Kingsford, *West Country Piracy: the School of English Seamen*, pp. 79-81, in *Prejudice and Promise in XVth Century England*.
[65] *Ordonnances des Rois de France*, ed. de Bréquigny, vol. xiv, p. 140.
[66] Balasque, op. cit., vol. iii, pp. 499-502.
[67] *Ordonnances*, op. cit., vol. xiv, p. 270. Ibid., p. 273.
[68] *Treaty Roll*, 30 Hen. VI, m. 10.
[69] *E.C.P.*, 64/345, cf. Commines, Book 4, Chapters 9 and 10. *G.R.B.*, f. 68. Ibid., f. 40, cf. *Treaty Roll*, 30 Hen. VI, m. 7; many similar licences are on these rolls.
[70] *E.C.P.*, 64/345, cf. *Wills*, ed. Wadley, p. 162, and *K.R. Memo. Roll*, Mich., 12 Hen. VI, m. 34. Troplong, op. cit., p. 521. *K.R. Cust. Acct.*, 19/14, cf. licences to ships of Caen in the *Treaty Rolls*, e.g. 31 Hen. VI, mm. 6, 7.
[71] Jullian, op. cit., p. 306; Troplong, op. cit., pp. 519, 521; Malvézin, op. cit., vol. ii, pp. 21, 23, 26. *K.R. Cust. Accts.*, 19/1, 3, and 4. *E.C.P.*, 27/383. *G.R.B.*, f. 97. *C.P.R.*, 1452-61, pp. 347, 608, 612, 614, 149.
[72] Troplong, op. cit., p. 521.
[73] *Libelle*, ed. Warner, p. 5.
[74] *K.R. Cust. Accts.*, 17/8 and 10.
[75] *E.C.P.*, 48/114.
[76] *K.R. Cust. Accts.*, passim; *C.P.R.*, 1401-5, pp. 437, 507. Ibid., 1446-52, p. 238. *Extracts from the Accounts Rolls of the Abbey of Durham*, ed. J. T. Fowler (3 vols., Surtees Society, Durham, 1898-1901), vol. iii, p. 616, cf. pp. 391, 697. Salzman, op. cit., pp. 251-2
[77] *Libelle*, ed. Warner, p. 4.
[78] *K.R. Cust. Acct.*, 19/14.
[79] *E.C.P.*, 30/40.
[80] *K.R. Cust. Accts.*, passim. *Tolzey Court Book*, 1487-97, ff. 157, 172. *Parliamentary and Council Proceedings: Exchequer*, roll. 28. A. Ashley, *The Mariners Mirrour* . . . Luke Wagenar (H. Hasselup, ? London), p. 12. *Treaty Roll*, 6 Hen. VI, m. 8, *Harleian MS.*, 433, ff. 171-2. *The Itineraries of William Wey*, pp. 153-5. *The Pilgrim's Sea Voyage*, quoted in Coulton, op. cit., p. 427.
[81] *K.R. Cust. Acct.*, 19/14. *Tolzey Court Book*, 1487-97, cf. *Cal. St. P. Span.*, vol. i, p. 4. *C.P.R.*, 1452-61, p. 440. *E.C.P.*, 64/459.
[82] *C.P.R.*, 1401-5, pp. 360, 363, 426-8.
[83] G. Daumet, *Étude sur l'alliance de la France et de la Castile au XIVe et au XVe siècles* (Bibliothèque de l'École des Hautes Études. Sciences Philologiques et Historiques, 118

fasc. Paris, 1898), p. viii. R. B. Merriman, *The Rise of the Spanish Empire in the Old World and in the New* (3 vols., New York, 1918–25), vol. i, p. 132.

[84] *C.P.R.*, 1401–5, pp. 360, 363, 426–8. See Kingsford, op. cit., p. 83 ff. for a full account of Hawley's career. *C.P.R.*, 1446–52, p. 215. Ibid., 1467–76, p. 599. Ibid., 1476–85, p. 271.

[85] Merriman, op. cit., p. 138. Daumet, op. cit., pp. 115–22. *Cal. St. P. Span*, vol. i, p. 112. Ibid., p. 57. Ibid., p. 136. Ibid., p. 250. Ibid., p. 255.

[86] V. M. Shillington and A. B. W. Chapman, *The Commercial Relations of England and Portugal*, pp. 13–14. Ibid., pp. 18, 49, 56, 68, 110 ff.

[87] *K.R. Cust. Accts.*, passim. "The Noumbre of Weyghtes," op. cit., f. 100d. *Cal. Fr. R., Hen. V*, p. 555.

[88] Shillington and Chapman, op. cit., p. 70. Ibid., p. 59, *Cal. Fr. R. Hen. V*, p. 549 ff. *K.R. Memo. Roll*, Mich., 12 Hen. VI, m. 34, cf. "The Noumbre of Weyghtes," op. cit., f. 100d.

[89] Shillington and Chapman, op. cit., pp. 46, 49.

[90] Ibid., p. 71.

[91] Ibid., p. 62. *C.P.R.*, 1452–61, p. 225. *Foedera*, vol. v, i, p. 37. Shillington and Chapman, op. cit., pp. 99, 307: "William Canis ... his ship La Mary Redclyff." This must refer to William Canynges.

[92] *E.C.P.*, 9/488.

[93] H. G. Richardson, *Illustrations of English History in the Mediaeval Registers of the Parlement of Paris*, in Trans. R. Hist. Soc., Fourth Series, vol. 10, pp. 55–85 (1927), p. 74.

[94] *Rot. Parl.*, vol. iii, pp. 662, 429.

[95] *K.R. Cust. Accts.*, 19/13.

[96] *C.P.R.*, 1416–22, p. 418. Ibid., 1452–61, pp. 438, 443.

[97] E.g. A. Abram, *Social England in the fifteenth century: a study of the effects of economic conditions* (1909), where it is stated that Sturmy "carried on a considerable trade in the Levant".

[98] J. Latimer, *The History of the Society of Merchant Venturers of the City of Bristol, with some account of the anterior merchants' guilds* (Bristol, 1903), p. 16.

[99] *L.T.R. Cust. Acct.*, 19, m. 6d. *K.R. Memo. Roll*, Trin. 20 Hen. VI, m. 2.

[100] *Treaty Roll*, 25 Hen. VI, m. 20.

[101] *L.T.R. Cust. Accts.*, 19, m. 7d. *Antiquities*, ed. Dallaway, pp. 78, 109.

[102] *G.R.B.*, ff. 17, 18, 186, 78, 93, *The Little Red Book*, ed. Bickley, vol. ii, p. 151, *E.C.P.*, 19/122, 24/221. *C.P.R.*, 1452–61, p. 156. *Rot. Parl.*, v, p. 245. *Paston Letters*, No. 208. *Antiquities*, ed. Dallaway, p. 112. See *P.C.C.*, Stokton, 14.

[103] *Foedera*, vol. v, ii, p. 67. *The Itineraries of William Wey*, p. 153.

[104] *K.R. Memo. Roll*, Easter, 36 Hen. VI, m. 37, *Treaty Roll*, 35 Hen. VI, m. 20. Ibid., m. 6. *P.C.C.* Stokton, 14.

[105] *Chronicles of London*, ed. C. L. Kingsford, p. 169. *Ricart's Kalendar*, p. 41; *Six Town Chronicles of England*, ed. R. Flenley, pp. 112, 161, Kingsford, op. cit., p. 169; *C.P.R.*, 1452–61, p. 517.

[106] *Letters of the Fifteenth and Sixteenth Centuries, from the Archives of Southampton*, ed. R. C. Anderson (Southampton Record Society; ed. H. W. Gidden, 1921), pp. 14–16.

[107] *Ricart's Kalendar*, pp. 41–2. In Flenley, op. cit., and Kingsford, op. cit., the sum is 6,000 marcs. *C.P.R.*, 1452–61, p. 517. *Wills*, Wadley, p. 137; Latimer, op. cit., p. 16.

[108] See *Wills*, ed. Wadley, passim.

[109] *Lambeth Palace MSS.*, vol. cccvi, f. 132, quoted in *Ricart's Kalendar*, Introduction.

[110] *Antiquities*, ed. Dallaway, p. 145.

[111] *Wills*, ed. Wadley, passim. *Ricart's Kalendar*, p. 46.

[112] *Wills*, ed. Wadley, pp. 42, 60, 87, 164, etc. *G.R.B.*, f. 248.

[113] *Wills*, ed. Wadley, passim; *A Calendar of Deeds (Chiefly relating to Bristol) collected by G. W. Braikenridge*, ed. F. B. Bickley, (Edinburgh, privately printed, 1899), p. 9. *Additional MS.* 29866. *E.C.P.*, 44/163.

[114] See above, p. 211.

[115] *Wills*, ed. Wadley, pp. 48, 77. *Var. Accts.; Ulnage*, 339/2. *K.R. Cust. Accts.*, 17/1 and 8, 19/14.

[116] *The Charm of the West Country*, ed. T. Burke (Bristol and London, 1913), p. 223. *E.C.P.*, 79/43, and cf. ibid., 19/263 and 64/42.

[117] Ibid., 64/345. Ibid., 59/22, 32/31. *Exchequer T.R., Council and Privy Seal*, File 46, 3 Hen. VI.

[118] *K.R. Cust. Acct.*, 19/14; Canynges had recently lent £333 6s. 8d. to the king, *K.R. Memo. Roll*, Easter, 3 Edw. IV, m. 6d.

NOTES TO OVERSEAS TRADE OF BRISTOL

[119] As shown by a comparison of the more reliable Ulnage Accounts with the *K.R. Cust. Accts.*

[120] *E.C.P.*, 16/473.

[121] W. J. Ashley, *The Early History of the English Woollen Industry* (Publications of the American Economic Association, Johns Hopkins University, Baltimore, vol. ii, No. 4, 1887), p. 62. Ibid., pp. 75, 80 ff. *E.C.P.*, 48/85, cf. *C.P.R.*, 1485-94, p. 447, for " merchant's " debts to " clothier ".

[122] Cf. *Var. Accts.: Ulnage*, 346/23, one of the more reliable accounts, with *K.R. Cust. Acct.*, 19/14.

[123] *Var. Accts.; Ulnage*, 339/2; *K.R. Cust. Acct.*, 17/1.

[124] *Wills*, ed. Wadley, p. 16. Ibid., p. 17. Ibid., p. 30.

[125] *Antiquities*, ed. Dallaway, pp. 114-15. *G.R.B.*, f. 78. *E.C.P.*, 24/211 and 217. Ibid., 26/474.

[126] *G.R.B.*, f. 331; *E.C.P.*, 64/533. Ibid., 64/533; *Additional MS.* 29866. *Var. Accts.; France*, 185/7; cf. W. Vogel, *Geschichte der deutschen Seeschiffahrt*, pp. 491-2, 498-9. See above, p. 228, *Rot. Parl.*, vol. v, p. 59.

[127] *Var. Accts.: France*, 184/19. Ibid., 193/4, 195/19. *G.R.B.*, ff. 38-161. C. L. Scofield, *The Life and Reign of Edward the Fourth* vol. ii, p. 417. Cf. prices paid by Edward IV for ships, from £80 to £600; Scofield, op. cit., vol. ii, pp. 410-14, and the cost of the *Margaret Cely* (? 200 tuns) £28, *Cely Papers*, pp. 176-7.

[128] *K.R. Cust. Accts., passim.* Vogel (op. cit., vol. i, p. 452) estimates only one man to 5 lasts (i.e. 10 tons). Worcester's tunnage figures are confirmed by the *K.R. Cust. Accts.*, e.g. the *Mary Bird* " of 100 tuns " carried 101 tuns in 1479; *K.R. Cust. Acct.*, 19/15.

[129] *E.C.P.*, 9/223; *Antiquities*, ed. Dallaway, p. 140; *Paston Letters*, No. 93; Scofield, op. cit., vol. ii, p. 416.

[130] *K.R. Cust. Acct.*, 19/14. F. I. Schechter, *The Historical Foundations of the Law relating to Trade Marks* (Columbia Legal Studies, I. New York, 1925), pp. 26-34.

[131] E.g. *E.C.P.*, 47/62, 68/200, cf. Michel, op. cit., vol. i, p. 72. *Ricart's Kalendar*, p. 47.

[132] *Churchwardens' Account Book*, Church of St. Ewen, Bristol, f. 61. *E.C.P.*, 29/390, 27/383 and 471, 64/131, 59/92. *Rot. Parl.*, vol. iii, p. 554.

[133] *E.C.P.*, 10/136. *Wills*, ed. Wadley, pp. 161, 162. Inscription on brass in Church of St. John, Bristol, and cf. *G.R.B.*, ff. 197-8.

[134] *K.R. Cust. Accts.*, 19/14 and 15. *E.C.P.*, 63/143.

[135] A. Abram, *English Life and Manners in the Later Middle Ages* (1913), p. 36.

[136] See above, p. 231; *The Little Red Book*, ed. Bickley, vol. ii, MSS. notes of Churchwardens' Accounts, Church of All Saints, Bristol. *E.C.P.*, 60/62.

[137] *G.R.B.*, f. 247.

[138] *E.C.P.*, 44/163.

[139] *Ricart's Kalendar*, p. 80 ff.

[140] See above, p. 236 and n. 118.

[141] *K.R. Memo. Roll*, Hil., 1 Hen. VII, m. 30 (see W. E. C. Harrison, *An Early Voyage of Discovery*, in *The Mariner's Mirror*, vol. xvi, (Cambridge, April, 1930), pp. 198-9. Nasmith, op. cit., p. 153. Lloyd was then usually spelt phonetically as " Thlyde ".

VI

THE GROCERS OF LONDON, A STUDY OF DISTRIBUTIVE TRADE

[1] J. A. Kingdon, *Facsimile of the first volume of the MS. Archives of the Grocers' Company*, vol. i, p. 9. (Henceforth referred to as *Grocers' Facsimile*, ed. Kingdon.)
[2] *L.Bk.*, D (MS.), f. 154v.
[3] *Cal. L. Bk.* C, p. 17; *Cal. L. Bk.*, E, pp. 53-4; A. B. Beaven, *The Aldermen of the City of London*, vol. i, p. 357.
[4] *Cal. L. Bk.*, C, p. 17; *Cal. L. Bk.*, E, p. 232; *Cal. L. Bk.*, G, p. 204.
[5] *Select Cases concerning the Law Merchant*, A.D. 1270-1628, vol. i, *Local Courts*, ed. C. Gross (Selden Society, vol. xxiii, 1908), p. 105.
[6] *Var. Accts.*; *Wardrobe and Household*, 395/8, 398/12.
[7] G. L. Kriegk, *Deutsches Bürgerthum im Mittelalter . . . mit besonderer Beziehung auf Frankfurt a. M.* (Frankfurt a. M., 1868), p. 60; G. Henslow, *Medical Works of the Fourteenth Century* (1899), pp. 9, 12, 67, 80; *The Paston Letters*, ed. J. Gairdner, vol. ii, p. 293; *Libelle*, ed. Warner, lines 354-67.
[8] *Memorials of London and London Life in the XIIIth, XIVth, and XVth Centuries*, A.D. 1276-1419, ed. H. T. Riley, pp. 273-4; G. Borel, *Les Foires de Genève au quinzième siècle* (Paris and Geneva, 1892), pp. 167, 178. See the Prologue, *Canterbury Tales*, lines 425-7, (*Poetical Works of Chaucer*, ed. W. Skeat, 1927); also *Stonor Letters*, vol. ii, pp. 107-8; *Var. Accts*; *Wardrobe and Household*, 402/18 and 19.
[9] *Calendar of Inquisitions Miscellaneous (Chancery)*, vol. ii, No. 451; W. Cunningham, *The Gild Merchant of Shrewsbury* (Trans. R. Hist. Soc., New Ser., vol. ix, pp. 95-117, 1895), p. 99.
[10] *Cal. of Early Mayor's Court R.*, p. 9; *Grocers' Facsimile*, ed. Kingdon, vol. i, pp. vii, 43.
[11] *Inquisitions Miscellaneous (Chancery)*, 160/24/2079; *Grocers' Facsimile*, ed. Kingdon, vol. i, pp. vii, 43.
[12] Beaven, op. cit., vol. i, pp. 336-8.
[13] *Grocers' Facsimile*, ed. Kingdon, vol. i, pp. 10-11, 13; *L. Bk.*, G, (MS.), f. 135v.
[14] *Cal. L. Bk.*, G, p. 204; *Grocers' Facsimile*, ed. Kingdon, vol. i, pp. 21, 118, vol. ii, pp. 174, 193.
[15] Ibid., vol. ii, pp. 323, vol. i, p. 18.
[16] Ibid., vol. i, p. 122.
[17] Ibid., vol. i, p. 15; *Wardens' Accts.*, Mercers, f. 4; *Grocers' Facsimile*, ed. Kingdon, vol. i, p. 112. The wardens in 1443-5 allowed the capital to diminish by £30, and were required to make up the loss. Later £20 was refunded to them, ibid., vol. ii, pp. 288, 290. Ibid., vol. i, p. 133.
[18] Printed in Baron Heath's *Some Account of the Worshipful Company of Grocers* (3rd ed., 1869, privately printed), pp. 410-12. See deeds 1 to 5, *Transcript and Translation of Deeds relating to the site of Grocers' Hall, contained in The Book of Register of Evidences of Lands, etc* (transcript, etc., by I. J. Churchill, privately printed, 1925), pp. 9-14. Exchequer K.R. *Subsidy Rolls*, Lay Series London and Middlesex, 238/90, 14 Hen. VI; *Grocers' Facsimile*, ed. Kingdon, vol. ii, p. 313; *Ord. Rem. and Accts.*, Grocers, f. 85. Ibid., f. 96.
[19] *Grocers' Facsimile*, ed. Kingdon, vol. ii, pp. 237, 273, loan of £266; *Ord. Rem. and Accts.*, Grocers, accounts 1493-7; *Grocers' Facsimile*, ed. Kingdon, vol. ii, p. 315; *Wardens' Accts.*, Grocers, 1460-71, ff. 13, 134 (1465); *Ord. Rem. and Accts.*, Grocers, accounts 1498.
[20] G. Unwin, *The Gilds and Companies of London*, p. 166; *Grocers' Facsimile*, ed. Kingdon, vol. i, p. 12; ibid., vol. ii, pp. 239, 258, 273; ibid., vol. i, pp. 68, 76; vol. ii, p. 228; *Wardens' Accts.*, Grocers, 1460-71, ff. 191, 193.
[21] *Register*, Grocers, f. 44; *Grocers' Facsimile*, ed. Kingdon, vol. ii, p. 177; ibid. vol. ii, p. 198; ibid., vol. ii, pp. 230, 299, 353.
[22] Ibid., vol. ii, p. 299. Will of John Oxneye, grocer, P.C.C., Marche, 20 (1409); *Memorials*, ed. Riley, p. 543. *Wardens Accts.*, Mercers, ff. 1, 48; *Report of the City of London Livery Companies' Commission*, vol. ii, p. 7; *The Mercers' Company Charters, Ordinances and Bylaws* (privately printed, 1881), p. 79. *Register*, Grocers, f. 52.

[23] Ibid., f. 16; *Cal. Plea and Memo. Rolls*, 1364-81, p. xlii; *E.C.P.*, 113/5; see also *E.C.P.*, 10/124, 46/226; *Cal. of Letters*, p. 170; *Memorials of the Goldsmiths' Company*, ed. W. S. Prideaux (2 vols., privately printed, 1896-7), *passim*.
[24] William Grantham, *P.C.C.*, Marche, 35; *L. Bk.*, H, (MS.), f. 297; Richard Hakedy, *P.C.C.*, Stockton 15.
[25] *Grocers' Facsimile*, ed. Kingdon, vol. i, p. 11; ibid., vol. i, p. 121. *Register*, Grocers, ff. 639-76, 194.
[26] *Journal*, 4, f. 36; *L. Bk.*, K, f. 173v; *E.C.P.*, 106/8, 108/42; *Calendar of Wills proved and enrolled in the Court of Hastings*, ed. R. R. Sharpe, vol. ii, pp. 119, 270. *Cal. Plea and Mem. Rolls*, 1364-81, p. 125; loans to the Master, *E.C.P.*, 96/64, 155/10; L. Verriest, *Les Luttes Sociales et le Contrat d'Apprentissage à Tournai jusqu'en 1424* (Mémoires ... Collection in-8°. Deuxième Série, Tome ix. Académie Royale de Belgique, Classe des Lettres [etc.], Brussels, 1913), p. 39.
[27] *The Reule of Crysten Religioun*, by Reginald Pecock, D.D., ed. W. C. Greet (E.E.T.S., Original Series, No. 171, 1927), pp. 321, 322; *Cal. Plea and Memo. Rolls*, 1323-64, pp. 268-9.
[28] *Plea and Memo. Rolls*, A. 69, m. 5 (MS. Cal.).
[29] Des Marez, *L'organisation du travail à Bruxelles au XVe siècle* (Mémoires Couronnés et autres mémoires. L'Académie Royale des Sciences des Lettres et des Beaux Arts de Belgique. Collection in-8°. Tome lxv, Brussels, 1903-4), p. 49.
[30] *Cal. L. Bk.*, A, pp. 224-5; *Mun. Gild.*, vol. ii (Lib. Cust.), i, pp. 107-8; sworn a broker in 1293; *Cal. L. Bk.*, C, p. 17; *Mun. Gild.*, vol. ii (Lib. Cust.) i, pp. 107-8; Andrew Godard, who served apprenticeship with a pepperer (*Cal. L. Bk.*, D, p. 97); appointment as weigher. *Cal. L. Bk.*, E, p. 37; *L. Bk.*, D, (MS.), f. 97; *Cal. L. Bk.*, C, pp. 137-9.
[31] *Cal. L. Bk.*, G, p. 204; *Cal. L. Bk.*, H, p. 22. Ibid., p. 385; *Grocers' Facsimile*, ed. Kingdon, vol. i, p. 75; ibid., p. 347.
[32] *Journal*, 2 f. 77v, 3, ff. 99-99v, 91, 6, f. 246.
[33] *L. Bk.*, D, f. 97 (MS.); *Grocers' Facsimile*, ed. Kingdon, vol. i, p. 87; *Wardens' Accts.*, Grocers, 1448-60, 1460-71; rent of £13 6s. 8d. paid for the weigh-house from 1458; *Cal. L. Bk.*, G, p. 304; *Journal*, 9, f. 42.
[34] *C.P.R.*, 1381-5, pp. 149, 299. Ibid., p. 359; ibid., 1377-81, p. 109; *Rot. Parl.*, iii, p. 129; *C.P.R.*, 1381-5, pp. 154, 299; *Cal. L. Bk.*, H, p. 385; the Cornhill site mentioned in *Wardens' Accts.*, Grocers, *passim*; *A Survey of London*, by John Stow, ed. C. L. Kingsford (2 vols., Oxford, 1908), vol. i, p. 192.
[35] *L. Bk.*, H, ff. 284v, 290 (MS.).
[36] *Rot. Parl.*, v, p. 332; Heath, op. cit., pp. 412-14; *Var. Accts: Miscellaneous*, 515/8, 9, and 12. *C.P.R.*, 1476-85, pp. 205, 311.
[37] *Grocers' Facsimile*, ed. Kingdon, vol. ii, p. 202; *C.P.R.*, 1452-61, p. 334, *Journal*, 4, f. 22; *Grocers' Facsimile*, ed. Kingdon, vol. ii, pp. 287, 291.
[38] *L. Bk.*, L, f. 5v (MS.), *Cal. L. Bk.*, L, p. 187; *Journal*, 9, f. 236.
[39] *Rot. Parl.*, ii, p. 276; ibid., pp. 277-8, repeated in abridged form as preamble to the statute following. *Select English Works of John Wyclif*, ed. T. Arnold (3 vols., 1869-71), vol. iii, p. 332. This sermon is discussed by R. H. Tawney, in *Religion and the Rise of Capitalism* (1926), p. 293. *Stat.* 37 Edw. III, c. 5. *Stat.* 38 Edw. III, c. 2.
[40] G. Unwin, *The Estate of Merchants*, 1336-65, p. 249, in *Finance and Trade under Edward III*, ed. G. Unwin, pp. 179-255.
[41] T. H. Marshall, *Capitalism and the Decline of the English Gilds*, p. 24, in The Camb. Hist. Journal, vol. iii, 1929, pp. 23-33.
[42] *C.P.R.*, 1364-7, p. 5; ibid., pp. 6-7; ibid., p. 4.
[43] *Cal. L. Bk.*, G, p. 179; ibid., p. 187. "... that every freman may cross the sea with any kind of merchandise he likes, and bring back to the city any kind of merchandise he likes, so that no one sell any kind of merchandise by retail except that which belongs to his mistery, but only in gross." *Cal. L. Bk.*, G, p. 203.
[44] See *Cal. L. Bk.*, E, pp. 291-6, and discussion by G. Unwin in *Industrial Organization in the Sixteenth and Seventeenth Centuries* (1904), p. 30.
[45] *Cal. L. Bk.*, E, p. 13; G. Norton, *Commentaries on the History, Constitution, and Chartered Franchises of the City of London* (1869), p. 334.
[46] William Lynne, see *Cal. L. Bk.*, K, p. 26; Thomas Broun, see his will, *Comm. Lon.*, More 216; John Crosby, see *C.P.R.*, 1452-61, p. 485; Jankyn Clerk, *Grocers' Facsimile*, ed. Kingdon, vol. ii, p. 175.
[47] *K.R. Cust. Acct.*, 142/3, and *Brokage Books*, *passim* (Archives of the Corporation of Southampton).

NOTES TO THE GROCERS OF LONDON 393

[48] Mercers, grocers, drapers, skinners, haberdashers, fishmongers, tailors—*Acts*, Mercers, f. 94.
[49] *Var. Accts.: Foreign Merchants*, 128/30 and 31.
[50] *K.R. Cust. Acct.*, 71/13.
[51] *K.R. Cust. Acct.*, 71/25.
[52] *Cal. L. Bk.*, H, p. 191.
[53] *C.P.R.*, 1364-7, p. 5; W. Herbert, *The History of the Twelve Great Livery Companies of London* (2 vols., 1836-7), vol. ii, p. 23.
[54] *Cal. Fr. R.*, Hen. VI, pp. 354, 349; Robert Pounde, Alan Johnson.
[55] *Brokage Books, passim*, Southampton.
[56] *E.C.P.*, 67/162; *Cal. Fr. R.*, Hen. VI, pp. 250, 252, 253, 254, 258; *C.C.R.*, 1419-22, p. 10; *C.P.R.*, 1429-36, p. 489; Kingsford, op. cit., vol. i, p. 109.
[57] F. Sargent, *The Wine Trade with Gascony*, p. 266, and G. Unwin, *The Estate of Merchants*, p. 250, in *Finance and Trade under Edward III*, ed. G. Unwin.
[58] *K.R. Cust. Accts.*, 73/23, 71/13; *E.C.P.*, 9/393, 11/303, 44/160, 44/220, 48/196, 64/705, 66/333, 80/65, 158/84. In a fleet of three wine ships arriving in 1446, were wines belonging to a grocer, an ironmonger, a draper, two mercers, and a fishmonger. The other fifty-seven shippers were presumably vintners, but their shares amounted to only seven casks apiece, while the grocer, Alan Johnson, had forty-nine. *K.R. Cust. Acct.*, 73/23. Licence to export old wine granted to "divers merchants, vintners and others of the city of London", *C.P.R.*, 1364-7, p. 107; *Var. Accts.: Foreign Merchants*, 128/30 and 31. Ibid., 128/31, m. 15, Simon Eyre; *Journal*, 10, f. 298.
[59] *E.C.P.*, 6/190; *Rot, Parl.*, vol. iii, p. 258; *E.C.P.*, 108/19.
[60] *E.C.P.*, 64/330; *E.D.*, 35/20, 47/25; *K.R. Cust. Acct.*, 97/8, John Blaunche; *Brokage Books, passim* (Southampton); *Var. Accts.: Foreign Merchants*, 128/30 and 31.
[61] J. E. Thorold Rogers, *A History of Agriculture and Prices in England* (4 vols., Oxford, 1866-82), vol. iv, p. 556.
[62] *Acts*, Mercers, ff. 35-6.
[63] *K.R. Cust. Acct.*, 71/13; Geoffrey Broke and Walter Newenton.
[64] *Port Books* and *Brokage Books, passim* (Southampton). Ibid., John Dowge; *Register of Edward the Black Prince*, part ii (Duchy of Cornwall), A.D. 1351-65, p. 170 (2 parts; the Deputy Keeper of the Records, 1930-1); *Cal. of Letters*, pp. 96-7. *Journal*, 3, f. 84; *Cal. L. Bk.*, K, p. 296.
[65] *Port Books* and *Brokage Books, passim* (Southampton); out of the eighty Londoners mentioned here, thirty-six were grocers.
[66] *Register*, Grocers, f. 43.
[67] *Rot. Parl.*, vol. iii, p. 662.
[68] *Grocers' Facsimile*, ed. Kingdon, vol. i, p. 66. Ibid., p. 82. Ibid., vol. ii, p. 225; *Register*, Grocers, ff. 48, 54; ibid., f. 4; *Grocers' Facsimile*, ed. Kingdon, vol. ii, p. 232; *Journal*, 2, f. 18; *Cal. L. Bk.*, L., p. 130.
[69] *Wardens' Accts.*, Mercers, f. 167; *Var. Accts.: Foreign Merchants*, 128/30 and 31; *K.R. Cust. Acct.*, 73/23; *E.C.P.*, 28/472, 46/119; *Journal*, 7, f. 113b; *Var. Accts.: Foreign Merchants*, 128/30.
[70] *Register*, Grocers, ff. 39, 4, 50, 51.
[71] *Wardens' Accts.*, Grocers, 1448-60, f. 30; *Grocers' Facsimile*, ed. Kingdon, *passim*. *Register*, Grocers, f. 47; *Journal*, 7, f. 112. *Journal*, 12, ff. 263-72.
[72] Herbert, op. cit., vol. i, p. 230; W. Cunningham, *The Growth of English Industry and Commerce during the Early and Middle Ages* (5th ed., 1922), p. 382. E. Lipson, *The Economic History of England*, vol. i. *The Middle Ages* (1929), pp. 384-5.
[73] C. Buecher, *Industrial Evolution*, trans. S. M. Wickett (1901), p. 125; G. von Below, *Probleme der Wirtschaftsgeschichte*, chapter 6; G. Des Marez, *L'organisation du travail à Bruxelles au XVe siecle*, pp. 323-5; see also, in support of von Below, H. Eckert, *Die Krämer in süddeutschen Städten bis zum Ausgang des Mittelalters* (Abhandlungen zur Mittleren und Neueren Geschichte, vol. xvi; Berlin and Leipzig, 1910), and for contrary view see F. Keutgen, *Der Grosshandel im Mittelalter*, in Hans. Gbl., Jahrgang, 1901 (1902), vol. ix, pp. 67-138.
[74] "The Noumbre of Weyghtes," *MS. Cotton Vesp.*, E, ix, f. 97d.
[75] *L. Bk.*, H, f. 284b (MS.).
[76] See *Cal. of Letters, passim*.
[77] *Report of the City of London Livery Companies Commission*, vol. ii, p. 20; *Wardens' Accts.*, Mercers, f. 2.
[78] *Grocers' Facsimile*, ed. Kingdon, vol. i, p. 139; ibid., vol. i, pp. 157, 158, 161; vol. ii, pp. 219, 239, 249.

2D

[79] Ibid., vol. ii, p. 259; *Register*, Grocers, f. 39.
[80] *Acts*, Mercers, ff. 34, 41-4, 56, 59; *Journal*, 8, f. 163.
[81] Ibid., 9, ff. 133v, 143; *Stat.* 3 Hen. VII, c. 10; *Rot. Parl.*, vi, p. 402.
[82] *Grocers' Facsimile*, ed. Kingdon, vol. ii, pp. 181, 201, 317.
[83] *Brokage Books, passim* (Southampton).
[84] *Chanc. Files, Tower Series*, G; *C.P.R., passim*; ibid., 1429-36, pp. 17, 91, 98, 161; *Roll of Outlawries*, m. 1; *Cat. Anc. Deeds*, vi, C. 6844; Robert Pounde, *Comm. Lon.*, Sharpe, 387; *C.P.R.*, 1461-7, p. 257; ibid., 1416-22, p. 18; ibid., 1452-6, p. 521; ibid., 1422-9, p. 311; *Roll of Outlawries*, m. 1, m. 12; *Chanc. Files, Tower Ser.*, G.; *C.P.R.*, 1467-72, p. 2; *Roll of Outlawries*, m. 1, 11d, 13; *C.P.R.*, 1461-7, p. 317; ibid., 1415-18, pp. 347, 355; ibid., 1429-36, p. 234; *Roll of Outlawries*, mm. 1, 11; *C.P.R.*, 1413-16, p. 81; *Roll of Outlawries*, m. 1, 1d.; *C.P.R.*, 1405-8, p. 401; ibid., 1422-9, pp. 307, 365; *Chanc. Files, Tower Ser.*, G.; *Plea and Memo. Rolls*, A. 33, m. 3v (MS. Cal.).
[85] *Journal*, 7, ff. 32-3.
[86] *Mun. Gild.*, vol. ii (*Lib. Cust.*), i, pp. 385, 404.
[87] *Memorials*, ed. Riley, p. 82; ibid., pp. 131-2; see also *E.C.P.*, 104/34. *Cal. Plea and Memo Rolls*, 1323-64, pp. 204, 245; *E.C.P.*, 1/208.
[88] *Journal*, 2, f. 18; *Cal. of Letters*, pp. 126-7. *P.C.C.*, Luffenham, 24; Stafford, 152 (Lambeth Palace MS.); *Plea and Memo. Rolls*, A. 66/10 (MS. Cal.).
[89] *Mun. Gild.*, vol. i (*Lib. Albus*), i, pp. 260-1, 433.
[90] *Cal. L. Bk.*, H, pp. 191-2; *Stat.* 7 Ric. II, c. 11. United with the other fishmongers by charter of incorporation, 11 Hen. VI. Herbert, op. cit., vol. ii, p. 24. Recited in charter of 1364, repeated in charters of 22 Rich. II and 6 Hen. IV, Herbert, op, cit., vol. ii, pp. 119, 123. *Journal*, 3, f. 6; 4, f. 111.
[91] *Memorials*, ed. Riley, pp. 516-18.
[92] *Cal. L. Bks., passim*; *C.C.R.*, 1354-60, p. 540; *Memorials*, ed. Riley, pp. 670-2. Ibid., pp. 341-2; *Cal. L. Bk.*, H, p. 74. *Plea and Memo. Rolls*, A. 26, m. 3d. (MS Cal.); *E.C.P.*, 66/228. *Report of the City of London Livery Companies Commission*, vol. ii, p. 649.
[93] *Cal. Plea and Memo. Rolls*, 1323-64, p. 237.
[94] *Mun. Gild.*, vol. ii (*Lib. Cust.*), i, p. 104; *Memorials*, ed. Riley, pp. 539-41, 570-3; *Mun. Gild.*, vol. i (*Lib. Albus*), i, p. 279; *Cal. L. Bk.*, K, p. 42; *Cal. L. Bk.*, H, pp. 366, 403, 418.
[95] *Memorials*, ed. Riley, p. 75.
[96] Ibid., p. 625.
[97] *Mun. Gild.*, vol. ii (*Lib. Cust.*), i, p. 103.
[98] *E.D.*, 46/17.
[99] "The Noumbre of Weyghtes," *MS. Cotton Vesp.*, E, ix, f. 97.
[100] *Cal. L. Bk.*, F, p. 179; *Cal. L. Bk.*, E, pp. 156-9; *Memorials*, ed. Riley, pp. 532-3; *Mun. Gild.*, vol. i (*Lib. Albus*), i, p. 261, vol. ii (*Lib. Cust.*), i, p. 96; *Cal. Plea and Memo. Rolls*, 1323-64, p. 1.
[101] *Var. Accts.*: *Foreign Merchants*, 128/30, plaster images sold to haberdashers; inventories of shops, *E.D.*, 24/28, *Memorials*, ed. Riley, p. 422.
[102] *C.P.R.*, 1364-7, p. 4.
[103] *E.D.*, 40/18; *E.D.*, 164, John Aubrey.
[104] *Mun. Gild.*, vol. ii (*Lib. Cust.*), i, p. 428; *Ancient Petition*, 168/8381; *Placita de Quo Warranto temporibus Edw. I, II, and III*, p. 457 (1818). *Stat.* 3 Edw. IV, c. 4. *Stat.* 1 Ric. III, c. 12.
[105] *E.D.*, 12/24, 38/17, 47/22, 62/1.
[106] *E.C.P.*, 66/345.
[107] *Cal. L. Bk.*, K, p. 89.
[108] *E.D.*, 12/24, 47/22, 47/25, 48/25, 46/19, 42/2, 62/1; *Wardens' Accts.*, Grocers, 1448-60, f. 117; *Wardens' Accts.*, Grocers', 1460-71, accts., 1470-1.
[109] *Cal. Plea and Memo. Rolls*, 1323-64, p. 118; *Wardens' Accts.*, Grocers, 1448-60, f. 70.
[110] *Grocers' Facsimile*, ed. Kingdon, vol. ii, p. 283, vol. i, *passim*.
[111] *K.R. Cust. Acct.*, 71/13; *Cal. Fr. R.*, Hen. VI, pp. 349, 401; *K.R. Cust. Accts.*, 73/20, 73/23; *Var. Accts.*: *Foreign Merchants*, 128/30; *Cal. Fr. R.*, Hen. VI, pp. 332, 340; *Plea and Memo. Rolls*, A. 71/11 (MS. Cal.); *Var. Accts.*: *Foreign Merchants*, 128/30.
[112] Ibid., 128/30 and 31; *Journals*, 9, ff. 240-1, 5, f. 233; *C.P.R.*, 1436-42, pp. 64-125.
[113] *P.C.C.*, Marche 8; *Hust. R.*, 133/84; *K.R. Cust. Acct.*, 71/13; *A Wardrobe Account of 16-17 Richard II, 1383-4*, ed. W. Paley Baildon, p. 508, in Archæologia, second series, vol. xii, (Soc. of Antiquaries, Oxford, 1911), pp. 497-514. G. Welch, *History of*

NOTES TO THE GROCERS OF LONDON

the Worshipful Company of Pewterers of the City of London (2 vols., 1902), vol. i, p. 25. *P.C.C.*, Stockton 8. *C.P.R.*, 1452-61, p. 155; *Var. Accts : Foreign Merchants*, 128/30; *Grocers' Facsimile*, ed. Kingdon, vol, ii, p. 323; *P.C.C.* Stockton 15.

[114] *Grocers' Facsimile*, ed. Kingdon, vol. ii, p. 181; ibid., pp. 175-6; *Wardens' Accts.*, Mercers, f. 101.

[115] *L. Bk.*, I, f. 153 (MS.); ibid., ff. 165, 204 (MS.); Beaven, op. cit., vol. i, p. 234; *Wills*, ed. Sharpe, vol. ii, pp. 428-9.

[116] *Cal. L. Bk.*, H, pp. 235, 257-60; *Journal*, 2, f. 21v; *Cal. L. Bk.*, K, pp. 163, 165; *Recognizance Rolls*, 13-24.

[117] *Journals*, 7, ff. 54, 193; 8, f. 27v; *L. Bk.*, L, f. 39 (MS.).

[118] *Acts*, Mercers, ff. 96, 108-9.

[119] *Cal. L. Bks., passim*.

[120] *Cal. L. Bk.*, H, pp. 442-3; ibid., p. 439; *Cal. L. Bk.*, I, pp. 215-16; *Acts*, Mercers, f. 58.

[121] Ibid., f. 96; *Register*, Grocers, ff. 1-2.

[122] Ibid., f. 54.

[123] *Grocers' Facsimile*, vol. ii, p. 186; *Cal. L. Bk.*, D, pp. 198-9.

[124] S. Kramer, *The English Craft Gilds. Studies in their Progress and Decline* (New York, 1927), p. 5.

[125] *C.P.R.*, 1364-7, pp. 15-17; *C.C.R.*, 1364-8, pp. 75-6.

[126] *K.R. Cust. Accts.*, 62/4, 13/1, 13/3, 6/2d, Roger Russel, John Whitfeld, Thomas Partrynton, William Brompton.

[127] *Port Books* and *Brokage Books, passim* (Southampton).

[128] *The Records of the Borough of Northampton*, ed. C. A. Markham (London and Northampton, 1898), vol. i, p. 235. *The Little Red Book of Bristol*, ed. F. B. Bickley vol. i, pp. 5, 47. *The York Mercers and Merchant Adventurers, 1356-1917*, ed. M. Sellers, (Surtees Soc., vol. cxxix, 1918), p. 92. Ibid., p. 91. Ibid., p. 92; *Extracts from the Records of the Merchant Adventurers of Newcastle-on-Tyne*, ed. F. W. Dendy (Surtees Soc., vol. xciii, 1895), pp. 5-6.

[129] *The Records of the City of Norwich*, ed. W. Hudson and J. C. Tingley (2 vols., 1906-10), vol. ii, p. 288, ibid., p. xlvi.

[130] Unwin, *The Estate of Merchants*, op. cit., p. 238; *Reading Records, Diary of the Corporation*, ed. J. M. Guilding (4 vols., 1892-1896), vol. i, p. 18. Barber fined in tiles.

[131] *Port Books* (Southampton), 18th March, 1451, William Barlowe.

[132] *E.D.*, 45/13.

VII

THE RELATIONS BETWEEN THE LANCASTRIAN GOVERNMENT AND THE MERCHANTS OF THE STAPLE FROM 1449 TO 1461

[1] M. Peake, *London and the Wars of the Roses*. Thesis presented for the degree of M.A. in the University of London, 1925 (deposited in the University of London Library), and W. I. Haward, *Economic Aspects of the Wars of the Roses*, in E.H.R., vol. xli, 1926, pp. 170–89.

[2] *Rot. Parl.*, vol. v, p. 144.

[3] *Rot. Parl.*, vol. iv, p. 503; vol. v, p. 144.

[4] *Rot. Parl.*, vol. v, p. 149. *Stat.* 27 Hen. VI, c. 2. The exemptions were in favour of Thomas Walsingham, Thomas Browne and John Pennycock, who were officials of the Royal Household, and the Prior of Bridlington. *Rot. Parl.*, vol. v, p. 183.

[5] For a study of the modification of the Staple regulations by royal licence and of the results of the legislation of 1449, see W. Haward, *The Transactions between the Merchants of the Staple and the Lancastrian Government*. Thesis presented for the degree of Ph.D. in the University of London, 1931 (deposited in the University of London Library), chapter iii.

[6] *C.P.R.*, 1446–52, p. 377.

[7] *C.P.R.*, 1446–52, p. 315. *Treaty Roll*, 26 Hen. VI, m. 15. *Treaty Roll*, 25 Hen. VI, m. 5.

[8] *Receipt Roll*, Mich. 29 Hen. VI; *K.R. Memo. Roll*, Hil. 29 Hen. VI, m. 9. *Issue Roll*, Mich. 29 Hen. VI. *C.P.R.*, 1446–52, p. 323.

[9] *Receipt Roll*, Easter 29 Hen. VI. *Treaty Roll*, 29 Hen. VI, m. 4. Ibid., m. 2. *Issue Roll*, Easter 29 Hen. VI (28th May). *C.P.R.*, 1446–52, p. 480.

[10] *E.C.P.*, 22/178.

[11] Thirty-two out of the seventy-nine who contributed to the loan of £10,700 in 1449 contributed also to that of £1,000 in 1450.

[12] *E.C.P.*, 22/178.

[13] *C.P.R.*, 1446–62, p. 315.

[14] *L.T.R. Cust. Accts.*, 19 m. 4d. (London); 19 m. 26 (Boston); 20 m. 17 (Hull); 19 m. 29d (Ipswich). It will be recalled that in 1449 the king had agreed to withdraw the licences to export elsewhere than to Calais for a period of five years, so that the merchants exporting in order to recover their loan had every reason to expect a good sale at Calais, since the market was not likely to be spoilt by competition elsewhere.

[15] Ibid. *L.T.R. Cust. Accts.*, 20 m. 1. *K.R. Memo. Roll*, Easter 31 Hen. VI, mm. 2, 4, ibid., Trin. m. 8.

[16] *K.R. Memo. Roll*, Easter 31 Hen. VI, m. 3. *L.T.R. Cust. Accts.*, 20 m. 2. The last sum (£127 15s. 5½d.) may not have been recovered within the four years.

[17] *L.T.R. Cust. Accts.*, 20 m. 26.

[18] *K.R. Memo. Roll*, Mich. 31 Hen. VI, m. 24. *L.T.R. Cust. Accts.* 20, mm. 18–23.

[19] Ibid., mm. 33d, 34.

[20] *L.T.R. Cust. Accts.*, 20 mm., 17, 18.

[21] *Rot. Parl.*, vol. v, p. 256. *C.P.R.*, 1452–61, p. 209. There are slight discrepancies between the figures given here and those we have given as the results of calculations from the customs accounts. Our figures for the first loan are £2,111 12s. 10¼d. instead of £2,113 0s. 1¾d., and £1,806 4s. 6½s. instead of £1,805 8s. 10¼d. of the 4,000 marks in Hull. But in a few cases it is not possible to be sure that a shipment was made before or after the petition was drawn up and, taking into consideration the rather elaborate calculations, the discrepancies are so slight that we have not attempted to explain them. The figures in the customs accounts have been used as the basis of later calculations because of the overlapping of dates, which is probably the cause of the differences.

[22] *L.T.R. Cust. Accts.*, 20, mm. 4, 21–3, 35. Ibid., m. 28d.

[23] *L.T.R. Cust. Accts.*, 21, mm. 1, 2.

[24] *C.P.R.*, 1452–61, pp. 423, 500.

[25] *L.T.R. Cust. Accts.*, 21, m. 2.

[26] *Issue Roll*, Easter 32 Hen. VI (12th July). *K.R. Memo. Roll*, Mich. 36 Hen. VI, m. 48.

[27] See pp. 304-5.

[28] *Var. Accts. France*. The Treasurer was responsible for the payment of wages and the Victualler for arms and ammunition as well as for provisions. His accounts contain entries for the purchase of corn, oxen, large quantities of bacon, wine, candles, tables, as well as guns, saltpetre, spades, hammers, " bulwerks," " squyrtes de laton," and arms of all kinds. Each received money from the Exchequer independently of the other, and kept separate accounts, but sometimes additional sums were paid by the Treasurer to the Victualler, whose accounts were balanced by entering the money as received for victuals " sold " to the Treasurer, or as a loan.

[29] J. Ramsay, *Lancaster and York*, vol. ii, p. 265.

[30] G. A. C. Sandeman, *Calais under English Rule*, p. 23, *Proc. and Ord. P.C.*, vol. v, p. 203.

[31] *Rot. Parl.*, vol. v, p. 207.

[32] *Rot. Parl.*, vol. v, p. 256.

[33] *Receipt Roll*, Easter 32 Hen. VI (24th and 29th May, 1st and 6th June); *Issue Roll*, Easter 32 Hen. VI (1st and 4th June, 12th July).

[34] *Var. Accts. France*, 195/3-5. The Duke of York is referred to as the " late " captain of Calais, although he did not give up his post until 1456.

[35] *Rot. Parl.*, vol. v, p. 295. *E.C.P.*, 32/246, 251. *Rot. Parl.*, v, p. 295.

[36] See below, p. 305.

[37] *K.R. Memo. Roll*, Easter 34 Hen. VI, m. 2.

[38] G. Schanz, *Englische Handelspolitik*, vol. ii, p. 565.

[39] *Treaty Roll*, 35 Hen. VI, m. 26. Ibid., 33 Hen. VI, m. 5.

[40] 25th May, 1450, £1,021 1s. 1½d.; 5th Aug., £1,000 to the Treasurer and £200 to the Victualler for " saltpetre "; 30th Oct., £3,333 6s. 8d. for wages and £1,266 13s. 4d. for victuals; 27th Feb., 1451, £4,533 6s. 8d. from the Staplers; 2nd Dec., 1452, £1,868 7s. 3¼d.; 24th and 25th July, 1453, £6,666 13s. 4d.

[41] There are frequent notes in the *Issue Rolls* of payments to messengers sent to communicate with the soldiers at Calais.

[42] *K.R. Memo. Roll*, 34 Hen. VI, Trin. m. 3.

[43] Sir James Ramsay says that it was " prompted by the wish to reconcile the soldiery to the authority of the Earl of Warwick, which, till then, had been defied "; *Lancaster and York*, vol. ii, p. 191.

[44] The sums are given in marks, shillings and pence. I have translated them into pounds, shillings and pence; the figures are more easily grasped and can be more readily compared with the Treasurer's accounts.

[45] *Issue Roll*, Easter 34 Hen. VI., ibid., Easter 35 Hen. VI (15th July).

[46] See above, pp. 74-5.

[47] See the interesting case as to his position, *Cartulaire de l'ancienne Estaple de Bruges*, ed. L. Gilliodts-van Severen, vol. ii, p. 36, *Treaty Rolls*, 33 Hen. VI, m. 5, 34 Hen. VI, m. 17.

[48] Two hundred sacks of Norfolk wool to be sent to any parts abroad by the Earl of Somerset and Lord Roos, *Treaty Roll*, 35 Hen. VI, m. 8.

[49] Probably on 16th Nov., 1457. See *C.P.R.*, 1452-61, p. 410.

[50] *K.R. Memo. Roll*, Mich. 36 Hen. VI, m. 48.

[51] *E.C.P.*, 26/341.

[52] *Treaty Roll*, 35 Hen. VI, m. 21.

[53] Ibid., 35 Hen. VI, m. 11; 36 Hen. VI, mm. 10, 29. Ibid., 35 Hen. VI, m. 4. Ibid., 36 Hen. VI, m. 23. Ibid., 36 Hen. VI, m. 4. Ibid., 35 Hen. VI, m. 22.

[54] Ibid., 36 Hen. VI, mm. 14, 16.

[55] *Cal. St. P., Ven.*, vol. i, p. 72. *E.C.P.*, 24/252. Ibid., 64/302 (Jury declare they will never hear the evidence of a Lombard against an Englishman), 64/638, 64/1011.

[56] R. Henley, *London and Foreign Merchants in the Reign of Henry VI*, in E.H.R., vol. xxv, (1910), pp. 644-55.

[57] *The New Chronicles* . . . *Fabyan*, ed. H. Ellis, p. 631. *Cal. St. P., Ven.*, vol. i, p. 84.

[58] *Cal. L. Bk.*, K, pp. 377-8.

[59] Here, and on many other occasions, Homobone Griti is described as " Homo Bonegriti ".

[60] The proceedings are recorded at length in the *K.R. Memo. Rolls*, Hil., Easter and Trin. 36 Hen. VI, Mich. 37 Hen. VI.

[61] *K.R. Memo. Rolls*, Hil. 36 Hen. VI, mm. 20-26, Trin. 37 Hen. VI, m. 32, *Cartulaire de l'ancienne Estaple de Bruges*, ed. L. Gilliodts-van Severen, vol. i, 703, 705, vol. ii, p. 36. *K.R. Memo. Roll*, Hil. 36 Hen. VI.

[62] *C.P.R.*, 1452–61, p. 444.
[63] *K.R. Memo. Rolls*, Trin. 37 Hen. VI, Mich. 38 Hen. VI.
[64] *Issue Rolls*, Easter, 35 and 36 Hen. VI.
[65] *Treaty Roll*, 37 Hen. VI, m. 11.
[66] *Receipt Roll*, Mich. 37, Hen. VI. *Treaty Roll*, 38 Hen. VI, m. 16.
[67] *L.T.R. Cust. Acct.* 21, m. 1.
[68] *Treaty Roll*, 37 Hen. VI, m. 10.
[69] *L.T.R. Cust. Acct.* 21. Ibid., m. 15.
[70] Ibid., m. 1.
[71] In 1458 the merchants of the Staple advanced £1,100 to Warwick as keeper of the seas, *C.P.R.*, 1452–61, p. 328.
[72] G. Dufresne de Beaucourt, *Histoire de Charles VI* (Paris, 1881), vol. vi, p. 260. "It is probable that from this moment, a secret agreement was reached by the Duke with the Yorkist party. Pourparlers were begun at Calais and London, and continued at Bruges in August."
[73] *Treaty Roll*, 36 Hen. VI, m. 12. Thrysk had succeeded White as Mayor of the Staple shortly before; ibid., m. 18. *Proc. and Ord. P.C.*, vol. vi, p. 253. G. Schanz, *Englische Handelspolitik*, vol. ii, p. 543.
[74] *The New Chronicles . . . Fabyan*, ed. H. Ellis, p. 633.
[75] *Treaty Roll*, 38 Hen. VI, m. 16. There is no such ordinance in the records of Parliament. The fact is mentioned incidentally in a mandate directing the Staplers to ship to any part abroad for the recovery of their loans. Several other persons receiving licences received similar directions, *Treaty Roll*, 38 Hen. VI, mm. 2, 6, 8. *The New Chronicles . . . Fabyan*, ed. H. Ellis, p. 636. *Rot. Parl.*, v, pp. 454–5.
[76] *Hist. MSS. Comm.*, Report V, App. 492, 522. *Foedera*, vol. v, p. 92. *Treaty Roll*, 38 Hen. VI, m. 9.
[77] *C.P.R.*, 1452–61, p. 598; the year for which the restriction of the Italian trade was imposed had expired four days before, and the Italians had evidently taken immediate advantage of the fact. *Cal. St. P., Ven.*, vol. i, p. 88. "Very great caution should be used in this matter, their release being sought in all suitable ways." The money does not appear to have been paid.
[78] For these negotiations, see C. L. Scofield, *Life and Reign of Edward IV*, vol. i, p. 48.
[79] *C.P.R.*, 1452–61, p. 600.
[80] *Treaty Roll*, 38 Hen. VI, m. 16.
[81] *The New Chronicles . . . Fabyan*, ed. H. Ellis, pp. 635, 652.
[82] *Select Cases before the King's Council*, 1243–1482, ed. I. S. Leadam and J. F. Baldwin, p. 112.
[83] H. G. Richardson, *Illustrations of English History in the Medieval Registers of the Parlement of Paris*, in Trans. R. Hist. Soc., Fourth Series, vol. 10, pp. 55–85 (1927).
[84] *Rot. Parl.*, vol. vi, p. 182.
[85] C. L. Scofield, op. cit., vol. i, p. 225.

APPENDIX A (TO ESSAY I)

VARIATIONS IN ENGLISH FOREIGN TRADE, 1446-1482. ANNUAL AVERAGES BY PERIODS

Period. Mich.–Mich.	Wool Exported by Denizens.	Wool Exported by Aliens.	Total.	Broadcloths Exported by Denizens.	%	Hansards.	%	Others.	%	Total.	Imports of Wine. Non-Sweet.	Imports of Wine. Sweet.	Value of Mdse. paying 3d. in the £ Hansards.[2]	Value of Mdse. paying 3d. in the £ Other Aliens.[2]	Value of Mdse. paying Poundage Share of Denizens.[3]	Total.
1446-1448	5947	1707	7654	29633	55	11289	21	12777	24	53699	10234	766	21794	32690	57162	121795
1448-1450	7266	1146	8412	18774	54	5929	17	10375	29	35078	8498	934	17981	26972	38846	91456
1450-1453	6560	1200	7760	22508	58	7420	19	9000	23	38928	6690	734	17038	25731	42770	91001
1453-1456	6347	2943	9290	19424	51	9650	26	8664	23	37738	6204	622	18824	28237	32636	82533
1456-1459	5493	2171	7664	19831	57	10289	29	4939	14	35059	3533	539	14725	22088	24653	59089
1459-1462	4117	859	4976	15950	50	9801	31	6181	19	31933	3628	562	14770	22156	27895	65503
1462-1465	6529	515	7044	15278	59	7157	27	3420	14	25855	6465	609	12274	18411	30488	57449
1465-1469	8066	1250	9316	20802[4]	52	6220	16	12642	32	39664	5452	490	20094	30141	32196	93942
1469-1471[1]	7049	762	7811	17532	64	3620	13	6458	23	27610	3249	162	10374	15562	21714	53421
1471-1476[1]	8109	982	9091	24927[4]	58	4721	11	13481	31	43129	4186	543	19685	29528	52245	115475
1476-1479	6374	1128	7502	33052[4]	64	9133	18	9704	18	51889	6580	307	13187	33662	62411	120333
1479-1482	8328	1456	9784	36728	59	13907	22	11951	19	62586	6570	357	26375	33061	116301	179340

[1] For wool these periods are 1469–1471 and 1472–1476.
[2] Estimated by assigning to Hansards 40 per cent and to other aliens 60 per cent of the total, except from 1476-1482, when the accounts themselves make the distinction.
[3] Estimated.
[4] The accounts for Bristol are missing from 8.2.1467 to Mich. 1467, and from Mich. 1471 to Mich. 1477. It may be estimated that in the first period 1600 cloths were imported, in the last period 5500 annually. The averages have been computed on this supposition.

401

APPENDIX B (TO ESSAY I)

TOTAL ENGLISH FOREIGN TRADE, 1446-1482.

Date.	Amount in Sacks of Wool Exported by Denizens. Wool. Fells.	Aliens. Wool.	Broadcloths Exported by Denizens.	Hansards.	Other aliens.	Total.	Value in £ of Alien Mdse. paying the Petty Custom of 3d. in the £.	Value in £ of Mdse. paying Poundage.	Tunnage. Tuns of wine. Non-sweet.	Sweet.
1446-1447	592 206	1614	31300	13157	10321	54778	59273	119563	9382	660
1447-1448	2412 9090 2006	1799	27966	9421	15232	52619	49693	124026	10042 11085	872
1448-1449	12895 126 55	1691	19516	6470	9604	35590	60372	80228	11957 12032	1207
1449-1450	1872 11390 2961	601	18033	5387	11146	34566	29523	102684	13239 4965	661
1450-1451	14952 5164 906	1126	22876	7349	10022	40247	45951	104455	5626 5114	562
1451-1452	7196 6225 1543	1547	15969	3279	12737	31985	24262	78529	5676 5919	877
1452-1453	9315 4717 1126	927	28678	11634	4241	44553	58094	90200	6796 9036	764
1453-1454	6770 749 492	3926	16665	8721	6344	31130	44082	61593 [1]	9800 5666	648
1454-1455	5167 9390 1487	1517	18123	7428	4211	29762	40549	75827	6314 8873	627
	12394								9300	

[1] Of which £1,492 is the value of aliens' tin.

APPENDIX B

Date	Amount in Sacks of Wool Exported by Denizens. Wool.	Fells.	Aliens. Wool.	Broadcloths Exported by Denizens.	Hansards.	Other aliens.	Total.	Value in £ of Alien Mdse. paying the Petty Custom of 3d. in the £.	Value in £ of Mdse. paying Poundage.	Tunnage. Tuns of wine. Non-sweet.	Sweet.
1455–1456	4518 2405	3385		24085	12800	15437	52323	56551	110178 [1]	4073	592
	10308									4665	
1456–1457	1549 695	2866		15653	7751	4359	27763	37215	63663 [2]	2428	435
	5110									2863	
1457–1458	6510 1215	1925		21522	12558	6492	40572	33377	57317 [3]	3703	441
	9650									4144	
1458–1459	4747 1765	1722		22317	10560	3966	36843	39847	56287 [4]	4468	742
	8234									5210	
1459–1460	89 1	780		10976	7214	8009	76199	31445	52699 [5]	4376	587
	870									4963	
1460–1461	5979 3600	1003		13875	10708	6525	31108	34391	63849 [6]	2879	338
	10582									3217	
1461–1462	1869 813	795		23000	11482	4010	38492	44943	79960 [7]	3630	762
	3477									4392	
1462–1463	3541 1015	732		18108	6256	1078	25442	28381	49753 [8]	4183	542
	5288									4725	
1463–1464	6329 2036	103		21029	10110	5198	36364	30216	69182	8257	859
	8468									9116	

[1] Of which £5,108 is the value of aliens' tin.
[2] Of which £363 is the value of aliens' tin.
[3] Of which £146 is the value of aliens' tin.
[4] Of which £463 is the value of aliens' tin.
[5] Of which £255 is the value of aliens' tin.
[6] Of which £1,513 is the value of aliens' tin.
[7] Of which £504 is the value of aliens' tin.
[8] Of which £2,033 is the value of aliens' tin.

APPENDIX B

Date	Amount in Sacks of Wool Exported by Denizens. Wool.	Fells.	Aliens. Wool.	Broadcloths Exported by Denizens.	Hansards.	Other aliens.	Total.	Value in £ of Alien Mdse. paying the Petty Custom of 3d. in the £.	Value in £ of Mdse. paying Poundage.	Tunnage. Tuns of wine. Non-sweet.	Sweet.
1464–1465	5265	1401	709	6696	5106	3984 [1]	15786	33457	53413 [2]	6956	427
		7375								7383	
1465–1466	5110	1279	1840	15132	8720	9875 [3]	33927	58606	91795 [4]	3948	490
		8229								4438	
1466–1467	7730	1336	880 [5]	12153	7261	20755	40169 [6]	54158	112933 [7]	4010	273
		9946								4283	
1467–1468	6772	1488	1096	20640	8033	10379	42738 [8]	45871	80247 [9]	7430	521
		9356								7951	
1468–1469	6662	1885	1182 [10]	33684	864	9560 [11]	40422	42305	90791 [12]	6416	677
		9729								7093	
1469–1470	6599	2673	328 [13]	16047	3898	6683 [14]	26571	31891	64928 [15]	3763	70
		9600								3833	

[1] Of which 398 rex per factores alienos.
[2] Of which £1,740 is the value of aliens' tin.
[3] Of which 6,777 rex per f.a.
[4] Of which £1,510 is the value of aliens' tin.
[5] Of which 19 rex per f.a., 344 rex ad partes exteras, 8 ind. ad p.e., 189 Duchess of York per f.a.
[6] Of which 7,314 by the king's denizen factors, 5,886 by the king's Hanseatic factors, 10,768 by other alien factors of the king, and 1,997 indigenae per f.a.
[7] Of which £16,901 is the value of king's cloths, £5,462 the value of denizens' cloths, and £6,630 the value of aliens' tin.
[8] Of which 11,333 by the king's denizen factors, 6,876 by the king's Hanseatic factors, 2,457 by other alien factors of the king, and 2,958 ind. per f.a.
[9] Of which £2,270 is the value of aliens' tin.
[10] Of which 646 rex per f.a., 201 ind. per f.a., 229 ind. ad p.e.
[11] Of which 1,931 rex per f.a., and 1,544 ind. ad p.e.
[12] Of which £6,049 is the value of aliens' tin.
[13] Of which 144 rex per f.a.; 44 Duchess of York per f.a., and 90 ind. ad p.e.
[14] Of which 2,216 rex per f.a.; 1,286 ind. ad p.e.
[15] Of which £2,339 is the value of aliens' tin.

APPENDIX B
405

Date.	Amount in Sacks of Wool Exported by Denizens. Wool. Fells.	Aliens. Wool.	Broadcloths Exported by Denizens.	Hansards.	Other aliens.	Total.	Value in £ of Alien Mdse. paying the Petty Custom of 3d. in the £.	Value in £ of Mdse. paying Poundage.	Tunnage. Tons of wine. Non-sweet. Sweet.
1470–1471	505 315 739		19016	3342	6232	38303	19980	41914 [1]	2734 254
	1559								2988
1471–1472	7605 3451 1219		14004	3202	16867 [2]	34073	57141	137562 [3]	5499 309
	12275								5808
1472–1473	5610 1051 788 [4]		22088	4087	12009 [5]	38184	57875	115513 [6]	4477 1179
	7449								5656
1473–1474	6066 1031 1414		21230	1949	20372 [7]	43551	41330	139775 [8]	3501 223
	8511								3724
1474–1475	6572 978 1372 [9]		16131	4217	10873 [10]	31221	53987	107604 [11]	3640 942
	8922								4582
1475–1476	7568 3562 356		23682	10152	7283 [12]	41117	35732	76919 [13]	3814 59
	11486								3873
1476–1477	775 211 2101 [14]		24321	8863	12815 [15]	45972	57650	120931 [16]	6702 118
	3807								6820

[1] Of which £1,142 if the value of aliens' tin.
[2] Of which 459 rex per f.a.
[3] Of which £2,138 is the value of aliens' tin and £2,741 the value of the king's tin.
[4] Of which 284 rex per f.a.; 284 ind. per f.a.
[5] Of which 1,341 were exported by Spaniards and 233 by merchants of Veer.
[6] Of which £300 is the value of aliens' tin, £1,138 the value of the king's tin.
[7] Of which 376 by Spaniards and 216 by merchants of Veer.
[8] Of which £765 is the value of the king's tin, £5,887 the value of aliens' tin and pewter vessels.
[9] Of which 558 ind. per f.a.
[10] Of which 1,667 by Spaniards and 106 by merchants of Veer.
[11] Of which £7,077 is the value of aliens' tin.
[12] Of which 976 by Spaniards and 111 by merchants of Veer.
[13] Of which £76 is the value of aliens' tin, £1528 the value of the king's.
[14] Of which 217 ind. ad p.c., 616 ind. per f.a.
[15] Of which 1,165 by Spaniards and 113 by merchants of Veer.
[16] Of which £3,766 is the value of aliens' tin, £1,240 value of the king's.

APPENDIX B

Date.	Amount in Sacks of Wool Exported by Denizens. Wool. Fells.	Aliens. Wool.	Broadcloths Exported by Denizens. Hansards. Other aliens. Total.				Value in £ of Alien Mdse. paying the Petty Custom of 3d. in the £.	Value in £ of Mdse. paying Poundage.	Tunnage. Tuns of wine. Non-sweet. Sweet.	
1477–1478	5400 3293	75 [1]	26481	6316	4271 [2]	37068	34879	112107 [3]	5423	70
	8768								5493	
1478–1479	6395 3047	1208 [4]	42854	12219	12027 [5]	67100	48019	127861 [6]	7614	732
	10650								8346	
1479–1480	6471 1500	869	33332	11581	11476 [7]	56589	49205	158936 [8]	7030	361
	8840								7391	
1480–1481	6857 3002	1529 [9]	38089	15567	10559 [10]	64215	65725	189784 [11]	7230	51
	11388								7281	
1481–1482	3819 3334	1969	38564	14573	13818 [12]	66955	63389	189300 [13]	5449	658
	9122								6107	

[1] Of which 17 rex per f.a., 58 ind. per f.a.
[2] Of which 903 by Spaniards, 79 by merchants of Veer, and 1,709 ind. per f.a.
[3] Of which £43 is the value of aliens' tin, £974 of the king's.
[4] Of which 282 ind. ad p.c. and 530 ind. per f.a.
[5] Of which 1,302 by Spaniards and 169 by merchants of Veer.
[6] Of which £2,115 is the value of aliens' tin, £1,150 of the king's.
[7] Of which 2,540 by Spaniards and 79 by merchants of Veer.
[8] Of which £3,410 is the value of aliens' tin, £884 the value of the king's.
[9] Of which 268 ind. per f.a.
[10] Of which 3,024 by Spaniards, 1,326 by Bretons, and 84 by merchants of Veer.
[11] Of which £2,212 is the value of aliens' tin, £1,645 the value of the king's.
[12] Of which 3,370 by Spaniards, 4,106 by Bretons, 24 by merchants of Veer.
[13] Of which £5,328 is the value of aliens' tin, £487 the value of the king's.

APPENDIX C (TO ESSAY III)

BROADCLOTHS EXPORTED BY THE HANSEATIC MERCHANTS, 1406–1480

Year (ending Michaelmas)	Broadcloths (to the nearest ten)	Year (ending Michaelmas)	Broadcloths (to the nearest ten)
1406	5560	1444	11470
1407	8730	1445	12980
1408	5710	1446	12020
1409	4830	1447	13160
1410	5970	1448	9420
1411	4340	1449	6470
1412	4990	1450	5390
1413	6050	1451	7350
1414	4660	1452	3280
1415	4890	1453	11630
1416	4430	1454	8720
1417	4390	1455	7430
1418	6020	1456	12800
1419	5940	1457	7750
1420	7650	1458	12560
1421	9410	1459	10560
1422	5380	1460	7210
1423	7490	1461	10710
1424	6820	1462	11480
1425	7090	1463	6260
1426	6200	1464	10110
1427	5500	1465	5110
1428	1720	1466	8720
1429	4754	1467	7260
1430	4300	1468	8026
1431	3070	1469	860
1432	2170	1470	3900
1433	3700	1471	3340
1434	5290	1472	3200
1435	5850	1473	4090
1436	2350	1474	1950
1437	12320	1475	4220
1438	12920	1476	10150
1439	9230	1477	8860
1440	10700	1478	6320
1441	8700	1479	12220
1442	12960	1480	11580
1443	11290	—	—

It has not been possible to begin the table earlier than 1406, owing to the fact that during the first six years of the reign the customs of Lynn (one of the principal centres of Baltic trade) were farmed by a group of private merchants and only imperfectly accounted for in the *L.T.R. Customs Rolls*. An estimate of Lynn exports based on later returns would be somewhat misleading, for the farming of customs was very unlikely to leave the position of Lynn unaffected.

It will probably be observed that some of the variations in the figures reflect changes in the administration of the customs, rather than fluctuations of the trade. For instance, it is quite probable that the drop in the figure for 1463 was due, at least in part, to the disorganization of the customs machinery in the year of civil war, while the spectacular rise of the amount for 1480 was due to the tightening up of exchequer control in the closing years of Edward IV's reign.

The most salient feature of the table is the striking rise of the Hanseatic exports after

1437, immediately following the conclusion of the Vorrath treaty. This, as all the other variations in the figures, reflects the fluctuations of Anglo-Hanseatic trade, but does not provide their correct measurement. The English-borne exports to the Hanseatic regions ran their own course and this movement sometimes failed to synchronize with that of the Hanseatic exports. Thus the circumstantial evidence of other records suggests that the English trade to Prussia flourished exceedingly between 1409 and 1418, the very period when German-borne exports were rather depressed (p. 113). If a general cause is to be assigned to this change after 1437, it is probably the definitive freeing of Hanseatic exports from all national and local taxation not provided for in their original charter, in exchange for a similar privilege to the English in Danzig (p. 119). Before 1437 the Hanseatic merchants were repeatedly subjected to local imposts and to tunnage and poundage (pp. 113, 114, 116).

Within these two main periods the important fluctuations reflected in the table are: (1) The drop in the year ending Michaelmas, 1428, which was probably due to the blockade of the Sund in 1427 and to the difficulties with Burgundy (pp. 113, 114). (2) The depression between 1431 and 1433 coincides with the critical years preceding the dispatch of the Vorrath delegation, while the figure for 1436 reflects both the effect and the relative ineffectiveness of Vorrath's temporary embargo on English trade (pp. 116–18). (3) The relative depression between 1449 and 1452 coincides with the capture of the Bay fleet and the period of friction which followed. The drop in the figure for 1452, however, is very much exaggerated in the table, and is largely due to the fact that the London accounts for 1451–2 cover only eight months, while the same accounts for 1452–3 cover the period of sixteen months. The corresponding amounts, when adjusted, are 5250 and 9350. A similar correction for the years 1455, 1456, and 1457 does away with the fictitious rise in 1456, and the amounts, thus corrected, are 9670, 9350, and 8870. (4) The drop of exports in 1465 reflects the temporary dislocation of the English cloth trade to Burgundy, in connection with the Burgundian embargo and the migration of the Merchant Adventurers to Utrecht. The Hanseatics affected were the Cologners, and even their trade recovered in the following two years, in common with the rest of English trade to the Low Countries (page 132, notes 71 and 108a). (5) The most spectacular change in the figures coincides with the "verdict" of 1468 and the difficulties of the next six years (pp. 132–7). The figures between 1469 and 1474 relate entirely to the Cologne exports, and the sudden rise in 1476 signals the official return of the rest of the Hanse to London.

LIST OF ABBREVIATIONS

USED IN THE NOTES

C.C.R.	Calendar of Close Rolls.
C.P.R.	Calendar of Patent Rolls.
Cal. Fr. R.	Calendar of French Rolls.
Cal. St. P., Ven.	Calendar of State Papers, Venetian.
Cal. of Letters	Calendar of Letters from the Mayor and Corporation of the City of London, ed. R. R. Sharpe.
Chanc. Misc.	Chancery Miscellanea.
Comm. Lon.	Registers of the Commissary Court of London.
Cust. Accts.	Customs Accounts.
Dipl. Norv.	Diplomatarium Norvegicum, ed. A. Bugge, C. C. A. Lange, and C. R. Unger.
E.C.P.	Early Chancery Proceedings.
E.D.	Chancery : Extents on Debts.
E.E.T.S.	Early English Text Society.
E.H.R.	English Historical Review.
G.R.B.	The Great Red Book (Bristol).
Hans. Gbl.	Hansische Geschichtsblätter.
Hust. R.	Hustings Rolls, Wills and Deeds (London).
Island. Ann.	Icelandic Sagas, Rolls Series, vol. iv (Appendix B, Icelandic Annals).
Journal	Journals of the Proceedings of the Court of Common Council (London).
K.R.	King's Remembrancer (of the Exchequer).
L.Bk.	Letter Books.
L.T.R.	Lord Treasurer's Remembrancer (of the Exchequer).
Mun. Gild.	Munimenta Gildhallæ Londoniensis, ed. T. R. Riley.
P.C.C.	Register of Wills proved in the Prerogative Court of Canterbury.
Plea and Memo. Roll	Plea and Memoranda Rolls of the City of London.
Proc. and Ord. P.C.	Proceedings and Ordinances of the Privy Council of England, ed. Sir H. Nicolas.
R. Hist. S.	Royal Historical Society.
R.S.	Rolls Series.
Rot. Parl.	Rotuli Parliamentorum.
S.P.D.	State Papers (Domestic).
Stat.	Statutes of the Realm.
Test. Ebor.	Testamenta Eboracensia, ed. J. Raine.
U.B.	Hansisches Urkundenbuch, ed. K. Höhlbaum, K. Kunze and W. Stein.
V.S.W.G.	Vierteljahrschrift für Social-und Wirtschaftsgeschichte.

USED IN THE TABLES

ind.	indigenae (denizens).
ad p.e.	ad partes exteras (abroad i.e. elsewhere than to Calais).
per f.a.	per factores alienos (by alien factors).
Mdse.	Merchandise.

BIBLIOGRAPHY[1]

MANUSCRIPT SOURCES

A. NATIONAL ARCHIVES

I. PUBLIC RECORD OFFICE

Chancery Brevia Regia or Files. Tower Series, G. (Statute Merchant and Statute Staple Certificates).
Chancery Miscellanea.
Early Chancery Proceedings.
Chancery. Extents on Debts.
Chancery. Inquisitions Miscellaneous.
Treaty Rolls. (Including those formerly known as Almain Rolls and French Rolls.)
Chancery and Exchequer, Ancient Correspondence.
Chancery and Exchequer, Ancient Petitions.
Chancery and Exchequer, King's Remembrancers [K.R.]. Parliamentary and Council Proceedings.
Exchequer, K.R. Customs Accounts.
Exchequer, K.R. Escheators' Accounts.
Exchequer, K.R. Extents and Inquisitions: General Series.
Exchequer, K.R., Memoranda Rolls.
Exchequer, K.R., Subsidy Rolls, Lay Series.
Exchequer, K.R., Various Accounts.
Exchequer, Lord Treasurer's Remembrancer [L.T.R.]. Enrolled Accounts: Customs.
Exchequer of Receipt. Issue Rolls.
Exchequer of Receipt. Receipt Rolls.

II. BRITISH MUSEUM.

Additional MS. 29866.
Cotton MS., Nero 27.
Cotton MS., Vespasian E. ix. (" The Noumbre of Weyghtes ").
Harleian MS. 433.

III. SOMERSET HOUSE
Principal Probate Registry

Registers of the Commissary Court of London.
Registers of Wills proved in the Prerogative Court of Canterbury.

B. ARCHIVES OF CORPORATIONS

I. BRISTOL

The Great Red Book.
The Great White Book.
Tolzey Court Book, 1480-81.
Tolzey Court Book, 1487-97.

II. IPSWICH

Waste Book of Henry Tooley, merchant, of Ipswich, 1524-48.

III. KING'S LYNN

Congregation Books I and II.
Entry Book.

---

[1] Works referred to only once or twice are not included in this Bibliography.

IV. KINGSTON-UPON-HULL

Bench Books II and III.
Chamberlain's Account Roll.

V. LONDON

City Archives (Guildhall)

Hustings Rolls, Wills and Deeds.
Journals of the Proceedings of the Court of Common Council.
Letter Books.
MS. Calendar of Plea and Memoranda Rolls.
Recognisance Rolls.
Roll of Outlawries.

Worshipful Company of Grocers

Ordinances, Remembrances, and Wardens' Accounts, 1463–1557.
Quires of Wardens' Accounts, 1448–60.
Quires of Wardens' Accounts, 1460–71.
Register of Freemen and Apprentices.

Worshipful Company of Mercers

Acts of Court. [First Volume.]
Register of Freemen.
Wardens' Accounts. [First Volume.]

VI. SOUTHAMPTON

Brokage Books : Fifteenth Century.
Port Books : Fifteenth Century.

PRINTED SOURCES

A. RECORDS OF THE CENTRAL GOVERNMENT

BERGENROTH, G. A. [Ed.]. Calendar of Letters, Dispatches, and State Papers, relating to the Negotiations between England and Spain. Vol. i. Henry VII. 1485–1509. 1862.
BROWN, R. [Ed.]. Calendar of State Papers and Manuscripts, relating to English affairs . . . in . . . Venice, and . . . Northern Italy. Vol. i, 1202–1509. 1864.
Calendar of the Close Rolls.
Calendar of the French Rolls, Henry V. The Forty-fourth Annual Report of the Deputy Keeper of the Public Records. Appendix No. 3. 1883.
Calendar of the French Rolls : Henry VI. The Forty-eighth Annual Report of the Deputy Keeper of the Public Records. Appendix No. 2. 1887.
Calendar of Inquisitions Miscellaneous (Chancery), vol. ii. 1916.
Calendar of the Patent Rolls.
DEVON, F. Issues of the Exchequer. 1837.
List of Various Accounts and Documents connected therewith. P.R.O. Lists and Indexes, No. 35. 1912.
NICOLAS, H. [Ed.]. Proceedings and Ordinances of the Privy Council of England, 7 vols. 1834–7.
Rotuli Parliamentorum, ut et Petitiones et Placita in Parliamento [etc.], 6 vols. Record Commission, 1767–77.
RYMER, T. [Ed.]. Foedera, conventiones, litterae et cujuscunque generis acta publica inter reges Angliae et alios quosvis imperatores, reges, pontifices, principes vel communitates (1101–1654), 3rd edition, 10 vols. The Hague, 1739–45.
TOMLINS, T. E., RAITHBY, J., CALEY, J., ELLIOTT, W. [Eds.]. The Statutes of the Realm, 9 vols. 1810–22.
The Statutes at Large, passed in the Parliaments held in Ireland, vol. i. Dublin. 1765.

B. RECORDS OF THE CORPORATION OF THE CITY OF LONDON

RILEY, H. T., H.A. [Ed.]. Memorials of London and London Life in the XIIIth, XIVth, and XVth Centuries, A.D. 1276–1419. Corporation of the City of London, 1868.

RILEY, T. R. [Ed.]. Munimenta Gildhallae Londoniensis ; Liber Albus, Liber Custumarum, et Liber Horn, 3 vols. Rolls Series, 1859–62.

SHARPE, R. R. [Ed.]. Calendar of Letter Books, A–L, *circa* A.D. 1275–temp. Henry VII. Corporation of the City of London, 1899–1912.

—— Calendar of Letters from the Mayor and Corporation of the City of London, *circa* A.D. 1350–70. Corporation of the City of London, 1885.

—— Calendar of Wills proved and enrolled in the Court of Husting, London, A.D. 1258–A.D. 1688. 2 parts. Corporation of the City of London, 1889–90.

THOMAS, A. H. [Ed.]. Calendar of Early Mayor's Court Rolls, A.D. 1298–1307. Corporation of the City of London, Cambridge, 1924.

—— Calendar of Plea and Memoranda Rolls, A.D. 1323–64. Corporation of the City of London. Cambridge, 1926.

—— Calendar of Plea and Memoranda Rolls, A.D. 1364–81. Corporation of the City of London. Cambridge, 1929.

C. OTHER ENGLISH AND IRISH RECORDS

BERRY, H. F. [Ed.]. Register of Wills and Inventories of the Diocese of Dublin, 1457–83. The Royal Society of Antiquaries of Ireland. 1898.

BICKLEY, F. B. [Ed.]. The Little Red Book of Bristol, 2 vols. Council of the City and County of Bristol. Bristol and London, 1900.

CAXTON, W. [Ed.]. Cronica Ranulphi Cistrensis Monachi (Caxton, Polychronicon), 1527.

City of London Livery Companies' Commission. Report and Appendix, 5 vols. 1884.

DALLAWAY, J. [Ed.]. Antiquities of Bristow in the Middle Centuries ; including the Topography by William Wyrcestre, and the Life of William Canynges. Bristol, 1834.

ELLIS, H. [Ed.]. The New Chronicles of England and France, in two parts ; by Robert Fabyan, 1811.

FLENLEY, R. [Ed.]. Six Town Chronicles of England. Oxford, 1911.

FOX, F. F. [Ed.]. Adams's Chronicle of Bristol. Bristol, 1910.

GAIRDNER, J. [Ed.]. The Paston Letters, A.D. 1422–1509. Intro. and 3 vols. Edinburgh, 1910.

HALL, H. and NICHOLAS, F. J. [Eds.]. Select Tracts and Table Books relating to English Weights and Measures [1100–1742]. In Camden Miscellany, vol. xv. Camden Third Series, vol. xli. Royal Historical Society, 1929.

HEARNIUS, Thomas. Wilhelmi Wyrcester Annales Rerum Anglicarum. In Liber Niger Scaccarii, vol. ii, pp. 522–41. Oxford, 2 vols., 1728.

KINGDON, J. A. [Ed.]. Facsimile of First Volume of MS. Archives of the Worshipful Company of Grocers of the City of London, A.D. 1345–1463, 2 parts. Printed for the Company, 1886.

KINGSFORD, C. L. [Ed.]. Chronicles of London. Oxford, 1905.

KINGSFORD, C. L., F.S.A. [Ed.]. The Stonor Letters and Papers, 1290–1483, 2 vols. Camden Third Series, vols. xxix, xxx. Royal Historical Society. London, 1919.

KINGSFORD, C. L. [Ed.]. Supplementary Stonor Letters and Papers (1314–1482). Camden Miscellany, vol. xiii. Camden Third Series, vol. xxxiv. Royal Historical Society, 1924.

LEADAM, I. S. and BALDWIN, J. F. [Eds.]. Select Cases before the King's Council, 1243–1482. Selden Society, vol. xxxv. Harvard, Mass. 1918.

MALDEN, H. E. [Ed.]. The Cely Papers. Camden Third Series, vol. i. Royal Historical Society, 1900.

NASMITH, J. [Ed.]. Itineraria Symonis Simeonis et Willelmi de Worcester. Cambridge, 1778.

POLLARD, A. F. [Ed.]. The Reign of Henry VII from Contemporary Sources, 3 vols. 1913–14.

RAINE, J. [Ed.]. Testamenta Eboracensia. A Selection of Wills from the Registry at York, vol. iv. Surtees Society, vol. liii. Durham, 1869.

The Royal Commission on Historical Manuscripts. Fifth and Eighth Reports. London, 1876, 1881.

BIBLIOGRAPHY

Roxburghe Club. The Itineraries of William Wey, Fellow of Eton College, 1857.
Seyer, Rev. S., M.A. [Ed.]. The Charters and Letters Patent . . . to the Town and City of Bristol. Bristol, 1812.
Smith, L. Toulmin [Ed.]. The Maire of Bristowe is Kalendar, by Robert Ricart. Camden Society Publications, New Series, vol. v. Royal Historical Society, 1872.
Stevenson, Rev. J. [Ed.]. Letters and Papers illustrative of the Wars of the English in France during the reign of Henry the Sixth, 2 vols. Rolls Series, 1862-4.
Tawney, R. H. and Power, E. Tudor Economic Documents, 3 vols. University of London Historical Series, No. 4, 1924.
Warner, G. [Ed.]. The Libelle of Englyshe Polycye. A poem on the use of sea-power, 1436. Oxford, 1926.
Wadley, Rev. T. P. [Ed.]. Notes or Abstracts of the Wills contained in the volume entitled The Great Orphan Book and Book of Wills, in the Council House at Bristol. Bristol and Gloucestershire Archaeological Society, Nos. i-v. Bristol, 1886.

D. FOREIGN SOURCES [1]

Archives Historiques du Département de la Gironde, vols. i and ii. Société des Archives Historiques du Département de la Gironde. Bordeaux and Paris, 1859-60.
Bréquigny, M. de [Ed.]. Ordonnances des Rois de France de la Troisième Race, vol. xiv. Paris, 1790.
Bruns, F. [Ed.]. Die Lübecker Bergenfahrer und ihre Chronistik. Hansische Geschichtsquellen. Neue Folge, Band ii. Verein für Hansische Geschichte. Berlin, 1900.
*Bugge, A. [Ed.]. Diplomatarium Norvegicum, Sambrig xx, Bind 2, Haefke.
Dasent, G. W. [Trans.]. Icelandic Sagas, vol. iv. Appendix B, Icelandic Annals. Rolls Series, 1894. Christiania. [See also under Lange, C.C.A.] 1915.
*Diplomatarium Islandicum. Hinu Islenzka Bókmentafélagi. Copenhagen, Reykjavik. 1857, etc.
Ducaunnès-Duval, G. and Brutalis, J.-A. Inventaire Sommaire des Archives Départementales antérieures, 1790. Gironde. Serie E supplément, Tome 2. Bordeaux, 1901.
*Höhlbaum, K., Kunze, K., Stein, W. [Eds.]. Hansisches Urkundenbuch, vols. i-iii, ed. Höhlbaum; iv-vi, ed. Stein. Verein für Hansische Geschichte. Halle (vols. i-iii); Leipzig (vols. iv-x), 1876-1907.
Keyser, R. and Munch, P. A. Norges Gamle Love indtil 1387, vols. i-iii. Den Kongelige Norske Videnskabers Selskab. Christiania [Oslo], 1846, 1848, 1849.
*Koppmann, K. [Ed.]. Die Recesse und andere Akten der Hansetage, von. 1256-1340. Hanserecesse, vols. i-viii. Die Historische Commission bei der Königliche Akademie der Wissenschaften. Leipzig, 1870-97.
*Kunze, K. Hanseakten aus England. 1275 bis 1412. Hansische Geschichtsquellen, vol. vi. Verein für Hansische Geschichte. Halle a.S., 1891.
*Kuske, B. [Ed.]. Quellen zur Geschichte des Kölner Handels und Verkehrs im Mittelalter, 3 vols. Gesellschaft für Rheinische Geschichtskunde, No. 33. 1923, 1918, 1923.
*Lange, C. C. A. and Unger, C. R. [Eds.]. Diplomatarium Norvegicum, vol. ii. Christiania [Oslo], 1852.
Macray, Rev. W. D. Report on the Royal Archives of Denmark, and Further Report on Libraries in Sweden. The Forty-fifth Annual Report of the Deputy Keeper of the Public Records. Appendix 2, No. 1, pp. 1-62, 1884. London, 1885.
Pagnini della Ventura, G. F. [Ed.]. Della decima et di varie altre gravezze imposte Comune di Firenze, etc. (Tomo terzo, contenente la Practica della Mercatura scritta da F. Balducci Pegolotti, etc. Tomo quarto . . . la Pratica della Mercatura scritta da G. di Antonio da Uzzano nel 1442.) 4 tom. Lisbona e Lucca [Florence], 1765-6.
Posthumus, N. W. [Ed.]. Bronnen tot de Geschiedenis van de Leidsche Textielnijverheid, 1333-1795. Rijks Geschiedkundige Publicatiën. 8, 14, 18, 22, 39, 49. The Hague, 1910-22.

---

[1] Under this heading are also included several collections of documents drawn wholly or partially from English archives and published in foreign series. These are marked with an asterisk.

*Ropp, G. von der [Ed.]. Hanserecesse 1431–76. Zweite Abtheilung, vols. i–vii. Verein für Hansische Geschichte, Leipzig, 1876–92.
*Scott, E. and Severen, L. Gilliodts-van [Transcriber and Ed.]. Le Cotton Manuscrit Galba B. 1. Commission Royale d'histoire de Belgique, Académie Royale des Sciences, des Lettres et des Beaux-Arts de Belgique. Quarto Series. Brussels, 1896.
Severen, L. Gilliodts-van [Ed.]. Cartulaire de l'ancienne Estaple de Bruges, 4 vols. Société d'Émulation. Bruges, 1904–6.
*Smit, H. J. [Ed.]. Bronnen tot de Geschiedenis van den Handel met Engeland, Schotland en Ierland. 1150–1485, 2 vols. Rijks Geschiedkundige Publicatiën, 65, 66. The Hague, 1928.
Storm, G. [Ed.]. Islandske Annaler indtil 1578. Den Norske Historiske Kildeskriftford. Christiania, 1888.

SECONDARY AUTHORITIES

Bahr, C. Handel und Verkehr der deutschen Hanse in Flandern während des vierzehnten Jahrunderts., Leipzig, 1911.
Balasque, J. Études historiques sur la ville de Bayonne, 3 vols. Bayonne, 1862–75.
Beaven, A. B. The Aldermen of the City of London, 2 vols. The Corporation of the City of London, 1908–13.
Below, G. von. Probleme der Wirtschaftsgeschichte. Tübingen, 1920.
Bens, G. Der deutsche Warenfernhandel im Mittelalter. Breslau, 1926.
Bugge, A. Handelen mellem England og Norge indtil Begyndelsen af det 15de Aarhundrede. Historisk Tidsskrift. Raekke iii. Bind 4. pp. 1–149. Den norske Historiske Forening. Christiania, 1898.
—— Den norske Traelasthandels Historie. Part 1. Fra de aeldste Tider indtil Freden i Speier 1544. Skien, 1928.
Cunningham, W. The Growth of English Industry and Commerce. The Middle Ages. 5th edit. Cambridge, 1905.
Daenell, E. R. Die Blütezeit der deutschen Hanse. Hansische Geschichte von der zweiten Hälfte des XIV. bis zum lezten Viertel des XV. Jahrhunderts, 2 vols. Berlin, 1905–6.
Daumet, G. Calais sous la domination Anglaise. Académie d'Arras. Arras, 1902.
—— Etude sur l'Alliance de la France et de la Castille au XIVe et au XVe siècles. Bibliothèque de l'École des Hautes Études. Sciences Philologiques et Historiques. 118 fascicule. Ministère de l'Instruction Publique. Paris, 1898.
Engel, K. Die Organisation der deutsch-hansischen Kaufleute in England im 14. und 15. Jahrhundert bis zum Utrechter Frieden von 1474. Hansische Geschichtsblätter, Band xix, pp. 445–517, Band xx, pp. 173–225. Verein für Hansische Geschichte. Munich and Leipzig, 1913–14.
Gjerset, K. History of Iceland, 1924.
Gras, N. S. B., Ph.D. The Early English Customs System. Harvard Economic Studies, vol. xviii. Cambridge, Mass., 1918.
Gray, H. L. The Production and Exportation of English Woollens in the Fourteenth Century. English Historical Review, vol. xxxix, pp. 13–35. 1924.
Hakluyt, R. The Principal Navigations Voyages Traffiques and Discoveries of the English Nation, vol. i. Glasgow, 1903.
Haward, W. I. Economic Aspects of the Wars of the Roses in East Anglia. English Historical Review, vol. xli, pp. 170–89. 1926.
Hirsch, T. Danzigs Handels-und Gewerbsgeschichte unter der Herrschaft des deutschen Ordens. Reissschriften gekrönt und herausgegeben von der Fürstlich Jablonowski'schen Gesellschaft zu Leipzig, No. vi. Leipzig, 1858.
Hunt, W. Bristol. Historic Towns. E. A. Freeman and Rev. W. Hunt [Eds.]. 1887.
Hurry, J. B. The Woad Plant and its Dye. A. R. Horwood [Ed.]. 1930.
Jullian, C. Histoire de Bordeaux depuis les origines jusqu'en 1895. Bordeaux, 1895.
Kingsford, C. L. Prejudice and Promise in Fifteenth Century England. Oxford, 1925.
Lipson, E. An Introduction to the Economic History of England, vol. i. The Middle Ages. 5th edit. 1929.
Magnusen, F. Om de Engelskes Handel og Foerd paa Island i det 15de Aarhundrede. Nordisk Tidskrift for Oldkyndighed, vol. ii, pp. 112–69. Kongelige Nordiske Oldskrift-Selskab. Copenhagen, 1833.

NORDENSKIÖLD, A. E. Periplus. An Essay on the Early History of Charts and Sailing-Directions. Translated by F. A. Bather. Stockholm, 1897.
OCHENKOWSKI, W. VON. Englands wirtschaftliche Entwickelung im Ausgange des Mittelalters. Jena, 1879.
POSTAN, M. Credit in Medieval Trade. Economic History Review, vol. i, pp. 234-61. The Economic History Society, 1928.
POSTAN, M. M. Private Financial Instruments in Medieval England. Vierteljahrschrift für Sozial-und Wirtschaftsgeschichte, Band xxiii, pp. 26-75. Stuttgart, 1930.
POWER, E. The English Wool Trade in the reign of Edward IV. Cambridge Historical Journal, vol. ii, pp. 17-35. Cambridge, 1926.
RAMSAY, J. H. Lancaster and York. A Century of English History, 2 vols. Oxford, 1892.
RICHARDSON, H. G. Illustrations of English History in the Medieval Registers of the Parlement of Paris. Trans. R. Hist. Soc. Fourth Series, vol. x, pp. 55-85. 1927.
SANDEMAN, G. A. C. Calais under English Rule. Oxford, 1908.
SCHÄFER, D. Die Hanse. Monographien zur Weltgeschichte, No. xix. E. Heyck [Ed.]. Bielefeld and Leipzig, 1903.
SCHANZ, G. Englische Handelspolitik gegen Ende des Mittelalters, mit besonderer Berücksichtigung des Zeitalters der beiden erstem Tudors, Heinrich VII. und Heinrich VIII., 2 vols. Leipzig, 1881.
SCHAUBE, A. Die Wollausfuhr Englands vom Jahre 1273. Vierteljahrschrift für Sozial-und Wirtschaftsgeschichte, Band VI, pp. 29-72. Berlin. Stuttgart, Leipzig, 1908.
SCHULTE, A. Geschichte der grossen Handelsgesellschaft, 3 vols. Stuttgart and Berlin, 1923.
SCHULZ, F. Die Hanse und England von Edwards III bis auf Heinrichs VIII. Zeit. Abhandlungen zur Verkehrs- und Seegeschichte, vol. v. D. Schäfer [Ed.]. Berlin, 1911.
SHILLINGTON, V. M. and CHAPMAN, A. B. W. The Commercial Relations of England and Portugal. 1907.
SCOFIELD, C. L. The Life and Reign of Edward the Fourth, 2 vols. 1923.
STEIN, W. Die Hanse und England beim Ausgang des hundertjährigen Krieges. Hansische Geschichtsblätter, Band XXVI, pp. 27-126. Lübeck, 1921.
TROPLONG, E. De la Fidélité des Gascons aux Anglais pendant le Moyen Age (1152-1453). Revue d'Histoire Diplomatique. Seizième Année, pp. 51-68, 238-66, 410-37, 481-521. Société d'Histoire Diplomatique. Paris, 1902.
UNWIN, G. [Ed.]. Finance and Trade under Edward III. Manchester, 1918.
UNWIN, G. The Gilds and Companies of London. The Antiquary's Books. Cox, J. C. [Ed.], 1908.
VARENBERGH, E. Histoire des relations diplomatiques entre le compté de Flandre et l'Angleterre au moyen âge. Brussels, Ghent, 1874.
VOGEL, W. Geschichte der deutschen Seeschiffahrt, vol. i. Von der Unzeit bis zum Ende des XV. Jahrhunderts. Berlin, 1915.

ATLASES

NORDENSKIÖLD, A. E. Facsimile-Atlas till Kartografiens Äldsta Historia. Stockholm, 1889.
BEEKMAN, A. A. Geschiedkundige Atlas van Nederland. Commissie voor den Geschiedkundige Atlas van Nederland. The Hague, 1914– (in progress).

INDEX

Abingdon, 57
Accounts, *see* Butler, Calais, Customs, Garbler, Household, Poundage, Subsidy, Tunnage, Ulnage
Admiralty, 193
Adour, river, 201, 202
Adventurer, *see* Merchant Adventurer
Agency, 147
Alabaster, 187, 216, 221, 243
Albertini, Co. of, 55
Albertis, Laurentius de, of Florence, 46
Alberton, John, of Bristol, 222
Albi, 206
Aldebrand, Angelo, of Florence, 314
Alderman: of English in Prussia, 150; of Hanse, 115, 149; of London, 249, 250, 252, 254, 263, 266, 373
Alfold, Piers, of London, 223
Alfonso I, king of Naples, 229
Algarve, 222
Alien, 4–7, 9–10, 12–15, 18–25, 30, 32–8, 47–9, 54–6, 58–60, 80, 82, 96, 98, 104, 112, 125, 257, 258, 267, 270, 273, 310, 311, 323, 324, 326–9, 402–5, 361, 364, 373. *See also* Foreigner, Hanse, and particular countries and towns
All Saints: Barking, parish of, 58; Bristol, 217, 231, 243
Almonds, 200, 207, 215, 224, 248, 283
Alnager, *see* Ulnager
Alum, 188, 200, 207, 269, 270, 272, 283, 290
Amber, 176, 268
Amsterdam, 87, 94, 171, 366
Anchors, 215
Andirons, 232
Anise, 200, 283
Antina, Petrus de, 224
Antwerp, 28, 41, 61, 64, 66, 70, 77, 143
Apothecaries: Geneva, 250; London, 248–250, 257, 271, 277, 279, 283 (*see also* Spicers); provincial, 276, 289
Apples, 266
Apprenticeship: Bristol, 196, 235, 236; Brussels, 256; London, 252, 254–6, 274, 276, 286, 287; Staple, 70, 83, 365, 367
Aquitaine, 97, 121, 140
Aragon, 179, 216
Aragon, Katherine of, 220
Aragon, Simon, 234
Ardson, William, of Delft, 370
Arms, 182, 224, 284, 398
Armourers, 279
Armstrong, Clement, 69, 70
Arnold, Thomas, of Cirencester, 53

Arras: 117, 121; canvas, *see* Canvas
Arthur, Prince, 220
Arsenic, 283
Ashes, 97, 135, 141, 207
Assignments, 67, 145, 299, 302
Astley, Sir John, 45
Atlantic, 155, 156, 174, 182, 183, 191, 221, 245, 246
Attorney, 236, 237. *See also* Factor
Aubrey: Andrew, Grocer, 250; John, Grocer, 277
Augsburg, 273
Aunsell, William, 259
Austyn, John, of Woodstock, 56
Avoirdupois, 248, 250, 258
Avon, river, 185, 187, 188, 190
Ayleward, John, of Bristol, 195
Ayr, 194

Bacon, 172, 198, 398
Bacon, Robert, 173
Badby, Thomas, of London, 16
Bags, leather, 283
Bagot, Clement, of Bristol, 195, 239
Bakers, 280
Baldwin Street, Bristol, 190, 229
Balance, 277, 283
Balinger, 238–240
Balls, tennis, 189
Balms mart, 66, 370
Baltic, 25–7, 29, 34, 36, 91, 93–5, 97, 99, 101, 107, 109, 120–3, 131, 133, 135, 138–142, 145, 146, 151–3, 157, 160, 191, 235, 245, 269, 380, 407
"Bame," 196
Banbury, 276, 367
Bann, river, 198
Bannebury, John, of Bristol, 193
Banners, 283
Banstead Down, 49
Barbarigo, Lorenzo, of Venice, 311, 312
Bardi, Co. of, of Florence, 58
Barge, 239, 240
Barking, 58, 286, 368
Barley, 169, 187
Barlowe, William, 395
Barnet, battle of, 136
Barnstaple, 188
Baron, —, of Bristol, 236
Barr, —, 380
Barrel staves, 221
Barromei, Benedict, of Florence, 44
Barrow, *see* Bergen op Zoom
Barry, —, 380

417

INDEX

Barter, 174, 189, 267
Barton: John, of Holme, Stapler, 41, 365; Thomas, 365
Base, Jacob van de, 69
Basinets, 200
Basins, 233, 283
Bataill, Thomas, Mercer, 285
Battery, 200
Bay of Bourgneuf, 26, 123, 127-131, 142, 221, 377, 378, 408
Bayonne, 201, 202, 204, 205, 207-9, 210, 211, 215, 234-6, 239, 242
Beads, 176, 281
Beam: 277; the King's, 56, 248, 257-9, 272, 285, 287
Beans, 216
Beauchamp, Richard, *see* Warwick
Beaufitz, William, 309
Beaufort, Cardinal, 85, 104, 119, 121, 125, 374, 376
Beaver skins, 207, 215
Beby, John, governor of the English in Danzig, 374
Beckington, 276
Bedford, 276
Bedford, John, Duke of, 162
Beds, 232, 233
Beef, 172
Beer, 139, 169, 172, 175, 176, 196, 200, 289, 371, 379
Behaim, 166
Bek, Raulyn de, 382
Bells, 189, 281
Belts, 291
Bensyn, Barnard, 211, 234
Bere, William, 363
Bergen: 93, 118, 143, 144, 151, 155, 157-9, 161-8, 171, 174, 177-9, 181, 182, 225, 372; *Bergenfahrer*, 130, 376
Bergen op Zoom, 41, 61, 66, 67, 69, 70
Berkeley, 195, 334
Berkeley Wood, 187
Berkeley, Sir Maurice, 234
Berkshire, 49, 50, 54
Bert, William, of Florence, 58, 327
Bertout, Jean, of Holland, 64
Berwick, 43, 330
Betson, Thomas, Stapler, 371
Beverley, 276
Beverston, 234
Bewdley, 188
Beyrout, 230
Bilbao, 216, 241
Bill (credit instrument), 17, 49, 67-9, 76-80, 85, 372
Bird, William, 233
Biscay, 216, 217
Black Death, 158, 259
Black Prince, 220
Black Sea, 143, 227
Bladesmiths, 291
Blakeney, 159, 172, 173, 381
Blankets, 199, 233, 283

Blaye, 203, 204, 210, 213
Bloxwich, John, Bishop of Hólar, 170
Blount, Sir Walter, 316
Bluett, Robert, of Southampton, 290
Boards, 215, 231
Bole, Richard, 308
Boleyn, Geoffrey, mayor of London, 312
Bolle, John, 16, 58, 363, 369
Bolt, John, Tailor, 369
Bolton, John, of York, 368
Bond, 76, 77, 243, 252, 286, 287
Bonegriti, Homo, *see* Griti, Homobone
Bonnets, 289
Bonville, Sir William, 126
Bonyfaunt, John, 195
Book of Rates, 362
Books, 244, 283
Boots, 281
Borax, 283
Bordeaux: 14, 82, 112, 176, 189-192, 201-213, 235, 237, 239, 240, 242; Archbishop of, 207
Boston, 41-3, 136, 137, 144, 148, 168, 188, 276, 295-300, 317, 330, 362
Bosworth, battle of, 1
Bourchier, Henry, Viscount, 296, 297
Bourgneuf, Bay of, *see* Bay of Bourgneuf
Bowell, —, 297
Bowstaves, 140, 152, 198, 207, 215, 283, 284, 378
Bowstrings, 281, 291
Boxes, 140, 281, 283
Brabant: cloth of, 41, 50, 60, 85; linen of, 379; trade of, 27, 29, 39, 44, 50, 60, 64, 84, 85, 97, 99, 121, 122, 135, 143, 144, 152, 294, 316, 376, 379, 380
"Braeschier" (? Berkshire) wool, 367
Brandenburg, 91
Brasiers, 55, 280, 369
Brasil, 270
Brasil, Island of, 245, 246
Brass, 199, 283
Bray, William, Draper, 369
Bread, 169, 196, 280
Bream, 197
Brecklings (broken wool), 51
Bremen, 91, 139
Breslau, 135
Breton, William, 57, 58, 369
Brewes, Walter, Woolman, 300, 363
Briddok(e), John, of Northleach, Woolman, 53, 366
Bridlington, Prior of, 397
Bridgenorth, 385
Bridgewater, 332
Bridport, 276
Brigandine, 215
Brimstone, 283
Bristles, 189
Bristol: 26, 28, 29, 133, 165 ff., 275, 276, 283, 290, 323, 332, 333, 372, 393; cloth of, 185, 187-9, 200, 237, 238, 283; Merchant Adventurers in, 229

INDEX

Bristol Channel, 190
Bristow, Childe of, 235, 236
Brittany: 103, 173, 191, 194, 198, 201, 205-7, 212, 221, 223, 242, 406; linen of, 175, 283
Broadcloth, *see* Cloth, of England
Brogger, *see* Broker
Broke, Geoffrey, Grocer, 264
Broker, 51, 249, 271
Brokerage, 61, 271
Brompton, William, 395
Brown, Stephen, Grocer, 266
Browne, Thomas, 397
Bruges: 41, 66, 69, 91, 143, 407; Hanseatic Factory in, 93, 94, 110, 375, 377; Merchant Adventurers in, 268, 269; trade and finance of, 12, 43, 44, 60, 65, 67-70, 82, 84, 85, 144, 312, 319, 366, 371
Brunswick: cloth of, 144; linen of, 379
Brushes, 291
Brussels, 256
Bücher, C., 273
Buckingham, 187, 277
Buckingham, Humphrey Stafford, Duke of, 104, 302, 374
Buckinghamshire, 57
Bullion regulations, 17, 40, 70, 73, 78-82, 87-9, 103, 293, 372
Bullok, John, 195
Burford, 53
Burgh, Sir William de, 194, 358
Burgundy: 26-8, 30, 60, 62, 73, 83-5, 87-90, 110, 117, 121, 122, 132, 133, 178, 296, 370, 376-8, 408; Duchess of, 316; Duke of, 27, 28, 84, 89, 296, 300, 301, 313-17
Burnham, 173
Burrishoole, 193
Burton, William, Grocer, 278
Bury St. Edmunds, 127, 276
Busshe: John, of Northleach, Wooldealer, 54, 56, 71, 367, 368; Thomas, 54, 368
Butler, 4, 13, 31-3, 361, 364
Butter, 172, 175, 196, 198, 289, 371
Buttons, 281

Cabbages, 266
Cabot, 182, 234, 246
Cade's Rising, 309
Caen, 212
Caenes, Margaret, of Chipping Norton, 52
Caerleon, 187
Calais: 20, 21, 37, 60, 85, 293-6, 302, 303, 308, 310, 311, 313, 314, 316, 319, 371, 399; garrison of, 40, 60, 72-5, 77-9, 89, 140, 294, 300-7, 311-15, 317-19, 372, 398; mint of, 66, 70, 80-2, 88, 89; officials of, 60, 73-5, 81, 296, 301-6, 309, 311, 316, 364, 372. *See also Calisvairders*, Staple
Calais pence, 327
Calcote, Hugh, of Calcote, Chapman, 53
Calf-hides, 198

Calisvairders, 66
Cambrai, 268, 269
Cambridge, 275, 276
Cambridge, William, Grocer, 285
Cambridgeshire, 363, 367
Camerik, *see* Cambrai
Campden, 52, 53-5
Campen, 118
Candelabra, 232, 283, 291
Candia, 229
Candles, 232, 398
Caniziani, Gerard, of Florence: 45, 48; widow of, 366
Canning, George, 235
Cantabrian Mountains, 207, 215
Cantelow(e): Thomas, 297; William, Stapler, 16, 64, 86, 87, 296-8, 311
Canterbury, 162, 192
Canterbury, Archbishop of, 133
Canvas: 59, 72, 139, 141, 249, 290; Arras, 59; Prussian, 283; dealers in, 268, 283. *See also* Corders
Canynges: John, mayor of Bristol, d. 1405, 234, 235, 238; John, son of William (the Great), 234, 236; Thomas, mayor of London, 235; Thomas, great nephew of William (the Great), 242; William, d. 1396, 234, 237, 238; William (the Great), Mayor of Bristol, d. 1474, 168, 178, 185, 190, 218, 222, 225, 229, 231, 232, 234-242, 244, 388; William, nephew of William (the Great), 242
Cappers, 280, 282
Caps: 175, 280-2; German, 281, 282
Caravel, 228
Cardiff, 187
Cardmakers, 280
Cards, 189, 200
Carlisle, 330
Carmarthen, 187
Carpenter, 231, 239
Carpenter, —, of London, 274
Carpets, 233
Carrack, 45, 224, 240, 326, 368
Carrickfergus, 194, 198
Carrier, 189
Carta Mercatoria, 98
Carts, 188
Cartographers, 174
Casks, 198
Castile, 215, 216, 218-220, 222
Castro, Diego de, of Spain, 371
Catalans, 227, 229
Cattle, 158, 161, 187, 198
Cat(ts)worth, Thomas, 16, 274
Caxton, William, Governor of Merchant Adventurers, 133
Cecily, Duchess of York, *see* York
Cely: firm, 12, 13, 49, 51, 52, 56-65, 68-71, 76-9, 297; George, 57, 59, 63, 67, 69, 76-9, 365, 366, 372; John, 52, 63; Richard, the Elder, 17, 46, 52, 62, 65, 66, 71, 365, 369, 377; Richard, the younger,

54, 57, 62, 63, 65, 67; Robert, 365; William, 365
Cely Papers, 48, 54, 59, 60, 67, 69, 70, 76–9, 369, 371
Cereals, 140
Chains, 281
Chancellor, Lord, 39, 46, 194, 196, 223, 282, 297, 303, 304, 308, 310
Chancery, 168, 170, 177, 192, 193, 195, 223, 242, 308, 369
Chandlers, 278, 279, 283, 287
Chapman, 53, 54, 176, 249, 273–6, 278, 280–2
Chapman, Richard, 194
Charcoal, 283
Charles, Duke of Burgundy, 28
Charles VII, king of France, 212, 229
Cheap (London), 248, 249, 280, 281
Cheddar, Robert, 234
Cheese, 141
Chepstow, 168, 187, 195, 205
Chester, 174, 187, 192, 195, 386
Chester: Alice, of Bristol, 231, 232, 243; Henry, of Bristol, 243; John, of Bristol, 242, 243; John, of London, 369
Chevisance, 75
Cheyne, Sir John, 303
Chichele, John, Grocer, 277
Chichester: 41, 276, 308, 335; Bishop of, 365
Chippenham, 189
Chipping Norton, 52
Chok, Richard, 229
Christ Church, Canterbury, Prior of, 192
Christian I, king of Denmark, 178, 180
Church, John, 126, 223, 380
Churcheman, John, Grocer, 258
Cineres, *see* Ashes
Cinnamon, 283
Cinque Ports, 185, 317
Cirencester, 53
Clapholt, 140
Claymond, John, Draper, 56
Cley, 49, 173
Cloth, of England: 6–9, 13, 19, 70, 139, 144, 145, 200, 249, 291, 322–5, 362–3; export of, 2–5, 7, 9–11, 13, 15, 16, 19–21, 23–38, 47, 48, 70, 85, 89, 96, 97, 101, 106–110, 114, 119, 122, 124, 129, 135–7, 139, 141–6, 152, 153, 168, 169, 175, 176, 181, 192, 193, 197, 201, 216, 217, 220, 221, 223, 224, 226–8, 237, 238, 243, 261, 263, 264, 265, 267, 270, 272, 278, 285, 291, 310, 314, 317, 327–9, 361, 364, 373–7, 379, 408; industry in, 7, 11–13, 25, 49, 52, 54, 58, 99, 133, 136, 141, 144, 145, 153, 185, 187–9, 200, 206, 207, 212, 214, 237, 238, 263, 270, 281, 286, 376, 390; prices of, 7–9, 19, 362, 363; trade in, 11, 88, 188–191, 247, 261–4, 281, 282, 284, 368. *See also* Kersey, Russet, Straits, Worsted
Cloth: foreign, 39, 43, 50, 144, 273; of gold, 268, 291

Clothier, 43, 52–6, 58, 237, 238
Clothman, 53. *See also* Clothier
Cloves, 283
Clyfton, Sir Gervase, Treasurer of Calais, 303
Coal: 48, 141, 187, 188, 190, 207; trade in, 291
Coal-scuttles, 291
Cobbler, 280
Cobham, Eleanor, duchess of Gloucester, 125, 126, 376
Cocket, 77, 80, 199, 299
Cod, 159, 172, 176, 197
Codir, William, 229, 244
Coffers, 140, 198
Cog, 239, 240
Coifs, 291
Coke: —, 380; Philip, Clothier, 237
Cokkes, James, 233
Colchester, 145
Cold mart, 66, 370
Cologne: 5, 6, 27, 35, 91, 96, 100, 101, 118, 123, 127, 130, 131, 135, 136, 139, 142, 143, 378, 379, 408; in London, merchants of, 98, 134, 143, 137, 318, 373. *See also* Hanse
Cologne thread, 139
Combines, 259, 260, 270
Combs, 175, 176, 200, 207, 215, 281
Commines, Philip de, 213
Commission trade, 146–8
Common Beam, *see* Beam, King's
Common Council, London, 261, 271, 275, 287
Company, City: 247, 248, 251–7, 261, 262, 263, 275, 280, 284–8; greater, 262, 284, 286, 287, 289; industrial, 247, 261, 262, 278, 279, 282, 287; minor, 249, 280, 283, 286, 287; monopoly of, 262, 265, 284; powers of, 279–281, 283, 284, 287; provincial merchants in, 276, 277, 286, 288 ff.; trade of, 247, 262, 263, 265, 268–270, 272–5, 277, 279–281, 284, 287; victualling, 266. *See also under* particular trades
Compass, 160, 381
Compostella, 193, 217, 227
Compton, John, 231
Concarneau, 212
Confections, 250
Conger, 197
Conquet, 212
Constance, Council of, 283
Constantinople, 227
Consumers, 99, 104, 136, 146, 260, 261, 278, 280, 284
Contarini: Jerome, of Florence, 45; Moses, of Gascony, 211, 214, 215, 234
Conterayn, *see* Contarini
Conton, Richard, Stapler, 371
Contor, *see* Factory
Contract, 51, 53, 55, 56, 57, 63, 231, 254–6, 277, 365–7, 369
Convoy, 59, 71, 75, 204, 371

INDEX

Conyhopelane (London), 23
Conyswaye (old fells), 61
Coolys, Richard, of Preston, 52
Copenhagen, 163
Copin, Richard, 319
Copper, 141, 175
Copperas, 283
Coppuldike, John, 308, 309
Corders, 248–250, 257
Cording, 53
Cordova, 215
Cordovan (leather), 207, 215
Cordwainer, 280
Cork : 221 ; white, 215
Cork (city), 193
Cork, John de, 231
Corn, 39, 97, 140, 152, 158, 173, 185, 188, 199, 201, 207, 208, 216, 221, 266, 375, 379, 398
Cornhill, 258, 280, 281, 392
Cornmongers, 266
Cornwall : 49, 168, 188, 189, 207, 216, 222, 226, 269, 362, 363, 367 ; Duchy of, 353 ; wool of, 49, 367
Corsey, Anthony, of Spain, 69
Corveser, 187, 198
Cosmetics, 250
Cotswolds : 46, 47, 49, 51–5, 57–9, 62, 188, 368 ; wool and woolfells of, 12, 45, 49, 51, 55, 57, 61, 71, 367, 370 ; wool and woolfells of, price of, 12, 45, 71, 367, 370
Cotton-wool, 283
Council, King's, 44–6, 77, 78, 100, 101, 104, 105, 119, 121, 122, 124–9, 130, 132, 133, 168, 189, 229, 300, 303, 307–9, 312, 314, 318–320, 374, 376
Counters, 140
Courteney, Sir Philip, 126
Coventry : 168, 169, 174, 187, 188, 243, 270, 275–7, 310, 311, 316, 317 ; Holy Trinity Guild of, 187
Coventry, William, Mercer, 284
Coverlets, 200, 232
Cowhides, 198
Cracow, 143
Craft, *see* Company
Crayer, 239
Credit : 44, 47, 53, 56, 57, 61, 63–70, 73, 76, 79, 80, 83, 84, 88, 145, 146, 369–371, 379. *See also* Exchange *and under* particular instruments of credit
Croft, Thomas, of Bristol, 245
Croke, John, Stapler, 57, 369
Cromer, 159, 168, 169, 172, 173
Crosby, Sir John, Grocer, 263, 366
Crossbows, 215
Crozon, 212
Cubebs, 283
Culgreve, Thomas, Alderman, 368
Culham, William, 257
Cumberland, 43, 330, 363, 367
Cummin, 283

Cunningham, W., 102
Cups, 223, 233
Curriers, of Bristol, 187, 198
Curteys, —, Stockfishmonger, 169
Customs : 4, 5, 9, 12, 13, 15, 18, 19–21, 34, 36, 37, 40, 42, 43, 45–8, 50, 51, 56, 58, 63, 71, 72, 74–82, 88, 97, 98, 107, 116, 124, 135–7, 142, 145, 176, 195, 199, 202, 203, 207, 209, 211, 213, 216, 219, 236, 237, 239–241, 304, 309, 313, 315, 317, 324, 326, 327, 361, 362, 363, 367, 372, 373, 408 ; accounts of, 3–9, 15, 16, 18–22, 30, 31, 41–3, 45, 47, 48, 68, 72 ff., 111, 142, 145, 152, 153, 168, 169, 175, 197, 209, 218, 221, 237, 243, 263, 264, 289, 290, 297, 299, 315, 321 ff., 361–4, 408 ; administration of, 72 ff,. 137, 366, 407, officials of, 27, 47, 48, 59, 60, 75, 80, 136, 168, 220, 228, 299, 301, 302, 303, 305, 308, 322, 324, 325, 327, 362, 372
Customs House : Bristol, 190 ; London, 258
Cutlery, 291
Cyflandia (*recte* Lyflandia), *see* Livonia
Cypressat, Lord of, 203
Cyprus, 229

Daggers, 291
Dalrymple, *see* Rumpyll, John de
Dalton, John, 78
Damask, 224, 268
Dammin, Balthasar van, 164
Daniell, Thomas, 128
Danzig : 26, 93, 100, 101, 106, 107, 108–111, 113, 114, 117–120, 123, 124, 126–8, 131–5, 137, 138, 140–3, 146, 147, 181, 373, 375, 377, 378, 408 ; English factory in, 97, 112, 115, 125, 148, 150, 152, 380
Daramayo, Ochoa, 216
Dartmouth, 169, 198, 205, 337
Dates, 214, 283
Dauphin of France, 315
Davy : Patrick, 208 ; William, 237
Dawes, Edward, 206
Dax, 209
Dayson, —, of Buckinghamshire, 57
Dean, Forest of, 187
Debenture, 75–7, 371, 372
Decasonn, Benynge, Lombard, 69
Deer Skins, 198
Defuye, Gabryell, of Genoa, 69
Delft : 60, 61, 79, 370 ; merchant companies of, 61, 370
Delopis, *see* Lopez, John de
Denham, John, Lord, 365
Denmark : 26, 93, 94, 114, 130, 133, 138, 143, 144, 151, 158, 159, 162, 164–9, 171–4, 178–182, 375, 378 ; king of, *see* Eric VII
Denton, Richard, 235, 236
Denys, William, Woolpacker, 58
Derby, 43
Derby, Walter, 238

INDEX

Dersingham, 173
Deryckson, Deryck, of Leyden, 370
Des Marez, G., 256, 273
Desers, Gomers, *see* Sore, Gomers de
Deva, 216, 219
Deventer, conference at, 129, 130
Devenysh, Nicholas, 195
Devonshire, 168, 188, 189, 226, 234, 269, 363, 367
Dickinson, John, 172
Diniz, king of Portugal, 222
Dishes, 281
Doctors, 250. *See also* Physicians, Surgeons
Dogger, 168, 172, 173. *See also* Fishing boat
Doo, Clarysse, of Leyden, 370
Dorchester, Abbot of, 52
Dordogne, 211
Dorset, 50, 363, 367
Douai, 366
Dounton, Thomas, Mercer, 285
Douro, river, 222
Dozen (of cloth) : 8, 199 ; price of, 362
Draper, 53
Draper, Peter, Ironmonger, 368
Drapers : Company of, 247, 260, 262, 277, 281, 282, 286, 287 ; as Merchant Adventurers, 393 ; trade of, 54-6, 58, 152, 263, 265-7, 270, 271, 277, 281, 282, 284, 369, 373 ; German merchants as, 250 ; of Bristol, 231 ; of Ludlow, 187, 228. *See also* Clothier
Drapery, 282, 286, 291. *See also* Cloth industry
Drayton, M., 190
Drogheda : 176, 194, 195, 198 ; Abbot of, 176, 177
Drugs, 248-250, 259, 271, 283
Dublin, 156, 195
Ducastet, John, 212
Dunstable, 276, 277
Dunwich, 173
Durham, 43, 215, 363, 367
Dye, 200, 206, 207, 215, 248, 262, 269, 270, 272, 276, 284, 289, 290
Dyers : 53, 54, 261, 277, 282, 283 ; provincial, 188, 276, 368
Dyke, Hugh, Stapler, 86, 87
Dynham, John, 318
Dyrholm, Isle, 161

Earnest money, 57, 62, 66, 67
East Anglia, 7, 144
Easterlings, 64, 189. *See also* Hanseatic League
Economic policy, 102, 105. *See also* Mercantilism
Edward : I, king of England, 10 ; II, king of England, 282 ; III, king of England, 10, 98, 102, 136, 381 ; IV, king of England, 6, 20, 22, 23, 24, 27, 29, 31, 32, 47, 70, 74, 132, 136, 153, 174, 177, 179, 180, 192, 212, 213, 216, 219, 230, 241, 243, 328, 362, 366, 368, 389, 407 ; IV, king of England, trade of, 24, 33, 34, 36, 47, 48, 50
Eels, 279
Egengton, John, 61
Egypt, 225
Eiderdown, 176
Elbe, river, 140
Elbing, 143
Elderbecke, —, 61
Eleanor of Aquitaine, queen of England, 201
Electuary, 250
Elizabeth, queen of England, 137, 199
Elmes, John, of Henley-on-Thames, 53, 54, 369, 371
Ely, 275
Elyngton, John, Stapler, 42
Elys, John, Mercer, 369
Embargo, 101, 107, 109, 118, 131, 135, 364, 375
Enamel, 233
Engel, K., 148
England : Eastern, 7, 12, 26, 27, 136, 144, 156, 162, 168, 173, 174, 196, 289, 290, 314, 323, 362, 363 ; Eastern, wool of, 12 ; Northern, 194, 289 ; Southern, 26, 28, 29, 144, 190, 191, 198, 314, 362 ; Southern, wool of, 12 ; Western, 29, 142, 144
English Channel, 26, 51, 172, 189, 205, 214, 224, 245, 317
Eric VII, king of Denmark, 113, 161, 162, 163, 164, 165, 166, 167
Erlandsson, Hauk, 160
Erlyngham, Thomas, 172, 173
Eskimo, 158
Essex, 363. *See also* Straits
Essey, John, 237
Esterfeld, John, 233, 244
Estfield, William, Stapler, 86, 87
Europe : Central, 137 ; Eastern, 91, 93, 96, 97, 137, 141, 189, 225-7 ; Northern, 9, 91, 93, 94, 96 ff., 101, 122, 130, 132, 133, 138, 141, 143, 145, 152, 172, 173 ; Southern, 97, 152, 188, 224, 273 ; Western, 93, 140, 143, 152
" Evechepynge," 281
Excestre, Philip, 234
Exchange, 62, 65, 66, 69, 77-9, 82, 363, 371, 373. *See also under* names of particular instruments of Exchange
Exchequer, 75, 77, 244, 259, 294-6, 299-303, 305, 306, 308, 321, 322, 327, 328, 361, 364, 368, 407
Exeter : 276, 337, 352 ; Duke of, 165, 166, 316, 317
Eyre, Simon, Draper, 271, 287
Eyton, John, 228, 229

Fabyan, 228, 310, 311, 316-320
Factor, 12, 21, 22, 37, 44, 45, 48, 50, 67, 89, 108, 147-9, 172, 176, 217, 236, 242, 267, 274, 276, 307-9, 311, 312, 314,

INDEX

315, 326, 327, 345, 346, 255, 358, 366, 404–6. *See also* Attorney
Factory, 46, 47, 93, 110, 149–150, 157, 375, 377. *See also* Company, trading, Hanse, Steelyard
Fairs, 131, 152, 153, 265, 266, 273–6, 291, 374, 376, 380
Fairford, 53, 54
Falcons, 176
Faldyng, 199
Falmouth, 192
Falsterbo, Diet at, 110
Farmer, 233, 278
Farnham, Silver de, Apothecary, 287
Faro, 222
Faroë Islands, 173
Farra, 173
"Farthing ware," 281
Fat, 5
Fauconberg, Thomas Neville, Bastard of, 104, 306, 374
Faukes, Thomas, Woolpacker, 57
Faunt, Philip, of Bristol, 195
Feathers, 181
Feld, John, Stapler, 67, 297, 300, 371
Feldyng, Geoffrey, Alderman, 368
Ferdinand II, king of Aragon, 220
Figs: 142, 214–16, 224, 283; price of, 272
Filongley: Henry, 309; Richard, 258
Finmark, 167, 173, 179
Firewood, 283
First-fruits, 170
Fish: 139, 157, 159, 161, 162, 164, 165, 167, 168, 170, 172, 175, 176, 181, 188, 190, 192, 198, 200, 201, 207, 216, 221, 265, 266, 268, 283, 289, 379; price of, 176, 266; trade in, 261, 265, 266, 269, 277–9, 284, 287, 289, 291; salt, 159, 172, 173, 176, 196, 278. *See also* Herring, Skania, Stockfish
Fish hook, 189
Fish wharf, 277
Fisher, 155, 159, 161–4, 172, 173, 182, 193, 196, 215, 265, 381
Fishery, 91, 93, 94, 161, 163, 174, 177, 182, 200
Fishing boat, 168, 169, 172, 182, 239
Fishmongers: Company of, 247, 260, 261, 265, 266, 277, 278, 285–7, 384; trade of, 99, 152, 189, 265, 266, 269–271, 277–9, 373, 393; provincial, 169, 174, 176, 276; of Brussels, 256. *See also* Stockfishmongers
Fitz-Walter, Lord, 253
Flanders, 12, 13, 27, 29, 41, 44, 50, 60, 61, 63, 64–8, 80–2, 84, 85, 89, 90, 93, 94, 97–9, 103, 110, 117, 118, 121, 122, 127, 128, 133–5, 139, 143–5, 189, 191, 198, 205, 207, 212, 214, 216, 224, 231, 243, 245, 250, 266, 268, 274, 309, 315, 317, 363, 365, 366, 370, 372, 375, 377, 378, 386; linen of, 175; wool of, 43, 50, 363

Flax, 144, 199, 283
Fleeces: 51, 55, 56, 370; refuse, price of, 368. *See also* Wool-fells
Fleet Prison, 46, 229
Fleming, John, 223
Flesh, wool, 51
Flock: 282; of Ireland, price of, 199
Florence: 44–6, 55, 226, 369; Companies of, in London, 46
Florijsson, Duic, of Holland, 64
Flour, rice, 283
Flushing, 67
Foddray, le Peele de, 48
Fogge, —, 378
Folbourne, —, 365
Food supply, London, 278. *See also* Victuals
Foreigner, 96–8, 260, 263, 265, 271–3, 280–2, 287, 376. *See also* Alien, *Gastenrecht*
Forest, 140, 198
Forster: John, 368; Stephen, Fishmonger, 168, 189, 271, 284, 285
Fortey: John, Dyer and Woolman, of Cirencester, 53, 54, 368; John, Woolman, of Northleach, 54, 366, 368; Nicolas, of Hamendon, 54; Thomas, of Hamendon, 54; William, of Harwell, 54
Foster, John, 241
Fouler, Roger, 173
Founde, Thomas, 214
Foundry, 188, 189
Founte, William de la, 241
Fowey, 168, 205, 222, 223, 229, 242, 352
Fox skins, 198
France, 2, 4, 6, 20, 25, 28, 29, 33, 36, 37, 39, 46, 103, 117, 121, 122, 135, 139, 140, 142, 153, 162, 172, 178, 179, 192, 198, 202, 205, 208, 209, 210, 212–15, 218–220, 224, 225, 229, 234, 235, 240, 242, 244, 266, 315, 378
Franchise, *see* Freedom
Frankfort-a-M., 135, 143
Fraternity, *see* Company
Freedom, 254, 256, 257, 261, 262, 263, 275, 286, 287, 290. *See also* Staple, membership of
Freight, 140, 238–240, 371. *See also* Transport
Freme, John, 212
Friars, Minor, Limerick, 193
Frieze, 188, 216. *See also* Wales, Ireland
Froissart, Jean, 208
Frome, river, 185, 190
Fruit: 142, 188, 200, 214, 215, 222, 224, 248, 263; trade in, 265, 266, 269, 276, 279, 285, 289, 290
Fruiterers, 266
Fuel, 175
Fuenterrabia: 216; Domingo de, 216
Fullers, 237, 261, 280, 282
Fur, 135, 141, 280, 283
Furness, Abbot of, 48
Furniture, 140, 198, 232, 233, 291

INDEX

Fustian, 69
Fylongley, Henry, see Filongley
Fynderne, Thomas, 309

Gadoid, 197
Galicia, 143, 217
Gall, 283
Galway, 193, 194
Gaming-tables, 281
Garbler, 257-9, 270, 273
Gardner, Thomas, 173
Garlic, 266, 278, 291
Garonne, river, 203, 209, 211
Garr, Robert, 147
Garveller, see Garbler
Gascony, 4, 14, 112, 140, 142, 152, 153, 187, 191, 201-3, 205-8, 211-14, 220-2, 227, 245, 261, 267, 269, 289
Gastenrecht, 112, 125
Gauntlets, 176
Gawge, John, 235, 236
Gaynard, Robert, 235, 236
Gaywode, John, 232, 233, 236
Geneva, Apothecaries of, 250
Genoa, 44, 57, 98, 99, 212, 218, 220, 222, 224, 225, 227-9, 234, 250, 268, 283, 290, 312, 315, 317
Gentile, Roger, 309, 310
Gentilis, Balthasar, 224
George, John, 219
Gerard, Ralph, Stapler, 42, 50
Geriksen, John, Bishop of Upsala, 170
Germany: 26, 38, 39, 64, 67, 91, 93, 95, 96, 98, 125, 133, 139, 140, 143, 144, 148, 152, 155, 157, 160, 164, 171, 176, 182, 250, 261, 273, 282; wool of, 144. See also Hanseatic League
Ghent, 69
Gibraltar, Straits of, 44, 45, 47, 50, 183, 225, 226, 228, 230, 295, 308, 314, 326, 366. See also Marrock, Morocco
Gile: Alphonso, 222; Gunsallo, 222
Ginger, 226, 250, 283
Girdlers, 55, 187
Girdles, 175, 198, 200, 281
Gironde, river, 201, 202, 210
Glass, 176
Glasses, 281
Glastonbury: 277; George Inn, 231
Gloucester: 136, 187, 188, 276; Abbot of, 52; Prior of, 52; Richard, Duke of, 104, 121, 125-7, 132, 374, 376
Gloucestershire, 53, 54, 189, 133; wool of, 49
Glover, Richard, 309
Glovers, 187, 276, 277, 281
Gloves, 175, 198, 281
Goat skins, 198, 215
Godard, Andrew, 392
Godell, William, 173
Godeman, John, 239
Gogh, John, 176, 195
Goldhap, 224

Goldsmiths, 224, 231, 255, 265, 267, 289, 373
Goodeer, Robert, Mercer, 287, 288
Gorgets, 200
Gower, John, 39
Gowns, taffeta and silk, 291
Grafton, John, 363
Grain (dye), 215, 221
Grantham, John de, Pepperer, 249
Grazier, see Wool-grower
Great Red Book (of Bristol), 189, 211, 212, 240, 241
Greece, 226, 268
Green, —, 380
Greenland, 156, 157, 381
Gregory's Chronicle, 310
Greipwald, 375
Grete, Homobone, see Griti, Homobone
Greyn, see Grain
Grimsby, 173, 191
Grindstones, 215
Griti, Homobone, of Venice, 311, 312, 314, 317, 398
Grocers: Aldermen, 373; Company of, 247-257, 259, 262, 264, 265, 276, 277, 285-7, 289-291; control of prices by, 272, 274, 287; corporate investment and trading of, 252, 253, 272, 284, 287, 391; powers of, 257-9, 270-2, 277, 284, 285, 287; trade of, 55, 152, 250, 258-260, 262-274, 282-9, 392
Grocers' Hall, 252, 253, 255
Grocery, 263, 265, 269, 271, 272, 285, 286
Guarande, 212
Guetaria, 216
Guiche, 204
Guienne, 2, 14, 25, 26, 28-33, 35, 208
Guildford, 276
Guildhall: London, commercial inquiry at, 311, 312, 368; Bristol, 185; Lynn, 165
Guilds, adulterine, 248
Guines, 75, 140, 298, 316
Guipuscoa, 216, 217, 218, 219
Gum arabic, 283
Guns, 188, 398
Gurnard, 197

Haakon, king of Norway, 161
Haarlem, 366
Haberdashers, 265, 275, 276, 280-3, 291, 393
Haberdashery, 268, 279, 286
Haburden, 197
Haddock, 197
Hafnarfjördur, 162, 169
Hainault: 85; linen of, 379
Hake, 176, 193, 197, 207, 216
Hakeday, Richard, Grocer, 259
Hakluyt, Richard, 192
Halgoland, 179
Hall, John, of Salisbury, 14
Halyards, 221
Hamburg, 91, 93, 131, 181, 377

INDEX

Hamendon, 54
Hammers, 398
Hammes, 75
Hamond, John, Grocer, 250
Hampshire, wool of, 49, 50
Hampton, *see* Southampton
Hanse, 112, 365
Hanseatic League, 2-6, 9, 10, 13, 18-21, 26, 27, 29, 30, 34-8, 64, 91 ff., 157, 158, 161, 163, 164, 166, 171, 177-183, 189, 224, 225, 234, 245, 246, 324, 328, 329, 361, 362, 364, 373-8, 381, 407, 408. *See also* Germany
Hanyagh, Thomas, 193
Hardware, 281, 291
Hare skins, 198
Harness, 198
Harpstrings, 291
Harrison, William, 233
Hartlepool, 181
Harwell, 54
Harz Mountains, 139
Hase, Godefry, Hanseatic, 361
Hastings: 289; William, Lord, 104, 374
Hatcliff, William, 104, 382, 378
Hats, 175, 221, 268, 281, 284, 290, 291
Hatterby, John, 376
Hauberks, 200
Haut Pays, 202, 204, 206, 208, 210
Haverford West, 187
Hawks, 198
Hawley, John, of Bristol, 219, 388
Hebrides, 156
Hedgeley, battle of, 177
Helgafell, monastery of, 165
Hemp, 141, 291
Henham, Thomas, 367
Henley-on-Thames, 53, 54, 369, 371
Henlove, John, of Bristol, 189
Henry: I, king of England, 197; II, king of England, 195, 201; IV, king of England, 11, 80, 109, 203, 361, 366; V, king of England, 113, 114, 162, 167, 192, 366, 381; VI, king of England, 1, 2, 11, 12, 21-3, 26, 27, 44, 45, 47-9, 51, 74, 116, 121, 122, 221, 230, 238, 293, 294, 300, 304, 316, 361, 377; VII, king of England, 173, 229, 364; VIII, king of England, 321-3, 364, 365, 370
Henry the Navigator, 220
Herber, le, in Walbrook, 258
Herbs, 250, 283
Hereford, 187
Herefordshire, wool of, 12, 49
Heron, Richard, Stapler, 318-320
Herrings, 97, 139, 141, 142, 172, 176, 196, 197, 207, 216, 291, 375
Hertford, 276
Hertfordshire, 276
Heryot, William, Alderman, 45, 366
Hexham, battle of, 177
Heyron, Richard, *see* Heron, Richard
Heyton, John, of Bristol, 194, 239

Hides, 3, 4, 6, 13, 14, 176, 187, 190, 194, 198, 200, 201, 207, 212, 216, 323, 328, 329, 361; price of, 198, 361
Higden, Ranulf, 200
Hólar, 169, 170
Holland, 24, 25, 27, 29, 33, 41, 47, 48, 58, 60, 63, 67, 69, 70, 81, 83-6, 88, 93, 94, 97, 101, 109, 110, 123, 124, 127, 128, 135, 138, 139, 141, 144, 152, 313, 316, 319, 366-8, 370, 378; wool of, 43
Holland, Lincs, wool of, 49, 367
Holm, Robert, of Hull, 163
Holme beside Newark, 41
Holt, William, 16, 363
Honey, 175, 176, 194, 207, 215, 250, 283, 289, 291
Hoo, Thomas, 308, 309
Hoper, Thomas, 236
Hops, 212, 216
Horn, 162
Horn, Adam, 173
Horne, Robert, Stapler, 16, 297
Horses, 49, 53, 172, 196, 198, 231, 232
Horseshoes, 175, 289, 291
Horsle, Richard, of Chichester, 308
Hostillers, provincial, 276
Hosts: of foreign merchants, 264, 271; views of, 52
Hound fish, 197
Household, buying for, 267, 273, 374. *See also* Household, royal
Household, royal: 299, 302, 307, 313, 314, 318, 327, 397; accounts of, 14
Howard, John, 126, 135, 374, 377
Huelva, 216
Hull, 41, 42, 99, 136, 137, 144, 163, 165-171, 174, 177, 181, 183, 191, 205, 206, 225, 276, 289, 295-9, 313, 317, 323, 361, 362, 397
Humber, river, 173, 183
Hundred Years' War, 1, 2, 14, 19, 20-2, 25, 28-31, 33, 34, 38, 39, 121, 208, 218, 219
Hungary, 139, 141, 143
Hunt, John, 233
Hurers, 280
Husbandman, 53, 54, 276
Hygdon, John, Grocer, 369

Iberian Peninsula, 97, 142, 152, 191, 214. *See also* Portugal and Spain
Iceland: 133, 140, 151, 155 ff., 190, 225, 229, 235, 239-241, 245, 266, 279, 284, 381; wool of, 158
Ilfracombe, 188
Images, 281
Incense, 283
Indenture, 55, 56, 255, 256, 303, 305, 369
Ink, 283, 291
Innkeepers, 259. *See also* Hostillers
Interest, 65, 66, 68, 75, 253, 300. *See also* Credit
Investment, 12, 13, 15-18, 37, 148, 233, 235, 252, 253. *See also* Credit

2F

426　INDEX

Ipswich, 42, 43, 78, 144, 148, 276, 295–300, 323, 361, 362
Ireland, 155, 156, 170, 171, 174, 175, 178, 187, 191, 192, 194–201, 207, 212, 216, 224, 234, 239, 245, 246, 316, 318, 381, 386; cloth of, 199; flock of, price of, 199; frieze of, price of, 199; linen of, 139, 175; Guild of English Merchants trading to, 195; wool of, 43; wool of, price of, 199
Irish Mead, Bristol, 195
Irishman, Patrick, 185, 234
Iron, 141, 152, 175, 187, 188, 193, 199, 200, 207, 215, 221, 235, 269, 284, 289, 290, 357, 363
Ironmongers, 248, 265–7, 269, 270, 285, 287, 291, 373, 393
Ironwiredrawers, 280
Isabella of Castille, 220
Italy, 9, 12, 19, 22–6, 32, 39, 40, 42–7, 50–2, 54–8, 81, 139, 140, 145, 160, 183, 189, 199, 217, 224–6, 228, 229, 258, 264, 267, 268, 270, 271, 294, 295, 307–312, 315, 317, 364, 369, 399
Ivarsson, Vigfus, 162
Ivory, 268, 281

Jakes: Elizabeth, 243; Robert, 234
James II, king of England, 200
Jay, John, of Bristol, 245
Jerkins, 198
Jerusalem, 157
Jeweller, 276, 291
John: Duke of Burgundy, 110, 133, 136; king of England, 185; I, king of Portugal, 220; the Irishman, Bishop, 156
John, Henry, Woolman, 57
Johnson, Alan, Stapler, 16, 284, 297, 363, 393
Johnson, John, Bishop of Hólar, 169
Johnson, John, of Delft, 370
Johnson, Peter, 370
Jonet, John, 196
Joppa, 226, 245
Jorsalafari, 157
Jutland, 91, 95, 122, 123

Kalmar, Union of, 158
Keling (fish), 172
Kendal: 188; frieze, 216
Kent: 129; wool of, 49, 50, 363, 367
Kent, Thomas, 104, 127, 130, 134, 374, 376
Kerchiefs, 291
Kermes, 221
Kersey (cloth): 7, 8, 145, 216, 283, 324, 325, 362; price of, 8
Keseby, Thomas, Brasier, 369
Kesteven, wool of, 49, 367
Kettles, copper, 175
Ketyll, Thomas, 87
Kid skins, 198, 215
Kidwelly, 187
Kilkenny, 198, 199

Kilmainham, Prior of, 192
King, trade of, 12, 21, 45, 48, 58, 267, 298, 307–311, 313–15, 317, 326–8, 346, 358, 371. *See also* Edward IV, Factor, Licence
King's beam, *see* Beam
Kingrode, 185, 196, 213, 226, 241
Kingston, *see* Hull
Kinsale, 193
Kirkeby, Sir Thomas, 304
Kirkjubaer, 171
Knappe, Thomas, 191
Knives, 175, 176, 200, 281
Knolles Alley (in Tower Ward), 58
Kymberley, Thomas, 376
Kyte: Edward, 233; Joan, 233

La Redo, 216
La Réole, 203, 209
Labour, 146, 233, 239, 247, 255, 280, 281, 303, 388. *See also* Servant, and under particular occupations
Laces, 215
Lamb-fells, 51, 141, 198, 347, 257, 368. *See also* Laslades, Mesands, Milk-fells, Morkins
Lamb-wool, 51, 368. *See also* Lamb-fells
Lamport, —, 378
Lancashire, 52, 276
Lancastrians, 103, 293, 300, 301, 314, 316, 318–320
Lances, 221
Land, investment in, 148, 233, 235, 253
Landes, the, 207
Langdon, Reginald, Girdler, 369
Languedoc, 206, 207
Lappenberg, J. M., 148
Lard, 198, 215
Laslades (diseased lamb-fells), 51
Laten, 232
Laths, 232
Laurencon, Garrad, of Leyden, 370
Laurencon, Peter, of Bergen-op-Zoom, 67
Law merchant, *see* Merchant law
"Lawgher Havyn" (Laugharne?), 187
Lawless, Patrick, 195
Lawn, 268, 269
Lead, 216, 221, 228, 283
Leadenhall, 56, 59
Leather, 185, 200, 215. *See also* Cordovan
Leather workers, 280
Lechlade, 53
Lee, Richard, Grocer, 274
Leghorn, 45
Leicester, 276, 291, 292, 294, 295
Lemberg, 143
Lemyng, William, Grocer, 369
Lenard, John, of Campden, 53, 369
Leominster, wool of, 49, 187
Letters of exchange, 66
Letters of payment, 67, 69
Levant, 224, 225, 227, 228, 245, 273, 388
Levyng, John, Stapler, 297
Lewys, William, 237

INDEX

Leyden, 43, 48, 60–2, 66–8, 73, 79, 85, 87, 365, 367, 371
Libelle of Englysche Polycye, 39, 44, 46, 47, 64, 65, 99, 102, 103, 128, 160, 163, 173, 174, 214, 217, 221, 250
Libourne, 203, 210
Licences, trading, 12, 43, 44, 47, 48, 50, 51, 76, 86–9, 161, 163, 164, 169, 170, 177–9, 196, 197, 208, 213, 225, 226, 228, 236, 237, 241, 271, 272, 274, 278, 279, 289, 293–5, 301, 302, 304, 306, 307, 311–15, 326–8, 357, 366, 369, 374, 387, 393, 397, 399
Licorice, 207, 215, 283
Ligger, 108, 148
Liguria, 327
Lille, 60, 61, 89, 370
Limerick, 193, 197
Lincoln, 156, 276
Lincolnshire, wool of, 43
Lindsey : 52 ; wool of, 49, 367, 368
Linen : 139, 144, 175, 176, 199, 207, 249, 268, 283, 284, 287, 289, 290, 379 ; price of, 199 ; workers, 185 ; yarn, 139, 199
Ling, 172, 197
Lisbon, 191, 193, 194, 220, 222, 223, 234, 239, 242, 243
Lithuania, 143
Litteræ de Cambio, *see* Letters of exchange
Liverpool, 192
Livery, 251, 252, 254, 264, 270, 277, 284, 285
Livestock, 198
Livonia, 93, 95, 106, 111, 124, 134, 143, 144, 149
Llafford's Gate, Bristol, 234
Llanstephan, 187
Lloyd, mariner, 245, 246
Loan, 15, 16, 45, 46, 73–7, 79, 89, 243, 244, 253, 256, 293, 295–305, 309, 313–16, 318–320, 371, 372, 389, 392, 397–9
Locks (wool) : 51, 56 ; price of, 368
Locksmiths, of Norwich, 291
Lodestone, 160
Lofoten Isles, 173
Loire, river, 209
Lombard, John, of Venice, 234
Lombard Street, 69
Lombard, William, 211
Lombardy, 44, 46, 47, 51, 53, 57, 58, 64, 66, 69, 80, 88, 229, 310, 368, 398
Londe, Robert, 195, 196
London, 3, 7, 8, 10, 21, 26, 28, 29, 41–5, 49, 55, 56, 58, 59, 66–71, 75, 77, 80, 81, 93, 98–101, 103, 104, 106–108, 112–15, 118, 119, 125, 126, 128, 129, 132–4, 136, 137, 142, 144, 145, 147, 148, 149, 152, 153, 162, 166–9, 174, 177, 180, 181, 183, 187, 189, 191, 203, 205, 206, 217, 218, 222, 223, 224, 227–9, 234, 235, 248 ff., 295–300, 308–312, 314, 315, 317, 321, 323, 325, 361–3, 368–71, 373, 376, 378, 408

London, Bishop of, 197
Longswords, 176
Lopez, John de, 60, 65, 69
Lopt, Thorvard, 171
Lorimers, of Norwich, 291
Louis XI, king of France, 3, 212, 213, 319
Low Countries, 6, 25, 29, 43, 48, 50, 67, 85, 95, 131, 133, 139, 141, 145, 151, 152, 153, 194, 201, 214, 326, 375, 377–80, 408
Lübeck, 26, 91, 93, 95, 96, 100, 101, 109, 110, 114, 116, 123, 127, 129–32, 134, 140, 181, 192, 376, 377
Lucca, 45, 46, 192, 314
Ludlow, 187, 188, 228, 234, 316
Lusk, 196
Luxembourg, 44
Lyneham, Lowes, 67, 371
Lydgate, John, 39
Lynn, 41, 99, 114, 136, 137, 144, 147, 148, 159, 163, 165–9, 174, 180, 205, 268, 276, 347, 362, 378, 407
Lynne, William, Grocer, 263

Mace, 283
Mackerel, 197
Madder, 69, 139, 189, 212, 216, 270, 291, 379
Madeira, 221
Magnus, alleged son of John Geriksen, Bishop of Skálholt, 171
Maidstone, 276
Maine, 126
Malahide, 196
Maldon, John, Grocer, 366
Malmesbury, 234
Malmesey wine : 14, 33–5, 38, 328, 361 ; price of, 363
Malpas, Philip, Draper, 284
Malt, 169, 175, 176, 187
Malta, 225, 228
Malvern, John, Stapler, 16, 363
Man, Isle of, 188
Manchester, 277
Mantles, Irish, 199, 216
Marble cloth : 8 ; price of, 362
March, Earl of, 316
March (of Wales), wool of : 49, 375 ; price of, 71
Marconovo, Laurence, of Venice, 52
Margaret, Duchess of Burgundy, 45
Margaret, queen of Denmark, 94
Margaret, queen of England, 1, 2, 136, 230, 295
Mariners : Fraternity of, in Bristol, 190 ; payment of, 239
Marrock, Straits of, *see* Gibraltar, Straits of
Marsh Gate, Bristol, 190, 243
Marshall, Robert, Grocer, 274, 278
Marten skins, 198
Maryon, William, 370
Maryot, John, of Bristol, 168
Mastic, 283
Masts, 140

INDEX

Matlok, John, 363
Mauléon, 204
Mauro, Fra, map of, 160
Maximilian, Emperor, 69
May, Colard de, 67, 371
May: Henry, 195, 196, 208, 222, 223, 234; Richard, 223
Mayor of London, 251, 258, 261, 272, 275, 278, 279, 287
Meal, 172, 175, 176
Mecklenburg, 91
Mede, Philip, mayor of Bristol, 229, 233
Medici, Co. of, 45, 307
Medicine: 221, 249, 250, 271, 279, 283; practice of, 250
Mediterranean, 12, 41, 45, 47, 97, 99, 159, 160, 183, 191, 224, 226, 228, 229, 240, 245, 273, 293, 314, 315, 326, 327
Medley cloth, price of, 8
Melcombe, 349
Memoranda Rolls, 46, 48, 55, 58, 172, 298, 304, 327
Mendips, 188
Mercantilism, 46, 103, 374
Mercers: Company of, 189, 250, 252, 268, 269, 274-6, 283, 285, 286, 287, 310, 311; provincial, 289-292; trade of, 17, 53, 54, 55, 66-8, 70, 152, 255, 263, 265-277, 279, 282, 283, 285, 289, 291, 292, 309, 310, 368, 369, 372, 373, 393
Mercery, 263, 265, 268, 283, 285, 286, 289, 290
Merchant Adventurers: 13-15, 17-19, 24, 28, 30, 32, 35-8, 70, 133, 146, 150-3, 189, 263-5, 268, 269, 315, 316, 377, 380, 408; of Bristol, 229; of York, 290
Merchant law, 73, 145
Mercury, 283
Merlawe, Richard, Alderman, 285
Meryell, William, Woolman, 187
Mesands (damaged lamb-fells), 51, 376
Metal, 142, 248, 262, 269, 272, 284
Metal goods, 139, 142, 188, 200, 207
Mettenye, Jean, 371
Michell, John, 363
Middleburgh, 43, 70, 143, 376
Middlemen, 51, 52, 55, 238, 260, 269, 278
Middlesex, wool of, 49
Middleton: Elizabeth, 234; Thomas, 234
Midlands, wool of, 12
Midwinter: Thomas, of Northleach, 54; William, of Northleach, 52, 54, 56, 62, 63, 368, 369
Milan, 45
Milan, Paul de, of Lucca, 46
Milford Haven, 187, 195, 205
Milk-fells, 51, 368. *See also* Lamb-fells
Milwell, 197
Minehead, 194, 195
Mint, 17, 66, 69, 70, 80-2, 87-9, 372
Mirrors, 268, 284
Modon: Bishop of, 226; Isle of, 226
Mold, John, 196

Moleyns, Adam, Bishop of Chichester, 365
Molyner, Nicholas, of the Hanse, 361
Monmouth, 187
Monopoly, 94, 96, 97, 100, 101, 104, 106, 112, 119, 125, 141, 215, 225, 227, 259-262, 265, 267-272, 277-282, 284, 287, 290, 291, 317. *See also* Staple
Montauban, 206, 207
Monte, Henry de, of Liguria, 327
Montendre, 202
Montferrant, Bertram de, 212
Morein, *see* Morling
Moresson, Gyesbryght, of Leyden, 370
Morgan, Stephen, Carpenter, 231, 232
Morkins (skins of dead lambs): 51; price of, 368
Morlings (skins of dead sheep): 51, 75, 328, 348, 350, 359, 360; price of, 367
Morocco, Straits of, *see* Gibraltar, Straits of
Mors, Ludovic, of Bristol, 206
Mortagne, 202
Mortar, 277
Motrico, 216, 217, 219
Mountayn, Alan, 48
Moy, Adam, 61
Muleyn, Nicholas de, of Venice, 46
Mulso, John, 310
Munster, 192, 193
Murrey cloth, price of, 8, 362
Muschangs, Thomas, Mercer, 369
Musk, 283
Mustard, 283
Mustrevillers, cloth, price of, 8, 362
Myrrour de Dames, le, 244

Nadale, Nicholas, 224
Nail (weight), 72
Nailers, 276
Nails, 175, 200, 215, 291
Nantes, 212
Napton, Thomas, of Coventry, 169, 174
Narbonne, 207
Navigation Acts, 103
Neckam, Alexander, 160
Needles, 175
Netherlands, 25, 26, 28, 29, 36, 39, 40, 43, 44, 49, 51, 59, 60, 66, 84, 93, 152, 153, 159, 199, 235, 242, 245, 310, 313, 315, 316. *See also* Low Countries
Nets, fishing, 175
New Found Land, 182
Newark, wool, of, 49
Newbury, 189, 276
Newcastle-on-Tyne, 12, 43, 47, 49, 51, 144, 168, 169, 173, 174, 205, 289-291, 350, 362, 368; wool of, 43
Newenton, Walter, Grocer, 264
Newgate Prison, 168
Newnham, 334
Newport, 187
Nicholas, servant of Walter Derby of Bristol, 238
Nieuport, 60

INDEX

Norfolk: 173, 196; wool of, 49, 363, 367, 398
Nori, Simon, 307, 312, 314, 315, 317, 368
Normandy: 2, 28, 35, 50, 103, 121, 201, 210, 212, 294; wool of, 50, 363
Norrell, John, of the Hanse, 361
North Channel, 194
North Sea, 91, 94, 97, 135, 152, 157, 183, 197, 224
Northallerton, wool of, 43
Northampton, 276, 290
Northbern, *see* Bergen
Northern Counties, wool of, 12, 43, 47, 49
Northleach, 52-4, 57, 367
Northumberland: Henry Percy, Earl of, 308, 309; John Neville, Earl of, 177, 374, 378
Northumberland, wool of, 43, 363, 367, 371
Norton, Thomas, of Bristol, 219
Norway, 93, 94, 106, 140, 142, 143, 144, 151, 155 ff., 169, 172-4, 180-2, 245, 374, 381
Norwich, 99, 145, 291
Nottingham, 187, 275
Nottingham, William, 312
Nottinghamshire, wool of, 43, 49, 367
Noumbre of Weyghtes, The, 45, 49, 70, 71, 76, 176, 196, 221, 273, 281, 367
Novgorod, 91, 93, 124, 143
Nuremburg, 135
Nutmegs, 283

Oak, 198, 232
Oars, 198, 240
Obligations, 61, 74-6, 78, 80-2, 299, 303-306, 308, 309
Oil, 139, 176, 181, 200, 215, 216, 218, 221, 242, 270, 272, 283, 290
Ointment, 250, 283
Old Corn Street, Bristol, 206
Olive Oil, 221
Olney, John, 16
Olof, Mistress, wife of Björn Thorleifsson, 180
Ombrière, l', castle of, 203
Onions: 145, 266, 278; seed, 266, 291
Oporto, 220, 222
Oranges, 266
Ordinances (Company), 254, 255, 261, 262, 265, 268, 270-2, 274-6, 282
Orkney Islands, 178
Örlyg, 156
Orwell, 173
Olwys, William, 77
Ore, 386
Oseney, Abbot of, 52
Osmund (iron), 141
Otteley, John, Grocer, 285
Otter skins, 198
Ottson, Henryck, of Leyden, 370
Outlaw, Richard, 380
Oxford, 274-6

Oxfordshire, 53-5, 276
Ox-hides, 198
Ozerio, Jerome de, 222

Packthread, 59
Padstow, 188
Page, Robert, Woolman, 52
Pale, the, 194, 200
Pallman, Gilbard, 371
Palmer, Nicholas, 214, 215
Pálsson, Hannes, 164, 165, 166
Pans, 175, 200, 279, 284
Papal Court, 318, 319
Paper, 175, 291
Parchment-maker, Bristol, 187
Parlement of Paris, 319
Parliament, 1, 12, 20, 26, 27, 49, 50, 57, 73, 81, 82, 86-8, 100, 101, 103-105, 114, 116, 125-7, 132, 133, 162, 167, 199, 204, 210, 227, 244, 257-260, 275, 282, 294, 299, 302, 303, 307, 310, 312, 316, 317, 327, 329, 362, 363, 373, 376, 399
Partition Ordinance (in the Staple), 61, 75, 76, 83-90, 372
Partnership, 55, 147, 236, 237, 254, 265, 285, 297-9, 368, 369
Partrynton, Thomas, 395
Pasdale, J., 382
Pask mart, 66, 380
Passage, 216
Paston, Margaret, 196, 197
Paul, Bishop, 156
Patrick, Bishop of the Hebrides, 156
Pavy, John, 242, 244
Payn, John, of Bristol, 219
Peacock, Bishop Reginald, 256
Pedlar, *see* Chapman
Pedlary ware, 200
Pelican, —, 380
Penmarch, 212
"Penny ware," 281
Pennycock, John, 397
Pepper, 226, 228, 248, 252, 270, 271, 285, 289
Pepperers, 248-250, 257, 276, 283
Pera, 227
Percy: Henry (*see* Northumberland, Earl of); John, 165; Thomas, 196
Perfume, 250
Pernau, 106
Perry, 200
Perschelettes (lamb-fells), price of, 368
Pestles, 277
Peterson, Claysse, of Delft, 370
Petronilla, wife of Bertram de Montferrant, 211, 212
Petty Custom, *see* Customs
Petyt, John, Mercer, 67
Pewter, 142, 145, 199, 323, 324, 328, 405
Pewterers, 269, 270, 285
Philip, Duke of Burgundy, 121, 122, 378
Physicians, 250
Picards (boats), 237
Picardy, wool of, 50, 363

Picquigny, Treaty of, 3, 29, 33, 213
Pinners, 280, 283
Pins, 175
Pinxstermarct, see Synchon mart
Piracy, 26, 107, 109, 110, 113, 122, 123, 126–131, 152, 164, 174, 178, 179, 192, 193, 205, 213, 217–19, 222, 227, 240, 241, 250, 285, 296, 397, 315
Pisa, 220, 226, 229
Pitch, 97, 135, 141, 175, 200, 207, 283, 284
Plague, 235
Plaice, 197
Plaster, 232
Plauen, Henry of, High Master of Prussia, 111, 113
Plymouth, 187, 188, 194, 205, 224, 227, 276, 337, 352
Points, 175, 176, 200, 281, 291
Pointmakers, 187, 215
Poland, 25, 93, 95, 97, 111, 137, 140, 141, 143, 145, 379
Pollack, 176, 197
Pons, Lord, 126
Ponte, John da, of Venice, 56, 214, 369
Poole, 41, 349, 356, 367
Porpoise, price of, 197
Portage, 59
Porter, William, 194
Porters, 59, 206, 287
Portugal, 152, 187, 188, 193, 201, 215, 218, 220, 221, 223, 224, 235, 240, 241, 245, 380
Portugalete, 216
Pots, 175, 200, 279, 283, 284
Pouchmakers, Bristol, 187
Pound-toll, 124
Poundage, subsidy of: 6, 9, 15, 18, 21, 30, 51, 294, 323, 324, 328–330, 361; accounts of, 3, 7, 14, 363. See also Subsidy
Pounte, John de, see Ponte, John da
Premage, 71
Premiums, of apprentices, 255, 256
Prest (loan in Staple), 74, 75, 304
Preston, 52
Prices, 164, 259–261, 266, 270, 272, 274, 278, 279, 287. See also under particular commodities
Prise, 197
Prussia, 25, 26, 29, 93, 95–7, 99–101, 107, 111, 113–120, 123–7, 129–131, 134, 138, 140–3, 145, 147–153, 163, 166, 241, 266, 374–9, 408
Puebla, De, Spanish ambassador, 220
Puke (Puyker), cloth, 8, 362, 367
Pulter, John, 363
Pursers, 281
Purses, 175, 198, 281, 291
Pynell, Ralph, of Genoa, 50
Pynner, Margaret, of Chipping Norton, 52
Pyrton, William, Lieutenant of Guines, 298, 300
Pyxes, 283

Quicksilver, 215

Quilts, 156, 268, 269, 283
Quimper, 212
Quimperle, 212, 221
Quivers, 371
Quyrke, John, 194

Rabbit-skins, 141, 198
Raisins: 142, 214–16, 224, 283, 291; price of, 272
Ray, 197
Reading, 125, 276, 291
Reame, Simon, 58
Reciprocity, 99, 100, 101, 104, 106, 111, 119, 129, 131, 137, 138, 146, 167
Redcliffe: Bristol, 231; Church of St. Mary, Bristol, 196, 206, 244; Mead, Bristol, 234; Street, Bristol, 185, 232
Rede, Thomas, Draper, 369
Redemption, admission by, 286, 287
Regulation, trade, 206, 248, 259, 270–2, 278–280, 282–4, 287, 290, 291, 311, 312, 368. See also Broker
Renamond, John, 217
Renteria, 216
Retail trade, 100, 146, 250, 260–2, 265, 272 ff., 287, 290, 392
Retailers, 100, 273, 277, 287
Retainer, Act of (1466), 74, 75
Reval, 106
Reynwell, John, mayor of the Staple, 86
Rhine: 25, 26, 29, 81, 91, 95, 143, 144; wine, 4, 267, 328
Ribbons, 291
Rice, 215, 248, 283
Richard: II, king of England, 80, 103, 106, 200, 205, 220, 238, 283, 362; III, king of England, 181
Richards, Alice, 189
Richeman, John, Stockfishmonger, 170
Richmond, wool of, 43
Rif, 179
Ripon, 276
Rivers, Richard Woodville, Lord, 316, 318
Rochelle, 205, 223
Rochester, Bishop of, 378
Roger of Dam, 242
Roger, William, 236
Rome, 170
Romsey, 270
Roos, Thomas, Lord, 104, 388
Ropers, see Corders
Ropery, 248, 249
Rosin, 207, 215, 284
Ross, 193
Rostock, 91, 144
Rotterdam, 94
Rouen, 357
Roumania, 143
Rowley: Joanna, 242; Margaret, 242; Thomas, 242; William, 242
Rugs: 198; price of, 199
Rumpyll, John de, 194
Russel, Roger, 395

INDEX

Russell: —, 104; John, Stapler, 52, 368; Margery, 243; Robert, 236
Russet (cloth): 187, 362; price of, 8, 9. *See also* Wales, cloth of
Russia, 93, 95, 97, 111, 140, 141, 143
Rye, 289
Rysbank, 75, 296

Sack (weight), 71, 72, 362
Saddlers, 231, 291
Saddles, 198
Saffron, 207, 215, 270, 271, 283
St. Albans: 277; battle of, 1, 325
St. Emilion, 203, 210
St. Ewen's Church, Bristol, 187
St. Ives, 188
St. Jean de Luz, 205
St. John the Evangelist, Chapel of, Bristol, 191
S. Lucar Barrameda, 216
St. Macaire, 203, 209
St. Mary's Church, Damme, 242
St. Mary's Church, Limerick, 193
St. Mary's Church, Redcliffe, Bristol, 196, 206. *See also* Redcliffe
St. Nicholas' Church, Bristol, 211, 228
St. Nicholas' Street, Bristol, 233
St. Peter's Church, Bristol, 196
St. Peter's Church, Cornhill, 310
S. Pol de Léon, 212
St. Stephen's Church, Bristol, 243
St. Thomas of Canterbury, shrine of, 162
St. Thomas' Spitell, Southwark, 170
St. Thomas' Street, Bristol, 185
St. Thorlak of Iceland, 156
St. Werburgh's Church, Bristol, 206
Sal-ammoniac, 283
Salettes, 176
Salimbene, Fra, 201
Salisbury, 232, 270, 274-6, 290, 291
Salisbury, Richard Neville, Earl of, 316
Salman, John, Mercer, 369
Salmon, 176, 195, 196, 200
Salt, 67, 142, 172, 175, 193, 194, 197, 199, 200, 215, 221, 232, 283, 290, 291, 386
Saltash, 168, 173
Salters, 265, 266, 269, 278, 279, 285, 289
Saltes, 216
Saltpetre, 398
Sampson: Joan, 238; Thomas, 238
San Domingo, Church of, Lisbon, 222
San Sebastian, 216
Sandwich, 41, 42, 44, 50, 51, 58, 169, 191, 217, 224, 229, 259, 276, 289, 310, 316-18, 323, 354, 361, 362, 368
Santander, 216, 217, 242
Sasiola, Godfred de, 218
Satin, 268
Sauly, Peter, of Genoa, 69
Saxby, —, 380
Saxony, 91, 95, 96, 110
Say, William, Lord, 104, 128
Scaldings (skins of scabby sheep), 51

Scalpin, 197
Scandinavia, 91, 93, 94, 97, 101, 142, 144, 151, 152, 157, 174, 178
Scarborough, 168, 173, 182, 341
Scarlet cloth: 7, 13, 200, 221, 324; grain, 270
Schanz, G., 7, 13, 40, 72, 321, 322-5
Schellendorp, Stephen, 164, 165, 171
Schiates, Bartholomew, of Lucca, 214
Schiedam, 171
Scotland: 156, 174, 179, 191, 194, 242; wool of, 43, 50, 84, 363
Scriveners, 142, 257
Scrope, Sir Stephen, 192
Sea coal, *see* Coal
Seal, price of, 197
Search: Customs, 48 (*see also* Smuggling); Municipal, *see* Regulation, trade
Seas, safeguarding of, 122, 126, 210, 227
Seeds, 283, 291
Seglysthorne, John, 242
Seine, river, 209
Selander, Hankyn, 222, 223
Selby, Richard, 16
Selly, David, 208
Sendeve, 147
Servant, 147, 169, 172, 177, 254, 255, 257. *See also* Factor
Sevedon Lane (Tower Ward), 58
Severn, river, 183, 187, 188, 190, 191, 224
Seville, 193, 215, 216, 217, 226, 242
Shadworth, John, Mercer, 258
Shaftesbury, 277
Shannon, river, 193, 198
Sharp: Richard, 16; William, 313
Sheep: 10-12, 25, 54, 57, 164, 188, 196, 209, 355 (*see also* Wool-growers); skins, *see* Fleeces, Wool-fells
Sheets, 156, 233
Shetland Islands, 178
Ship-boards, 198
Ship-building, 140, 141, 159, 160
Ship-owners, 239 ff., 284
Shipward, John, mayor of Bristol, 218, 233, 236, 243
Shirburn, 188
Shirts, 199
Shoemaker, 201
Shoes, 175, 176, 198
Shop, 108, 112, 206, 231 ff., 255, 256, 261, 270, 277-9, 281-3, 287, 288, 290-2
Shopkeepers, 249, 254, 273, 281
Shorlings: 51, 75, 141, 328-330, 347, 359, 360; price of, 367
Shrewsbury, 187, 276; Earl of, 211, 308, 309, 311, 312
Shropshire: 276; wool of, 12; March of, wool of, 49
Sigismund, Emperor, 113, 365
Silesia, 144
Silk, 156, 189, 224, 268, 281, 284, 287, 291
Silver, 176, 283
Simples, 250

INDEX

Skagafjörd, 170
Skálholt, 155, 162, 169–171
Skania, 91, 93, 94, 97, 106, 107, 109, 142, 364
Skiff, 172, 193
Skins, 51, 141, 198, 215, 269, 280, 291, 347
Skinners, 55, 265, 280, 283, 289, 373, 393
Skyrmot, William, 219
Skyvile, Adrian, 296
Sligo, 193, 196
Sluys, 43, 366
Smigmates (soap), 215
Smiths, 291
Smuggling, 46–8, 50, 56, 58, 73, 86–8, 135, 168, 169, 179, 294, 295, 313, 366, 368
Snaefellness, 156
Soap, 200, 215, 269, 270, 272, 283, 284, 289–291. See also *Smigmates*
Sombart, W., 146
Somerset, 50, 168, 188, 189, 234, 276
Somerset, Henry Beaufort, Duke of, 303, 309, 316, 398
Somme, river, 209
Soper, William, 357
Sopers Lane, London, 248
Sore, Gomers de, 69
"Sotill ware," 271, 272, 274. See also Spices
Soulac, 213
Sound, the, 91, 114, 123, 130, 131, 133, 136, 138, 408
Southampton, 3, 7–9, 26, 28, 29, 41, 44, 45, 57, 144, 185, 189, 191, 206, 217, 218, 224, 229, 259, 266, 268, 269, 270, 276, 277, 290, 291, 304, 314, 315, 317, 321, 323, 326, 349, 356, 361, 362, 366, 370
Southray, wool of, 49
Southwark, 170, 268
Southwold, 173
Spades, 398
Spain: 6, 33, 39, 40, 69, 110, 139, 152, 174, 192, 193, 201, 202, 205–208, 214–221, 224, 231, 234, 235, 240–2, 245, 269, 343, 371, 405, 406; wine of, 267; wool of, 43, 84, 353, 357, 365
Spaynell: Soneta, 238; William, 238
Spectacles, 281
Speed, John, 183
Spencer, John, 257
Spenser, Edmund, 191, 192, 199
Spicers: 248–250, 279, 280; provincial, 276, 289
Spices, 200, 224, 226, 228, 248, 250, 257–9, 269–272, 274, 278, 282–5, 289, 290. See also "Sotill ware"
Sponges, 283
Spoons, 233, 283
Sprats, 196
Spryng, Jordan, 217
Spurs, 281
Squirrel fur, 198
Staffordshire, 276
Stanes, William de, apothecary, 249

Stanton Drewe, 234
Staple: 40, 141, 143, 153; Bergen, 163, 164, 178, 179; Bristol, 187, 216, 217, 234; Calais, 40, 41, 64, 65, 73, 74; Middleburgh, 43
Staple, Calais, Fellowship of the Company of the: 43, 73, 77, 253; administration of customs and loans by, 27, 41, 46, 47, 72 ff., 293–300, 309, 313–15, 317–320, 370, 371, 399; membership of, 41, 55, 70, 83, 86, 365; officials of, 41, 44, 59, 60, 75, 76, 78, 79, 81, 84, 86, 87, 89, 302, 306, 311, 312; privileges of, 40, 44, 72, 89, 293, 299, 301, 307, 309, 312, 313; negotiations by, 61, 62, 64, 67, 68, 70, 73, 83–5; regulation of bullion and credit sales by, 17, 62, 64–6, 68, 70, 73, 78–82, 84, 86, 88, 89; regulation of wool prices by, 49, 63–5, 70, 71, 83, 84, 86, 88–90, 305, 365; regulation of wool trade by, 47, 48, 50, 51, 57–62, 72, 73, 83–6, 88–90; seal of, 75, 78, 83, 379; wool trade of, 40–4, 46–51, 64, 226, 262, 300–302, 306–308, 314, 315–17, 319, 326, 327, 363, 368, 369, 371, 397, 398
Staple, Treatise concerninge the, 70
Staplers: 12, 13, 15–19, 21, 22, 35–8; as wool merchants, 51, 53, 57, 58, 59, 62, 63, 66–8, 70–2, 77, 80, 82, 83, 85, 86; as financiers, 17, 62, 65, 67–9, 70, 79, 81, 82, 85, 86; as general merchants, 17, 63, 82, 263–5, 311. See also Staple, Wool
Statute staple, 67
Statutes, parliamentary, 53, 55, 56, 58, 74, 75, 125, 167–9, 177, 260, 275, 279, 282, 290, 294, 295, 304, 314, 327, 329, 362, 369, 364. See also Bullion Regulations, Partition
Steel, 207, 221, 222, 269, 283, 291
Steelyard, 93, 98, 100, 112–18, 124, 127–9, 133, 137, 148, 149
Stephen, king of England, 185
Stevenson, Garrad, of Leyden, 370
Stocker, Sir William, mayor of the Staple, 78, 366
Stockfish, 155, 168–170, 172–4, 176, 266, 279, 284
Stockfish rows, Bristol, 174
Stockfishmongers, 152, 174, 278, 284
Stockings, 291
Stokes, John, of Ceryngnorton, 53
Stokker, Sir William, see Stocker, Sir William
Stone, John, 195
Stone, Robert, Mercer, 369
Stonor: Elizabeth, 232, 371; Sir William, 367
Stonor Papers, 54
Stourbridge fair, 274
Stourton, Sir John, 229, 313
Straits: cloth, 7, 145, 362; price of, 8; Essex, 362

INDEX

Straits of Dover, 194
Stralsund, 107
Strange, Thomas, 239, 240
Straps, 281
Strosse (? Strozzi), Ludovic, 214
Strossy (? Strozzi), Maxy, of Spain, 69
Sturgeon, Sir John, Stapler, 372
Sturmy : Ellen, 227 ; Robert, 225, 226, 227, 228, 229, 230, 240
Stychemersh, Stephen, 223
Subsidy : of Tenth and Fifteenth, 20, 295, 302; of Tunnage and Poundage: 324, 328, 334, 361; accounts of, 7, 321 ff. Subsidy on wool: 12, 13, 27, 40, 42, 43, 45, 46, 48, 50, 51, 59, 63, 71, 74 ff., 81, 87, 106, 107, 116, 119, 294, 295, 299–307, 313, 315, 324, 326, 327, 330, 334, 363, 372; accounts of, 41
Sudeley, Ralph, Lord, 296
Suffolk : 173, 196 ; wool of, 49, 363, 367
Suffolk, William de la Pole, Duke of, 1, 104, 121, 125, 126, 128, 210, 241, 295, 309, 374, 376
Sugar, 207, 221, 242, 248, 271, 283, 284
Sulphur, 176
Sund, *see* Sound, the
Sunday closing, 290
Surgeons, 250, 283
Surplusage, 77, 78
Surrey, wool of, 363, 367
Sussex, wool of, 50, 363, 367
Sutton, Hamo, mayor of the Staple, 86, 87, 89
Swans, 381
Swansea, 169
Sweden, 93, 141, 144, 158, 179
Swords, 175
Swyn, 107
Syger, William, of Camden, 52
Symondes, William, 237
Synchon mart, 66
Syrup, 250, 283

Tables, 232, 233, 291, 398
Taffeta, 291
Tagus, river, 222
Tailors, 231, 265–7, 285–7, 289, 393
Tallow, 141, 181, 198, 215
Tallies, 295, 303, 304, 305
Talmont, 205
Tannenberg, battle of, 111
Tanners, 187, 198, 200
Tanworth, John, 365
Tapestry, 232, 233, 268, 291
Tar, 97, 135, 141, 175, 215, 216, 283, 284, 291
Tariff, *see* Customs, Subsidy
Tassells, 189
Taunton, Prior of, 243
Taverner, Hugh, 126
Taverner, John, 225, 240
Taverners : 277, 279 ; provincial, 276
Tame, 54. *See also* Thame

Teazles, 200, 291
Tees, wool of, 43
Temple : Church, Bristol, 185 ; Cross, Bristol, 230 ; Gate, Bristol, 230 ; Street, Bristol, 185, 233
Tenby, 187, 205
Tenement, Bristol, 233–5
Tenth and Fifteenth, *see* Subsidy of Tenth and Fifteenth
Teutonic Order, *see* Prussia
Teviotdale, wool of, 43
Tewkesbury, 187, 276
Thame, John, of Fairford, 53. *See also* Tame
Thames, river, 58, 311
Thames Street, *see* Ropery
Thorgunna, 156
Thorkill, Robert, 382
Thorlak, St., 156
Thorleifsson, Björn, Governor of Iceland, 179, 180
Thread, 59, 175, 268, 269, 281, 283, 289, 290, 379
Thrums, 141
Thrysk, John, mayor of the Staple, 300, 306, 311, 315, 319, 399
Thurland, Thomas, mayor of the Staple, 87
Tilbury, 310, 311
Tiles, 284, 291, 395
Timber, 97, 135, 140–2, 145, 146, 158, 187, 190, 198, 224, 226, 228, 231, 232, 262, 284, 291, 379
Tin : 5, 48, 82, 188, 190, 216, 269, 270, 284, 304, 309, 323, 324, 329, 353, 363, 402–406 ; price of, 270
Tintern, Abbot of, 187
Tod, 362
Tolls, 44, 138, 157, 161, 162, 189, 192, 193, 198, 202–204, 206, 366. *See also* Customs
Tolsey Court, 190, 215, 227, 239, 244
Tooley, Henry, 172
Touker Street, Bristol, 185
Toulouse, 206
Tower Ward, 58
Townsend, John, of Lechlade, 54, 369
Towton, battle of, 177, 183
Transport, 13, 45, 49, 50, 53, 56, 59 ff., 71, 237, 274 ff. *See also* Freight
Treacle : 250 ; -mongers, 283
Treasurer, 229, 295, 318–320
Trenchers, 140
Trevelyan, John, 128
Trollope, Andrew, 316
Tron, 258
Tronage, 56, 258
Tucker, 189
Tudor period, 120, 137, 153, 220, 229, 320
Tunnage : 294, 328, 361 ; accounts of, 4, 13, 363. *See also* Subsidy of Tunnage and Poundage
Tunny-fish, 215

INDEX

Turks, 226, 227, 229. *See also* Sultan
Turner, Henry, Grocer, 369
Turpentine, 283
Tweed, wool of, 43
Tymanson, Jacob, of Leyden, 370
Tyre (Tire), wine of, 361

Ulnage, accounts of, 8, 9, 238, 362
Ulnager, 8, 238, 249
Ulster, 194
Umlandfahrt, 95
Upsala, Bishop of, 170
Upholsterers, 287
Usk, 187
Usury, 47, 65. *See also* Credit
Utrecht: 3, 5, 28, 29, 121, 130, 136-8, 377, 408; Bishop of, 133
Uvedale, Henry, 369, 370
Uzzano, da, Giovanni, of Florence, 366

Vache, John, 166
Vaðmál, *see* Wadmole
Vannes, 212
Varnish, 283
Varrole, John de, 217
Vasqueannus, 222. *See* Vasquez
Vasquez, Sir John, 221
Vaughan, Henry, 216
Veer, 362, 405, 406
Vegetables, 265, 266, 279
Veilho, John, 222, 223
Velvet, 268
Venice, 44-7, 52, 98, 224, 225, 227, 234, 284, 287, 309, 310, 317, 365
Verdict, the (1468), 132, 134, 137, 374, 408
Vermilion, 375
Vestmann Isles, 161, 162, 164, 172, 177
Viana, 222
Victuallers, 260, 265, 266, 268, 278
Victuals, 141, 144, 170, 173, 175, 248, 259, 260, 262, 266, 272, 278, 279, 398
Views of Hosts, *see* Hosts
Vigfusson: Ivar, 171; Margaret, 171
Vikings, 155, 157, 159
Vinegar, 215, 283
Vines, 201, 211, 214, 220, 222
Vintners: 247, 260-2, 265-7, 276, 277, 287, 289, 373, 393; provincial, 289
Vintry Ward, 58
Voet, Bartholomew, 166
Vorrath, Heinrich, burgomaster of Danzig, 116-120, 123, 124, 126, 132, 137, 408
Vyell Place (Bristol), 231

Wadmole, 158, 175, 176, 215, 283
Wainscot, 140, 212, 216, 232, 283
Walberswick, 173
Walbrook (London), 258
Walcomstraso, John, 311, 312
Walden, John, mayor of the Staple, 298, 300, 319

Wales: 163, 187-9, 205, 224, 234; cloth of, 175, 187, 217, 334; frieze of, 8, 216; March of, wool of, 367, 368
Wallachia, 143
Walsingham, Thomas, 397
Walton, 195
Wardrobe, King's, 76, 249, 285
Warehouse, 45, 59, 71, 277
Warner, Robert, of Wallington, 369
Warrant, 75-9, 295, 308, 372
Wars of the Roses, 1, 2, 11, 20-2, 24, 25, 28, 29, 36, 104, 105, 136, 177-9, 245, 293, 300, 304, 407
Warwick: 188, 240; Earl of, 130, 132, 177, 188, 229, 240, 242, 303, 304, 307, 315-18, 374, 376, 398. *See also* Beauchamp, Richard
Warwickshire, wool of, 367
Waterford, 192, 193, 276
Waver, Henry, 368
Wax: 3, 4, 18-20, 32, 34, 36, 37, 69, 141, 175, 188, 198, 207, 215, 221, 242, 248, 258, 270, 272, 283, 284, 290, 323, 329; price of, 19, 364
Waxchandler, 276
Weavers, 175, 185, 189, 196, 244, 261, 266, 282, 286
Weighing, 45, 56, 59-61, 72, 248, 257, 258, 277, 283, 287, 290, 392. *See also* Beam, Sack
Wells, 234
"Welsh Back," the (Bristol), 190, 191, 229, 233, 243
Wendish Towns, 91, 95, 110, 111, 114, 116-19, 130, 132, 144, 161, 178, 181
Wesel, Gerard von, 134
Westbury on Trym, 234, 244
Westfalia, 91, 95, 96, 98, 100, 134, 139, 149, 379
Westminster, 126, 318, 320
Westmoreland: 276; wool of, 43, 363, 367
Weston, Robert, Stockfishmonger, 169, 170
Weston Stowe, 362
Whaddon, 276
Whale, price of, 197
Wharfage, 59
Wharfager, 59
Wheat, 48, 156, 169, 170, 175, 187, 214
Whetehill, Richard, 305
Whitby, 173
White, Robert, mayor of the Staple, 295, 296, 298, 300, 311, 314-16, 369
Whitfeld, John, 395
Whitsun mart, 67
Whittington, Richard, 81, 366, 369
Whityngham, John, 214
Whiting, 197
Whittawers, 187, 198
Whittles (Irish blankets), 199
Wight, Isle of, 128, 205, 276
Wild, —, of Drogheda, 176
Willey, William, of Campden, 54, 55

INDEX

William: Bishop of Skálholt, 155; of Worcester, 226, 231, 239-241, 244; Richard, 222
Williamson: Jacob, of Delft, 370; John, of Leyden, 370; John, of Louth, 306; John, Bishop of Hólar, 170
Wiltshire: 54, 189; James Butler, Earl of, 318-320; wool of, 49, 50, 363, 367; Clement, 231, 233
Winchcombe, Abbot of, 52
Winchelsea, 217
Winchester: 270, 274, 276, 290, 310; Bishop of, 357, 376
Windsor, Treaty of, 220
Wine: 3, 4, 6, 11-16, 18-21, 31-7, 116, 140, 142, 152, 169, 170, 175, 176, 188, 192, 194, 200-216, 218, 221, 222, 232, 239, 240, 242, 247, 261-3, 265-9, 276, 277, 279, 283, 284, 289-291, 322, 327-9, 361-4, 393, 398; non-sweet, 363, 364; price of, 14, 279, 363; red, 363, 364; Rumney, 361; sweet, 116, 328, 363, 364; white, 4
Wine Street, Bristol, 233
Winnington, Robert, 127, 128, 376
Winter, Hans, 376, 377
Wismar, 91
Withiford, Hugh, 234
Woad, 139, 187-9, 206, 207, 212, 215, 232, 235, 242, 270, 290
Wode: John, 242; Thomas, 242
Wodehouse, John, 305
Wolf-skins, 198
Wolfe, John, 178
Wolleman, Godfrey, 366
Women, trading in Bristol, 243
Wood, 48, 158, 172, 175, 187. *See also* Firewood, Timber
Woodwork, 198
Wool: bearding of, 46, 56, 58, 312, 369; clacking of, 46, 56, 58, 369; clift, 51, 68, 367, 368; coarse, 43, 50, 58, 363, 367; "end," 68, 367; fine, 43, 50, 55, 57, 65, 367; forcing of, 56; good, 50, 51, 56, 368, 375; grades and kinds of, 12, 39, 43, 47, 49, 50, 51, 56, 57, 68, 83, 141, 187, 282, 367, 368 (*see also* under place names *and* Locks); unwinding of, 56; middle, 51, 55-7, 59, 71; pell, 51, 368; price of, 12, 13, 19, 50, 65, 71, 363, 367, 368, 371, *and see also* Staple; refuse, 51, 56, 367, 368; stowing of, 59, 370; tithe, 53; trade in, 3-5, 10-23, 25, 32, 41 ff., 141, 144, 147, 153, 185, 187, 188, 190, 214-16, 224, 226, 228, 229, 245, 258, 294, 301-314, 316, 319, 322, 323, 326-330, 348, 359, 360, 362 ff., 398, *and see also* Staple, Staplers; trade in, profits of, 13, 45, 50, 70-2, 83, 371;

young, 49, 51, 55. *See also* Lamb-fells, Lamb-wool, Wool-fells
Wool-combers, 43, 215
Wool-fells: 51, 58, 61, 62, 72, 141, 291, 326, 357, 368, 370, 371; grey or black, 62; price of, 83, 88, 368; summer, 61, 370; tellers of, 59, 61. *See also* Fleeces, Morlings, Scaldings, Shorlings, Wool
Wool-growers, 40, 51-5, 57, 58, 63, 85, 104, 313, 363. *See also* Sheep
Woolmen, 40, 43, 50-5, 57, 62, 63, 250, 257, 263
Woolpackers, 51, 56-60, 308, 312, 369
Woolquay, 58, 59
Woolwharf, 258
Wool Oil, 221
Worcester: 187, 188; William of, 226, 231, 239, 240, 241, 244
Worcestershire, 235, 236
Worsop, John, 368
Worsted (cloth): 4, 6, 13, 142, 145, 200, 324, 325, 329, 347, 359, 361, 363; price of, 361
Wyclif, John, 259, 260
Wych, Hugh, mercer, 368
Wyche, John, of Bristol, 168, 193
Wye, fair of, 274
Wyfold, Nicholas, Grocer, 274
Wykes, John, Draper, 368
Wylly, John, 242
Wylliamson, Adryan, of Leyden, 370
Wymark, Thomas, 315, 316
Wynne, John, 238
Wynsbarge, Gyesbryght van, of Bruges, 60

Yarmouth, 41, 142, 144, 291, 325, 359, 361, 362
Yarn, 139, 144, 175, 199, 364
Yeomen, 53, 54
Yong, John, Grocer, 257, 368
Yonge, Thomas, 235, 244
York: 99, 145, 165, 167, 183, 276, 289-291; Adam of, 205; Archbishop of, 378; Cecily Neville, Duchess of, 45, 47, 358, 404; Richard Plantagenet, Duke of, 2, 235, 242, 309, 316, 318, 398
Yorkists, 2, 21, 22, 31, 33, 38, 132, 135, 293, 300, 310, 311, 314, 316-320, 374, 378, 399
Yorkshire: 144; wool of, 49, 50; wold, wool of, 43, 52
Youghal, 193
Ypres, 256, 273

Zealand, 41, 47, 48, 59, 84, 85, 87, 88, 97, 121, 122, 135, 242, 310-13, 316, 378
Zuider Zee, 91, 95, 100, 118, 143

Printed and bound in Great Britain by
TJ International Ltd, Padstow, Cornwall